THE IMPACT OF NEAR-INFRARED SKY SURVEYS ON GALACTIC AND EXTRAGALACTIC ASTRONOMY

ASTROPHYSICS AND SPACE SCIENCE LIBRARY

VOLUME 230

THE IMPACT OF NEAR-INFRARED SKY SURVEYS ON GALACTIC AND EXTRAGALACTIC ASTRONOMY

Proceedings of the 3rd EUROCONFERENCE
on Near-Infrared Surveys held at Meudon Observatory, France,
June 19–20, 1997

Edited by

N. EPCHTEIN

Observatoire de la Côte d'Azur, Nice, France,
and
Département de Recherche Spatiale,
Observatoire de Paris, France

KLUWER ACADEMIC PUBLISHERS

DORDRECHT / BOSTON / LONDON

Library of Congress Cataloging-in-Publication Data

ISBN 0-7923-5025-1

Published by Kluwer Academic Publishers,
P.O. Box 17, 3300 AA Dordrecht, The Netherlands.

Sold and distributed in North, Central and South America
by Kluwer Academic Publishers,
101 Philip Drive, Norwell, MA 02061, U.S.A.

In all other countries, sold and distributed
by Kluwer Academic Publishers,
P.O. Box 322, 3300 AH Dordrecht, The Netherlands.

Printed on acid-free paper

Printed in the Netherlands.

TABLE OF CONTENTS

IV-Star forming regions and Interstellar medium

V-Extragalactic

VI-Miscellaneous

FOREWORD

Thirty years after the pioneering enterprise of Neugebauer and collaborators, the astronomical sky is surveyed anew in the near infrared range with a gain in sensitivity greater than 4 orders of magnitude. Data have started to come through the "pipelines" routinely and at the turn of the century, the astronomical community will be provided with immense databases that will eventually contain accurate positions and 3- colour (or even 4-colour after merging DENIS and 2MASS data) photometry for hundreds million of stars and millions of galaxies.

This fantastic harvest of data will eventually result of the huge effort that has been deployed on both sides of the Antlantic to promote 2 major projects, 2MASS and DENIS.

The basic aim of this 3rd Euroconference (and last in the series), was to put in close contact the scientific teams of 2MASS and DENIS in order to present and discuss the first significant results of the two surveys and to start promoting possible future plans of collaboration. It was preceded by a workshop, with a smaller attendance, sponsored by a NSF-CNRS action, that was dedicated to the technical aspects of the data processing and database implementation and management. The Euroconference itself, although short (2 days) has been rather dense and animated, and real advances in various fields were presented that promise a final great success.

After several months of operations in *proto-phase* or in routine phase, and having archived a good deal of data, we are now in a better position to start answering some of the key questions that were addressed at the beginning of the projects. What are we going to learn with the 2 micron survey data ? What will be the size of the final catalogues (stars and galaxies)? How homogeneous, complete, and reliable will they be ? What are the most appropriate algorithms for image processing, source extraction, star/galaxy separation, photometric calibration of point sources and low surface brightness objects. Finally, how to manage to the best the astrophysical exploitation and follow–up of the surveys, while 8–10 meter class telescopes are flourishing around the world, while ISO is about to end up

after a very successful mission, and while future space missions such as
SIRTF are in preparation phase. Some answers are extremely exciting. We
will eventually find hundreds of brown dwarfs and thousands of very low
mass stars, improve the local luminosity function and several basic parameters of the galactic structure, probe the stellar populations of the Magellanic
clouds and of the bulge. The largest photometric catalog of galaxies will be
produced, superseding in reliability and photometric accuracy the catalogs
based on digitised photographic material. This will lead to unprecedented
statistical works on the local structure of the Universe and the census of
galaxies in the zone of avoidance, just to cite a few exemples.

   This conference has, indeed, been very fruitful in exchanging information between the American and European teams. It has been also a good
opportunity to compare our working technics and methods, and to note
that the European Science needs to be better organised to manage middle–
size projects that are not fully sponsored by official institutions such as
ESO.

   The European Commission (DGXII) that supported this cycle of EU-
ROCONFERENCE and the early phase of DENIS is thanked for its in-
valuable contribution. I sincerely regret that it did not pursue its support
while the programme is entering its active phase of scientific exploitation.

   It is a great pleasure for me to warmly thank all the participants to this
conference, the Scientific and Local Organising Committees, and especially
those who have presented excellent talks and provided me with outstanding written contributions. I am also greatly indebted to Eric Copet, Chris-
tine Denis, Constance Imad, Jacqueline Thouvay, Jean–Jacques Poisot and
Suzanne Berton, from Observatoire de Paris and Josette Schmidt from Institut d'Astrophysique de Paris for the fine organisation of the logistics of
the conference sessions and dinner.

   Finally, I thank Alain Omont for having taken the responsibility of this
cycle of EUROCONFERENCE during the last 3 years.

                                    Nicolas Epchtein

LIST OF PARTICIPANTS

Alard, Christophe *alard@iap.fr*	Observatoire de Paris, DASGAL	France
Alvarez, Pedro *alvarez@graal.univ-montp2.fr*	GRAAL Montpellier	France
Bartlett, James *bartlett@cdsxb6.u-strasbg.fr*	Observatoire de Strasbourg	France
Barucci, Maria-Antonella *barucci@obspm.fr*	Observatoire de Paris, DESPA	France
de Batz, Bertrand *debatz@obspm.fr*	Observatoire de Paris, DASGAL	France
Baudrand, Anne *baudrand@obspm.fr*	Bureau des Longitudes, Paris	France
Becker, Robert *bob@igpp.llnl.gov*	University of California-Davis	USA
Berend, Zsolt *berend@ogyalla.konkoly.hu*	Konkoly Observatory, Budapest	Hungary
Bertin, Emmanuel *ebertin@eso.org*	ESO, Garching	Germany
Bienaymé, Olivier *bienayme@ cdsxb6.u-strasbg.fr*	Observatoire de Strasbourg	France
Cambrésy, Laurent *cambresy@obspm.fr*	Observatoire de Paris, DESPA	France
Carpenter, John M. *carp@pegasus.ifa.hawai.edu*	University of Hawaï	USA
Copet, Eric *copet@obspm.fr*	Observatoire de Paris, DESPA	France
Cioni, Maria-Rosa *cioni@strw.leidenuniv.nl*	Sterrewacht Leiden	The Netherlands
Cornelisse,Remon *cornelisse@ strw.leidenuniv.nl*	Sterrewacht Leiden	The Netherlands
Cutri, Roc *roc@ipac.caltech.edu*	IPAC/CALTECH	USA
Delfosse, Xavier *delfosse@gag.observ-gr.fr*	Observatoire de Grenoble	France
Deul, Erik *deul@strw.leidenuniv.nl*	Sterrewacht Leiden	The Netherlands
Epchtein, Nicolas *epchtein@obspm.fr*	Observatoire de Paris, DESPA	France
Forveille, Thierry *forveille@gag.observ-gr.fr*	Observatoire de Grenoble	France
Garzón, Francisco *fgl@ll.iac.es*	Instituto de Astrofisica de Canarias	Spain
Gonzalez-Solares, Eduardo *eglez@ll.iac.es*	Instituto de Astrofisica de Canarias	Spain
Groenewegen, Martin A.T. *groen@MPA-Garching.MPG.de*	MPI für Astrophysik, Garching	Germany

Hammersley, Peter *plh@iac.es*	Instituto de Astrofisica de Canarias	Spain
Holl, Andras *holl@ogyalla.konkoly.hu*	Konkoly Observatory, Budapest	Hungary
Hron, Josef *hron@astro.ast.univie.ac.at*	Institüt für Astronomie Wien	Austria
Jarrett, Tom H. *jarrett@ipac.caltech.edu*	IPAC/CALTECH	USA
Kimeswenger, Stefan *Stefan.Kimeswenger@uibk.ac.at*	Universität Innsbruck	Austria
Kraan-Korteweg, Renée *kraan@norma.astro.ugto.mx*	Observatoire de Paris, DAEC	France
Lafon, Jean-Pierre *lafon@obspm.fr*	Observatoire de Paris, DASGAL	France
Lopez-Corredoira, Martin *martinlc@iac.es*	Instituto de Astrofisica de Canarias	Spain
Loup, Cécile *cloup@eso.org*	Institut d'Astrophysique de Paris	France
Mamon, Gary A. *gam@iap.fr*	Institut d'Astrophysique de Paris	France
Mobasher, Bahram *b.mobasher@ic.ac.uk*	Imperial College, London	UK
Montmerle, Thierry *montmerle@.cea.fr*	SAp/CEA, Saclay	France
Omont, Alain *omont@iap.fr*	Institut d'Astrophysique de Paris	France
Paturel, Georges *patu@adel.univ-lyon1.fr*	Observatoire de Lyon	France
Price, Stephan *price@plh.af.mil*	Air Force Phillips Lab., Hanscom, Mass.	USA
Rosenberg, Jessica *rosenber@fcrao2.phast.umass.edu*	University of Massachusetts, Amherst	USA
Ruphy, Stéphanie *stephanie.ruphy@larecherche.fr*	Observatoire de Paris, DESPA	France
Schneider, Stephen E. *schneide@wilt.phast.umass.edu*	University of Massachusetts, Amherst	USA
Schultheis, Mathias *schultheis@astro.ast.univie.ac.at*	Institüt für Astronomie Wien,	Austria
Simon, Guy *Guy.Simon@obspm.fr*	Observatoire de Paris, DASGAL	France
Skrutskie, Michael *skrutski@north.phast.umass.edu*	University of Massachusetts, Amherst	USA
Unavane, Mukund *munavane@ast.cam.ac.uk*	IoA, Cambridge	UK
Van Driel, Willem *vandriel@mesioq.obspm.fr*	Observatoire de Paris, Nançay	France
Van Eck, Sophie *svaneck@astro.ulb.ac.be*	Inst. Astron. Astrophys., Bruxelles	Belgique
Vauglin, Isabelle *isa@altair.univ-lyon1.fr*	Observatoire de Lyon	France

I- Infrared Survey Status

THE DEEP NEAR INFRARED SURVEY OF THE SOUTHERN SKY (DENIS):

Progress report, and scientific results overview

N.EPCHTEIN
Observatoire de la Côte d'Azur
Département Fresnel, BP 4229, F06304 Nice cedex
and DESPA, Observatoire de Paris

Abstract. I present the status of achievement of DENIS operations and data processing in November 1997, and summarise the main scientific results obtained so far based on the analysis of the first set of observations. Prospects for the coming years are briefly outlined.

1. Introduction

Although 2MASS and DENIS have followed different development plans, they are basically aimed at similar objectives: mapping the all (southern, in the case of DENIS) –sky primarily at 2 micron (filter K_s), and in 2 accompanying wavelengths, Gunn-I and J for DENIS, J and H for 2MASS. This difference in spectral coverage makes each project slightly better adapted to investigate different astrophysical problems. DENIS is better suited to pick up cool isolated red (and brown) dwarfs, while 2MASS is better adapted to probing star forming regions, since highly extinguished objects are generally not detectable in the I band. In addition, the slightly higher sensitivity of 2MASS in K_s, obtained thanks to a larger telescope aperture and a fully cooled instrument, will undoubtedly provide an advantage in the detection of galaxies and low surface brightness objects.

2. Performances of DENIS

The main specifications of DENIS have been described several times (e.g. Epchtein, 1997a; Epchtein, 1997b; Copet 1996; Ruphy 1996) and are just briefly outlined here. The DENIS survey aims at covering the all–southern sky ($-88°$ to $+2°$ of declination) simultaneously in the I, J, K_s bands at

3

N. Epchtein (ed.),
The Impact of Near-Infrared Sky Surveys on Galactic and Extragalactic Astronomy, 3-9.
© 1998 *Kluwer Academic Publishers. Printed in the Netherlands.*

arcsecond resolution using the ESO 1 meter telescope at La Silla, Chile. Mapping of the sky is performed by scanning the telescope along strips of 30° in declination and 12′ wide in RA in a step–and–stare mode. Each elementary image of 12′ × 12′ is acquired in ≈ 10s. The main characteristics and performances are summarised in Table 1.

TABLE 1. DENIS characteristics and performances

Channel	I	J	K_s
Central wavelength			
(μm)	0.8	1.25	2.15
Arrays	CCD Tektronix	NICMOS3	NICMOS3
Size of the arrays	1024×1024	256×256	256×256
Pixel size (*arcsec*)	1	3	3
Exposure time (*second*)	9	10	10
Limiting mag.			
(point source, 3σ)	18.5	16.5	14.0
Saturation (mag.)	9.5	8.5	6.5

Several improvements of the focal instrument have been designed and set up in 1997. The CCD dewar has been replaced by a new one with a much longer hold-time (more than 32 hours), and most importantly, an air-conditioning system of the focal instrument has been installed. The aim of this device is to reduce the thermal emission background of the *warm* optics and thus to improve the sensitivity of the instrument by at least 0.5 magnitude in the K_s band in Summer time. The temperature of the instrument is stabilized around 5°C by blowing a continuous flow of dry and cool air in an envelope encompassing the whole focal box (Fig 1). The thermal background emission is now independent of the variations of the room temperature. Background emission is reduced by a factor of ≈ 2 with respect to the former worse conditions. The homogeneity of the survey has now considerably improved.

3. Present status of the observations

Since the beginning of the operations, more than 2000 strips have been scanned and reduced, covering about 30 % of the objective. Fig 2 shows the progression of the survey during the first 18 months of operations. The large plateau in southern Winter 1997 corresponds to the interruption of the survey caused by the mechanical modifications described above and a period of particularly bad meteorological conditions. Not all the data are

Figure 1. The DENIS instrument in its new thermalization envelope

good enough to pass the quality criteria and it is expected that a fraction of the strips will have to be reobserved.

4. Status of the Data Processing

The data processing is performed routinely in the 2 data analysis centres (DACs) at Paris (PDAC) and Leiden (LDAC), according to the data stream displayed in Fig. 4 of Epchtein (1997a). The description of the pipelines has been detailed in the previous *Euroconferences* by Borsenberger (1997) and Deul *et al.* (1995) and are not repeated here. Most of the images taken during the *protosurvey* period and the first year and half of operations have been processed, archived, and delivered to LDAC for source extraction. Information concerning the DENIS database status at PDAC can be retrieved

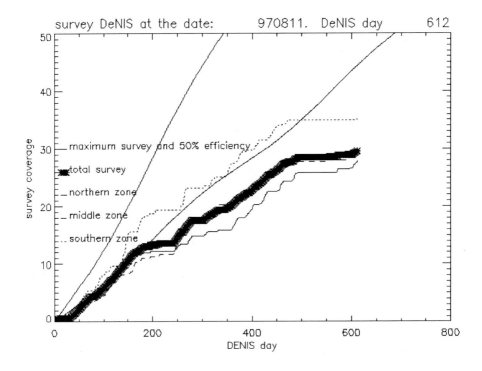

Figure 2.   Status of the observations in August 1997(from P. Fouqué)

on the website:

`http://www-denis.iap.fr`

At this time are available, the database containing the history of the observations, (called *FOURBI*) and several utilitary routines that allow, for instance, to check if a given area of the sky has been surveyed and where the relevant data are stored. Access to the database is provisionally restricted to DENIS consortium members, but will be opened soon for general release. Image data are stored in a jukebox of 52 DLTs which contain more than 1000 Gbytes of data (some 25 % of the southern sky).

LDAC has started to perform routinely source extraction and calibration only since September 1997, and a still limited number of strips (a hundred or so as of Nov. 1997) have been processed. Lists of sources per strip can be sorted out (with the same access restriction as for PDAC) at the following web address:

`http://www.strw.leidenuniv.nl/denis/index.html`

5. Science with DENIS, an overview

This Euroconference is essentially dedicated to presenting the scientific analysis of the first data sets of the 2–micron surveys, and the purpose of this book is to summarize these first results, and to try to prepare the best exploitation and follow–up observations of the huge amount of new data soon to come. The main areas in which significant results have been obtained so far are the regions of star formation, the galactic structure, the low mass stars and brown dwarfs and the galaxies. In this section, I briefly mention some of the most prohemINENT results obtained with DENIS and refer to papers included in the present book for further details.

5.1. STAR FORMING REGIONS

The near-infrared range is one of the most appropriate to detect young stellar objects inside or close to their parental molecular cloud and to derive the luminosity function, as well as the variations of the dust extinction (see Carpenter in this volume). For the first time, square degrees of regions of intense stellar formation activity such as the Orion, Chameleon and ρ Ophiuchus molecular clouds are mapped in this spectral range providing panoramic overviews and very large samples of YSO candidates that will lead to improve the initial luminosity and mass functions, as well as the possible variations of the star forming rate within the cloud.

A DENIS/ISO collaboration has begun which is aimed at exploring the most nearby regions of star formation. Persi et al. (this volume) present the first cross–identified ISOCAM/DENIS data in the Chameleon I cloud. Cambrésy (this volume) analysing the J counts across the Chameleon cloud made a detailed mapping of the extinction in this region and has discovered a number of new faint YSOs, that are likely to be classical T Tau candidates (Cambrésy et al., 1998).

5.2. STAR COUNTS AND GALACTIC STRUCTURE

Massive star counts in the NIR allow exploring the distribution of the stellar populations in highly extinguished regions, and probing the basic parameters that describe the structure of the Milky Way (e.g., Bienaymé, this volume; Robin, 1997). The immense gain with respect to optical surveys is a consequence of the good transparency of the interstellar dust at 2 μm, that allows to unveil hidden populations of the Galactic disc and bulge.

The combination of the DENIS near–IR and mid–IR observation provided by ISO (7 and 15 μm) in the framework of the ISOGAL survey (Omont et al., this volume) allows a good discrimination between the var-

ious species of objects, and in particular easily breaks out AGB stars and YSOs.

Ruphy (1996), using the first release of DENIS data has studied the galactic anticentre direction and analysed strips in these directions. Althouh, in most directions, infrared star counts and models (Robin, 1997; Cohen, 1997 and ref. therein) of stellar populations are in good agreement, toward the anticentre there are significant discrepancies with all models. There are fewer stars observed than the models predict (Ruphy et al.,1996). Moreover, colour diagrams have been used to attempt to separate giant and dwarf populations. An excellent separation is obtained at low latitudes. Based on a comparison between DENIS star counts and models, new revised values of the scale length of the late type giant stars and of the cut–off distance of the Galaxy have been derived and an investigation on the stellar content and shape of the ring at 4 kpc has been initiated (Ruphy et al., 1997).

A full coverage of the Magellanic Clouds is essentially completed that will lead to the construction of an exhaustive catalogue of mass–losing AGB stars and allow an easy discrimination between their various species (Carbon/Oxygen rich star separation) (see Loup et al., this conference)

5.3. RED AND BROWN DWARFS

One of the most spectacular results of DENIS in 1997 has been the discovery of the first isolated brown dwarf (see Forveille et al., this volume). This exciting result, based on the analysis of about 1 % of the DENIS data, is extremely promising for the future, since hundreds of brown dwarfs and thousands of M dwarfs later that M7 will come out of DENIS (and 2MASS). After the completion of the surveys, the first statistically significant catalog of nearby late red dwarfs and brown dwarfs will be available and will usefully complete the former catalogs towards the low end of the luminosity fcunction. The cross–identification of the DENIS and 2MASS observations made at different epochs will be useful to measure large proper motions.

6. Extragalactic

Analyses of the first DENIS and 2MASS data show that the 2 surveys will have a considerable impact on statistical extragalactic atstronomy thanks to the production of huge complete and reliable catalogs providing linear photometry. This last point is obviously a great advantage compared to catalogs based on digitized photographic plate catalogs such as APM or COSMSOS. Clearly, 2MASS thanks to a better sensitivity in K_s, a better homogeneity of the PSF across the frame, and a larger sky surface coverage will produce a much larger K_s catalog of galaxies than DENIS will do (more

than 1 million in the all-sky compared to a few tens of thousands in the Southern Sky). One advantage of DENIS, however, is its very sensitive I channel with a 1 arcsec resolution which makes easier the star/galaxy separation. A million galaxies are expected in that band.

7. The future

There is no doubt that the case for a 2-micron all sky survey that were made out almost ten years ago to support the project were good. Most of the objectives will be reached. In the coming years, we will be provided with the largest photometric and astrometric star catalog (one billion star with position better than 1 arcsec and photometry better than 10 %) ever produced, and a large, homogeneous and reliable catalog of galaxies . An unbiased sample of hundreds of brown dwarfs will be probably available for the first time, several large molecular clouds will reveal all their content of relatively young embedded objects (surveys at longer wavelengths, partly done by ISO will be necessary to pick up even younger objects). It is worth mentionning that this extraordinary harvest of data will have been obtained with really little money and small (old–fashion for DENIS) telescopes. I do hope that for the maximum benefit of both surveys, their databases will be easily interconnected, and look forward to prepare the next all–sky survey in the still uncovered spectral domain that spans between 2 and 10 microns.

References

Cambrésy L., Epchtein N., Copet E., de Batz B., Kimeswenger S., Le Bertre T., Rouan D., Tiphène D. (1996) A&A, **Vol. no. 265**, pp. 145–332
Cambrésy L., Copet E., Epchtein N. (1998) A&A, in press
Borsenberger J., (1997), Proc. of the 2nd Euroconference on *The impact of Large Scale near-infrared sky surveys*, Puerto de la Cruz, Spain, eds. F. Garzon, N. Epchtein, A. Omont, W.B. Burton, P. Persi, Kluwer ASSL series **vol. no. 210**, pp 181–186
Deul E. (+17 authors) (1995) Proc. 1 st Euroconference on *Near-Infrared Sky Surveys*, San Miniato, Italy in *Mem. Soc. Astron. Ital.* **vol. no. 66**, pp 549–566
Copet E., (1996) *Thèse de Doctorat, Université de Paris 6,*
Epchtein N. (+ 47 authors)(1997a) *The Messenger*, **Vol. no. 87**, pp. 27–34
Epchtein N. (1997b) Proc. of the 2nd Euroconference on *The impact of Large Scale near-infrared sky surveys*, Puerto de la Cruz, Spain, eds. F. Garzon, N. Epchtein, A. Omont, W.B. Burton, P. Persi, Kluwer ASSL series **vol. no. 210**, pp 15–24
Robin A.(1997) Proc. of the 2nd Euroconference on *The impact of Large Scale near-infrared sky surveys*, Puerto de la Cruz, Spain, eds. F. Garzon, N. Epchtein, A. Omont, W.B. Burton, P. Persi, Kluwer ASSL series **vol. no. 210**, pp 57–61
Ruphy S. (1996) *Thèse de Doctorat, Université de Paris 6,*
Ruphy S., Robin A.C., Epchtein N., Copet E., Bertin E.,Fouqué P. , Guglielmo F. (1996) A&A, **Vol. no. 313**, pp. L21–L24
Ruphy S., Epchtein N., Cohen M., Copet E., de Batz B., Borsenberger J., Fouqué P., Kimeswenger S., Lacombe F., Le Bertre T., Rouan D., Tiphène D., (1997) A&A, **Vol. no. 326**, pp. 597–607

THE TWO MICRON ALL SKY SURVEY (2MASS): STATUS REPORT NOVEMBER 1997

M.F. SKRUTSKIE

University of Massachusetts
Department of Physics and Astronomy
Box 3-4525, Amherst, MA 01003

Abstract. The Two Micron All Sky Survey (2MASS) began regular survey observations at the Northern Hemisphere 2MASS facility at Mt. Hopkins, Arizona in June 1997. At the time of this writing approximately 10% of the entire sky has been observed. The Southern Hemisphere facility at Cerro Tololo is scheduled to begin taking data in February 1998. 2MASS hopes to release its first increment of data to the community in the first half of 1999.

1. Introduction

The Two Micron All Sky survey will map the entire celestial sphere in the near-infrared J ($1.13 - 1.37\mu$m), H ($1.50 - 1.80\mu$m), and K_s ($2.00 - 2.32\mu$m) bands through the year 2000. Table 1 summarizes the general survey characteristics. One survey facility, which includes a dedicated 1.3m telescope and a three-color infrared camera, began full operations at Mt. Hopkins, Arizona in June 1997. A second facility will come on line in the Southern Hemisphere at Cerro Tololo, Chile in early 1998. On a typical night one of these telescopes automatically observes approximately 60 square degrees of survey area, calibrating once an hour throughout the night. The Infrared Processing and Analysis Center (IPAC) has developed the 2MASS Production Processing System which, running on a Sun Enterprise server, can process an entire night's data to photometrically and astrometrically calibrated point and extended source lists and finished Atlas Images in less than 24 hours. The prototype version of this pipeline currently monitors observatory and camera health and has demonstrated that the survey requirements outlined in Table 1 can be met. IPAC is currently developing the final production version of the pipeline which will begin operating in

11

N. Epchtein (ed.),
The Impact of Near-Infrared Sky Surveys on Galactic and Extragalactic Astronomy, 11-15.
© 1998 *Kluwer Academic Publishers. Printed in the Netherlands.*

early 1998. The production pipeline will generate the initial 2MASS data catalogs and images which are targeted for general release in the first half of 1999. 2MASS plans to release data incrementally throughout the life of the survey, typically within 12-18 months of the date of observation. At the completion of survey operations in the year 2000 all data will be fully reprocessed to produce a final uniform set of catalogs and images. The final 2MASS point source catalog, which will have a data volume of ~300GBy, will contain approximately 300 million entries. The 2MASS extended source catalog will consist of an extended source list containing about 1 million entries (100 MBy) and postage stamp images of all extended sources (10 Gby). Finally, 2MASS will produce an image atlas (1″ pixels) of the entire sky. The uncompressed full resolution image data will span 14 Tby. A more manageable ~20-times lossy compressed version of the images will be available for general distribution.

TABLE 1. 2MASS Characteristics

Property	Requirement
Arrays	256×256 NICMOS3 (HgCdTe)
Pixel Size	2.0″
Wavebands	J, H, and K_s (2.00 – 2.32μm)
Telescopes	1.3-meter Equatorial Cassegrain
Integration time	6 × 1.3s/frame = 7.8s total
Sensitivity (3σ)	17.1, 16.4, 15.6 mag for J, H, and K_s
Photometric Accuracy	5% for bright sources
Photometric Uniformity	4% over the sky
Positional Accuracy	0.5″
Completeness / Reliability at 10σ	0.99 / 0.9995

The 2MASS observing hardware has been described in other contributions (Skrutskie *et al.* 1997, Milligan *et al.* 1996). Current details about the project's hardware/software development and status are available at the project's websites -
http://pegasus.phast.umass.edu/ and
http://www.ipac.caltech.edu/2mass/
This contribution focuses on the project's sky coverage and planned data releases during the survey lifetime. Since the sky coverage proceeds in a systematic fashion one can approximate the portion of sky which will be released as a function of time.

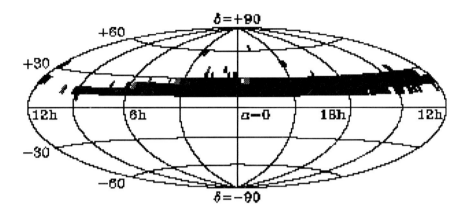

Figure 1.   2MASS Northern Hemisphere sky coverage through November 21, 1997 in equatorial coordinates.

2. Observing Strategy/Schedule

Figures 1 and 2 show the 2MASS sky coverage as of November 21, 1997. Only the Northern Hemisphere facility was in operation during this period. Northern Hemisphere sky coverage begins at $+12°$ declination and progresses northward during the lifetime of the survey. The boundary between hemispheres is located at $\delta = +12°$ because weather statistics suggest that sky coverage will be more efficient from the Southern Hemisphere.

The fundamental unit of 2MASS coverage is the $6°$ by $8.5'$ tile. Approximately 60,000 tiles cover the entire sky. Scheduling software at the telescope automates and optimizes the selection of tiles. Tiles must be within 0.2 airmasses of the transit airmass to be candidates for observation. Priority is assigned on the basis of available observing time in the future which largely dictates the strategy of progressing from equator to pole. The Northern hemisphere survey began by mapping the $+12$-$18°$ declination band. When no more tiles were available at a given time of night the survey scheduler began covering the $+18$-$24°$ declination band. Figure 1 reflects the coverage obtained in June through October. The Northern Hemisphere facility does not operate in August due to the Arizona summer monsoon. The coverage map represents all observations obtained to date. Some fraction (probably 30 to 50%) of these observations will be scheduled for repeat coverage

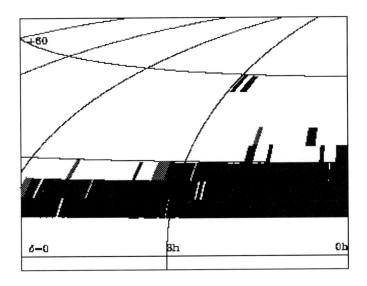

Figure 2. A magnified view of one equatorial quadrant showing detail at the level of individual 2MASS tiles.

because of poor photometric, airglow, or seeing conditions.

3. Calibration Strategy

2MASS calibration tiles are observed at one hour intervals throughout the night. Calibration observations begin and end the night. Calibration data is obtained in the same manner as regular survey data with the exception that calibration tiles are 1 degree in length rather than 6 degrees long. Each calibration tile is repeatedly observed 6 times during a calibration observation. Since each calibration tile yields 6 apparitions of the star, a single calibration series produces 36 apparitions of all of the stars in the 1-degree by 8.5-arcminute region. The majority of the calibration tiles contain a classical calibration standard, most of which were measured for the NICMOS standards program. Ultimately 2MASS will to internally calibrate the survey using all of the hundreds of stars which appear in each of these calibration strips.

Adjacent 2MASS survey tiles overlap their neighbors by 10% in right ascension. The survey scheduling software makes every effort to obtain tiles in contiguous blocks so that the comparison of photometry in the overlapping regions provides an additional test of photometric quality. At high galactic latitudes the number of stars in this overlap region will be suffi-

cient to photometrically register adjacent strips to 0.01 magnitude. Global reprocessing of the survey data at the completion of operations will include an effort to internally photometrically register all of the survey data using these redundant observations.

4. Data Products

IPAC will begin production processing of the survey data taken to date (1.5 Terabytes at the time of this writing) in early 1998. The 2MASS project aims to distribute the first incremental release of survey data in mid-1999. The exact format and and volume of this release are still under discussion, but the project will aim to make these preliminary data products – point and extended source catalogs and images – largely resemble the final release products. Given the scheduled survey coverage, this first release should largely come from the declination range +12-24° in a band which completely circles the sky and thus covers a full range of galactic and extragalactic environments. The release may include some southern hemisphere data depending on the timing of the commissioning of that facility. The first sky coverage in the "southern" hemisphere will be the +6-12° declination band.

References

Milligan, S., Cranton, Brian W., Skrutskie, Michael F. 1996, "Development of a three-channel SWIR camera, for ground-based astronomical imaging", Proceedings of the SPIE, **2863**, pp 2-13.

Skrutskie, M.F., *et al.* 1997, in "The Impact of Large Scale Near-IR Sky Surveys," F. Garzon et al. (eds.), Kluwer (Netherlands), pp 25-32.

MIDCOURSE SPACE EXPERIMENT SURVEYS

STEPHAN D. PRICE, MICHAEL P. EGAN AND RUSSELL F. SHIPMAN
Air Force Phillips Laboratory
Geophysics Directorate/GPOB
29 Randolph Rd.
Hanscom AFB, MA 01731-3010
USA

MARTIN COHEN
Radio Astronomy Laboratory
University of California at Berkeley
Berkeley, CA 94720
USA

AND

MEHRDAD MOSHIR
IPAC
California Institute of Technology
MS 100-22
Pasadena, CA 91125
USA

Abstract. The Midcourse Space Experiment (MSX) conducted several infrared surveys during its 10 month mission which began in April 1996. We report on the progress in the analysis of these survey observations with an initial estimate of the instrument performance parameters. Initial results indicate that the surveys are at least as sensitive as the Infrared Astronomy Satellite (IRAS) survey, and have higher spatial resolution.

1. Introduction

The Midcourse Space Experiment (MSX) surveyed the entire Galactic Plane to a latitude of $\pm 5°$. In addition to the survey scans, raster scan observations toward selected directions probed Galactic structure more deeply.

N. Epchtein (ed.),
The Impact of Near-Infrared Sky Surveys on Galactic and Extragalactic Astronomy, 17-27.
© *1998 Kluwer Academic Publishers. Printed in the Netherlands.*

Band	Isophotal λ (μm)	λ (μm) 50% peak Intensity	Isophotal BW $\Delta\lambda(\mu m)$	0 mag flux (Jy)	Absolute Phot. Accuracy	Point Source Survey Sensitivity (Jy)
A	8.28	6.8 - 10.8	3.36	58.55	8%	0.1 - 0.2 - 0.4
B_1	4.29	4.22 - 4.36	0.104	194.5	12%	2.0 - 4.0 - 8.0
B_2	4.25	4.24 - 4.45	0.179	188.8	13%	2.5 - 4.0 - 8.0
C	12.13	11.1 - 13.2	1.72	26.51	5%	0.15 - 0.3 - 0.6
D	14.65	13.5 - 15.9	2.23	18.29	5%	0.1 - 0.2 - 0.4
E	21.41	18.2 - 25.1	6.34	8.75	13%	0.4 - 0.7 - 1.2

TABLE 1. SPIRIT III Spectral Bands

MSX also surveyed the sky not covered by IRAS both the inertial gaps and the zodiacal background.

1.1. INSTRUMENT

The infrared telescope on MSX is an off-axis, aspheric re-imaging optical system with an unobscured primary aperture of about 33 cm diameter. The five line-scanned focal plane arrays each consist of 8 in-scan columns and 192 cross-scan rows of detectors (pixels). (Band B has two slightly different narrow band filters, one spanning the upper half of the array, the other the lower.) Each detector is approximately square and is about 18.3" in extent. Four of the columns are offset in cross-scan with respect to the other four, providing critical (Nyquist) sampling in cross-scan for a single observation. To reduce telemetry requirements only half the columns are active. (All eight columns in band A, two on either side of the stagger in bands C and D, and two staggered columns in bands B and D.) Table 1 lists the band designation, the wavelength at half peak response, the isophotal wavelengths and bandwidths. The source function in the isophotal calculations is the Kurucz model Vega spectrum in Cohen et al. (1992); MSX used the Vega and Sirius spectrum in this article plus the calibrated spectra of the six additional standards published by Cohen et al. (1995) for in-flight calibration.

The MSX photometric bands have several major astronomically relevant properties. Bands B and D are centered on the 4.2 and 15 μm CO_2 atmospheric features; besides MSX, only the ISO camera is currently capable of doing photometry at these wavelengths. Band A is the most sensitive (having all 8 columns active) and covers a spectral region not previously well surveyed. Band C is a narrower analog of the IRAS 12 μm filter and the COBE/DIRBE band 5. Band E is a good analog of the COBE/DIRBE

band 6, which is commonly taken as a comparison with the IRAS 25 μm band.

Owing to the diverse experimental objectives, MSX operations bear little resemblance to typical space-based astronomy missions such as IRAS or ISO. For a variety of reasons (see Mill et al., 1994) data acquisition was limited for infrared observations to 2-2.5 hours a day for a duty cycle of about 10%. Other spacecraft constraints limited continuous infrared observations to 36 minutes or less. Furthermore, observations were routinely made against the hard Earth. Thus, the astronomy observations were subject to the tail end of start up transients and small temperature variations from the thermal pulses caused by the Earth looking observations. These short term thermal variations were superimposed on a systematic increase in the operational temperature of the system as the solid hydrogen in the cryostat sublimed away from the thermal straps.

In spite of the dynamic state of the telescope, the uncertainties quoted in Table 1 are conservative. Three independent means of calibrating the instrument were used: a ground calibration in a vacuum chamber with sources which were well quantified and traceable to NIST standards; stellar standards; and well characterized black emissive reference spheres ejected from the MSX spacecraft. More than half of the on-orbit observations were in support of calibration and performance assessment experiments used to quantify the photometry as a function of instrument parameters. The conservative absolute photometric accuracies listed in Table 1 contain a few percent bias between calibrations and the estimated error in transferring the high signal to noise calibrations throughout the dynamic range of the sensor. The latter dominates the uncertainty. These uncertainties will be reduced within the next year by a global calibration which cross-ties the three methods and extends the calibration over the entire dynamic range. Relative accuracy, or the agreement of repeated observations on a source, is 2-3%. This is consistent with the fact the response of the pixels are uniform within 5% across an array.

1.2. EXPERIMENTS

The basic surveys were composed of scans between 130° and 180° in length, nominally at a scan rate of 0.125 deg/sec. The combination of scan rate, pixel size and the 72 sample/sec telemetry rate yields 2.8 samples/dwell. The scan rate was decreased somewhat toward the end of the cryogen life to partially compensate for the increase in dark current noise as the focal plane temperatures rose. In addition to the long scans, fifteen raster scans were made at various locations in the Galactic plane in the inner Galaxy and one in the anticenter direction.

The scan pattern was tailored for the objectives of each of the surveys. The Galactic plane was covered by 75 scans in longitude at constant latitude. The first survey began at the Galactic plane with subsequent scans offset by increments of 0.45° in latitude. This pattern produces a single survey in each of the B bands and redundant coverage in remaining bands. A second set of scans was interleaved with the first survey to provide four pass redundancy. There was inadequate time to complete the overlapping survey scans so quadruple coverage in the first and fourth quadrants is missing two of scans at $> +4°$ latitude and extends to $|b| < 3°$ in the second and third quadrants. Similarly, four pass redundancy was obtained by 64 scans over the two IRAS gaps. The geometry used to survey the IRAS gaps was that of a defined rotation pole, a zenith angle and azimuth limits; the scans were roughly along ecliptic longitude. The 64 scans required to cover the gaps four times spanned a range of sun centered longitudes from 60° to 173° . To this are added five ecliptic pole to pole scans spanning sun centered longitudes 25° to 30°, providing global observations of the zodiacal emission.

The raster scans of selected regions along the Galactic plane consisted of 21-25 legs, each spanning approximately 3° in latitude, centered at constant longitude, with a scan rate of 0.05 deg/sec. Successive raster legs were offset by a quarter to a third of a pixel. The longer dwell time and redundancy increases the sensitivity by about a factor of about eight compares to the survey scans. Alternatively, one could take advantage of the oversampling and use image enhancement techniques to resolve sources in those regions where even MSX is confused. The observations from the deep raster scans will be used to provide truth tables to assess completeness and reliability of the larger area survey.

1.3. DATA PROCESSING

One of the primary data products from the survey will be the point source catalog. For point source identification and parameter estimation, a two dimensional source extraction algorithm is used because the point response functions have about the same support in both cross-scan and in-scan. Since dark current subtraction errors and other sources of pattern noise are correlated in-scan more than cross-scan, a form of pseudo-median estimator was used to filter the data stream for each pixel. An average of the cascaded MINIMAX and MAXIMIN operators, $\frac{1}{2}[MINIMAX(MAXIMIN\{S_L\})+ MAXIMIN(MINIMAX\{S_L\})]$ where S_L is the data in the window around the current point (see Pratt 1991), separates point sources from the background. This filter was chosen because it not only eliminates the striping from dark current subtraction residuals and other pattern noise in the data

but also because it has superior characteristics in crowded regions and at inflection in the data. As with all (pseudo-) median filters, low amplitude (SNR ≤ 3) sources are biased by a small amount (5-8%) to lower values.

Two data streams resulting from the filtering (low frequency background, and high frequency, containing point sources). The background data is averaged into $0.25°$ square pixels and written to a file which provides the basis for analyzing the zodiacal background and the emission from interstellar dust along the galactic plane without the bias of point sources. The high frequency data is processed to extract the point sources .

The point source data is first convolved with a model of the point response function (PRF), a B_3 or cubic B-spline with the same full width at half maximum (FWHM) as the measured PRF. This model is used rather than the position dependent PRF to increase computational speed for the search step. The convolution almost realizes the visibility gain of matched tuned filtering of the data with the system response to a point source . The visibility is the co-add increase in signal to noise ratio (SNR) over that from the single sample. Dead and anomalous pixels (<5% of the total of 3840 pixels) are removed as a first step which make the visibility a weak function of cross-scan position. Potential sources have amplitudes of 4.5 times the noise after filtering, which equates to a SNR of 2.7 for the final extracted point sources, which do not have the matched-filter gain. The flux and position of each potential source are determined using a three parameter simultaneous χ^2 minimization of the data and a point source model, as follows:

$$\chi^2 = \sum_{i=1}^{N} \left[\frac{\rho_i - \sum_{k=1}^{M} f_k H(x_i - \xi_k, y_i - \eta_k)}{\sigma_i} \right]^2 .$$

Here ρ_i is the data value at point i while (x_i, y_i) is the detector position and σ_i^2 is the variance of the noise in the data (detector and Poisson). The data model consists of M point sources of flux and position f_k, (ξ_k, η_k) convolved with the PRF, H. The PRF is band dependent and has been determined on orbit. (The initial results presented in the next section use an averaged PRF for each band. The next step is to include the position dependent PRFs.).

2. Results

2.1. POINT SOURCES

This section constitutes a progress report which provides the realistic estimates of the survey sensitivities which appear in Table 1. Figures 1 through

STEPHAN D. PRICE ET AL.

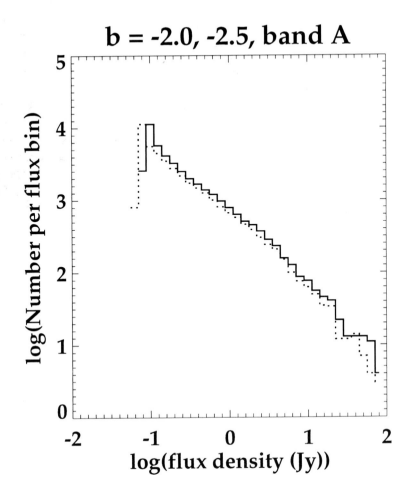

Figure 1. dLog N vs log F histogram of point sources extracted from MSX band A data. The solid line plots the data for the 180° long scan centered on b = -2.0°, while the dotted line shows results for the scan centered at b = -2.5°. The flux cutoffs are 96 and 80 mJy, respectively.

5 show the dLog N vs. Log F plots in dLog F increments of 0.1 for each of the radiometer bands in two first-fourth quadrant scans at b = -2.00° and -2.5°. These scans form the basis of our early analysis and estimation of the survey performance. At these latitudes, the complex background from interstellar dust is considerably reduced compared to the scan at b = 0. Also, these scans avoid the highest source density regions so an estimate of the performance can be obtained from the source distribution plots without the added complication of confusion.

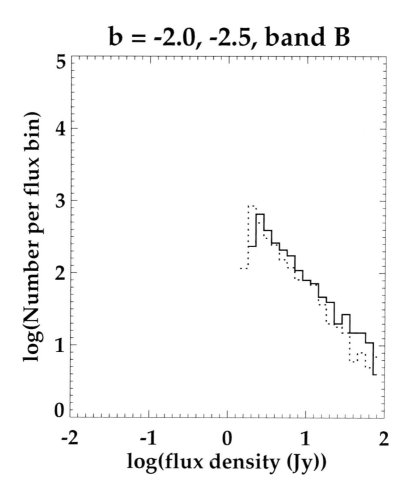

Figure 2. dLog N vs log F histogram of point sources extracted from MSX band B data. The solid line plots the data for the 180° long scan centered on b = -2.0°, while the dotted line shows results for the scan centered at b = -2.5°. The flux cutoffs are 2.0 and 2.4 Jy, respectively.

The turnover in each Figure is defined by the SNR criterion. However, spurious sources evidently increase the number of objects in the last one or two flux bins well marking the statistical limit for real sources. Note, that the flux at the limits are underestimated by 5-8% as the background filter bias has not been removed in these plots. Anomalous pixels have been removed from the process which by definition includes those with response is greater than 5% of the mean. Therefore, the SNR cutoff is a good representative for an absolute cutoff in flux. Note that in all cases

the cutoff for the later scan (taken 5 September 1996) is at about 20% higher flux than the earlier scan (taken 19 July). This reflects the increase in dark current noise as the focal plane temperature gradually rose as the solid hydrogen cryogen sublimed away. The first and second flux limits for extracted sources in Table 1 are representative for the beginning and end of the first and fourth Galactic quadrant survey and for the IRAS gap at ~342° ecliptic longitude. The highest flux limit in Table 1 is for the highest noise levels observed during the surveys of anti-center region and the IRAS gap at ecliptic longitude ~162° .

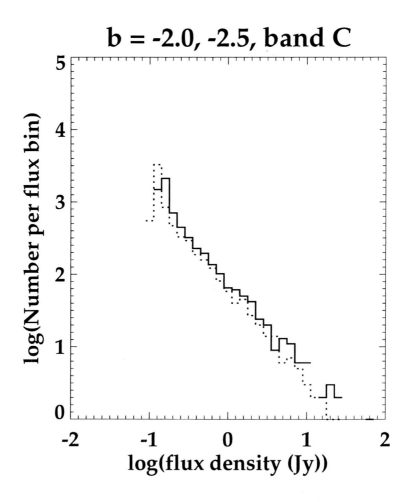

Figure 3. dLog N vs log F histogram of point sources extracted from MSX band C data. The solid line plots the data for the 180° long scan centered on b = -2.0°, while the dotted line shows results for the scan centered at b = -2.5°. The flux cutoffs are 150 and 120 mJy, respectively.

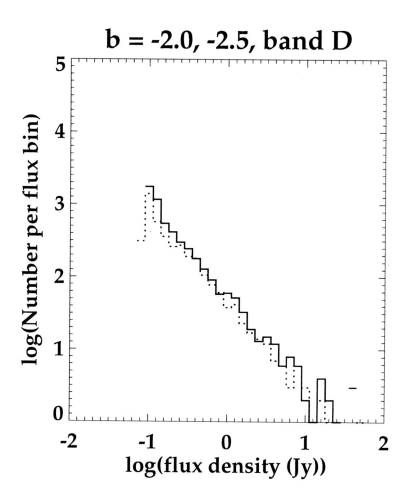

Figure 4.   dLog N vs log F histogram of point sources extracted from MSX band D data. The solid line plots the data for the 180° long scan centered on b = -2.0°, while the dotted line shows results for the scan centered at b = -2.5°. The flux cutoffs are 100 and 110 mJy, respectively.

The MSX survey of the inner Galaxy is about as sensitive in Bands C and E as the IRAS instrumental limits at 12 and 25 μm , Band A is about 4 times more sensitive. Thus, one of the original goals of the astronomical experiments on MSX will be realized: to complete the census of the mid-infrared sky to the IRAS flux limits. The MSX point response is about 30 times smaller than those in the IRAS 12 and 25 μm bands. Consequently, MSX can probe 3 to 5.5 times more deeply into the IRAS confused areas.

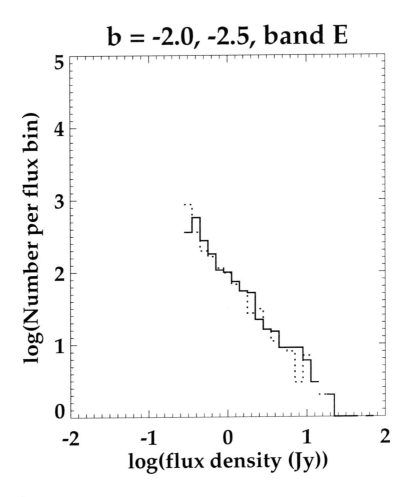

Figure 5.   dLog N vs log F histogram of point sources extracted from MSX band E data. The solid line plots the data for the 180° long scan centered on b = -2.0°, while the dotted line shows results for the scan centered at b = -2.5°. The flux cutoffs are 370 and 320 mJy, respectively.

2.2. IMAGE DATA

In addition to the point source data, image data is produced for every scan. The increased resolution of MSX data over the IRAS data shows that there is highly structured IR emission throughout the galactic plane. Most striking is the complexity of the interstellar dust emission in Band A above a radiance threshold of several MJy/sr. The background in this band is undoubtedly enhanced by the strong 6.6, 7.7 and 8.3 micron PAH/HAC emission features associated with interstellar dust. In addition to the struc-

tured emission, we have found over two thousand dark clouds silhouetted against this bright background within half a degree of the plane (the latitude limits we have searched to date). The clouds are sharp edged, dark (implying large optical depth) and cold ($\leq 10K$ as deduced from the absence of emission in the IRAS bands). The extinction edges of the clouds do not change across the MSX wavebands, which means that the extinction properties of the dust do not change between 7 to 25 μm. This implies that the dust grains are quite large, which is consistent with a very low temperature and grain mantle growth due to freeze-out of molecules onto grains. The clouds appear to be a new population of very cold, dense, molecular cores.

3. Conclusions

The MSX survey data will serve to complete the census of the mid-infrared sky begun by the IRAS satellite. In addition to completing observations in the IRAS gaps, the enhanced resolution of the MSX infrared instrument allows accurate cataloging of stars in the Galactic plane, where the IRAS data products suffered from confusion due to high source density and large detector size. Viewed as images, the MSX data has shown complex extended emission structures along the plane, and reveals a population of cold, dense, cores in the interstellar medium.

References

Cohen, M., Walker, R.G. , Barlow, M.J. and Deacon, J.R. (1992) Spectral Irradiance Calibration in the Infrared. I. Ground-Based and IRAS Broadband Calibration, *Astron. J.*, **Vol. 104**, pp. 1650-1657

Cohen, M., Witteborn, F.C., Walker, R.G., Bregman, J.D., and Wooden, D.H. (1995) Spectral Irradiance Calibration in the Infarared. IV. 1.2-35 μm Spectra of Six Standard Stars, *Astron. J.*, **Vol. 110**, pp. 275-289

Mill, J.D., O Neil, R.R., Price, S., Romick, G.J. , Uy, O.M., Gaposchkin, E.M., Light, G.C. , Moore Jr., W.W. , Murdock, T.M., and Stair jr., A.T. (1994) Midcourse Space Experiment: Introduction to the Spacecraft, Instruments and Scientific Objectives, *J. Spacecraft and Rockets*, **Vol. 31**, pp. 900-907

Pratt, W.K. (1991) *Digital Image Processing*. John Wiley and Sons, New York.

II- Galactic Structure

THE IMPACT OF IR SURVEYS ON GALACTIC STRUCTURE

O. BIENAYMÉ
Observatoire de Strasbourg,
11 rue de l'Université, F-67000 FRANCE

Abstract. Most of the galactic stellar mass is in the galactic disc and IR observations allow one to observe through nearly the entire disc, giving access in detail to its morphology, from the inner bar-bulge, the arms and inner ring, the outer limit of the exponential discs to the dependence of the scale lengths with stellar populations, while the brightest halo giants completely probe the stellar halo morphology and structure.

Kinematic observations can be performed to complete IR multicolour star counts. Such complementary data will strongly constrain the morphology of the stellar components and give clues to the scenario of galactic formation and evolution. Some of the expected results concerning the internal dynamics of our Galaxy are constraints on the galactic potential in the halo, a direct measure of the rotation of the inner bar, kinematic gradients in the stellar discs and dependence with age.

The local stellar Luminosity Function can be much better determined using proper-motions, separating discs and halo Luminosity Functions. It will also be the only means to accurately identify existing intermediate populations like the thick disc, as well as other hypothetical populations (extended bulge or accreted satellites).

1. Galactic components and Parameters of the Milky-Way

The main constituents of the Milky Way galaxy are the stellar populations, the ISM and the dark matter. The stellar component is usually separated into three populations with different morphology, kinematics and also ages and abundances; evolutionary links between these quantities are far from fully understood. Stellar populations are the thin and thick discs, with a total mass $M_d \sim 4\,10^{10}\ M_\odot$, rapidly rotating with low internal dispersion, vertical dispersions in the range of $5\,\mathrm{km\,s^{-1}}$ to $18\,\mathrm{km\,s^{-1}}$ for the thin disc

31

N. Epchtein (ed.),
The Impact of Near-Infrared Sky Surveys on Galactic and Extragalactic Astronomy, 31-40.
© 1998 *Kluwer Academic Publishers. Printed in the Netherlands.*

(Gomez et al, 1997) and $40 \, \text{km} \, \text{s}^{-1}$ for the thick disc. The bulge population is in a slightly flattened spheroid of mass $M_b \sim 2 \, 10^{10} \, M_\odot$, rapidly rotating ($\sim 100 \, \text{km} \, \text{s}^{-1}$) and with a high internal rotation ($\sim 100 \, \text{km} \, \text{s}^{-1}$). The Metal-Poor Halo has a mass $M_h \sim 10^9 \, M_\odot$ and low rotation, its contribution to the dynamical mass of the Galaxy is negligible. Finally, at large radii the main contributor to the mass is the dark matter component: at large R the mass is proportional to R, $M_{D.M}(R) \sim V_c^2 \sim 10^{10} \, R$ if the rotation curve ($=V_c$) remains flat.

Thus the stellar mass is essentially in the discs and mainly in the lowest mass stars. Most of the stellar mass is then emitting in IR and in the galactic plane, strongly obscured in visible band. As a consequence, IR observations are necessary for both reasons that low mass stars are bright in the IR and that in IR bands the extinction by interstellar matter is minimal.

Therefore DENIS, 2MASS, ISOGAL or MSX are the most promising surveys for the development of new and global views on the structure of our Galaxy (and of external galaxies).

2. Photometry and galactic morphology

2.1. SURFACE PHOTOMETRY

To study the galactic structure, wide field surface brightness surveys were obtained during the Pioneer and, more recently, COBE/DIRBE experiments. The line-of-sight integral of luminosity distribution maps are interpreted using models and fitting free parameters. The lowest galactic latitude fields (less than 20°) are affected by interstellar obscuration, while at higher latitudes interstellar extinction is less serious. Infrared observations reduce the difficulties of extinction. The recent DIRBE observations have been investigated by numerous groups leading to detailed parameterization of the Galaxy: however some of the structural properties deduced from surface photometry data alone are fully model dependent, and it can be shown that very different 3D models can produce nearly identical surface densities on the sky (Zhao, 1997).

2.2. IR COUNTS

IRAS sources gave a deep and large-scale view of the Galaxy. Sources are dominated by late type giants AGB and dust shell stars; they form two (thin and thick) discs and the very identifiable bulge. From IRAS, Garwood and Jones (1987) have shown that the halo is consistent with a $R^{1/4}$ law and with the local density of Population II subdwarfs.

Much better resolution of IR counts from DENIS and 2MASS will provide wide digital sky surveys with reliable photometric calibrations and

uniform acquisition and reduction (visible bands photometric surveys from Schmidt plates are under progress, however the final photometric accuracy will not be so accurate).

Counts compared to surface photometry carry information on the density distribution along the line-of-sight, and the distances can be statistically determined as long as the luminosity function is effectively known everywhere. In practice, galactic structure parameters are found through models with building blocks having the relevant astrophysical ingredients. The necessary ingredients for such models are: parametric density laws for the different stellar populations; accurate Luminosity Functions that are now achievable from Hipparcos or similar data; calibration of the colour or magnitude dependence with metallicity; modeling of the absorption either by some regular absorption law or by ad hoc structures to mimic clouds or arms.

Comparison of models to stellar counts allows one to determine the morphology of components. While counts in three colours are necessary to accurately discriminate the effect of metallicity from morphology, extinction must be calibrated with more colours. For instance at least IJH and K colours should be used.

Converging results are now obtained; for example, from the TMGS (Hammersley et al, 1995), the Sun is at $15.5 \pm 3\,\mathrm{pc}$ above the plane and there is a possible tilt of the local old disc with respect to the average HI or stellar disc of the inner Galaxy. Stanek et al (1997), using red clump stars towards the bulge, determine the inner bar orientation. Ruphy et al (1996), with DENIS data, find a scale length for the disc, $2.3 \pm 0.1\,\mathrm{kpc}$, and the cutoff radius of stellar discs at $R = 15 \pm 2\,\mathrm{kpc}$; and Ruphy (1996) obtains results concerning the morphology of inner arms and ring. Other determinations concerning the disc, thick disc scale height and halo should be obtained.

3. Kinematics and dynamics

The analysis of stellar kinematics and Galactic potential is linked to the study of the spatial distribution of stars in the Galaxy, since they are related through the Boltzmann and Poisson equations. Measuring all the visible density and mass distribution from general star counts and the gas cloud density gives only a small fraction of the total amount of the dynamical mass that is deduced from the kinematics of the galactic constituents. As in many spiral galaxies, most of the Galactic mass is unseen and unknown.

We could classify the main potential, or mass, "tracers" as 1) those related to the determination of the rotation curve: HI and CO clouds, young disc populations like cepheids or young open clusters... 2) those related to

the study of the density distribution perpendicular to the galactic plane
and the determination of the plane galactic density: gas flaring and stellar
samples up to 1 or 2 kpc towards the Galactic poles... 3) samples related
to a 3D halo analysis, such as RR Lyrae or BHB stars, globular clusters
and at larger distances galactic satellites (see reviews by Fich & Tremaine,
1991 and Crézé, 1991).

It is important to find tracers corresponding to very different scales in
order to obtain an accurate determination of the potential at each scale.
This will help to clarify some unsolved questions: what is the exact mass
density at large galactic radius; what is the shape of the dark matter distribution -spherical dark halo or flat-; is it triaxial; is there a stellar population
with intermediate angular momentum? In particular, many observational
efforts linking deep star counts to radial velocities and proper motions measurements are still needed.

Another essential question is the determination of the evolutionary relationship between stellar populations in the different components of the
Galaxy. Links between kinematics, stellar ages and chemical abundances
allow one to build the dynamical history of the Galaxy from the old, metal-
poor stars of the stellar halo to the present, young disc stars (Gilmore et al,
1989). Such studies provide the opportunity to understand the formation,
evolution and structure of galaxies in general and to discriminate between
formation scenarios: 1) Halo stars formed during a free-fall collapse of the
proto-Galaxy and disc stars formed later with enriched gas in a rapidly
rotating disc (Eggen et al, 1962); 2) An alternative model is that the halo
formed as a merger of dwarf galaxies over several Gyr (Searle & Zinn, 1978).
Reality looks certainly much more like a combination of these two scenarios.

It is more fruitful to combine kinematics and morphological analysis
of stellar populations that are strongly correlated in the case of nearly
steady state systems. Solutions of dynamical systems given by the Boltzmann equation allow one to quantify the relations between the density
distribution and the velocity distribution. For instance, explicit solutions
are known in the case of the determination of the force perpendicular to the
galactic plane. A good approximation is a one dimensional problem and the
general solution for an isothermal population (constant velocity dispersion
σ) is known: the vertical density is $\rho(z) = \rho(0) \ exp(-\Phi(z)/\sigma^2)$ where $\Phi(z)$
is the potential. More generally, the virial theorem relates the velocities,
the scale lengths and the potential (through the mass M): for a rotating
disc, $M \sim V^2/R^2$, or for a non-rotating population, $M \sim \sigma^2/R^2$.

In conclusion, it is more constraining to analyse simultaneously galactic
morphology and kinematics. A straightforward example is the kinematical
determination of the scale length ($2.5 \pm^{0.8}_{0.6}$ kpc) of the Galaxy that can be
deduced from a local sample of stars with known velocities (Fux & Martinet,

1994). Important results are obtained in the study of the galactic bulge-inner bar (see below) using the kinematics to discriminate between models that were compatible using star counts or surface photometry alone. An essential by product is the measure of the potential and of total (dynamical) mass.

Concerning the galactic potential, it can be recovered from the rotation curve assuming the shape of the mass distribution (spherical, flat...). The rotation curve at a given radius constrains mainly the amount of mass inside this radius. Forces from dark matter account for half of this mass at the solar radius. This estimate depends slightly on the mass assigned to the stellar disc and its scale length.

3.1. NEED FOR A LARGE KINEMATICS SAMPLE

The second important aspect of kinematic study is the need for a large sample of stars with radial velocities or, more easy to obtain, with proper motions. The necessity for large set of data is closely related to the (numerically unstable) inverse Laplace transform at least implicitly faced in dynamical analysis. A simple example is the splitting of a velocity distribution into a summation of various gaussians: very different solutions may coexist having the same statistical meaning unless a sufficient quantity of data is available. Large surveys will soon be available by combining proper motion surveys like PMM or others to IR survey. They would help to clarify the identification of kinematic populations.

4. Galactic components

4.1. BAR-BULGE

From a qualitative comparison of the optical and radio properties of our Galaxy with spirals, de Vaucouleurs & Pence (1978) classified it as an SAB(rs) with an inner bar (see their fig. 6). A tilted bar was proposed to explain the kinematics of the HI and CO at the Galactic center. High latitude parts of the bulge are accessible in visible bands, but only IR surveys allow one to explore in more detail the inner structure of the Galaxy. The bar was detected in the 2.4-micron observations of the Galactic center of Matsumoto et al (1982).

A large amount of work using COBE/DIRBE data confirmed an inner bar (Dwek et al, 1995, see also a recent review by Weinberg, 1996) that is tilted relative to the line-of-sight, and also the presence of arms or an inner ring (Binney et al, 1997). These results are strongly model dependent and it has been shown (Zhao, 1997) that the differences between the inner bar properties obtained by various authors is just due to the non-unique depro-

jection of the Galactic bar. A bar with various orientations and axis ratios would produce the same projected surface brightness. Stanek et al (1997) identified red clump stars from V, I magnitudes in 12 fields obtained by the OGLE collaboration and presented a more accurate description of the density along the line of sight constraining more tightly the inner structures (bar oriented at $20° - 30°$ to the line of sight and axis ratio 3.5:1.5:1).

On the other hand, kinematic data give independent measurements and radial velocities (Tiede & Terndrup, 1997), or proper motions from Spaenhauer et al (1992), used by Zhao et al (1996), allow one to determine the bar properties. Anisotropy of proper motions are compatible with an axis ratio c/a of 0.7, while the rotational velocity and tangential dispersion where deduced from the radial velocity sample. Both methods find a bar pattern speed of $70 - 77 \, \mathrm{km \, s^{-1}}/\mathrm{kpc}$ (model dependent), while we remark that a really direct determination of the pattern speed can be obtained with accurate (1 mas/y) proper motions measured at the extremity of the bar, since we just have to wait and "see" the bar rotating.

The most powerful analyses are a combination of available information, photometric and kinematic, in a unique self-consistent dynamical description to take full advantage of correlations. It will give the full 3D mass and potential distribution and define the part of random to periodic or regular stellar motions.

Finally, microlensing detections towards the bulge can certainly give the bulge stellar mass function and consequently the total stellar mass in the bulge.

4.2. STELLAR DISCS

According to external spiral galaxies, stellar discs are exponential. The Galactic thin disc is a continuum of discs with varying age, metallicity, kinematics and morphology. Scale-heights range from 75 pc to 250 pc, and vertical velocity dispersions from 5 to $20 \, \mathrm{km \, s^{-1}}$. Most recent optical scale length determinations favour short values $\sim 2.5 \, \mathrm{kpc}$ (Robin et al, 1992).

It is very difficult to find evidence from star counts in the galactic plane for ellipticity of the stellar disc at the solar galactic radius, particularly if we are on one of the symmetry axes. Signatures from kinematics give more reliable constraints (Kuijken & Tremaine, 1994): Oort's constants C and K, the LSR radial velocity, show no evidence for non-axisymmetry, while recent analysis (Gomez et al, 1997) from Hipparcos data favours a null vertex deviation (velocity ellipsoid pointing towards the galactic centre). Likewise the axis ratio σ_u/σ_v is observed to be about ~ 0.5 and can be a signature of ellipticity (Kuijken & Tremaine, 1994), but may also simply be explained if the rotation curve is slightly decreasing locally, or if the kinematic and

density scale lengths are very different (Bienaymé & Séchaud, 1997).

A global analysis of the stellar discs is possible with OH/IR stars and Planetary Nebulae that can be identified near the plane at large distances and for which radio observations supply accurate radial velocities. Such data give a unique opportunity to measure stellar density, orbital structure and kinematic gradients over large areas of the Galactic disc (te Lintel Hekkert, 1990; Sevenster et al, 1995; Durand et al, 1996). Systematic searches closer to the Galactic plane are possible (Kistiakowsky, 1995) and are promising for the study of younger populations and kinematic-gradient.

The identification of OH/IR stars has largely been done with IRAS and improvements of the detection and identification very close to the plane is expected with new IR surveys, while systematic searchs in radio (OH) are done in the bulge region (Sevenster et al, 1997).

OH/IR stars with known radial velocities can probe the disc dynamics if the sample is complete, and without determining the distance of individual stars. Bulge-to-disc links and their extensions are thus kinematically accurately defined. Kinematical scale lengths of disc and thick disc were measured. More extended surveys will allow one to define the relation between kinematical scale lengths and ages to understand the dynamical heating, both with age and galactic radius.

4.3. K_Z FORCE PERPENDICULAR TO THE GALACTIC PLANE

Comparing scale heights of stellar discs to the vertical velocity dispersions σ_w of their constituents gives direct access to the vertical potential. In the academic case of a stellar sample distribution, $\rho_*(z)$, where σ_w does not vary with height and when distances are below 1 kpc, we have $\Phi(z) = \sigma_w^2 log(\rho_*(z)/\rho_*(0))$. Then, the local dynamical mass ρ_{dyn} may easily be deduced from the potential. There has been a long controversy as to whether the dynamical mass is in excess of the total "observed" mass density $(0.09\,M_\odot pc^{-3})$, the main discussion being concerned with the quality of used samples. A summary of the most recent results are given by Crézé (1991) and Kuijken (1995), where it appears that the most accurate samples indicate no need for a flat disc of dark matter. Though less constraining, vertical HI gas dynamics favour this conclusion (Boulares & Cox, 1990; Malhotra, 1995).

The most recent result is obtained with Hipparcos data providing the first, volume limited and absolute limited homogeneous tracer of stellar density and velocity distributions in the solar neighbourhood. Crézé et al (1997), from A-F dwarf samples, find the local dynamical density as $\rho_0 = 0.076\pm0.015\,M_\odot pc^{-3}$, a value well below all previous determinations leaving no room for any disc shaped component of dark matter.

4.4. THICK DISC

The thick disc (TD) is identified by star counts at high galactic latitude
(Reid & Majewski, 1993) and also by distinctive kinematic signatures that
are constant at various heights above the galactic plane (Soubiran, 1993).
The TD has a large rotational velocity, looking more like the thin disc
populations than those of the halo, but its kinematics remain fully separate
from the disc. This is very probably the signature of a merging event in the
early phase of the Galactic disc's formation (Robin et al, 1996; Ojha et al,
1996). This may explain also the absence of a vertical abundance-gradient
(Gilmore et al, 1996).

The thick disc vertical velocity dispersion ($38\,\mathrm{km\,s^{-1}}$, Beers et al, 1996)
and scale height (750 pc, Robin et al, 1996; Ojha et al, 1996) can be used to
estimate the K_z force at large z (1-2 kpc). We estimate that it is consistent
with no massive disc of dark matter (the plane-parallel approximation is
no longer valid so far from the plane and a complete 3D modeling would
be necessary).

4.5. THE GALACTIC HALO

Understanding and modeling the 3-dimensional dynamics of halo stars has
progressed rapidly during the last few years; see, for example, models like
the Stäckel potential with three explicit integrals of motion or models
with action integrals (Dehnen & Binney, 1996) or with orbit computations
(Flynn et al, 1996).

The quantity of available kinematic data for distant halo stars is surprisingly low, and most of our knowledge is based on local kinematics.

Halo samples with 3-D kinematics seem to show substructures that
could be fragments of destroyed globular clusters or else... (Majewki et
al, 1996). In fact, the mixing time for halo stars is a few Giga-years and
relaxation is not fully achieved (Tremaine, 1993). We expect partial mixing
to leave traces of initial formation or accretion period. Non-stationarity will
limit the description of the Galactic potential, but it is also a unique chance
to find explicit and "still" living traces of Galactic formation.

4.6. LOCAL KINEMATICS

Proper motions can be obtained with an accuracy of 6-8 mas/year by reasonable means. Combined with photometric IR surveys, this is sufficient to
differentiate distant giants and close dwarfs. Difference in absolute magnitudes between the reddest giants and dwarfs is large and consequently, at a
given apparent magnitude, the difference in proper motions is large. Thus

a detailed description of the local kinematics could be obtained from the kinematics of neighbouring dwarfs.

The local kinematics describe the continuous range of thin discs the thick disc and the halo. Possible links between these components and intermediate populations would be revealed by groups of stars with intermediate properties, velocities dispersions and velocity lags. To find unknown and faint new populations is certainly one important goal: the existence of a possible bulge-like (metal rich) population (Grenon, 1990) or (metal poor) accreted satellite (Preston et al, 1994) with rotation around $100 \, \text{km s}^{-1}$ at the solar galactic radius could be established more clearly.

Metal-poor Blue Main Sequence stars near the solar circle have been discovered by Preston et al (1994) as a new kinematic population. These stars have an isotropic velocity dispersion and relatively large mean rotational velocities of about $128 \, \text{km s}^{-1}$. Preston et al suggest they are probably accreted from dwarf spheroidal satellites. It will be essential to check and extend the detection of this population out of the galactic plane, since it will be the best potential tracer at intermediate distances around 3-6 kpc out of the Galactic plane.

The kinematics from a very large data base is certainly the only tool for identifying accurately such faint populations that could be the remnant of an intermediate, rapid and important event during the formation or evolution of the Galaxy. The practical analysis of such data will need to establish definite IR-LF for each population. Multicolour calibrations must first be obtained from close red stars over a large range of metallicity. Inversely, kinematic signatures can be used to distinguish stellar populations and to determine more accurately their LF. Analysis of kinematics and the LF cannot be separated, but the counter part is that such an analysis will provide a more definite and exact separation between populations.

References

Beers T.C., Sommer-Larsen J., 1996, *Ap.J. Suppl.* **96**, 175
Bienaymé O., Séchaud N., 1997, *A. & A.*, **323**, 781
Binney J., Gerhard O., Spergel D., 1997, *M. N. R. A. S.* **288**, 365
Boulares A., Cox D.P., 1990, *Ap. J.* **365**, 544
Crézé M., 1991, *The Interstellar Disk-Halo Connection in Galaxies*, IAU Symp. **144**, 313
Crézé M. et al, 1997, *A. & A.*, (in press) *astro-ph/9709022*
Dehnen W., Binney J., 1996, *Formation of the Galactic Halo .... Inside and Out*, ASP
    Conf. Series **92**, eds. H. Morrison & A. Sarajedini, 391
de Vaucouleurs G., Pence W.D., 1978, *A. J.* **83**, 1163
Durand S., Dejonghe H., Acker A., 1996, *A. & A.* **310**, 97
Dwek E., Arendt R.G., Hauser M.G. et al., 1995, *Ap. J.* **445**, 716
Eggen O.J., Lynden-Bell D., Sandage A., 1962, *Ap. J.* **136**, 748
Fich M., Tremaine S., 1991, *Ann. Rev. Astron. Astrophys.* **29**, 409
Flynn C., Sommer-Larsen J., Christensen P.R., 1996, *M. N. R. A. S.* **281**, 1027
Fux & Martinet, 1994, *A. & A.* **287**, L21

Garwood R., Jones T.J., 1987, *P. A. S. P.* **99**, 45

Gilmore G., Wyse R., Jones J.B., 1996, *A. J.* **109**, 1095

Gilmore G., Wyse R., Kuijken K., 1989, *Ann. Rev. Astron. Astrophys.* **27**, 555

Gomez A.E., Grenier S., Udry S., Haywood M., 1997, Hipparcos Venice'97 (ESA)

Grenon M., 1990, *ESO/CTIO Workshop on bulges of galaxies*, 150

Hammersley P.L., Garzon F., Mahoney T., Calbet X., 1995, *M. N. R. A. S.* **269**, 753

Kistiakowsky V., Helfand D., 1995, *A. J.* **110**, 2225

Kuijken K., 1995, *Stellar Populations*, IAU Symp. **164**, 198

Kuijken K., Tremaine S., 1994, *A. J.* **421**, 178

Majewski S.R., Munn J.A., Hawley S.L., 1996, *Ap. J.* **459**, L73

Malhotra S., 1995, *Ap. J.* **448**, 138

Matsumoto T. et al, 1982, in the Galactic Center ed. G. Riegler & Blandford (New York: AIP), 48

Ojha D. K., Bienaymé O., Robin A. C. et al, 1996, *A. & A.* **311**, 456

Preston G.W., Beers T., Shectman S.A., 1994, *A. J.* **108**, 538

Reid N., Majewski S.R., 1993, *Ap. J.* **409**, 635

Robin A.C., Crézé M., Mohan V., 1992, *A. & A.* **265**, 32

Robin A.C., Haywood M., Crézé M. et al, 1996, *A. & A.* **305**, 125

Ruphy S., 1996, *Thesis*, Université de Paris VI

Ruphy S. et al, 1996, *A. & A.* **313**, L21

Searle L., Zinn, 1978, *Ap. J.* **225**, 357

Sevenster M.N., Dejonghe H., Habing H.J., 1995, *A. & A.* **299**, 689

Sevenster M.N. et al, 1997, *A. & A. Suppl.* **122**, 79

Soubiran C., 1993, *A. & A.* **274**, 181

Spaenhauer A., Jones B.F., Whitford A.E., 1992, *A. J.* **103**, 297

Stanek et al, 1997, *Ap. J.* **477**, 163

te Lintel Hekkert P., 1990, *Ph D Thesis The evolution of OH/IR stars and their dynamical properties*, Leiden University

Tiede G.P., Terndrup D.M., 1997, *A. J.* **113**, 321

Tremaine S., 1993, *Back to the Galaxy*, AIP Conf. Proc. **278**, eds. S.S. Holt et al, 599

Weinberg M. D., 1996, *Barred galaxies* ASP Conf. Series **91**, ed. R. Buta et al, 516

Zhao H.S., 1997, *astroph9705046*

Zhao H.S., Rich R.M., Biello J., 1996, *Ap.J.* **470**, 506

RESOLVED DENIS AND UKIRT INFRARED STELLAR OBSERVATIONS TOWARDS THE GALACTIC CENTRE

M. UNAVANE, G. GILMORE

Institute of Astronomy,
Cambridge CB3 0HA, UK

Abstract.

IJK$_s$ DENIS images, in a crowded region towards the centre of the Galaxy, covering 17.4 deg^2 in $|\ell| < 5°$, $|b| < 1.5°$, result in $\sim 750\,000$ sources per colour. An investigation of the completeness and systematic effects present in these crowded images suggests that the standard DENIS magnitude limits of $\sim$18, 16 and 14 in I,J and K$_s$ were not achieved due to crowding – 80% completeness falls about 2 magnitudes brighter than these limits.

We convolve a detailed model of the systematic and random errors in the photometry with a simple model of the Galactic disk and dust distribution, to simulate expected colour-magnitude diagrams. These are in good agreement with the observed diagrams, allowing us to isolate those stars from the inner disk and bulge. After correcting for local dust-induced asymmetries, we find evidence for longitude-dependent asymmetries in the distant J and K$_s$ sources, consistent with the general predictions of some Galactic bar models. Complementary nbL-band (3.6μm) observations taken at UKIRT at $b = -0.1°$ and $\ell=\pm4.3°$ and $\ell=\pm2.3°$ are also presented. The magnitude limit ($\sim$12) and low coefficient for interstellar extinction at this wavelength (A_{nbL}=0.047A_V), allows us to observe bulge giants. We successfully match 95% of nbL sources with DENIS K$_s$ sources. Dereddened number counts show an excess of $\sim$15% and $\sim$5% in source counts at $\ell = -4.3°$ and $\ell = -2.3°$ compared to $\ell = +4.3°$ and $\ell = +2.3°$ respectively. This is in the same sense as predicted by many bar models, with our results favouring gas dynamical models and the recent deconvolution of surface photometry data (e.g. Binney et al. 1991; Binney et al. 1997), over earlier treatments of photometric data (e.g. Dwek et al., 1995).

N. Epchtein (ed.),
The Impact of Near-Infrared Sky Surveys on Galactic and Extragalactic Astronomy, 41-47.
© 1998 *Kluwer Academic Publishers. Printed in the Netherlands.*

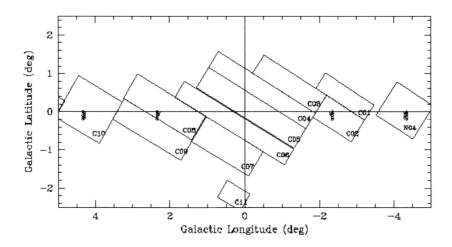

Figure 1. The observed DENIS IJK$_s$ *rasters* (large boxes). The small marked regions near $b = 0°$ and at $\ell = \pm 4.3°$, $\ell = \pm 2.3°$ are the locations of the supplementary nbL observations.

1. Introduction

Evidence for the existence of a kiloparsec-scale bar in the centre of our Galaxy has been accumulating. Many disparate observational techniques point to the conclusion that there is a bar with a scalelength of 2–5 kpc, with its major axis in the first quadrant – Binney et al. (1991) and Blitz & Spergel (1991) find a striking parallellogram in the observed longitude-velocity for gas motions, just as expected for motions in a rotating bar-like potential; Nakada et al. (1982) use IRAS Miras as tracers and again find the same result; OGLE event frequencies disagree with axisymmetric bulge models, but agree with bar models (Paczynski et al. 1996); COBE/DIRBE surface photometry modelling and deconvolutions (Dwek et al. 1995; Binney et al. 1997) also suggest a similar bar.

To detect the bar, however, by means of its stellar population is more difficult. We are limited by the dust which hampers the optical view of the central regions. Turning to near infra-red wavelengths, the effects of dust are much diminished. At K-band (2.2μm) the $\sim$40 magnitudes of optical extinction are reduced to only $\sim$4 magnitudes, and at 3.6μm, to only $\sim$2. The work of Hammersley et al. (1994) has used a K-band stellar survey, but was severely limited by working in only one waveband, where the effects of patchy dust clouds cannot be unambiguously disentangled from those of Galactic structure.

Multicolour surveys such as DENIS allow some attempt to be made to separate these two effects.

2. DENIS data reduction and completeness

The DENIS images used, taken between April and September 1996, cover the regions shown in figure 1. The images were prepared according to the standard pipeline reduction (Borsenberger, 1997). Each image is 768×768 pixels, which, in the case of the J and K_s images is the result of microscanning with a 256×256 detector. Source extraction and aperture photometry with an aperture of 7 arcseconds diameter were carried out using the SExtractor program (Bertin & Arnouts 1996). Standard stars observed just before and after each *raster* (see caption of figure 1) were used for photometric calibration. A thorough investigation of photometric errors and completeness was carried out. Random photometric errors were deduced by comparison of photometry in overlapping images. The addition of artificial stars to crowded DENIS images in each of the three colours, at various magnitudes, allowed a characterisation of the systematic offset of magnitude which results from flux from other sources entering the aperture. These artificial star experiments also allowed completeness levels to be deduced. Finally, two-dimensional maps of completeness levels for $J-K_s$ and $I-J$ colour-magnitude diagrams were constructed by use of a Monte-Carlo process based on the completeness levels. Faint and bright end cut-offs were imposed in I,J and K_s at 17,15,13 and 11,9,8 respectively. Absolute astrometry was carried out by a step-up process from optical sky survey images.

3. Disk Model

A very simple model to represent only the disk of the Galaxy, in the presence of a strong dust layer was constructed. The model consists of a stellar disk, with an exponential scale-length and scale-height (taken from Kent et al. 1991), together with a local luminosity function (Garwood & Jones, 1987). The dust layer is specified by its scale-length, scale-height, the strength of dust extinction, and the displacement of the sun from the plane. The model output is a list of sources generated by a streamlined Monte-Carlo method for given lines of sight, using these model parameters. The output is subsequently convolved with a parametrisation of the derived completeness limits. The dust parameters are refined by a fit to the data.

4. Bulge Models

Figure 4 shows the number count asymmetries expected according to various bar models of the Galactic central regions. For a centrally concentrated bar with its major axis in the quadrant $90° > \ell > 0°$, we expect, at relatively large longitudes ($\gtrsim 10°$) that the number counts for tracer objects should

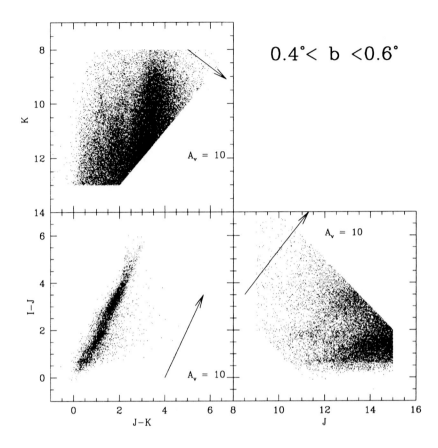

Figure 2. A typical set of colour-magnitude diagrams (for b=0.5°). Shown are (J)-(J−K), (I)-(I−J) and (I−J)-(J−K) diagrams, each constructed separately. The direction of the reddening line is shown in each diagram. Notice the rotated (I)-(I−J) axes. The most striking feature of these diagrams is the strong reddening. The limits of unreddened I−J and J−K$_s$ colours are between ∼0 and ∼1 for most main-sequence and giant stars, yet the ranges we see here are much large, and are consistent with stars seen through heavy reddening. We use the reddening as a filter to separate local and distant sources, and to investigate inner disk/bulge asymmetries.

be larger at a positive longitude +ℓ than at the corresponding negative longitude −ℓ. However, at smaller longitudes ($\lesssim$ 10°), the bar geometry dictates that this contrast will be reversed with greater number counts being seen at *negative* longitudes. (see Blitz et al. 1991). We choose a few representative bar models from the literature – we use two of the best fitting models (E3 and G2) and from Dwek et al. (1995) based on a fit to DIRBE 2.2μm surface photometry; we use two dynamical models, those

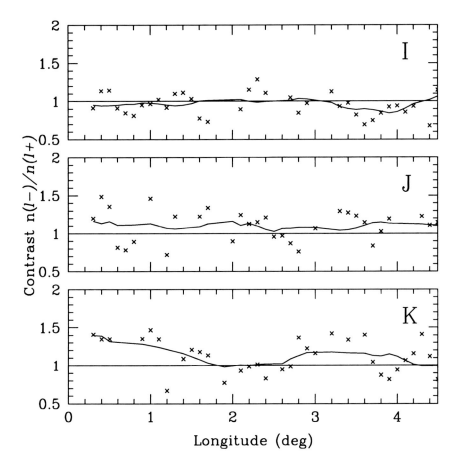

Figure 3. The expected number count asymmetries from various bar models. The points correspond to the results of the nbL observations after dereddening, with Poisson counting errors indicated.

of Binney et al. (1991) and Blitz et al. (1991); and we use a recent three-dimensional deconvolution of the DIRBE near-IR photometry by Binney et al. (1997). According to most of these models, we typically expect a peak in the number count contrast around 4–6°.

5. Counting experiment

By means of our disk model, we can delimit regions in the CM diagrams dominated by near-disk, and also by far-disk/bulge sources. At the bright magnitudes corresponding to nearby disk objects, a fit is made between equal negative and positive longitude pairs, to remove the effects of local

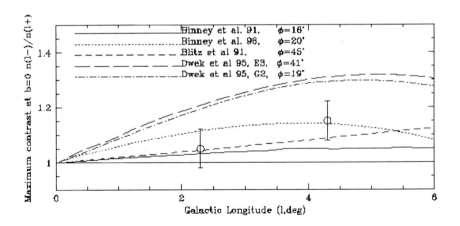

Figure 4. The expected number count asymmetries from various bar models.

asymmetries. Any additional asymmetries remaining at fainter magnitudes will (in the case of the J band and K_s band) contain some signal of asymmetries in the inner disk or in the bulge. The I band, according to the model distances, should serve as a control, since it is expected to penetrate no more than a few kpc – the number counts seen should, after this correction for differences in local extinction, show equal values at positive and negative longitudes. This is what we see (see figure 3). The deviation of the mean ratio from unity is no more than 1.5σ. However, for the J and K_s bands, the deviation from unity is $\sim 3\sigma$. Note that the signal is not clean. The method we use, although removing local asymmetries in the disk, does not remove asymmetries which may be caused by dust nearer the centre.

6. nbL-band data

The noisy results from IJK_s data led to the use of a wavelength with an even lower coefficient of extinction. It was clear, according to the model distances, that while DENIS K–band observations were likely to penetrate, DENIS J-band observations might not reliably penetrate the most severe extinction towards the central regions of the galaxy.

Thus complementary nbL (3.6μm) observations were made covering a total of 277 arcmin^2 equally distributed between fields at $\ell = \pm 4.3°$ and $\ell = \pm 2.3°$ were taken at UKIRT in July 1996. (The field positions are shown in figure 1) The observation mode required the co-adding of multiple very short exposures, since the sky background at 3.6μm is very bright and easily saturates the detectors. Data reduction was carried out in the standard way, with a flat field constructed by the median filtering of several survey images. The small pixel size (0.286 arcseconds) meant that severe confusion, as in

the DENIS images, was not a problem. The astrometry was carried out by matching images to the DENIS K_s catalogue (see above). The resulting 95% match of K_s and nbL sources suggests that the penetration by neither K_s and L band data is severely limited by dust. We deredden the stars by assuming the majority of the stars to be K_s and M giants displaced at 8 kpc. A calculation based on a simple galactic model (Binney et al. 1997) suggests that the inner Galaxy (within 3 kpc from the centre) has a 10–12% disk contamination for $|b| < 0.1°$. The difference in distance to the two sides of the putative bar for lines of sight at $\ell = \pm 4°$ is less than a few tenths of a magnitudes, and we use the dereddened nbL-band stars as tracers. The resulting number count contrast is shown in figure 4. We see that the gas dynamical (Blitz et al 1991; Binney et al. 1991) and the more recent photometric model (Binney et al. 1997) is preferred over the earlier photometric work by Dwek et al. (1995).

References

Bertin E., Arnouts S., 1996, A&AS, 117, 3

Binney J., Gerhard O.E., Stark A.A., Bally J., Uchida K.I., 1991, MNRAS, 252, 210

Binney J., Gerhard O., Spergel D., 1997, MNRAS, 288, 365

Blitz L., Spergel D.N., 1991, ApJ, 379, 631

Borsenberger J., 1997, in *The Impact of Large Scale Near-IR surveys*, eds. F.Garzón et al., (Kluwer), p181

Dwek E. et al., 1995, ApJ, 445, 716

Freudenreich H.T., 1996, ApJ, 468, 663

Garwood R., Jones T.J., 1987, PASP, 99, 453

Hammersley P.L., Garzón F.,Mahoney T., Calbet X., 1994, MNRAS, 269, 753

Kent S.M., Dame T.M., Fazio G., 1991, ApJ, 378, 131

Nakada Y., Deguchi S., Hashimoto O., Izumiura H., Onaka T., Sekiguchi K., Yamamura I., 1991, Nature, 353, 140

Paczynski B. et al., 1996, in Blitz L., Teuben P., eds., IAU 169, *Unsolved Problems of the Milky Way*, Kluwer, Dordrecht, p93

MASS-LOSING AGB STARS AND YOUNG STARS IN THE ISOGAL SURVEY

A. OMONT AND B. CAILLAUD,
Institut d'Astrophysique de Paris-CNRS, France

P. FOUQUE,
Observatoire de Paris, DESPA, France and European Southern Observatory, Chile

G. GILMORE,
Institute of Astronomy, Cambridge, U. K.

D. OJHA,
TIFR, Bombay, India

M. PERAULT, AND P. SEGUIN,
Laboratoire de Radioastronomie Millimétrique, ENS and CNRS, Paris, France

G. SIMON,
Observatoire de Paris, DASGAL, France

R.F.G. WYSE,
John Hopkins University, Baltimore, USA

AND

THE ISOGAL-DENIS TEAM

ABSTRACT

ISOGAL is the first near+mid-infrared, high-resolution imaging survey of the inner disk and bulge of the Milky Way Galaxy (Pérault et al. 1996). The ISO satellite, and especially ISOCAM, allows a quantum jump in observational analyses of Galactic structure and stellar populations, star formation and infrared properties of the interstellar medium, especially in the most obscured regions of the inner Galactic disk. The combination of ISOCAM data with DENIS (Epchtein et al. 1997) IJK data allows characterisation of the stellar populations.

N. Epchtein (ed.),
The Impact of Near-Infrared Sky Surveys on Galactic and Extragalactic Astronomy, 49-56.
© 1998 Kluwer Academic Publishers. Printed in the Netherlands.

We illustrate the scientific capabilities of ISOGAL with an analysis of the stellar sources in a field in the inner Galactic bulge/disk ($\ell, b = 0, +1$). ISOGAL+DENIS has sufficient sensitivity resolution to be almost complete to the RGB tip in the inner Galactic bulge at all of $2\mu m$, $7\mu m$ and $15\mu m$, allowing analysis of bulge mass-losing AGB stars. In this field the relative number of mass-losing stars with respect to non-mass-losing AGB stars of similar luminosity is larger than in the solar neighbourhood. The scientific ramifications of these observations are uncertain – is this a metallicity effect?

The study of stellar formation at Galactic scales is another major goal of ISOGAL. The analysis of the first results confirm the expectations derived from the IRAS results on YSOs in nearby giant molecular clouds: ISOGAL is able to detect solar mass YSOs (of "type I and II") up to a few kpc, and those of intermediate mass up to the Galactic Center. The combination with the near infrared data of the DENIS survey allows to discriminate YSOs from other ISOGAL sources, mainly red giants. From the detection of more than 10 000 YSOs, one can expect a detailed and global view of star formation in the different environments of the most obscured regions of the inner Galaxy.

1. WHAT IS ISOGAL?

ISOGAL is the first near+mid-infrared, high-resolution imaging survey of the inner disk and bulge of the Milky Way Galaxy, combining ISOCAM $7\mu m$ (LW2) and $15\mu m$ (LW3) images with DENIS IJK$_s$ images. These data allow the determination of the distribution of interstellar extinction on small angular scales, and hence deduction of intrinsic stellar colours and spatial distributions, thereby facilitating a broad range of analyses of Galactic structure. Additionally, from the reddening-corrected photometric data, one may search for and identify any remarkable individual stars. The ISOCAM sensitivity allows us to detect dusty low-mass young stars up to several kpc from the Sun, and regions of current or recent star formation, and individual bright M giants, to beyond the Galactic Center. The central parts of the Milky Way are of considerable intrinsic interest; the inner disk and bulge contain most of the stars and interstellar medium, most active star-formation regions, the greatest number of products of the late stages of stellar evolution, most rare and short-lived stages of stellar evolution (which can dominate the infrared luminosity of galaxies), and exotic objects. The most important manifestations of spiral arms and of large-scale dynamical asymmetries may be studied in unique detail, and with unprecedented reliability.

With these goals in mind, we have selected fields distributed along the

inner Galactic disk, to optimise the range of studies outlined above – the inner Galactic bulge is densely sampled, with less dense sampling of the disk out to longitude $| \ell | = 60°$. We discuss here the results from two ISOGAL fields of the inner Galaxy, with an emphasis on the RGB and AGB stars and young stars. The results illustrate the capabilities of the ISOGAL data and provide an indication of the scientific returns from this survey.

2. THE DATA

The fields analysed here are the one at $\ell=-45°$ described in Pérault et al. (1996), and a small field at $(\ell, b) = (0.0, 1.0)$ with area 0.038 sq deg.

The DENIS source density is approximately 50000 per sq deg, being confusion limited (~ 30 pix/source) by the DENIS $3''$ pixels. The completeness limits are K$\sim$10.5, J$\sim$12.5 and I$\sim$13.5. The K/J-K colour-magnitude diagramme (Fig.1) shows a well-defined bulge red giant sequence, shifted by fairly uniform extinction of $A_V=6\pm1$ mag. with respect to the reference K_o vs $(J - K)_o$ of Bertelli et al. 1994) with Z=0.02.

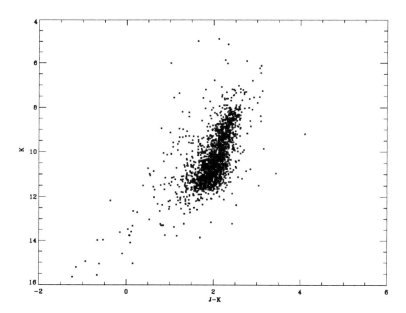

Figure 1. K versus $J - K$ magnitude color diagram of the DENIS sources

ISOGAL observed this field with the broad filters LW3 (12-18 microns) and LW2 (6-8.5 microns) with $6''$ pixels in a (4×7) raster. Since this field is one of the smallest observed by ISOGAL, edge effects are relatively large, with only $\sim 60\%$ of the field observed twice. The images have been pro-

A. OMONT ET AL.

cessed by the ISOCAM team IA software, with some enhancements. Source extraction and photometry is based on a maximum-likelihood analysis optimised for crowded fields and under-sampled data.

Source counts are displayed in Figures 2 and 3. With source densities typically ∼10000 per sq. deg. (∼40 pixels per source), point-source identification is again confusion limited. Quantification of ISOCAM data completeness is underway.

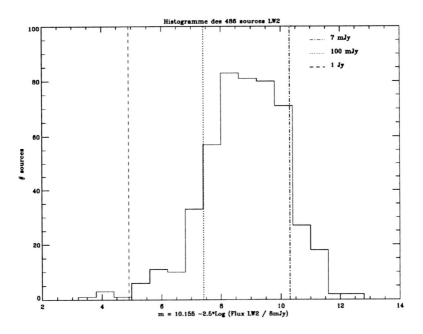

Figure 2. Magnitude distribution of the 486 LW2-ISO sources (central field)

A substantial fraction of the ISO sources can be identified in the DENIS J and K data: 85% of all LW3 and 90% of all LW2 sources are cross-matched, with the fractions increasing to 97% for LW3 sources with $S_{15} > 10$ mJy and 98% for LW2 sources with $S_7 > 15$ mJy. Note also that ∼80% of LW3 sources with $S_{15} > 5$ mJy have an LW2 counterpart.

We now restrict discussion to point sources above the completeness limits, considering the 216 sources detected in both the LW3 and LW2 bands with $S_{15} > 5$ mJy and $S_7 > 7$ mJy.

3. THE MANY MASS-LOSING AGB STARS IN THE INNER BULGE/DISK

The striking feature of the colour-colour and magnitude-colour diagrams derived in the $\ell=0$ b=1 field from the ISOGAL and DENIS data of the 216

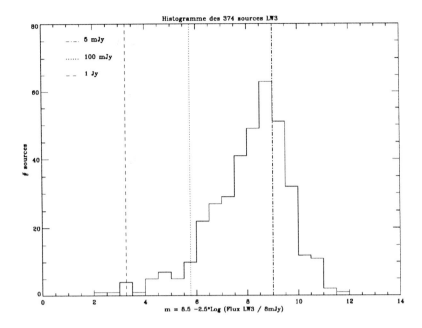

Figure 3. Magnitude distribution of the 374 LW3-ISO sources (central field)

bright sources is the large range of K-[15] and K-[7] colours. Interstellar extinction in this line of sight is $A_K \sim 0.6$, $A_7 \sim 0.2$ and $A_{15} \sim 0.1$. The photospheric colours of normal late-type red giants are $(K-[15])_o < 0.3$ and [7]-[15]< 0.3. More than 40% of the sources under discussion here have observed K-[15] colours redder than K-[15]~1, and very red [7]-[15] and K-[7]colours. Thus these data suggest these are mass-losing stars.

Further, most of these bright ISO sources have apparent K magnitudes $(K_o + 0.6)$ which are above the RGB tip $(K_{o,tip} \sim 8.3$ in the bulge, see e.g. Tiede et al. 1995). Almost all the very red stars are above the RGB tip, and are thus AGB stars. What fraction of all AGB stars are this red? Our LW3 completeness limit is such that we would detect only $\sim 50\%$ of non-mass-losing AGB stars just above the RGB tip. However, DENIS is complete in K to significantly below the RGB tip. Thus, the number of non-red excess AGB stars this luminous in K is derivable from the ~ 300 DENIS sources with K< 9 (foreground disk contamination is negligible in this field).

We conclude that at least 25% of the AGB stars above the RGB tip are losing mass, from their very red ISO colours. This high proportion of mass-losing red giants above the RGB tip is larger than the value in the solar neighbourhood (see e.g. Wainscoat et al. 1992 and Glass et al. 1995)).

Our conclusion of a large mass-losing fraction is robust, since the large

spread of ISOGAL colours is certainly real. However the exact source counts are sensitive to our completeness corrections, which remain under development.

AGB models (Justtanont and Tielens 1992, M. Groenewegen in preparation) suggest that our observed colours correspond to mass-loss rates of order a few $10^{-7} M_\odot yr^{-1}$. The $\sim 10\%$ of the sources with the largest $15\mu m$ excesses probably have larger mass-loss rates, of order a few $10^{-6} M_\odot yr^{-1}$. These most extreme sources also have detectable J-K excess, with a correlation between J-K colour and K-[15] colour, further establishing the physical validity of our identification of them as AGB stars with large mass-loss.

We have begun to analyse the red giant population in other ISOGAL fields. For instance in the symmetric field ($\ell=0$ b=-1), the content of red giants seems quite similar, but the extinction is much larger and variable which makes the estimate of intrinsic colours more difficult. Farther in the bulge (b=-2.17), their density is about twice smaller while their infrared colours look relatively similar. In the central disk (b$\sim$0°), the extinction is even larger (up to $A_v \sim$35).

A first analysis of a field at ℓ=-45° has been given in Pérault et al. (1996). About half (180) of the 395 $15\mu m$ sources have a clear identification with a bright K source (K < 11) with a matching radius 6". Most of them have a J counterpart. The colour-colour diagrams (J-K)/(K-[15]) (Pérault et al. (1996) and (J-K)/(K-[7]) show that most of these bright K sources are luminous red giants with a large interstellar extinction (up to $A_v \sim$30). Many of them should be mass-losing AGB stars.

4. DUSTY YOUNG STARS

In this field at ℓ=-45° in addition to such relatively well defined sequence of red giants, there are also a number of 15 μm sources associated with relatively faint K sources and large values of K-[15], or without any K association (Pérault et al. 1996).

With a 6" matching radius, 52 ISOGAL sources are associated with a weak DENIS K source (12.5>K>11), among them 27 have also a J counterpart. Most of these sources have large values of K-[15] and relatively small values of J-K, i.e. typical colours of T Tauri stars. However, more than half of them should be pure chance associations, and one has to wait for a better ISOGAL astrometry to confirm the nature of the others. The number of 15 μm sources without K association is $\sim$160. Thus almost half the total number of 15 μm sources have no K association. The only plausible candidates for such a large number of cold sources are dusty young stars. The expected numbers of detectable galaxies and asteroids in our 0.144 deg^2 field are less than 1 and 5 respectively.

As discussed by Pérault et al. (1996), the observed density of 15 μm sources without K counterpart ($\sim 1300/\text{deg}^2$) is just in the range of the expected number of young sources in a giant molecular cloud (GMC) a few kpc away, inferred from the IRAS results in nearby clouds such as L1641 in Orion (Strom et al. 1989). From this detailed study of Strom et al., it appears that "Type II" YSOs should have typically K-[15]>4, while "Type I" YSOs should have K-[15]> 8. Most similar objects detected at $15\mu m$ should not be detectable in the K band at 3-5 kpc with our sensitivity. But many class II sources could be detectable with a slightly better sensitivity, as possibly observed in another ISOGAL field (Testi et al. in preparation) with TIRGO data ($K_{LIM} \sim 14.5$).

In conclusion, the ISOGAL survey presents a major interest for the study of stellar formation at Galactic scales. The analysis of the first results confirm the expectations derived from the IRAS results on YSOs in nearby giant molecular clouds: ISOGAL is able to detect solar mass YSOs (of "type I and II") up to a few kpc, and those of intermediate mass up to the Galactic Center. The combination with the near infrared data of the DENIS survey allows to discriminate YSOs from other ISOGAL sources, mainly red giants. From the detection of more than 10 000 YSOs, one can expect a detailed and global view of star formation in the different environments of the most obscured regions of the inner Galaxy: disk, disk-bulge transition region, bar, molecular ring, spiral arms, inter-arm foreground regions, etc.

However, the reality of all the weak sources detected by ISOGAL without K association still needs to be confirmed, and their nature should be determined by follow-up observations such as deeper K images (used with an improved ISOCAM astrometry) and visible and infrared spectrometry. It should also be stressed that in addition to such individual YSOs, ISO-GAL will also bring various other information related to star formation in the inner Galaxy: (young) open clusters and other groups of young stars, supergiants, young bright red giants, rich diffuse IR emission by PAHs and dust in regions of stellar formation, dark cloud condensations of various sizes traced by high IR extinction, etc.

References

Bertelli G. et al. 1994 A&AS 106, 275

Epchtein N. et al. Messenger 87, 27

Glass I.S., Whitelock P.A., Catchpole R.M. & Feast M.W. 1995 MNRAS 273, 383

Justtanont K. & Tielens A.G.G.M. 1992, ApJ 389, 400

Pérault M., Omont A., Simon G., Séguin P., Ojha D., Blommaert J., Felli M., Gilmore G., Guglielmo F., Habing H., Price S., Robin A., de Batz B., Cesarsky C., Elbaz D., Epchtein N., Fouqué P., Guest S., Levine D., Pollock A., Prusti T., Siebenmorgen R., Testi L., Tiphène D., 1996, AA 315, L165

Strom K.M., Newton G., Strom S.E., Seaman R.L., Carrasco L., Cruz-Gonzalez I., Serrano A. 1989, ApJS 71, 183

Tiede G.P., Frogel J.A. & Terndrup D.M. 1995, AJ 110, 2788
Wainscoat R.J. et al. 1992, ApJS 83,111

GALACTIC BULGE FROM TMGS STAR COUNTS

M. LÓPEZ–CORREDOIRA, F. GARZÓN, P. L. HAMMERSLEY,
T. J. MAHONEY AND X. CALBET
Instituto de Astrofísica de Canarias
E-38200 La Laguna, Tenerife, Spain

Abstract. The bulge of the Galaxy is analysed by inverting K-band star counts from the Two-Micron Galactic Survey in a number of off-plane regions. Assuming a non-variable luminosity function within the bulge, we derive the top end of the K-band luminosity function, which shows a sharp decrease brighter than $M_K = -8.0$ when compared with the disc population, and the stellar density function, whose morphology is fitted to triaxial ellipsoids with the major axis in the plane at an angle with line of sight to the Galactic centre of 12° in the first quadrant. The axial ratios are 1 : 0.54 : 0.33 and the distance of the Sun from the centre of the triaxial ellipsoid is 7860 pc.

We use some off-plane regions in the Galactic bulge ($10° > |b| > 2°$, $|l| < 15°$) taken from TMGS (Two-Micron Galactic Survey; Garzón et al. 1993) up to nineth K magnitude. The total sky coverage is some 75 deg^2 of sky. In the areas considered, the contribution to the star counts will be primarily from the disc and bulge and the extinction is low (between 0.05 to 0.5 mag at K) and not too patchy (Garzón et al. 1993).

In order to isolate the bulge component a model disc was subtracted from the total counts: Wainscoat et al. (1992; hereafter WCVWS), which has been used because it provides a good fit to the TMGS counts in the region where the disc dominates (Cohen 1994). So $N_{K,\mathrm{bulge}}(m_K) = N_K(m_K) - N_{K,\mathrm{disc}}(m_K)$ and (in rad^{-2})

$$N_{K,\mathrm{bulge}}(m_K) = \int_0^\infty \Phi_{K,\mathrm{bulge}}(m_K+5-5\log_{10} r - a_K(r)) D_{\mathrm{bulge}}(r) r^2 dr, \quad (1)$$

where $\Phi_{K,\mathrm{bulge}}(M) = \int_{-\infty}^M \phi_{K,\mathrm{bulge}}(M) dM$, ϕ is the normalised luminosity function ($\int_{-\infty}^\infty \phi(M) dM = 1$), D is the density, and a_K is the extinction in the line of sight according to WCVWS.

N. Epchtein (ed.),
The Impact of Near-Infrared Sky Surveys on Galactic and Extragalactic Astronomy, 57-61.
© 1998 *Kluwer Academic Publishers. Printed in the Netherlands.*

With the change of variables $\rho_K = 10^{0.2 a_K(r)} r$ and $\Delta_K = D(r) \frac{r^2 dr}{\rho_K^2 d\rho_K}$
we transform the equation (1) of counts in the bulge into

$$N_K(m_K) = \int_0^\infty \Phi_K(m_K + 5 - 5\log_{10}\rho_K)\Delta_K(\rho_K)\rho_K^2 d\rho_K. \qquad (2)$$

The density is obtained by inverting this equation: Δ is the unknown
function and Φ is the kernel of a Fredholm integral equation of the first
kind.

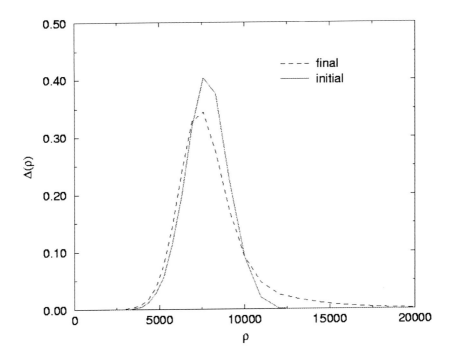

Figure 1. Recovery of the theoretical luminosity function through the inversion proccess.

When the luminosity function Φ, is the unknown instead of Δ, then
we can make a new change of variable $M_K = m_K + 5 - 5\log_{10}\rho_K$ and we
obtain a new first kind of Fredholm equation:

$$N_K(m_K) = 200(\ln 10)10^{\frac{3m_K}{5}} \int_{-\infty}^\infty \Delta_K(10^{\frac{5+m_K-M_K}{5}})10^{\frac{-3M_K}{5}}\Phi_K(M_K)dM_K,$$
$$(3)$$

where Φ is now the unknown function and Δ_K is the kernel.

Both integral equations are inverted using Lucy's statistical method (Lucy 1974). This method is fairly insensitive to the high-frequency fluctuations and in our tests with known functions, which are similar to that of the bulge, gave good results (note: this method would not be applicable to the disc as a whole). Fig. 1 shows the outcome of a numerical simulation where we introduce an initial Δ function, obtain the counts through (2) adding a Poissonian equivalent noise over a square degree of sky and invert by Lucy's algorithm: the final Δ is similar to the initial Δ in spite of noise.

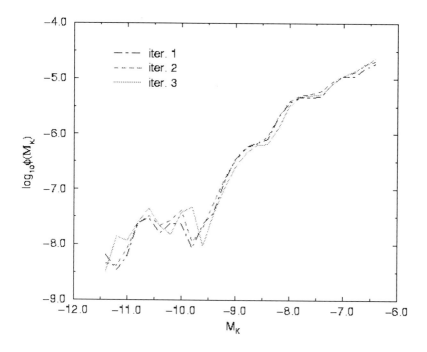

Figure 2. Luminosity function in the first three iterations.

We solved first for the luminosity function for each region using the WCVWS bulge density. Then, assuming that the luminosity function is independent of the position (while our assumption may not be not strictly true, it is still a reasonable approximation between about 250 pc and 1200 pc from the galactic plane) we average it and use for inverting (2) to derive a new density distribution. The new density was then used to improve the luminosity function, etc. The whole process was iterated three times which

was enough for the results to stabilize as can be seen in the Fig. 2: we see
how the result of the third iteration is very close to the first; i.e. stabilization
is reached in the first iterations.

The obtained luminosity function is shown in the Fig. 3 and it is accurate
enough (the number of bulge stars is large enough compared with possible
sources of contamination) down to $M_K \sim -9.5$. The coincidence of our
luminosity function with that of WCVWS for the faintest stars is due to
the fact that we used their luminosity function to initiating the iteration
process. Practically speaking, this overlapping corresponds to an effective
normalization to the WCVWS luminosity function in the range $M_K > -7$.

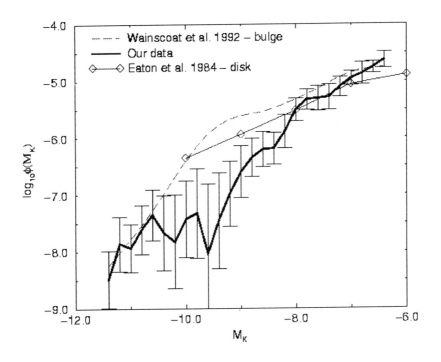

Figure 3.   Luminosity function of the bulge stars in the K band: the thick solid line is
the third and final iteration. Comparisons with the same luminosity function in the first
iteration, WCVWS in the bulge and Eaton et al. (1984) in the disc are also provided.

Fig. 3 shows that for $-10 < M_K < -7$ the bulge luminosity function is
significantly lower than that of the disc (Eaton et al. 1984). The discrepancy
with WCVWS could arise from their not having taken into account that
the brightest stars in the bulge are up to 2 magnitudes fainter than the disc

giants (Frogel & Whitford 1987). This would shift the luminosity function to the right.

The morphology of the bulge can be examined by fitting the isodensity surfaces to $D(\vec{r}) = D(r, l, b)$. We fitted three-dimentional ellipsoids with two axes in the Galactic plane, x and y (we have ignored a possible tilt out of the plane), to 20 isodensity surfaces (from 0.1 to 2.0 star pc^{-3}, in steps of 0.1) with four free parameters: R_0, the Sun-Galactic centre distance; K_z and K_y, the axis ratios with respect the major axis x; and α the angle between the major axis of the triaxial bulge and the line of sight to the Galactic centre.

The four averaged parameters have been fitted for the 20 ellipsoids and the results are: $R_0 = 7860 \pm 90$ pc, $K_z = 3.0 \pm 0.9$, $K_y = 1.87 \pm 0.18$ and $\alpha = 12 \pm 6$ deg. We can also express the axial ratios as 1 : 0.54 : 0.33. The errors are calculated from the average of the ellipsoids, and so do not include possible systematic errors. Hence, the true errors are larger that stated but tests suggest that they do not alter the general findings of this paper. These numbers indicate that the bulge is triaxial with the major axis close to the line of sight towards the Galactic centre. The error in K_z is quite large and is due to a non-constant axial ratio of the ellipsoids. There is a trend towards increasing K_z with proximity to the centre, i.e. the outer bulge is more circular than the inner bulge.

References

Cohen M., 1994, Ap&SS, 217(1), 181

Eaton N., Adams D. J, Gilels A. B., 1984, MNRAS, 208, 241

Frogel J. A., Whitford A. E., 1987, ApJ, 320, 199

Garzón F., Hammersley P. L., Mahoney T., Calbet X., Selby M. J., Hepburn I. D., 1993, MNRAS, 264, 773

Lucy L. B., 1974, AJ, 79(6), 745

Wainscoat R. J., Cohen M., Volk K., Walker H. J., Schwartz D. E., 1992, ApJSS, 83, 111 (WCVWS)

IR STAR COUNTS IN THE INNER DISC

P.L. HAMMERSLEY, F. GARZÓN, T. MAHONEY AND
M. LÓPEZ-CORREDOIRA

Instituto de Astrofísica de Canarias E-38200 La Laguna

Abstract. New small-scale JH star counts are presented for 4 regions on the plane between $l=31°$ and $l=15°$. The colour-magnitude diagrams clearly show that there is a major giant branch at $l=27°$ which is not present at $l=31°$. The distance to this feature is about 7.5 kpc with a total extinction of $A_V=7$ mag. This giant branch is also seen at $l=21°$ and $l=15°$ and is consistent with there being a major bar at an angle of about 75° to the line of sight. At $l=31°$ only features attributable to the disc can be seen and show that the extinction within the molecular ring is significantly higher than along the rest of the line of sight.

1. Introduction

Currently there is no satisfactory explanation for the distribution of stars near the plane for $l=33°$ to 15° and $l=-15°$ to –30°. Between $l=27°$ and 15° the Two Micron Galactic Survey (TMGS, Garzon et al. 1992) is finding a high concentration of very luminous sources within about 0.5° of the plane, which is not seen in any other area surveyed by the TMGS (Hammersley et al. 1994). This is clearly a young population related with the inner Galaxy. The more usual suggestion is that it could be a ring. However, the DIRBE 2.2 and 3.5 μm data show that a uniform circular ring is not feasible, and that if it were a ring it must be highly elliptical. Furthermore, the TMGS data would imply that this elliptical ring only has a significant density of stars near the tangential line of sights, with very few stars towards $l=7°$ or $l=-1°$. In Hammersley et al. (1994) the problems with the ring were discussed and it was suggested that this feature could be related to the bar, however more information was required.

63

N. Epchtein (ed.),
The Impact of Near-Infrared Sky Surveys on Galactic and Extragalactic Astronomy, 63-68.
© 1998 *Kluwer Academic Publishers. Printed in the Netherlands.*

TABLE 1. The lines of sight for areas covered. All lines of sight cross the disc and the Sagittarius and Scutum spiral arms

Position	Crosses		Comment
	stellar bar	3 kpc dust ring	
$l=31°$			Nearly tangential to the Scutum arm
$l=27°$	X		End of bar
$l=21°$	X	X	
$l=15°$	X	X	

2. The Data

Maps at J and H were made of number of small areas in the Galactic plane ($b = 0°$) at strategic positions determined from the TMGS and the DIRBE maps (Table 1). CAIN, the facility IR camera, on the 1.5 m TCS (Tenerife) was used to obtain the images. The 5 σ limiting magnitudes were about $H=16$ mag and $J=16$ mag, and the pixel scale, of 0.4" per pixel, was sufficient for confusion not to be a significant problem. In Figure 1 is presented the $J-H$ vs. H colour-magnitude diagrams for the regions at $l=31°, 27°, 21°$ and $15°$. The area covered at each region is given in the plots.

In order to help interpret these colour-magnitude diagrams Figure 2 shows the $l=31°$ region with the position of giants and dwarfs for various distances and total extinctions along the line of sight marked.

3. Results

The main difference between the $l=31°$ and $27°$ regions is the presence of a major giant branch in the latter region.

3.1. THE DISC

The $l=31°$ region is dominated by disc sources. The dwarf stars are less luminous than the giants and even with the magnitude limit of around $H=+16$ mag, the maximum distance for a G dwarf is around 2 kpc. Therefore the amount of reddening will be limited and hence the dwarfs form the clump with $J-H$ between 0 and 1.

The disc giants, which have their peak space density near K0III to K3III, form the diagonal stripe which can be seen in the $l=31°$ region between ($J-H=1,H=12$) and ($J-H=2,H=14$). This feature is visible in all the areas, although the actual gradient depends on the extinction. However this stripe does not form a smooth shallow curve as is predicted by the model;

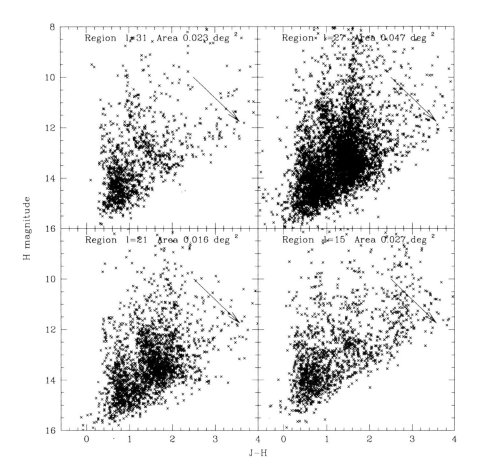

Figure 1. The $J - H$ vs. H colour-magnitude diagram for the regions at $l=31°, 27°, 21°$ and $15°$. The arrow indicates the reddening vector for 10 magnitudes of visual extinction.

rather, there is a significant dog-leg at ($J-H=1.2$, $H=12.5$). The only reasonable explanation for this is that the level of distributed extinction along the line of sight jumps suddenly by a factor three. If it is assumed that the stars causing the stripe are K2III then the dog-leg is at a Galactocentric distance of about 5 kpc (assuming $R_o=8$ kpc) and extends inwards to at least 4 kpc (the data is not sufficiently deep to determine what happens inside this distance). The location of this increased extinction is coincident with the molecular ring, which shows up prominently in radio maps (see e.g. Clemens, Sanders & Scoville 1988). The increase in extinction is consistent with the recent result from the analysis of DIRBE data (Sodroski et al.

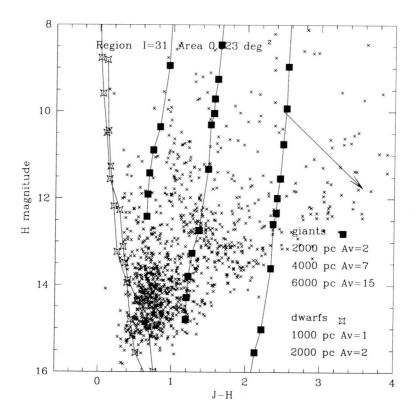

Figure 2. The $J - H$ vs. H colour-magnitude diagram for the $l=31°$ regions with the position of the dwarfs and giants at various distances and extinctions. The faintest giant marked in each case is G5III. The arrow indicates the reddening vector for 10 mag of visual extinction.

1997).

3.2. THE GIANT BRANCH

The giant branch at $l=27°$ and $l=21°$ runs from about $(J-H=1.6, H=14)$ to $(J-H=1.8, H=8)$. There are a number of important features

- From the $J-H$ colour, the total extinction to the feature is about $A_V=7$ mag.
- Assuming that the disc stripe is formed by K2III then the distance to the feature is about 7.5 kpc.
- The small spread in $J-H$ for sources within the giant branch indicates that there is little extinction within the feature, and that the feature does not extend significantly along the line of sight. The spread that

does exist can be attributed principally to the errors in the measured magnitudes.

– Over the H magnitude range covered by the plot the giant branch contributes some 50% sourced detected at $l=27°$.

– the giant branch is present at $l=21°$ and $15°$ and so extends significantly along the plane.

– The H star counts at $l=27°$ and $l=21°$ fainter than $H = +10$ are identical within the errors, whereas there are far more young stars at $l=27°$ than $l=21°$ (Hammersley et al. 1994).

4. Discussion

The giant branch indicates the presence of a major old feature in the inner Galaxy. However its location and extent are consistent with the very young feature discussed by Hammersley et al. (1994) and strongly suggest that the young and old sources stem from the same feature in the inner galaxy.

There is no evidence for either the giant branch or the excess of very young stars at $l=31°$ which is almost tangential to the Scutum spiral arm. Hence this feature is definitely not related to a spiral arm or young stars trailing off the arms, as $l=31°$ would be the position where it should be strongest. Similarly, the lack of the giant branch at $l=31°$ rules out the thick ring proposed by Kent, Dame and Fazio (1991), which would require the ring to extend to about $l=35°$.

Both the bar proposed in Hammersley et al. (1994) and an elliptical thin ring with the tangential points at $l=27°$ and $l=-22°$ could explain the presence of the giant branch and young stars at the same location, However, a bar and a ring should produce a difference distribution for the young and old star.

– A bar would be expected to have the young stars concentrated towards the end of the bar with far fewer in the middle of the bar (i.e. more at $l=27°$ than at $l=21°$), whereas the older stars would be spread more evenly down the bar.

– In principle a ring would have a similar distribution for both the old and young stars; i.e. a major peak for both young and old sources at the tangential point but falling rapidly inwards.

The evidence from this data set supports a bar far more than a ring. The bar would be expected to give the distribution of young and old sources that is seen. Only a very *ad hoc* patchy arrangement of young stars in a ring could give observed distribution.

It is now widely acknowledged that the Galaxy is barred. However, the bar that is normally referred to is that at a position angle of about $15°$ to the sun Galactic Centre line of sight (see, for example, Dwek et al. 1995) and

is in reality a triaxial bulge. However, this cannot be causing the features at $l=21°$ and $27°$. If the features at $l=27°$ and $l=21°$ are associated with a bar then it is distinct from the triaxial bulge and would have to have a position angle of about $75°$. Hence the Galaxy would in effect be a double barred spiral.

5. Conclusions

New JH star counts are presented for various directions on the Galactic plane looking towards the inner disc. The analysis of the disc counts shows that the extinction in the region of the molecular ring ($R=4.5$ kpc) is some three times higher than would be expected from a simple extrapolation from the solar circle.

The colour-magnitude diagrams show the presence at $l=27°$ $21°$ and $15°$ of a major giant branch which is not present at $l=31°$. This giant branch accounts for some 50% of the detected H sources at $l=27°$ and the feature causing the branch is at a distance of about 7.5 kpc. A bar provides the simplest explanation for the distribution in the inner disc of both the old stars detected here and young stars detected in the TMGS. A ring could be made to fit the data but the distribution of sources would be *ad hoc* and patchy. If the bar does turn out to be the explanation, then the Galaxy is a two barred spiral.

References

Clemens D. P., Sanders D. B., Scoville N.Z. 1988, ApJ,327, 139

Dwek E et al. 1995, ApJ. 445, 716.

Garzón F., Hammersley P. L., Mahoney T., Calbet X., Selby M. J., Hepburn, I., 1993, MNRAS, 264,773

Hammersley P.L., Garzón F., Mahoney T. ,Calbet X. 1994, MNRAS, 269 753

Kent S.M., Dame T. M., Fazio, G., 1991, ApJ 378 131.

Sodroski.T.J., Odegard,N., Arendt R.G., Dwek E., Weiland J.L., Hauser M.G., Kelsali T., 1997, ApJ 480, 173

SPATIAL DISTRIBUTION OF EVOLVED GIANT STARS IN THE GALACTIC DISC USING DENIS DATA

STÉPHANIE RUPHY
Observatoire de Paris, DESPA, 92190 Meudon, France
stephanie.ruphy@larecherche.fr

Abstract. I will present the analysis of 3-colour (IJK$_s$) near infrared star counts obtained during the commissioning phase of the Deep Near Infrared Southern Sky Survey (DENIS) project. Nine strips of 12' of RA $\times 30°$ in declination crossing the galactic plane at different longitudes ranging from 217 °to 385 °, covering approximately 50 square degrees are analyzed. One strip has been measured in 3 colours, the others in J and K only. More than 250 000 objects are detected and calibrated. The completeness limits are 17.5, 15.5 and 13.5 in the I, J and K$_s$bands, respectively. Colour-colour diagrams are shown to be efficient tool for breaking out dwarf and giant star populations especiall y at low latitude, where the interstellar extinction strongly affects the far away red giants. Source counts are compared to the SKY model developed by Cohen (1997). This small sample of DENIS data is tentatively used to investigate the existence and the spatial distribution of the stellar populations associated with the molecular ring at R = 4 kpc. The detail of my work has been published in Ruphy et al., (1996), Ruphy, (1996) and Ruphy et al., (1997).

References

Cohen M. (1996) Proc. of the 2nd Euroconference on *The impact of Large Scale near-infrared sky surveys*, Puerto de la Cruz, Spain, eds. F. Garzon, N. Epchtein, A. Omont, W.B. Burton, P. Persi, Kluwer ASSL series **vol. no. 210**, pp 67–70

Ruphy S. (1996) *Thèse de Doctorat, Université de Paris 6*

Ruphy S., Robin A.C., Epchtein N., Copet E., Bertin E., Fouqué P., Guglielmo F. (1996) *A&AL*, **Vol. no. 313**, pp. L21-L24

Ruphy S., Epchtein N., Copet E., de Batz B., Borsenberger J., Fouqué P., Kimeswenger S., Lacombe F., Le Bertre T., Rouan D., Tiphène D. (1997) *A&A*, **vol.326**, pp. 597-607

N. Epchtein (ed.),
The Impact of Near-Infrared Sky Surveys on Galactic and Extragalactic Astronomy, 69.
© *1998 Kluwer Academic Publishers. Printed in the Netherlands.*

III- Stars

INFRARED EMISSION OF CARBON STARS

M. A. T. GROENEWEGEN
Max-Planck-Institut für Astrophysik,
Karl-Schwarzschild-Straße 1, D-85748 Garching, Germany

Abstract.
This review addresses the infrared emission from the most important classes of carbon-rich objects: the N- and R-type carbon stars, the carbon dwarfs and the CH-stars. Examples of carbon rich objects in the Galactic halo and the Magellanic Clouds are discussed. Discrimination of carbon-rich objects against red oxygen-rich objects is investigated. The detectibility of N-type carbon Miras in the DENIS and 2MASS near-infrared surveys is discussed.

1. Introduction

The organisers had asked me to review the infrared emission of carbon stars. They may not have realised that this is a formidable task indeed as there are actually many types of carbon-rich objects. Here, I will not discuss the R CrB stars, hydrogen deficient carbon (HdC) stars and carbon-rich post-AGB stars. The latter two classes have no or very little present-day mass loss and their near-infrared emission (most important for the kind of infrared surveys that are the topic of this conference) is therefore dominated by the stellar photosphere. Instead, I will concentrate on the more well-known classes of carbon-rich objects, namely the N- and R-type carbon stars, the CH-stars and the carbon dwarfs. In particular, I would like to discuss the spectral characteristics of these classes of carbon-stars.

As will be discussed below, the near-infrared DENIS and 2MASS surveys have the potential to discover carbon stars with near-infrared emission to large distances. In addition, the related question how to distinguish the different types of carbon-rich objects amongst each other and from red oxygen-rich objects from the data of these surveys will be investigated using colour-colour diagrams.

N. Epchtein (ed.),
The Impact of Near-Infrared Sky Surveys on Galactic and Extragalactic Astronomy, 73-86.
© 1998 *Kluwer Academic Publishers. Printed in the Netherlands.*

2. Different kinds of carbon stars

2.1. THE N-TYPE CARBON STARS

The N-type carbon stars are formed on the Asymptotic Giant Branch
(AGB) after one or more third dredge-up events where carbon is mixed
into the convective envelope. For a comprehensive scenario see Groenewegen et al. (1995), for a general review on AGB stars, see Habing (1996).

Characteristic of this class of stars is their variability and heavy mass
loss, which are related to each other. As is the case for oxygen-rich Miras,
there are correlations between the pulsation period and luminosity (Feast
et al. 1989, Groenewegen & Whitelock 1996), and period and mass loss rate
(Groenewegen et al. 1997b) for carbon miras.

2.2. THE R-TYPE CARBON STARS

The R-type carbon stars are hotter and less luminous than the N-type
(Scalo 1976) and can not be on the AGB. These, or very similar hot and
low luminosity carbon stars, have been found in the Galactic bulge (Lloyd
Evans 1985, Westerlund et al. 1991) and the Magellanic Clouds (Westerlund
et al. 1992, 1995).

McClure (1997) monitored 22 R-stars and found no evidence for radial
velocity variations in any of them.

The classical explanation for the formation of these carbon stars considers an extraordinary mixing event at the Helium core flash (e.g. Dominy
1984). Based on the lower than expected 20% binary frequency McClure
(1997) proposes that these stars may be coalescing binaries.

Significant cold and hot dust is known in only one case (Parthasarathy
1991). For the general absence of significant IR excess in R-, CH- and Ba
II-stars see Dominy (1986).

2.3. THE CH-TYPE CARBON STARS

These stars, recognised as a separate class by Keenan (1942), are typically
metal-poor objects with the kinematics of Population II objects. They are
in binary systems (McClure & Woodsworth 1990). They are hotter than
the N-type, with equivalent spectral types in the range G-K. Their near-
infrared colours are of photospheric origin.

2.4. THE CARBON DWARFS

Currently, there are nine of these peculiar objects known. Their space density exceeds that of N-type carbon stars (Green et al. 1992). The prototype
carbon dwarf G77-61 was discovered twenty years ago (Dahn et al. 1977)

and long remained the only example known. Then, eight more were discovered by Green et al. (1991, 1992), Heber et al. (1993), Warren et al. (1993) and Liebert et al. (1994). Three carbon dwarfa are known binaries; this was established for the prototype from radial velocity measurements, for the two others from composite spectra. In the latter cases the companion is a white dwarf. The absolute V-magnitude is in the range +9.7-10.8.

3. Carbon stars in different environment

3.1. HALO CARBON STARS

Carbon stars in the Galactic halo have been long known (Sanduleak 1980, Margon et al. 1984). They are sometimes designated faint high-latitude carbon (FHLC) stars. Margon et al. (1984), Mould et al. (1985), Bothun et al. (1991), Green et al. (1992) and Moody et al. (1997) contain in total 41 such stars, some of which turned out to be dwarf carbon stars (Green & Margon 1994), or are known CH-stars. Originally, the interest in them was as tracers of the outer halo.

In a recent paper, Totten & Irwin (1997) present the results of an optical survey (a byproduct of the APM survey) for FHLC stars covering about 6500 sq. degrees. Thirty-two are definitely N-type, and some of them may be 'dusty'.

Interestingly enough, some FHLC stars are losing mass at a considerable rate. Two were serendipitously discovered by Cutri et al. (1989) and Beichman et al. (1990), namely IRAS 08546+1732 and IRAS 12560+1656. Both are Miras with a 390 day period (Joyce et al. 1997). A more detailed analysis is performed by Groenewegen et al. (1997a). From the period-luminosity relation of Groenewegen & Whitelock (1996) a luminosity of 5800 $L_\odot$ is derived for a period of 390 days, measured for both stars. A model fit with a dust radiative transfer model to the spectral energy distributions then gives the distances of 8.0 and 20 kpc from sun, and 7.8 and 11 kpc from the Galactic plane.

CO J = 2-1 emission was detected in the nearest object (IRAS 12560) after ten hours of integration using the IRAM 30m telescope. The expansion velocity is low at only 3.2 km s^{-1}, and stellar LSR velocity is +88 km s^{-1}. Combining the CO and dust observations and the modelling, Groenewegen et al. (1997a) derive for this star a mass loss rate of 1.3 $\times$ 10^{-6} M$_\odot$yr^{-1}, and a dust-to-gas ratio of 0.0014. The abundance of CO w.r.t H$_2$ is found to be 2 $\times$ 10^{-4}, indicating an underabundance of oxygen by –0.7 dex. w.r.t. solar.

The colours of these two stars are as follows: M_K = –6.8 and –7.6, I_C = 14.3 and 18.7, J = 10.4 and 14.0, H = 8.6 and 11.8, K = 7.0 and 9.7. With such colours and a K-survey down to 14th magnitude one could probe the

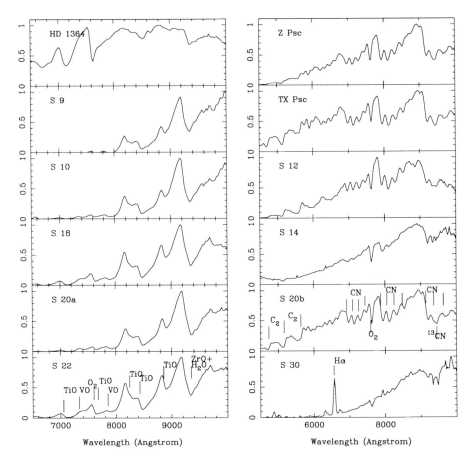

Figure 1. Optical spectra of AGB stars in the SMC (identified by S <number>), the M3.5 IIIa MK standard star HD 1364 and the known carbon stars TX Psc and Z Psc. Well known lines are identified, including telluric O_2 and H_2O lines. From Groenewegen & Blommaert (1997).

halo out to distances of at least 150 kpc. It is expected that 2MASS and DENIS will identify many more mass-losing halo carbon stars.

3.2. CARBON STARS IN THE MAGELLANIC CLOUDS

This is a long standing research topic dating back to the first surveys in the 1960's by Westerlund (1960). I had the opportunity to review this subject recently, including a discussion of the first ISO results on AGB stars in the Magellanic Clouds (Groenewegen 1997b). I will therefore be brief on this topic. Just as a reference: the total estimated number of carbon stars in the LMC is about 11 000 (Blanco & McCarthy 1983), while about 2 900 are known in the SMC (Blanco & McCarthy 1983, Rebeirot et al. 1993).

The last few years saw a number of interesting papers (WEG: taking a look at this subject) from the point of view of IRAS detected AGB stars in the Clouds (Whitelock et al. 1989, Reid et al. 1990, Reid 1991, Wood et al. 1992, Groenewegen et al. 1995, Zijlstra et al. 1996, van Loon et al. 1997a, b, Loup et al. 1997, Groenewegen & Blommaert 1997). The first and last paper in this list specifically deal with the SMC, the other papers concentrate on the LMC. The important outcome of these papers is that mass-losing AGB stars exist in the Clouds. However, as the 12 μm fluxes are close to the detection limit, the IRAS view is far from complete. For a given mass loss rate, the IRAS detection probability increases with increasing luminosity, and vice versa. An almost complete census of AGB stars in the Clouds will be provided by DENIS and 2MASS.

4. Spectral characteristics of carbon stars

In this section I will describe the emission and absorption features one can observe in carbon stars, starting in the optical and then turning to the near- and mid-infrared.

In the optical the absorption bands that identify a carbon star are the C_2 bands at e.g. 4737, 5165 and 5636 Å, and the stronger CN bands longwards of 7000 Å. As an example, Fig. 1 shows low resolution optical spectra of carbon (and oxygen-rich AGB stars for comparison) stars in the SMC, together with some well known objects (Groenewegen & Blommaert 1997).

A comprehensive atlas of carbon star spectra can be found in Barnbaum et al. (1996; at moderate resolution) and Barnbaum (1994; at high resolution).

Although one could have thought that the optical spectra of carbon stars are well understood almost a century since their discovery, the recent paper by Sarre et al. (1996) provides the first accurate vibrational band assignments of the SiC_2 molecule. This molecule has prominent bands in the 4750-5050 Å region (also called Merrill-Sanford bands). Figure 2 is an adaptation of Fig. 1 of Sarre et al. (1996) where details can be found. See Barnbaum et al. (1996) for more examples.

Green et al. (1992) find unusually strong C_2 6191 Å bandheads in the carbon dwarfs, which is not seen in any of the other FHLC stars they observed, and suggest this may be a spectroscopic way of identifying carbon dwarfs.

Moving towards the near-infrared there are two prominent absorption bands that identify carbon stars: a C_2 band at 1.77 μm at the edge of the H-band, and a blend of HCN and C_2H_2 lines (see Ridgway et al. 1978 for a high resolution spectrum) near 3.1 μm at the edge of the L-band.

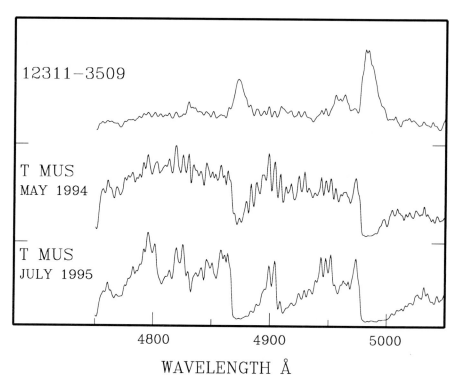

WAVELENGTH Å

Figure 2.   Spectra between 4750 and 5050Å of IRAS 12311-3509 and the semiregular variable T Mus in May 1994, when the SiC₂ absorption spectrum was abnormal, and July 1995. The spectra are flux-calibrated on an arbitrary intensity scale. The absorption bands at 4872, 4911 and 4982 Å are clearly visible in the bottom spectra. The spectrum of 12311–3509 illustrates that these bands can also be observed in emission. Adopted from Sarre et al. (1996), where more details can be found.

An example of the 1.77 μm feature is shown in Fig. 3 (from Lançon & Wood 1997). More near-infrared spectra of carbon stars are shown in Lázaro et al. (1994).

An example of the shape of the 3.1 μm feature is shown in Fig. 4 (from Groenewegen et al. 1994; also see Yamamura et al. 1997b). Substructure is clearly visible due to the fact that this feature is a blend. More 3 μm spectra of carbon- and oxygen-rich stars can be found in Merrill & Stein (1976a,b,c).

Recently, the Japanese IRTS and ESA's ISO satellite provided a wealth of new information, because of the coverage of wavelengths not observable from the ground, and the higher spectral resolution. IRTS/NIRS-MIRS spectra of carbon stars are shown in Fig. 5 (adopted from Yamamura et al. 1997a). ISO SWS spectra are shown in Fig. 6 (adopted from Yamamura et al. 1997b). The following lines can be identified: HCN + C₂H₂ features

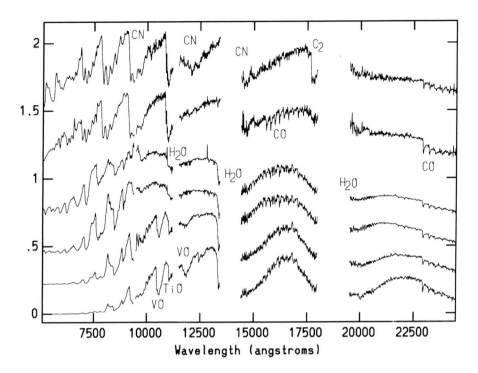

Figure 3. Near-infrared spectra of a carbon star (top spectrum) compared to oxygen-rich spectra. Note the strong C_2 absorption at 1.77 μm. From Lançon & Wood (1997).

at 3.1 μm (see above), 3.9 μm (also observable from the ground, e.g. Bregman et al. 1978), 7.5 μm and 13.7 μm, a C_3 feature at 5.2 μm, and the well-known silicon carbide (SiC) dust emission feature at 11.3 μm. I will not discuss features longward of 20 μm. The SiC feature can be observed from the ground (e.g. Treffers & Cohen 1974, Speck et al. 1997) and is present in the wavelength range covered by the IRAS low resolution spectrograph, and is thus studied extensively (e.g. Lorentz-Martins & Lefèvre 1994, Groenewegen et al. 1997b)

The SWS spectra have revealed so much detail that the theoretical interpretation is lacking behind the observations at the moment. Recent attempts to remedy this, and e.g. to predict the strength of the various absorption features as a function of phase in the pulsation cycle, can be found in Loidl et al. (1997) and Hron et al. (1997).

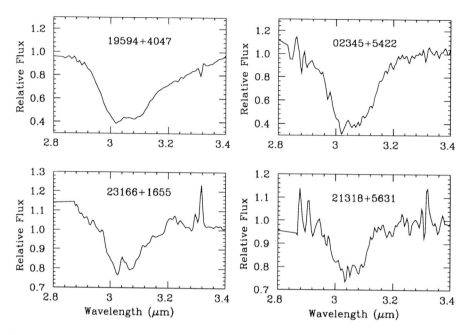

Figure 4. Normalised 3 μm spectra of carbon stars. IRAS names are indicated. From Groenewegen et al. (1994).

5. Carbon stars in relation to DENIS and 2MASS

Let us first estimate to which distances carbon Miras can be detected in the DENIS and 2MASS surveys. As the K-band seems the most suitable filter in terms of sensitivity and intrinsic brightness of the objects in question, I concentrate on that filter. In Groenewegen & Whitelock (1996) the following period-K-relation is derived from stars in the LMC, scaled to the galaxy: $M_K = -3.56 \log P + 1.14$.

In Table 1 the relevant numbers are collected for a typical 'short' period of 200 days, an 'average' period of 400 days and a typical 'long' period of 700 days. The respective absolute K-magnitudes based on the P-K-relation are listed, as well as the range in distances carbon miras can be observed based on saturation and 10σ detection limits for DENIS (Epchtein 1997) and 2MASS (Skrutskie et al. 1997). The conclusion is that the near-IR surveys have the potential to detect carbon stars out to several hundred kpc.

Can the different types of carbon-rich objects be distinguished from each other, and from oxygen-rich objects?

Figure 7 shows *IJK* and *JHK* colour-colour diagrams from Groenewegen (1997a). Oxygen-rich and carbon-rich AGB stars are compared to

IRTS/NIRS-MIRS Spectra of Carbon Stars

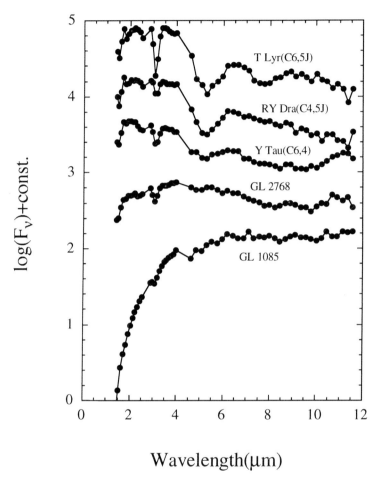

Figure 5. IRTS spectra of carbon stars. Note the strong features at 3.1 μm and 5.2 μm. Adopted from Yamamura et al. (1997a).

galaxies, M-dwarfs, Herbig Ae/Be stars and T Tau stars. For the construction of these samples see Groenewegen (1997a). Note that the sequence for the oxygen-rich AGB stars (the filled squares) does not appear continuous. This is an artifact of the type of templates used.

Additional information comes from Green et al. (1992, their Fig. 1) who present a colour-colour diagram which includes the carbon dwarfs. It appears that in a $(J - H), (H - K)$ diagram they are off-set with respect to other FHLC-stars and the low luminosity carbon stars in the Galactic

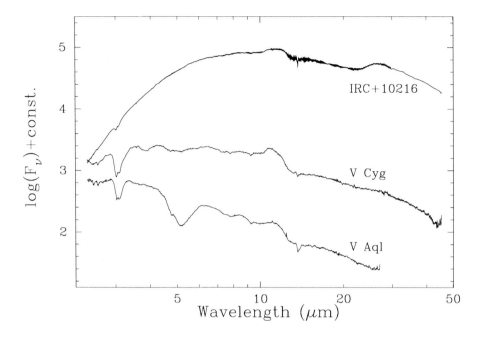

Figure 6.   ISO SWS spectra of carbon stars. Adopted from Yamamura et al. (1997b).

TABLE 1. How far can carbon miras be detected ?

	survey	$P = 200$	400	700 days
M_K		−7.05	−8.12	−8.95
Range	DENIS[a]	5.1-90	8.4-145	12.5-220
(kpc)	2MASS[b]	1.6-190	2.7-300	3.9-450

[a]Based on a saturation limit of $K = 6.5$ and a 10σ detection limit of 12.7. Interstellar extinction is neglected.
[b]Based on a saturation limit of $K = 4.0$ and a 10σ detection limit of 14.3. Interstellar extinction is neglected.

bulge. The colours of the carbon dwarfs are blue: $0.25 \lesssim (H - K) \lesssim 0.36$, $0.35 \lesssim (J - H) \lesssim 0.65$.

Furthermore, Feast & Whitelock (1992, their Fig. 5) present a $(J - H), (H - K)$ colour-colour diagram that includes CH-stars in the LMC, carbon dwarfs in dwarf spheroidals, Galactic CH- or related stars, CH-stars in ω Cen and the dwarf carbon stars. Apart from the dwarf carbon stars that stand out as mentioned above, there is a large overlap between the classes. They also show that there is a significant overlap with normal oxygen-rich giants.

For comparison, Fig. 8 shows colour-colour diagrams for a relatively

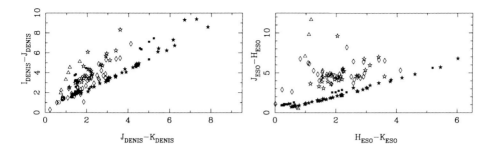

Figure 7. IJK and JHK colour-colour diagram. Symbols: carbon stars = filled stars; oxygen-rich AGB stars = filled squares; galaxies = open circles; M-dwarfs = open triangles; He Ae/Be stars = open diamonds; T Tau stars = open stars. The limits of the IJK plot are set based on the saturation and 5σ detection limits of DENIS; very red AGB objects outside the plot limits do exist. For the AGB stars the colours are dereddened. From Groenewegen (1997a).

unbiased sample of carbon stars in the LMC (Costa & Frogel 1996). The larger scatter in the bottom panel is in all likelihood due to the fact that the I- and JK photometry was not taken simultaneously.

The conclusion I draw from all these data is that, based on IJK and JHK colour-colour diagrams alone, (a) it is extremely difficult to separate unreddened carbon stars (mainly CH-stars, R-stars) from normal oxygen-rich giants, as exception possibly being the carbon dwarfs, (b) for moderate red colours there is the danger of overlap with other red sources. This danger appears to be less for the 2MASS system, (c) mass-losing AGB stars with very red colours are easily identified but this will be a minority of sources amongst the 10^8 that are expected to be detected, as demonstrated in Fig. 7.

As discussed in Groenewegen (1997a) additional information may be used to make a more clear-cut discrimination, e.g. optical colors or IRAS fluxes. However the latter only provides such information for a few 10^5 sources only.

6. Conclusions

Carbon stars display a rich absorption and emission spectrum. The recent satellite missions ISO and IRTS have unveiled parts of the spectrum that are inaccessible from the ground, the 5-8 μm and the $\gtrsim 20$ μm region.

The upcoming near-infrared surveys have the potential to detect carbon stars out to large distances. However, except for the reddest sources, it will prove difficult to separate the different classes of carbon stars from colour-colour-diagrams alone and there is the potential of confusion with oxygen-rich sources, or other red sources. Conclusive identification could be done using narrow-band filters in the optical (e.g. Richer et al. 1984)

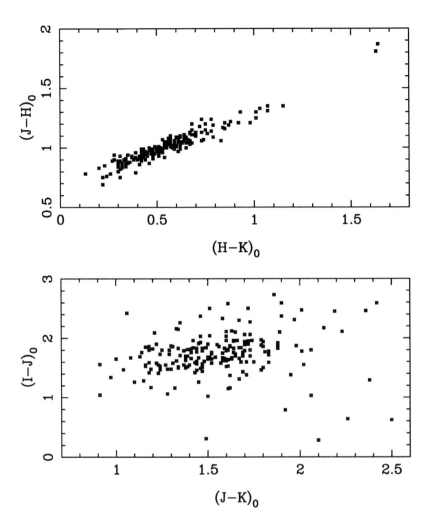

Figure 8.　Colour-colour diagram for a sample of carbon stars in the LMC. Based on data from Costa & Frogel (1996).

or the near-infrared (not yet attempted). This should be possible even for distant objects with the new generation of 10m class telescopes.

ACKNOWLEDGEMENTS

I would like to thank the people who granted me permission to include (modified) version of published figures and for their effort in making these figures: P. Sarre, T. Lloyd Evans, J. Blommaert, A. Lançon, I. Yamamura, and their collaborators.

References

Barnbaum C., 1994, ApJS 90, 317

Barnbaum C., Stone R.S., Keenan P.C., 1996, ApJS 105, 419

Beichman C.A., et al., 1990, AJ 99, 1569

Blanco V.M., McCarthy M.F., 1983, AJ 88, 1442

Bothun G., et al., 1991, AJ 101, 2220

Bregman J.D., Goebel J.H., Strecker D.W., 1978, ApJ 223, L45

Costa E., Frogel J.A, 1996, AJ 112, 2607

Cutri R.M., et al., 1989, AJ 97, 866

Dahn C.C., Liebert J., Kron R.G., Spinrad H., Hintzen P.M., 1977, ApJ 216, 757

Dominy J.F., 1984, ApJS 55, 27

Dominy J.F., 1986, AJ 91, 951

Epchtein N., 1997, in: "The impact of large-scale IR surveys", eds. F. Garzón et al., p. 15

Feast M.W., Glass I.S., Whitelock P.A., Catchpole R.M., 1989, MNRAS 241, 375

Feast M.W., Whitelock P.A., 1992, MNRAS 259, 6

Green P.J., Margon B., 1994, ApJ 423, 723

Green P.J., Margon B., Anderson S.F., MacConnell D.J., 1992, ApJ 400, 659

Green P.J., Margon B., MacConnell D.J., 1991, ApJ 380, L31

Groenewegen M.A.T., 1997a, in: "The impact of large-scale IR surveys", eds. F. Garzón et al., p. 165

Groenewegen M.A.T., 1997b, in: "ISO's view on stellar evolution", eds. L. Waters, C. Waelkens and K. A. van der Hucht, Kluwer Academic Publishers, p. TBD

Groenewegen M.A.T., Blommaert J.A.D.L., 1997, A&A, submitted

Groenewegen M.A.T., van den Hoek L.B., de Jong T., 1995, A&A 293, 381

Groenewegen M.A.T., de Jong T., Geballe T.R., 1994, A&A 287, 163

Groenewegen M.A.T., Oudmaijer R.D., Ludwig H.-G., 1997a, MNRAS in press

Groenewegen M.A.T., Smith C.H., Wood P.R., Omont A., Fujiyoshi T., 1995, ApJ 449, L119

Groenewegen M.A.T., Whitelock P.A., 1996, MNRAS 281, 1347

Groenewegen M.A.T., Whitelock P.A., Smith C.H., Kerschbaum F., 1997b, MNRAS in press

Habing H., 1996, A&AR 7, 97

Heber U., Bade N., Jordan S., Voges W., 1993, A&A 267, L31

Hron J., Loidl R., Jørgensen U.G., Kerschbaum F., in: "ISO's view on stellar evolution", eds. L. Waters, C. Waelkens and K. A. van der Hucht, Kluwer Academic Publishers, p. TBD

Joyce R.R., Merrill K.C., Gillett F.C., 1997, in preparation

Keenan P.C., 1942, ApJ 96, 101

Lançon A., Wood P.R., 1997, in : "Poster proceedings of IAU Symp. 189 on Fundamental stellar properties: The interaction between Observation and Theory", p.168, ed. T.R. Bedding, School of Physics, University of Sydney

Lázaro C., et al., 1994, MNRAS 269, 365

Liebert J., et al., 1994, ApJ 421, 733

Loidl R., Höfner S., Hron J., Aringer B., Jørgensen U.G., in: "ISO's view on stellar evolution", eds. L. Waters, C. Waelkens and K. A. van der Hucht, Kluwer Academic Publishers, p. TBD

Lloyd Evans T., 1985, MNRAS 216, 29P

van Loon J. Th., Zijlstra A.A., Whitelock P.A., Waters L.B.F.M., Loup C., Trams N.R., 1997a, A&A 325, 585

van Loon J. Th., Zijlstra A.A., Whitelock P.A., te Lintel Hekkert P., Chapman J.M., Loup C., Groenewegen M.A.T., Waters L.B.F.M., Trams N.R., 1997b, A&A in press

Loup C., Zijlstra A.A., Waters L.B.F.M., Groenewegen M.A.T., 1997, A&AS, in press

Lorentz-Martins S., Lefèvre J., 1994, A&A 291, 831

Margon B., Aaronson M., Liebert J., 1984, AJ 89, 274

McClure R.D., 1997, PASP 109, 256

McClure R.D., Woodsworth A.W., 1990, ApJ 352, 709

Merrill K.M., Stein W.A., 1976a, PASP 88, 285

Merrill K.M., Stein W.A., 1976b, PASP 88, 294

Merrill K.M., Stein W.A., 1976c, PASP 88, 874

Moody J.W., Gregory S.A., Soukup M.S., Jaderlund E.C., 1997, AJ 113, 1022

Mould J.R., Schneider P., Gordon G.A., Aaronson M., Liebert J., 1985, PASP 97, 130

Parthasarathy M., 1991, A&A 247, 429

Rebeirot E., Azzopardi M., Westerlund B.E., 1993, A&AS 97, 603

Reid N., 1991, ApJ 382, 143

Reid N., Hughes S.M.G., Glass I.S., 1995, MNRAS 275, 331

Richer H.B., Crabtree D.R., Pritchet C.J., 1984, ApJ 287, 138

Ridgway S.T., Carbon D.F., Hall D.N., 1978, ApJ 225, 138

Sanduleak N., 1980, PASP 92, 246

Sarre P.J., Hurst M.E., Lloyd Evans T., 1996, ApJ 471, L107

Scalo J.M., 1976, ApJ 206, 474

Skrutskie M.F., et al., 1997, in: "The impact of large-scale IR surveys", eds. F. Garzón
    et al., p. 25

Speck A.K., Barlow M.J., Skinner C.J., 1997, MNRAS 288, 431

Treffers R., Cohen M., 1974, ApJ 188, 545

Totten E.J., Irwin M.J., 1997b, MNRAS, submitted

Warren S.J., Irwin M.J., Evans D.W., Liebert J., Osmer P.S., Hewett P.C., 1993, MNRAS
    261, 185

Westerlund B.E., 1960, Uppsala Astron. Obs. Ann. 4, No. 7

Westerlund B.E., Azzopardi M., Breysacher J., Rebeirot E., 1992, A&A 260, L4

Westerlund B.E., Azzopardi M., Breysacher J., Rebeirot E., 1995, A&A 303, 107

Westerlund B.E., Lequeux J., Azzopardi M., Rebeirot E., 1991, A&A 244, 367

Whitelock P.A., Feast M.W., Menzies J.W., Catchpole R.M., 1989, MNRAS 238, 769

Wood P.R., Whiteoack J.B., Hughes S.M.G., Bessell M.S., Gardner F.F., Hyland A.R.,
    1992, ApJ 397, 552

Yamamura, I. and the IRTS team, 1997a, in "Infrared Diffuse Radiation and the IRTS",
    eds. H. Okuda, T. Matsumoto, and T. L. Roellig, PASP 124, 72

Yamamura I., de Jong T., Justtanont K., Cami J., Waters L.B.F.M., 1997b, in: "ISO's
    view on stellar evolution", eds. L. Waters, C. Waelkens and K. A. van der Hucht,
    Kluwer Academic Publishers, p. TBD

Zijlstra A.A., Loup C., Waters L.B.F.M., Whitelock P.A., van Loon J. Th., Guglielmo
    F., 1996, A&A 279, 32

AGB STARS IN THE GALACTIC BULGE
OBSERVED BY DENIS

M. SCHULTHEIS
Institut für Astronomie der Universität Wien, Austria

G. SIMON
Observatoire de Paris, France

AND

J.HRON
Institut für Astronomie der Universität Wien, Austria

Abstract. We present first results of DENIS photometry for semiregular variables (SRVs) and Miras in field #3 of the Palomar-Groningen survey (PG3, $l = 0^0, b = -10^0$). The PG3 Miras and SRVs are located in the colour-colour diagram (CCD) in both colours at the reddest end. PG3 variables show a large scatter in $(I - J)_0$ while in a $K_0^S/(J - K^S)_0$ diagram they are situated at the top of the red giant branch. In contrast to the LMC we do not find any carbon star sequence which is due to the different age and metallicity of the Bulge. PG3 variables follow a PC relation as well as a period-luminosity relation.

1. Introduction

PG3 (field #3 of the Palomar-Groningen Variable Star Survey; $l = 0^0$, $b = -10^0$) is well searched for variable stars (Plaut 1971, Wesselink 1987). Blommaert (1992) studied the properties of the PG3 Miras while Schultheis et al. (1997) the properties of the SRVs. Besides near-Infrared photometry (JHKL'M) obtained at the 1 m ESO telescope (now dedicated to DENIS), spectra and radial velocities are available. Schultheis et al. (1997) found that the PG3 SRVs are not the analogs of the field SRVs. The PG3 SRVs form a short period extension to the Miras PK and PC relations. This indicates that the PG3 Miras and SRVs are both pulsating in the same

87

N. Epchtein (ed.),
The Impact of Near-Infrared Sky Surveys on Galactic and Extragalactic Astronomy, 87–94.
© 1998 Kluwer Academic Publishers. Printed in the Netherlands.

mode, possibly the fundamental. The metallicity of PG3 is between half solar and solar. Both PG3 Miras and SRVs follow the SgrI PK relation which again stresses the metallicity independence of the PL relation. Ng & Schultheis (1997) found for a few faint AGB stars evidence that they are members of the Sagittarius dwarf galaxy. Two carbon stars found in PG3 might be member of the Sagittarius darf galaxy as well (Ng, 1997).

The main aim of this work is to obtain DENIS photometry for those well-known AGB stars. Their position in a colour-colour and a colour-magnitude diagram will help to search for more AGB stars candidates. Further on, DENIS will offer a good tool to study the stellar population related to the Sagittarius dwarf galaxy.

2. Selection of DENIS strips

Based on the coordinates of the PG3 variables we looked for 77 Miras and 78 SRVs in the DENIS archive. 21 PG3 Miras and 15 PG3 SRVs have been observed by DENIS up to now. At least two measurements for 6 Miras and 2 SRVs were obtained. Fig. 1 shows the observed DENIS strips of PG3. In

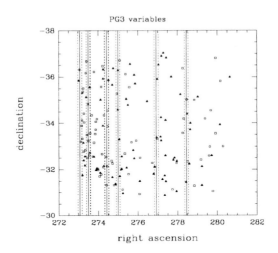

Figure 1. Distribution of the PG3 variables in α and δ. PG3 SRVs are indicated by triangles, PG3 Miras by squares. Solid lines mark the centre of the observed DENIS strips, the dashed ones indicate each 6'.

total 8 strips were observed by DENIS where two of them were reobserved (see table 1), which gives a total number of ~ 80 frames. For two strips the quality is very poor and have to be reobserved. Note that we do not deal with full strips but with single frames.

strip number	Date obs.	α	comments
2801	26/08/95	18 33 50	I channel not available
2887	14/09/95	18 20 00	
4099	19/05/96	18 17 41	
4109	22/05/96	18 27 41	
4423	14/08/96	18 12 18	
4438	16/08/96	18 13 04	
4485	22/08/96	18 33 50	different epoch as 2801
4721	11/10/96	18 20 00	different epoch as 2887

TABLE 1. Observed DENIS strips for PG3

3. Reduction procedure

The whole reduction procedure was done with the PDAC pipeline. For each strip two standard stars were used in order to derive the photometric zero point. In the subsections below the reduction procedure is described roughly. For a more detailed description I refer to Ruphy (1996).

3.1. ABSOLUTE ASTROMETRY

For the absolute astrometry the individual DENIS frames were cross-correlated with the Guide Star Catalog in each channel. As we are dealing with crowded fields the automatic correlation failed and it had to be done manually. The corresponding offset has been applied to the frames. Afterwards for each frame the distortion matrix was calculated. The absolute astrometry is accurate in the order of ~ 0.5".

3.2. SOURCE EXTRACTION

The Sextractor software written by E.Bertin was used for extracting the sources. For a description of the Sextractor itself I refer to Bertin and Arnouts (1996). In the remaining catalog, bad sources have been removed. Near the edge of the frame some sources are not extracted to avoid border problems. Fig. 2 demonstrates the difference in the extraction procedure as well as the systematic shift in the astrometry. LDAC extracts in total more sources than we found, using the whole frame and extracting deeper in magnitude (due to different cuts used).

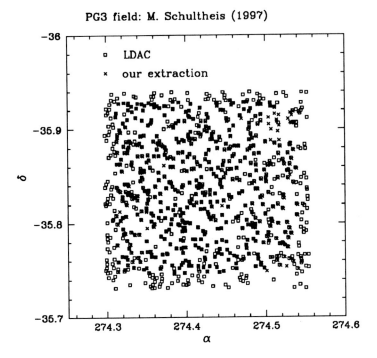

Figure 2.   Comparison of the LDAC and our source extraction for frame Nr. 531977. The sources are detected in all three channels. Open squares indicate the LDAC source extraction, crosses our source extraction.

3.3. PHOTOMETRY

As we used only two standard stars for the determination of the zero point a standard extinction coefficient has been applied. For some strips the standard star was clearly saturated, mostly in the I channel, so that only one star was used for the definition of the zero point. The standard deviation of the 8 single measurements taken for the standard PHOTO is typically of the order of a few hundreths of a magnitude. The mean over the 8 values was taken for the zero point. Between the different strips the zero point can deviate up to $0^m.8$ which is most likely due to different atmospheric conditions for the various strips.

3.4. PAIRING

The pairing procedure determines the reliability of the colours one gets and is therefore very important, especially for crowded fields where misidentifications lead to wrong colours. In our case the pairing was done between the three channels for each frame separately. In an iterative procedure the

best match between all channels has been obtained. The resulting accuracy
of the pairing is of the order of 0.1".

3.5. IDENTIFICATION OF THE PG3 VARIABLES

The PG3 variables were identified mainly based on their coordinates and
their known magnitudes in J and K. In a few cases, there were a few possible
candidates very close to the position. In this case finding charts helped to
identify the correct object. Especially, some PG3 Miras are saturated and
could not be used for further analysis.

3.6. QUALITY ANALYSIS

For each strip separately a colour-colour diagram was obtained and compared with each other. For some strips the colour-colour diagrams look
very broad and show a significantly large offset which is mostly due to the
quality of the night. Those strips have been excluded. They further show
in contrast to the others a very broad magnitude distribution. In total four
strips were taken into account for further analysis. Between the four strips
there is a noticeable shift in the magnitude distribution. We shifted the
remaining strips with regard to the reference strip. The magnitude distribution observed here comes from the gaussian peaked shape of the bulge
population superimposed to the non-gaussian distribution of the disk population. The faint FWHM is approximately the place where the combined
field stars and bulge RGB contribution ought to become dominant. Since
this is not the case we assume that this hints for a large incompleteness
in the stellar sample or the detection limit of the survey due to increased
crowding. Our detection limits are therefore $I = 14^{m}.8$, $J = 14^{m}.3$ and
$K^{S} = 13^{m}.8$ respectively. We only regarded sources where the photometric
error in each channel is less than $0^{m}.1$. All sources have been corrected for
interstellar extinction according to Wesselink (1987).

4. Results

Fig.3 shows the $(I - J)_0 / (J - K^S)_0$ diagram. The AGB stars cover in both
colours the reddest end. In $(I-J)_0$ the colour range is very large and goes up
until $4^m.0$. Especially the AGB stars show a large variation of $(I-J)_0$. Loup
(see her contribution at this conference) shows very nicely two branches in
the colour-colour diagram for the LMC.

One is related to the oxygen-rich stars while the other correspond to
the c-rich objects. Her result is very well in agreement with our fig. 3
where we clearly miss the c-rich branch. The absence of carbon stars in
the Bulge is due to a different age and metallicity compared to the LMC.

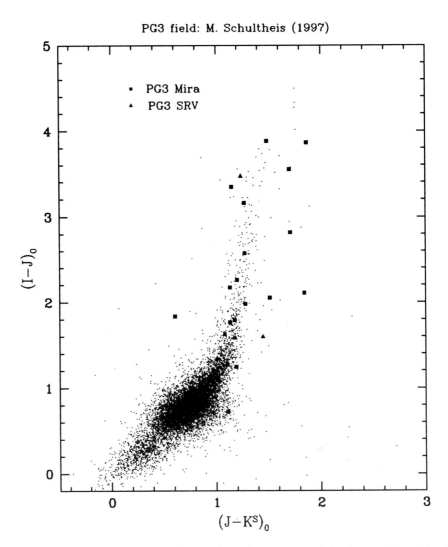

Figure 3.   CCD of PG3 stars. All stars have been corrected for interstellar extinction according to Wesselink (1987). PG3 SRVs are indicated by triangles, PG3 Miras by squares.

In a $K_0^S/(J - K^S)_0$ diagram one can clearly see the tip of the horizontal branch, the red giant branch and the AGB (see fig. 4). The PG3 Miras and SRVs are situated at the tip of the red giant branch. A closer look shows that the AGB is separated from the RGB. This separation is not very clear due to the variability of those stars. The upper limit of the scatter in J–K due to variability is ~ 0.2 mag for Miras and ~ 0.1 mag for SRVs. The variation in K is about 1 mag for Miras and 0.5 mag for SRVs (Hron &

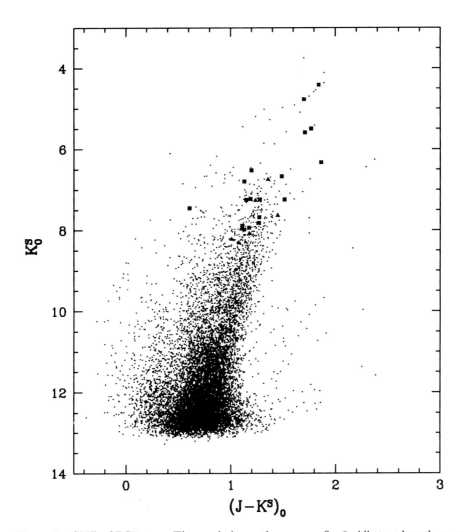

Figure 4. CMD of PG3 stars. The symbols are the same as fig. 3. All stars have been corrected for interstellar extinction according to Wesselink (1987).The limiting magnitudes are $I = 14^{m}.8$, $J = 14^{m}.3$ and $K^{S} = 13^{m}.8$ and $\sigma_{I} < 0^{m}.1$, $\sigma_{J} < 0^{m}.1$ and $\sigma_{K} < 0^{m}.1$

Kerschbaum 1994). Again in comparison to the LMC we miss the branch of the carbon stars. The PG3 variables follow a PK_{0}^{S} relation. The slope of the PK_{0}^{S} relation is the same as the PK relation. As a first approach we determined the shift between K and K^{S} assuming that the slope remains the same. We obtained a $\Delta(K - K^{S})$ of ~ 0.4. Further on PG3 variables follow in J–K, I–J and I–K a period-colour relation.

5. Outlook

DENIS CMDs and CCDs will enable us to find new AGB star candidates.
Isochrones from the Padova group (e. g. Bertelli et al. 1994) will allow us
to derive metallicities and ages. Further on with DENIS we will be able
to study in detail the stellar populations related to the Sagittarius dwarf
galaxy.

Acknowledgements

The authors thank Y. K. Ng, A. Omont, C. Loup, M. R. Cioni and D. Ojha
for constructive suggestions. M. Schultheis thanks the Institut d' Astrophysique where part of this research was carried out, for their hospitality.
We are especially grateful to F. Tanguy and J. Borsenberger for their help
in using the DENIS data. The research of M. Schultheis is supported by
the Austrian Science Fund projects P9638-AST and S7308.

References

Bertin, E., Arnouts, S., (1996) A&AS Sup. 117, 393
Blommaert, J.A.D.L (1992), phD thesis, Leiden University, the Netherlands
Hron J., Kerschbaum F., (1994), ApSS 217, 137
Ng, Y.K. (1997), A&A, in press
Ng, Y.K., Schultheis, M. (1997), A&AS 123, 115
Plaut, L., A&AS 4, 75
Ruphy, S. (1996), phD. thesis, University Paris 6
Wesselink, Th. J. H (1987), Ph. D. thesis, Catholic University of Nijmegen, the Nether-
     lands.
Willems,F.J, (1987), Ph. D thesis, University of Amsterdam, the Netherlands

ANALYSIS OF DENIS DATA IN ISOGAL FIELDS

C. ALARD

DASGAL, 77 avenue Denfert Rochereau, Observatoire de Paris.
and Institut d'Astrophysique de Paris.

1. Introduction

We present here DENIS color magnitude diagrams for 3 different fields in the Milky Way. One field is situated in a window at only 2 degrees from the Galactic Center, the two others are in the Galactic plane at longitudes l=15 and l=25. We first show that it is possible to probe the extinction law along the line of sight using K vs. (J-K) color magnitude diagrams, and we also demonstrate that the shape of the giant branch is changing with Galactic latitude. For these fields ISO data from the ISOGAL project are also available. These ISOCAM data have been reprocessed using the CIA package (see acknowledgements), allowing reconstruction of a high quality mosaic image from the raw ISOCAM data. Magnitude and positions of stars are extracted from the ISOCAM mosaic image and associated to DE-NIS K band point sources. These DENIS K magnitudes are an important asset to our ISO 7 and 15 micron fluxes, especially in the case of AGB stars.

2. Probing the extinction law along the line of sight.

The field close to the Galactic Center, is a new window closer to the Galactic Center than previous studies in Baades's Window (Tiede *et al.* 1995). But the extinction in this field is too low to probe with some efficiency the extinction law. However the color magnitude diagrams for the two others fields located in the Galactic plane at longitudes l=15, and l=25 (see Fig. 1) indicate a significant reddening, quite variable with distance. Three sequences are visible in the diagrams(from left to right): a main sequence, the sequence traced by the giant clump associated with this main sequence, and finally an upper giant branch from stars in the central region of the Galaxy. The Second sequence, the clump of giant stars is especially useful because its absolute magnitude and unreddened colors lie within a narrow range. Consequently, measuring the colors and magnitudes of this clump will give immediatly the extinction law. Looking back at the diagrams, we

95

N. Epchtein (ed.),
The Impact of Near-Infrared Sky Surveys on Galactic and Extragalactic Astronomy, 95-100.

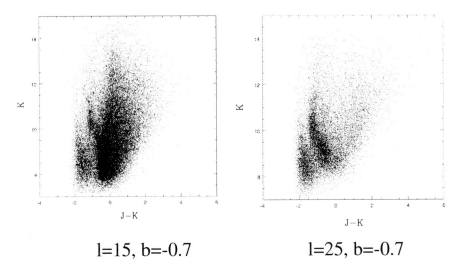

l=15, b=-0.7   l=25, b=-0.7

Figure 1. The variations of extinction with distance. Note the sudden change in the foreground giant clump color. Magnitudes are not calibrated, zero points remain to be estimated.

see that the color variation with distance of the clump is very similar for the two diagrams. A sudden variation of the clump color occurs at a distance that we estimate to be about 3 Kpc (we wait until making a real absolute calibration to be more specific). It means that a large amount of extinction, and consequently of interstellar material is concentrated at this distance. This feature could be associated with the Sagittarius arm, but might also be related to the molecular ring. At this time, it is difficult to guess what the right interpretation is. Although, further investigations with more DENIS data, and especially a selection of new fields evenly sampled from the center to a longitude of about 45 deg. would be very helpful. The new ISOGAL/DENIS reductions which will be achieved soon will certainly provide us with a suitable material.

3. Changes in the giant branch shape with Galactic longitude.

The DENIS I,J,K data it is possible to derive a magnitude and a color which are independent of reddening. We have only to assume a reddening law (Frogel and Withford, 1987) to derive the correction to reddening, we derive: $K' = K - 0.538 \times (J - K)$ and, $(I - J)' = (I - J) \times 2.15(J - K)$. In figure 2 we plot the K' vs. (I-J)' diagrams for our three fields. We immediately notice a tail on the right of the diagram, for bright magnitudes in the Galactic center diagram. This tail is not found in the two other diagrams. Note also that the upper part of the diagram is more and more depopu-

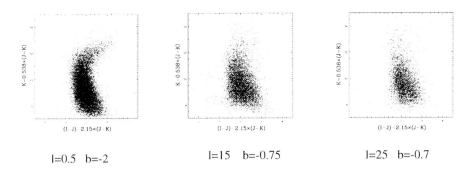

l=0.5 b=-2   l=15 b=-0.75   l=25 b=-0.7

Figure 2.   We plot here the color/magnitude diagrams corrected for extinction in 3 different Galactic fields. Note the change with latitute observed in the region of the diagram situated at bright magnitude and red colors. Magnitudes are not calibrated, zero points remain to be estimated.

lated with increasing longitude. This feature, which exists only close to the Galactic Center shows that a particular population is present in the central region. It is tempting to relate these giants with redder colors to a metal rich population, which we expect to find in the Galactic Bulge. Mapping the extension of this population by counting the stars in the region occupied by the feature would provide us with an interesting insight concerning the structure of the Galactic Bulge. Such mapping is essential in order to understand the formation and chemical evolution of our Galaxy. It would require to get DENIS data for all the central region.

4. The ISO data.

The ISOGAL project is a survey of the Galactic plane and central regions of the Milky Way. We made observations at 7 and 15 microns for a few hundreds fields evenly sampled along the Milky Way. The ISOCAM infrared camera of the satellite makes a series of 32x32 images for each field. Each $32 times 32$ small image is repated about 15 to 10 times in order to create a time series, and from the whole stack of images a mosaic image of the field is constructed. The image reconstruction process is not simple, and require different corrections, the most difficult beeing the transient correction. These transients are due to the detector memory effect, if an area of the detector is illuminated with a source, the relevant pixels will not drop to zero immediately after the source is off. This memory effect will create ghost images of a previously seen source, which will take long to disappear. This is especially annoying for our crowded Galactic fields, and is the main limitation to the depth of our images. An illustration of this memory effect

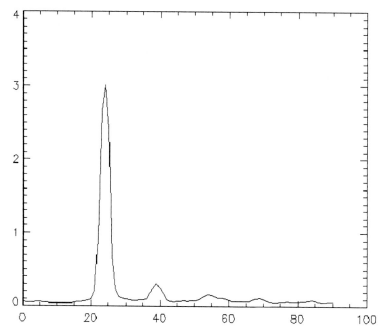

Figure 3.   Memory effect of ISOCAM. The detector sees first a bright source on the left of the diagram. Note the decreasing ghost images of this bright source visible as a periodic sequence.

is given in Fig. 3. Another important issue is that this difficult processing is not completely satisfactory in the standard ISO/ESA pipeline. The data had to be reprocessed using the CIA package, and in particular the J.L. Starck wavelet method was used for correction of the memory effects. A dramatic improvement of the point source photometry and repeatability was achieved using CIA. This improvement is also obvious just by looking at the images (see Fig. 4).

4.1. CROSS IDENTIFICATION WITH DENIS SOURCES

Each ISO source is searched for a DENIS source within a small radius around the ISO source. We start with a radius of 10 arcsec, which allows us to find a first list of candidate associations. A differential fit is then performed, and a new search for DENIS sources is conducted. We iterate the process until convergence. Our typical resulting rms error in the ISO/DENIS associations is about 1.5 arcsec. We perform the final associations at 3 σ, which gives an eventual association radius of 4.5 arcsec. The resulting diagram is given in Fig. 5. for a field near the Galactic Center. Note that the density of DENIS sources is so high that it is difficult to avoid false associations like the clump of faint stars on the right of the diagram. However, the likelihood of associations with bright DENIS sources is much

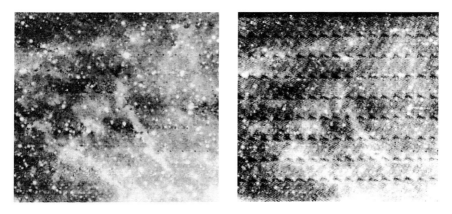

Figure 4. Comparison of data processing methods. Left is the original mosaic image from the ISO/ESA pipeline, and right is the newly processed image, using the CIA package.

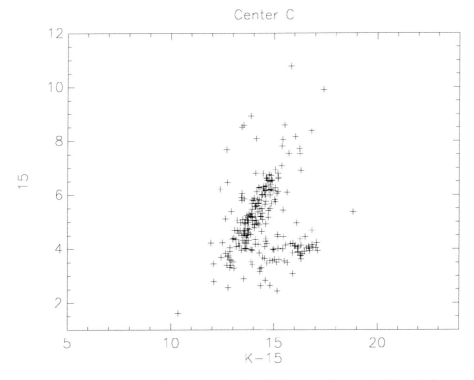

Figure 5. The ISO vs. DENIS associations for a field situated near the Galactic Center. See text for discussion.

higher, and the sequence on the left of the diagram is real. This sequence is associated with bright giants, most of them beeing probably AGB stars. We estimate that about 70 % of ISO sources are found in real associations

with DENIS sources.

5. Conclusion.

We demonstrate here that interesting results can be derived from the DE-NIS observations of the ISOGAL fields. It would be certainly interesting to pursue these investigations with DENIS data covering a more extended region around the Bulge. We also show that these DENIS data can be well completed with ISO data at 7 and 15 micron. Processing of ISO data is now efficient and reliable, and we demonstrate that most of ISO source are retrieved in DENIS with excellent positions and magnitude correlation.

Acknowledgements

The ISOCAM data presented in this paper was analysed using "CIA", a joint development by the ESA Astrophysics Division and the ISOCAM Consortium led by the ISOCAM PI, C. Cesarsky, Direction des Sciences de la Matiere, C.E.A., France.

References

Alard, C. 1997, in preparation
Frogel, J. and Withford, A.E., 1987, ApJ, 320,199
Tiede, G., et al., 1995, AJ, 110, 2788

IN QUEST OF VERY LOW MASS STARS AND BROWN DWARFS WITH NEAR-IR SURVEYS

T. FORVEILLE, X. DELFOSSE
Observatoire de Grenoble
Université de Genoble, France

AND

N. EPCHTEIN
Observatoire de la Côte d'Azur, France

1. Introduction

Deep large scale near-infrared surveys have started revolutionizing the study of very low mass stars and brown dwarfs (hereafter VLMS and BD) by producing, for the first time, statistically significant samples. They represent the most efficient observational method to discover the so called *free-floating* BDs that for decades have been looked for, as well as large unbiased samples of VLMS of spectral types later than M6.5V, whose mass and luminosity functions are still poorly known and understood.

The efficiency of deep near–IR surveys simply results from their probing the 1-2 micron spectral window, where objects with effective temperature in the 1500-3000K range radiate the bulk of their bolometric luminosity. Based on a black-body reasoning, red and brown dwarfs would be expected to have extreme infrared colours for any bandpass combination, but the deep molecular absorption bands that characterize these very cool stars mean that this is not always true. For well chosen filter combinations however, like the I−J colour provided by DENIS, red and brown dwarfs do show up in uncrowded areas of near IR colour–colour diagrams. The only other stellar populations that exhibit similar colours are the late giants (red giants, AGBs stars, extreme carbon stars, etc..). As they are more luminous by 5 to 10 orders of magnitudes, and have a rather flat galactic distribution, this confusion is not difficult to remove at least outside a 40 degrees band around the galactic equator. There is on the other hand no obvious way, to distinguish between BDs and VLMS on the sole basis of the infrared colours, except for the very coolest BDs. Spectroscopic follow up observation is

N. Epchtein (ed.),
The Impact of Near-Infrared Sky Surveys on Galactic and Extragalactic Astronomy, 101-108.
© 1998 *Kluwer Academic Publishers. Printed in the Netherlands.*

thus an essential step to definitely confirm a colour selected candidate as a genuine brown dwarf. The so-called *Lithium test*, which consists in detecting the 6807 Å absorption of Li in the atmosphere of the star, is at present the most conclusive confirmation of a candidate as a *bona fide* brown dwarf (Martín et al., 1995).

The two ongoing large scale near infrared surveys, are likely to produce a wealth of exciting data on BDs. The discovery of a sample of good candidates and the confirmation of at least one BD in a small sample of DENIS data is extremely encouraging for the future. Hundreds of BDs are likely to be effectively singled out in the coming years. They will for the first time yield a statistically significant set of such stars and the first direct measurement of the low-end of the solar neighbourhood luminosity function. The parallel intense modeling activity (e.g., Tsuji, Allard et al., 1997, Chabrier and Baraffe, 1997) will undoubtedly also provide breakthroughs in this exciting area of astrophysics.

2. The quest for brown dwarfs

Not so long ago, brown dwarfs were still considered as hypothetical objects (Tinney, 1995) although stellar evolution theories have long predicted the existence of astronomical objects whose mass spans the range between a few Jupiter masses (hereafter M_J) and some 70 M_J, and whose luminosity is smaller than $10^{-4}L_\odot$. They fill the mass and luminosity gaps that separate giant planets orbiting around a star (such as Jupiter, about 1/1000th of solar mass) and low mass stars (of a few hundredth of solar mass). They are not massive enough to initiate the combustion of hydrogen in their core, hence their chemical composition has not varied much along their evolution. For this simple reason, one of the most efficient test to confirm an object as a brown dwarf is the Li test. Objects with masses lower than some $60M_J$ must have kept their Li since the very efficient proton collision reaction $[Li^7(p, \alpha)He^4]$ easily destroys the Li in some 10^7 yrs, at temperatures lower than are needed to initiate hydrogen burning.

As brown dwarfs have extremely low luminosities, all early searches used indirect methods and looked for the reflex astrometric or radial velocity motion induced on a brighter binary companion star. All of these early attempts actually failed to single out any serious candidate (e.g., Stevenson, 1991), but recent radial velocity searches with much improved technology have isolated several unseen brown dwarf companions to bright nearby stars (Mayor, private communication). The quest for brown dwarf was revived in the mid 1980s by the development of panoramic IR detectors and high spatial resolution technics such as speckle interferometry and coronography, which have to a large extent taken over the indirect detection methods.

Since that time, several authors have claimed to discover genuine brown dwarf candidates. They almost invariably turned out to be VLMS rather than BDs, with only GD165B (Becklin & Zuckermann, 1988) remaining as an undecided borderline case.

2.1. CONFIRMED BROWN DWARFS: PRESENT STATUS

A good overview of the early and recent searches for BDs has been recently published by Kulkarni (1997). Here we will only briefly summarize the status of presently known BDs and update his compilation with the most recent results. Known BDs can be observationally split into two groups, young BDs (younger than roughly 0.3 Gyear) found near their formation site, and old BDs (older than roughly 1 Gyear) found in the field or around a bright nearby star.

2.1.1. *Young BD's,*
Young BDs are characterised by much higher luminosities (by several orders of magnitude) than old BDs, because they haven't yet had time to cool down. They can consequently be searched for at much larger distances, in nearby star forming regions and stellar associations. Searches in regions of recent star formation such as the Taurus or Ophiuchus clouds have essentially failed, mainly because the strong dust extinction that characterize these regions hampers accurate luminosity determination. In addition the Li test is inadequate there, since *all* low mass stars retain a large fraction of their Li for the first 10^7 years of their life. For this reason, BD searches have now concentrated on the nearby Pleiades open cluster, whose age is $\sim 10^8$ years. A systematic deep CCD survey (with an 80 cm telescope !), followed up by high resolution spectroscopy on the Keck 10m telescope resulted in the discovery of the first confirmed young BD (Teide 1), with an estimated mass of 55 $\pm$15 M_J (Rebolo et al., 1995; Rebolo et al., 1996). This has now been followed by the detection of a wealth of new BDs and VLMS (Zapatero-Osorio et al., 1997).

2.1.2. *Old BD's*
Gliese 229B, was the first confirmed BD and was found during a search for low-mass companions to nearby stars ($\leq 15pc$) (Nakajima et al., 1995). This program used a specially designed coronographic instrument on the 60" telescope at Palomar Observatory. Gl 229B remains, by a large margin, the BD with the coolest known effective temperature ($\sim$1200 K). Its near-infrared spectrum is characterized by extremely strong CH_4 absorption bands, and is in many respects intermediate between those of warmer BDs and of the giant planets.

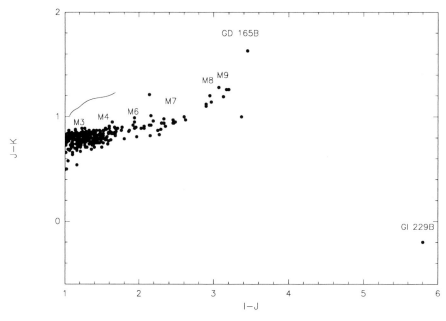

Figure 1. The I–J:J–K colour-colour diagram for previously known very low mass-stars. The short continuous line shows the giant sequence.

2.2. THE DENIS BROWN DWARFS AND VERY LOW MASS STARS

The set of DENIS colours (IJK) is particularly well suited to identify VLMS and BD (Reid, 1994). As illustrated in Figure 1, the [I-J] colour has large variations over the relevant spectral type range, when [J-K] (and [J-H], not shown here) have a much smaller dynamical range, and even become bluer beyond the spectral type of GD 165B (Gl 229B has the same J-K colour as a B star). It is thus relatively easy to single out BDs and VLMS even from relatively noisy measurements near the DENIS sensitivity limit, while from JHK measurements this would only be possible, if at all, from accurate photometry of well detected sources. For such a program the DENIS sensitivities at I and J are in addition quite well matched, as they cross-over at spectral type M6V-M7V.

Using some of the first DENIS data, a program aimed at selecting extreme red dwarfs, the *"DENIS brown dwarf mini-survey"*, was carried out (Delfosse, 1997; Delfosse et al., 1997). The analysed area consists of a set of 52 strips totalizing 230 square degrees. Their distribution on the sky is largely random, except that their distance from the galactic plane is always greater than 20 ^{o} to avoid crowding and contamination by red giants, AGB stars, and distant reddened objects. Image processing was performed in the standard DENIS pipeline (Borsenberger, 1996), but source extraction was

done using SExtractor package. A 3 colour catalog of objects brighter than I = 18.5, J = 16 and K = 13.5 was produced, in which some 50 sources have [I-J] $\geq$ 2.5.

Follow-up near IR spectroscopy of all objects redder than [I-J] $\geq$ 2.8 was then obtained at AAT using the IRIS spectrograph. This confirmed that the three reddest objects, namely DENIS-P J0205.4-1159, 1058.7-1548 and 1228.2-1547, were indeed good BD candidates. Further optical spectroscopic observations were then performed at the Keck telescope (Martin et al., 1997) and at the AAT (Tinney et al., 1997) for last two objects. They show a spectacular LiI absorption line in 1228.2-1547, but not in 1058.7-1548. DENIS-P J1228.2-1547 thus became the first *bona-fide* isolated (or free-floating) BD, together with Kelu 1, which was simultaneously discovered by Ruiz et al. (1997) during a proper motion survey aimed at cool white dwarfs. Another isolated BD candidate, called 296A, has also passed the Li test (Thackrah et al., 1997), but its status should nonetheless probably still be regarded as uncertain: if it is indeed a brown dwarf, its relatively high effective temperatures implies an uncomfortably young age for a field object.

The three DENIS BD candidates, Kelu-1, and GD 165B have optical spectra which are unlike those of the late M dwarfs, without the strong TiO and VO bands that characterize the M spectral type. This is presumably due to condensation of these refractory molecules onto dust grains (Allard, 1997), and leads Martín et al. (1997) to suggest that these spectra should be attributed a new spectral class, for which they propose L.

TABLE 1. Properties of confirmed brown dwarfs. *(Notes in col. 6, 1: Nakajima et al. 1995; 2: Rebolo et al., 1996; 3: Ruiz et al., 1997; 4: Delfosse et al., 1997; 5: Tinney et al., 1997; 6: Thackrah et al., 1997)*

Name	Type	d (pc)	Mass (MJ)	Teff (K)	Réf.
Gl229B	Companion	5.7	$\leq$ 50	$\leq$1200	1
Teide 1	Pleiades	125	55 $\pm$ 15	2600$\pm$150	2
Calar 3	Pleiades	125	55 $\pm$15	2600 $\pm$ 150	2
Kelu 1	isolated	12	$\leq$ 75	1900 $\pm$ 100	3
DENIS-P J1228-1547	isolated	?	$\leq$ 60	1600 $\pm$ 300	4,5
296A	isolated	?	65 $\pm$ 25	2800 $\pm$ 200	6

TABLE 2. M dwarfs later than spectral type M7V in de DENIS minisurvey (from Delfosse, 1997).

Name	I	I–J	J–K	I–K
DENIS-P 0909 − 0658	17.21 ±0.08	3.20 ±0.09	1.50 ±0.09	4.70 ±0.12
DENIS-P 0912 − 0414	16.71 ±0.06	2.46 ±0.07	1.10 ±0.12	3.56 ±0.13
DENIS-P 0910 + 0019	18.40 ±0.20	2.65 ±0.26	-	-
DENIS-P 0944 − 1305	16.72 ±0.05	2.59 ±0.06	0.76 ±0.17	3.35 ±0.18
DENIS-P 0940 − 2257	17.02 ±0.10	2.79 ±0.11	0.99 ±0.16	3.78 ±0.19
DENIS-P 0944 − 0900	18.30 ±0.18	2.69 ±0.24	-	-
DENIS-P 0944 − 1310	18.50 ±0.21	2.80 ±0.24	-	-
DENIS-P 1007 − 1706	17.73 ±0.14	2.84 ±0.16	-	-
DENIS-P 1154 + 0135	16.03 ±0.04	2.77 ±0.04	1.09 ±0.06	3.86 ±0.07
DENIS-P 1227 + 0114	16.96 ±0.10	2.88 ±0.11	1.29 ±0.15	4.17 ±0.17
DENIS-P 1228 − 1547	18.19 ±0.27	3.76 ±0.27	1.70 ±0.16	5.46 ±0.31
DENIS-P 1228 − 2415	18.00 ±0.20	3.11 ±0.21	-	-
DENIS-P 1058 − 1548	17.80 ±0.17	3.72 ±0.17	1.37 ±0.15	5.09 ±0.22
DENIS-P 1026 − 0637	18.00 ±0.11	2.99 ±0.14	-	-
DENIS-P 2052 − 5512	17.52 ±0.13	2.70 ±0.15	0.74 ±0.23	3.44 ±0.26
DENIS-P 0142 − 4715	18.40 ±0.16	2.86 ±0.23	-	-
DENIS-P 0142 − 3952	17.80 ±0.16	2.72 ±0.18	-	-
DENIS-P 0020 − 4414	18.32 ±0.16	3.35 ±0.17	1.37 ±0.16	4.72 ±0.22
DENIS-P 0021 − 4244	16.83 ±0.05	3.20 ±0.05	1.38 ±0.06	4.58 ±0.08
DENIS-P 0151 − 6430	17.39 ±0.12	2.93 ±0.13	1.03 ±0.21	3.96 ±0.23
DENIS-P 0429 − 6649	17.32 ±0.13	2.89 ±0.14	1.33 ±0.17	4.22 ±0.21
DENIS-P 0430 − 8314	18.33 ±0.23	3.31 ±0.29	-	-
DENIS-P 0205 − 0653	16.83 ±0.06	2.89 ±0.07	1.27 ±0.11	4.16 ±0.12
DENIS-P 0205 − 1159	18.30 ±0.24	3.67 ±0.25	1.63 ±0.21	5.30 ±0.31
DENIS-P 0205 − 1637	18.64 ±0.22	3.04 ±0.27	-	-
DENIS-P 0449 − 0228	17.50 ±0.10	3.00 ±0.11	1.23 ±0.23	4.23 ±0.24
DENIS-P 0449 − 2225	18.70 ±0.20	2.84 ±0.26	-	-
DENIS-P 0247 − 1055	18.37 ±0.18	3.00 ±0.19	-	-
DENIS-P 0205 − 4313	17.95 ±0.15	2.78 ±0.21	-	-
DENIS-P 0205 − 3357	17.13 ±0.08	2.80 ±0.09	0.87 ±0.21	3.67 ±0.22
DENIS-P 2146 − 2153	18.40 ±0.27	2.98 ±0.29	-	-
DENIS-P 2143 − 8337	16.21 ±0.05	2.77 ±0.06	1.00 ±0.11	3.77 ±0.12
DENIS-P 2040 − 5700	18.14 ±0.17	2.90 ±0.20	-	-
DENIS-P 2040 − 3245	17.86 ±0.16	2.97 ±0.17	-	-
DENIS-P 0426 − 5735	18.45 ±0.20	3.17 ±0.22	-	-

3. And many more to come

In addition to the three BD candidates (including the confirmed BD DENIS-P J1228-1547) which are discussed above, the DENIS mini-survey has also provided a large sample of VLMS, and Table 2 lists the 35 dwarfs whose

spectral type is later than M7V. Five of them have spectral types of M9V or later, doubling the size of the known inventory of such late objets.

From scaling of the DENIS mini-survey results (based on only 1% of the southern sky), it is clear that applying the same strategy to the full DENIS survey will eventually identify a few thousand M dwarfs later than M7V, a few hundred M dwarfs later than M9V, and perhaps 150 objects with the new L spectral type. Many more will only be detected in the more sensitive band, J, but from the DENIS data alone they will be very difficult to separate from the unavoidable cosmic ray hits and electronic glitches. With additional optical data, for instance from the Sloan Digital Sky Survey, they could be validated. This would then either yield some isolated equivalents of Gl 229B, whose colour would prevent a detection at I and K, or a significant upper limit on their local density. For 2-colour late dwarf detection (as opposed to identification), 2MASS has a significantly better sensitivity at J+H than DENIS has at I+J. Given the low discriminating power of [J-H] and [H-K], they however have to use additional data. Their initial plan is to use digitized Schmidt plates to separate late M dwarfs and BDs from earlier type stars, but combination with either DENIS data or the Sloan CCD survey will eventually have greater discriminating power.

Even for the smaller DENIS I+J catalog, the necessary follow-up will be a large work. High resolution optical spectroscopy will be needed for all objects to apply the Li test, and due to the optical faintness of these objects can probably only be obtained on 8m class telescopes. Parallaxes will also have to be obtained for a significant fraction of the sample, to, at last, obtain a reliable and unbiased low end of the local stellar luminosity function.

References

Allard F., Hauschildt P.H., Alexander D. R., Starrfield S. (1997) *ARAA*, **Vol. no. 35**, pp. 137-177
Becklin E.E, Zuckermann B. (1988) *Nature*, **Vol. no. 336**, pp. L656–659
Borsenberger J., (1996), Proc. 2nd Euroconfeence on Near-IR surveys (Tenerife), Kluwer ASSL Ser. **vol.210** pp. 181-186
Chabrier G., Baraffe I. (1997) *AA* **in press**
Delfosse X., (1997), Thèse de doctorat, Université de Grenoble 1
Delfosse X., Tinney C.G., Forveille T., Epchtein N., Bertin E., Borsenberger J., Copet E., de Batz B., Fouqué P., Kimeswenger S., Le Bertre T., Lacombe F., Rouan D., Tiphène D. (1997) *AAL*, **Vol. no. 327**, pp. L25-L28
Kirkpatrick D. (1998) This volume
Kulkarni S.R. (1997) *Science*, **Vol. no. 276**, pp. L1350–1354
Martin E.L., Basri G., Delfosse X., Forveille T. (1997) *AAL*, **Vol. no. 327**, pp. L29-L32
Nakajima T., Oppenheimer B.R., Kulkarni S.R., Golimowski D.A., Matthews K., Durrance S.T. (1995) *Nature*, **Vol. no. 378**, pp. 463–465
Rebolo R., Zapatero–Osorio M.R., Martin E.L. (1995) *Nature*, **Vol. no. 377**, pp.129–131
Rebolo R., Martin E.L., Basri G., Marcy G.W., Zapatero–Osorio M.R. (1996) *ApJ*,

Vol. no. 327, pp. L53–L56

Reid N. (1994) *ASpSc.*, **Vol. no.217**, pp.57-62

Ruiz M.T., Leggett S.K., Allard F. (1997) *ApJL*, **Vol. no. 491**, pp. L107–L110

Thackrah A., Jones H., Hawkins M. (1997) *MNRAS*, **Vol. no. 284**, pp. 507–512

Stevenson D.J. (1991) *ARAA*, **Vol. no. 29**, pp. 163–193

Tinney C., Delfosse X., Forveille T. (1997) *ApJ*, **Vol. no. 490**, pp. L95–L98

Tinney C.(1995) *Mem. Soc. Ast. It.*, **Vol. no. 66**, pp. 611–618

Zuckermann B., Becklin E.E (1987) *ApJ*, **Vol.no. 319**, pp.L99–L102

SEARCHING FOR LOW-MASS STARS AND BROWN DWARFS WITH 2MASS

J. DAVY KIRKPATRICK
Infrared Processing and Analysis Center
California Institute of Technology
M/S 100-22, Pasadena, CA 91125, USA

MICHAEL F. SKRUTSKIE
Univ. of Massachusetts
Five College Astronomy Department, Dept. of Physics and
Astronomy, Amherst, MA 01003, USA

JAMES LIEBERT, KEVIN LUHMAN AND MATT FISHER
Univ. of Arizona
Steward Observatory, Tucson, AZ 85721, USA

ROC CUTRI, CHARLES BEICHMAN AND CAROL LONSDALE
Infrared Processing and Analysis Center
California Institute of Technology
M/S 100-22, Pasadena, CA 91125, USA

NEILL REID
California Institute of Technology
M/S 105-24, Pasadena, CA 91125, USA

AND

DAVE MONET AND CONARD DAHN
U.S. Naval Observatory
P.O. Box 1149, Flagstaff, AZ 86002-1149, USA

1. Introduction

We have begun to look for low-mass stars and brown dwarfs using data from the 2MASS Prototype Cameras. Reported here are some very early, yet very encouraging, results which demonstrate the ease with which 2MASS will uncover missing, very cool members of the solar neighborhood.

N. Epchtein (ed.),
The Impact of Near-Infrared Sky Surveys on Galactic and Extragalactic Astronomy, 109-113.
© 1998 *Kluwer Academic Publishers. Printed in the Netherlands.*

2. Search Method

Our search of the 2MASS databases thus far has been restricted to $b > 20°$ (to avoid confused regions near the plane) and to $K_s < 14.5$ (to insure brighter targets which could be followed up spectroscopically in the optical). Known brown dwarfs and brown dwarf candidates have colors as red as $J - K_s \approx 1.7$ for GD 165B and as blue as $J - K_s \approx -0.1$ for Gl 229B. Thus, $J - K_s$ color alone cannot be used as a selection criterion since most of the stars on the main sequence *also* fall in this range. However, a combination of colors from the optical and the near-infrared provide excellent criteria — known low-mass stars and brown dwarfs follow a monotoncially increasing sequence (e.g., in $R - K_s$) as temperatures decrease. Low-mass M dwarfs like LHS 2924 (M9 V) have $R - K_s \approx 7.5$ and the brown dwarf Gl 229B has $R - K_s \approx 10.8$.

Therefore, we have been pairing up the 2MASS database with digitizations of optical sky surveys in an effort to find 2MASS sources with no optical counterparts. For the data from the Prototype Cameras, we have used the APM digitization of the POSS-I plates, which have $R_{lim} \approx 20.0$. (For the actual survey, we will be using USNO digitizations of the POSS-II plates, which probe to $R_{lim} \approx 22.0$).

The pairing is done by position only, generally using a $3''$ matching radius. Thus, 2MASS targets with no matching sources in the optical fall into two categories: (1) proper motion objects which have moved more than $3''$ during the time interval between the optical and 2MASS surveys, and (2) infrared sources lacking *any* optical counterparts, even after possible motion matches were considered. Sources were retained if their $R - K_s$ colors or color limits exceeded 6.00, corresponding very roughly to a spectral type of M7 V.

3. Preliminary results

Using this search method, we have chosen a handful of low-mass star and brown dwarf candidates from the Protocam data. As of the date of this conference, we have obtained optical spectroscopy of sixteen sources. These are listed in Table 1 along with spectral types, K_s magnitudes, and estimated distances. Figure 1 shows the optical spectra of the objects obtained at the 5m Palomar and 4.5m MMT Observatories. A note on a few of the more interesting objects is given below.

3.1. 2MASP J1716586+451216AB

This object was first announced by Chester et al. (1992), where it was shown at higher resolution to be a close ($\sim 0.5''$), equal-magnitude binary. Our

TABLE 1. Protocam Sources with Follow-up Spectroscopy

Object Name[a]	Spectral Type	K_s mag	Estimated Distance (pc)
2MASP J1007435+113432	M4.5 V	12.77	102
2MASP J1244316+254720	M5.5 V	13.62	100
2MASP J1716586+451216AB	M6 V	13.14	83
2MASP J0152095+340037	M6.5 V	13.58	67
2MASP J0338549+223153	M6.5 V	14.34	83
2MASP J1246094+291603	M6.5 V	13.62	64
2MASP J1254369+253850	M7.5 V	13.24	48
2MASP J1524248+292535	M7.5 V	10.18	11
2MASP J1256227+283047	M7.5 V	13.53	55
2MASP J0339527+245728	M8 V	11.61	22
2MASP J0354012+231635	M8 V	11.79	24
2MASP J2234330+291850	M8: V	13.99[b]	37
2MASP J1242464+292619	M8: V	13.23	45
2MASP J1519431+260937	M8 V	14.33	73
2MASP J1520477+300210	M8.5 V	13.85	53
2MASP J0345432+254023	$\geq$M10 V	12.68	$\leq$21

[a]   Source designations for 2MASS discoveries are given as "2MASx Jhhmmss[.]s±ddmmss." The "x" in the prefix will vary depending upon the catalog from which the object is taken; "P" is used for sources from the Prototype Camera data. The suffix conforms to IAU nomenclature convention and is the sexigesimal J2000-equinox RA and Dec, which for Protocam ("2MASP") sources is epoch 1993.5.
[b] This is the J-band magnitude.

joint spectrum of the pair is typed as M6 V. At the estimated distance of 83 pc, the physical separation on the sky is ~40 AU, meaning that this pair is, regrettably, too wide to provide an orbital determination and dynamical mass measures on a short timescale.

3.2. 2MASP J0338549+223153

As reported in Kirkpatrick, Beichman, & Skrutskie (1997), this object has a distance of ~83 pc assuming that it has an age comparable to an average field M dwarf (~1 Gyr). However, it lies in the direction of the Pleiades, and if it's a member of this cluster (age ~75 Myr), then it will be more luminous than a field M6.5 dwarf by ~0.8 mag at K_s. Its derived distance would then be ~125 pc, which is consistent with the distance to the Pleiades. Thus, this object may be a Pleiad lying near the cluster's stellar/substellar break, much like PPl 15 (Stauffer, Hamilton, & Probst 1994; Basri, Marcy, & Graham 1996).

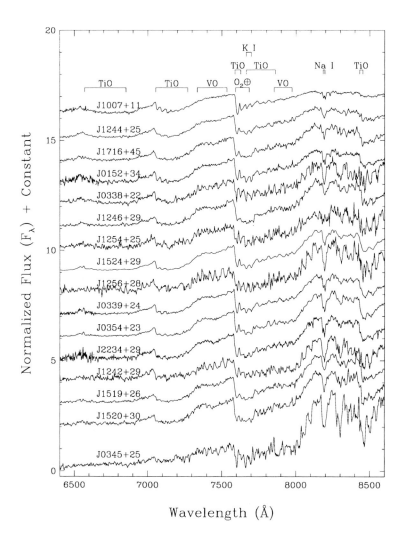

Figure 1.   Spectra from 6400 to 8600 Å of 2MASS Protocam sources. The sources are in the same order as that shown in Table 1, with the M4.5 dwarf at the top and the ≥M10 dwarf at the bottom. Note the increasingly red continuum at cooler and cooler temperatures along with the strengthening of the vanadium oxide (VO) bands. The 2MASS names have been shortened here for ease of plotting.

3.3. 2MASP J1524248+292535

Of the objects so far uncovered by 2MASS, this one — at an estimated distance of only 11 pc — is the closest new discovery to the Sun. Though it is easily detected on the POSS-I plates ($R \approx 17.5$) and has a large motion ($\mu \approx 0.61''/yr$), it was missed by Luyten during his proper motion survey

of the northern sky (Fisher et al. 1997). This is the first of many such "missing" members of the solar neighborhood that 2MASS will uncover during the course of the survey.

3.4. 2MASP J0345432+254023

As of the date of this conference, this dwarf — of type $\geq$M10 — is the coolest object so far detected by 2MASS (Kirkpatrick, Beichman, & Skrutskie 1997). Though located toward the Pleiades, it is almost certainly a foreground object. The distance estimate, based on the trigonometric parallax for the slightly warmer ($\geq$M9) dwarf LP 944-20, places it at $\leq$21 pc.

4. Discussion

The results reported here are all based on Prototype Camera observations. As a first test, we have primarily chosen brighter objects for follow-up and thus have yet to probe into the deeper 2MASS data. Despite this, we have shown that 2MASS is already detecting extremely cool dwarfs, brown dwarf candidates toward the Pleiades, and missing low-mass members of the nearby stellar census.

The actual 2MASS survey is now underway. As we continue to build up data over larger areas, we will continue to scour them for late dwarf and brown dwarf candidates. Access to the Keck 10m telescope and low-resolution spectrograph will allow us to scrutinize even the faintest 2MASS sources. Follow-up on some of our early survey candidates will allow us to better understand our selection criteria, and our goal is to produce an all-sky catalog of "rare object" targets — including late-type M dwarfs, brown dwarf suspects, obscured carbon stars, IR-bright QSO candidates, etc.

Stay tuned for increasingly more exciting science from the Two-Micron All-Sky Survey.

References

Basri, G., Marcy, G. W., & Graham, J. R. 1996, ApJ, 458, 600
Chester, T., Beichman, C., Evans, T., Kopan, G., Schombert, J., Kleinmann, S., Lysaght, M., Skrutskie, M., Armus, L., Matthews, K., Neugebauer, G., Reid, N., Soifer, T., Tinney, C., & Hawley, S. L. 1992, BAAS, 181, 6809
Fisher, M., Liebert, J., Kirkpatrick, D., Cutri, R., Beichman, C., Reid, N., Djorgovski, G., & Monet, D. 1997, BAAS, in press
Kirkpatrick, J. D., Beichman, C. A., & Skrutskie, M. F. 1997, ApJ, 476, 311
Stauffer, J. R., Hamilton, D., & Probst, R. G. 1994, AJ, 108, 155

DENIS SURVEY OF AGB AND TIP-RGB STARS
IN THE LMC BAR WEST AND OPTICAL CENTER FIELDS

C. LOUP
Institut d'Astrophysique de Paris (IAP), CNRS

P.A. DUC, P. FOUQUÉ AND E. BERTIN
European Southern Observatory (ESO)

AND

N. EPCHTEIN
DESPA, Observatoire de Paris

Abstract. We have observed with the DENIS instrument two regions of $22' \times 23'$, located in the Bar of the LMC, and overlapping the Bar West and Optical Center fields studied by Blanco et al. (1980, BMB) in a prism-objective survey. Observations were performed simultaneously in the I, J, and K_S bands. There were 376 AGB stars identified in previous studies in these 2 fields. We typically find back 97% of them in the DENIS data. We show that the BMB's M and C stars follow two different sequences in the (I–J,J–K_S) colour-colour diagram. For M stars, the [I–J] colour is an indicator of the M subtype, increasing from 0.9 to 1.8 as one goes from M0 to M7 spectral types, while the [J–K_S] colour remains almost constant (from 1.0 to 1.35). Conversely, C stars are located on a "reddening" branch, with [J–K_S] ranging from 1.0 to about 2.2. M and C stars discovered by BMB have no or faint mass-loss. The (I–J,J–K_S) diagram allows to define a simple criterion to select stars of spectral types M and C. With this criterion, we find a total of 1177 new AGB and tip-RGB stars candidates, and have calculated the bolometric luminosities of all of them as well as previously known stars, assuming a distance modulus of 18.55. 90% of the new candidates are blue sources, not searched for in a complete way by BMB. Their luminosity distribution shows a very clear peak at $M_{bol} \simeq -3.5$, that we interpret as the tip of the Red Giant Branch. A second group is formed by stars for which the BMB survey should have been complete (i.e. relatively red C stars and M stars with spectral type later than M5.5). We find, however, 23% and 38% more such stars than they do in the Bar West and Optical Center, respectively.

N. Epchtein (ed.),
The Impact of Near-Infrared Sky Surveys on Galactic and Extragalactic Astronomy, 115-127.

Finally, we also discover in this study 42 red sources, with $2.2 < [J-K_S]$ < 4.2. These stars experience mass-loss at significant rates. Note that there might be redder obscured AGB stars in the fields, but that the DENIS limiting magnitudes do not allow to detect sources with $[J-K_S]$ larger than about 4. Only 4 of them have an IRAS counterpart. It is interesting to note that we discover 42 mass-loosing AGB stars in 0.14 square degrees, while only about 50 have been discovered in the whole LMC using the IRAS data. The luminosity distribution of these red sources is very similar to the one of the BMB's C stars, ranging from $M_{bol} \simeq -3.5$ to -6.

1. Introduction

Searches for AGB stars and red supergiants in the Magellanic Clouds have started in the sixties, through optical/I photographic and prism-objective surveys. One of the most fundamental one is the work of Blanco et al. (hereafter BMB) in 1980. Compared to previous works which were (almost) spatially complete, they observed only 3 small regions in the Large Magellanic Cloud (LMC), and 2 in the Small Magellanic Cloud (SMC), of 23' in diameter. However, their I limiting magnitude was 17 instead of 14 in previous works, so that they typically found 50 times more AGB stars than previously known. Their survey was later extended to 52 regions in the LMC (Blanco & McCarthy 1990, BM). The main result of their surveys was to derive the true luminosity function of LMC carbon stars (see e.g. Richer 1981, and Costa & Frogel 1996), while only the brightest tail was known before. This brought a very serious problem to the theoreticians as theories predicted much too high a luminosity for C stars. The problem is getting solved by taking into account physical phenomena like high mass-loss rates and "overshotting" (see e.g. Bertelli et al. 1985).

This type of surveys, as well as surveys devoted to the search for Long-Period Variables (LPVs, see e.g. Hughes 1989), does not allow to find AGB stars with high mass-loss rates as they become invisible in the optical/I. Actually, these surveys picked up only AGB stars without, or with faint, mass-loss. One of the first assumption for the lack of high luminosity C stars predicted by theories was that they could all loose mass at a high rate, and so have been missed by BMB. The JHK survey of Frogel & Richer (1983) however failed to find such very luminous obscured sources. Later, searches for "dust obscured" AGB stars and red supergiants became more intensive with the use of the IRAS data. At the moment, about 50 obscured AGB stars have been discovered thanks to IRAS data (see e.g. Reid et al. 1990, Wood et al. 1992, Zijlstra et al. 1996). It shows that some very luminous

obscured AGB stars exist, but they are rare. The main limitation of IRAS observations in the Magellanic Clouds is that source fluxes are very close to the detection limit. As a consequence, only the most luminous and reddest sources have been found, and even for such sources IRAS is not complete (Loup et al. 1997). Between optical/I and IRAS surveys, we still end up with a very incomplete view of the AGB population in the Magellanic Clouds. First, the whole optically thin population, including M and C stars, is actually well known in only 1 BMB field, the Bar West field (Frogel & Blanco 1990). Second, all the population with intermediate mass-loss rates is missing as it has not been seen neither in optical/I surveys, nor by IRAS.

The goal of the present work was to estimate to which extent the IJK_S DENIS survey could provide us with a much more complete knowledge of the LMC AGB population. It has been concentrated on two fields observed by BMB : the Bar West (BW) and Optical Center (OC) fields. In section 2 we briefly present the DENIS observations. In section 3, we present the cross-identification between BMB and DENIS sources, and the location of these stars in the $(I–J,J–K_S)$ colour-colour diagram as a function of spectral type. In section 4, we present new DENIS AGB star candidates not found by BMB, in particular those with significant mass-loss, and the resulting luminosity distribution. Finally, in section 5, we give the main conclusions.

2. Observations

Observations have been performed with the 3 cameras of the DENIS instrument mounted at the ESO 1m telescope (la Silla), simultaneously in the I, J, and K_S bands, in December 1995. The field of view is $12'$, the pixel size $1''$ in I and $3''$ in J and K_S. Integration times were 9s in J and K_S, and only 1s in I (it is 9s too in the normal survey mode). Our goal was to observe two fields previously surveyed by BMB in the Bar of the LMC : the Bar West and the Optical Center fields. For each field, we performed a mosaic of 6 images, 2 images Est-West and 3 North-South, with an overlap of $2'$, so that the total mapped area is 22x32'. The mosaic has been repeated 3 times within 15 minutes the same night on both fields. The DENIS fields do not overlap perfectly with the BMB fields : we miss a few of their sources in the North-East and North-West directions. Magnitudes of point sources have been determined with the "Sextractor" software (Bertin & Arnouts 1996). Confusion limit is not reached in Bar West (except in globular clusters), nor in K_S in the Optical Center; some parts of the field are rather crowded in I and J in the Optical Center.

In this study, we only kept point sources which are, at least, detected in the K_S band (so sources detected only in I and J are excluded), not blended, confirmed in the 3 repeated mosaics, and with an uncertainty on magnitudes

better than 0.15 mag. This last requirement, and the short integration time in the I band, limits the sensitivity of this study to magnitudes 15.5 in I, 15 in J, and 12.8 in K_S.

3. Previously known AGB stars

In the following we limit the discussion to stars in the fields commonly observed by BMB and DENIS, i.e. to two fields of 22x23'. In the Bar West (BW) field, BMB found 40 M stars with spectral types later than M5.5, and 65 C stars. Later, Frogel & Blanco (1990, FB) found 96 M stars with spectral types earlier than M5.5, 1 additional C star, and finally 50 other M stars in a third, more complete, search performed in 30% of the BMB-BW field. The BW field also contains 2 M stars (Rebeirot et al. 1983), and 4 Mira and 2 SRa variables (Hughes 1989, spectral type unknown) which were not found by BMB. In the Optical Center (OC) field, BMB found 32 M stars with spectral type later than M5.5, and 73 C stars. There are 5 additional M stars (Rebeirot et al. 1983, Westerlund et al. 1981, 1975), and 3 Mira and 6 SRa variables of unknown spectral type (Hughes 1989), not found by BMB. In total 186 and 37 M stars, 65 and 73 C stars, and 6 and 9 LPVs of unknown spectral type, were known in the BW and OC fields respectively.

Cross-identifications of these stars with DENIS sources were done on the basis of coordinates (when available) and finding-charts (especially in crowded parts). Excluding the third more complete search for M stars of FB, we find back 99% and 96% of the previously known sources in the BW and OC fields respectively. The few sources not recovered are located in crowded parts or coincide with bad pixels. For the third search of FB, the recovering rate is only 64%. The M stars of FB which are not recovered are fainter and not detected in the K_S band; they are however detected in the I and J bands.

DENIS allows for the first time to study the location of AGB stars in the (I–J,J–K_S) colour–colour diagram as observations are performed simultaneously in the 3 bands. Such a diagram made with previous non-simultaneaous observations actually suffers from a large spread (Loup & Groenewegen 1994), due to the variability of AGB stars, and due to the differences between the photometric systems. The (I–J,J–K_S) DENIS diagram is presented in Figure 1, for both BW and OC fields together as no differences in the source locations were found. Fig.1a shows the location of all the DENIS sources selected as defined in section 2. One can see already that the stars are located on two branches. The main branch starts at about (0,0), goes towards increasing values of both colours and ends up with a vertical branch, [J–K_S] beeing almost constant while [I–J] increases. The

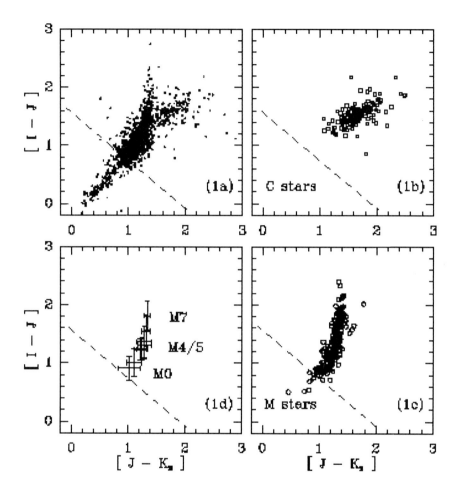

Figure 1.   The DENIS (I–J,J–K$_S$) colour–colour diagram. Fig.1a shows the location of all the DENIS sources in both BW and OC fields, with an error on the magnitude smaller than 0.15 in the 3 bands. Fig.1b and 1c show the location of the BMB's C and M stars, respectively. Fig.1d presents the mean colours of the BMB's M stars, derived for each M subtype (see also Table 1). The dashed line in the 4 plots indicates the criterion used to select AGB and tip-RGB stars from the DENIS data (section 4).

second branch, located in the reddest part of the diagram, seems to follow a redening sequence. In Fig.1b and 1c, we show the location of the BMB C and M stars, respectively. Clearly, the red branch is formed by C stars, while M stars form the vertical branch. However, the two branches have a limited overlap around I-J=1.5 and J-K=1.4. It has been shown (Groe-

C. LOUP ET AL.

newegen private communication, Loup & Groenewegen 1994) that the main branch of the diagram is a spectral type sequence, starting with A/B type until M type stars. The vertical part of the main branch is also a spectral type sequence, from M0 to M8/10. As one goes towards later M spectral types, the TiO and VO molecular bands included in the I filter becomes deeper. On another side, there are no such huge molecular bands contained in the J and K_S filters. J and K_S are mainly affected by a small decrease of the effective temperature. So what we mainly see is a decrease of the I flux, while the J and K_S fluxes remains almost constant. The fact that $[J-K_S]$ ranges in a so narrow interval of values also means that none of the M stars found by BMB is loosing mass at a significant rate, i.e., if they loose mass, the amount of dust formed is so small that its contribution to J and K_S is negligible compared to the photospheric contribution. The work of BMB and FB provides enough stars from spectral types M0 to M7.5 to allow us to make statistics on the $[I-J]$ and $[J-K_S]$ colours as a function of the M subtype. The mean colours for each M subtype are presented in fig.1d, and in Table 1. It confirms that $[I-J]$ increases as one goes towards later M spectral types. In the future, this could be helpful to determine, statistically, the M spectral type index.

TABLE 1. Observed mean values of $[I-J]$ and $[J-K_S]$ as a function of the M subtype. The second column gives the number of sources used to calculate the averages.

Spectral type	Number	$< I - J >$	$< J - K_S >$
M0/0.5	14	0.91 ± 0.21	1.02 ± 0.20
M1/1.5	33	1.01 ± 0.23	1.11 ± 0.13
M2/2.5	20	1.23 ± 0.19	1.22 ± 0.11
M3/3.5	17	1.24 ± 0.19	1.25 ± 0.09
M4/4.5	13	1.31 ± 0.24	1.29 ± 0.12
M5/5.5	27	1.37 ± 0.27	1.29 ± 0.13
M6/6.5	34	1.55 ± 0.27	1.32 ± 0.07
M7/7.5	22	1.81 ± 0.25	1.34 ± 0.05

C and M stars are distributed almost in opposite ways, in the sense that C stars exhibit a larger range of colours in $[J-K_S]$ than in $[I-J]$. At first glance (see also Loup & Groenewegen 1994), the C stars seems to follow a reddening sequence which could be attributed to circumstellar dust extinction. However, if it would be so, it would mean that many C stars discovered by BMB loose mass at a significant rate, while M stars do not. We have not seen any systematic bias in their observations which

could explain that. It is not in agreement with observations in our Galaxy where M stars are observed with all the range of mass-loss rates. Finally, M and OH/IR stars loosing mass at significant and high rates have been discovered in the LMC (Wood et al. 1992, Zijlstra et al. 1996). It is thus probably not the right hypothesis to assume that the red C star branch is due to mass-loss. We now take as an assumption that C stars seen by BMB do not loose more mass than the BMB's M stars. $[J-K_S]$ ranges from 1.0 to 2.2 (plus 3 objects between 2.2 and 2.5). The first effect one can think of is the influence of the effective temperature. We have calculated, using the real DENIS passbands (Fouqué et al. 1997), that blackbodies with temperatures of 2500 and 2000 K would have $[J-K_S] = 1.4$ and 1.9, respectively. So, assuming that C stars may have effective temperatures as low as 2000 K, their $[J-K_S]$ values may be as large as 2. However, as shown by Cohen et al. (1981), the effect of blanketing by molecules like C_2, CN, and CO, between 1 and 3 μm, has a large influence on the resulting $[J-K]$ colour. They demonstrate that, for an effective temperature of 3000 K, one can easily reach $[J-K]$ of the order of 2. Hence, we conclude that both C and M stars discovered by BMB have no or faint mass-loss, and that the red branch formed by C stars in the $(I-J, J-K_S)$ diagram is due to the combined influence of the effective temperature and carbon molecule blanketing. The few C stars with $[J-K_S]$ larger than 2.2 might start to be also affected by circumstellar dust.

We finally would like to end this section with a remark. Figure 1 could give the impression to the reader that the "C" branch contains only C stars. Let say for instance that all the stars with $[J-K_S] > 1.6$ would be C stars. This would be equivalent to similar conclusions derived in the past from (J–H, H–K) diagrams. We think, however, that using the diagram in that way might be erroneous because it neglects the effect of the mass-loss. As soon as an M star starts to loose mass at a significant rate, its location in the diagram will be shifted to the red part, following a reddening line which is almost parallel to the C star branch (at least for not high mass-loss rates). One example of such a source with $[J-K_S] > 1.6$ is displayed in Figure 1c. This star is a known supergiant, WOH-SG 264 (Westerlund et al. 1981), with an IRAS counterpart, showing that the star does loose mass. In Figure 2, one can see also that we find quite a few new AGB stars candidates with $1.6 < [J-K_S] < 2.2$, not found by BMB (see section 4). They can be *a priori* C stars, or M stars with some mass-loss. Spectroscopic follow-up is of course required for these sources. The only conclusion that we may draw out is that stars located on the vertical branch and above the C star branch are very likely to be of late M–type (Fig.1a).

4. New DENIS AGB star candidates

Figure 1 allows to define a simple criterion to select new AGB star candidates from the DENIS data. We have taken all the sources located above the dashed line, and not identified in previous studies (see section 3, mostly from BMB and FB). We put the line a little below the mean colours of M0 spectral types. It means that we have in principle selected most M stars, and all the C stars. As seen in Fig.1c, we have probably missed a few M0/1 stars. We have also probably selected a few late K type stars. In addition to AGB stars, our selection has also picked up a number of RGB stars close to the RGB tip. In total, following this selection criterion, we find 369 and 808 new AGB or tip–RGB star candidates in the BW and OC fields, respectively.

These DENIS candidates can be divided in three groups. In the first group we put all the "blue" sources. According to figure 1, they might have spectral types from late K to M4/5, or they could be blue C stars with $[J-K_S] < 1.4$. About 90% of the new candidates belong to this group. In the second group we put the DENIS sources located on the C star branch defined by the BMB C stars with $1.4 < [J-K_S] < 2.2$, as well as stars located on the last part of the vertical branch formed by their M stars, i.e. sources expected to have spectral types later than M5.5 ($[I-J] > 1.5$). According to BMB, their survey should be complete for such objects. We find, however, 26 and 50 new DENIS candidates belonging to this second group in the BW and OC fields, respectively. Comparing with the BMB stars having the same properties, they missed 23% and 38% of the stars in the BW and OC fields.

Finally, we have put in the third group all the DENIS candidates with $[J-K_S] > 2.2$, i.e. AGB stars supposed to experience a significant mass-loss, that hampers optical/I surveys detection (except a few, see Figure 1). There are 10 in the BW field, and 32 in the OC field. Most of them have not been detected in the I band, because of circumstellar dust extinction, but also because our integration time in I was only 1s. The reddest $[J-K_S]$ colour is about 4.2. It does not mean that redder sources do not exist in the field. The limiting magnitudes are such that redder sources would not be detected in the J band. Very obscured AGB stars with $[J-K]$ as large as 6 have been found among the IRAS sources (Reid 1991, Zijlstra et al. 1996).

We have calculated the bolometric magnitudes of all the DENIS sources, including previously known BMB stars and new candidates, detected at least in the J and K_S bands. We assume a distance modulus of 18.55. Bolometric magnitudes have been calculated by integrating over the IJK_S fluxes with spline interpolation. To take into account the energy radiated at

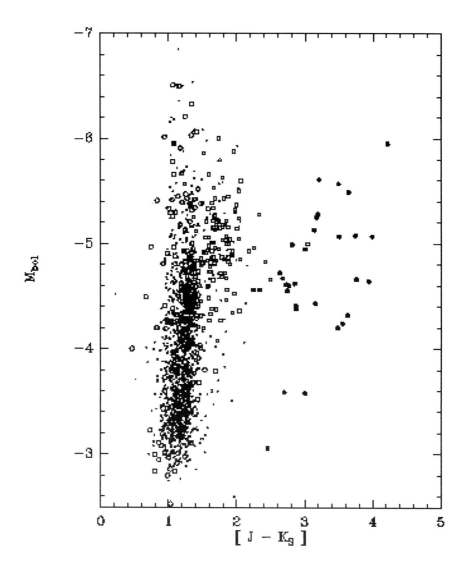

Figure 2.   Bolometric magnitudes as a function of the [J–K$_S$] colour. Open circles are previously known M stars, open squares previously known C stars, and open triangles previously known LPVs of unknown spectral type. Filled circles are the new AGB and tip-RGB DENIS candidates. Bolometric magnitudes have been calculated as explained in section 4, with a distance modulus of 18.55.

shorter wavelenghts than I and longer than K$_S$, a blackbody was fitted and integrated from 0.1 to 0.75 and from 2.2 to 60 μm. For sources with [J-K$_S$] > 2.7, we have however used the bolometric correction of Groenewegen (1997)

to better take into account the energy radiated by the circumstellar dust. Groenewegen shows that the correction is negligible for smaller values of [J–K_S]. Finally, for the 4 IRAS sources, the flux was integrated by splines until 7.5 μm, and the IRAS contribution was calculated following the method of Loup et al. (1993).

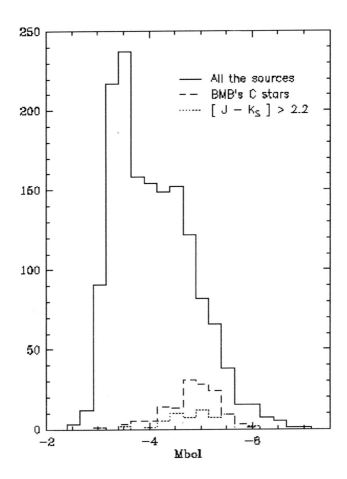

Figure 3.   Luminosity distribution of the DENIS sources. Bolometric magnitudes have been calculated as explained in section 4, with a distance modulus of 18.55. The peak at $M_{bol} \simeq -3.5$ corresponds to the tip of the RGB sequence. The distribution of the new DENIS sources with significant mass-loss rates is very similar to the one of the optical BMB's C stars.

The results are shown in Figures 2 and 3. Figure 2 displays the (J–K_S,M_{bol}) colour-magnitude diagram. It can be compared to the diagram shown by Costa & Frogel (1996) for a sample of more than 800 C stars

(mostly from BMB and BM). The distributions of the optical C stars in our diagram and Costa & Frogel's one are slightly different. In their Fig. 2, the average luminosity increases from [J–K] = 1.0 to 1.7, and decreases for larger values of [J–K], up to about 2.7. We find that the luminosity of most optical C stars is essentially independant of [J–K$_S$]. In addition, there are a few C stars with faint luminosities (M$_{bol}$ < −4) and 1.0 < [J–K$_S$] < 1.7, which are not found by Costa & Frogel, although they do include these C stars in their sample. We think that the difference comes from their calculation of the bolometric fluxes derived from a bolometric correction based on [J–K] and a relatively small sample of stars. The main new feature in our colour-magnitude diagram is of course the presence of stars with large values of [J–K$_S$]. Figure 2 shows that their range of luminosities is similar to the one of the BMB's C stars. There are 3 stars with [J–K$_S$] > 2.2 and faint luminosities (M$_{bol}$ ∼ −3.5). Their nature is still unclear; we do not exclude the possibility that they are RGB stars experiencing a phase of mass-loss (see below, and Fig.3).

In Figure 3, we present the luminosity distribution of all the DENIS sources, the BMB's C stars, and our new candidates with [J–K$_S$] > 2.2. In the distribution of all the sources, there is a very clear peak at about M$_{bol}$ = −3.5. The most likely interpretation is that we find the tip of the Red Giant Branch, so that a non negligible percentage of our new "blue" DENIS candidates (first group) are tip-RGB stars rather than AGB stars on the E-AGB branch. The drop of the distribution at lower luminosities only reflects the limits of our study. It will be interesting in the future to also keep sources detected only in I and J, as one should thus find faint AGB stars at the very begining of the E-AGB branch, as well as fainter RGB stars. The brightest tail of the distribution is mainly formed by M0 to M2 stars (see also FB). These stars probably belong to luminosity classes I or II. The luminosity distribution of the BMB's C stars is in good agreement with previous studies (see e.g. Cohen et al. 1981). More interestingly, we show that the distribution of the new DENIS candidates experiencing large mass-loss ([J–K$_S$] > 2.2) have essentially the same distribution than the BMB's C stars, and that none of them is more luminous than M$_{bol}$ ≃ −6, including the 4 IRAS sources. This bring us back to the closing remark of section 3. Does it means that all these red sources are C stars ? If yes, it would mean that there are very few M stars loosing mass at significant rates in the LMC, and that most M stars in a certain range of initial masses would become C stars before to reach the stage of mass-loss. If not, it means that M and C stars experiencing mass-loss have very similar luminosity distributions. Spectroscopy of the red stars discovered in this study must be definitely performed.

5. Conclusions

We show that DENIS is the most powerful tool we ever had to study the AGB and RGB populations in the Magellanic Clouds. Including sources detected only in I and J, or only in J and K_S, DENIS allows to discover most of the optically thin AGB population, as well as a large fraction of the RGB population. We show that the tip of the RGB branch occurs at $M_{bol} \simeq -3.5$, assuming a distance modulus of 18.55. On the side of obscured AGB stars, DENIS allows to find them up to $[J–K_S]$ of the order of 4.0. More optically thick AGB stars will not be detected and should be searched for using other instruments, in particular the ISO satellite.

Optical C and M stars previously found by Blanco et al. (1980, BMB) and Frogel & Blanco (1990) in the so-called Bar West and Optical Center fields in the Bar of the LMC, appear well separated in two branches in the $(I–J, J–K_S)$ DENIS colour-colour diagram. For M stars, the $[I–J]$ colour is an indicator of the M subtype. This diagram also allows to define a simple criterion to select M and C stars. We find a total of 1177 new AGB and tip-RGB star candidates in both BMB's fields (excluding sources not detected in the K_S band), to be compared with 376 stars identified in previous studies. Though BMB reasonably thought to be complete in their survey of relatively red C stars and M stars with spectral types later than M5.5, we find 23% and 38% more such sources in the Bar West and Optical Center fields, respectively. The main new feature of this study is the discovery of 42 sources with $[J–K_S]$ ranging between 2.2 and 4.2, experiencing mass-loss at non-negligible large rates. Their luminosity distribution is very similar to the one of the BMB's C stars, ranging from $M_{bol} \simeq -3.5$ to -6. Only 4 of them have an IRAS counterpart, the brightest ones as expected. Their chemical type is still unknown, and spectroscopic follow-up should be performed.

References

Bertin E., Arnouts S., 1996, A&AS 117, 393
Blanco V.M., McCarthy M.F., 1990, AJ 100, 674 (BM)
Blanco V.M., McCarthy M.F., Blanco B.M., 1980, ApJ 242, 938 (BMB)
Cohen J.G., Frogel J.A., Persson S.E., Elias J.H., 1981, ApJ 249, 481
Costa E., Frogel J.A., 1996, AJ 112, 2607
Epchtein N., et al., 1997, The Messenger 87, 27
Fouqué P. et al., 1997, in preparation
Frogel J.A., Blanco V.M., 1990, ApJ 365, 168 (FB)
Frogel J.A., Richer H.B., 1983, ApJ 275, 84
Groenewegen M.A.T., 1994, A&A 288, 782
Hughes S.M.G., 1989, AJ 97, 1634
Hughes S.M.G., Wood P.R., 1990, AJ 99, 784
Loup C., Forveille T., Omont A., Paul J.F., 1990, A&AS 99, 291
Loup C., Groenewegen M.A.T., 1994, Ap&Sp.Sci. 217, 131

Loup C., Zijlstra A.A., Waters L.B.F.M., Groenewegen M.A.T, 1997, A&AS 125, 419

Rebeirot E., Martin N., Mianes P., Prévot L., Robin A., Rousseau J., Peyrin Y., 1983, A&ASS 51, 277

Reid I.N., 1991, ApJ 382, 143

Reid I.N., Glass I.S., Catchpole R.M., 1988, MNRAS 232, 53

Richer H.B., 1981, ApJ 243, 744

Westerlund B.E., Olander N., Hedin B., 1981, A&AS 43, 267 (WOH)

Westerlund B.E, Olander N., Richer A.B., Crabtree D.R., 1978, A&ASS 31, 61

Wood P.R., Bessel M.S., Paltoglou G., 1985, ApJ 290, 477

Wood P.R., Whiteoack J.B., Hughes S.M.G., Bessell M.S., Gardner F., Hyland A.R., 1992, ApJ 397, 552

Zijlstra A.A., Loup C., Waters L.B.F.M., Whitelock P.A., Guglielmo F., 1996, MNRAS 279, 32

DENIS AND HIPPARCOS:
LUMINOSITY AND KINEMATIC CALIBRATIONS

R. ALVAREZ AND M-O. MENNESSIER
GRAAL (ESA 5024/CNRS), Université Montpellier II,
F-34095 Montpellier Cedex 05, France

Abstract. The homogeneous set of apparent magnitudes in the three photometric bands that the DeNIS survey will provide may be fruitfully combined with the astrometric and kinematical data of the Hipparcos satellite in order to apply a maximum-likelihood method and derive absolute magnitudes, kinematics and spatial distribution for extensive samples of stars.

1. Introduction

The DeNIS survey and the Hipparcos mission both provide us a considerable amount of data. Sophisticated statistical treatments are necessary to fully exploit all this information and thus improve our knowledge on Galactic structure, populations classification, HR diagram calibration, etc. One of this possible treatment is the LM method (Luri, Mennessier et al. 1996) specifically developed to exploit the Hipparcos data to its full extent for luminosity calibrations and distance determinations. The DeNIS survey is of prime interest for the application of the LM method as it provides homogeneous photometry for a large sample of stars with available astrometric and kinematical data. Furthermore, the observational censorship used to define a sample is known (Hipparcos selection function + DeNIS selection function): this permits to derive almost unbiased estimates of absolute magnitudes and distances (Luri & Arenou 1997).

2. The LM method

The reader is referred to Luri, Mennessier et al. (1996) for a thorough description of the LM method. We outline here its most important features. This method, based on the maximum-likelihood principle, allows us to si-

N. Epchtein (ed.),
The Impact of Near-Infrared Sky Surveys on Galactic and Extragalactic Astronomy, 129-133.

multaneously calibrate the luminosity and determine the mean kinematic characteristics and spatial distribution of a given sample. This sample is specifically modeled with appropriate distribution functions corresponding to the absolute magnitudes, kinematics and spatial distributions. Sampling effects, the galactic differential rotation and observational errors are rigorously taken into account by including appropriate functions in the density law describing the sample. The method is able to use inhomogeneous samples, i.e. samples composed of a mixture of groups of stars with different luminosities, kinematics or spatial distributions. In this case the method identifies and separates the groups. Moreover, the LM method assigns each star to a group and estimates its most probable distance.

3. Hipparcos stars with available DeNIS photometry

As any statistical method, the need for sufficiently large sample is essential. Relying on V magnitudes and V−I colours taken from the Hipparcos Catalogue (ESA 1997), we have counted how many stars among the over 120 000 Hipparcos Catalogue entries are fainter than 9.5 mag in I (DeNIS limit of saturation). The number of such stars was counted per spectral type and luminosity class. More than half the Hipparcos stars have not been attributed a luminosity class. Nevertheless, for each spectral type, we randomly dispatch the unclassified stars among the luminosity classes according to their relative weights. Finally, as an approximation of the southern-sky coverage of DeNIS, the number in each class was divided by two. The results are shown in Table 1. The B to M giants and B to G dwarfs appear to be the samples which contain enough stars (≥ 100) to apply the LM method. If TYCHO data were used, these numbers should be multiplicated by a factor ≈ 8. The larger available samples would then compensate for the less accurate proper motion measurements.

4. Example of application of the LM method

We have considered a sample of 103 oxygen-rich Miras and 129 Semi-Regular variables (Alvarez et al. 1997) with available Hipparcos trigonometric parallaxes and proper motions (ESA 1997); radial velocities from the Hipparcos Input Catalogue (Turon et al. 1992); and apparent K magnitudes from Catchpole et al. (1979), Fouqué et al. (1992), Whitelock et al. (1994), Kerschbaum & Hron (1994) and Kerschbaum (1995). In order to describe the sample, the following distribution functions have been adopted:

1. **Distribution of absolute K magnitudes:** a gaussian law with mean M_0 and standard deviation σ_M

TABLE 1. Estimates of the number of Hipparcos stars with available DeNIS photometry per spectral type and luminosity class

Spectral Type	Dwarfs & Subdwarfs	Giants & Subgiants	Supergiants & Bright giants
O	9	2	4
B	211	140	56
A	353	127	20
F	919	144	28
G	360	278	21
K	94	386	9
M	43	126	7
R N S C	–	7	–

2. **Velocity distribution:** a Schwarzschild ellipsoid with means (U_0, V_0, W_0) and dispersions $(\sigma_U, \sigma_V, \sigma_W)$
3. **Spatial distribution:** an exponential disc with scale height Z_0

Three distinct classes of stars with different kinematics and scale heights have been identified. Table 2 gives the estimates of the model parameters in the columns marked θ and the corresponding errors are given in the columns marked σ.

Two significant populations are well separated. Group 1, which is the main one (about 81 % of the sample), has the kinematics of late disk stars. The scale height is characteristic of the old disk population. This group can be interpreted as the standard disk population which has an exponential scale height of $\sim$ 300 pc (Jura & Kleinmann 1992).

Group 3 (about 17 % of the sample) has a larger velocity ellipsoid. The scale height is much more important. The large velocity ellipsoid and the important scale height characterize a population older than the group 1. The stars of this group might belong to the extended/thick (E/T) disk or they might be halo stars.

Group 2 is a very small group with very low velocity dispersion. It might be formed by a sub-population of younger stars. The small number of stars prevents further interpretation.

The individual absolute magnitudes of the Miras are also obtained with the LM method. They are plotted against the periods (Fig. 1). The three

TABLE 2. Model parameters using m_K (103 Miras and 129 Semi-Regulars)

		group 1		group 2		group 3	
		θ	σ	θ	σ	θ	σ
M_0	(mag)	-6.3	0.7	-6.1	1.6	-6.7	0.9
σ_M	(mag)	1.0	0.4	0.4	0.4	0.8	0.5
U_0	(km.s^{-1})	-11	6	-53	17	-33	40
σ_U	(km.s^{-1})	37	8	1	7	93	34
V_0	(km.s^{-1})	-23	6	-57	74	-93	53
σ_V	(km.s^{-1})	22	4	15	30	75	24
W_0	(km.s^{-1})	-12	4	-33	10	-2	33
σ_W	(km.s^{-1})	20	5	3	4	58	31
Z_0	(pc)	260	40	370	180	820	240
%		81	7	2	1	17	7

groups are distinguished by different symbols. For the two most significant groups (1 and 3), least-square linear fits are obtained: two parallel period–luminosity relations are found in K, one for each population.

Figure 1 also shows the M_K—P relation that Van Leeuwen et al. (1997) have calibrated for Galactic oxygen–rich Miras by using Hipparcos parallaxes and adopting *a priori* the slope of the Large Magellanic Cloud (LMC) relation. Its slope is in very good agreement with ours. This is a very remarkable result: we find that the slopes of the Galactic period–luminosity relations in K are the same as the LMC one.

It has been discussed for a long time as to whether metallicity effects in Miras might generate different period–luminosity relations. The results of the present work tend to demonstrate that Galactic Miras follow different period–luminosity relations in K, according to the two distinct populations that we have separated: the slopes are the same and only the zero points differ by about 0.5 mag. The shift between the period–luminosity relations is interpreted as the consequence of the effects of metallicity abundance on the luminosity.

5. Conclusion

Hipparcos has provided a large number of trigonometric parallaxes and proper motions. DeNIS and 2MASS will provide precise and homogeneous photometric data allowing to define specific classes of stars, constituting homogeneous samples to which the LM method may be applied. This will

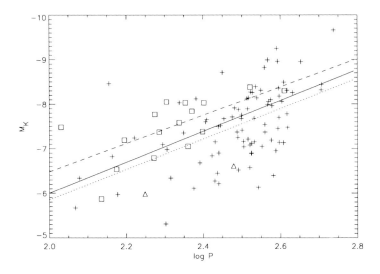

Figure 1.   Period–luminosity relations in K band. Crosses represent Miras belonging to group 1, triangles to group 2 and squares to group 3. Dotted line and dashed line are the period–luminosity fit relations for group 1 and 3 respectively. Solid line is the period–luminosity relation determined by Van Leeuwen et al. (1997)

enable us to calibrate the luminosities of large number of B to M giants and B to G dwarfs, as was done for the Long Period Variables.

References

Alvarez R., Mennessier M-O., Barthès D., Luri X., Mattei J.A., 1997, A&A in press

Catchpole R., Robertson B., Lloyd Evans T., Feast M., Glass I., Carter B., 1979, SAAO Circ 1, 61

ESA, 1997, The HIPPARCOS Catalogue, ESA SP-1200

Fouqué P., Le Bertre T., Epchtein N., Guglielmo F., Kerschbaum F., 1992, A&AS 93, 151

Jura M., Kleinmann S., 1992, ApJS 79, 105

Kerschbaum F., 1995, A&AS 113, 441

Kerschbaum F., Hron J., 1994, A&AS 106, 397

Luri X., Arenou F., 1997. *Utilisation of Hipparcos Data for distance determinations: error, bias and estimation.* In: Perryman M.A.C. (ed.) The Hipparcos and Tycho Catalogues, ESA-SP 402, in press

Luri X., Mennessier M-O., Torra J., Figueras F., 1996, A&AS 117, 405

Turon C., Crézé M., Egret D. et al., 1992, The HIPPARCOS Input Catalogue, ESA SP-1136

Van Leeuwen F., Feast M., Whitelock P., Yudin B., 1997, MNRAS 287, 955

Whitelock P., Menzies J., Feast M., Marang F., Carter B., Roberts G., Catchpole R., Chapman J., 1994, MNRAS 267, 711

MAXIMUM LIKELIHOOD ESTIMATION OF THE SCALE HEIGHT OF MIRA VARIABLES.

ZSOLT BEREND AND LAJOS G. BALÁZS

Konkoly Observatory, Budapest

Abstract. Based on the DENIS data observed in a strip passing near to the Galactic anticenter ($l=182^o$ - 209°, $b=-2^o$ - 13°), and using photometric selection criteria, we extracted a sample of Mira variables. Assuming a spatial distribution in the form of an exponential disk we estimated the scale height using the Maximum Likelihood technique. The procedure also yielded the confidence interval of the estimated parameter.

1. Introduction

The Mira variables are pulsating red giants with high luminosity, lying on the Asymptotic Giant Branch of the H-R diagram. The DENIS project has important role in their studying because they are brightest in the infrared bands. From DENIS strips a sufficient number of red variables can be extracted for statistical studies. Their spatial distributions can help in understanding the structure of the Galactic Disk.

We have to be acquainted with the scale heights of the populations in order to know their distributions. The aim of this work is to give a Maximum Likelihood estimation of scale height of Mira variables.

2. Maximum Likelihood estimation

The spatial distribution of Mira variables can well be approximated assuming exponential distribution (Wainscoat (5)) in z and R (distance from the Galactic plane and centre, respectively). Consider the following function:

$$L = \tilde{A}(m_1, l_1, b_1; z_0)\tilde{A}(m_2, l_2, b_2; z_0) \ldots \tilde{A}(m_n, l_n, b_n; z_0), \qquad (1)$$

135

N. Epchtein (ed.),
The Impact of Near-Infrared Sky Surveys on Galactic and Extragalactic Astronomy, 135-138.
© 1998 *Kluwer Academic Publishers. Printed in the Netherlands.*

where $\tilde{A}$ is the probability density function of stars

$$\tilde{A}(m,l,b,S) = \frac{A(m,l,b,S)\Psi(m)\Xi(l,b)}{\int_{-\infty}^{\infty} A(m,S)\Psi(m)\Xi(l,b)dmdldb}, \qquad (2)$$

A gives the amounts of stars in one square degree depending on distance and direction referring to a given spectral type, m_i, l_i, b_i are the apparent magnitude and galactic coordinates of stars of the sample, $\Psi(m)$, $\Xi(l,b)$ are the truncation functions in m, l, b and z_0 is the exponential scale height of the population, and the unknown parameter of the likelihood function. This function takes its maximum at some $\tilde{z}_0 = \tilde{z}_0(m_i, l_i, b_i)$. This $\tilde{z}_0$ value is considered to be the estimation of the real scale height value. The likelihood function (1) gives the probability density of obtaining the available sample in the course of the sampling of $\tilde{A}(m,l,b;z_0)$. It means, that the z_0 value is estimated by that special $\tilde{z}_0$ value, which if it were the real value of our parameter, then exactly the given sample would the most likely ensue among the possible samples of n elements.

If $\tilde{z}_0$ is the Maximum Likelihood estimation of the z_0 parameter, then assymptotically

$$2(L_{max} - L_0) \approx \chi^2 ,$$

where L_{max} is the maximum of the likelihood function (1), and L_0 is the value taken at the real parameter, an d χ^2 has the degree of freedom of the parameters estimated.

The first confidential area can be obtained by subtracting 0.5 from the likelihood function at maximum and drawing at that point a horizontal line (see Figure 2). The two extremities of the confidential area will be where this line intersects the curve.

By the process written above we obtain the 1 σ probability of $\tilde{z}_0$. This value can be reduced by increasing the number of elements of the sample.

We have written a programme estimating scale height making use of the outlined process. Firstly we tested the programme with simulated data. We produced the samples with Monte Carlo method, and the estimated scale heights were all consistent to the simulated values within 1 σ.

3. Application to DENIS data

The available sample contains the right ascensions, declinations and I, J, K colours of 25054 stars (Field: l=182° - 209° ; b=−2° - 13°).

In order to extract the Mira variables from this strip we plotted the J-K colour indexes in function of I-K (see Figure 1) using the literature data (Bessel & Brett (1); Feast et al. (2)). 77 Mira type variables have been left after the selection. Miras can be classed into populations according to

Figure 1.   Field: l=182° - 209° ; b=−2° - 13°

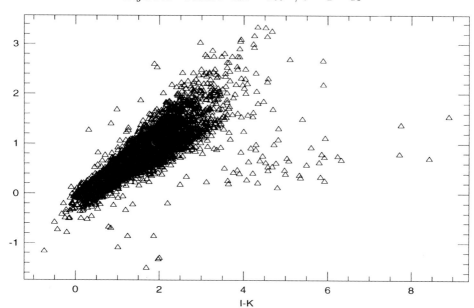

Distribution of the sample in the $J - K$, $I - K$ plane. Mira variables can be found in the range: $3.3 < I - K < 6$ and $1 < J - K < 1.4$.

their periods, and each population represent a different subsystem of the Galactic Disk with different scale height (Jura & Kleinmann (4) ; Hron (3)). However we have not got any information of the periods we only know the apparent magnitudes. Therefore the estimated scale height of this sample is a mean value of the populations. In order to calculate the maximum of the likelihood function we used numerical methods. We increased the z_0 parameter by 10 pc from a chosen initial value, and calculated its likelihood function at every step with numerical integration. The point at which the value of the likelihood function is the highest is considered to be the estimated scale height of the sample.

The likelihood function obtained by this method is in Figure 2. The scale height is <u>510</u> pc and the region surrounded by solid lines represent the 1 σ confidence interval.

Acknowledgements

Special thanks to Stéphanie Ruphy for providing us with the DENIS strip data (private communication 1996).

Figure 2.   Likelihood Function

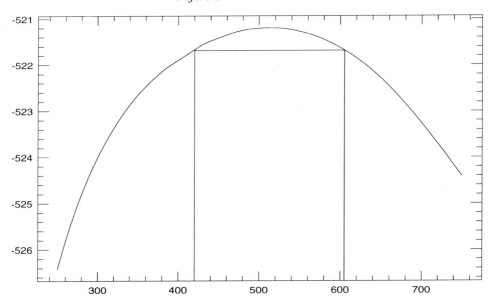

The maximum of the Likelihood Function is at z_0=510 pc, the selected region represents the first confidence interval.

References

Bessel, M.S., & Brett, J.M. 1988, PASP, 100, 1134

Feast, M. W., Robertson, B. S. C., Catchpole, R. M., Lloyd Evans, T., Glass, I.S., & Carter, B. S. 1982, MNRAS, 201, 439

Hron, J. 1991, A&A, 252, 583

M. Jura & S. G. Kleinmann : 1992, ApJS 79, 105-121

Wainscoat, R. J., Cohen, M., Volk, K., Walker, H. J, & Schwartz, D.E. 1992, ApJS, 83, 111

IV- Star forming regions and Interstellar medium

2MASS OBSERVATIONS OF MOLECULAR CLOUDS

JOHN M. CARPENTER
California Institute of Technology
Department of Astronomy, MS 105-24, Pasadena, CA 91125

1. Introduction

A major goal of star formation studies is to characterize the conditions and "mode" under which most stars form in our Galaxy (see, e.g. Lada, Strom, & Myers 1993). That is, among the continuum of stellar systems found in molecular clouds, how are most stars created? Are they formed primarily in rare, but densely populated clusters, or among smaller clusters and isolated star forming regions? Do most stars form uniformly in time throughout the lifetime of a molecular cloud, or in sporadic bursts? What causes one portion of a molecular cloud do form rich clusters, but not other regions? How (and if at all) do the properties of the stars (e.g. lifetime of protoplanetary disks, the stellar initial mass function, etc...) vary among the different stellar systems? While answering these questions requires substantial photometric and spectroscopic observations, the first crucial step requires determining the size and spatial distribution of the stellar population within molecular clouds.

Determining whether most stars form in isolation or in clusters has far broader implications than merely establishing the predominant morphological distribution of young stellar objects. First, it establishes the environmental conditions most stars form under, which in turn may influence the resultant stellar properties. For example, the stellar densities observed in some clusters imply that the initial protostars may have undergone substantial gravitational and tidal interactions (Zinnecker, McCaughrean, & Wilking 1993). Such interactions may alter the mass accretion rate onto a star, the lifetime of protoplanetary disks, the final stellar mass, and the formation of binary systems (Ostriker 1994; Kroupa 1995; Price & Podsiadlowski 1995; Jensen, Mathieu, & Fuller 1996; Bonnell et al. 1997). The spatial distribution of stars can also potentially constrain various evolutionary scenarios for molecular clouds. Dense clusters are easily recognized

141

N. Epchtein (ed.),
The Impact of Near-Infrared Sky Surveys on Galactic and Extragalactic Astronomy, 141-153.
© 1998 *Kluwer Academic Publishers. Printed in the Netherlands.*

as a group of stars forming in a localized region of space. Many clusters are
localized in time as well in that they represent "bursts" of star formation
where hundreds of stars or more are formed on time scales of less than a
few million years (Hillenbrand et al. 1993; Greene & Meyer 1995; Meyer
1996; Hillenbrand 1997). Dynamical considerations also suggest that compact clusters constitute relatively young stellar systems (Lada, Margulis,
& Dearborn 1984). Thus a stellar population consisting largely of clusters
would suggest that star formation has not taken place over long periods of
time, either since the cloud is young, or because star formation has been
inhibited over most of the cloud lifetime. On the other hand, a molecular
cloud containing primarily a large scale, uniformly distributed population
of stars is more difficult to interpret, as such a population may result from
numerous isolated star forming events or small, old clusters that have since
dispersed over large spatial scales. While these scenarios do not exhaust all
possible situations and interpretations, it is clear that the observed spatial
distribution of stars provides an important initial step toward establishing
how star formation proceeds within molecular clouds.

The primary difficulty in determining the spatial distribution of stars in
clouds is identifying young stellar objects actually associated with the cloud
amongst the population of unrelated field stars. Classically this has been
accomplished by selecting individual stars based on the presence of an emission feature associated with young stellar objects (e.g. Hα, near-infrared
excesses, far-infrared emission, x-rays, etc...). While these methods generally have a high reliability in finding young stellar objects, they have severe
selection biases in that these emission features (except x-rays) are generally associated with pre-main-sequence stars surrounded by optically thick
accretion disks. Since the evolution of these disks and emission features as
a function of time and stellar mass is unknown, it is not possible to infer
the extent of the stellar population that has already passed through this
phase of stellar evolution and is not detectable by these methods. While x-
rays surveys probe chromospheric activity and can detect older stars, these
surveys often provide a vastly incomplete census of the stellar population.
In the Orion region, for example, the *ROSAT* All Sky Survey detected 850
x-ray sources in a 450 deg^2 area centered on the Orion molecular cloud
(Alcalá et al. 1996). The total stellar population in Orion, however, exceeds at least 5000 stars as inferred from near-infrared observations (Lada
et al. 1991; Strom, Strom, & Merrill 1993; Ali & DePoy 1995).

As an alternative to definitively identifying each individual star associated with a cloud, the underlying stellar population can be inferred statistically using star counts. This method attempts to establish the stellar population by determining the excess number of stars observed toward the cloud
with respect to the field star population. This approach is particularly ad-

vantageous for near-infrared wavelength observations. As indicated above, near-infrared observations are often more sensitive to the embedded stellar population than peculiar emission surveys. Further, near-infrared emission generally probes the stellar photosphere (except for heavily accreting objects). Thus the sensitivity of these surveys as a function of stellar mass and age are easier to estimate. While optical observations also possess these advantages, the lower extinction at near-infrared wavelengths have enabled these surveys to probe deep into molecular clouds and discover stars not detectable at optical wavelengths. Thus at the cost of uniquely identifying young stars, near-infrared star count studies can potentially obtain a more complete census of the embedded stellar population.

In the following discussion, I examine the potential that the current generation of large scale near-infrared surveys – and 2MASS in particular – have for extending our understanding of the stellar population in molecular clouds through star count studies. I will begin by reviewing in §2 recent results on characterizing the stellar population within clouds, and indicate the need for surveys such as 2MASS to answer many of the outstanding questions. In §3, I examine the sensitivity of 2MASS to young stars as a function of stellar mass, age, distance, and extinction, and identify regions in the Galaxy that are particularly well suited for star count studies with the 2MASS data base. Details of a star count analysis are considered in §4, and well as some of the numerical methods that hold promise to objectively analyze the data. A summary of my conclusions is provided in §5.

2. Recent Results

Much of our understanding of the distribution of stars within molecular clouds comes from studies of two regions: Taurus and Orion. Taurus has been studied at nearly every available part of the electromagnetic spectrum, and a compilation of these studies shows that the known stellar population in Taurus consists of ~185 stars (Kenyon & Hartmann 1995), at least half of which can be assigned to six small groups of ~15 stars each (Gomez et al. 1993). Interestingly, spectroscopic observations have shown that stars in Taurus generally have ages of $\lesssim$3 Myr (Kenyon & Hartmann 1995), and that a widespread population of old stars does not appear to be present. Since molecular clouds typically have lifetimes in excess of 10 Myr (Leisawitz, Bash, & Thaddeus 1989; Elmegreen 1991), these results suggest that unless the Taurus region is much younger than the average molecular cloud, star formation has occurred only in its recent history. These conclusions remain controversial, however, as there has been much debate on the completeness of current surveys in sampling the total stellar population in molecular clouds (Feigelson 1996; Briceño et al. 1997).

One complication in generalizing the above results is that most of the molecular mass in the Galaxy is contained in Giant Molecular Clouds (GMCs) that have masses an order of magnitude or more larger than Taurus (Sanders, Scoville, & Solomon 1985). Logically one assumes that most stars form in GMCs as well, although it remains to be demonstrated that this is actually the case. The nearest example of a GMC is the Orion molecular cloud, which like Taurus has been the subject of numerous studies at multiple wavelengths. The most sensitive and systematic of these surveys designed to address the importance of cluster and distributed stellar populations in Orion have been conducted in the near-infrared. These surveys indicate that the stellar population in the northern half of Orion (L1630) is contained almost exclusively in 4 rich, dense clusters (Lada et al. 1991; Li, Evans, & Lada 1997). The southern half of Orion (L1641) contains roughly an equal number of stars, however, they are distributed uniformly throughout the cloud (Strom, Strom, & Merrill 1993) and not in rich dense clusters that characterize the northern half of Orion. The implications of these disparate conclusions concerning the spatial distribution of stars for different parts of the same molecular cloud are unclear. These results might suggest that no dominant mode of star formation exists, and that the evolution of clouds and their star formation content depends strongly on the local conditions. Alternatively, perhaps clusters are the dominant mode of star formation, and the distributed stellar population found in L1641 represents clusters formed long ago but have since dispersed. Note, however, that these two studies have imaged just 4% of the projected surface area of the Orion molecular cloud (Maddalena et al. 1986). Further, neither survey encompasses the Trapezium region, which has a total stellar population that exceeds what has been inferred so far in L1630 and L1641 combined (Ali & DePoy 1995).

Clearly any conclusions concerning the stellar population within molecular clouds remain speculative. Existing surveys often do not cover entire clouds, and the number of clouds that have been observed are so few in number that any generalized statements are not possible. The primary difficulty in this endeavor of course is the inordinate time required to map entire molecular clouds to sensitive levels at near-infrared wavelengths. These limitations, however, will soon be lifted by the 2 Micron All Sky Survey (2MASS), which has begun to scan the entire sky to a 10σ completeness limit of 15.8^m, 15.1^m, and 14.3^m at J, H, and K_s band respectively. The large area coverage, the uniform sensitivity, and the multi-wavelength observations inherent to 2MASS provide powerful tools to infer the underlying stellar population in molecular clouds. In the remainder of this contribution, I investigate the practical aspects involved in conducting star count analyses with the 2MASS data base.

3. Sensitivity to Young Stellar Objects

Before discussing the computational aspects of analyzing star count data, it is important to establish how well 2MASS can probe the underlying stellar population associated with a molecular cloud. The primary factors to consider are *(i)* the sensitivity of 2MASS to young stellar objects as a function of stellar mass, age, distance, and extinction; and *(ii)* the constraints imposed by field stars in inferring the stellar population associated with the cloud. I discuss these issues below and demonstrate that the stellar population can be constrained to interesting limits for clouds in the solar neighborhood. This discussion also serves to underscore subtle aspects that must be considered in the data analysis in order to accurately characterize the stellar population.

3.1. STELLAR AGES, MASSES, AND DISTANCES

Since most stars associated with molecular clouds are in the pre-main-sequence phase of stellar evolution, their brightness will depend sensitively on the stellar age and mass. The range of stellar masses and ages that 2MASS can probe is illustrated in Figure 1 for four well-known star forming regions that span a range of distances from the sun: Taurus (distance = 140 pc), Orion (450 pc), W3 (2200 pc), and W51 (7000 pc). The solid curves in Figure 1 represent K_s band isomagnitudes calculated using the pre-main-sequence evolutionary tracks from D'Antona & Mazzitelli (1994) assuming zero extinction, and the grey shaded region highlights the parameter space that 2MASS can probe at the 10σ K_s band completeness limit (14.3^m). For example, Figure 1 shows that at the distance of Taurus, 2MASS will be able to detect all stars younger than 10^8 years that are now on the cloud surface (i.e. $A_V = 0^m$). Even for visual extinctions as large as 20^m, the 2MASS survey will be able to detect nearly all stars within this age range ($A_K \approx A_V/10$). Given that the age of a typical cloud is thought to be less than 10^8 years (Leisawitz, Bash, & Thaddeus 1989; Elmegreen 1991), 2MASS will be able to detect nearly all stars in Taurus with $A_V < 20^m$ that have formed throughout the cloud lifetime. At the distance of Orion, 2MASS will be able to detect a surface population of stars more massive than 0.4 $M_\odot$ that have formed over the cloud lifetime, and at the distance of W3, a surface population of 1.4 $M_\odot$ stars is readily detectable. Beyond a couple of kiloparsecs, only young, massive stars will be easily detected.

Besides the obvious decrease in sensitivity with increasing distance, Figure 1 also emphasizes that for a given stellar mass, the sensitivity decreases with increasing stellar age. To illustrate the effect time evolution has on the detectability of the underlying stellar population within a cloud, Figure 2 shows the fraction of stars in a model molecular cloud that are brighter

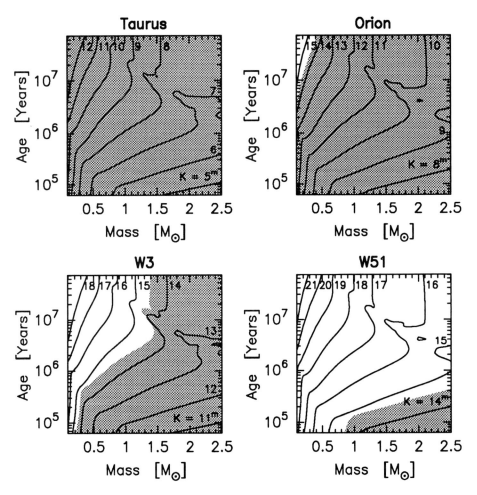

Figure 1. K_s band isomagnitude contours as a function of stellar age and mass for stars at the distance of Taurus (140 pc), Orion (450 pc), W3 (2200 pc), and W51 (7000 pc). The magnitudes were computed using the pre-main-sequence evolution tracks from D'Antona & Mazzitelli (1994; model 1 with CM convection and Alexander opacities) assuming $A_V = 0^m$ and that no excess near-infrared emission is present. The shaded area highlights the parameter space that 2MASS can probe at the 10σ K_s band completeness limit (14.3^m). Since clouds are thought to have ages of less than 10^8 years, 2MASS can detect all stars now on the surface of Taurus that have formed throughout the cloud lifetime. For Orion, a surface population of stars more massive than 0.4 $M_\odot$ that have formed over the cloud lifetime will be detectable. One challenge in inferring the size of the underlying stellar population within a cloud is to take into account the sensitivity of 2MASS to stars of various masses, ages, and extinction.

than the 2MASS K_s band completeness limit assuming that stars have been forming at a constant rate over time with a Miller-Scalo stellar initial mass function (Miller & Scalo 1979). Three different time periods for

the star formation episode are indicated in the figure. At the distance of Orion, for example, if star formation has occurred only in the past 10 Myr, then ~90% of the stars will be detectable with 2MASS. (Note, however, that extinction has been ignored for this illustration.) Only about half of the stars will be visible though if star formation has taken place over a time period of 70 Myr. Since a distributed population of stars might be expected to be older on average than stars found in clusters, the sensitivity functions shown in Figure 1 must be considered when evaluating the relative significance of cluster and distributed stellar populations.

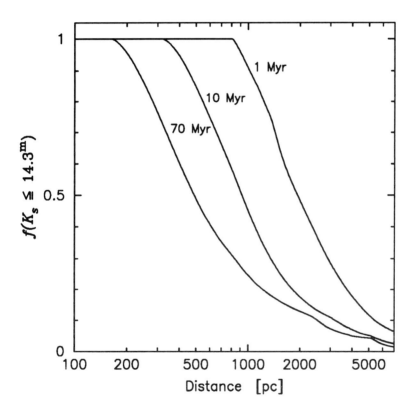

Figure 2. The solid curves represent the fraction of stars brighter than the 2MASS K_s band completeness limit (14.3^m) in a model molecular cloud that has been forming stars at a constant rate over time with a Miller-Scalo initial mass function. The results are shown for when star formation has occurred constantly over three different time periods: 1 Myr, 10 Myr, and 70 Myr. No extinction has been added to the models, and the stellar mass range spans from 0.1 $M_\odot$ to 20 $M_\odot$. At a distance of 500 pc, for example, 2MASS can detect anywhere from 100% of the stars if star formation has persisted for only 1 Myr, to as low as 48% of the stars if star formation has continued for as long as 70 Myr.

3.2. EXTINCTION

Besides the stellar mass, age, and distance, extinction will have important consequences for determining the visibility of a star. For most regions, extinction will come primarily from dust associated with the parental molecular cloud and not from dust in the general interstellar medium. To illustrate the effect that extinction has on the sensitivity of 2MASS to young stellar objects, Figure 3 shows the lowest mass star that can be detected at J, H, and K_s bands for the 10σ completeness limits as a function of depth (i.e. visual extinction) into a cloud. The stellar magnitudes were computed using the pre-main-sequence evolutionary tracks from D'Antona & Mazzitelli (1994) assuming stellar ages of 1 Myr (left panel) and 20 Myr (right panel) and a distance of 450 pc (corresponding to the Orion molecular cloud). Figure 3 shows that for an age of 1 Myr, the J, H, and K_s band surveys are sensitive to $0.1\,M_\odot$ stars (and the more massive brown dwarfs) on the cloud surface. The J band surveys quickly lose sensitivity to the low mass stars as the extinction increases, and for $A_V > 10^m$, K_s band is the most sensitive probe of embedded stars regardless of the age. Even for $A_V = 30^m$, the 2MASS K_s band survey will detect 1 Myr stars more massive than $0.4\,M_\odot$ at the distance of Orion. For $A_V < 10^m$, H band is generally more sensitive than K_s band.

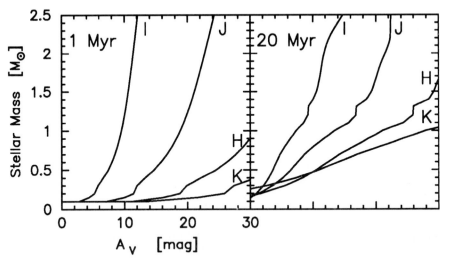

Figure 3. The lowest mass pre-main-sequence star that can be detected at various depths into the cloud (as measured by visual extinction) at the distance of Orion (450 pc) for the 10σ completeness limits of 2MASS at J (15.8^m), H (15.1^m), and K_s (14.3^m) bands. The magnitudes were computed using the pre-main-sequence evolutionary tracks from D'Antona & Mazzitelli (1994). The left panel shows the results for stars with an age of 1 Myr and the right panel for an age of 20 Myr. These curves show that the 2MASS H band survey is generally the most sensitive probe of young stellar objects for $A_V < 10^m$, and the 2MASS K_s band survey is more sensitive for $A_V > 10^m$.

For actual molecular clouds, the visual extinction for a random line of sight is typically $A_V \lesssim 5^m$ and for a star forming dense core, $A_V \gtrsim 10^m$ (Carpenter, Snell, & Schloerb 1995; Heyer, Carpenter, & Ladd 1996). Thus the most sensitive probe of stars randomly situated throughout a molecular cloud are the 2MASS H band observations. These data are particularly important for tracing a widespread distributed stellar population since many of these stars are expected to be old and have low visual extinctions. In dense cores, however, the 2MASS K_s band data are best used to detect embedded objects. Thus while I emphasize analysis of the K_s band data in this discussion, the most complete analysis of the stellar population will actually be obtained from an aggregate star count map constructed from the J, H, and K_s band 2MASS data.

3.3. FIELD STARS

The calculations presented above demonstrate that 2MASS is quite sensitive to young stellar objects in nearby molecular clouds within ~1 kpc of the sun (see Fig. 1). However, since the stellar population associated with a cloud will be inferred from star counts (see §4 for details), an additional criteria is that the number of stars associated with the cloud significantly exceeds the random fluctuations among the field star population. These constraints are particularly important for any uniformly distributed stellar population since these stars may be significant in number but low in surface density. The number of field stars (N_f) projected against a circular cloud with angular radius θ_c immersed in a field star backdrop with surface density D_f is $N_f = D_f \pi \theta_c^2$. For Poisson statistics, the minimum *detectable* distributed population associated with the cloud (N_{min}) is

$$N_{min} \propto \sqrt{N_f} \propto \sqrt{D_f} \, \frac{R_c}{d_c},$$

where R_c is the cloud radius and d_c the cloud distance. As an example, the Orion molecular cloud has a projected surface area of ~48 deg^2. The estimated field star surface density is ~0.35 stars arcmin^{-2} for $K_s \leq 14.3^m$ (Jarrett 1992), implying that the 3σ minimum detectable stellar population is ~750 stars for an assumed distance of 450 pc. Since this limit is less than the number of stars found in the various clusters in Orion (Lada et al. 1991; Ali & DePoy 1995), interesting limits on the relative importance of the distributed and clustered populations can indeed be obtained for Orion and nearby clouds. Note that this analysis only considers stars brighter than the photometric completeness limit. As emphasized in Figure 1, old, low mass stars may be present at fainter magnitudes. The number of such stars will depend on the cloud distance and frequency distribution of stellar ages and masses, and is necessarily model dependent.

4. Data Analysis

It was shown in §3 that 2MASS will be able to detect a substantial fraction of the stellar population in nearby molecular clouds and establish the relative contributions of clustered and distributed stellar populations to interesting limits. Since the methods to actually extract this information from the star count data are diverse, I sketch only a general outline here that attempts to analyze the data in a self-consistent manner. In addition, I briefly discuss some of the numerical methods that can be used to objectively identify stellar clusters.

4.1. STAR COUNTS

The observed star counts toward a molecular cloud consists of three components: *(i)* field stars foreground to the cloud; *(ii)* background field stars reddened primarily by dust associated with the cloud; and *(iii)* stars embedded in the cloud. The cloud stellar population can therefore be obtained by subtracting the foreground stars and reddened background objects from the observed star counts. The practical difficulty in this procedure is that near-infrared colors and magnitudes cannot completely distinguish field stars from the stellar population associated with the cloud. Stars with red near-infrared colors can either by reddened background objects or stars embedded within the cloud, and unreddened stars may either be foreground objects, young stars on the cloud surface, or background stars appearing through holes in the cloud. While stars with a near-infrared excess can be unambiguously assigned to the cloud, such a selection criteria only identifies objects surrounded by optically thick accretion disks, which may represent a small fraction of the total stellar population. Also, many stars will be detected at only one or two wavelengths, further limiting the information that can be inferred from the colors and magnitudes.

Rather than attempt to definitely identify each young stellar object, the stellar population associated with a cloud can be statistically determined by subtracting the expected distribution of field stars from the observed star counts. The systematic and random angular variations in the field star surface density can be established quite accurately from the 2MASS observations of the regions surrounding the molecular cloud. A semi-empirical model of the background field star population can then be constructed by using Galactic star count models to estimate the fraction of the observed field stars that are likely background objects. Star count models already provide an accurate description of the near-infrared sky (e.g. Bahcall & Soneira 1984; Garwood & Jones 1987; Jarrett 1992), and they will be even further refined with the extensive 2MASS data base. Next, the semi-empirical background field stellar population needs to be reddened using

an extinction map of the cloud. Such maps are now readily obtained from molecular line observations, most notably CO and its isotopes.[1] While it is well established that molecular clouds contain substructure down to the smallest observable spatial scales, the high resolution, fully sampled maps now available resolve the large scale filaments, shells, and sheets of gas within molecular clouds (e.g. Bally et al. 1987; Carpenter, Snell, & Schloerb 1995) and accurately trace large scale extinction variations. Thus after subtracting off the model distribution of unreddened foreground field stars and reddened background field stars, a two dimensional map of the stellar population associated with the cloud is obtained.

4.2. CLUSTER IDENTIFICATION

In many respects, identifying clusters is one of the more difficult parts of the analysis since a cluster is not well defined mathematically. In addition, a cluster in one cloud may not be classified as such in another cloud if, for example, the field star surface density is larger. By most definitions, clusters represent a "significant" enhancement in the stellar surface density with respect to the fluctuations in the field star surface density, and the distributed population consists of stars not found in clusters. Most star formation studies have identified clusters by choosing a stellar surface density threshold in a binned star count map. The difficulty with this analysis is that the surface density threshold and the binning cell size are arbitrary parameters biased against finding compact clusters smaller than the cell size, extended low density regions, and clusters not conforming to the adopted axes for the binned star count map.

Recently, non-parametric algorithms (e.g. wavelets, maximum penalized likelihood estimators, kernel density estimation) have been developed and applied to astronomical problems that avoid arbitrary binning of data and provide a more objective measure of the underlying density distribution (Silverman 1986; Scott 1992; Pisani 1996; Fadda, Slezak, & Bijaoui 1997). An illustration of adaptive kernel density estimation is shown in Figure 4 for a simulated stellar population consisting of 5 clusters superimposed on a random distribution of field stars. In this technique, each star is represented by a kernel function (e.g. a gaussian – the results do not depend sensitively on the actual kernel used as long as it has rapidly falling tails). The kernel size for any individual star is computed based on the local stellar density, and the density estimate for the total stellar population is given by the sum of the individual kernels. This procedure contains a number

---

[1] The star counts cannot be used to determine the extinction (e.g. Lada et al. 1994) since this method assumes that none of the stars are associated with the cloud, which is exactly the stellar population that one is attempting to measure.

of highly desirable features for identifying clusters: *(i)* the method is non-parametric and requires no binning of the data; *(ii)* the individual kernel sizes are computed objectively by minimizing the mean integrated square error of the difference between the kernel density estimate and the observed data (Silverman 1986); *(iii)* the probability that each cluster could result from a random distribution of objects can be readily computed (Materne 1979; Pisani 1996); *(iv)* extension of this technique to n-dimensions (e.g. right ascension, declination, magnitude, etc..) is straight forward. The best manner in which to employ these techniques still needs to be explored, but preliminary results are encouraging.

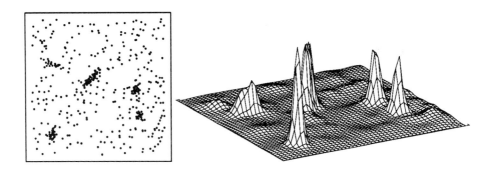

Figure 4. Left panel: The spatial distribution of a simulated stellar population containing 5 clusters superimposed on a random distribution of field stars. *Right panel:* Adaptive kernel density estimate of the model stellar population shown in the left panel (viewed at an angle for clarity). The five clusters are evident as peaks in the density estimate. The number of stars inferred for these clusters agree rather well with the input parameters for the model simulation.

5. Summary

Throughout this discussion I hoped that I have conveyed the excitement and promise that 2MASS provides for investigations into the stellar population of molecular clouds. For nearby objects in particular, 2MASS will be able to determine the distribution of stars that have formed over nearly the entire expected lifetime of molecular clouds. The biggest improvements over existing observations is that for the first time, our understanding of the stellar population in star forming regions will be based on studies of entire ensembles of entire molecular clouds encompassing of range of environments and masses. I look forward to presenting the results of this research at the next Euro conference!

References

Alcalá, J. M. et al. 1996, A&AS, 119, 7

Ali, B. A., & DePoy, D. L. 1995, AJ, 109, 709

Bahcall, J. N., & Soneira, R. M. 1984, ApJS, 55, 67

Bally, J., Langer, W. D., Stark, A. A., & Wilson, R. W. 1987, ApJ, 312, L45

Bonnell, I. A., Bate, M. R., Clarke, C. J., & Pringle, J. E. 1997, MNRAS, 285, 201

Briceño, C., Hartmann, L. W., Stauffer, J. R., Gagné, M., Stern, R. A., & Caillault, J.
    P. 1997, AJ, 113, 740

Carpenter, J. M., Snell, R. L., & Schloerb, F. P. 1995, ApJ, 445, 246

D'Antona, F., & Mazzitelli, I. 1994, ApJS, 90, 467

Elmegreen, B. G. 1991, in The Physics of Star Formation, eds. C. J. Lada & N. Kylafis,
    (Dordrecht:Kluwer), 35

Fadda, D., Slezak, E., & Bijaoui, A. 1997, A&A, in press

Feigelson, E. D. 1996, ApJ, 468, 306

Garwood, R., & Jones, T. J. 1987, PASP, 99, 453

Gomez, M., Hartmann, L., Kenyon, S. J., & Hewett, R. 1993, AJ, 105, 1927

Greene, T. P., & Meyer, M. R. ApJ, 450, 233

Heyer, M. H., Carpenter, J. M., & Ladd, E. F. 1996, ApJ, 463, 630

Hillenbrand, L. A. 1997, AJ, 113, 1733

Hillenbrand, L. A., Massey, P., Strom, S. E., & Merrill, K. M. 1993, AJ, 106, 1906

Jarrett, T. H. 1992, Ph.D. thesis, University of Massachusetts–Amherst

Jensen, E. L. N., Mathieu, R. D., & Fuller, G. A. 1996, ApJ, 458, 312

Kenyon, S. J., & Hartmann, L. 1995, ApJS, 101, 117

Kroupa, P. 1995, MNRAS, 277, 1522

Lada, C. J., Margulis, M., & Dearborn, D. 1984, ApJ, 285, 141

Lada, C. J, Lada, E. A., Clemens, D. P., & Bally, J. 1994, ApJ, 429, 694

Lada, E. A., DePoy, D. L., Evans, N. J. II, & Gatley, I. 1991, ApJ, 371, 171

Lada, E. A., Strom, K. M., & & Myers, P. C. 1993, in Protostars and Planets III, ed. E.
    H. Levy & J. Lunine (Tucson: University of Arizona Press), 245

Leisawitz, D., Bash, F. N., & Thaddeus, P. 1989, ApJS, 70, 731

Li, W., Evans, N. J. II, & Lada, E. A. 1997, ApJ, in press

Maddalena, R. J., Morris, M., Moscowitz, J., & Thaddeus, P. 1986, ApJ, 303, 375

Materne, J. 1979, A&A, 74, 235

Meyer, M. R. 1996, Ph.D. thesis, University of Massachusetts

Miller, G. E., & Scalo, J. M. 1979, ApJS, 41, 513

Ostriker, E. C. 1994, ApJ, 424, 292

Pisani, A. 1996, MNRAS, 278, 697

Price, N. M., & Podsiadlowski, PH. 1995, MNRAS, 273, 1041

Sanders, D. B., Scoville, N. Z., & Solomon, P. M. 1985, ApJ, 289, 373

Scott, D. W. 1992, Multivariate Density Estimation, (New York: Wiley)

Silverman, B. W. 1996, Density Estimation for Statistics and Data Analysis, (London:
    Chapman & Hall)

Strom, K. M., Strom, S. E., & Merrill, K. M. 1993, ApJ, 412, 233

Zinnecker, H., McCaughrean, M. J., & Wilking, B. A. 1993, in Protostars and Planets
    III, eds. E. H. Levy & J. I. Lunine, (Tucson: University of Arizona Press), 429

STAR FORMING REGIONS AND NEAR-IR SURVEYS

T. MONTMERLE
Service d'Astrophysique, CEA/DAPNIA/SAp
Centre d'Etudes de Saclay
91191 Gif-sur-Yvette Cedex
France
montmerle@cea.fr

Abstract.
    The traditional way to find young, low-mass stars has been to do deeper and deeper near-IR surveys of molecular clouds, and to look for objects with excess IR flux over a blackbody photosphere. We thus expect to find many low-luminosity young objects with surveys such as DENIS and 2MASS. However, taken in isolation, such surveys cannot be conclusive in two cases: (i) young objects without near-IR excess (such as the "weak-line T Tauri stars": WTTS); (ii) background cool main-sequence stars or red giants, which dominate the faint population of IR sources. One of the best ways to select young stars without IR excess is to use their X-ray emission properties. As X-ray observations done with ROSAT show, many WTTS are present at a distance from star-forming regions. The spectroscopic determination of their age then allows in particular to trace the past history of star formation of these regions. In this context, I will also discuss the new possibilities offered by the next generation of X-ray satellites, AXAF and XMM

N. Epchtein (ed.),
The Impact of Near-Infrared Sky Surveys on Galactic and Extragalactic Astronomy, 155.
© 1998 *Kluwer Academic Publishers. Printed in the Netherlands.*

A STUDY OF EXTINCTION AND STAR FORMATION IN THE CHAMAELEON I CLOUD WITH DENIS

L. CAMBRESY

Observatoire de Paris, DESPA, F-92195 Meudon Cedex, France

Abstract.

   I present the first massive star count in the J band (1.25 μm) provided by DENIS in the Chamaeleon I dark cloud. These data are used to derive a high resolution map (2') of an area of 1.5° × 3° around the centre of the cloud using an original processing which involves an adaptive grid for counting and a wavelet decomposition for noise filtering of the extinction map. The maximum extinction in this cloud is found to be 10 Av, using a normal law. Preliminary results on the study of the star formation improve our knowledge about the stellar population of the cloud. In particular, the K_s luminosity function allows the estimation of the age of the stellar population of the cloud.

1. Introduction

The Chamaeleon I cloud is the most obscured region of the Chamaeleon dust-molecular complex. Near infrared (1-2 μm) star counts are more appropriate to probe regions where $A_V \gtrsim 4$ since an extinction of 10 visual magnitudes drops to only ≈ 3 magnitudes in the J band at 1.25 μm. The aim of this paper is to investigate in detail the extinction toward the Cha I cloud using this new wealth of data.

   The Cha I dark cloud is located at $b = -16°$ and its current distance estimate is 140 pc (Whittet et al., 1987). Its high galactic latitude implies a small number density of background stars which limits the spatial resolution of the extinction estimation, but, on the other hand, the probability of crossing several clouds on the line of sight is low.

157

N. Epchtein (ed.),
The Impact of Near-Infrared Sky Surveys on Galactic and Extragalactic Astronomy, 157-163.

2. Star count method

Usually, the extinction is evaluated by comparison of star counts in the absorbed region and a nearby area assumed to be free of obscuration (Wolf diagram method). Star counts are performed by adding up the stars up to a given magnitude (or in a given magnitude range, e.g., $\pm\frac{1}{2}$) within a grid of fixed squares. The step of the grid is a compromise between the stellar density and the spatial resolution. In other words, the spatial resolution is underestimated wherever the extinction is low, while in highly obscured areas, the content of several cells must be merged, in order to pick up enough stars. Moreover the poissonnian error resulting from star counts depends on the extinction.

I have developed a new method to investigate the extinction across a cloud which consists in replacing usual star counts by an estimation of the local projected star density obtained by measuring the mean distance of the x nearest stars. The most important advantage of this method is to match the local extinction: it corresponds to a star count with adaptable square size (Fig. 1).

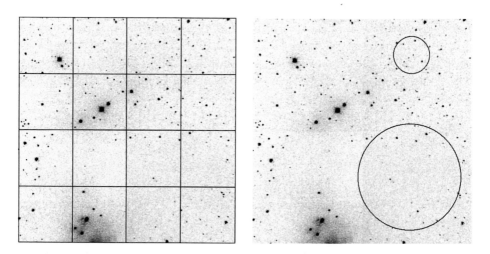

Figure 1.   Classical (left) and adaptive (right) star counts method

Another very interesting advantage of the method is to provide a map with white noise. Therefore, we can simply estimate the noise by computing the standard deviation σ of the mean distance on a part of the map with no signal.

I obtain a map where each point represents the square root of the local

density. The extinction is then easily derived by the relation :

$$A_\lambda = \frac{1}{a} \log \left(\frac{\overline{d_{cl}}}{\overline{d_{cp}}} \right)^2 \qquad (1)$$

where a is defined by :

$$\log \left(\overline{d_{cp}} \right)^{-2} = a \times m_\lambda + b \qquad (2)$$

where m_λ is the magnitude, $\overline{d_{cl}}$ the mean distance of the x nearest stars in the cloud and $\overline{d_{cp}}$ the mean distance of the x nearest stars in a comparison field supposed unobscured. I verified that the relation (2) is correct up to $J = 16$, i.e. our limit of completeness. Then we convert A_J into visual extinction using the extinction law of Cardelli et al. (1989) for $R_V = \frac{A_V}{E_{B-V}} = 3.1$. So $\frac{A_J}{A_V} = 0.282$.

I can consider the map as a digitized *image* which allows to use current technics of image processing such as the wavelet transform to restore the image and to filter the noise (Starck & Murtagh, 1994). I apply the *à trous* wavelet transform algorithm to split-off the image into 4 wavelet planes (Fig. 2). The decomposition is made by convolving the image by a low–pass filtering matrix. The difference between the original image and the result of the first convolution gives the first plane of the wavelet transform which corresponds to the high frequency plane. Further iterations of this process provide the 4 wavelet planes and the final smooth plane.

Thus, we can use the high frequency plane to identify aberrant points and remove them in the final image in order to eliminate their contribution in all the planes, by replacing the bad pixels by the average of the surrounding 8 pixels. The fact that this plane contains only noise indicates that the extinction measurement are over sampled.

Lastly, we filter each wavelet plane at $3\sigma_i$, where σ_i corresponds to the standard deviation of the plane i. It could be estimated in a part of the image without signal, or it could be simulated. The simulation is very easy since the number of stars in each cells is fixed to x. So, a Poisson noise is generated and we replace in the equation (1) the expression $\left(\frac{\overline{d_{cl}}}{\overline{d_{cp}}} \right)^2$ by $\left(\frac{x}{P(x)} \right)$ where $P(x)$ is a Poisson distribution of mean x. I apply the wavelet transform to this simulated noise and we obtain the σ_i for each plane.

3. Results

The final result is the extinction map presented in Fig. 3. This map results from the recombination of the 4 wavelet planes.

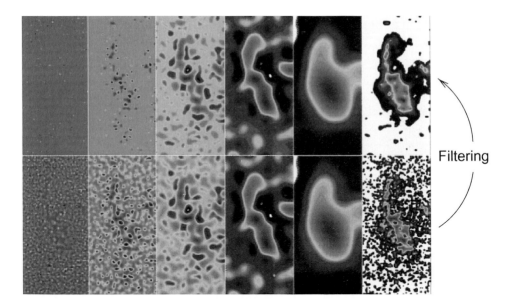

Filtering

Figure 2. Wavelet decomposition of the extinction map. The five first images represent
the wavelet planes and the last smooth plan. The lower right image is the raw map, the
upper right image is the filtered extinction map

Comparison between near–infrared extinction and IRAS 100 μm emission has been discussed in Cambrésy et al. (1997). In particular, the excellent correlation suggests that the J extinction and the *cold* 100 μm emission
have the same origin, a result in agreement with the Désert at al. (1990)
dust model which shows that the 100 μm emission and the near infrared
extinction are both caused by big grains. The relation between IRAS emission near–infrared extinction is constrained by two parameters : the evolution of the temperature inside the cloud and the extinction efficiency ratio
$\frac{Q_e(100\mu m)}{Q_e(J)}$.

This accurate mapping of the extinction is very useful to study the star
formation in the cloud. Assuming that the majority of the stars are behind
the cloud, we can use the extinction map to deredden them. According to
the *Besançon* model (Robin and Crézé, 1986), 98% of the sample consists
of background stars. The dereddening applied to the associated members
of the cloud is an upper limit. Then we represent each star in a colour–
magnitude diagram (K_s vs $J - K_s$) and we select stars which are separated
from the main sequence by a distance corresponding to 8 magnitudes of visual extinction, at least. After removing the brightest sources which probably correspond to background giant stars and faintest sources for which the
photometric errors are too large, we obtain a sample of 58 good candidates
of young stars (Cambrésy et al., in preparation). The number of known

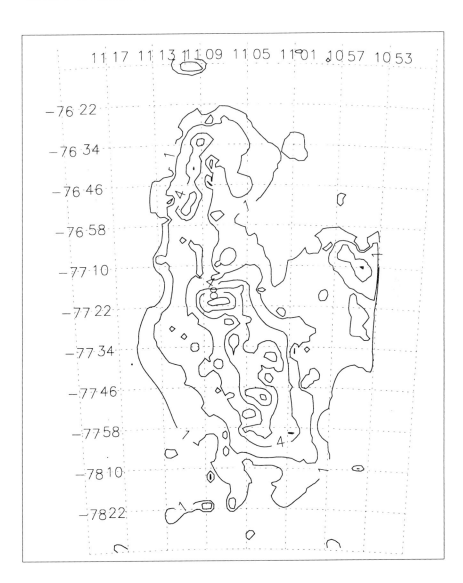

Figure 3.   Extinction map derived from J band stellar counts. Isocontours correspond to 1, 2, 4, 6, 8 and 10 magnitudes of visual extinction

T–Tauri stars in the Chamaeleon I cloud is 125 (Feigelson and Kriss 1989; Schwartz 1991; Gauvin and Strom 1992; Hartigan 1993; Lawson et al. 1996), so after confirmation we would increase significantly the size of this sample. A spectroscopic diagnosis is now required to confirm the nature of these objects, but their concentration near the cores of the cloud is in favour of their association with the cloud. Another explanation could be the presence of

small highly extinguished globules in the cloud which would strongly affect the colour of background stars. These globubes should have a size smaller than $1'$ to escape detection in the star count process and thus, extinction should be greater than 15 visual magnitudes. Finally, the selection board only on a colour criterion can confuse unresolved binaries. A forthcoming work will present a thorough study of the star formation in the Chamaeleon I cloud. Preliminary results based on theoretical model by D'Antona and Mazzitelli (1994) show that most sources would have an age ranging from $4\,10^5$ to $3\,10^6$ years.

4. Conclusion

The extinction map of the Chamaeleon I cloud has been significantly improved for extinction greater than $4A_V$ with respect to previous maps obtained from star counts on Schmidt plates. Four distinct maxima are detected and we reach 10 visual magnitudes of extinction without degradation of the resolution. This result has been obtained both by exploiting the massive star counts in the J band provided by DENIS, and by applying a variant of the classical star count method which is adapted to large variations of extinction and a wavelet analysis of the extinction map.

Moreover, DENIS gives us the opportunity to investigate the young stellar population of the cloud at a larger scale than the earlier investigations which were limited to small regions around the visible reflection nebulae. This homogeneous large scale observations will be very useful to investigate the star formation history of the whole cloud. The depth of the survey allows an estimation of the age of the stellar population thanks to the delimitation of a peak in the K_s luminosity function of the cloud members. The age estimate for the stellar population of the cloud is about 10^6 years.

Acknowledgements

The DENIS team is warmly thanked for making the observations available for scientific analysis.

References

Boulanger F., Bronfman L., Dame T.M., and Thaddeus P. (1997), *submitted*
Cambrésy L., Epchtein N., Copet E., de Batz B., Kimeswenger S., Le Bertre T., Rouan D. and Tiphène D. (1997), *A&A*, **324**, pp.L5-L8
Cardelli J.A., Clayton C. and Mathis J.S. (1989), *ApJ*, **345**, pp.245
D'Antona, F. and Mazzitelli, I. (1994), *ApJS* **90**, 467
Désert F.-X., Boulanger F. and Puget J.L. (1990), *A&A*, **237**, pp.215
Feigelson, E. and Kriss, G. (1989), *ApJ*, **338**, pp. 262
Gauvin, L. and Strom, K. (1992), *ApJ*, **385**, 217
Gregorio Hetem J.C, Sanzovo G.C. and Lépine J.R. (1988), *A&AS*, **76**, pp.347

Hartigan, P. (1993), *AJ*, **105**, 1511
Jones T.J., Hyland A.R., Harvey P.M., Wilking B.A. and Joy M. (1985), *AJ*, **90**, pp.1191
Laureijs R.J., Clarck F.O. and Prusti T. (1991), *ApJ*, **185**, pp.372
Lawson, W. A., Feigelson, E. D., and Huenemoerder, D. P. (1996), *MNRAS*, **280**, 1071
Robin, A. and Crézé, M. (1986), *A&A* **157**, 71
Schwartz R.D. and Henize K.G. (1983), *AJ*, **88**, pp.1665
Schwartz, R. (1991), in B. Reipurth (ed.), *Scientific Report*, No. **11**, p. 93, ESO
Starck J.L. and Murtagh F. (1994), *A&A*, **288**, pp.342
Whittet D.C.B., Kirrane T.M., Kilkenny D., Oates A.P. and Watsonf G. (1987), *MNRAS*, **224**, pp.497

DENIS AND ISOCAM OBSERVATIONS OF CHAMAELEON I CLOUD

P. PERSI
Istituto Astrofisica Spaziale, CNR, CP.67,00044 Frascati, Italy

E. COPET
Observatoire de Paris, DESPA, F-92195 Meudon Cedex, France

AND

A.A. KAAS
Stockolm Observatory, S-133 36 Saltsjöbaden, Swenden

Abstract. We present the results of the observations of the Chamaeleon I molecular cloud, in DENIS near-infrared (I, J and K_s) and ISOCAM mid-infrared (LW2, LW3).

1. Observations

1.1. ISOCAM DATA

The Chamaelon cloud has been surveyed with the ISOCAM instrument (Césarsky et al, 1996) in the two broad band filters LW2 (6.75 μm) and LW3 (15 μm). The PFOV was 6 arsec and $T_{int} = 2.1$ seconds, but for some sub-regions wich contain bright sources, $T_{int} = 0.28$ seconds. Then, the dataconsist of 5 rasters map but not uniformly limited in sensitivity.

303 sources have been detected in a region of approximately 1964 sq. arcmin in Cham I including the two B9 stars HD 97300 (North) and HD 97048 (South) which is associated with the bright reflection nebulae Ced 112 and Ced 111. 64% of the sources have been detected only in LW2, 33% show emission in both LW2 and LW3, while approximately 3% have been found only in LW3. The spatial distribution of the sources is shown in Fig. 1. We could detect two clusters, a cluster of very red ISOCAM sources (m(6.75)-m(15) > 1.2) is lovated in the northern part of the cloud (Cham I North), and the other around the star HD 97048. The superimposition on the extinction map of the cloud (Cambrésy et al, 1997) shows that both

N. Epchtein (ed.),
The Impact of Near-Infrared Sky Surveys on Galactic and Extragalactic Astronomy, 165-170.
© 1998 *Kluwer Academic Publishers. Printed in the Netherlands.*

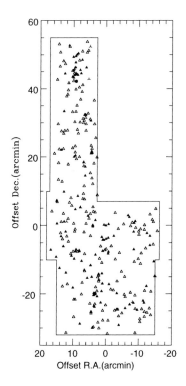

Figure 1.   Spatial distribution of the 303 sources found with ISOCAM. The symbols are: open triangle, source detected only in LW2; filled circle, detected only in LW3; filled triangle sources detected in both bands. The (0,0) correspond to R.A.(1950)= 11h05m34s Dec(1950)=-77d02'

YSO clusters are located in the densest part of the cloud.

The comparaison of the LW2 and LW3 luminosity functions with the "SKY Model" (Cohen, private communication) shows a cutoff at about 2 mJy for LW2 and 5 mJy for LW3, corresponding roughly to the limits of sensitivity of the ISOCAM survey. In addition, the observed LW3 star count shows an excess and a peak at about 77 mJy with respect to the SKY model, indicating that in Cham I YSO's population is brighter probably than 8th magnitudes (12 mJy) at 15 μm.

1.2. DENIS DATA

The DENIS (Epchtein et al, this issue) images were acquired in survey mode, with $T_{int} = 9$ seconds in I (0.8 μm), $T_{int} = 9\times1$ seconds in both

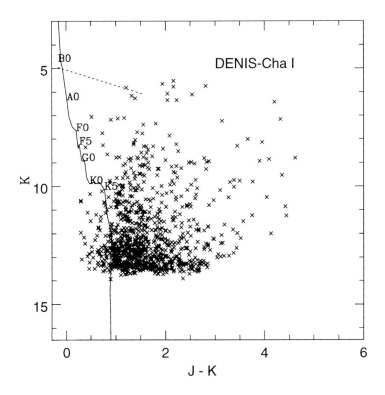

Figure 2. K_s, $(J-K_s)$ diagram the 1172 sources detected by DENIS. the main-sequence is draw in solid line.The dashed line indicate the reddening vector for $A_V = 10$

J (1.25 μm) and K_s(2.16 μm). 13 DENIS "strips" were used to cover the full ChamI cloud. Limiting magnitudes are 18, 16 and 14 at 3 σ level in I, J and $K_s$bands, respectively. 1172 sources have been detected by DENIS in the $K_s$band at a limit of 14 mag in the same ISOCAM surveyed region, 975 have been found also in J.

The color-magnitude K_s, $(J-K_s)$ of the DENIS sources is shown in Fig. 2. Most of the sources common to DENIS and ISOCAM are located in the region $(J-K_s) > 1.5$ and $K_s < 13$ of the diagram. The color magnitude diagram in a reference area (not shown) present a concentration in the K=13.5-14, J-K=0.5-1.5 region, then we make the assumption than these sources with $J-K_s > 2$ are background stars. The extinction of Cham I is in the range between 1 and 8 (peak at 10) (Cambrésy, this issue), then, sources between K_s=8 and K_s= 13 and $(J-K_s)$=1-2 could be T Tauri stars without IR excess while sources with a (J-K)>2 and brighter than K_s=13 could be T-Tauri with a strong IR excess.

2. Discussion

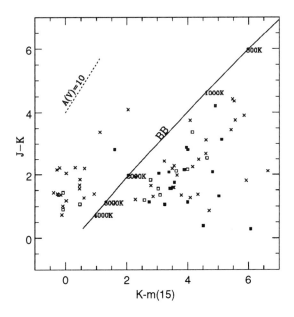

Figure 3. (J-K), (K-LW2) diagram the common sources detected both by DENIS and ISOCAM. The positions of the known CTT (filled square) and WTT(open square) are reported. This diagram separates two distinct groups of sources (see text)

2.1. COLOR-COLOR DIAGRAMS

The J-K vs K-m(15) diagram presented in Fig. 3, shows two distinct groups of sources: *i*) K-m(15)=0 (only WTT fill this part of the diagram); *ii*) K-m(15)>2. indicate an IR excess at 15 μmfor these sources (presence of a dust circumstellar disk ?). CTT and WTT are located in this region of the diagram. This suggests that WTT can be either Class II sources with IR excess, or Class III sources. The same conclusion is drawn out using J-K vs m(6.75)-m(15) diagram.

2.2. SPECTRAL ENERGY DISTRIBUTION

Using the two instruments we can derive a spectral energy distribution (SED) on a large spectral domain. The SED of the known CTTs and WWTs detected by DENIS and ISOCAM are presented Fig. 4. We remark 3 differents groups: CCTs which are class II sources with a spectral index n $(0 < n < 1)$, WTTs with and without IR excess.

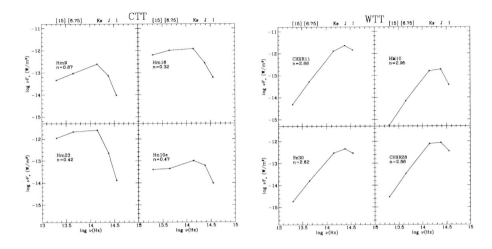

Figure 4. Left: Energy distribution of known CTTs. right: SED of WTTs with infrared excess.

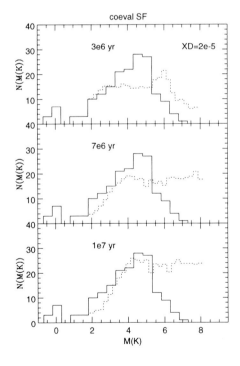

Figure 5. Observed LF in K of the ISOCAM-DENIS sources (solid line), the dashed line shows the model for a coeval SF modele computed for a deuterium abundance XD=2e-5

2.3. AGE OF THE CHAM I YSO

We have derived a K luminosity function for coeval star formation model (shown in Fig. 5) and continous SF models from the stellar evolution tracks computed for different deuterium abundances (D'Antona, private communication), and taking a distance d=140pc for the cloud and a mean A_V = 4. From the comparaison of these different models, it appears that the young stellar population has an age not younger that 10^7 year.

Acknowledgements

We thank F. D'Antona for providing the stellar evolution models in K band, and the La Silla DENIS team for making the observations.

References

Cambrésy L., Epchtein N., Copet E., De Batz B., Kimeswenger S., Le Bertre T., Rouan D. and Tiphène D. (1997) *A&A*, **324**, p.L5
Cesarsky C (+ 20 authors) (1996) *A&A*, **315L**, p. 32
Nordh L (+20 authors) (1996) *A&A*, **315L**, p. 185

PLANETARY NEBULAE WITH DENIS

S. KIMESWENGER

Institut für Astronomie der Leopold–Franzens Universität
Technikerstraße 25, A-6020 Innsbruck, AUSTRIA

1. Introduction

The last, and only, attempt to survey the sky in the near infrared range was the TMSS (Neugebauer & Leighton, 1969). This survey contains mainly bright stars. The Deep Near Infrared Southern Sky Survey (DENIS) is the first attempt to survey all the southern sky in the near infrared (NIR) range in three bands; I, J and Ks (Epchtein et al., 1994). Planetary nebulae (PNe) were investigated by means of aperture photometers (e.g. Whitelock 1985, Kwok et al. 1986, Pena & Torres–Peimbert 1987, Preite–Martinez & Persi 1989, Phillips & Cuesta 1994) in the past. These investigations often use J, H and K bands. Thus the DENIS survey will lead, due to different bands and the total sky coverage, to a new view on PNe in this wavelength domain. We show here the capabilities of investigations of PNe with the DENIS data, being comparable in spatial resolution, will also support investigation at longer wavelengths (Kimeswenger et al., 1997a) done with the ISOCAM instrument (Cesarsky et al., 1996). Spatially resolved observations also provide better information about the contamination of the red (or highly reddened) foreground stars. The survey also will uncover the nature of several objects suspected to be PNe by means of their IRAS colors, but having no optical identification yet.

2. Individual objects

The objects here were selected from the pool of already observed PNe with diameters greater than 15 arcseconds. A set of them have NIR information in the literature already. The objects here were selected to show the main advantages of NIR imaging.

N. Epchtein (ed.),
The Impact of Near-Infrared Sky Surveys on Galactic and Extragalactic Astronomy, 171-174.
© 1998 *Kluwer Academic Publishers. Printed in the Netherlands.*

2.1. NGC 2440 (= PN G234.8+02.4)

This object is given with $m_J = 10^m.33$ and $m_K = 9^m.68$ (Whitelock, 1985) and is one of the classical bipolar systems (sometimes even classified as quadrupolar). The nebula has 16" in diameter (Acker et al. (1992)). The DENIS images of NGC 2440 (Fig. 1) show the main nebula being already significantly larger (22" × 28").

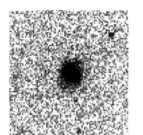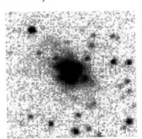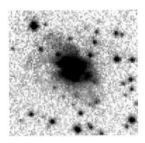

Figure 1. Images of NGC 2440 by the DENIS survey at the ESO 1m (from left to right: Ks, J, I) with a resolution of 1"/pixel and an exposure time of 10 seconds.

The photometrical result obtained with DENIS in the K band is somewhat fainter than the values listed in the literature. The J band corresponds extremely well. The total I band flux had to be slightly corrected for stellar contamination ($0^m.08$). To avoid confusion due to different aperture sizes, we obtained not only the total flux, but also that one of the apertures used in the photometers in other studies.

TABLE 1. Results of the photometry for NGC 2440 obtained with DENIS and found in the literature

band	aperture ["]	DENIS [mag]	from lit. [mag]	ref.
K/Ks	total	9,38		
	27	9,52	9,39	Persson & Frogel (1987)
	24	9,63	9,68	Whitelock (1985)
	14	10,22	10,07	Pena & Torres–Peimbert (1987)
J	total	9,99		
	24	10,21	10,33	Whitelock (1985)
	14	10,71	10,67	Pena & Torres–Peimbert (1987)
I	total	11,21		

2.2. NGC 3918 (= PN G294.6+04.7)

This system is a "classical" round system without any structure at a scale of a few arcseconds. The ring structure is hardly visible. It is more likely a

uniform brightness object. Persi et al. (1987) have given $m_K = 8^{m}\!.85$ and $m_J = 9^{m}\!.13$ for this object. The aperture used there is not clear to us, but taking into account the size of the object of 19" only, we assume that the whole object was within the aperture. We find $8^{m}\!.71$, $9^{m}\!.18$ and $10^{m}\!.58$ for K, J and I respectively.

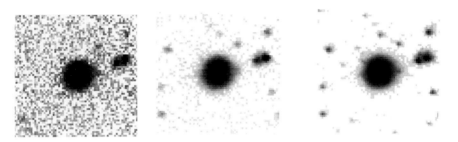

Figure 2.   Images of NGC 3918 by the DENIS survey (from left to right: Ks, J, I).

2.3. KFL 14 (= PN G002.5-05.4)

This nebula is claimed to be a bulge sample object (Acker et al., 1992). The membership investigations of the bulge sample are of importance for the calibration of many "global" properties of PNe. The extinction towards the nebulae is known (by Balmer decrements). It is found to be less than $E_{B-V}=1^{m}$. Comparing the red DENIS images with the (deeper !) sky survey clearly shows, that the extinction towards the bulge is significantly higher than $E_{B-V}=1^{m}$. Thus, this kind of investigations of the "surrounding" of PNe gives us a new tool to better select the real bulge sample.

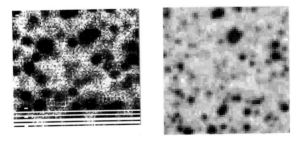

Figure 3.   The images of KFL 14 (left: DENIS J, right: optical sky survey).

2.4. SAKURAI'S OBJECT (= PN G010.4+04.4)

This object, first claimed by Y.Sakurai in Feb. 1996 to be a nova, is a born–again PNe undergoing a very late He-flash. The DENIS images allowed

174

(together with spectra from the LasCampanas 100" telescope) to monitor the dust formation phases (Kimeswenger et al., 1997b).

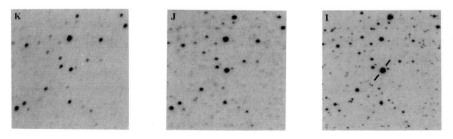

Figure 4. The images of Sakurai's Object obtained in spring 1996.

Acknowledgements

This project was supported by the FWF projects P8700-PHY and P10036-AST. The DENIS project is partly funded by the European Commision through *SCIENCE and Human Capital and Mobility* plan grants. It is also supported, in France by the Institut National des Sciences de l'Univers, the Education Ministery and the Centre National de la Recherche Scientifique, in Germany by the State of Baden–Württemberg, in Spain by the DGI-CYT, in Italy by the Consiglio Nazionale delle Ricerche, in Austria by the *Fonds zur Förderung der wissenschaftlichen Forschung und Bundesministerium für Wissenschaft und Forschung*, in Brazil by the Fundation for the development of Scientific Research of the State of São Paulo (FAPESP), and in Hungary by an OTKA grant and an ESO C & EE grant.

References

Acker, A., Ochsenbein, F., Stenholm, B., et al: 1992, The Strasbourg-ESO Catalogue of Galactic Planetary Nebulae, ESO, Munich, Germany
Cesarsky C.J., Abergel A., Agnèse P., et al., 1996, A&A, 315, L32
Epchtein, N., de Batz, B., Copet, E., et al., 1994, Ap&SS 217, 3
Neugebauer G., Leighton R.B., 1969, Two Micron Sky Survey, NASA, SP 3047
Kimeswenger, S., Kerber, F., Gratl, H., et al.: 1997, IAUC 6608
Kimeswenger, S., Kerber, F., Weinberger, R.: 1997, MNRAS, submitted
Kwok, S., Hrivnak, B.J., Milone, E.F.:1986, ApJ, 303, 451
Pena, M., Torres–Peimbert, S.: 1987, RMexAA, 14, 534
Persi, P., Preite–Martinez, A., Ferrari–Toniolo, Spinoglio, L.: 1987, ApSS Library, 135, 221
Persson, E.S., Frogel, J.A.: 1973, ApJ, 182, 503
Phillips, J.P., Cuesta, L.: 1994, A&AS, 104, 169
Preite–Martinez, A., Persi, P.: 1989, A&A, 218, 264
Whitelock, P.A.: 1985, MNRAS, 213, 59

V- Extragalactic

GALAXIES WITH DENIS:

Preliminary star/galaxy separation and first results

GARY A. MAMON

Institut d'Astrophysique de Paris & DAEC, Obs. de Paris
98 bis Bd Arago, F–75014, Paris, FRANCE

AND

JEAN BORSENBERGER, M. TRICOTTET AND V. BANCHET

Institut d'Astrophysique de Paris

Abstract. The numerous extragalactic and cosmological motivations of the DENIS and 2MASS near infrared surveys are outlined. The performance of the DENIS survey is estimated from $50 \, \mathrm{deg}^2$ of high galactic latitude data ($20° < |b| < 60°$). Simple star/galaxy separation methods are presented and comparison with 300 visually classified objects as well as COSMOS and APM classifications. We find that the peak intensity over isophotal area is an excellent star/galaxy separation algorithm, fairly robust to variations of the PSF within the frames, achieving 98.5% completeness and 92.5% reliability for $I < 16.5$, in comparison with visual classification. A new estimate of the photometric accuracy for galaxies is presented. The limiting factors for homogeneous galaxy extraction at high galactic latitudes are completeness and photometric accuracy in K, photometric accuracy in J and star/galaxy separation in I (also used for classification in J and K). Galaxy counts are presented on $50 \, \mathrm{deg}^2$. The I counts are in excellent agreement with a Euclidean extrapolation of the published counts around $I = 16 - 17$ (more so than in all previous studies), and thus point to a high normalization at the bright end, in contrast with the counts published from the APM and COSMOS plate scans. The J-band differential galaxy counts follow the relation $N(J) = 12 \pm 1 \, \mathrm{dex}(0.6 \, [J - 14]) \, \mathrm{deg}^{-2}\mathrm{mag}^{-1}$. Extrapolation of these high latitude counts suggest that DENIS will produce highly homogeneous catalogs of $\simeq 6000$ ($K < 11$), $\simeq 700\,000$ ($J < 14.8$) and, $\simeq 1\,000\,000$ ($I < 16.5$) galaxies, respectively with photometric accuracy of 0.08^m in I and 0.20^m in J and K. Larger highly homogeneous samples are expected with improvements to the camera and the algorithms.

N. Epchtein (ed.),
The Impact of Near-Infrared Sky Surveys on Galactic and Extragalactic Astronomy, 177-192.
© 1998 *Kluwer Academic Publishers. Printed in the Netherlands.*

1. Introduction

The DENIS consortium has been imaging the southern sky in the I (0.8μm), J (1.25μm) and K_s (2.15μm) wavebands since December 1995. When the survey is complete, around 2000–2001, we expect to have extracted tens of thousands of galaxies in K, roughly one million in J, and a few million in I (see § 7 below for our estimated sizes of homogeneous, highly complete, reliable and photometrically accurate galaxy catalogs).

Much of the information in this review has been given elsewhere (Mamon et al. 1997b). The notable improvements here are improved reliability estimates from a much larger visually classified sample, a first-order optimization of star/galaxy separation yielding a one-half magnitude improvement in the high completeness/reliability magnitude limit and a more accurate estimate of the photometric accuracy.

2. Prospective scientific impact

Wide-angle near infrared (hereafter NIR) galaxy surveys, such as DENIS and 2MASS (see Schneider, Jarrett, Rosenberg and Cutri, all in these proceedings) will have a wide array of scientific prospects, of which a few are listed below. The two important advantages of NIR selection are 1) the near transparency of interstellar dust in our foreground Galaxy and within external galaxies, and 2) the low sensitivity of NIR light to recent star formation in galaxies (see Mamon et al. 1997b), hence a better estimation of the stellar mass content of galaxies in the NIR.

Statistics of NIR properties of galaxies: DENIS and 2MASS will provide the first very large galaxy databases with NIR photometry. Photometry of the brighter galaxies will be coupled with redshift measurements, either already made, or performed during spectroscopic followups (see, e.g., Mamon 1996; Paturel, in these proceedings) to be used for distance estimates and computation of precise parameters of the fundamental plane and Tully-Fisher relations (see Vauglin et al. 1997; Rosenberg, in these proceedings).

Cross-identification with other wavelengths: The extragalactic objects extracted by DENIS and 2MASS will be cross-identified with analogous samples at other wavelengths, such as optical galaxy samples, for example in the Zone of Avoidance (see Kraan-Korteweg et al., in these proceedings), IRAS galaxies (Saunders et al. 1997), quasars (see Cutri, in these proceedings), radio-galaxies, galaxies found in blind HI surveys (see Kraan-Korteweg et al., in these proceedings), etc. The NIR properties (mainly their location in color-color diagrams) of such objects will be targeted for discovering new

large samples of such objects. One should expect followups at non-NIR wavelengths of DENIS and 2MASS galaxies.

Galaxy counts: There has been a debate on the level of galaxy counts at the bright end, as first estimates (Heydon-Dumbleton et al. 1989; Maddox et al. 1990) found a depletion relative to the extrapolation of the faint-end counts, while later work (e.g. Bertin & Dennefeld 1997) disputed this. This debate has consequences on galaxy evolution and on whether the environment of the Local Group is underdense on very large scales ($z \lesssim 0.1$).

Zone of avoidance There are two main applications for studying galaxies behind the Galactic Plane (see Kraan-Korteweg et al., in these proceedings): 1) Mapping the large-scale distribution of galaxies in this still poorly known region. Indeed, the Zone of Avoidance contains interesting structures such as the largest large-scale concentration of matter in the local Universe, the Great Attractor (at the intersection of the Supergalactic Plane and the Galactic Plane, Kolatt, Dekel & Lahav 1995) and within the Great Attractor, the Norma cluster, Abell 3627, richer and closer than the Coma cluster (Kraan-Korteweg et al. 1995). 2) The fluxes and angular sizes of galaxies are affected by extinction from dust in the Galactic Plane, and one can measure this extinction from galaxy counts (Burstein & Heiles 1982), colors (Mamon et al. 1997a), and color-color diagrams (Schröder et al. 1997, and Kraan-Korteweg et al., in these proceedings).

Small-scale structures of galaxies Only a few catalogs of clusters (Lumsden et al. 1992; Dalton et al. 1997; Escalera & MacGillivray 1995, 1996) and compact groups (Prandoni, Iovino & MacGillivray 1994) are based upon automatically selected galaxy samples, which happen to be optical and photographic (hence subject to photometric non-linearities). Because star formation is probably enhanced by galaxy interactions, one expects that the statistical properties of pairs, groups and clusters of galaxies built from NIR selected galaxy catalogs will be different from those built from optical catalogs. DENIS and 2MASS will thus have the double advantage of using a NIR galaxy sampled based upon linear (non-photographic) photometry. The applications of such NIR-based samples of structures of galaxies are numerous (e.g. Mamon 1994) and include understanding the dynamics of these structures, their bias to projection effects, their constraints on Ω_0 and the primordial density fluctuation spectrum, their use as distance indicators, and the environmental influences on galaxies.

Large-scale structure of the Universe: The NIR selection and the linear photometry will also benefit the measurement of statistics (two-point

and higher-order angular correlation functions, counts in cells, topologi-
cal genus, etc.) of the large-scale distribution of galaxies in the Universe.
For example, the (3D) primordial density fluctuation spectrum of galaxy
clustering can be obtained from the two-point angular correlation function
(Baugh & Efstathiou 1993) or from the 2D power spectrum (Baugh & Efstathiou 1994). Moreover, by the end of DENIS and 2MASS, large-scale
cosmological simulations with gas dynamics incorporated (thanks to which
galaxies are properly identified) will provide adequate galaxy statistics in
projection that will be compared with those obtained from the surveys,
iterating over the cosmological input parameters of the simulations.

3. Galaxy extraction and current galaxy pipeline

The current galaxy pipeline consists of the following steps:

1) Bias subtraction, flat-fielding, bad pixel mapping and astrometric
calibration (standard DENIS Paris Data Analysis Center pipeline, Borsenberger 1997); 2) Cosmic ray removal; 3) Extraction of photometric zero-
points and airmasses from relevant files; 4) Galaxy extraction using the
SExtractor (Bertin & Arnouts 1996) object extraction software, version
1.2b6a (which includes a neural-network star/galaxy separator, Bertin 1996,
whose input parameters are 8 isophotal areas, the maximum intensity and
as a control parameter, the FWHM of the PSF), with detection and Kron
(1980) photometry parameters optimized from simulated images.

4. Star/galaxy separation

Nevertheless, star/galaxy separation is intrinsically difficult because, at the
galaxy extraction limits $I \simeq 16.5$ (see below), DENIS will extract roughly
5.5 times as many stars as galaxies in I, at very high galactic latitude
($|b| \simeq 70°$, see Lidman & Peterson 1996), and the ratio worsens considerably
at lower galactic latitudes and at brighter magnitudes.

We discuss below the steps towards an efficient star/galaxy separation
method. For this, we extracted in the I band (which has the best angular
resolution) classical star/galaxy separation diagnostics such as isophotal
area, peak intensity, and FWHM, as well as the neural-network based stellarity parameter, in a direct fashion, or using a suitably modified version
of SExtractor that includes a two-dimensional modeling of the PSF that is
used as input to the neural network.

Figure 1 shows how these quantities vary with magnitude for all objects
at least 20 pixels from the frame edges on a high latitude strip.

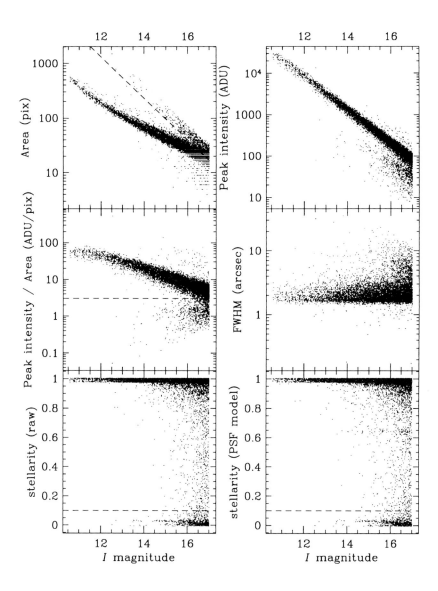

Figure 1.   Diagnostics of star/galaxy separation over one DENIS ($6\,\mathrm{deg}^2$) strip. The *dashed lines* are the critical lines for selection of candidates for visual classification (see § 4.1).

4.1. TESTS OF AUTOMATIC STAR/GALAXY SEPARATION

One of us (G.A.M.) has classified by eye a set of 329 galaxy candidates on 109 DENIS *I* band images (of which 33 appeared on consecutive images,

leaving 296 unique candidates). These candidates were chosen with $I \leq$ 16.5, centers at least 20 pixels from the image borders. Furthermore, they met *at least one* of the following loose (to ensure completeness) galaxy criteria (*dashed lines* in Fig. 1):

- Isophotal area: $A \geq 40 \, \mathrm{dex}[-0.38(I - 16)]$ pixels
- Pseudo surface brightness: $\Sigma = I_{\mathrm{peak}}/A \leq 3$ ADU/pixels
- Neural-network stellarity before PSF modeling: $s_0 \leq 0.1$
- Neural-network stellarity after PSF modeling: $s \leq 0.1$

We've used 5 sets of truth tables:

- Visual DENIS I (see above)
- COSMOS b_J
- APM b_J
- APM r_F
- A mix of the previous 4

The COSMOS and APM lists were obtained through the World Wide Web (`telnet://catalogues apm3.ast.cam.ac.uk` for the APM and `telnet://cosmos cosmos.aao.gov.au` for COSMOS).

We've optimized each of the 6 algorithms plotted in Figure 1 for a linear star/galaxy separator in these plots (slope and normalization, except that we forced a zero slope for the two neural network algorithms). The results are showed in Figure 2, which plots the completeness-reliability plots for 4 of the 5 truth tables. The different points in Figure 2 for a given algorithm correspond to different cuts through the algorithm versus magnitude diagram and we only plotted the optimal slope, varying the normalization.

Figure 2 shows that the pseudo-surface brightness criterion is slightly superior to the peak intensity, which, in turn, is slightly superior to the isophotal area (except for the COSMOS-based truth table, for which isophotal area does best). The other three algorithms (FWHM, and neural network stellarity before and after PSF modeling), are far inferior to the first three algorithms. For the visually classified DENIS I sample, we achieve 92.5% reliability at 98% completeness, and for the global sample we obtain 96% reliability at 96% completeness. The poor results of the neural networks is probably due to the variations of the PSF across the frames, and for this particular DENIS strip (number 5570), PSF modeling worsened the results!

4.2. COSMOS AND APM VERSUS VISUAL STAR/GALAXY SEPARATION

Table 1 shows the comparison between the visual classification and the classification obtained from the COSMOS and APM lists.

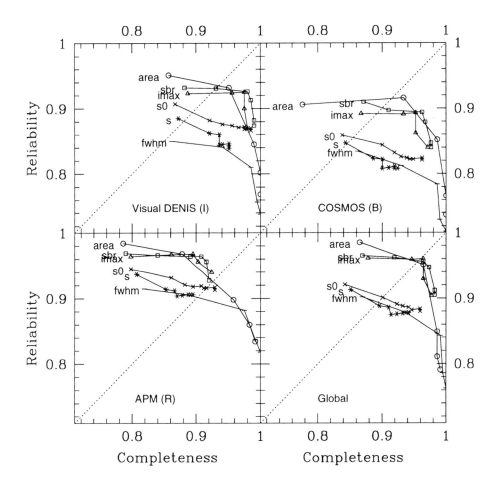

Figure 2. Completeness versus reliability of different automatic star/galaxy separation algorithms using 4 different truth tables. The algorithms are isophotal area (`area`), peak intensity (`imax`), pseudo-surface brightness (`sbr`), star/galaxy separation without PSF modeling (`s0`), star/galaxy separation with PSF modeling (`s`), and full-width half maximum (`fwhm`).

Of the 11 objects termed as junk, 3 were fragments of a bright galaxy, two were deemed optical flaws, but according to both APM and COSMOS, one of those was a star.

The numbers in Table 1 do not permit to establish which star/galaxy separation is best between visual DENIS, APM or COSMOS. However, if one assumes that visual DENIS star/galaxy separation is perfect, one would then conclude that APM and COSMOS both have a completeness of $193/203 = 95\%$ at $I = 16.5$ (this also assumes that the DENIS I extraction

TABLE 1. Visual DENIS I versus COSMOS and APM star/galaxy separation

| Visual DENIS I | | COSMOS b_J | | | APM b_J | | | |
Type	Total	Galaxy	Star	Notfound	Galaxy	Star	Faint	Notfound
Galaxy	203	193	10	0	193	5	3	2
Star	53	6	46	1	9	42	1	1
Star+Star	8	4	3	1	4	3	0	1
Faint	21	7	11	3	10	10	0	1
Junk	11	0	2	9	2	3	3	3
Total	296	210	72	14	218	63	7	8

is 100% complete, which remains to be proven). The reliability of the extraction would then be $193/210 = 91\%$ for COSMOS and $193/218 = 89\%$ for APM.

If one assumes that APM or COSMOS are complete, than the incompleteness of the DENIS galaxy extraction can be estimated from the objects too faint for DENIS visual classification but called galaxies by the optical surveys. One obtains completeness levels of 95% or 97% at $I = 16.5$ using APM or COSMOS, respectively. Of course, if the visual classification were imperfect and that objects classified as stars or double stars are in fact galaxies, the completeness of DENIS visual classification would decrease to levels of 90% or 92% using APM or COSMOS, respectively. Moreover, DENIS may not have detected objects at $I = 16.5$ that are seen in the optical surveys, and this issue will be addressed in a forthcoming publication.

4.3. QUICK AND DIRTY AUTOMATIC STAR/GALAXY SEPARATION

Since the pseudo-surface brightness criterion seems to produce the best star/galaxy separation, we have adopted the following preliminary algorithm for each DENIS strip:

We adopt a constant critical pseudo surface brightness (independent of magnitude — the optimal slope with respect to the visual DENIS I, COSMOS B, APM B, and global classifications was 0.05), by fitting with a cubic polynomial the histogram of the values of $\Sigma = I_{\mathrm{peak}}/A$ for $I \leq 16.5$, in a range chosen to exclude the peak due to the stars. Although $k\sigma$ curves down from the stellar locus have negative slope, the higher slope of the galaxy counts relative to the star counts leads us to believe that a given reliability will be achieved with a cut of k that decreases with magnitude, i.e., with a lower slope for Σ_{crit}. This may explain why the optimal slope

is non-negative.

For the J and K bands, we rely on the star/galaxy separation performed in the I band. Because the I band has better angular resolution and is more sensitive than J or K (except at very low galactic latitudes, corresponding to visual extinction $A_B > 3$, see Kraan-Korteweg et al., in these proceedings), using I-band star/galaxy separation is superior to doing star/galaxy separation directly in J or in K.

Our star/galaxy separation, relying only on pseudo surface brightness is simpler than in our previous work (Mamon et al. 1997b), where we required out galaxies to satisfy both neural network stellarity (after PSF modeling) and isophotal area algorithms, and our former star/galaxy separation method had the disadvantage of using a fixed critical isophotal area line, whereas strip to strip variations of the PSF lead to variations of this critical line from one strip to another.

We have thus analyzed a little over $50 \, \mathrm{deg}^2$ of DENIS data, restricting ourselves here to $I < 17$.

5. Photometry

We estimate below the accuracy of DENIS galaxy photometry using objects within image overlaps and comparing with APM and COSMOS, and we use color-magnitude diagnostics as an additional test on the reliability of star/galaxy separation.

5.1. PHOTOMETRIC ACCURACY FROM OVERLAPS

Figure 3 shows the magnitude differences on unflagged overlap objects extracted from $50 \, \mathrm{deg}^2$ of high galactic latitude data.

Contrary to the analogous figure in Mamon et al. (1997b), we have high certainty on the extragalactic nature of the J-band and K-band overlap objects (since again, we rely on I-band star/galaxy separation). For this reason, the photometric accuracy is worse than given in Mamon et al. (1997b): The rms error on a single measure is 0.05 at $I = 15$, 0.10 at $I = 17$, 0.10 at $J = 13.7$, and 0.20 at $J = 14.8$. There are too few K overlaps to conclude strongly, but indications (based upon only 4 points!) are that the rms photometric accuracy for a single measure is roughly 0.20 at $K \simeq 12.2$. The J-band photometric accuracy was considerably better in our previous study (Mamon et al. 1997b), but unreliable direct (using neural network stellarity in J lower than 0.2) star/galaxy separation had been used for the photometric accuracy study of that work, and the inclusion of stars tends to improve the photometric accuracy.

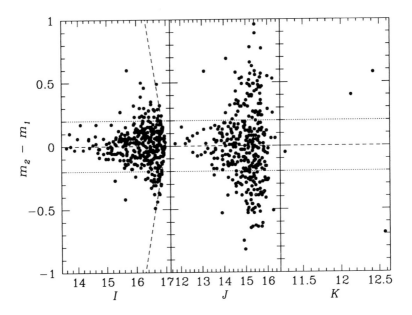

Figure 3. Photometric accuracy for galaxies lying within overlaps of 2 images, extracted within $50\,\mathrm{deg}^2$ of high galactic latitude ($20° < |b|60°$) DENIS data. Objects closer than 20 pixels to the frame edges are excluded). The *tilted dashed line* represents an $I \leq 17$ selection, whose effects are also seen in the J band.

5.2. COMPARISON OF DENIS GALAXY PHOTOMETRY WITH COSMOS

For the $3.6\,\mathrm{deg}^2$ region in which we visually classified our extracted objects, we plot in Figure 4 the color-magnitude relation obtained with COSMOS b_J photometry, taken from the World Wide Web. This figure shows the difficulties in star/galaxy separation, as a number of points lie far off the $B - I \simeq 2 - 3$ region. Part of this difficulty lies in poor star/galaxy separation from COSMOS. Moreover, there is a trend for bluer galaxy colors at brighter magnitudes, which we interpret as poor photometry on the COSMOS side, because of inaccurate compensation for plate saturation.

We also attempted the same with APM data from the World Wide Web, but that photometry suffers from unusually strong systematic errors at the bright end (up to 6 mag difference with COSMOS!), as the photometric calibration has been optimized for stars that saturate at these magnitudes (Maddox, private communication).

5.3. COLORS OF DENIS GALAXIES

Figure 5 shows the color-magnitude diagram for the galaxies. The bluest two points turn out to be galaxies! Visual inspection shows that they are

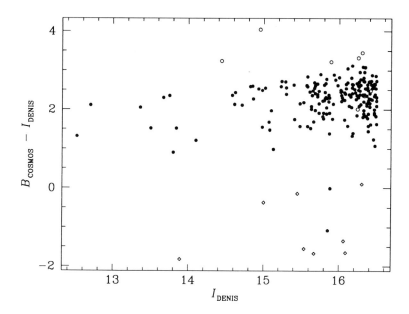

Figure 4. Color-magnitude diagram for galaxies extracted within 3.6 deg^2 of high galactic latitude ($20° < |b| 60°$) DENIS data. *Diamonds* refer to objects classified as stars by COSMOS, but as galaxies by APM, DENIS visual inspection and all DENIS automatic star/galaxy separation algorithms. *Open circles* are objects classified as galaxies with low certainty by the DENIS visual classification and that were not stars in COSMOS.

low surface brightness galaxies that are barely visible in J (and invisible in K). The use of adaptive aperture photometry to define colors makes such objects appear very blue. We checked that their central colors are normal.

Figure 5 shows that at the limit $J = 14.8$ for $\Delta J = 0.20$ mag photometric accuracy, the star/galaxy separation performed in I should be roughly as reliable as at $I = 16.5$, and could be made even more reliable by culling out the reddest objects for which $I > 16.5$.

In Figure 6, we plot the color-color diagram for extracted galaxies. The galaxy colors cluster around $I - J = 1.2 \pm 0.3$, $J - K = 1.1 \pm 0.5$, but there are indications for fairly bright objects with red $J - K \simeq 2$ colors, which upon visual inspection are confirmed as galaxies. An important fraction of the points off the central cluster lie near the frame edges where the PSF is larger. The large open circle refers to an object too faint in I for reliable star/galaxy separation, and indeed, visual inspection shows it to be a star blended with a faint galaxy.

6. Galaxy counts

Figure 7 illustrates our IJK galaxy counts. The K-band counts become

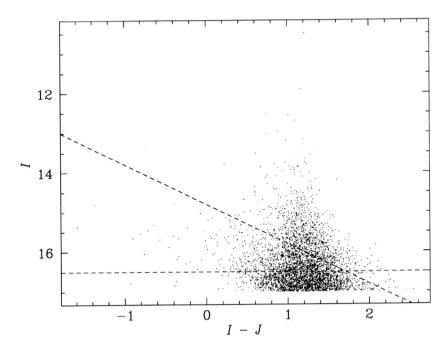

Figure 5. Color-magnitude diagram for galaxies extracted within 50 deg² of high galactic latitude (20° < |b| < 60°) DENIS data. Objects closer than 20 pixels to the frame edges are excluded. The *horizontal line* represents $I = 16.5$ (the and the dashed line represents $J = 14.8$ (the limit for 0.20 mag J-band photometry and reliable star/galaxy separation).

incomplete at $K \simeq 11$, in comparison to both published counts by Gardner et al. (1996) and to the expected Euclidean 0.6 slope (the completeness is still roughly 50% at $K = 12$).

The I band counts match well the published data, although Lidman and Peterson (1996) find fewer counts at the bright end, while Gardner et al. find more counts at the bright end (the two sets of published data differ by a factor of 3 at $I < 15$). Note that DENIS, Gardner *et al.* and Lidman & Peterson all work with the Cousins I band, so no conversion was made from another I filter. Also, our survey has smaller error bars at the bright end as it covers 4 to 5 times the solid angle of the two cited surveys. Our bright-end I-band counts are more consistent with the extrapolation of the faint counts with a Euclidean slope than either two sets of published data (our high value at $I = 16.5$ is caused by important stellar contamination in the fainter half of the bin; also, at $I > 18$, the published counts become lower than the Euclidean line because of significant k-correction at these magnitudes). In this sense, although not as high as Gardner et al.'s counts, *the DENIS I-band counts argue for a high bright-end normalization, consistent with little*

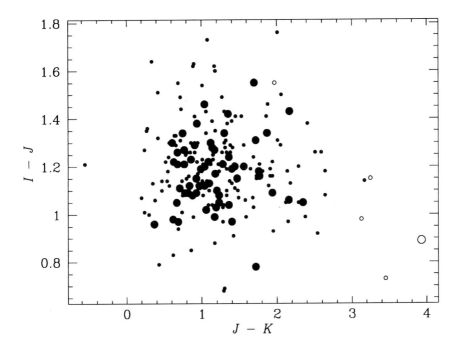

Figure 6. Color-magnitude diagram for galaxies extracted within 50 deg² of high galactic latitude (20° < |b| < 60°) DENIS data. Objects closer than 20 pixels to the frame edges are excluded. *Large* and *small circles* are for objects brighter or fainter than $K = 12$ (the limit for fairly accurate K photometry, see § 5.1), respectively. *Filled* and *open circles* correspond to objects brighter and fainter than $I = 16.5$ (the rough limit for reliable star/galaxy separation, see § 4.1), respectively.

galaxy evolution at the bright end, in line with analogous findings by Bertin and Dennefeld (1997) using blue counts.

The J counts are new (although they were already shown in Mamon et al. 1997b). They are highly complete to $J = 15$, follow very well the Euclidean slope of 0.6, and are well described by the relation $N(J) \simeq 12 \times \mathrm{dex}[0.6\,(J - 14)]\,\mathrm{deg}^{-2}\,\mathrm{mag}^{-1}$.

7. Discussion

From the results of the preceding sections, we can establish limits for the homogeneous extraction of galaxies from DENIS, as given in Table 2.

The limiting factors turn out to be star/galaxy separation in I, photometry and star/galaxy separation in J, and detection in K (assuming that I-band star/galaxy separation is used to classify objects detected in the other bands).

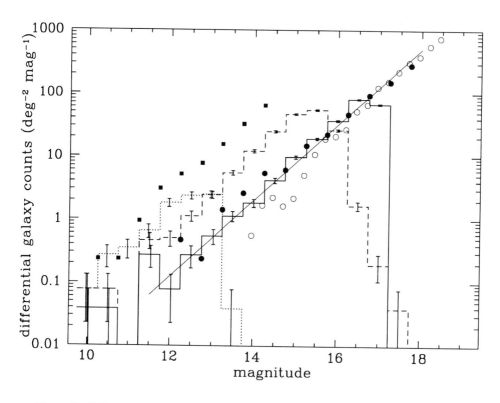

Figure 7. Differential galaxy counts over 50 deg^2 of high galactic latitude ($20° < |b| 60°$),
$I < 17$ DENIS data. Objects closer than 20 pixels to the frame edges are excluded. *Solid,*
dashed, and *dotted histograms* refer to the DENIS I, J, and K counts, respectively. The
squares represent K-band counts from Gardner et al. (1996), while the *open* and *filled*
circles represent the I-band counts from Lidman and Peterson (1996), and Gardner et al.
(1996), respectively. The *thin oblique line* represents an eye-fit Euclidean count function
(0.6 slope).

TABLE 2. Estimated DENIS limits from 50 deg^2 of reduced data

	I_c	J	K
completeness ($\simeq$ 80%)	17.25	15.25	11
star/galaxy separation (90% reliability, from I)	16.5	14.8	13.5
photometry (0.20 mag accuracy)	>18?	14.8	12.2?
photometry (0.10 mag accuracy)	17.4	13.7	<11?

Using the counts from Figure 7 to extrapolate to the entire survey area
(roughly a hemisphere), we infer that our homogeneous catalogs will have
sizes of 6000 at $K < 11$ (0.2 mag photometry), 100 000 to 500 000 at $J <$

13.7 and 14.8 (with 0.2 and 0.1 mag photometry, respectively), and 900 000 galaxies at $I < 16.5$ (0.1 mag photometry). The recent installation of an air conditioning system on the K band optics has decreased the instrumental background by 0.7 magnitude, which should bring the extraction limit to $K \simeq 11.7$, and thus increase the size of the homogeneous K sample to roughly 15 000 galaxies.

Moreover, there is still room for progress on star/galaxy separation. C. Alard has devised a new algorithm to accurately model the variations of the PSF across the frame, which need no longer be an elliptical gaussian (fitting the asymmetric coma of the images), and tests on visually classified data are about to be performed.

Acknowledgements

We thank Emmanuel Bertin for supplying recent updates of his SExtractor software package, Steve Maddox for useful comments on the APM data, Nicolas Epchtein for a careful reading of the manuscript, and Pascal Fouqué and the DENIS operations team.

References

Baugh C.M. & Efstathiou G. (1993) *MNRAS*, **Vol. no. 265**, pp. 145–332
Baugh C.M. & Efstathiou G. (1994) *MNRAS*, **Vol. no. 267**, pp. 323–332
Bertin E. (1996) *PhD thesis*, University of Paris 6
Bertin E. & Arnouts S. (1996) *A&AS*, **Vol. no. 117**, pp. 398–404
Bertin E. & Dennefeld M. (1997) *A&A*, **Vol. no. 317**, pp. 43–53
Borsenberger J. (1997) in *The Impact of Large-Scale Near-IR Surveys*, eds F. Garzón *et al.*, Kluwer, pp. 181–186
Burstein D. & Heiles C. (1982) *AJ*, **Vol. no. 87**, pp. 1165–1189
Dalton G.B., Maddox S.J., Sutherland W.J. & Efstathiou G. (1997) *MNRAS*, **Vol. no. 289**, pp. 263–284
Epchtein N. *et al.* (48 authors) (1997) *ESO Messenger*, **Vol. no. 87**, pp. 27–34
Escalera E. & MacGillivray H.T. (1995) *A&A*, **Vol. no. 298**, pp. 1–21
Escalera E. & MacGillivray H.T. (1996) *A&AS*, **Vol. no. 117**, pp. 519–555
Gardner J.P., Sharples R.M., Carrasco B.E. & Frenk C.S. (1996) *MNRAS*, **Vol. no. 282**, pp. L1–L6
Heydon-Dumbleton N.H., Collins C.A. & MacGillivray H.T. (1989) *MNRAS*, **Vol. no. 238**, pp. 379–406
Kolatt T., Dekel A. & Lahav, O. (1995) *MNRAS*, **Vol. no. 275**, pp. 797–811
Kraan-Korteweg R.C., Woudt P.A., Cayatte V., Fairall A.P., Balkowski C. & Henning P.A. (1995) *Nature*, **Vol. no. 379**, pp. 519–521
Kron R.G. (1980) *ApJS*, **Vol. no. 43**, pp. 305–325
Lidman C.E. & Peterson B.A. (1996) *MNRAS*, **Vol. no. 279**, pp. 1357–1379
Lumsden S.L., Nichol R.C., Collins C.A. & Guzzo L. (1992) *MNRAS*, **Vol. no. 258**, pp. 1–22
Maddox S.J., Sutherland W.J., Efstathiou G., Loveday J. & Peterson B.A. (1990) *MNRAS*, **Vol. no. 247**, pp. 1P–5P
Mamon G.A. (1994) *Astrophys. & Sp. Sci.*, **Vol. no. 217**, pp. 237–242
Mamon G.A. (1996) in *Dark Matter in Cosmology, Quantum Measurements, Experimen-*

tal Gravitation, eds. R. Ansari, Y. Giraud-Héraud & J. Trân Thanh Vân, Frontières, pp. 225-232 (astro-ph/9608076)

Mamon G.A., Banchet V., Tricottet M. & Katz D. (1997a) in *The Impact of Large-Scale Near-IR Surveys* eds. F. Garzón *et al.*, Kluwer, pp. 239-248 (astro-ph/9608077)

Mamon G.A., Tricottet, M., Bonin, W. & Banchet, V. (1997b) in *Extragalactic Astronomy in the Infrared*, eds. G.A. Mamon, T.X. Thuan & J. Trân Thanh Vân, Frontières, pp. 369-380 (astro-ph/9711281)

Monet D. (1997) *Bull. A.A.S.*, **Vol. no. 188**, 54.04

Prandoni I., Iovino A. & MacGillivray H.T. (1994) *AJ*, **Vol. no. 107**, pp. 1235-1244

Saunders W. et al. (15 authors) (1997), in *Extragalactic Astronomy in the Infrared*, eds. G.A. Mamon, T.X. Thuan & J. Trân Thanh Vân, Frontières, pp. 415-424

Schröder A., Kraan-Korteweg R.C., Mamon G.A. & Ruphy S., (1997) in *Extragalactic Astronomy in the Infrared*, eds. G.A. Mamon, T.X. Thuan & J. Trân Thanh Vân, Frontières, pp. 381-386 (astro-ph/9706093)

Vauglin I., Paturel G., Marthinet M.C., Petit C. & Borsenberger J. in *Extragalactic Astronomy in the Infrared*, eds. G.A. Mamon, T.X. Thuan & J. Trân Thanh Vân, Frontières, pp. 387-392

EXTRAGALACTIC ASTRONOMY WITH 2MASS

S. E. SCHNEIDER AND J. L. ROSENBERG
UMass Astronomy Program, Amherst, MA 01003 USA

T. H. JARRETT AND T. J. CHESTER
IPAC, Caltech 100-22, Pasadena, CA 91125 USA

AND

J. P. HUCHRA
Harvard–Smithsonian CfA , Cambridge, MA 02138 USA

1. Introduction

Observations for the Two–Micron All Sky Survey (2MASS) have recently begun at the northern hemisphere site. The project is now in the final phases of tuning the data analysis software in preparation for running the "pipeline" at full bore. The path to completing the extragalactic portion of the pipeline, called *GALWORKS*, was complicated. It required an enormous number of ideas, compromises, and decisions to generate as accurate and as useful a set of data as we possibly can from the raw survey data.

At this meeting and the previous ones, we have described some of the particular software developments for extragalactic astronomy with 2MASS (Chester & Jarrett 1995; Schneider et al. 1997; Jarrett et al. 1997; Jarrett 1998; Rosenberg 1998). In this paper, we will review these developments more generally. By reviewing *GALWORKS* and its development, we can shed some light on how it came to take its particular final form, and perhaps aid future users of 2MASS data.

To put the 2MASS *GALWORKS* project in context, we begin with a brief review of earlier cataloging projects. We then turn to the goals and implementation of the survey, and consider a number of the issues involved in designing the software. Finally, we give some initial results for galaxy counts from the 3–channel survey camera.

N. Epchtein (ed.),
The Impact of Near-Infrared Sky Surveys on Galactic and Extragalactic Astronomy, 193-208.
© 1998 *Kluwer Academic Publishers. Printed in the Netherlands.*

2. A Brief History of Galaxy Cataloging

Actually, although most of our discussion focuses on galaxies, the 2MASS "galaxy" catalog will include all sources that are detectably extended. Early extended-source catalogs included a large fraction of Galactic sources: 32% of the 103 sources in Messier's (1781) list are galaxies, approximately 85% of the New General Catalog/Index Catalog (Dreyer 1888, 1895, 1908) objects are galaxies. At the faint levels 2MASS will reach, we expect the extended source counts will be overwhelmingly dominated by extragalactic sources. It will certainly include many nearby extended sources like planetary nebulae and HII regions, but we do not have enough experience at low Galactic latitudes yet to predict how many of these sources we will identify.

We face almost identical problems as the earliest extended source catalogs. Like Messier, we have to worry about accidental duplication (M102 = M101), double stars (M40), tight groupings of a few stars (M73), and spurious sources (M91). (Note that today M102 is sometimes assigned to NGC 5866 and M91 to NGC 4548.) In modern parlance, Messier's list was about 96% reliable. Messier also "missed" seven sources which subsequent observers felt should be added to bring up the overall list to 110. Thus he was 93% complete. Our targets for the 2MASS extended source completeness and reliability are actually quite similar as we discuss later.

The completion of the Palomar Observatory Sky Survey (POSS) in the 1950's marked a new degree of uniformity in sky coverage. A number of new galaxy catalogs soon followed based on direct inspection of the POSS Schmidt plates: The Catalogue of Galaxies and of Clusters of Galaxies carried out by Zwicky et al. (1961–1968) for 31,000 galaxies brighter than $B \approx 15.7$ mag in the northern hemisphere; The Morphological Catalog of Galaxies (Vorontsov–Velyaminov et al. 1962–1968), a somewhat less uniform survey of 29,000 galaxies north of $\delta = -33°$; and the Uppsala General Catalogue (Nilson 1973) of 13,000 northern galaxies, which is diameter limited to about $1'$. In addition, Lauberts (1982) generated a catalog of 18,000 southern galaxies ($\delta < -18°$) from the ESO(B) Schmidt plates. These surveys remain the primary all-sky optical catalogs of galaxies even though the subjective aspect of human inspection of the images leaves much to be desired.

In recent years galaxy cataloging has entered a transitional period from photographic to digital data, and from subjective "eyeball" to more objective computer software schemes. In certain ways these transitions are linked, since the nonlinear response of photographic plates has many subtleties that are difficult to define in terms of a set of straightforward computer algorithms. Star/galaxy separation has become automated by using automatic plate scanning machines like COSMOS and APM (see, for exam-

ple, Maddox et al. 1990) and developing classification methods like FOCAS
(Jarvis & Tyson 1981). These approaches define a variety of parameters for
each source, often keyed to the idea that at a given magnitude an extended
source will cover a larger area of the image (to some fiducial surface brightness limit) and will have a smaller peak flux density. A variety of other
measures like 2nd, 3rd, 4th moments, degree of elongation, and measures
of asymmetry or multiple peaks (to exclude multiple stars) were added to
further aid in discrimination. These were compared to the locus of parameters for stars as a function of magnitude, and a measure of the deviation
from being star-like was used to set the catalog boundaries.

In recent years, neural network schemes (Odewahn et al. 1992) and decision tree methods (Weir et al. 1995) have been developed that can more
effectively adapt to unusual circumstances like seeing, plate sensitivity, and
image artifacts. While the approaches are somewhat different, both use
training sets to "teach" the algorithm how to recognize galaxies. These
approaches identify the combinations of parameters that best distinguish
between the different types of real and artificial sources, and can even be
used to classify different morphological types of galaxies. A drawback, however, is that the flexibility of the selection criteria can make it difficult to
understand the completeness of the sample.

The 2MASS extended source catalog is based on a rigid star/galaxy
separator primarily. It is probably fair to say that the need for neural
networks and decision trees grows in direct proportion to the messiness
of the raw data. Thus photographic surveys are especially well served by
them. Because the 2MASS raw data are so uniform, we believe we can meet
survey goals without them. Still, close to the flux limit of the survey, it may
be possible to extract significantly more useful data, and we are currently
investigating a decision tree approach to see what results it yields.

We do not currently plan to attempt any morphological classifications
for the galaxies, in part because the cues for these distinctions are much
weaker in the infrared. Actually, such parameters as color differences may
be powerful discriminators between galaxy types (and between other non-
galaxian sources), but we do not plan to build those kinds of distinctions
into the catalog other than to provide the basic data.

3. 2MASS Extragalactic Objectives

Even before the final design of the 2MASS telescopes and cameras, we set
a number of goals for the extragalactic parts of the survey. These Level–1
specifications are listed in Table 1, and were based on early assessments
of detector sensitivity, telescope size, and survey duration. The flux limits
were estimated on the basis that we ought to be able to detect an extended

source distributed over roughly twice the diameter of a seeing-convolved point source. Thus the integrated background noise would be approximately two times worse, which would allow us to detect a source about 0.8 mag brighter than the point source limit.

TABLE 1. Level–1 Specifications for Extended Sources

Sensitivity:	J<15.0 H<14.2 K_s <13.5
Photometric Uniformity:	< 10%
Photometric Precision:	< 10% (for H<13.8)
Reliability:	> 99% ($|b| > 20°$)
	> 80% ($|b| > 10°$)
Completeness:	> 90% ($|b| > 30°$)
	(for galaxies with scale lengths > 0.5″)

These photometric limits allow us to make some quick estimates of the likely number of sources we should detect based on the optical catalogs. Assuming an average color of B − K_s = 4, the K_s–band sensitivity limit of 13.5 is comparable to an optical limit of ~17.5. The CGCG includes ~31,000 galaxies in northern hemisphere to about 1.8 mag brighter than this, so there would be a factor of ~ 12× more galaxies. Correcting for the whole sky and zone of avoidance suggests that roughly a million galaxies will be detected by 2MASS. We will revisit this estimate at the end of the paper.

It is also important that the galaxy photometry be adequate for the kind of science one might envision doing with a near-infrared survey. One of the more important directions for follow-up studies will be to use the infrared Tully–Fisher relation (IRTF) to determine galaxy distances (see Rosenberg 1998). Since the IRTF is at best accurate to about 15% (see, for example, Willick et al. 1996), the survey photometry and calibration should be more accurate than this.

The specification on calibration uniformity is 10% over the whole sky. We expect to maintain at least this degree of uniformity by frequent re-observation of the same set of calibration fields, by comparison of stellar photometry in overlap regions of the survey, and by comparisons to observations made with other instruments in an assortment of fields chosen to represent a wide range of Galactic longitudes and latitudes. One of the biggest concerns is that the photometry be well matched between the northern and southern telescopes. We hope to assure this by observing the same calibration fields along the equator, by overlapping the coverage at the

boundary between north and south, and by cross–observing selected fields in the other telescope's hemisphere.

The photometric precision required for repeated observations of the same source is also set at 10%, but for sources about half a magnitude brighter than the sensitivity requirement. The brighter sources will also generally be the larger sources for which other important parameters for the IRTF like the inclination will be well measured. The specification is listed in terms of the H–band sensitivity since, at the time, the H–band IRTF was favored. It appears that K_s–band may be as good or better, and we expect to have a similar precision for galaxies half a magnitude brighter than the limiting sensitivity at K_s as well.

Finally, we set completeness and reliability values for the galaxy catalog. We cannot detect some galaxies that meet the catalog's nominal magnitude cutoff because they are too small, too nucleated, or too low in surface brightness. We try to summarize such problems by a scale-length requirement, which specifies a fraction of the flux that should extend into the wings of the PSF to make a source detectably extended. Based on repeated observations of the same field and by comparisons to other infrared and optical images of the same fields, we appear to be meeting the completeness requirement of 90% quite readily. The reliability limit of 99% is a much greater challenge, especially at Galactic latitudes approaching 20°, where the number of double and triple stars, which can look like extended sources, grows large. Much of the final tuning of the $GALWORKS$ pipeline is directed at this problem.

4. Hardware Requirements and Limitations

The ability to carry out a near infrared sky survey has been provided by the development of NICMOS–3 detector arrays for the Space Telescope. These 256×256 pixel arrays provide excellent sensitivity to beyond 2μ, and allow us to reach sufficiently faint levels for galaxy cataloging in short integrations even with a relatively small telescope. The extragalactic goals of the 2MASS project place some serious requirements that ultimately affect the duration (and cost) of the survey: (1) we need to sample the sky on scales small compared to the point spread function, so that stars and galaxies can be separated; and (2) we need long enough integrations to provide surface brightness sensitivity to the outer parts of galaxies.

The compromise we have reached, which allows the survey to be completed within about 3 years, is to design the optics to have a plate scale of $2''$ per pixel and integrate about 8 seconds on each point of the sky. The $2''$ pixel size is not ideal for star/galaxy separation, but by collecting the data in six 1.3 s integrations, offset by a fraction of a pixel ("dithering"), an

adequate sampling is achieved. The total integration is sufficiently long to detect K_s surface brightnesses of about 20 mag arcsec^{-2}. This value sounds surprisingly faint compared to the K_s–band point source sensitivity of 14.3, but it should be kept in mind that that is a 10–σ precision limit for point sources that may be spread over up to four $2'' \times 2''$ pixels. The rms noise in an individual pixel is closer to 19 mag arcsec^{-2}, and for isophotal fits to extended sources, many pixels can be averaged. The resulting images are close to the sensitivity of the POSS when the color differences in galaxies are taken into account. Fig. 1 shows some sample galaxies detected with 2MASS compared to their blue images as found on the digitized POSS.

Unlike DENIS, the 2MASS frames are dithered "on the fly." As the telescope swings along fixed-R.A. scans, a slight tilt of the detector array shifts the image center a fraction of a pixel to the side from frame to frame. (See Fig. 2.) Each frame is frozen for 1.3 s by a tip–tilt secondary mirror, and the exact timing determines the fractional pixel offset along the direction of the scan. By an appropriate combination of R.A. and Dec. offsets, for example 1/6th of a pixel in R.A. and 42 2/3rd pixels in Dec., the pixel centers can be quite evenly spaced on the sky, providing good PSF sampling. The actual offsets chosen are slightly complicated by the need to provide good sampling for all three of the J, H, and K_s arrays, which do not have precisely the same plate scale.

Since galaxies are extended, and since measuring their fluxes and sizes across frames is difficult and inaccurate, the extragalactic portion of 2MASS also puts a requirement on frame overlap. The in-scan frames overlap by 5/6ths, and a continuous image 8.5' wide by 6° in declination is generated. The scans are overlapped by 10% (0.85') in R.A. so that sources of this size and smaller will be entirely on a single frame. We also measure galaxies which are at least 75% on the frame, so that we will include all galaxies up to about 1.7'. These galaxies should have fairly accurate parameters since most of the light comes from the center, and the blocked outer portions will be corrected by isophotal substitution based on the fits to the interior regions.

This leaves a fairly small number of large galaxies out of the catalog. The UGC has 3465 galaxies 1.7' or larger in the northern hemisphere. Assuming these galaxies fall randomly on the array, only about 400 would fall so close to the edge that less than 75% was on either of two neighboring scans. Over the whole sky this number would double, and correcting for zone of avoidance effects might double it again. Thus the catalog should be incomplete for only the largest ∼14,000 galaxies, and of these, only ∼1600 will be caught so close to the scan edge that they cannot be measured.

The overlap between scans creates a different problem. Between 5 and 10% of the sources will be duplicated. One of the reasons we identify the

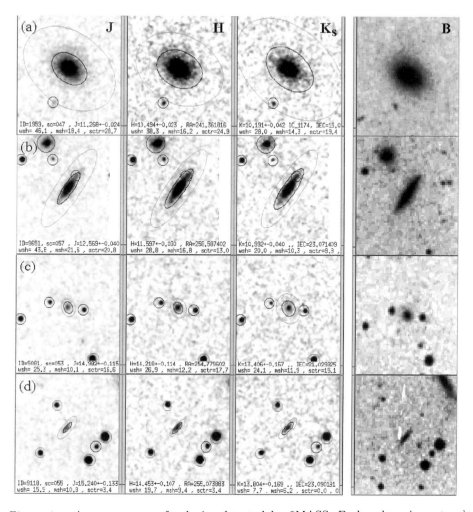

Figure 1.   An assortment of galaxies detected by 2MASS. Each galaxy is centered in a $100'' \times 100''$ box. The dark ellipse surrounding each galaxy indicates where the surface brightness has dropped to 20 mag arcsec^{-2}. The fainter ellipse is a Kron elliptical aperture. Small circles surround other sources that were blanked from the image. The top two objects are examples of "bright" galaxies. Galaxy (a) is IC 1174, with $K_s = 10.2$, and a photographic magnitude of 14.5. Galaxy (b) is optically uncataloged at $K_s = 11.0$. The bottom two galaxies are close to the nominal sensitivity limit of the survey. Galaxy (c) has $K_s = 13.4$; galaxy (d) at $K_s = 13.8$ demonstrates that edge-on galaxies can be clearly detected to beyond the 2MASS sensitivity limit.

location of sources by their brightest point (as opposed to a centroid) is that it is a uniquely defined position. The centroid of a source that is cut off at the edge of a frame will be quite different from one frame to the next, making it difficult to cross–identify.

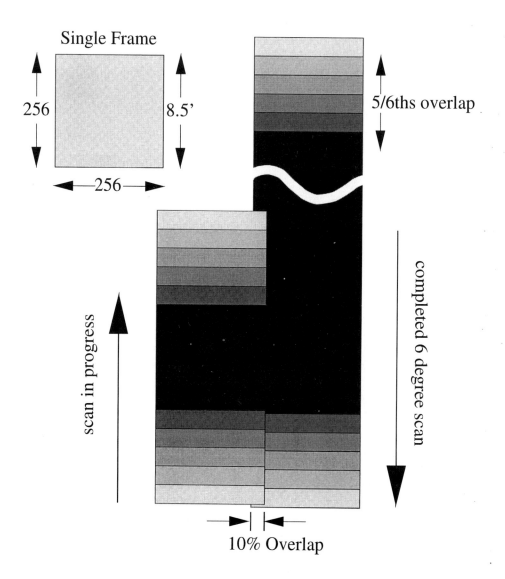

Figure 2. 2MASS is constructed from a series of 256×256 image frames strung together in 6°-long declination scans. The frames are overlapped by 5/6ths so that each spot on the sky is observed for 1.3 s six times. The scans are overlapped by 10% so that galaxies as large as 0.85′ are always contained on a single scan.

5. Extended Source Identification

The method for identifying galaxies from the 2MASS data was developed during experimentation with prototype camera images. We tested various

parameters like those discussed in section 2 to find the ones that did the best job of separating stars and galaxies. The problem is somewhat more difficult for a near-infrared survey like 2MASS because the effective sensitivity is not quite as good as that of optical surveys, and in particular, the blue color of spirals' disks make them weaker relative to the nucleus.

We began by examining several fields, particularly in the direction of galaxy clusters to study which parameters best discriminated between stars and galaxies. These results were based on a comparison to optical determinations from the POSS. The parameters that proved the most powerful in broadly identifying extended sources were a basic maximum surface brightness vs. magnitude comparison $(MXDN)$, and a more complicated "radial shape discriminant" parameter (SH) based on fitting a generalized exponential to the distribution. This latter parameter is determined by fitting to the azimuthally averaged radial distribution defined by:

$$f(r) = f_0 e^{-(r/\alpha)^{1/\beta}} \tag{1}$$

where α is a scale length and β is the rate of exponential decay. These parameters allow the distribution to take on a variety of forms ranging from Gaussian $(\beta = 1/2)$ to an exponential disk $(\beta = 1)$ to a de Vaucouleurs $r^{1/4}$ law $(\beta = 4)$. Our original hope was that this might also prove to be useful for determining morphological types of galaxies, but perhaps because spirals are bulge dominated in the infrared, this does not appear to be the case. In fact, α and β tend to be strongly correlated, so we have defined a single parameter (SH) as the product $\alpha \times \beta$, which ranges from small values for stars to larger ones for galaxies.

The camera optics provide an essentially uniform PSF across the arrays, but one thing that became clear in the testing phase of 2MASS was that the star/galaxy separation depends critically on the seeing. Thus we cannot choose fixed cutoff values for the star/galaxy separation parameters because that would either reject too many galaxies when the seeing is good or accept too many stars when the seeing is poor. In fact, the star/galaxy separation depends on knowing the seeing to better than 0.1″. This at first appeared to be a serious problem, but we discovered we could reverse the situation by using the shape parameter to track the seeing. We use the large number of stars—even at high Galactic latitude and even while passing through a galaxy cluster—to provide us with a large number of point sources which all have consistently low SH scores that depend only on the magnitude and seeing. Then, using a running average over a timescale of minutes, we determine which sources are extended based on their score relative to the lower envelope of SH scores.

On the initial pass, we accept sources that pass a very weak SH or $MXDN$ test, then we tighten up the requirements with a set of tests to re-

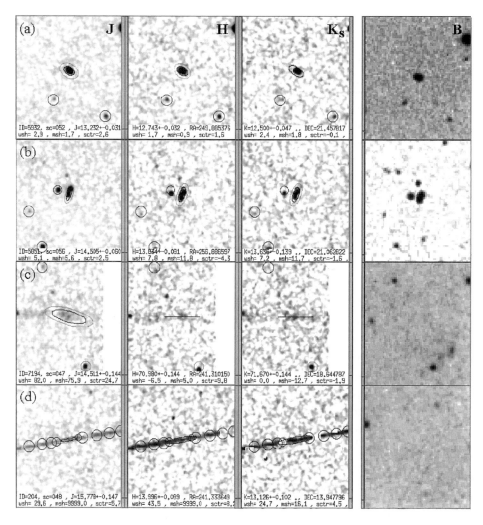

Figure 3. Examples of false extended sources. Images are displayed as in Fig. 1. Source (a) is a double star, and (b) is a triple star. Both have values in the modified shape tests that allow them to be distinguished from galaxies. Object (c) is an unmasked diffraction spike of a star. It was picked up in the J–band image, probably because of a faint star that is superimposed, but undetected at H and K_s. Object (d) is a portion of a meteor trail. Despite its obvious appearance to the eye, these trails have proved "expensive" to detect in *GALWORKS*.

ject various false sources. The primary contaminants are double and triple stars with increasing frequency at lower Galactic latitudes. We also have to struggle with meteor trails and diffraction spikes from bright stars, especially when the star is off the frame. (See Fig. 3.)

An assortment of parameters are being used to identify and reject false

sources. Several of our tests examine the shape score over limited portions of a source in order to eliminate the contribution from isolated secondary sources. For example, we can examine the values of the shape parameter in wedge-shaped "pie slices" (where the vertex of the wedge is centered on the point of peak flux density). A galaxy should show a consistently large SH score in each wedge, but a binary star will have small scores except in the wedge that contains the secondary star. Similarly, we can find the SH score for the *median* flux level in annuli at each radius. Again, this should not change much for a galaxy, but it will tend to eliminate contributions from secondary sources that contribute a significant amount of light over less than half of the azimuthal distribution about a source.

Our current strategy is to accept potential sources to about a magnitude fainter than the Level–1 specifications in any of the bands. These sources become part of a working survey database, which we then pare back to generate the "official" database based on a much larger set of acceptance and rejection criteria that we carry along with each source (including several that we are not currently implementing). This allows us to experiment with modifications to the galaxy selection procedure without having to rerun the extended source processor on the raw data.

6. Magnitude and Surface Brightness Issues

Up to this point we have cheated a little by talking about galaxy magnitudes as though they were well defined. One of the major problems in galaxy cataloging is the difficulty in measuring anything remotely resembling a "total flux." Even with effective surface brightness limits substantially fainter than in 2MASS, total magnitudes can only be approximately extrapolated from magnitudes measured within fixed bright isophotes, and this introduces large errors. Isophotal magnitudes, on the other hand, may be more consistent, but they are somewhat arbitrary. This is part of the reason that there is such a proliferation of techniques for measuring galaxy magnitudes.

Since galaxies fade to unmeasurable surface brightnesses while still missing a significant fraction of their total of light, we are forced to select between methods that are accurate but imprecise, and others that are precise but inaccurate. For example, circular apertures are less likely to introduce biases due to the exigencies of ellipse fitting. They also should introduce a similar level of faint star contamination in edge-on versus face-on galaxies. However, elliptical apertures, having less contamination and a smaller background noise contribution will tend to be more precise. For statistical studies, it is better to be accurate, but in studies of an individual galaxy where color comparisons are being made, precision is better.

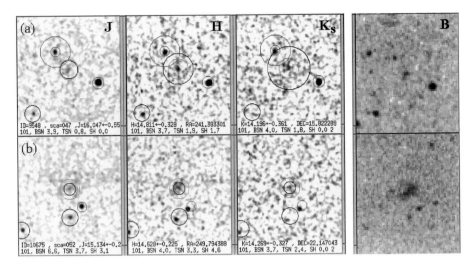

Figure 4.   Low central surface brightness galaxies detected by Algorithm 2. Plotted as in Fig. 1. At $K_s = 14.2$ and 14.3, these objects are outside of the sensitivity limit requirements, but they demonstrate the potential of the survey for deeper "mining."

These conflicting needs are reflected in the 2MASS database. We are recording a large assortment of magnitudes in the working survey database, although only a few of them are likely to appear in the released catalog. Currently we determine magnitudes in a series of fixed circular apertures, isophotal magnitudes for circular and elliptical isophotes, Kron magnitudes as is done in DENIS, and Petrosian magnitudes. The Petrosian magnitudes are determined by finding the isophote at a fixed fraction of the mean surface brightness interior to the isophote. Such a magnitude is unbiased in principle, but it has proved very imprecise, possibly because of the limited dynamic range of our survey. In principle, we could determine each kind of magnitude in each band, and then find the corresponding magnitude in the other bands, but we have decided to treat the K_s–band as the fiducial as much as possible since this is foremost a 2μ survey.

Another concern for any imaging survey is the problem of overlooking sources with large integrated fluxes whose light is too broadly distributed to be picked out at the early stages of image processing. For example, the 2MASS extended source processor begins by looking around local maxima in the images. Since most galaxies are strongly centrally condensed, this is a reasonable operative approach, but we know of some galaxies that never exceed the local maximum requirement, yet have a large integrated flux.

To search for these objects, we have developed a second algorithm to examine the images after first subtracting point and extended sources detected earlier in the pipeline. This "Low Central Surface Brightness"

(LCSB) processor smooths the residual images and searches for significant peaks. This process picks up some surprisingly faint sources (see Fig. 4), but it does not appear to add a large enough number to indicate that our Level–1 specification on completeness might otherwise be compromised. We plan to continue running this processor, however, since it detects some very interesting sources. The LCSB processor is discussed in much more detail by Jarrett (1998) elsewhere in this volume.

7. Image Masking and Blanking

Even though the 2MASS data are very uniform, there are an assortment of situations that force us to excise data in various ways. In some cases we need to mask out data from any consideration in the extended source processor, while in others we need to manipulate the image, for example, blanking out stars that overlay a galaxy.

One of the consequences of our stringent reliability criterion is that we need to avoid regions that are likely to generate false extended sources. One such area is in the wings of the PSF of bright stars. Bright stars also generate bright diffraction spikes, persistence "ghosts" that may take up to 10 s to fade from the image, and "horizontal stripes," an electronic read-out problem in rows offset by 128 pixels from a bright star. All of these artifacts represent a sort of high-dynamic-range PSF, which is not well enough understood to allow us to simply subtract it from the data. This is frustrating, because we have already encountered many examples of fairly bright galaxies that were clearly visible, but lay on these features, making them unreliable. The amount of area masked can also grow very large as the star density increases near the Galactic plane.

To minimize these problems, we are trying to determine worst-case levels for these various features relative to the brightness of the source so that we can mask them only where necessary. Our goal is to establish the highest safe level for these features relative to the image background noise. The background noise includes an estimate of the effective noise caused by stellar confusion so that deep in the Galactic plane where the bright star artifacts are swamped by other stars, we do not mask out regions that might prevent us from detecting a bright galaxy.

Large galaxies and HII regions also present a problem for the extended source processor, which tends to break them up into a large number of smaller sources. This is another annoying problem, although it includes a relatively small number of sources. Our strategy is to use outside catalogs to flag such regions. For the largest of these regions we simply turn off the processing because it becomes extremely inefficient, and "expensive" computationally speaking. For other cataloged sources we merely flag the

source or sources that are detected within its boundaries.

For the data that survives the blanking process, there are still sources present that interfere with making isophotal fits and magnitude measurements. We identify sources that are within about 1 mag of the galaxy's brightness. These are then blanked out for isophotal fitting procedures, and an isophotal substitution is performed before determining magnitudes.

This procedure was debated before the survey began because there is a risk that nearby, large galaxies will be handled differently than poorly-resolved distant galaxies. For example, an obviously-extended HII region in a nearby galaxy might be treated as a contaminating star if the galaxy were farther away. Similarly, it might seem more accurate to determine the local background level in an annulus surrounding a galaxy *without* removing the stars. This is because it is much more difficult to identify stars against the galaxy itself, so leaving the stars in the annulus biases it in the same way. In the prototype camera tests, though, we found that if we did not work on removing stars, the magnitudes simply became unacceptably imprecise, and they did not show any significant improvement in the biasing.

8. The Real Beginning

As of this writing (October 1997), 2MASS has already surveyed 7% of the northern sky. We expect a fairly large fraction of this data to survive the quality-assurance tests and to become part of the final survey data. The software is essentially complete, except for some parameter tuning, and we are examining fields so that we can reach some final decisions on the best choices for these parameters.

Based on our work to this point, we have offered a quick look at some of the individual source images, and how they are handled. We are also now in a better position to say something about the probable size of the 2MASS catalog based on these early analyses. In Fig. 5, we plot the extended source counts from two essentially random regions at high Galactic latitudes. The regions cover about 6 and 10 sq deg after we have eliminated some apparent clusters in each.

The figure shows the differential source counts in half magnitude bins. The dashed line shows the simple volume increase, and indicates that the counts are complete to $K_s = 13.5$, and almost complete to $K_s = 14$. The counts in these regions indicate that there are about 26 sources per sq deg, or about 1.1 million sources over the whole sky to $K_s = 13.5$. This is close to our initial extrapolations from the optical catalogs. Our counts are in good agreement with the values found by Gardner et al. (1996) as is shown if Fig. 5.

These counts are slightly higher than values found with our prototype

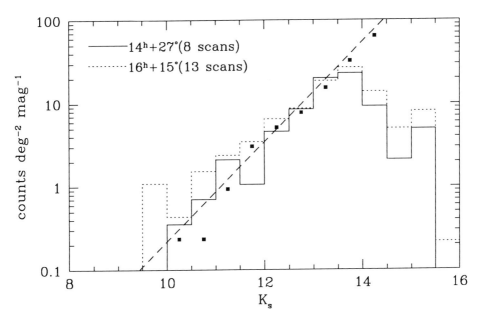

Figure 5.   Galaxy counts drawn from two fields at high Galactic latitude. Counts are
per half-magnitude bins in K_s, normalized to one mag interval. The dashed line shows
the simple increase with volume of a complete sample, and the square symbols show the
values found by Gardner et al. (1996) in an 8.5 sq deg region.

camera. The 3–channel camera is more successful at detecting galaxies close
to and beyond our sensitivity limit, at least in part because it has three
opportunities to catch them. We had been cautious in interpreting our
earlier counts because we thought they might be *over*estimates since most
of the prototype fields were targeted on rich galaxy clusters. Still, it was
apparent in the redshift results from the Abell 262 region, for example, that
most of the galaxies detected were not members of the cluster (Schneider
et al. 1997). It is clear now that the total counts will be even higher.

Actually, if we do not exclude clusters, the total counts we will find
will be significantly higher. We chose the fields in Fig. 5 at random, and
they have no major clusters in them, but there were high density regions in
each that would have raised the average counts by more than 50% in each
case. (We note that Gardner et al. also excluded a cluster in their region.)
If the regions we examined are representative, it seems likely that 2MASS
may detect closer to 1.5 million extended sources with K_s <13.5. With
sources also meeting the J and H sensitivity criteria, the 2MASS catalog
will balloon to several million sources, and it seems clear that their will be
several million more galaxies beyond our official completeness limit.

References

Chester, T. J., & Jarrett, T. 1995, Proc. Euroconference on Near Infrared Sky Surveys, San Miniato, Italy, eds. P. Persi et al., Mem. S. A. It., 66, 567

Dreyer, J. L. E. 1888, Mem R Astr Soc, 49, 1

Dreyer, J. L. E. 1895, Mem R Astr Soc, 51, 185

Dreyer, J. L. E. 1908, Mem R Astr Soc, 59, 105

Gardner, J. P., Sharples, R. M., Carrasco, B. E., & Frenk, C. S. 1996, MNRAS, 282, L1

Jarret, T. 1998, this proceedings.

Jarret, T., Chester, T., Schneider, S. & Huchra, J. 1997, in "The Impact of Large Scale Near-IR Sky Surveys," p. 213, F. Garzon et al. (eds.), Kluwer (Netherlands).

Jarvis, J. F., & Tyson, J. A. 1981, AJ, 86, 476

Maddox, S. J., Sutherland, W. J., Efstathiou, G., & Loveday, J. 1990, MNRAS, 243, 692

Messier, C. 1780, in "Connoissance des Temps pour l'Année bissextile 1784," p. 227, l'Imprimerie Royale (Paris).

Nilson, P. 1973, Uppsala General Catalogue of Galaxies, Uppsala Astr Obs Ann, 6

Odewahn, S. C., Stockwell, E. B., Pennington, R. L., Humphreys, R. M., & Zumach, W. A. 1992, AJ, 103, 318

Rosenberg, J. L. 1998, this proceedings.

Schneider, S. E., Huchra, J. P., Jarrett, T. H., & Chester, T. J. 1997, in "The Impact of Large Scale Near-IR Sky Surveys," p. 187, F. Garzon et al. (eds.), Kluwer (Netherlands).

Vorontsov–Velyaminov, B. A., et al. 1962, 1963, 1964, 1968, Morfologiceskij Katalog Galaktik, I–IV, Moscow State University (Moscow).

Weir, N., Fayyad, U. M., & Djorgovski, S. 1995, AJ, 109, 2401

Willick, J. A., Courteau, S., Faber, S. M., Burstein, D., Dekel, A., & Kolatt, T. 1996, ApJ, 457, 460

Zwicky, F., et al. 1961, 1963, 1965, 1966, 1968, Catalogue of Galaxies and of Clusters of Galaxies, I–VI, California Institute of Technology (Pasadena).

LARGE-SCALE STRUCTURES BEHIND THE MILKY WAY FROM NEAR-IR SURVEYS

R.C. KRAAN-KORTEWEG
DAEC, Observatoire de Paris, Meudon, France, and
Dept. de Astronomia, Universidad de Guanajuato, Mexico

A. SCHRÖDER
Institute of Astronomy, NCU, Chung-Li, Taiwan

G.A. MAMON
IAP, Paris, France, and
DAEC, Observatoire de Paris, Meudon, France

AND

S. RUPHY
DESPA, Observatoire de Paris, Meudon, France

Abstract. About 25% of the optical extragalactic sky is obscured by the dust and stars of our Milky Way. Dynamically important structures might still lie hidden in this zone. Various approaches are presently being employed to uncover the galaxy distribution in the Zone of Avoidance (ZOA) but all suffer from (different) limitations and selection effects.

We investigated the potential of using the DENIS NIR survey for studies of galaxies behind the obscuration layer of our Milky Way and for mapping the Galactic extinction. As a pilot study, we recovered DENIS I_c, J and K_s band images of heavily obscured but optically still visible galaxies. We determined the I_c, J and K_s band luminosity functions of galaxies on three DENIS strips that cross the center of the nearby, low-latitude, rich cluster Abell 3627. The extinction-corrected $I - J$ and $J - K$ colours of these cluster galaxies compare well with that of an unobscured cluster. We searched for and identified galaxies at latitudes where the Milky Way remains fully opaque ($|b| < 5°$ and $A_B \gtrsim 4 - 5^m$) — in a systematic search as well as around positions of galaxies detected with the blind H I-survey of the ZOA currently conducted with the Multibeam Receiver of the Parkes Radiotelescope.

N. Epchtein (ed.),
The Impact of Near-Infrared Sky Surveys on Galactic and Extragalactic Astronomy, 209-220.
© 1998 *Kluwer Academic Publishers. Printed in the Netherlands.*

1. Introduction

Some of the results of this study have already been reported in Schröder *et al.* 1997 (Paper I). For a comprehensive description, the goals and earlier results of this project are repeated here, but the reader is referred to paper I for details on earlier presented results.

About 25% of the optically visible extragalactic sky is obscured by the dust and stars of our Milky Way. Dynamically important structures — individual nearby galaxies (*cf.* Kraan-Korteweg *et al.* 1994) as well as large clusters and superclusters (*cf.* Kraan-Korteweg *et al.* 1996) — might still lie hidden in this zone. Complete whole-sky mapping of the galaxy and mass distribution is required in explaining the origin of the peculiar velocity of the Local Group and the dipole in the Cosmic Microwave Background.

Various approaches are presently being employed to uncover the galaxy distribution in the ZOA: deep optical searches, far-infrared (FIR) surveys (*e.g.*, IRAS), and blind H I searches. All methods produce new results, but all suffer from (different) limitations and selection effects. Here, the near infrared (NIR) surveys such as 2MASS (Strutskie *et al.*, 1997) and DENIS in the southern sky, (Epchtein, 1997; Epchtein *et al.*, 1997) could provide important complementary data. NIR surveys will:

- be sensitive to early-type galaxies — tracers of massive groups and clusters — which are missed in IRAS and H I surveys,
- have less confusion with Galactic objects compared to FIR surveys,
- be less affected by absorption than optical surveys.

But can we detect galaxies and obtain accurate magnitudes in crowded regions and at high foreground extinction using NIR surveys? To assess the performance of the DENIS survey at low Galactic latitudes, we addressed the following questions:

(1) How many galaxies visible in the B_J band ($B_{\lim} \approx 19\overset{m}{.}0$) can we recover with DENIS in I_c (0.8μm), J(1.25μm) and K_s(2.15μm)? Although less affected by extinction (45%, 21% and 9% as compared to B_J), their respective limits for highly complete, reliable and photometrically accurate galaxy extraction with DENIS are lower (16$\overset{m}{.}$5, 14$\overset{m}{.}$8, and $\simeq$ 11, Mamon *et al.* 1998).

(2) Can we determine the I_c, J, and K_s band luminosity functions?

(3) Can we map the Galactic extinction from NIR colours of galaxies behind the Milky Way?

(4) Can we identify galaxies at high extinction ($A_B > 4 - 5^m$) where optical surveys fail and FIR surveys are plagued by confusion?

(5) Can we recover heavily obscured spiral galaxies detected in a blind H I search and hence extend the peculiar velocity field into the ZOA via the NIR Tully – Fisher relation?

We pursued these questions by comparing available DENIS data with results from a deep optical survey in the southern ZOA (Kraan-Korteweg & Woudt 1994, Kraan-Korteweg *et al.* 1995, 1996, and references therein). In this region ($265° \lesssim \ell \lesssim 340°$, $|b| \lesssim 10°$), over 11 000 previously unknown galaxies above a diameter limit of $D = 0\!'\!2$ and with $B \lesssim 19\!.\!^{m}0 - 19\!.\!^{m}5$ have been identified (*cf.* Fig. 1 in Paper I). Many of the faint low-latitude galaxies are intrinsically bright galaxies. Within the survey region, we investigated DENIS data at what seems to be the core of the Great Attractor (GA), *i.e.*, in the low-latitude ($\ell = 325°$, $b = -7°$), rich cluster Abell 3627, where the Galactic extinction is well determined (Woudt *et al.*, 1997), and in its extension across the Galactic Plane where the Milky Way is fully opaque.

2. Expectations for DENIS galaxy extraction in the ZOA

What are the predictions for DENIS at low latitudes? In unobscured regions, the density of galaxies per square degree is 110 in the blue for $B_J \leq 19\!.\!^{m}0$ (Gardner *et al.*, 1996), and 30, 11, and 2 in the I_c, J and K_s bands for their respective completeness limits of $I_{\lim} = 16\!.\!^{m}0$, $J_{\lim} = 14\!.\!^{m}0$, $K_{\lim} = 12\!.\!^{m}2$ (see Mamon *et al.* 1997b). The number counts in the blue decrease with increasing obscuration as $N(< B) \simeq 110 \times \text{dex}(0.6\,[B - 19])\,\text{deg}^{-2}$. According to Cardelli *et al.* (1989), the extinction in the NIR passbands are $A_{I_c} = 0\!.\!^{m}45$, $A_J = 0\!.\!^{m}21$, and $A_{K_s} = 0\!.\!^{m}09$ for $A_B = 1\!.\!^{m}0$, hence the decrease in number counts as a function of extinction is considerably slower. Figure 1 shows the predicted surface number density of galaxies for DENIS and for $B < 19$, as a function of Galactic foreground extinction.

The NIR becomes notably more efficient at $A_B \simeq 2 - 3^{m}$. At an extinction of $A_B \simeq 3 - 4^{m}$, J becomes superior to I_c, while at $A_B \simeq 10^{m}$, K_s becomes superior to J. We can expect to find galaxies in J and K_s, even at $A_B = 10^{m}$. These are very rough predictions, do not take into account the most recent expected DENIS high-latitude limits (Mamon *et al.*, 1998), which are more favourable for the I and J bands, but less favourable for the K band (see § 1). Moreover, we have not yet taken into account any dependence on morphological type, surface brightness, orientation and crowding, which may lower the counts of actually detectable galaxies counts (Mamon, 1994).

In April 1997, a new cooling system for the focal instrument of DENIS has been mounted. This appears to increase the K_s band limiting magnitude by ~ 0.5 magnitude and therewith the number of galaxies detectable in the deepest obscuration layer of the Milky Way by a factor of about 2. Consequently, the *long dashed curve* representing the K_s counts in Figure 1 should be moved up by roughly a factor of 2, which would make the K_s

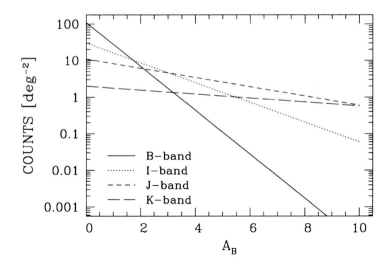

Figure 1. Predicted galaxy counts in B, I_c, J and K_s as a function of absorption in B, for highly complete and reliable DENIS galaxy samples and a $B_J \leq 19^{\mathrm{m}}$ optical sample.

passband competitive with J starting at $A_B \simeq 7^{\mathrm{m}}$.

3. DENIS data in the Norma cluster A3627

3.1. RECOVERY OF GALAXIES FOUND IN THE B BAND

Three high-quality DENIS strips cross the cluster Abell 3627 practically through its center. We inspected 66 images which cover about one-eighth of the cluster area within its Abell-radius of $R_A = 1°75$ (each DENIS image is 12′x12′, offset by 10′ in declination and right ascension). The extinction over the regarded cluster area varies as $1^{\mathrm{m}}2 \leq A_B \leq 2^{\mathrm{m}}0$.

We cross-identified the galaxies found in the optical survey with the DENIS I_c, J, and K_s images. An example of a DENIS image in the central part of the cluster is given in Figure 3 of Paper I. On the 66 images, 151 galaxies had been identified in the optical. We have recovered 122 galaxies in the I_c band, 100 in the J band, and 74 in the K_s band (not including galaxies visible on more than one image). As suggested by Figure 1, the K_s band indeed is not optimal for identifying obscured galaxies at these latitudes due to its shallow magnitude limit. Most of the galaxies not rediscovered in K_s are low surface brightness spiral galaxies.

Surprisingly, the J band provides better galaxy detection than the I_c band. In the latter, the severe star crowding makes identification of faint galaxies very difficult. At these extinction levels, the optical survey does remain the most efficient in *identifying* obscured galaxies.

3.2. PHOTOMETRY OF GALAXIES IN THE NORMA CLUSTER

We have used a preliminary galaxy pipeline (Mamon *et al.*, 1997b, 1998), based upon the SExtractor package (Bertin & Arnouts, 1996) on the DENIS data in the Norma cluster to obtain I_c, J and K_s Kron photometry. Although many of the galaxies have a considerable number of stars superimposed on their images, magnitudes derived from this fairly automated algorithm agree well with the few known, independent measurements.

Magnitudes could be determined for 109, 98 and 64 galaxies of the 122, 100, 74 galaxies re-discovered in I_c, J, and K_s. Figure 2 shows the luminosity function (LF) of these galaxies together with the B band LF of the 151 galaxies visible on the same 66 DENIS images. The histograms are normalised to the area covered by the 66 images. The hashed area marks the 60 galaxies common to all 4 passbands. This subsample is mainly restricted by the K_s band. The magnitudes in the bottom row are corrected for extinction. The corrections are derived from Mg_2-indices of elliptical galaxies in the cluster (Woudt *et al.* in prep.) and interpolations according to the Galactic H I distribution.

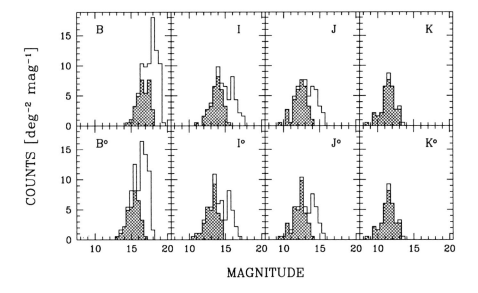

Figure 2.   The luminosity function for the observed Norma galaxies in B, I_c, J, and K_s. The bottom panels display magnitudes corrected for foreground extinction. The *hashed histograms* represent the sample common to all 4 passbands ($N = 60$).

To assess whether the LFs displayed here are, in fact, representative of the cluster as a whole — and therefore the extinction corrected NIR I_c, J, and K_s band LFs displayed in the lower panels characteristic for

rich clusters — we compared the B band LF of the 151 galaxies on the 66 DENIS-images with the cluster LF as a whole (*cf.* Woudt, 1997). The extinction-corrected blue cluster LF of the 609 galaxies within the Abell radius, scaled to the Abell area, actually has lower number counts than the B^o band LF displayed in the bottom panel of Figure 2. This is explained by the fact that our three strips cross the center of the cluster and therewith the region of highest density. The comparison indicates that we are fairly complete to a magnitude of $B^o = 16{.}^m5$, which is more or less the shaded area, and that the shape of the total LF is very similar to the distribution of the common subsample.

Even though these LFs are still preliminary (we have so far covered only a small area of the Norma cluster and will have missed dwarf galaxies and other LSB galaxies due to the foreground obscuration) the here determined extinction-corrected LFs of the galaxies common to all passbands can be regarded as a first indication of the bright end of the NIR I_c, J, and K_s band LFs in rich clusters.

From the below discussed colours of the Norma galaxies, we know that the extinction corrections are of the correct order. Adopting a distance to A3627 of 93 Mpc (Kraan-Korteweg *et al.*, 1996), thus $m-M = 34{.}^m8$, the 60 galaxies cover a luminosity range in K_s of $-25{.}^m3 < M_K^o < -21{.}^m8$. This compares well with the bright end of the K_s band LF of the Coma cluster core derived by Mobasher & Trentham (1997), although it remains puzzling why the number counts derived by them (*cf.* their Table 1) are so much lower compared to the A3627 cluster.

The NIR magnitudes have been used to study the colour–colour diagram $I - J$ versus $J - K$. This has been presented and discussed in detail in Paper I. Here it suffices to state that the extinction-corrected colours of the cluster galaxies match the colours of galaxies in unobscured high latitude regions (Mamon *et al.* 1997b, 1998) extremely well, suggesting that our preliminary photometry is reasonably accurate. Moreover, the shift in colour can be fully explained by the foreground extinction or, more interestingly, the NIR colours of obscured galaxies provide, in principle, an independent way of mapping the extinction in the ZOA (see also Mamon *et al.*, 1997a).

4. 'Blind' search for galaxies

The GA is suspected to cross the Galactic Plane from the Norma cluster in the south towards the Centaurus cluster in the north. In this region, we performed a search for highly obscured galaxies on the so far existing DENIS survey images. The search area within the GA-region — marked as a *dashed box* in Figure 3 — is defined as $320° \leq \ell \leq 325°$ and $|b| \leq 5°$.

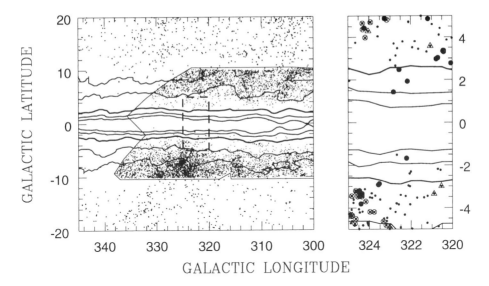

Figure 3. Galaxy distribution in the GA region displaying Lauberts galaxies ($D \geq 1\overset{'}{.}0$, Lauberts 1982) and galaxies from the deep optical search ($D \geq 0\overset{'}{.}2$, outlined area). The superimposed *contours* represent absorption levels of $A_B = 1\overset{m}{.}5, 2\overset{m}{.}5, 5\overset{m}{.}0$ (*thick line*), $7\overset{m}{.}5$ and $10\overset{m}{.}0$, as determined from H I column densities and assuming a constant gas/dust ratio. The *box* marks the DENIS blind search area with the results shown enlarged in the right panel: optical galaxies re-identified on DENIS images ($N=31$, including 3 uncertain identifications) as *large encircled crosses*, optical galaxies not seen by DENIS ($N=6$) as *triangles*, and newly identified, optically invisible galaxies ($N=15$) as *filled dots*.

Of the 1800 images in this area we have inspected 385 by eye (308 in K_s). 37 galaxies at higher latitudes were known from the optical survey. 28 of these could be re-identified in the I_c band, 26 in the J band, and 14 in the K_s band. They are plotted as *encircled crosses* in Figure 3. In addition, we found 15 new galaxies in I_c and J, 11 of which also appear in the K_s band (*filled circles*). The ratios of galaxies found in I_c compared to B, and of K_s compared to I_c are higher than in the Norma cluster. This is due to the higher obscuration level (starting with $A_B \simeq 2\overset{m}{.}3 - 3\overset{m}{.}1$ at the high-latitude border of the search area, *cf. contours* of Fig. 3).

On average, we have found about 3.5 galaxies per square degree in the I_c band. This roughly agrees with the predictions of Figure 1, although the number of the inspected images and detected galaxies are too low to allow a statistical conclusion. Since we looked in an overdense region we expect *a priori* more galaxies. On the other hand, we do not expect to find galaxies below latitudes of $b \simeq 1° - 2°$ in this longitude range (Mamon, 1994). The visual impression of the low-latitude images substantiates this — the images are nearly fully covered with stars.

Figure 4 shows a few characteristic examples of highly obscured galaxies

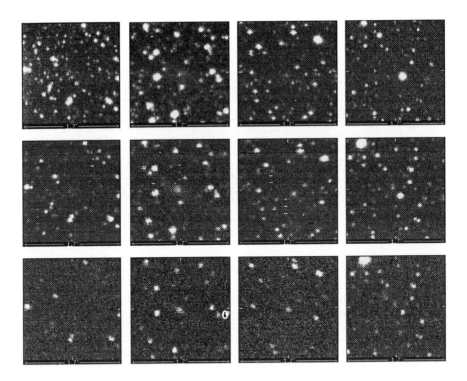

Figure 4. DENIS survey images (before bad pixel filtering) of four galaxies found in the deepest extinction layer of the Milky Way; the I_c band image is at the *top*, J in the *middle* and K_s at the *bottom*.

found in the DENIS blind search. I_c band images are at the top, J in the middle and K_s at the bottom. The left-most galaxy is located at $(l,b) = (324°6, -4°5)$, with $A_B = 2^m8$ as estimated from H I-column densities (Kerr *et al.*, 1986) following the precepts of Burstein & Heiles (1982). It is barely visible in the J band, although its B band image is similar to the B of the second galaxy. This galaxy at $(l,b) = (324°7, -3°5)$ is, however, subject to heavier extinction $(A_B = 3^m7)$ and hence easier to recognise in the NIR. The most distinct image is the J band. The third galaxy at even higher extinction $(l, b, A_B) = (320°1, +2°5, 4^m6)$ is not visible anymore in the B band. Neither is the fourth galaxy: at $b = +1°9$ and $A_B = 6^m3$ this galaxy is not even visible in the I_c band and very faint in J and K_s.

The most important result from this search is that *highly obscured, optically invisible galaxies can indeed be unveiled in the NIR* and — as indicated with the distribution in the right panel of Figure 3 — found at lower latitudes than the deep optical survey. The lowest Galactic latitude at which we found a galaxy is $b \simeq 1.5°$ and $A_B \simeq 7^m5$.

5. Galaxies detected in H I

NIR surveys are the only tools that will identify early-type galaxies and therewith uncover the cores of massive groups and clusters at very low-latitudes. In addition, highly obscured spiral galaxies should be detectable with these surveys as well. Such identifications will proof important in connection with the systematic blind H I survey currently conducted with the Multibeam Receiver (13 beams in the focal plane array) at the 64 m Parkes telescope: a deep survey with a 5σ detection limit of 10 mJy is being performed in the most opaque region of the southern Milky Way ($213° \lesssim \ell \lesssim 33°$; $|b| \lesssim 5°$) for the velocity range of $-1000 \lesssim v \lesssim 12000$ km s^{-1} (Staveley-Smith, 1997). Roughly 3000 detections are predicted. Hardly any of them will have an optical counterpart. However, at these latitudes many might be visible in the NIR. The combination of data from these two surveys, *i.e.*, NIR photometry with H I-data (velocity and linewidth) will proof particularly interesting because it will allow the extension of peculiar velocity data *into* the ZOA via the NIR Tully–Fisher relation.

Only a few cross-identifications were possible with the data available from both surveys by June 1997. But we could identify thirteen galaxies detected blindly in H I on existing DENIS images. Four of them are visible in the B, I_c, J, and K_s bands. The other galaxies are only seen in the NIR. Four of them need further confirmation.

Figure 5 shows four examples of the candidates. The first galaxy is a nearby ($v = 1450$ km s^{-1}) ESO-Lauberts galaxy (L223-12) at $b = +4°8$ and $A_B = 3^m2$. It is very impressive in all three NIR passbands (note the larger image scale for this galaxy, *i.e.*, $3'3$ instead of $1'7$). The second galaxy at $(l, b, A_B) = (306°9, +3°6, 3^m3)$ is slightly more distant ($v = 2350$ km s^{-1}). This galaxy has also been identified in B and is quite distinct in I_c and J. The third galaxy at $(b, A_B) \simeq (-2°9, 4^m6)$ had been detected by us as an OFF-signal at $v = 2900$ km s^{-1} during pointed H I observations in the ZOA. It has no optical counterpart but can be clearly seen in all three NIR passbands. The last example is an uncertain NIR counterpart at $(b, A_B) \simeq (+1°5, 7^m5)$ of a galaxy detected in H I at $v = 1450$ km s^{-1}. It is barely visible in the I_c band.

Although the present data is scarce, NIR counterparts of H I detected, highly obscured galaxies certainly seem to merit a systematic exploitation for large-scale structure investigations.

6. Conclusion

Our pilot study illustrates the promises of using the NIR surveys for extragalactic large-scale studies behind the ZOA as well as for the mapping of the Galactic extinction.

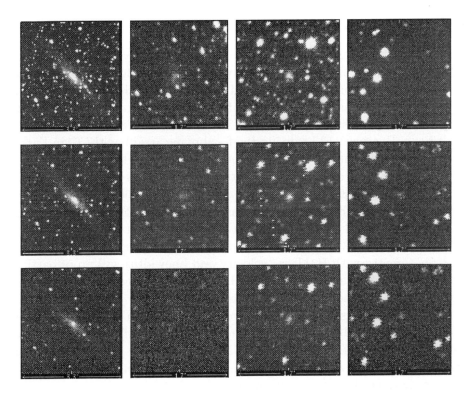

Figure 5. DENIS survey images (before bad pixel filtering) of four galaxies detected blindly in H I at $|b| \leq 5°$; the I_c band image is at the *top* , J in the *middle* and K_s at the *bottom*.

At *intermediate latitudes and extinction* ($5° < |b| < 10°$, $1^m \lesssim A_B \lesssim 4 - 5^m$) optical surveys remain superior for identifying galaxies. However, the NIR luminosities and colours together with extinction data from the NIR colours will prove invaluable in analysing the optical survey data and their distribution in redshift space, and in the final merging of these data with existing sky surveys. Despite the high extinction and the star crowding at these latitudes, I_c, J and K_s photometry from the survey data can be successfully performed at these low latitudes and lead, for instance, to the preliminary I_c^o, J^o and K_s^o galaxy luminosity functions in A3627.

At *low latitudes and high extinction* ($|b| < 5°$ and $A_B \gtrsim 4 - 5^m$) the search for 'invisible' obscured galaxies on existing DENIS-images implicate that NIR-surveys can trace galaxies down to about $|b| \simeq 1°\!.5$. The J band was found to be optimal for identifying galaxies up to $A_B \simeq 7^m$, although this might change in favour of K_s with the new cooling system. NIR surveys can hence further reduce the width of the ZOA. This is furthermore the only tool that permits the mapping of early-type galaxies — tracers of density

peaks — at high extinction.

The combination of two different surveys, *i.e.*, NIR data for highly obscured spiral galaxies detected in a systematic blind H I survey — a fair fraction could indeed be re-identified on DENIS-images — allows the mapping of the peculiar velocity field in the ZOA through the NIR Tully – Fisher relation. This will be pursued as well at intermediate latitudes ($5° < |b| < 10°$) with pointed H I observations of optically identified spiral galaxies. About 300 spiral galaxies have already been detected (Kraan-Korteweg *et al.* 1997).

Whether the systematic identification of ZOA galaxies from the DENIS survey must be performed by visual examination or whether galaxies can be successfully extracted using classical algorithms (Mamon *et al.* 1997b, 1998) or artificial neural networks (Bertin & Arnouts 1996, Bertin, in these proceedings) or a combination of both requires further exploration.

Acknowledgements

We thank Jean Borsenberger for providing bias subtracted, flat fielded DENIS images, Emmanuel Bertin for supplying recent updates of his SExtractor software package, and Eric Copet for providing software to display Figures 4 and 5.

References

Bertin, E., Arnouts, S., 1996, *Astr. Astrophys. Suppl. Ser.* **117**, 398
Burstein D., Heiles C., 1982, *Astron. J.* **87**, 1165
Cardelli J.A., Clayton G.C., Mathis J.S., 1989, *Astrophys. J.* **345**, 245
Epchtein, N., 1997, in *The Impact of Large Scale Near-Infrared Surveys* p. 15, eds. F. Garzon, N. Epchtein, A. Omont, W.B. Burton, B. Persi, Kluwer, Dordrecht
Epchtein, N., *et al.*, 1997, *Messenger*, **87**, 27
Gardner, J.P., Sharples, R.M., Carrasco, B.E., Frenk, C.S., 1996, *MNRAS* **282**, L1
Kerr, F.J., Bowers, P.F., Jackson, P.D., Kerr, M., 1986, *Astr. Astrophys. Suppl. Ser.* **66**, 373
Kraan-Korteweg, R.C., Woudt, P.A., 1994, in *Unveiling Large-Scale Structures Behind the Milky Way*, p. 89, eds. C. Balkowski, R.C. Kraan-Korteweg, ASP Conf. Ser. 67
Kraan-Korteweg R.C., Loan A.J., Burton W.B., Lahav O., Ferguson H.C., Henning P.A., Lynden-Bell D., 1994, *Nature* **372**, 77
Kraan-Korteweg, R.C., Fairall, A.P., Balkowski, C., 1995, *Astr. Astrophys.* **297**, 617
Kraan-Korteweg R.C., Woudt P.A., Cayatte V., Fairall A.P., Balkowski C., Henning P.A., 1996, *Nature* **379**, 519
Kraan-Korteweg, R.C., Woudt, P.A., Henning, P.A., 1997, *PASA* **14**, 15
Lauberts, A. 1982, The ESO/Uppsala Survey of the ESO (B) Atlas, ESO, Garching
Mamon G.A., 1994, in *Unveiling Large-Scale Structures Behind the Milky Way*, p. 53, eds. C. Balkowski, R.C. Kraan-Korteweg, ASP Conf. Ser. 67 (astro-ph/9405056)
Mamon, G.A., Banchet, V., Tricottet, M. Katz, D., 1997a, in *The Impact of Large-Scale Near-Infrared Surveys*, p. 239, eds. F. Garzon, N. Epchtein, A. Omont, W.B. Burton, B. Persi, Kluwer, Dordrecht (astro-ph/9608077)

Mamon, G.A., Tricottet, M., Bonin, W., Banchet, V., 1997b, in XVIIth Moriond Astrophysics Meeting on *Extragalactic Astronomy in the Infrared*, p. 369, eds. G. A. Mamon, Trinh Xuân Thuân, and J. Trân Thanh Vân, Frontières, Paris (astro-ph/9711281)

Mamon, G.A., Borsenberger, J., Tricottet, M., Banchet, V., 1998, in these proceedings

Mobasher, B., Trentham, N., 1997, *MNRAS* , in press (astro-ph/9708226)

Schröder, A., Kraan-Korteweg, R.C., Mamon, G.A. Ruphy, S., 1997, in XVIIth Moriond Astrophysics Meeting on *Extragalactic Astronomy in the Infrared*, p. 381, eds. G. A. Mamon, Trinh Xuân Thuân, and J. Trân Thanh Vân, Frontières, Paris, (paper I, astro-ph/9706093)

Staveley-Smith, L., 1997, *PASA* **14**, 111

Strutskie, M.F., *et al.* 1997, in *The Impact of Large Scale Near-Infrared Surveys*, p. 25, eds. F. Garzon, N. Epchtein, A. Omont, W.B. Burton, B. Persi, Kluwer, Dordrecht

Woudt, P.A., 1997, *Ph.D. thesis, Univ. of Cape Town.*

Woudt, P.A., Kraan-Korteweg, R.C., Fairall, A.P., Böhringer, H., Cayatte, V., and Glass, I.S., 1997, *Astr. Astrophys.*, in press

RAPID EXTRACTION OF GALAXIES FROM DENIS

G. PATUREL, I. VAUGLIN, M.C. MARTHINET AND C. PETIT

CRAL-Observatoire de Lyon
69561 Saint-Genis Laval, France
patu@obs.univ-lyon1.fr

AND

J. BORSENBERGER, L. PROVOST

Institut d'Astrophysique de Paris, France

1. Introduction

In order to face the challenge of collecting data for deep extragalactic samples it is necessary to identify new galaxies and to collect the main information on them: coordinates, magnitudes, diameters and axis ratios, position angles and morphological types. The DENIS project is a great opportunity to do that. It is the first time that such a survey is undertaken by getting CCD images directly at the telescope for an entire hemisphere. This new way of making a survey provides us with incredibly high quality images compared with photographic counterparts.

The Lyon-Meudon Extragalactic database (LEDA) was built in 1983 with the aim of collecting the main astrophysical parameters for the principal galaxies. Presently, LEDA contains more than 140,000 galaxies for which we collected the most important astrophysical parameters (Paturel et al., 1997). Our task in the DENIS consortium is to perform cross-identifications between DENIS and LEDA galaxies. This will allow us to recognize new galaxies for which it is important to follow kinematics up.

We present here the reduction of the first part of this quick look on the DENIS Survey. The raw data will be available through LEDA, while the provisional catalogue of mean data will be distributed to the DENIS consortium.

N. Epchtein (ed.),
The Impact of Near-Infrared Sky Surveys on Galactic and Extragalactic Astronomy, 221-227.
© *1998 Kluwer Academic Publishers. Printed in the Netherlands.*

Figure 1.   A matrix of pixels for a new galaxy identified in I-band

2. Quick Data Reduction

2.1. PIPE-LINE OF DATA

All raw images send from Chile to France by P. Fouqué are pre-processed at the Institut d'Astrophysique de Paris by J. Borsenberger for cleaning purposes. The routines warn us when an image is ready to be analyzed. Then, each I-image is reduced (averaged 2x2 pixels), thresholded, compressed and send to Lyon by ftp. Each night about 3600 I-band images are received via this pipe-line. This flow is daily controlled in Lyon by C. Petit and J. Rousseau. The source extraction may start.

2.2. SOURCE EXTRACTION AND GALAXY RECOGNITION

The main method for source extraction is described in Paturel et al.(1996). Each object (star or galaxy) is represented by a matrix of pixels (Fig.1) from which a set of parameters is extracted: surface, total flux, peak flux, axis ratio, diameter, etc...

These parameters are used in a conventional discriminant analysis in order to perform a separation between stars and galaxies. The program was trained on a sample of 511 objects (239 stars and 272 galaxies) for which the discrimination between stars and galaxies was made by an human expert (F. Gallet and R. Garnier). The ratio of $maximum - intensity/surface$ appears as one of the most efficient parameter for such a discrimination. The principal component allows the recognition of 99.2% of objects from a test sample. Two levels of probability are chosen. The range between these levels define the uncertainty zone (see Fig.2 for illustration).

Both levels are chosen in such a way that 0% of stars will be identified as galaxy and that 10% of galaxies may be identified as stars. This choice will avoid the contamination of LEDA by stars.

The astrometry is made using the GSC as described in Paturel et al. (1996) and/or using the telescope coordinates registered in the header of each image. The accuracy is generally better than 10 arcsec.

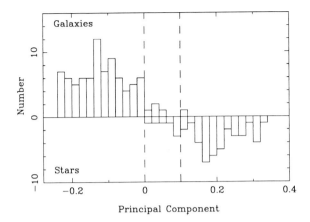

Figure 2. Galaxy/star recognition from a discriminant analysis. Histogram of the principal component obtained for our test sample. The two vertical lines define the uncertainty zone.

The final step of this treatment consists in checking visually all frames recognized as galaxies. This tedious part allows us to reject artefacts (a few percent) like those produced by star halos truncated by the edge of the frame. Such tuncated halos look like an elongated, low-surface brightness object, easily accepted as galaxy. This cleaning part is made by J.Rousseau and R. Garnier.

2.3. PROVISIONAL CALIBRATION

Flux are calibrated by comparison with the measurement in I-band photometry made by Mathewson et al. (1992, 1996). This comparison allows us to correct for seasonal variation of the zero-point. Fig.3 shows such a variation. After correction the zero-point distribution is quite Gaussian with an standard deviation of 0.20 magnitude (Fig.4).

In Fig.5, the comparison between Mathewson et al. and DENIS I-band magnitudes is shown. The standard deviation is 0.18 magnitude. If we assume that the error is identical for both systems we conclude that the mean error on DENIS extragalactic I-band magnitude is about 0.13 magnitude.

3. Cross–Identification with LEDA

3.1. AUTO-CROSS-IDENTIFICATION

Our first archive includes 52800 individual measurements. Some galaxies are measured twice because they are in the overlapping zone of the images.

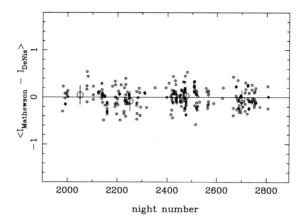

Figure 3. Zero-point variation obtained by comparison with Mathewson's I-band photometry.

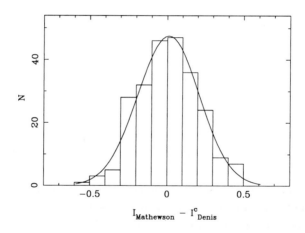

Figure 4. Zero-point distribution after a tiny seasonal correction

In the first step, we perform what we call the auto-cross-identification.
This will consist in identifying measurements concerning a same object.
This is done by a hiearchical method in which we merge step by step the
closest measurements. The definition of the distance of two measurements
i and j is taken as:

$$d_{ij} = \frac{1}{N} \sum_{k=1}^{N} \frac{|m_{ik} - m_{jk}|}{2\sigma_i}$$

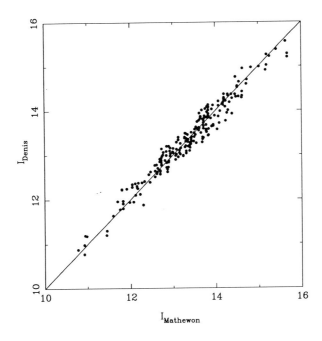

Figure 5. Comparison of extragalactic I-band magnitudes from Mathewson et al. and from DENIS

where, N is the number of parameters (coordinates, diameters magnitudes...) of a given measurement, m_{ik} is the k-th parameter of measurement i, m_{jk} is the k-th parameter of measurement j. σ_i is the standard error of the $i-th$ parameter. When d_{ij} is smaller than a given limit d_{limit} both measurements are merged and are replaced by a single one made of the mean of both. The final result does not depend on the order the original file is read. Note that, special care must be taken for periodic parameters, like right ascension and position angle (e.g., $p.a. = 0$ deg is identical to $p.a. = 180$ deg).

The distance d_{limit} is chosen from the distribution of all distances (Fig.6). We adopted $d_{limit} = 0.55$.

3.2. CROSS-IDENTIFICATION WITH LEDA GALAXIES

The previous step leads to the construction of a catalogue of mean parameters. Each galaxy of this catalogue must then be cross-identified with LEDA galaxies. This is done by calculating the distance between a DENIS galaxy (distance in the mathematical sense, as defined by the previous equation) and a LEDA galaxy. The cross-identification is performed if the distance is smaller than a limit d_{limit}. From a distribution of distances between LEDA

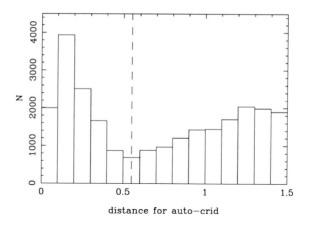

Figure 6. Distribution of "distances" d_{ij} between two DENIS measurements (i and j). This graph is used to chose d_{limit} in the auto-cross-identification phase (see text).

and DENIS measurements similar with the one shown in Fig.6, we adopted $d_{limit} = 1.00$. This limit is voluntarily severe (i.e., small) because we prefer to miss a cross-identification than to merge two distinct galaxies. Finally, we rejected every galaxy which could be cross-identified with more than one LEDA galaxy.

3.3. DATA DISTRIBUTION

The raw data are available through LEDA database using either a telnet access or the World Wide Web.

```
telnet leda.univ-lyon1.fr
login: leda    (no password needed)
```

    or

```
http://www-obs.univ-lyon1.fr/leda/leda-consult.html
```

This way allows the user to retrieve I-band raw parameters (including the matrix) for galaxies observed during the first year of the survey. These galaxies are identified with the provisional acronym RED for "Rapide Extraction DENIS" (e.g., RED1000). According to the "Data Release Policy Group" a code is required to access DENIS parameters. This code may be asked to denis@obs.univ-lyon1.fr.

On the other hand, the whole catalogue of 36246 galaxies (among which 21956 are new ones) is now available with all I-band mean parameters. This catalogue is available for DENIS Co-Investigators on request. To get it, send a mail to denis@obs.univ-lyon1.fr.

4. Follow–up

A galaxy without redshift is not very useful. Fortunately, for many DENIS galaxies identified with LEDA galaxies the redshift is already available (in LEDA more than 120.000 redshifts are collected). However, for the 21956 new galaxies detected after one year of the DENIS project, it is urgent to get at least the redshift and more detailed information if possible. In fact, this is the justification of this "Rapide Extraction". Thanks to this catalogue we may start redshift and HI follow-up's of the DENIS survey.

5. Acknowledgments

This work would have been impossible without technical help by F. GALLET, R. GARNIER, and J. ROUSSEAU from the Observatoire de Lyon. They are fully associated with this work.
The DENIS team is warmly thanked for making this work possible and in particular the operations team at La Silla headed by P. FOUQUE.

References

Paturel G., Garnier R., Petit C., Marthinet M.C. (1996) *A. & A.*, **311**,12
Paturel G., Andernach H., Bottinelli L., et al. (1997) *A.& A.* **124**,109
Mathewson D.S., Ford V.L., Buchhorn M. (1992) *Astrophys. J. Suppl. Ser.*, **81**,413
Mathewson D.S., Ford V.L. (1996) *Astrophys. J. Suppl. Ser.*, **107**,97

WIDE-ANGLE NEAR-INFRARED SURVEYS OF LOCAL GALAXIES

BAHRAM MOBASHER
Astrophysics Group,
Blackett Laboratory, Imperial College, Prince Consort Road,
London SW7 2BZ, U.K.

1. Introduction

Recently, it has become possible to perform wide-angle galaxy surveys at near-infrared ($2.2 \mu m$) wavelengths. Such surveys cover limited areas to magnitude limits similar or fainter than that achieved by the DENIS or 2MASS projects. Therefore, the resulting number-magnitude counts can be used to calibrate these datasets. Also, due to the relatively bright magnitude limit of these wide-angle surveys, spectroscopic observations are straightforward and hence, one could construct the local near-ir luminosity function (LF) of galaxies. This could be used to predict the space density of galaxies expected from DENIS or 2MASS, providing reliable control samples for these larger studies.

The infrared LF is also required to model the counts of galaxies. This is particularly useful since the near-ir ($2.2 \mu m$) light is less affected by the evolutionary processes (due to the dominance of the near-infrared light by old, near-solar mass stars) and can be more securely modeled. Also, at these wavelengths the galaxy spectral energy distributions are similar for all galaxy types, leading to similar K-corrections for all galaxies. Therefore, the near-infrared number-magnitude counts of galaxies are less affected by the mix of galaxy types or uncertainties due to evolution, compared to other wavelengths.

In this article, I present a brief review of the available infrared surveys which are most comparable to those conducted by the DENIS and 2MASS teams. Using the recent wide-angle surveys, the LF of local galaxies at this wavelength will then be constructed.

N. Epchtein (ed.),
The Impact of Near-Infrared Sky Surveys on Galactic and Extragalactic Astronomy, 229-237.
© 1998 *Kluwer Academic Publishers. Printed in the Netherlands.*

2. Near-infrared Surveys of Field Galaxies before DENIS and 2MASS

The main problem in performing infrared surveys is the small field of view of near-infrared detectors. Because of this, galaxy surveys at this wavelength require a trade-off between the area they cover and the depth of the survey. Therefore, previous near-ir galaxy surveys are either constructed from optically selected samples, covering relatively larger areas (Mobasher et al. 1993) or, are mainly pencil beam surveys (Glazebrook et al 1995; Cowie et al 1996), covering small solid angles to deeper levels. However, the former surveys suffer from optical selection criteria, making it difficult to convert to an infrared limited survey because of changes in the type mix with redshift whereas, the latter are affected by uncertainties due to small number statistics of galaxies of a given luminosity.

With the advent of large format near-ir detectors, wide-angle surveys at this wavelength have become possible. These provide the closest available surveys to DENIS and 2MASS (i.e. wide-angle, relatively shallow). There are three independent such programs currently in progress, including, a survey complete to K=15 (Gardner et al 1997), a deeper survey, covering a smaller area and complete to K=16 (Szokoly et al 1998) and a larger survey (with not yet available spectroscopic measurements) to K=16 (Huang et al 1997).

Partial redshift information are available for both Gardner et al (1997) and Szokoly et al (1998) surveys. Work is currently in progress to complete the spectroscopic observations of Szokoly et al (1998) survey to K=16.5. Moreover, spectroscopic observations are planned to measure redshifts for galaxies in Huang et al (1997). The list of different wide-angle, near-infrared galaxy surveys (with available or planned spectroscopic data) is presented in Table 1. These provide the control samples to compare with the much larger DENIS and 2MASS projects.

However, there are a number of other surveys which extend much deeper over a smaller area (Cowie et al 1996; McLeod et al 1995; Djorgovski et al 1995; Moustakas et al 1997). For example, the survey by Cowie et al (1996) employs the LRIS spectrograph on the Keck to measure the spectra of galaxies to K=20 mag., using two of the Hawaii Deep Fields, to establish the near-ir LF of galaxies at high redshifts. These deep surveys are not comparable with the DENIS and 2MASS and hence, will not be further discussed here.

3. Near-infrared Field Luminosity Function

Near-infrared redshift surveys of galaxies, complete to a given magnitude limit, are needed to construct the luminosity function at this wavelength.

TABLE 1. The wide-angle infrared surveys currently available

Survey	Area	K_{lim}	Spect. completeness	Telescope (Detector)
Mobasher et al 1993	41.56 deg^2	12.25	98%	UKIRT (UKT9)
Glazebrook et al 1995	551.9 arcmin^2	16.5	59%	UKIRT (IRCAM)
Gardner et al 1997	4.4 deg^2	15	90%	1.3m KPNO (IRIM)
Szokoly et al 1997	0.8 deg^2	16	30%	1.3m KPNO (IRIM)
Huang et al 1997	9.8 deg^2	16	—	0.6m/2.2m UHT (NICMOS)

This is carried out using the surveys presented in Table 1. Over the years, different techniques have been developed to construct the LF of galaxies, correcting for various effects such as the incompleteness due to selection criteria (Mobasher et al 1993), inhomogeneities in galaxy distribution (Efstathiou et al 1988) and spectroscopic incompleteness (Sandage, Tamman and Yahil 1979).

In this section, a wide-angle near-ir survey, carried out in collaboration with my colleagues at Johns Hopkins University is presented. While the DENIS and 2MASS surveys will eventually constrain the bright-end of the local infrared LF, this survey is designed to establish its faint-end slope. A brief discussion of two different methods for constructing the LF of galaxies is carried out in sections 3.1.1 and 3.1.2. These will then be applied on this survey to estimate the local near-ir LF. A comparison between differnt measurements of the near-ir LF for field galaxies will then be carried out in section 4.

3.1. A WIDE-ANGLE MEDIUM DEEP NEAR-INFRARED SURVEY

The near-ir survey here is carried out using the NICMOS 3 (HgCdTe) 256×256 array (IRIM) on the 1.3m telescope at KPNO. Two fields with existing multi-colour photometric ($UB_J R_F I_N$) and spectroscopic data ($Lynx2$ and $SA68$) are observed to $K_s = 17$ mag (at 5σ detection). The filter used for these observations (K_s at $\lambda = 2.15\mu m$; $\Delta\lambda = 0.33\mu m$) is similar to that of the 2MASS. Details of the observation and data reduction are given in Szokoly et al (1998). The number counts from this survey is compared with other studies in Figure 1, showing agreement within errors. As the spectroscopic observations here are based on an optically selected sample, it is likely that at fainter K_s magnitudes, the survey becomes incomplete in redshift space. The incompleteness, defined as the change with magnitude of the ratio of the number of galaxies with measured redshift to the total

number of galaxies to a given K_s limit, is corrected by assuming a Fermi-Dirac distribution for the selection function (Sandage, Tammann & Yahil (1979)), $\left(\exp\left(\frac{m-m_l}{\Delta m}\right)+1\right)^{-1}$. This parametric function is then fitted to the observed data in Figure 2.

We find $m_l = 15.25$, $\Delta m_l = 0.80$ for SA68 and $m_l = 14.86$, $\Delta m_l = 0.54$ for Lynx2. For the luminosity function analysis in this study, we select a redshift completeness limit of 30% in Fig. 2, corresponding to limiting magnitudes of $K_s = 16$ and $K_s = 15.25$ in the SA68 and Lynx2 fields respectively. There are a total of 110 galaxies brighter than these limits. The redshift distribution for the complete sample, containing both the fields, are presented in Figure 3. The redshift distributions show that most of the near-ir selected galaxies are local objects ($z < 0.4$) and reveal the presence of a cluster in the Lynx2 field at $z \sim 0.05$, which could affect estimates of the luminosity function. To explore the sensitivity of the LFs to density enhancement in the Lynx2 field, we employ two different methods for estimating the LF from this survey.

3.1.1. *The Traditional Method*

For each galaxy in the survey, the maximum comoving volume, V_{max}, within which it remains in the sample by satisfying its apparent magnitude and redshift limits is calculated as

$$V_{max} = (c/H_0)\Omega_i \int_{z_1}^{z_2} \frac{d_L^2\, dz}{(1+z)^3(1+2q_0z)^{0.5}}$$

where Ω_i is the solid angle of the field containing the galaxy and $z_1 = max(z_L, z_l)$ and $z_2 = min(z_U, z_u)$. z_L and z_U are, respectively, the lower and upper redshift limits of the survey and z_l and z_u correspond to the redshifts the galaxy would have when shifted, respectively, to the brighter and fainter apparent magnitude limits of the survey. The luminosity distance of the galaxy, d_L, is given as

$$d_L = (c/H_0q_0^2)(q_0z + (q_0 - 1)((1 + 2q_0z)^{0.5} - 1)))$$

The luminosity function is then estimated by summing contributions of galaxies in different absolute magnitude bins

$$\phi(M) = \Sigma_i\left(\frac{1}{V_{max}^i}\right)$$

Applying this method on the survey in section 3.1, we construct the K-band LF and fit it to a Schecter form, using a χ^2 technique. The resulting Schecter LF parameters are given in Table 2 and shown in Figure 4. This LF is sensitive to the presence of density enhancements in the sample.

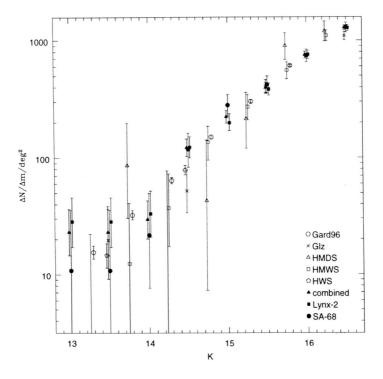

Figure 1.   K-band differential number counts in the $K = 13 - 16.5$ range. The data are compiled by Gardner et al (1993). our SA-68 and Lynx-2 fields are also shown. Errors are 1σ estimates from the raw counts.

3.1.2. *The C-method*

The C-method is a non-parametric technique for constructing the LF of galaxies, insensitive to density inhomogeneities (Lynden-Bell 1971). This calculates the cumulative LF which is then differentiated to give the more familiar differential form. The cumulative LF, $\Psi(M_0)$, is defined as the density of galaxies with $M < M_0$. However, in reality we measure the cumulative distribution $X(M_0)$ which is the same as $\Psi(M_0)$ subject to a set of observational constraints (i.e. surface brightness limit). The C-method constructs the function $C(M)$, a subset of $X(M)$, for which the following relation satisfies:

$$\frac{d\Psi}{\Psi} = \frac{dX}{C}$$

In principle, $C(M_0)$ is the number of galaxies brighter than M_0 which would be observed if their absolute magnitude were M_0. Solving for $\Psi(M)$ leads

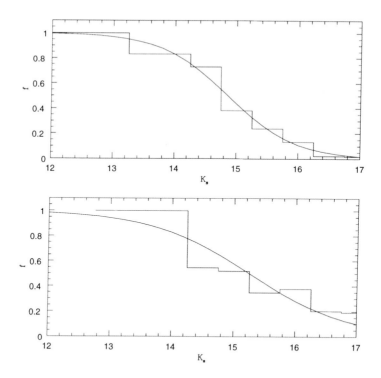

Figure 2. The redshift completeness, f, in each of the fields. The sample used in the luminosity function is cut at $K_s = 16$ in SA68 and $K_s = 15.25$ in Lynx2.

to

$$\Psi(M) = A \; exp \; \left(\int_{-\infty}^{M} \frac{dX}{C} \right)$$

Differentiating this relation gives the differential LF.

The quantities dX, are series of Dirac Delta functions $dX = \Sigma_i \delta(M - M_i)$. Using the redshift information of galaxies in the sample, the functions $C(M)$ and $X(M)$ are calculated as explained in SubbaRao et al (1996). Knowing these functions, the differential LF can be calculated from the above relation.

Applying the C-method to our data, the near-ir LF is constructed and presented in Figure 4 (open circles). The errors are estimated using bootstrap re-sampling simulations. A parametric fit to the data, using the cluster-free maximum likelihood method gives the Schecter LF parameters, as listed in Table 2. This also shows that the shape of the infrared LF here is consistent with the Schecter form.

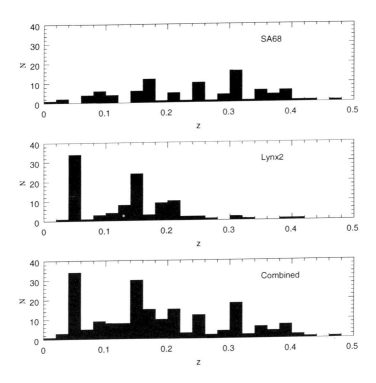

Figure 3.   The redshift distribution of each sample of galaxies that were used in the luminosity function derivation.

4. Comparison of the Infrared LFs

The near-ir LF parameters, estimated from the traditional and the C-method, are compared in Table 2. Also listed in this table are the *local* LFs from other independent studies, converted to the same scale as explained in Szokoly et al (1998). All the estimates here are corrected to $H_0 = 50$ Km/sec/Mpc and $q_0 = 0.5$. It is clear that, at a given α, the M_K^* values from different methods are in close agreement. However, the space density of local galaxies (ϕ^*) in the present sample is slightly smaller than others (~ 1.5).

Compared to a similar study by Gardner et al (1997), the LF found here has a steeper faint-end slope (Figure 4) while the two LFs are in close agreement at the bright-end. This result is currently being investigated by measuring redshifts for the fainter galaxies in our sample.

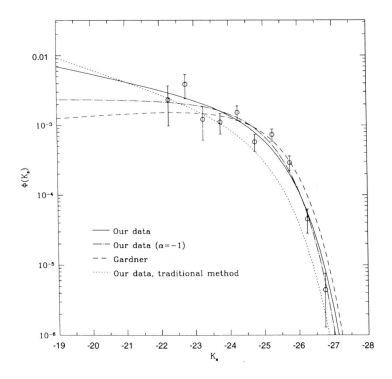

Figure 4. Differential luminosity function from the C-method (open circles) is compared with the fits to the LFs from the traditional method and Gardner et al (1997)

TABLE 2. Schecter infrared luminosity function parameters

Survey	M_K^*	α	Φ^*	n
This study (C-method)	-25.09	-1.27	0.15×10^{-2}	110
This study (conventional method)	-24.94	-1.42	0.95×10^{-3}	110
This study $\alpha = -1$	-24.84	-1	0.15×10^{-2}	110
Gardner et al 1997	-24.87	-1.03	0.22×10^{-2}	532
Glazebrook et al 1995	-24.55	-1.04	0.33×10^{-2}	98
Mobasher et al 1993	-24.88	-1	0.14×10^{-2}	95

5. Discussion

The local near-infrared surveys discussed in this article provide reliable control samples for both DENIS and 2MASS. Also, the near-ir LFs here provide estimates of the space density of galaxies in the local Universe expected from these surveys.

The steep faint-end slope of the local infrared LF, if confirmed, will have important implications towards constraining the models for formation of nearby, low-luminosity field galaxies (ie. the mergers scenarios). This is because the infrared LF is mainly sensitive to the mass function and not the star formation (i.e. young population) in galaxies. Also, this implies the existence of a large population of evolved, metal rich galaxies in the local Universe. The colour distribution of the K-selected surveys shows that the faint blue galaxies start to contribute to the galaxy counts at about $K \sim 18$ mag. (Gardner et al 1995). Such near-infrared surveys will then reveal if the faint blue galaxies have an underlying population of old stars. The surveys selected in the K-band are mainly dominated by normal massive galaxies. Therefore, the characteristic magnitude (M_K^*) found for the IRLF here implies that the very red galaxies with $M_K \sim -27$ mag. (Egami et al 1996) have a space density of $\leq 5 \times 10^{-5}$ Mpc^{-3} and hence, are not likely to be local objects $(z < 0.4)$.

References

Cowie, L. L., Songaila, A., Hu, E. M., Cohen, J. G. 1996, Astron.J. 112, 839

Djorgovski, S. et al. 1995, Ap.J., 438, L13

Efstathiou, G.; Ellis, R. S.; Peterson, B. A. 1988, MNRAS, 232, 431

Egami, E.; Hu, E; Cowie, L.L 1996 Ap.J. 112, 73

Gardner, J. P., Sharples, R. M., Carrasco, B. E., Frenk, C. S. 1997, Ap.JL 480, L99

Glazebrook, K., Peacock, J. A., Collins, C. A. and Miller, L. 1994, MNRAS 266, 65

Huang, J. S., Cowie, L. L., Gardner, J. P., Hu, E. M., Songaila, A., Wainscoat, R. J., 1997, Ap.J. 476, 12

Lynden–Bell, D., 1971, MNRAS, 155, 95

Mobasher, B., Ellis, R. S. and Sharples, R. M. 1986, MNRAS 223, 11

McLeod, B.A., Bernstein, G.M. Reike,M.J., Tollestrup,E.V. & Fazio, G.G. 1995. Ap.JS 96, 117

Moustakas, L.,A., Davies, M., Graham,J.R., Silk,J., Peterson,B.A. & Yoshii, Y. 1997, Ap.J. 475, 44

Sandage, A., Tammann, G.A., & Yahil, A., 1979, Ap.J. 232, 352.

Saracco,P., Iovino,A.,Garilli,B., Maccagni,D. & Chincarini, G. 1997, AJ. 114, 887

SubbaRao, M.U., Connolly, A.J., Szalay, A.S. & Koo, D. C. AJ. 112, 929

Szokoly, G.P., Subbarao, M. U., Connolly, A.J. & Mobasher, B. 1998, Ap.J. 492 (in press)

DETECTION OF LOW SURFACE BRIGHTNESS GALAXIES IN 2MASS

T. JARRETT
IPAC — Caltech/JPL
Pasadena, CA 91125

Abstract. The study of low surface brightness galaxies (LSB) has become popular in recent years owing to their extreme properties (e.g., mass to light ratio) which make them attractive as the harbingers of the so called "missing" dark (baryonic) matter in the universe. The Two Micron All Sky Survey (2MASS) is expected to detect 1 million galaxies, a fraction of which will be LSB type galaxies. We have carried out a preliminary study of LSB galaxies using near-infrared data acquired with the 2MASS prototype camera. We report the results from a study of the Coma cluster and a field located near the north galactic pole.

1. Introduction

What is a low surface brightness galaxy (LSB)? Historically low surface brightness galaxies are delineated from their more "normal" cousins by their central surface brightness. In general, LSB galaxies have a central surface brightness fainter than 22 - 23 mag per sq. arcsec at B band (cf. Bothun et al. 1991). This loose definition allows a wide variety of objects classified as such, including spirals, ellipticals, dwarf ellipticals (probably the most numerous), dwarf irregulars and in the deepest studies, globular clusters (associated with massive galaxies). Because they are (possibly) abundant in number and their mass to light ratio is large, LSB galaxies may provide enough mass to cluster systems (e.g., Coma) to close or significantly narrow the "missing" dark matter gap. The true nature of these objects remains a mystery, including their stellar population(s), metallicity, star formation efficiency and evolution, and as noted, their overall mass. A number of large-area coverage studies have been carried out to address these issues (to cite just a few: Sandage et al. 1985; Schombert et al. 1992; Impey et al. 1996;

N. Epchtein (ed.),
The Impact of Near-Infrared Sky Surveys on Galactic and Extragalactic Astronomy, 239-246.
© 1998 *Kluwer Academic Publishers. Printed in the Netherlands.*

Bothun et al. 1993; Bernstein et al. 1995; Ulmer et al. 1996; Sprayberry et al. 1996; O'Neil et al. 1997; for a review, see Impey and Bothun 1997).

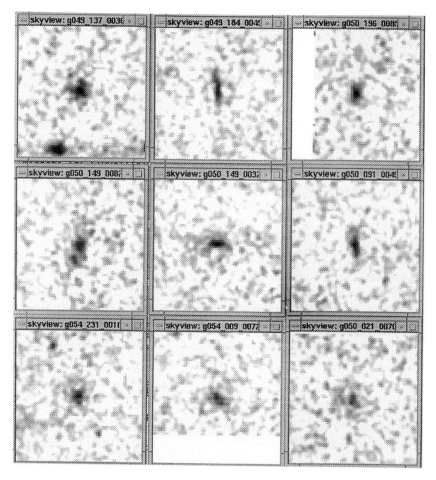

Figure 1.   J-band "postage stamp" images of a representative sample LSB galaxies toward the Coma cluster. The images are about 1 arcmin in width. Integrated mags range from 14 to 15.

Adopting the central surface brightness criteria of 22 mag per sq. arcsec at B as the working definition of an LSB galaxy, we can estimate the surface brightness in the near-infrared using a color of (B-K) = 3 or 4 (B-I ranges from 2 to 3 for LSBs, O'Neil 1997, private comm). Thus, our definition of an LSB galaxy in the near infrared becomes

```
>19.0 - 20.0 mag per arcsec2 at J
>18.5 - 19.5 mag per arcsec2 at H
>18.0 - 19.0 mag per arcsec2 at K
```

The 2MASS survey will cover the entire sky, north and south, at the near-infrared bands of J, H and K, with a limiting J magnitude of about 15.0 for galaxies. 2MASS sacrifices depth for areal coverage, but still should be sensitive to the bright end of the LSB spectrum. For example, the typical sky noise in a 2MASS coadd image is:

```
J:
        1-sigma = 21.2 mag per sq. arcsec
        2-sigma = 20.5 mag per sq. arcsec
    K:
        1-sigma = 19.9 mag per sq. arcsec
        2-sigma = 19.2 mag per sq. arcsec
```

Based on the flux limits of the survey and the typical background noise, 2MASS should be sensitive to LSBs with central surface brightness up to 20 mag per sq. arcsec, or equivalent to a B surface brightness of 23 to 24 mag per sq. arcsec. This corresponds to "bright" LSB galaxies, easily detected in deep photographic and CCD optical limited-coverage surveys now underway, but far from the state of the art (e.g., Rlim $\sim$27, O'Neil et al. 1997). Nevertheless, 2MASS should detect a wealth of LSB type galaxies due to the all sky coverage. This paper provides some preliminary information on what we should expect to see in 2MASS with LSB galaxies using data acquired for the Coma cluster (z=0.023), and the galactic pole region SA 57 .

Questions we address: How many LSB galaxies do we detect? Can these galaxies be well fit by an exponential (thus suggesting a population type)? How do their colors compare with normal galaxies? Outstanding Issues: Are normal or high surface brightness galaxies (HSB) and LSB galaxies distinct populations? Or, are LSB galaxies that 2MASS is likely to detect simply a "faint" extension of the HSB – normal – galaxy population? The latter point does not preclude the importance of LSB galaxies, it simply means that 2MASS may not have the sensitivity to address outstanding issues with regard to LSBs.

2. Data

The data was acquired with the 2MASS prototype camera (single channel mode), during observing runs at KPNO during spring of 1995. Five square degrees, comprising the SA57 region (NGP) and one square degree, centered on the Coma cluster, were examined in detail.

JHK 2MASS scans cover about 1 sq. degree (in 6 degree strips). One scan through Coma contains over 150 galaxies down to J$\sim$15.

The sensitivity and depth of the 2MASS image product is demonstrated in Figure 1, in which we show some J-band examples of LSB galaxies found in the Coma cluster. The integrated J mag for the set ranges from 14 to 15.

3. Central Surface Brightness and Color

The central surface brightness was computed from the center or peak pixel value of the galaxy (for 2MASS, the pixel size is 1 arcsec, but the true resolution is closer to 2 arcsec). Figure 2 shows the central surface brightness vs. integrated mag for LSB galaxies, normal (or HSB) galaxies and for stars. The horizontal dashed lines denote the limit for LSB candidacy, as given by the adopted definition given in section 1. Note that LSB galaxies need only satisfy the limit in at least one band (thus, for example, a galaxy may satisfy the limit in K band, but not in J band).

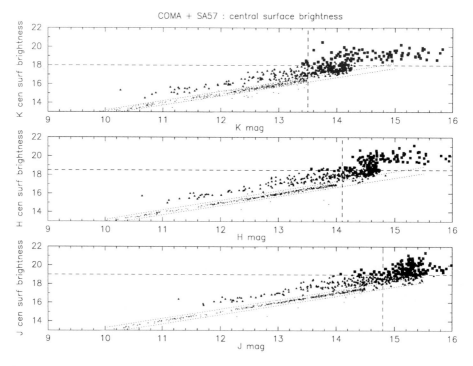

Figure 2. Central surface brightness vs. the integrated flux. LSB galaxies are denoted by the filled squares, HSB galaxies by small triangles and stars by small points. The horizontal dashed lines represent the defined limit for LSBs – they need only satisfy the limit in at least one band. The vertical dashed lines represent the sensitivity (completeness) limit of the 2MASS survey.

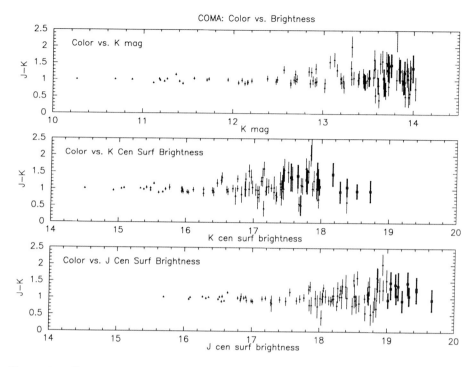

Figure 3.   Color vs. brightness for Coma galaxies: LSBs are denoted by filled square symbols (and thicker error bars) and HSBs by small triangles.

There are a number of LSBs that are situated well above the HSB population, but they tend to be very faint (low SNR) subject to significant distortion from background noise. For the brighter LSB galaxies, the central surface brightness is not significantly different than HSB galaxies with comparable integrated flux (see J band results in particular).

Do LSB galaxies detected in 2MASS form a distinct population? It appears more likely that the Coma+Sa57 LSBs are simply an extension of the HSB or normal galaxy surface brightness curve. Moreover, the colors of LSB galaxies (see Figure 3) are typically about 1.0 in J-K, similar to HSB galaxies – particularly if you take into account the scatter in the color measurement.

We find that the peak intensity over

4. Radial Surface Brightness

An exponential function was fit to the mean surface brightness profile (per band) for each LSB galaxy. For the brighter galaxies in which the elliptical parameters are well determined, the radial profile was constructed from elliptical annuli. For most of the remaining LSB galaxies, the annuli were

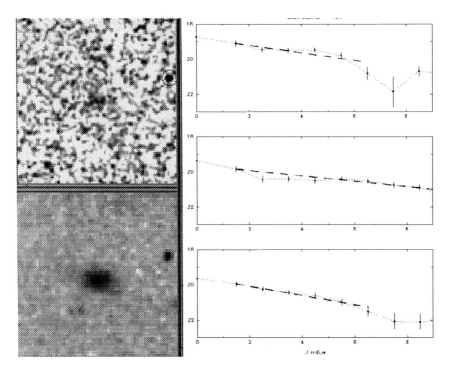

Figure 4. (a) SA57 galaxy as seen in K (upper panel), and optical DSS (lower panel). The integrated J mag is ~14.9. (b) Radial surface brightness. K (top panel), H (middle) and J (lower panel). The dashed lines represent the best fit exponential. The derived scale length is ~5 arcsec.

circular.

The exponential was fit over a range of 2 to 10 arc seconds – comprising most (if not) all of the area that is not lost in the background noise for a typical LSB galaxy. We avoid the inner 2 arc seconds to minimize the effect of the PSF. Only points with >2*sigma values were used in the fit, where sigma represents the uncertainty in the mean surface brightness measurement (poisson statistics). Figure 4 shows a typical LSB galaxy and its radial profile.

The derived scale length for Coma galaxies, Figure 5, ranged from a low of ~1 arcsec (typical of the fainter LSBs – indicative of our lack of sensitivity), corresponding to about 500 pc (assuming $H0 = 75$ km/s/Mpc and DM = 34.9 for Coma) to 10 arcsec for bright LSBs with a very flat profile, corresponding to ~4.6 kpc for Coma galaxies. No redshift data is available for the SA57 galaxies so the distance is unknown. Based on their scale lengths, however, the brighter SA57 galaxies are probably closer than the Coma cluster.

A simple exponential appears to fit the profiles very well in most cases.

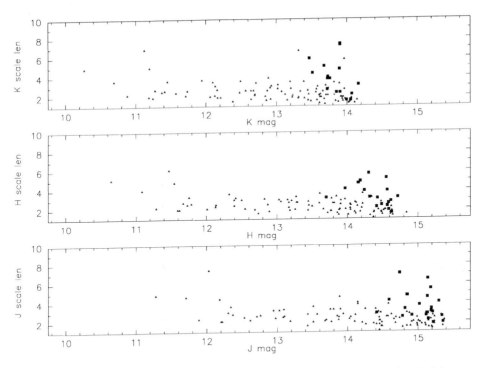

Figure 5. Derived radial profile scale lengths (in arcseconds) for low surface brightness galaxies (large squares) and high surface brightness galaxies (denoted by small triangles).

The results suggest that we are either measuring the "disks" of the LSB galaxies, as opposed to a "spherical" or "bulge" component in which we would expect a profile more similar to a r**1/4 law or at least a departure from a simple exponential , or it may suggest a selection effect: 2MASS is more sensitive to spirals than to dwarf ellipticals. In any case, this result is consistent with that seen in the optical for Coma LSB galaxies (Bernstein et al. 1995).

5. Summary

In this study, we examined fields centered on the Coma and SA57 regions (near the north galactic pole). Nearly 20% of all galaxies detected in 2MASS have a central surface brightness faint enough to be classified as type LSB, but most are in the faintest integrated flux bins (near the sensitivity limit of the study) and thus their true number density is incomplete.

Based on the Coma and SA57 preliminary results, the central surface brightness for LSBs appears to be a faint extension of the normal galaxy surface brightness curve. In addition, the J-K color for the LSB galaxies is undistinguishable from that of HSB galaxies. There is no compelling

evidence here to suggest that LSB galaxies detected at the 2MASS survey limits belong to a different galaxy population. We caution, however, that the LSB sample is too small to draw any definitive conclusions at this time.

Simple exponential functions are well fit to most radial profiles, suggesting that we are either measuring the "disks" of the LSB galaxies, as opposed to a "spherical" or "bulge" component which we would expect profiles departing from simple exponentials, or it reflects a kind of selection effect – LSBs at the bright limit (of the definition threshold) are well fit by exponentials, regardless of their morphology (i.e., we are not sensitive to the bulge/disk differences). In any case, these results are consistent with that seen in the optical for Coma LSB galaxies.

2MASS (and DENIS) should easily detect low surface brightness galaxies in the local group and the brighter population in clusters at least as far as the Coma cluster (z = 0.02). The archive, however, will be far from complete given the sensitivity limits of both all sky surveys.

References

Bernstein, G., Nichol, R., Tyson, J., Ulmer, M., and Wittman, D. 1995, *AJ*, 42, 565.
Bothun, G. *et.al.* 1991, *ApJ*, 376, 404.
Bothun, G. *et.al.* 1993, *AJ*, 106, 530.
Impey, C. *et.al.* 1996, *ApJS* , 105, 209.
Impey, C. and Bothun, G. 1997, *ARAA*, in press.
O'Neil, K., Bothun, G., and Cornell, M. 1997, *AJ* , 113, 1212.
Sandage, A., Binggeli, B. and Tammann, G. 1985, *AJ* , 90, 1759.
Schombert, J. *et.al.* 1992, *AJ* , 103, 1107.
Sprayberry, D. *et.al.* 1996, *ApJ* , 463, 535.
Ulmer, M. *et.al.* 1996, *AJ* , 112, 2517.

2MASS AND THE TULLY-FISHER RELATION

JESSICA L. ROSENBERG

Department of Physics and Astronomy, UMass

1. Introduction

The major advantage of studying galaxies in the near infrared (NIR), is the minimization of dust extinction. The NIR is the region of the stellar emission spectrum which is least affected by both dust emission and extinction. Dust emission becomes more of a factor at longer wavelengths while dust extinction is more significant at shorter ones. The other important advantage of a NIR study is that it probes the bulk of the stellar mass in the galaxies. Since Tully-Fisher (T-F) is a relationship between a galaxy's total stellar content and its rotation speed, minimizing the biases in the measurement of the bulk of the stellar emission provides a significant advantage.

One of the projects that can be carried out with NIR data is determining the peculiar motions of a large number of galaxies. With this information, the derivation of the three dimensional potential and hence the mass density field and the cosmological parameter Ω (Bertschinger *et. al.*, 1990) should be possible. Constraining Ω and studying peculiar motions over the entire sky is one of the core projects for the 2MASS data set.

2. Why Use 2MASS for a Tully-Fisher Study?

One of the 2MASS survey's major advantages over other large T-F studies is sample consistency. 2MASS will provide a uniform sample of galaxies over the entire sky which surpasses the number of sources in all previous catalogs by an order of magnitude. In addition, all of the galaxies observed with 2MASS will also have simultaneous measurements in three NIR bands, J, H, and K. With such a large survey and so many objects to choose from we have the additional advantage that subsamples of the survey will also be large. With the availability of large subsamples, we will be able

N. Epchtein (ed.),
The Impact of Near-Infrared Sky Surveys on Galactic and Extragalactic Astronomy, 247-253.

to apply stringent constraints to the data without harming our sample statistics. There is also a hidden benefit for 2MASS in using the data in a large T-F project; the driving force behind this and the other 2MASS core science projects is database validation. In order to generate a well tested catalog for public consumption, the data must be exercised through careful scientific investigation. A project of this scope requires the use of much of the information generated in the extragalactic database.

One of the most obvious and most basic concerns in any project of this sort is the limitations due to signal-to-noise (S/N). Some of the concerns related to signal-to-noise, such as our ability to measure the disk of the galaxies, will be discussed in later sections. As with any observational project, one has to consider the observational unknowns which include the variability of the point spread function and photometric calibration. These are concerns which will continue to be addressed as the project continues and we obtain more survey data.

Another general concern for any all-sky T-F survey is the effects arising at low Galactic latitude. As we have noted, the NIR minimizes the effects of extinction, but it is still a concern at the lowest Galactic latitudes. In the plane the selection criteria for galaxies is going to be different because of the effect of dust and the fact that we are confusion limited. In particular, more galaxies will be selected at K since it is less affected by extinction than at J which selects most of the objects at high galactic latitude because it is more sensitive.

A more technical concern for the use of the 2MASS survey is how we choose to automate the selection of objects. We have the advantages of a large survey, but with that comes the difficulty of managing the data. We must cull the sample so that we are only analyzing spiral galaxies, since they are the only ones to which the T-F relation applies. We must also eliminate distorted spirals from the data set. Separating morphological types has proved to be a difficult task since it is hard to determine morphology in the NIR. Ideally we would like to have a parameter, or set of parameters, in the database which could be used to distinguish morphological types. To test parameters for this purpose, we have selected a sample of the 2MASS objects and, from the Digitized Sky Survey (DSS) data, have determined the morphology by-eye. It is the by-eye determination which is the only way we have to obtain "truth." It should be noted that even by-eye, using the optical DSS data, it was often difficult to determine a galaxy's morphology. When using this sample, we were not able to find any parameters (we tested many of those in the database, but in this preliminary investigation we did not test them all) which separated out spiral galaxies. If we are not able to find parameters which do distinguish morphological types, we have the option of applying an axis ratio limit to the galaxies used. Since ellipticals do

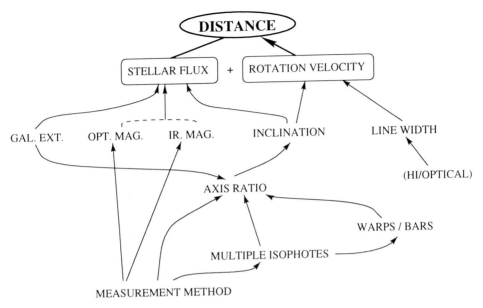

Figure 1. A diagram of the relationship between the parameters which enter into the determination of the T-F distance

not normally have an intrinsic flattening greater than E7, choosing galaxies with axis ratios b/a < 0.3 should guarantee a spiral dominated sample.

3. The Components of the Distance Determination

At the heart of determining mean mass density of the Universe is determining an independent distance to a very large number of galaxies, because individual galaxies may have peculiar motions associated with very localized dynamics, and the accuracy of the T-F method requires large numbers of galaxies in a region to "beat down" the noise. The T-F method to determine a distance requires a stellar flux for a galaxy and its rotation velocity. Figure 1 is a diagram of the interdependence of the various parameters which enter into the derivation of the stellar flux and rotation velocity and hence the distance.

A line width, either optical or HI, is necessary for deriving rotation velocity. The T-F core project will use previously measured line widths and obtain new measurements for galaxies over the entire sky. We have no choice but to obtain additional data in order to determine line widths, but we would prefer to derive the inclination from the existing database. Using optical data would pose the problems of obtaining all of the necessary images, and the impossibility of obtaining those images in the Galactic plane, and potential biases depend on the source of the data.

Deriving an accurate inclination for all of the galaxies is one of the most critical parts of T-F analyses as it feeds into sample selection, rotation velocity determination, and corrections to the stellar flux. We would like to derive the inclination, i, directly from the axis ratio using the standard assumption that the disk has an intrinsic axis ratio (r_o) when seen edge-on so that:

$$cos^2i = \frac{(\frac{b}{a})^2 - r_o{}^2}{1 - r_o{}^2}$$

where we let $r_o = 0.2$. Peletier & Willner (1991) point out that this is not necessarily the best method for the determination of the inclination, but it is the only one for which we have enough information.

The utility of 2MASS data for finding inclinations obviously depends on our ability to measure the disks of spiral galaxies, which in turn translates into a surface brightness sensitivity. One test of the K-band sensitivity is to compare the axis ratios to optical determinations. In particular we must confirm that we are observing far enough out that we are measuring the disk of the galaxy and that we are not dominated by measurements of the bulge. We have compared the axis ratios as derived at the 3-sigma level in the 2MASS images and the Digitized Sky Survey optical images. If 2MASS is measuring the bulge or is not measuring far enough out in the disk we would expect to be biased in our measurements of the axis ratio relative to the optical values growing worse at small values of b/a. Figure 2 shows the comparison between the NIR and optical measurements of the axis ratios. The lines on the plots are 1-1 lines, not fits to the points. Note that the galaxies represented by the open triangles in the NIR axis ratio (J, H, K, and S which is the super co-add or sum of the three bands) versus visual, V, axis ratio plots are within 0.2 magnitudes of the official survey limit or fainter (most are fainter than the limit). For many of these faint objects, the axis ratio cannot be well determined so a value of 1.0 is assigned. Most of the points follow the 1-1 line with some associated scatter. We will be expanding these comparison samples and testing the accuracy of them for T-F distance comparisons as more data are collected.

The axis ratio of a galaxy is a combination of the galaxy's intrinsic shape and its inclination, but it can also be effected by warps, bars, or the presence of star-formation in the galaxy. An additional advantage of K-band that it is less strongly affected by the star formation regions than are optical wavelengths. Figures 3a and 3b demonstrate the variability of the axis ratio at different points in the K-band images of Messier 64 and 66 respectively. These figures demonstrate how we can be affected by our choice of the position at which we measure the axis ratio. For Messier 64 the vertical lines on the plot represent the 3-sigma and 1-sigma isophotes while for Messier 66 they show the position of the rapid change in axis ratio due

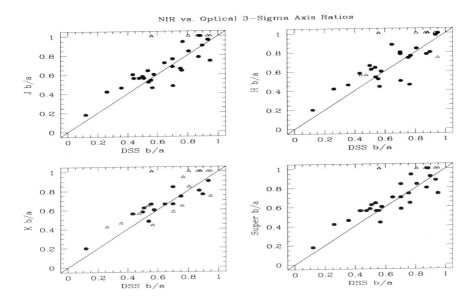

Figure 2. Comparison between NIR and optical measurements of axis ratio determined at the 3-sigma level. The open triangles represent the galaxies whose magnitudes are within 0.2 magnitudes or fainter of the official survey limit. The lines represent the 1-1 relationship between the axis ratios and are not fits to the points.

to the bar, and the 1- and 3-sigma isophotes. The measurement methods need to be studied in detail to determine the most robust axis ratio. We are also testing the use of axis ratio measurements at two separate isophotes for weeding out the warped and irregular objects.

As with determining the axis ratio, we must determine the best way to measure the magnitude for the galaxies. We need to consider whether to use circular magnitudes, which are less biased, or elliptical magnitudes, which are less noisy. In addition, we have to select isophotal magnitudes (and which isophote) extrapolated total magnitudes, or Petrosian magnitudes, or any other type of magnitude. Because of the tight correlation between the T-F parameters, we can invert the relation and minimize the scatter in order to test these magnitudes (Fouqué *et. al.*, 1990).

4. Preliminary Results

We have plunged ahead to make a first stab at testing the 2MASS data using the T-F relation in Hercules. The first caveat is that this was done using prototype camera data. We think that the improvements in the survey camera will improve the data quality and hence these measurements. In addition, all available HI data were used to determine line widths; there

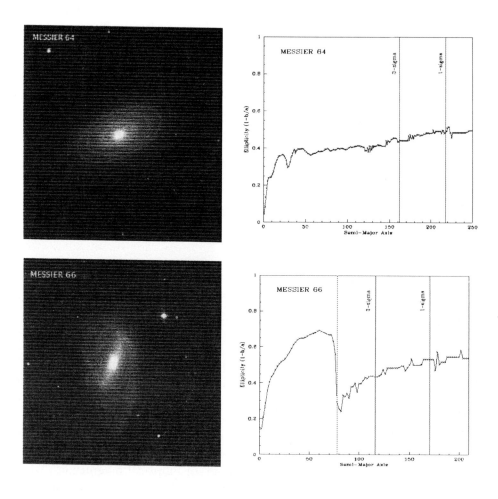

Figure 3.   K-band images and the corresponding plots of ellipticity as a function of
position on the semi-major axiw. For M64 we show the axis ratio at the 1- and 3- sigma
isophotes. For M66 we show the axis ratio as it changes near the bar as well as the 1-
and 3-sigma isophotes

were not enough galaxies to cull the sample and use only the best measurements. To measure the magnitudes of the galaxies we used the K-band
elliptical measurements. Some discussion has taken place about whether

it is better to use circular or elliptical measurements (Peletier & Willner, 1993; Bothun & Mould, 1987). This magnitude is determined in an aperture which is allowed to grow until the surface brightness in the aperture undergoes and inflection or reaches a predetermined surface brightness cutoff. This is probably not the most robust method for determining the magnitude, but we have not yet tested all of the magnitudes to determine which is best. The relationship between magnitude and the logarithm of the rotation velocity for this data showed a lot of scatter because of the difficulties with the data stated above. Even with the scatter, we do find that the data follow a slope of 9.94 with an RMS of 0.19 when one outlier is eliminated, consistent with previous T-F measurements (eg. Kraan-Korteweg *et. al.*, 1988; Aaronson *et. al.*, 1980; Malhorta *et. al.*, 1996).

5. Summary and Conclusions

There is still much work to be done regarding the testing of the 2MASS parameters for use in the T-F relation. The testing will provide us with the best possible parameters to use for determining distances while also exercising the database. In the end we will improve upon the T-F relation described above and use the result to study peculiar velocities over the entire sky. The result of the mapping will be a better understanding of the large-scale flows in the local Universe, a measurement of the mean mass density, and an improved 2MASS dataset.

References

Aaronson, M., Mould, J., and Huchra, J. 1980, ApJ, **237**, 655

Bertschinger, E., Dekel, A., Faber, S. M., Dressler, A., & Burstein, D. 1990, ApJ, **264**, 370

Bothun, G. D., Mould, J. R. 1987, ApJ, **313**, 629

Fouqué, P., Bottinelli, L., Gouguenheim, L., & Paturel, G., 1990 ApJ, **349**, 1

Kraan-Korteweg, R. C., Cameron, L. M., Tammann, G. A. 1988, ApJ, **331**, 620

Malhorta, S., Spergel, D. N., Rhoads, J. E., Li, Jing 1996, ApJ, **473**, 687

Peletier, R. F. & Willner, S. P. 1991, ApJ, **382**, 382

Peletier, R. F. & Willner, S. P. 1993, ApJ, **418**, 626

QSOS IN THE 2 MICRON ALL-SKY SURVEY

ROC CUTRI, B.O., NELSON, C.J. LONSDALE
Infrared Processing and Analysis Center/JPL Pasadena, USA

AND

H.E. SMITH
Center for Astrophysics and Space Science, UCSD

Abstract. The Two Micron All-Sky Survey (2MASS) will detect QSOs. For example, all of the PG QSOs will be detected by 2MASS in J, H and K_s at a $SNR > 10$. During prototyping observations for 2MASS, 40 QSOs with redshifts in the range $0.1 < z < 3.1$ were serendipitously detected in at least one of the survey bands. Thus, 2MASS will produce a highly uniform set of near infrared photometry for a wide variety radio, optical, ultraviolet and X–ray detected QSOs. 2MASS also has the potential to reveal large numbers of previously unknown AGN. Because QSOs occupy distinct regions of near infrared and infrared-optical color space, it will be possible to carry out highly efficient automated searches of the 2MASS databases in combination with newly available digitized optical sky survey databases for candidates. We review the near IR and optical/IR properties of "conventional" QSOs from UV and optical samples, and estimate the number that will be detected by 2MASS. At minimum, it should be possible to find the southern hemisphere equivalents of the UV-excess PG QSOs (≈ 100 new QSOs in the area $b < 30$ *deg*. There is growing evidence for the existence of a significant population of highly reddened QSOs from IRAS and radio–based surveys (*e.g. Low et al. 1988, ApJ, 327, L41; Webster et al. 1995, Nature, 375, 469; Gregg et al. 1996, AJ, 112, 407*). The infrared and radio surveys suggest that UV–selected searches for QSOs, such as the PG-survey, underestimate by factors of 2-5 the space density of even nearby QSOs. Thus, 2MASS may reveal between several hundred and several thousand new, red QSOs. We discuss 2MASS's ability to test for such new populations of QSOs based on a variety of models of their space density and luminosity function. Finally, we discuss preliminary infrared/infrared-optical color searches and spectroscopic follow-up of new QSO candidates drawn from the 2MASS Prototype Camera database.

N. Epchtein (ed.),
The Impact of Near-Infrared Sky Surveys on Galactic and Extragalactic Astronomy, 255.
© 1998 *Kluwer Academic Publishers. Printed in the Netherlands.*

THE FIRST-VLA SURVEY:

The First 5000 Square Degrees

R. BECKER

University of California-Davis, and IGPP/LLNL, USA

Abstract.

The VLA FIRST survey now encompasses 5000 sq. deg., mostly in the north Galactic Cap. The First survey generates images of the sky at 1400 MHz with a sensitivity to point sources down to 1 mJy with positions accurate to 1 arcsec (90% confidence). The survey finds approximately 85 discrete sources per sq. degree. Detailed information about the FIRST survey can be obtained at http://sundog.stsci.edu. At the level of the POSS 1, 15% of FIRST sources have optical counterparts. While these are primarily galaxies, there are significant numbers of quasars and stars detected in the survey. This presentation will highlight some of the research being pursued by the FIRST science team.

N. Epchtein (ed.),
The Impact of Near-Infrared Sky Surveys on Galactic and Extragalactic Astronomy, 257.
© *1998 Kluwer Academic Publishers. Printed in the Netherlands.*

FIRST-VLA RADIOSOURCES IN ELAIS AREAS

E. A. GONZÁLEZ–SOLARES AND I. PÉREZ-FOURNON
Instituto de Astrofísica de Canarias
C/ Via Lactea
38200 La Laguna
Tenerife, Spain

AND

ELAIS COLLABORATION

Abstract. ELAIS (*European Large Area ISO Survey*) is a project that has carried out a deep wide angle survey with ISO at 7, 15 and 90 μm over an area of $\sim$13 square degrees of high latitude sky. The value of the ELAIS survey will be enhanced by carrying photometry at 7 wavelengths on $\sim$300 sources at 4.5, 6.7, 7.8, 15, 25, 50, 90, 135 and 180 microns. We present a cross-correlation of the ELAIS sources and the FIRST-VLA radio sources in the CAM test survey area.

1. Introduction

The Infrared Astronomical Satellite (IRAS) had enormous success arising principally from its survey products (particularly the Point Source Catalog and the Faint Source Catalog). Perhaps most significant was the discovery of a whole new class of objects with enormously high far infrared luminosity [notably F10214+4724 (Rowan–Robinson *et al.*, 1991a) and P09104+4109 (Kleinmann *et al.*, 1988)]. As well as discovering new objects, IRAS demonstrated the benefit of selecting objects in the far infrared. This wave band is not sensitive to dust obscuration which biases optically selected samples. The emission arises from thermally heated dust and thus complements studies of emission directly from starlight, gas or AGN engines.

The Infrared Space Observatory (ISO) is the successor to IRAS and is providing unparalled observations in the mid and far infrared. The sensitivity of ISO is orders of magnitude better than IRAS.

N. Epchtein (ed.),
The Impact of Near-Infrared Sky Surveys on Galactic and Extragalactic Astronomy, 259-263.
© *1998 Kluwer Academic Publishers. Printed in the Netherlands.*

2. ELAIS survey

The European Large Area ISO Survey (ELAIS) is a project that has now surveyed ∼13 square degrees of the sky at 15 and 90 μm and ∼7 square degrees at 6.7μm with the Infrared Space Observatory (ISO). ISO photometry will be carried out on around 300 sources.

The ELAIS survey areas have been carefully selected to be at high galactic latitude and also in regions of the lowest dust column density and cirrus emission. The survey regions consist of 4 regions ∼ 2° × 2° and 6 smaller regions 20′ × 20′ in extent (see table 1).

The choice of where to distribute these areas on the sky was governed by a number of factors. Firstly we decided not to group these all in a single contiguous region of the sky. Had we done so, we may have difficulty distinguishing evolutionary effects from local large scale structures. Cirrus confusion is a particular problem, so we selected regions with low IRAS 100 μm intensities using the maps of (Rowan–Robinson et al., 1991b). To avoid conflict with other ISO observations we further restricted ourselves to regions of high visibility over the mission lifetime (> 25%). To avoid high zodiacal backgrounds we only selected regions with high ecliptic latitudes ($|\beta| > 40°$). Finally it was essential to avoid saturation of the CAM detectors so we had to avoid any bright IRAS source.

At our survey limit ∼ 50 mJy at 90 μm, ISO may be confusion limited by galaxies and galactic cirrus emission and hence our survey will be the deepest far infrared survey possible with the ISO satellite. The 15 μm survey shall reach a 5 sigma sensitivity of 2 mJy. The survey is detecting objects 5-10 times fainter than IRAS in the 50-100 μm range and 20-50 times fainter than IRAS in the 10-20 μm range.

2.1. ELAIS SCIENTIFIC AIMS

While it is impossible to predict all the scientific benefits of such a large project, below is outlined some of the key issues that we hope to address. A major theme is the detection of high redshift galaxies, the derivation of the star formation history of the Universe between now and a redshift 1 and the compilation of unbiased samples of active galaxies.

2.1.1. *Epoch of Galaxy Formation*

Ly-alpha searches have failed to find the epoch of galaxy formation. If elliptical galaxies underwent an intense period of star formation accompanied by prodigious quantities of dust they may be undetectable in the optical but detectable in the far infrared

2.1.2. *Star Formation in Spiral Galaxies at High Redshift*

The main extra-galactic population detected by IRAS was galaxies with high rates of star formation. The far infrared emission arises from dust heated by young stellar populations. The sensitivity of ISO will allow us to detect these objects at much higher redshifts and thus abtain greater understanding of the cosmological evolution of star formation.

2.1.3. *Ultra and Hyper-Luminous IR Galaxies at high redshift*

IRAS uncovered a population with enormous far infrared luminosities. Exploration of these objects at higher redshift will have particular significance for models of AGN/galaxy evolution.

2.1.4. *Emission from dusty tori around AGN*

Unified models of AGN suggest that the central engine is surrounded by a dusty torus. Optical properties are then dependent on the inclination angle of this torus. The far infrared emission from the torus will be less sensitive to the viewing angle. The far infrared properties of these will place important constraints on unification schemes.

2.1.5. *Dust in normal Galaxies to Cosmological Distances*

Faint optical redshift surveys find surprisingly few galaxies beyond z=1. One possible explanation for this is a dust fraction that increases with z. Emission from the cool interstellar 'cirrus' dust in normal galaxies will be detectable in our survey to much grater distances than were accesible with IRAS, so we will be able to examine the dust content to higher z.

2.1.6. *Circumstellar Dust Emission from Galactic Halo Stars*

The deep stellar number counts provided by this survey will be relatively unaffected by Galactic extinction and may provide improved estimates of the halo/disk population ratios.

2.1.7. *New classes of objects*

F10214 was discovered at the limit of the IRAS capability and it is reasonable to hope that equally unexpected and exciting objects will be discovered at the limits of this survey.

2.1.8. *Clustering Properties*

The volume of this survey is comparable to that surveyed by the entire IRAS Point Source Catalog. The median redshift will be much higher. We will thus be in a position to examine the evolution of clustering strength, giving perhaps the most direct test of gravitational instability picture of structure formation.

TABLE 1. Summary of Areas. The first four areas comprise the main survey made up from $40' \times 40'$ rasters. One raster in N3 will be repeated. The final 6 areas are single smaller rasters $20' \times 20'$

Area	Rasters	Nominal Coordinates J2000		$\langle I_{100} \rangle$ /MJysr^{-1}	Visibility /%	β
N1	3×3	$16^h 08^m 44^s$	$+56°26'30''$	1.2	98.0	73
N2	4×2	$16^h 39^m 34^s$	$+41°15'34''$	1.1	58.7	62
N3	3×3	$14^h 28^m 26^s$	$+32°25'13''$	0.9	26.9	45
S1	4×3	$00^h 38^m 24^s$	$-43°32'02''$	1.1	32.4	-43
Lock. 3	1	$13^h 34^m 36^s$	$+37°54'36''$	0.9	17.3	44
Sculptor	1	$00^h 22^m 48^s$	$-30°06'30''$	1.3	27.5	-30
TX1436	1	$14^h 36^m 43^s$	$+15°44'13''$	1.7	22.2	29
4C24.28	1	$13^h 48^m 15^s$	$+24°15'50''$	1.4	16.8	33
VLA 8	1	$17^h 14^m 14^s$	$+50°15'24''$	2.0	99.8	73
Phoenix	1	$01^h 13^m 13^s$	$-45°14'07''$	1.4		36

3. Needs for radio data

The spatial resolution of ISO is insufficient to unambiguously identify many of the faintest ISO sources. Even at 15 μm, the survey resolution is $\sim 10''$ and at 90 μm it is $\sim 2'$ so there will be multiple optical counterparts within each error ellipse. Complementary radio data will play a crucial role in identifying many of the most interesting objects.

In addition, combining deep radio and optical data with the ISO survey fluxes will provide information on the trivariate IR-radio-optical luminosity function and its evolution and the contribution of starburst galaxies to the sub-mJy radio source counts. The ratio of the FIR emission and radio emission will also allow us to investigate the physical origin and spatial distribution of the energy sources in the detected objects in the same way that the VLA maps have been central to our understanding of the origin of IRAS sources.

We expect that most of the ISO sources will be detected at the 0.1-0.5 mJy level at 20 cm. The physical basis for this is the well established FIR/radio correlation (Helou et al., 1985).

3.1. THE FIRST SURVEY

The VLA FIRST (*Faint Image of the Radio Sky at Twenty-cm*) survey is a survey of the sky obtained with the VLA at a wavelength of 20 cm. Images are produced with 1.8″ a typical rms of 0.15 mJy and a resolution of 5″

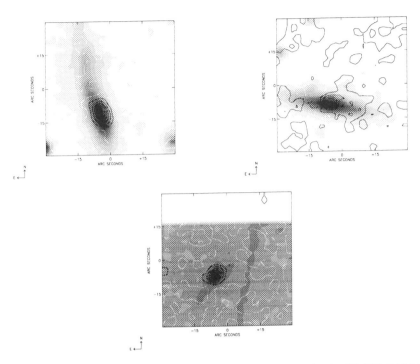

Figure 1. FIRST radio sources with 15μm counterpart in the ELAIS CAM test region. Radio contours are plotted over an optical DSS image.

(Becker *et al.*, 1994).

The ELAIS test region is a $43' \times 43'$ area in N2 centered on $\alpha(2000) = 16\ 35\ 45$, $\delta(2000) = +41\ 06\ 00$. This region was the first one observed with CAM and the first one to be analyzed.

The ISO data at 15 μm of the CAM test region has 53 sources detected with a nominal reliability of 95% and a flux limit 0.5 mJy. There are 94 FIRST radio sources in ELAIS CAM test raster, 20 of them are point-like and 74 extended. Only 3 of them are also detected at $15\mu m$ (2 are known IRAS galaxies). Figure 1 shows optical images of these 3 sources with radio contours from FIRST.

References

Becker, R.H. *et al.*, 1994, ApJ, **450**, 559
Helou *et al.*, 1985, ApJ, **298**, L7-L11
Kleinmann *el al.*, 1988, ApJ, **328**, 161
Rowan–Robinson *et al.*, 1991a, Nature, **351**, 719–721
Rowan–Robinson *et al.*, 1991b, Mon. Not. R. Astron. Soc., **249**, 729–741

VI- Miscellaneous

THE SOM-FITTING METHOD

E. BERTIN

Sterrewacht Leiden
(presently at ESO-Garching, Germany)

Abstract. We present a new astronomical image analysis method based on Self-Organizing Maps (SOMs). The SOM-fitting method allows one to perform accurate photometry, astrometry and classification using a morphologically-ordered set of codebook image patterns. The prototype software and some preliminary results on DeNIS simulations and real survey images are presented.

1. Introduction

Profile-fitting has proven to be one of the most accurate methods for deriving astrometrical and photometrical measurements of sources in astronomical images. When the Point Spread Function (PSF) can be considered as constant, it is fairly easy to apply profile-fitting to stellar fields. Comparison with the PSF can also provide an efficient star/galaxy classification.

Unfortunately, in large, ground-based imaging surveys one often has to deal with a PSF that is strongly variable with time and position. Variations with time may originate from changes in the seeing and/or uncompensated mechanical flexures. Variations with position, due to imperfect optics, are very common on large-field instruments. Among other aberrations, coma is then generally most obvious to the eye. Figure 1 shows two samples of the DeNIS instrumental PSF from the same K-band image. How shall we handle such sources?

In all DeNIS bands, aperture-magnitude growth curves prove to be stable (at the 1% level) for radii $\gtrsim 5$". Such aperture magnitudes can therefore be used to normalize the PSF, but will not be optimum for measuring directly faint stars (contribution of the background noise) or in crowded fields (contamination by neighbours). On the other hand, fitting with an inadequate profile yields significant photometric biases: up to $\approx 10-20\%$ for the DeNIS PSF variations. These biases are not easy to handle, as they may not

267

N. Epchtein (ed.),
The Impact of Near-Infrared Sky Surveys on Galactic and Extragalactic Astronomy, 267-276.
© 1998 *Kluwer Academic Publishers. Printed in the Netherlands.*

Figure 1.   Left: a star near the center of a DeNIS K frame. Right: in a frame's corner.

only depend on the position of the source in the image, but also on its flux (the pixel-to-pixel ratios of appropriate weights are a function of the flux in the régime of the DeNIS image noise model). In addition, star/galaxy separation needs proper modeling of the PSF (see Mamon, these proceedings), which encourages us to search for a global method for representing the shapes of sources as they appear throughout the images.

2. General concept

Looking at any astronomical image, it is obvious that detections — to a certain degree of precision — come in a fairly limited number of shapes. Let's suppose that we find suitable prototypes for representing most of these objects. We may sort these prototypes in some low-dimensional space in such a way that we can locally interpolate them to give a "fair" representation of most sources that we may encounter in our image (or set of images). We might then assign to any detected and catalogued source a "feature vector" that gives the position of the source in this "feature-space". Doing so, we have achieved some kind of lossy image compression by providing a mapping from pixel-space to feature-space. We should then be able to use this low-dimensional feature-map as simply as, for instance, a colour-magnitude diagram, with the possibility to isolate groups of objects that share similar morphologies, study correlation with position, etc.

3. Self-Organizing Maps (SOM)

The Self-Organizing Map algorithm (Kohonen 1987) is precisely intended to provide such a mapping from some input space to a feature space. SOMs, as a neural network model, share similarities with the organization of neural functions found in the brain. I will only describe here the basics of the method and my own modifications done to it. See Kohonen (1997) for more details. Some preliminary attempts of classification of astronomical images with SOMs can be found in Mähönen & Hakala (1995) or Naim *et al.* (1997).

3.1. THE BASIC ALGORITHM

Each prototype i is a node (sometimes called neuron) of a lattice which can be given different topologies; for simplicity we have adopted here (hyper)cubic meshes. Each node is assigned a characteristic vector $\mathbf{m}_i$, initialized to some random direction and module. "Learning" will consist in adjusting iteratively and both competitively and cooperatively these weight vectors so that they converge to a state where they provide a (self-) organized map of prototype vectors for a given set of input data.

Basically, each iteration consists of picking a new input vector $\mathbf{x}$ and computing for each node the Euclidean distance

$$d_i = ||\mathbf{x} - \mathbf{m}_i|| \tag{1}$$

A "winning" node c with the lowest distance d_c is then found and node vectors are updated according to

$$\mathbf{m}_i(t+1) = \mathbf{m}_i(t) + h_{ci}(t).(\mathbf{x} - \mathbf{m_c}), \tag{2}$$

where h_{ci} is a kernel function which specifies the domain around the winning node where the update should be made. A common choice is the gaussian kernel:

$$h_{ci} = \eta(t)e^{-(r_c-r_i)^2/2\sigma^2(t)}, \tag{3}$$

where $\eta(t)$ and $\sigma(t)$ specify, respectively, the learning rate and the kernel width (both decreasing functions of time). Because of the finite range of h_{ci}, "pockets" rapidly emerge in the lattice, where groups of similar patterns can be found. These groups tend to organize their relative positions in such a manner that a large-scale ordering appears. As $\eta(t)$ and $\sigma(t)$ decrease, the system slowly "freezes" in a state where nodes have become faithful prototypes of input patterns. The SOM algorithm indeed tends to minimize the so-called "average distortion measure":

$$\sum_j \sum_i h_{c(j)i}||\mathbf{x_j} - \mathbf{m}_i|| \tag{4}$$

3.2. MODIFICATIONS

For astronomical purposes, several important modifications had to be made to the original SOM algorithm. In particular, handling of *weighted* input vector components was added; and instead of normalizing the *variance* of input vectors (which is done, when possible, to speed-up convergence), we normalize their modulus.

3.3. DIMENSIONS OF THE SOM

Before learning, the number D of dimensions, and the number of nodes along each dimension have to be specified. For the examples shown here $D = 2$ is used, with 5 to 20 nodes per axis. For large practical applications featuring strongly variable PSFs and galaxies, it is better to use $D = 3$. This avoids a "folding" of the map in the input space.

4. Input and output spaces

What information should be put in the input pattern vectors to describe the detections? Although there are many interesting ways of describing a profile (fitted sets of parameters, principal components,...), the current choice is to use directly an array of pixel values centered around each detection. This has many advantages: linearity (no bias when S/N becomes low); weights are easy to assign to each component (bad or saturated pixels for instance get zero weight); any shape can be handled; all the information up to a given scale is kept, etc... The main problems are that: (1) only partial information is available for very extended objects, and (2) the patterns are not shift-invariant, even for well-sampled images. Problem (1) is not critical for the DeNIS sources because the main interest lies in stars and faint galaxies. Problem (2) is bypassed by recentering each detection prior to learning, using sinc-interpolation. Subtraction of a Gaussian core is applied to remove most of the aliased component when dealing with moderately undersampled data (1 pixel < FWHM < 2.3 pixels). After learning, two extra-dimensions are added to the "pure" feature-map, with prototypes regularly resampled over the pixel grid using an appropriate step[1]. Figure 2 shows the content of a typical SOM.

---

[1] Any Gaussian feature can be recovered through linear interpolation, with a maximum fractional error $< \epsilon$, if the step used is smaller than FWHM $\times \sqrt{\epsilon/\ln 2}$.

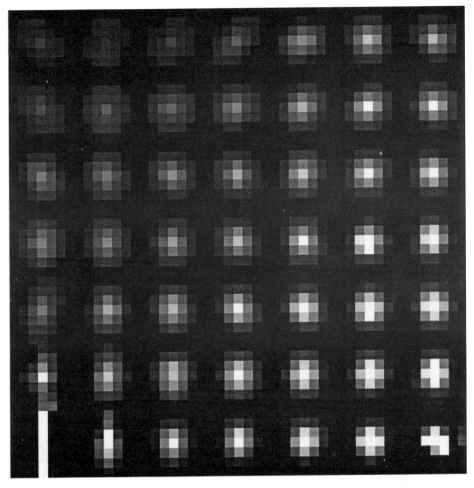

Figure 2. Small 2-dimensional feature-map with 7 × 7 nodes, produced after training on a CCD image. Each prototype vector is represented here in grey levels (logarithmic scale). Note the "cosmic-ray" (lower right) and "bad column" (lower left) prototypes. Galaxy shapes can be found in the upper left part of the array.

5. SOM-fitting

5.1. IMPLEMENTATION

The prototype of a "SOM-fitting" code has been implemented in the SExtractor detection software (Bertin & Arnouts 1996). Once learning is accomplished (on a good workstation this generally takes no more than a few minutes for several thousands of sources), the module containing the m_i is loaded in SExtractor and used to interpret each source detected on the current images. Given a source, one can define its "error landscape" in feature-space: a χ^2 estimator based on expected photon-statistics defines

the intensity of the error as a function of position in feature (+position) space. A typical error landscape, in two feature dimensions, is shown in Fig. 3. As it can be seen, a minimum with a reduced error of ≈ 1 can be found for this object. Currently, the χ^2 minimization is done through a combination of grid-search and conjugate-gradient methods over the linearly-interpolated grid of prototypes.

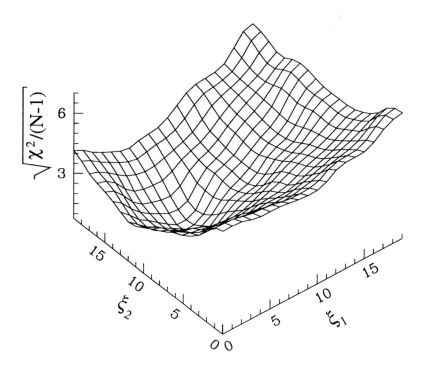

Figure 3. Typical χ^2 error landscape in a simple case. Flux is a free parameter, which explains the "$\chi^2/(N-1)$" label for the vertical axis. The ξ_1 and ξ_2 axes are feature-space coordinates. The two resampling coordinates have been dropped here for clarity.

5.2. CROWDED FIELDS

In I-band DeNIS images where the source density is low, SOM-fitting generally gives reduced errors close to 1, even for fairly bright stars (in the

microscanned J and K channels, this is not so good because of the jitter of the atmospheric PSF between the short sub-exposures). In crowded fields the situation degrades significantly, because of blending. One may therefore occasionally allow for n prototypes to be fitted simultaneously, which implies adjusting n times more parameters. As a first step for the prototype considered here, the program limits itself to two passes through the data, one to remove the best-fitting prototypes; and a second one where each prototype is temporarily added back and the fitting done again. As Fig. 4 shows, this method already yields fairly good results in crowded fields. In the meanwhile, SOM-fitting provides position estimates of prototypes which are much more accurate than usual barycentering: improvements in astrometric precision of about 4× are not uncommon.

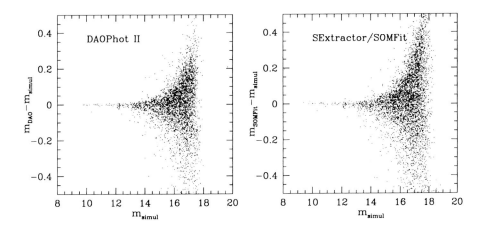

Figure 4. Photometric comparison between DAOphot2's "allframe" and SExtractor's SOMfit prototype on a DeNIS-I band simulated image of a galactic bulge field produced with SkyMaker2[2]. The seeing FWHM is 2 pixels. With the detection parameters set here for DAOphot and SExtractor, the latter detects 30% more stars, mostly on the faint side. Note the trend seen on both plots towards faint magnitudes: it can be explained as an artifact of the cross-identification process with the simulated catalog, due to the strong density of background sources.

5.3. VARIABLE PSFS

From what has been seen so far, the handling of variable PSFs with SOMs should be straightforward. Indeed, as Fig. 5 demonstrates, the SOM-fitting method maps PSF distorsions along the field in a rather efficient way. What is needed now is a mapping from x, y positions (and possibly time t) to

[2] ftp://ftp.iap.fr/pub/from_users/bertin/skymaker/

feature-space. In the current prototype, this is done by adding *explicitely* x, y to the input vector. This has, however, the disadvantage of generating unnecessary prototypes, especially for image zones where the PSF stays stable. Tests are currently underway to find a more general method which would also be able to deal with brutal PSF changes, like those that can be found in coadded images.

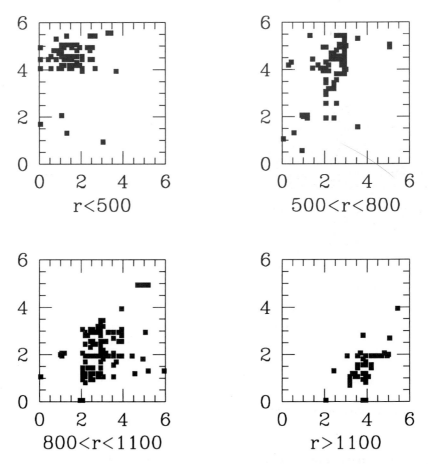

Figure 5. (Two-dimensional) feature-space coordinates of sources extracted in 4 different zones of an image with variable PSF. The image is a simulated DeNIS I-band, crowded, stellar field to which a variable coma aberration component has been added. The purely "atmospheric" FWHM is 1.5 pixels, and the d80 (diameter of the disk within which 80% of the light is enclosed) of the coma component varies radially across the field from 0 (at radius $r = 0$) to 2 pixels ($r = 1500$). Only stars with I< 13 are plotted.

5.4. CLASSIFICATION AND STAR/GALAXY SEPARATION

Figures 6 and 7 show how different kind of objects can be selected in a feature map. It is important to stress that the SOMfitting method is not more than an abstraction tool for classification: all it does is reducing dramatically the dimensionality of pattern vectors. A discriminant analysis is still required to perform the classification itself. A star/galaxy separation method based on SOM-fitting is currently under development. Preliminary tests indicate a net increase in performance in comparison to SExtractor's CLASS_STAR classifier, especially in crowded regions, which is of prime importance for studies of the Zone of Avoidance.

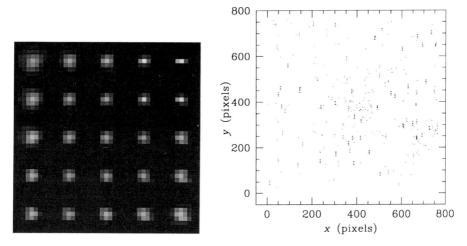

Figure 6. Left: Typical feature map obtained for a DeNIS J-band image. Right: x, y positions, for a full DeNIS strip, of sources that were identified as the upper rightmost prototype in the same feature map. Note the peculiar arrangement of bad pixels, due to microscanning.

6. Conclusion and perspectives

We have shown that SOM-fitting is a promising tool for handling morphological information in imaging surveys. Photometry and astrometry, as well as classification are likely to benefit from this new technique. Work is currently underway to implement it as a module ("SOMfit") in the SExtractor package. Many improvements are still necessary to make the system fully general, though. This includes the handling of large objects. In addition, only shift- and flux-invariances are implemented yet. Rotation and possibly scale invariances would be of great interest for analysing data with a high image quality (isotropic PSF, highly-resolved sources).

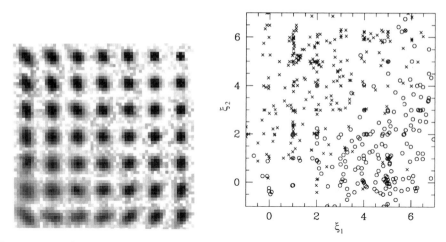

Figure 7. Left: Feature map obtained from a deep NTT image (negative, logarithmic scale). Note the prefered orientation of elongated galaxy prototypes along the diagonals, due to the square shape of the selection-window. Right: position, in the same feature-space, of sources classified with SExtractor's CLASS_STAR parameter as stars (crosses) and galaxies (circles).

Acknowledgments   I would like to thank Pascal Fouqué for interesting discussions and Erik Deul for helpful suggestions made on the manuscript of this paper.

References

Bertin E., Arnouts S. 1996, *A&AS*, **117**, 393
Kohonen T., 1987, *Self-Organization and Associative Memory*, 2nd edition, Springer
Kohonen T., 1997, *Self-Organizing Maps*, 2nd edition, Springer
Mähönen P.H., Hakala P.J., 1995, *ApJ* **L77**, 452
Naim A., Ratnatunga K.U., Griffiths R.E., 1997, *ApJS* **111**, 357

NEAR INFRARED OBSERVATIONS OF ASTEROIDS

TO IMPROVE THE ASTEROID CLASSIFICATIONS.

A. BAUDRAND
Bureau des longitudes, URA CNRS 707, Paris
Observatoire de Paris, Meudon, DESPA

A. BEC-BORSENBERGER
Bureau des longitudes, URA CNRS 707, Paris

A. BARUCCI
Observatoire de Paris, Meudon, DESPA

AND

G. SIMON
Observatoire de Paris, DASGAL

Abstract. In the frame of the Deep Near Infrared southern sky Survey (DENIS), our program is to recover all the asteroids observed during the survey and to determine their I, J and K magnitudes. The aim of our work is to enlarge the asteroid colorimetry data base to the near-infrared in order to improve the knowledge of the compositional structure of the asteroid population.

1. Introduction

Classification allows to investigate the compositional structure of the whole asteroid population. A better knowledge of the chemical composition of asteroids can help in understanding the origin and the evolution of this population. These small bodies contain a large amount of information regarding some of the primordial processes which governed the evolution of the Solar System, immediately after the collapse of the protoplanetary nebula and before the formation of planets. Small differences between objects imply different histories (undisturbed survival, differenciation, collisional fragmentation...). Therefore, each taxonomic unit may record the final stages of one of these histories. It follows that a good model for the evolution of the Solar

277

N. Epchtein (ed.),
The Impact of Near-Infrared Sky Surveys on Galactic and Extragalactic Astronomy, 277-280.
© 1998 *Kluwer Academic Publishers. Printed in the Netherlands.*

System has to take into account, as boundary conditions, the multiplicity of asteroid types and their physical implications.

The recent classifications of asteroids obtained by means of statistical analysis (Tholen 1984, Barucci et al. 1987 and Tedesco et al. 1989) are based essentially on colorimetry over the wavelength range of 0.3 to 1.1 microns and the albedo obtained by IRAS (Tedesco et al. 1992). The asteroids have been grouped according to their spectral characteristics in several classes which are connected to heliocentric distance and compared to meteorites.

Enlarging the asteroid colorimetry data base to the near infrared field will allow to improve the existing classification. Indeed, the infrared colors add new dimensions to the parameter space used, which may lead to refine the distinctions between existing classes or even to recognize new ones.

2. Utilization of DENIS data and first results

At present, 2000 strips (a strip is composed of 180 images of 12'x12') have been observed. The possibility of retrieving asteroids in the strips has been studied. It can be envisaged in two different ways using the DENIS data base called FOURBI, which provides information on the observed areas characterized by their geocentric equatorial coordinates and their epoch of observation:

1) when the position of one given asteroid at a given epoch is known, we search the strips in which observed areas correspond to the calculated one;

2) more generally, we have to determine the asteroids which are in each observed area. For this, we have to create a good interface between asteroid ephemerides and the FOURBI data base.

In this preliminary study, we have considered only the first point and we have obtained the magnitudes of the following asteroids: 253 Mathilde, 423 Diotima, 669 Kypria, 633 Zelima, and 1515 Perrotin, as reported in the Table 1.

TABLE 1. Apparent magnitudes (* beyond DENIS limits)

Asteroid	Epoch	I	J	K
253	96-03-26	14.29 ± 0.02	14.11 ± 0.04	13.54 ± 0.29
423	96-03-27	not observed	11.10 ± 0.03	10.57 ± 0.03
633	96-03-28	14.03 ± 0.03	13.58 ± 0.04	13.13 ± 0.15
669	96-03-26	14.21 ± 0.07	15.01 ± 0.48	*
1515	96-03-29	16.94	*	*

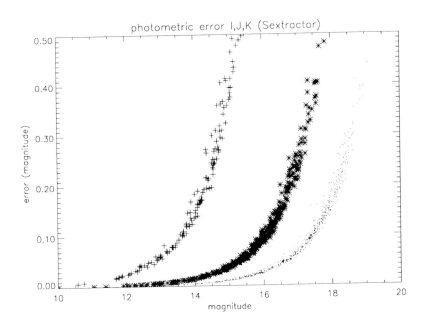

Figure 1. Limits of the three filters with the relative errors. Points, stars, crosses mark the filters I, J and K, respectively.

As it is showed by the Table 1, the apparent magnitude of some observed asteroids will be beyond the DENIS limits. Therefore we will have to select the most favorable period of observations. Figure 1 shows the limits of the three filters with the relative errors.

3. Conclusion

The statistical method of classification that will be used, called the G-mode method (Coradini et al., 1977), allows the user to obtain an automatic classification of the asteroids in spectrally homogeneous groups. The role of infrared colours in separating the various groups has already been studied (Birlan et al., 1996) and the results obtained with IR data are encouraging for continuing the observations in this region.

Up to now, the asteroid investigation in the near infrared is still poor. Therefore, the DENIS survey is a good opportunity to get such information, especially as it offers a large and homogeneous amount of data. Indeed, homogeneity and largeness of the data base used are both crucial qualities for all the statistical classifications.

In this way, the DENIS contribution to the asteroid classifications will be both quantitative and qualitative. On one hand, it will increase the number of asteroids used. On the other hand, the increase of the number of

measured parameters describing the sample will better describe the nature of the studied objects.

References

Barucci M. A., Capria M. T., Coradini A. and Fulchignoni M., 1987, Icarus, 72, 304-324.

Birlan M., Barucci M. A. and Fulchignoni M., 1996, A&A, 305,984-988.

Coradini A., Fulchignoni M., Fanucci O. and Gavrishin A. I., 1977, Comput. Geosci. 3, 85.

Tedesco E., Williams J. G., Matson D. L., Veeder G. J., Gradie J. C. et al., 1989, Astronom. J., 97, 580.

Tedesco E., Veeder G. J., Fowler J. W., Chillemi J. R., 1992, IRAS Minor planets survey-final report, Phillips Laboratory.

Tholen D. J., 1984, Ph. D. Asteroid taxonomy from cluster analysis of photometry, Doctoral thesis, Univ. of Arizona.

INDEX of AUTHORS

282

SCARLET LETTERS

Also by Naomi Segal

THE BANAL OBJECT: Theme and Thematics in Proust, Rilke, Hofmannsthal and Sartre

THE UNINTENDED READER: Feminism and *Manon Lescaut*

NARCISSUS AND ECHO: Women in the French *Récit*

FREUD IN EXILE: Psychoanalysis and its Vicissitudes (*co-editor with Edward Timms*)

THE ADULTERESS'S CHILD: Authorship and Desire in the Nineteenth-Century Novel

Scarlet Letters

Fictions of Adultery
from Antiquity to the 1990s

Nicholas White

Department of French
Royal Holloway, University of London

and

Naomi Segal

Department of French Studies
University of Reading

First published in Great Britain 1997 by
MACMILLAN PRESS LTD
Houndmills, Basingstoke, Hampshire RG21 6XS and London
Companies and representatives throughout the world

A catalogue record for this book is available from the British Library.

ISBN 0–333–65460–9 hardcover
ISBN 0–333–68430–3 paperback

First published in the United States of America 1997 by
ST. MARTIN'S PRESS, INC.,
Scholarly and Reference Division,
175 Fifth Avenue, New York, N.Y. 10010

ISBN 0–312–17307–5

Library of Congress Cataloging-in-Publication Data
Scarlet letters : fictions of adultery from antiquity to the 1990's /
Nicholas White and Naomi Segal.
p.   cm.
Includes bibliographical references and index.
ISBN 0–312–17307–5
1. Adultery in literature.   2. Fiction—History and criticism.
I. White, Nicholas, 1967–   . II. Segal, Naomi.
PN3352.A38S29 1997
809.3'9353—dc21   96–51669
                                                           CIP

This book is printed on paper suitable for recycling and made from fully managed and
sustained forest sources.

10   9   8   7   6   5   4   3   2   1
06   05   04   03   02   01   00   99   98   97

Printed in Great Britain by
The Ipswich Book Company Ltd
Ipswich, Suffolk

This book is dedicated to the memory of Marie Maclean

Contents

Notes on the Contributors

Joan DeJean (University of Pennsylvania, USA), author of *Tender Geographies* (Columbia University Press) and *Fictions of Sappho 1546–1937* (Chicago).

Felicia Gordon (Anglia University, UK), author of *The Integral Feminist: Madeleine Pelletier 1874–1939* (Polity) and *A Preface to the Brontës* (Longman).

Elizabeth Guild (University of Cambridge, UK), author of articles on feminist theory and Renaissance literature, e.g. 'The Abbé de Choisy' in *Romanic Review* (1994).

Mary Hamer (University of Cambridge, UK), author of *Signs of Cleopatra: History, Politics, Representation* (Routledge) and *Trollope's Serial Fiction* (Cambridge University Press).

Sarah Kay (University of Cambridge, UK), author of *Subjectivity in Troubadour Poetry* (Cambridge University Press) and *Framing Medieval Bodies* (Manchester University Press).

Jo Labanyi (University of London, UK), author of *The Politics of the Family in the Spanish Realist Novel* and *Myth and History in the Contemporary Spanish Novel* (Oxford University Press).

Claire Lamont (University of Newcastle, UK), author of many articles and editions, e.g. *Sense and Sensibility*, *Waverley* and *The Heart of Midlothian* (Oxford University Press).

Maria Manuel Lisboa (University of Cambridge, UK), author of *Machado de Assis* (Edwin Mellen) and articles on lusophone literature and critical theory.

Marie Maclean (Monash University, Australia), author of *Narrative as Performance: The Baudelairean Experiment* and *The Name of the Mother: Writing Illegitimacy* (Routledge).

Naomi Segal (University of Reading, UK), author of *Narcissus and Echo* (Manchester University Press) and *The Adulteress's Child* (Polity).

Alison Sinclair (University of Cambridge, UK), author of *The Deceived Husband: a Kleinian Approach to the Literature of Fidelity* (Oxford University Press).

Jonathan Smith (University of Manchester, UK), author of articles on social, ethnic and sexual identities, eg. 'Realism and post-structuralism' in *Italian Studies* (1994).

Nicholas White (University of London, UK), author of editions of *L'Assommoir* (Everyman) and *A Rebours* (Oxford University Press).

D.A. Williams (University of Hull, UK), author of *Les Scénarios de l'Education sentimentale* (Corti) and *The Monster in the Mirror* (Oxford University Press).

Michael Wood (Princeton University, USA), author of *America in the Movies* and *The Prisons of Paradise* (Columbia University Press).

Was I a mere imitator and fool that I needed that *third person* in order to write about the fate of two people who were making life hard for each other? How easily I fell into the trap! I should have known, of course, that this third person who pervades all life and literature, this ghost of a third person, who never existed, does not mean a thing and ought to be denied. He is one of the pretexts of nature, which is always trying to distract people's attention from its deepest secrets. He is the folding-screen behind which a drama is played out. He is the noise at the entrance to the voiceless site of a real conflict. You might say that everyone has simply found it too difficult to speak of the two people who really mattered; the third, precisely because he is so unreal, is the easy part – the part they could all manage. From the very beginning of their plays one can feel their impatience to get on to that third person, they can hardly wait for him. The moment he appears all is well. But how tiresome if he is late, nothing can happen without him, everything halts, hesitates, waits. And what would happen if that was where it stayed, stock-still and blocked? What would you do then, Mr Dramatist, or you, the enlightened public who know all about life, if he just went missing, the popular man-about-town or arrogant youth who fits into every marriage like a master-key? What if the devil took him, for example? Let's just see. All at once the theatres become unnaturally empty; they are bricked up like dangerous holes; only the moths from the edges of the boxes tumble unstoppably through the empty space. Playwrights no longer enjoy their villas in the smart suburbs. All the public Detective Agencies are busy searching far-flung corners of the world for the indispensable one without whom there was no plot.

Rainer Maria Rilke, *The Notebooks of Malte Laurids Brigge*, 1910
(trans. Naomi Segal)

Introduction:
The Present State of Affairs

Nicholas White

Popular interest in the issue of adultery during the 1990s has revolved around the extra-marital transgressions of male politicians in various western countries. These include Conservative scandals in the United Kingdom and the alleged profligacy of Bill Clinton and of François Mitterrand. Nowhere has the powerful mythology of the adulterous child been orchestrated more skilfully than in Mitterrand's arrangements for his own funeral attended by wife, mistress and illegitimate daughter. In the photographs, which were flashed around the world, of these three standing behind the president's coffin we see the classic family portrait reconstructed by the absent father. Mitterrand's immaculate conception of his own mortal end was thus presented as a final moment of candour from the master of self-deification, a moment when that particularly French division of the public realm of politics and the private domain of sexuality could be breached honourably.

As a result of the alleged Jennifer Flowers affair Bill Clinton's desire for the reflected glory of an analogy with John F. Kennedy proved all too appropriate ... or perhaps it didn't. For what is so striking about the allegations is the fact that they preceded his election to the White House, and it is hard to imagine earlier post-war electorates accepting such moral failings on the part of a candidate. Kennedy's sexual notoriety is, obviously, part of an *ex post facto* demythologisation – and remythologisation – of the fallen hero. In the meantime the concept of the family has been subject to sufficient revision to make the sexually reckless presidential candidate plausible (this remythologisation of Kennedy is clearly part of that process of revision). Aware of the relevant stereotype, Hillary, the politician's savvy wife – or rather the savvy politician as wife – appeared on national television claiming not to be 'standing by her man' in Tammy Wynette fashion. This nostalgia for the indestructibility of the couple is, however, precisely the kind of mythology to which she was appealing.

This nostalgia needs, however, to be read in the context of the perpetual transgression of the Seventh Commandment in and by fictional narratives of sexual infidelity. Here at the heart of the Judaeo-Christian tradition, from which the exemplary cases studied in this book are drawn, we find a primary warning against the dangers of adultery. To live within the bounds of this prescription is to live an unnarratably blithe existence. In the famous words of Denis de Rougemont, 'Happy love has no story.'[1] To enter the realm of adultery is, it seems, to move from the biblical genre of the prescriptive dictum, which is morally and rhetorically self-enclosing, to the narratable forms of desire analysed in this volume. This cynicism about a literally indescribable conjugal bliss is no less visible in forms of popular culture. But even though before as well as since the saga of Charles and Diana the instability of the marriage tie is readily recognisable as a tabloid commonplace, the sanctity of marriage retains the status of an ideal to which couples still aspire in vast numbers. Indeed, it could be argued that it is this which is most conspicuous in the context of the social and sexual transformations witnessed in post-war Europe and North America.

The focus of conflict between the idealism of such social practice and the cynicism of cultural forms is most often the wife. Just as she is passed between father and husband in the traditional wedding ceremony, so she is offered up on the dissection table of narrative and passed within the homosocial contract of patriarchal culture between a male author and what might be termed his desired male readers, as opposed to the female readers pathologised in so many classical accounts of adultery. Author and desired reader stand either side of the heroine's dissected corpse like the priest and the pharmacist at the end of *Madame Bovary*, Bournisien and Homais. Such a wife is stereotypically strait-jacketed within the familiar double postulation of purity and sexuality (dis)embodied in the figure of the Virgin Mother. These fictions of adultery may be read as both reactionary and subversive, stressing at once the perceived necessity and the feared implausibility of this dual female role. In contemporary versions of adultery, where husbands take the role of the adulterous spouse, the position of the wife seems at least momentarily to have been refashioned. No longer the feared and desired adulteress, the figure of the wife is reinscribed within the family structure as a good mother and homemaker.

Meanwhile though, there is also evidence of recent reform in society's definitions of the very concepts of fidelity and monogamy. In societies where unwanted pregnancies and births from illegitimate couplings can often be avoided (and the division of sex for pleasure and sex for reproduction thereby asserted), the issue of legitimacy no longer functions in quite the same way as in those nineteenth-century texts which belong to what we have termed the High Age of Adultery. By means of another aspect of sexual technology, sexual legitimacy itself is not the site of uncertainty it once was. In a longer historical perspective, the development of divorce laws in the nineteenth century is important not only because in practical terms it frees unhappy couples and redefines the liberational quality sometimes ascribed to adultery, but also because it signals the fragility of state-sponsored idealism about the indestructibility of the married couple. All of these events determine a cultural shift beyond this High Age of Adultery, but they have to be understood in the context of a modernist culture keen to valorise and not merely pathologise all manner of perversions. It has become clear that fidelity can operate as a parameter within a vast range of contexts, including for instance a long-term unmarried couple. What seems to happen in this case, though, is that the sense of a public institution being violated by adultery is replaced by the contravention of a private contract of trust within the binary unit. There are, moreover, grey areas foregrounded by certain patterns of behaviour: for example, is monogamy a concept which can operate within short-term couplehood? Can you be a 'serial monogamist'? For a year? a month? a night? The transformation of social practices does not merely contradict the normative criteria for ethical behaviour; it also helps to redefine those very criteria. So adultery is not what it once was.

Beyond this, sexual fidelity can also be said to compete with other forms of loyalty – to friends to whom we might feel we owe some of our time but whom we abandon for the intoxication of passion; to children from a previous relationship used (or perhaps just structurally positioned) as a way of not being able to commit oneself fully to a new partner, if commitment is demanded in its more obsessive form as the complete erasure of one's past. In the final section of this book Jonathan Smith's piece 'Dissolving adultery: domesticity and obscenity in *The Game*' introduces readers to a 1994 novel which in spite of its apparently mainstream status within popular culture puts into question our very definitions of adulterous transgression; in the story

of Genevieve we are invited to work through the paradox that 'sexual
fidelity is her offence'.

To understand this present state of affairs it would seem wise to
consider the history of western representations of adultery. *Scarlet
Letters* aims to chart the shifting terms by which dominant cultural
forms in the traditions of English-language and European culture have
depicted sexual infidelity. Ranging from the classical myth of
Amphitryon and a medieval tale of King Arthur to *Fatal Attraction*,
The Piano and *Sommersby* via a multiplicity of literary instances, this
volume of essays draws upon a range of disciplines and provides
analytical 'snapshots' at symptomatic moments in the long history
of the representation of adultery. The scope of this gallery of texts is
itself testament to the ubiquity of such a cultural obsession.

Grouped together these essays serve to highlight particular
confluences of interest, and as a general principle we adopt the
assertion of both Judith Armstrong and Tony Tanner[2] that the
nineteenth-century bourgeois novel represents a moment where
concern about wifely adultery in particular is represented in fiction
in especially conspicuous forms. In the broadest of terms it might be
suggested that the peculiarly frequent and intense occurrence of representations of adultery coincides with the rise of middle-class culture
in much of the western world and precedes the disarming of some
of the patriarchal family's constraining powers. For such a culture,
'1789 And All That' represents not so much an actual moment of origin
within the causal mechanisms of history but rather a symbolic
retrospective focus for western democracy. At one level the analogical
power of the notion of legitimacy is undeniable for a developing
class obsessed with the assertion of its own political authority. Prior
to the logic of analogy though, the family is clearly at the root of social
organisation within the bourgeoisie's conception of the organic
'naturalness' of the sociocultural order it dominates. So at the level
of argument (which from a modern perspective might be said to
conceal the rhetoric of argument or the demon of analogy), threats
to the authority of the *paterfamilias* bespeak a fear of more general
transgressions – and of the bourgeois insecurity that its own notion
of order is the fruit of political transgression. As is revealed by the
contexts and texts from this High Age of Adultery, analysed in the
two central sections of the book, the mentality of a bourgeois regime
borne of the revolutionary transgression of the Old Order is haunted
by a fear of social and sexual transgressions whose origins are
mythically twinned with the advent of modernity.

What needs to be addressed is a conflict between on the one hand the perennial cultural significance of adultery and on the other its historical specificity. Is adultery best viewed in Denis de Rougemont's terms as one of the great universal themes of literature? In which case, are psychoanalytically defined archetypes the most persuasive source of explanation for this cultural obsession? We could argue against this that sexual permutations are bound to colour cultural concerns and that interest in adultery is simply the most palatable case of cultural curiosity about perversion represented in domestic form as an encounter between consenting heterosexual adults. From this perspective it is the variations and transformations in the representation of adultery to which we should pay greatest attention. Clearly arguments over explanations of the cultural predominance of the adultery motif belong to a wider conflict between psychoanalysis and history which is manifestly not resolved by any reductive notion of psychohistory. Readers of this book will find particular emphases in different chapters, not merely as a gesture of eclecticism but as a way of inviting comparisons between methods as well as topics.

The issues of legitimacy (framed psychoanalytically by Freud's 'family romance'[3]) and legality (best mapped as a process of historical change) which underpin Tony Tanner's influential account are shown to have distant echoes in the book's first section, 'Before Modernity'. The motif of the legal trial recurs in Sarah Kay's 'Adultery and Killing in *La Mort le roi Artu*' and Elizabeth Guild's 'Adultery on Trial: Martin Guerre and his Wife, from Judge's Tale to the Screen'. In the medieval text 'Launcelot and the queen are never legally required to defend themselves as adulterers, only as killers. The killings, it seems, function as a displacement of the crime of adultery, and also as a narrative metaphor for it.' As such 'we are offered the trials as metaphors for our inquiry into adultery; and yet they don't lead very far'. The Renaissance account of Jean de Coras, one of the judges presiding at the infamous trial of Martin Guerre's impostor, sees the wife as 'a victim of imposture, therefore an innocent adulteress, and her honour thus preserved (possibly at the cost of "truth")' in contrast with two film versions, *Le Retour de Martin Guerre* and *Sommersby* which 'celebrate her adultery as affirmation of autonomy, authenticity, and desire'.

Joan DeJean and Claire Lamont offer contrasting yet complementary examples of female-authored fictions of transgression. In her account of 'Marriage and the Novel in Crisis in France 1690–1715' DeJean analyses how *'fin-de-siècle* women writers' such as Madame de

Lafayette, the Comtesse de Murat and Anne-Marguerite Du Noyer 'turn the novel into a notoriety trial' by 'show[ing] the grounds on which a woman was proclaimed notorious and the consequences of this verdict'. Lamont argues that 'in creating her female characters Austen is in Wollstonecraft's camp rather than Johnson's [...] Austen's novels offer a woman the chance to be valued for non-sexual virtues.' Maria Bertram's adultery in *Mansfield Park* 'offends against her creator's view of how responsible autonomy in a woman might manifest itself'. In both cases the metaphor of women on trial is reflected in the debates on divorce in France and England. Mr Rushworth unusually procures a divorce, presumably by Act of Parliament. More generally, the debate in France over a century earlier focuses upon the power of the State to grant the dissolution of a marriage no longer viewed as a sacrament but as a contract.

This question of the contractual basis of modern marriage is explored in 'The High Age of Adultery: Contexts' which unpicks the ideological stakes in the nineteenth century's renowned obsession with adultery in the novel. As Tony Williams suggests in 'Patriarchal Ideology and French Fictions of Adultery 1830–57', narratives of the adulterous wife 'provid[e] something of a test-case for theories about the relationship between ideology and literature'. His examples from Balzac, Sand and Flaubert highlight the conspicuous 'latitude' in the relationship between the two. Naomi Segal's 'The Adulteress's Children' goes on to distinguish between, on the one hand, the adulterous mothers of sons who 'stand as they are put, as the channel or seedbed that, once itself transferred from father to husband, carries *le nom du père* from husband to son', and on the other hand, mothers of daughters: 'the very fact of self-reproduction in a mother seems a scandal that can only be read as punishment. Women in male-authored fiction do not have daughters unless they are already transgressive.'

In 'Adultery and the Exchange Economy' Jo Labanyi uses the novels of Galdós to analyse the function of adultery as 'an ambivalent image which presents the newly established capitalist system [in Spain] as a gain in freedom at the expense of commodification', and it is the problematic relationship between women and contract theory which 'exposes the contradictions in the system'. In terms which she borrows from Carole Pateman's *The Sexual Contract*[4] Labanyi asks, 'What is this contract made by women who cannot make contracts?' Felicia Gordon's 'Legitimation and Irony in Tolstoy and Fontane' again foregrounds a broad ideological context by viewing canonical European novels 'in relation to the issue of democratic legitimacy'.

Here female adultery appears as 'an instance of reality breaking through ideology' with ambivalent effects, which can be read 'simultaneously as a construction of legitimation or an ironic undermining of the ethical double standard on which marriage rested'. This concept of ambivalence is developed in Nicholas White's 'Carnal Knowledge in French Naturalist Fiction' which suggests that 'adultery as a literary theme is perhaps always already tired of itself, only too aware of the "decadence" it betrays'. As such 'this kind of self-conscious cultural fatigue characterises a form of the novel which is written in spite of itself'.

'The High Age of Adultery: Texts' pinpoints the precise textual effects generated by three nineteenth-century novelists and addresses questions of textual and sexual identities. In 'No Fairy-tale: the Story of Marriage in Trollope's *He Knew He Was Right*' Mary Hamer analyses the comparison between Louis Trevelyan and a statue of Apollo which stands for purification in the face of an adulterous 'pollution' of masculinity: 'in living with a woman a man's notion of masculinity, his confidence in that male identity he has been brought up in, risks coming under threat'. In Maria Manuel Lisboa's account of 'Machado de Assis and the Beloved Reader: Squatters in the Text' this intertextual nuancing which already 'adulterates' the identity of any single text is exemplified in *Dom Casmurro*, a novel which 'dislocates the Brazilian Positivist moment [by] gesturing [...] backward, to a (now unstable) Realist certainty, and forward, to Modernist uncertainty, to disturbing lost possibilities in Sophocles and Aeschylus, in Genesis and Shakespeare'. In 'The Need for Zeal and the Dangers of Jealousy: Identity and Legitimacy in *La Regenta*' Alison Sinclair uses Klein's account of the three-person relationship characteristic of jealousy to explore the characterisation of Fermín de Pas. 'The problem with these triangles', she concludes, 'is their number, their complexity, and their lack of absolute geometric integrity, since repeatedly there are possible substitutes at different angles. This, added to the degree to which they overlap, will dictate the inaccessibility of desire. As structures to construct or allow desire, triangles in *La Regenta* are decidedly unsafe.'

Such triangular structures located at the heart of traditional tales of adultery have been redefined within the convoluted geometries of modern films and fictions. In the final section on 'Films and Fictions' (which includes Smith's chapter discussed above) Naomi Segal draws a contrast between the 'powerfully negative myth of contemporary

masculinity' in *Fatal Attraction* and the 'equally powerful positive myth of contemporary femininity' in *The Piano*. Whereas the former is 'true to the tradition of adulterous plots' as 'the story of an outsider breaking in and breaking up', the latter 'reverses the triangulation which sees the "third" element as invasive, and presents it instead as a putting out, a means towards the other. Where Beth's daughter was a possession that could be stolen from her, Ada's daughter is an extension of herself that is broken from her.'

What emerges from these analyses is the historically mutable form of triangular structures whose geometry is articulated most eloquently in the psychoanalytical forum. The necessarily ternary patterns of adulterous desires and jealousies have been shown by René Girard's classic study *Deceit, Desire, and the Novel* to have an almost irresistible narratological force.[5] Such narratives are invariably modelled on the indirection of desire which is endemic to both the happy ending of comedy (usually marriage) and the mini-tragedy of oedipal resolution in which we must accept that adult love will always be second-best and that we can never have the one we wanted. Indirection, as Lacan warns us, enters us when we enter language, and the symbolic is that system of systems where every love is adulterous and every sexual feast is inevitably populated with ghosts. This same triangle can be read through a sexual–political argument as in Eve Kosofsky Sedgwick's *Between Men* which explores the homosocial bond of patriarchy which links those male 'rivals', husband and lover.[6] Here the paradoxical identification which same-sex jealousy engenders is shown to be grounded in the ideological solidarity of the group as well as in an individual psychic structure.

Not only do theoretical models of the triangle change; so do the mechanisms of triangulation within particular historical situations (like our definitions of fidelity and monogamy). The classic seducer of nineteenth-century fiction (the 'stranger in the house', or the 'third person' of our epigraph from Rilke) is an invasive force that disrupts the privacy of the bourgeois household. Or put another way, adultery is a wife's way to puncture the private/public divide which defines feminine middle-class roles in the post-revolutionary period in spatial terms, such that a woman cannot be both public and respectable. Rodolphe's seduction of Emma during a riding lesson when he leads her into the woods echoes a medieval model of triangular desire offered by, for example, Beroul's *Tristan et Yseut*, but rather in the manner of an inverted image reflected in the intertextual mirror. For Yseut's domestic realm, the palace, does not represent a private realm

of intimacy but an all too public domain where transgression is vulnerable to prying eyes. The forest to which she and Tristan escape represents an extra-domestic assertion of privacy in keeping with the spatial logic of courtly life as symbolic spectacle, whereas Emma's crime is to act in the only way a woman of her historical moment and social class is permitted to act (that is, privately) beyond the socially sanctioned realm of privacy, the home.

The final section on 'Films and Fictions' opens with Michael Wood's 'No Second Chances: Fiction and Adultery in *Vertigo*', which considers Hitchcock's thriller as the study of a man 'in love with his own reinvention of another man's wife'. In a dizzying play of identities and simulacra, adultery becomes 'something like the fiction of the fiction, that [Scottie] was in love not only with another man's wife, but with another man's invention'. It is perhaps in such an assertion of the 'meta' quality of the adulterous motif that we circle most closely around a convincing explanation of narrative's enduring desire for and love of adultery. As Wood suggests, 'the cinema itself seems to be talking to us' through *Vertigo* and 'it says not that there are only fictions but that fictions are often what we need, that there is a place where secondariness is home'.

The history of cultural representations may well be the second home of those who explore the secret history of private life, and a history of the representations of adultery has a particular vitality because adultery enjoys a doubly enigmatic status. In terms of individual experience, on the one hand, adultery may be understood as an enigma to be resolved or concealed, depending on one's position within the cognitive triangle of dramatic irony. The victim of adultery is, in the first instance, usually a victim of ignorance too, whereas lovers share the knowledge of a sexual secret. In this sense we might say that the pleasures of *connaître* equate to the power of *savoir*. As such, adultery hides its face as one of the most private moments in any history of intimacy, whereas marriage is the public face of private life whose official status is articulated in both religious and civil services. So in addition to the enigma of knowledge adultery poses another enigma, this time for the retrospective writing of that private history. We might define this as the enigma of referentiality. We must therefore ask: how is it possible to divine the secret history of a society's desires if not by reference to that society's cultural projections of those desires, however convoluted their modes of referentiality might be? So desire in fiction offers not so much simple historical examples as an exemplary mode of writing history.

This collection opens with a fresh perspective offered in an essay by the late Marie Maclean. 'The Heirs of Amphitryon: Social Fathers and Natural Fathers' elaborates the theory of an Amphitryon complex to which future researchers may well choose to return. This complex explains the 'recurrence, over centuries, of stories and fantasies of parenting a child not one's own flesh and blood but a separate entity'. By 'extend[ing] the triangle from that of sexual desire to that of philo-progenitive desire', Maclean suggests that this narrative of 'borrowed paternity' 'enacts both a deep-laid masculine fear, the uncertainty of biological fatherhood, and an equally deep-laid desire, to father the perfect or miraculous child'. This model of male ambivalence could be applied to the Don Juan figure so central to the adulteress's tale and the contemporary political narratives of adultery, but also to the history of paternity suits which revolves around the much-feared uncertainty of paternity. This uncertainty would presumably be interpreted in a rather less negative light by the male seducer who, of course, has as long a past as the adulteress whom he partners within this unfolding history of heterosexual transgression.

Notes

1   Denis de Rougemont, *L'Amour et l'Occident* (Paris: Plon, 1939), p.2. Unless otherwise stated, translations are my own. According to the original version of this seminal formulation, 'L'amour heureux n'a pas d'histoire.'
2   Judith Armstrong, *The Novel of Adultery* (Basingstoke: Macmillan, 1976); Tony Tanner, *Adultery in the Novel* (Baltimore/London: The Johns Hopkins University Press, 1979).
3   See Sigmund Freud, 'Family Romances', in *The Penguin Freud Library*, 15 vols (Harmondsworth: Penguin, 1991–93), VII: *On Sexuality*, ed. by Angela Richards, pp. 217–25.
4   Carole Pateman, *The Sexual Contract* (Cambridge: Polity, 1988).
5   René Girard, *Deceit, Desire, and the Novel*, trans. by Yvonne Freccero (Baltimore: The Johns Hopkins University Press, 1972). Available in the original as *Mensonge romantique, vérité romanesque* (Paris: Grasset, 1992).
6   Eve Kosofsky Sedgwick, *Between Men* (New York: Columbia University Press, 1985).

Part I
Before Modernity

1

The Heirs of Amphitryon: Social Fathers and Natural Fathers

Marie Maclean

pater semper incertus est, mater sed certissima

When Freud first used the adage which contrasts the uncertainty of fatherhood with the certainty of motherhood, he used it as a basis for the edification of the 'family romance'.[1] In the fantasy of the 'family romance' the young child imagines itself a foundling or bastard in order to lay claim to a more illustrious paternity than nature has provided for it.

The family romance has a special place in Freud's work because it is a fantasy which does not and cannot go back to the experiences of infancy. We can only construct stories of this nature when we are already conscious of the nature of stories. What is more, these are not just anecdotes of everyday life. A child of six becomes, as Freud says, aware of the uncertainty of fatherhood and may have heard stories of local bastards or foundlings. But the attempt to fabricate a more satisfying paternity stems from a more literary source, whether oral or written (as I endeavoured to show in *The Name of the Mother*).[2] It is from the early performances or readings of folktale or myth (the most obvious of which used to be the weekly ration of Christian observance) that the child of six is most likely to have acquired the idea of another and more illustrious paternity. The family romance is often in fact the first fiction of adultery.

It is also the first example of what René Girard calls mimetic desire. If the shepherd boy of folktale can be revealed to be a king's son, then why cannot I? The myth of Heracles, which begins when Zeus decides to find the perfect woman in order to create one last perfect son (Hesiod, cited in Lindberger, 1956:21), can be read in this light; we can all dream of being offspring of Zeus.

'It is human to desire an immortal child'
Giraudoux, *Amphitryon 38*, II,2

Yet there is another less recognised variation which can be given to
the 'family romance'. It is not only children who dream of divine or
royal parents. Parents too may be sadly dissatisfied with the hand
which fate has dealt them. There is a parental fantasy which
complements that of the unhappy child, a fantasy of the perfect
offspring, physically beautiful, mentally a genius, strong and adept,
immortal in fame and repute. Like the child, the parent may be
prepared in imagination to sacrifice biological certainty to the
promptings of desire.

In 1961, in *Mensonge romantique, vérité romanesque*, René Girard
formulated the theory of triangular desire, the notion that the object
of our desire is always something or someone we know to be wanted
by a third person. Girard takes a very bleak, and particularly in the
case of love, a very masculine view of his discovery of mimetic desire.
He starts with the simple case of the man who desperately desires
his best friend's lover or wife, only to lose interest in her the moment
she reciprocates his interest. As he applied it to the novel, and as others
have used his idea, it has come to be associated almost exclusively
with sexual desire: 'I want her because he wants her'. It has been a
theory less universally adopted than the Oedipal story, perhaps
because, unlike Freud, Girard does not allow absolution by the
unconscious. His mimetic desire occurs at the age of responsibility
and can be condemned as based on 'envy, malice and all unchari-
tableness'. Yet we have only to observe the devastating effects of
peer group pressure from a very early age to see the power of Girard's
observations. I should make it clear that I find certain aspects of both
Freud's and Girard's theory both dubious and antipathetic,
particularly their misogyny. Yet this cannot invalidate the force of their
master narratives, especially in their applicability to patriarchal
society. Indeed, it is fascinating to compare the force of two different
patriarchal ideologies meeting head on, as developed by thinkers who
differed in almost every way.

From its base in his work on the novel, Girard gradually develops,
particularly in *A Theater of Envy* (1991), a whole range of mimetic
desires, for sex, for wealth, for power, even for literary success, fuelled
by envy and doomed to disappointment in the very moment they are
fulfilled. To this his only answer seems to be – if a reign of
scapegoating, sacrifice and revenge is to be averted – the religious

doctrine of humility and renunciation. It seems to me that there is another possible outcome, namely that a genuine love can be born even from the seemingly impropitious soil of mimetic fantasy. By inverting the usual terms of the argument, and of the famous nature/nurture debate, in other words by looking at the effects of parental desire not on the child but on the parent, we can perhaps find an alternative outcome to the most unfortunate aspect of Girard's theory, whereby the acquisition of the object of the desire of the other automatically brings an end to that very desire. Centuries of cultural conditioning have produced this deplorable result of a certain form of male vanity, which views the female as trophy. Yet if we extend the triangle from that of sexual desire to that of philoprogenitive desire we see a new pattern emerging, in which the object of desire is not merely icon or trophy, but the potential base of a new triangle, which involves not only power, but love and nurture.

This makes it all the more strange that Girard does not deal with the one human desire which is as deep-seated, yet different, as that for a sexual partner and complement: namely, the desire for a child. This desire has two components, firstly the generally recognised need to reproduce oneself, one's family line, one's blood, but secondly the yearning to produce something better, more perfect than oneself or than the originary biological partners. Offered the choice between your child and a potential Einstein or Mozart, which would you take? It is this second desire of the other which founds certain fantasies of paternity. Just as Girard developed his theory of the desire of the other before Lacan, so he also gave it a religious as well as a purely human dimension. A higher desire than that provided by human mediation is, for the religious mind, provided by divine mediation. Countless shrines festooned with phallic symbols bear witness to this marriage of the human other and the divine Other.

To have a child is to be blessed, but twice blessed if it is also miraculous. In modern days the myth finds a new life in artificial insemination by donor. In a way this enables you to take a ticket in a lottery for a child who may surpass your expectations. There are even those who endeavour to obtain the sperm of Nobel prize winners: the latest version of the divine birth and inversion of the family romance? It is, I think, at least one of the possible readings of the Amphitryon legend. The child, at first desired mimetically as an exemplar of perfection, can then become in due course the object of genuine care and affection for its own sake. The desire of the desire of the Other may

not simply produce humiliation or the momentary satisfaction of the chase. It may also be the basis for a lasting relationship.

In one version of this 'romance' of parenting the adulterine child may be seen as providing not the punishment but the prize.[3] In this study I am not looking at sources, or except in a general way, at intertexuality, but rather at the recurrence, over centuries, of stories and fantasies of parenting a child not one's own flesh and blood but a separate entity. We find, in these narratives, a necessary complement and corrective to the suggestion that the Oedipus Complex is universally applicable. Indeed, one may well ask, whatever happened, in the psychoanalytic version of the story of the tragedy of Thebes, to Periboea and Polybus, the loving 'parents' who raised Oedipus? So the question arises, what would an Amphitryon complex be?

The myth of Heracles is one of the most pervasive and undying of all. As with all great myths its variants are endless and its potential unlimited.[4] But equally enduring, and for less obvious reasons, is the myth of Heracles' social father, Amphitryon. This begins with the story of Heracles' conception and Zeus' impersonation of Amphitryon in order to seduce his faithful bride, Alcmene. In its origin it is not so much a parable of sexual gratification as a myth of parenting. It originates in Zeus' plan to create a hero son, of which his selection of the perfect woman as mother forms only a part. It is complemented by Amphitryon's acceptance of the desire of Zeus, the Other, a desire in this case for a child rather than for mere seduction, as in other of his rapes and liaisons. The will of Zeus fulfils Amphitryon's own, mortal, wish for a divine son. Hence the emphasis in the second part of the myth, often forgotten in comic or modern variants, on Amphitryon as parent and on the upbringing of Heracles.

The myth of Amphitryon was given many different treatments in classical times, although only when it slipped from belonging to a corpus of belief to becoming merely another fiction did it change its focus from the birth of Heracles to the cuckolding of his father. Even in the version of Plautus, which used both the tragic and comic Greek dramatic sources, such as the tragedy of Euripides and the contemporaneous satyr plays,[5] the culmination of the play is the birth of the divine child. The parallel with other miraculous births is still frequently perceived until the mid seventeenth century, after which the emphasis, following Molière, moves to the comic. The enduring appeal of the story is shown by the fact that, when Giraudoux came to write a version in 1929, he called it *Amphitryon 38*, his calculation of the

number of previous versions, though in fact they total nearer 60 (see Passage and Mantinband). They divide roughly into three types: those that emphasise the miraculous birth, those which stress the Zeus/Alcmene relationship, and those which focus on the comedy of errors involved in the doubling of masters and servants.

In his *The Greek Myths*, Robert Graves quotes from 16 different Greek and Roman variants of the story (II:87–8), and these are, of course, merely the written ones (there were hundreds more in the oral tradition). In these recorded variants we can glimpse many different Amphitryons. The very name, according to Graves, means 'harassing on either side', an apt description of fundamental ambiguity. A few of the possible readings of the story include:

He may be seen as a loving husband, unfairly cheated by Zeus, but ready to accept both wife and adulterine child, since his love helps him to believe in Alcmene's innocence.

He may be seen as complicitous in the rape of his wife, in exchange for the chance to add a divine child to his line. Amphitryon is an unusually devoted father. Indeed he is remarkable in the classical myths where attentive parents are the exception rather than the rule, and Graves allots several pages to his fatherly activities.

He may be completely overawed by the divinity of Zeus. In one version of the story, the poor man never gets to sleep with his wife at all. She tells him he must first avenge her brothers, and when he returns successful, only to find that Zeus has taken his place in the marriage bed, he is so terrified of the god's possible jealousy that he does not dare consummate his marriage.[6]

On the other hand, the most common version of the tale has Amphitryon sleep with his wife immediately on his return. No wonder the poor woman complained, after a night on which Zeus had stretched both the time and his sexual prowess over 36 hours (Graves,II:86). The result of these unions, the mortal and immortal, were the twins, Iphicles and Heracles, of whom the bastard Heracles was naturally the stronger and finer.

In one version of the incident in which the infant Heracles strangles two snakes which attack him in his shield/cradle it is Amphitryon himself who introduces the snakes (see Graves, II:91, 93), in order to see which baby is the son of Zeus and which his own. After making sure, he seems to devote himself to the upbringing of the divine child in preference to his own flesh and blood.

It is neither just the story of a divine birth nor that of miraculous impersonation which gives the tale its attraction, but the fact that it

enacts both a deep-laid masculine fear, the uncertainty of biological fatherhood, and an equally deep-laid desire, to father the perfect or miraculous child. The fear, that of 'the hazards of all husbands/ That marry wives' (*King John*, I, i, 119–20), has led, in life as in literature, to tragedy and comedy in equal parts. The ribaldry at the expense of the cuckold is in direct proportion to man's fear at his uncertain control over the name of the father. The comic versions of Amphitryon are all rooted in the depth of this fear, and have tended to preoccupy criticism, even feminist criticism, to the exclusion of the more ancient narrative, that of the drama of parenting.

In both tragic and comic depictions of cuckoldry, adulterine children arouse excesses of passion. Too often the excess is one of hate. But it must be remembered that it may also be one of love. One of the saddest figures in literature is Alexei Karenin, sitting silently, hopelessly and lovingly by the cradle of the baby daughter who is his and yet not his. Caught in the toils of the patriarchal system he must lose either his wife or his child, but in any case his self-esteem.

> Sometimes he would sit gazing for half an hour at a stretch at the downy, wrinkled, tomato-coloured little face of the sleeping baby, watching the frowning forehead and the chubby little hands with their curled-up fingers, rubbing the tiny eyes and nose with the backs of its fists. At such moments especially Karenin felt quite calm and at peace with himself, and saw nothing abnormal in his position, nothing that need be changed.
>
> But as time went on he saw more and more clearly that, however natural his position might appear to him now, he would not be allowed to remain in it. He felt that besides the blessed spiritual force that guided his soul, there was another force, brutal and as powerful, or more powerful, which controlled his life, and that this second force would not allow him the humble peace he longed for. (1971:445)

Tolstoy's Karenin had no chance of defeating the brutal forces of social prejudice and enjoying his unconventional family on his own terms. As social and legal father of the little Anna he does win her in the end, but only at the price of tragedy. Yet his longings point a way. There can be deep fulfilment in fathering the child of another, or even of the transcendent Other, and that is what will preoccupy me here.

**Son, why hast thou thus dealt with us? behold, thy father and I have sought thee sorrowing.
And he said unto them, How is it that ye sought me? wist ye not that I must be about my Father's business?**

Luke III:48–9

It is important to see such stories as part of an even larger corpus, dealing with the birth of the miraculous child, and the frequency of double fathering associated with the tale.[7] Special cases of double fathering are those which pair a divine father and a social father: of these the best known are Zeus and Amphitryon as the fathers of Heracles, and God and Joseph as the fathers of Jesus. Both social fathers accept the divine will. Any doubts about fathering the child of another are assuaged in Amphitryon's case by Zeus himself and in Joseph's by an angel of the Lord (Matthew I:20–1).

However, in both cases the divine child is also inscribed in the genealogy of the social father, Heracles in Amphitryon's descent from Perseus and Niobe,[8] Jesus in that of David. In fact Jesus' inscription in Joseph's family genealogy, the so-called Tree of Jesse (Matthew I), was an important factor in establishing his claim to be the Messiah.[9] The honouring of the social father in myth can be read as recognition of the fact that in most cultures, and unless he takes formal steps to disavow them, the mother's husband is accepted as the father of her children despite any underlying uncertainty. In the bible, as in the Greek myth, the child of the god is given mortal brothers and the human family is lovingly represented.

There exists an extraordinary play dating from the early seventeenth century which makes explicit the parallels between these two stories of the divine birth of a saviour child, the clearing of the name of the virgin mother, and the acceptance of the divine favour by the social father. I quote at some length from Lindberger (1956):

> One of the strangest adaptations of Plautus' *Amphitruo* belongs to this category. It is Johannes Burmeister's *Sacri Mater Virgo*, printed in Lüneburg in 1621. The author was a priest, and it was his ambition to create a 'comedy converted from Plautus to Christ' – as he says in the dedication to Adolph Friedrich, Duke of Mecklenburg.
>
> The basic principle of Burmeister's 'conversion' is that Mary has been substituted for Alcumena and Jesus for Hercules. Jupiter's part has been assumed by the Holy Ghost, Amphitruo's by Joseph. The part of Mercury has been divided among the Arch-Angel Gabriel,

who [...] reads the prologue, and Asmodes, a devil, who executes
the more malevolent tricks.

...

Burmeister has turned Plautus' play into a miracle play about the
virgin birth. Gabriel has announced to Mary that she will be made
with child without any man and give birth to Messiah. But Asmodes
wants that the child to be born will not be believed to be the son
of God, an[d] he therefore tries to arrange for Mary to be suspected
of adultery. Though appearing as Sosia he succeeds in arousing
suspicion in the real Sosia and in Joseph. But Gabriel appears to
Joseph in a dream and relates to him the truth of the matter. Joseph
is reconciled with Mary and with her sets out for Bethlehem. But
Asmodes has not yet given up. He deludes the clergy into believing
that Mary has committed adultery. When a priest arrives at Mary's
home to conduct an investigation, Asmodes has locked the door
and in the shape of Sosia insults the priest. The result is that the
true Sosia is made the object of the priest's anger. However, the child
is born, and after the birth the midwife testifies that Mary is still a
virgin. There follows the chorus of angels and the adoration of the
shepherds. (43–4)

Lindberger points out that, in making this strange transposition,
Burmeister has actually brought the Amphitryon myth closer to its
origin, ending with a point of view somewhere between Hesiod and
the lost tragedy of Euripides (45).

One thing that this naive rendition shows clearly is the difference
between living myth as part of a corpus of faith and the same story
viewed as mere entertainment. The original Amphitryon was given
a noble and worthy reputation similar to that of the Joseph figure,
whose high status in the Christian tradition gives one some clue as
to what the Greek myth might have represented in the days of the
worship of Heracles. One can contrast the unkind ridicule reserved
for Amphitryon in later days with the worship of the nurturing social
father, Joseph, portrayed as both strong and kind in countless iconic
and verbal texts dedicated to the Holy Family.

As Janet Lungstrum (1992) remarks, we have a very unusual
inversion in the Heracles story in which the father is defined in the
name of the son, rather than the son in the name of the father. The
same inversion marks the story of Joseph. Instead of the father
presuming that the son exists to carry on his name into further
generations, in these myths we see the situation reversed. It is the father

who will carry retrospectively the name of the son. Joseph will only be known because he is the 'father' of Jesus, Amphitryon will only be known because he is the 'father' of Heracles.

The cult of myths of miraculous birth and divine adultery follows the patterns of cultural mutations. For example, most prevalent in the Middle Ages were the models of the Arthurian cycle, with its plethora of royal/divine bastards, starting with Arthur himself. In the legends of the birth of Arthur, the Amphitryon figure is split into two parts. Count Gorlois plays the role of the deceived husband whose shape is assumed by Uther Pendragon. His deluded wife, Ygraine, the Alcmene figure, thus conceives the future king and saviour of England.[10] On the other hand, the role of the non-biological nurturing parent is played by the ambivalent figure of Merlin, the celibate, who raises and trains the child for the role he is to assume. We will be looking at other such figures, if less august ones.

With the resurgence of classical myths in the Renaissance the emphasis shifted from the models of the Arthurian cycle back to those of Olympus. Heracles, as adulterine saviour figure and rather ambiguous figure of hyper-virility (see Loraux, 1989), then renewed his role as the authorising figure of bastardy (see *Name*). The myth of the absent royal or divine father and the natural son's relegitimation by extraordinary valour was adopted as inspiration for their life story by such royal bastards as William the Conqueror, Don Juan of Austria (who used the figure of Heracles as his bowsprit at the battle of Lepanto). Such figures then went on, in their turn, to acquire mythical dimensions for future generations.

'Look here upon this picture, and on this;
The counterfeit presentment of two brothers.'
Hamlet, III, iv

When I speak of the heirs of Amphitryon, I am looking not just at the avatars of the figure of the social father but also, quite literally, at the question of inheritance. This includes inheritance in the genetic sense, but also inheritance of property, status and name. The question arises with one of the more intriguing Amphitryon avatars, Sir Robert Faulconbridge, who features in the opening scene of Shakespeare's *King John*.[11] The interest of this variant of the story is that Sir Robert has just died, and what the scene relates is the dispute between his two sons over the inheritance of his name and his property. The Heracles figure, Philip Faulconbridge, is in fact adulterine and the son

of the previous king, Richard Cœur de Lion, who seduced Lady Faulconbridge, having exercised his royal/divine prerogative after sending her husband off to foreign wars. The Iphicles figure, Robert, is the legitimate son, born after his father's return.[12]

It is precisely the question of legitimacy which is foregrounded, and in a very ambiguous way. Although Sir Robert has apparently had a change of heart on his deathbed and bequeathed all his property to the son of his blood, the legal fact remains that, while husband and wife remain married, any adulterine children are treated as legitimate. They have both the rights and the penalties of legitimacy. On the one hand they cannot be excluded from the right to inheritance:

King John:

> Sirrah, your brother is legitimate;
> Your father's wife did after wedlock bear him,
> And if she did play false, the fault was hers;
> Which fault lies on the hazards of all husbands
> That marry wives. Tell me, how if my brother,
> Who, as you say, took pains to get this son,
> Had of your father claim'd this son for his?
>   …
> My brother might not claim him; nor your father,
> Being none of his, refuse him: this concludes;
> My mother's son did get your father's heir;
> Your father's heir must have your father's land.

Robert:

> Shall then my father's will be of no force
> To dispossess that child which is not his?

Bastard:

> Of no more force to dispossess me, sir,
> Than was his will to get me, as I think. (I,i, 116–33)

On the other hand, adulterine children remain subject to the rule of their social father, bear his name and not even their biological father can loosen these social fetters. It is a situation which can be used to the advantage of the social father, as in *Anna Karenina*, to the advantage of the child, as here in *King John*, where Philip cannot be legally disinherited, or even to procure the double advantage of both the real father's prestige and the social father's name and lineage.

In *King John,* Philip the bastard solves his father's posthumous dilemma by opting to delegitimate himself, lose the Faulconbridge manor and fortune, but lay claim to his royal descent. He is promptly rewarded by being relegitimated by his grandmother and his 'cousin' King John and given the title of Sir Richard Plantagenet, but he remains in the play a somewhat less than heroic figure, more brains than brawn. The text cannot escape that ambiguity surrounding bastardy, its whiff of evil, fully developed in Edmund in *King Lear.* The ambivalence remains, even in the Elizabethan context, for Elizabeth herself was declared illegitimate at the age of two and a half, when her mother was beheaded for adultery. While Mary and Elizabeth were named as heirs to the throne in Henry's will, this was not signed, and they were never officially relegitimated (Marcus: 403).[13] Thus authors in Shakespeare's time had to handle the topic with kid gloves, or find they were in danger of casting aspersions on the queen herself.

Shakespeare sets us an interesting conundrum in his Amphitryon figure. We are left to decide why Sir Robert did not repudiate the wife and son he found on his return from the wars. There is, of course, the possibility that he made this choice because he loved his wife and was unwilling to divorce her. This suggestion is given even more validity if we suppose, à la Girard, that wife and child were made more desirable by the desire of the other, and not just any other, but that of the king himself. In the light of the 'divinity which hedge[s] a king', the regal adultery had added lustre both to Sir Robert's conjugal relations and to his family tree.

But there is another factor to be taken into consideration, and it is one which recurs in many of these stories. The adulterine child is the stronger, handsomer and cleverer of the two sons:

Bastard:

> Madam, and if my brother had my shape,
> And I had his, Sir Robert his, like him;
> And if my legs were two such riding-rods,
> My arms such eel-skins stuff'd, my face so thin
> That in mine ear I durst not stick a rose
> Lest men should say, 'Look, where three-farthings goes!'
> And, to his shape, were heir to all this land,
> Would I might never stir from off this place
> I'd give it every foot to have this face: (I,i, 138–67)

This contrast is the common pattern in Heracles/Iphicles pairs, and Philip the bastard is quite deliberately linked to Heracles in the text (II,i, 136–48). So the other choice Sir Robert may have made was that of retaining the more lusty handsome son, even when that son showed his true lineage, 'a trick of Cœur-de-Lion's face' (I,i, 85) in every feature.[14] In fact Sir Robert is an enigma, and like all our Amphitryons, readable in many ways, as 'harassing from both sides'.

'60 francs for my woman guiding humanity, on condition that I changed her into a holy virgin.'[15]

There is a watershed which occurs in 1668, with the production of a truly great comic version of the myth by Molière. This has had a double effect. It has skewed future variants towards the brilliant surface play of the themes of doubling and cuckoldry and has turned people away from questions of fathering. My present concern is with later versions and subversions of paternity, and leads away from the comic aspect.

Of later versions of the play, *Amphitryon* (1828) by Heinrich von Kleist probably remains closest to the classical ideal of conforming to the will and the desire of the transcendent Other, at least in its ending. The play was consequently misunderstood by a generation accustomed to a romantic view of sexual relationships and a socially conventional view of the way in which a husband should defend his honour. Kleist's is one of a group of Amphitryons which centre mainly on the Jupiter/Alcmene relationship, the humanisation of the divine and the divinisation of the human. I am currently exploring another form of love to show, rather, the humanisation of the divine father which accompanies the divinisation of his apparently human son.

Kleist does, however, draw heavily – and ironically – on the parallels between the Christian story and the Greek one. Goethe, perhaps distrustful of a younger talent, certainly commented on the change into a holy virgin. In his diary of 14 July 1807, he wrote: 'Das Stück *Amphitryon* von Kleist enthält nichts Geringeres als eine Deutung der Fabel ins Christliche, in die Überschattung der Maria vom Heiligen Geist' – 'Kleist's play *Amphitryon* offers nothing less than a Christian interpretation of the fable, Mary overshadowed by the Holy Spirit' (Wittkowski: 59, cited by Lungstrum: 74). If we take into account this deliberate use of the sacred, the ending of the play is not so surprising as it may appear.[16]

When Zeus reveals himself, Amphitryon, like Joseph, immediately submits to the right and the law of the divine Father. What makes Kleist's play almost unique, however, is that the birth of Heracles is the result of Amphitryon's own request for a son to outdo all others. In other words, the divine conception is initiated by Amphitryon's desire, not by that of Zeus. In this way Kleist has produced perhaps the clearest example of the inversion of the 'family romance'. In exchange for the union of his wife with the Other he asks as recompense the perfect child. As always with Kleist, one is never entirely sure whether one's reading should be straight or ironic.

My own feeling is that Kleist's Amphitryon is ambiguous. He is returning to the original myth, 'harassing from both sides'. His Amphitryon is apparently in the archetypal mould, ready to cherish both wife and child all the more because they have been the target of the desire of the Other, not just any other, but that transcendent Other, the divine Father himself. The ending of the play, Amphitryon's humble acceptance of the situation in return for the gift of a son, was seen as ridiculous when it first appeared (see Lungstrum), but this meant the hero's submission was being interpreted as the wimpishness of the cuckold, as customary in the historical and social context of the play's own time. Viewed in terms of the inversion of paternity, where the earthly mortal father is touched by the immortality of the child he shares and where he desires to be remembered in the name of his son, Kleist's *Amphitryon* presents us with a very ambivalent comment on the law of the Father, a kind of reverse genealogy.

There is, however, no ambiguity whatsoever about the political intentions or the subversive inversions of the Amphitryon/Joseph myth produced by Flora Tristan, ten years after Kleist, in her novel *Méphis* (1838). Better known as a feminist revolutionary and the author of utopian socialist visions such as *The Workers' Union*, she did write this one piece of fiction, so convoluted as to have been considered unreadable for the last 150 years. A bastard herself, she produced an absolute compendium of the fantasies of bastardy.[17]

I will not even attempt to tell the full story, but merely give an account of the parodic and proto-feminist way in which it overturns the law of the Father and the patriarchal traditions of the divine birth. The hero, Méphis, the Zeus figure, is marked as an inverted divinity by the name given him, which marks both his ambivalence and his status as fallen angel. Méphis is of course short for Méphistopheles, which means 'he who hates the light or lover of darkness'.[18] Méphis is a revolutionary, a proletarian and a feminist. As Lord of Darkness,

he is not only seeking justice for his own family but for all the dispossessed. He is from the working class, yet blessed with every traditional attribute of nobility.

At one stage, Méphis, secretary to a duke who is desperate for a child, is persuaded to enact the 'divine' role of inseminator in one more comedy of the Holy Family, engendering the heir his noble patron is impotent to produce, and leaving the child to take the ducal name. When the duke actively encourages his duchess to sleep with Méphis, his social inferior but superior in every other respect, he is adopting what was quite a common method of bringing new vigour to depleted stock. There was often agreement that 'the lusty stealth of nature' produced 'More composition and fierce quality / Than doth, within a dull, stale, tired bed, / Go to the creating a whole tribe of fops' (*King Lear*, I, ii). The love children of the nobility were often seen as bringing a secret transfusion of energy to exhausted stock.[19] What particularly marks the duke as an Amphitryon figure is his adoration of the miraculous and adulterine child, to whom he devotes the rest of his life. His Alcmene, however, is not so lucky and conveniently dies in childbirth.

But the second episode, the culmination of the book, is even more revealing. This time Méphis, again the Zeus figure, definitely plans to impregnate his Beloved, the already married Maréquita, in order to produce not only the perfect adulterine child but the new woman who will be the saviour of mankind. After the conception, Méphis dies a martyr's death, and Maréquita follows him to the grave soon after giving birth to the child. Here the Amphitryon part is taken, not by Maréquita's husband, a villain of the darkest dye, but by another social father, the painter, Albert. He is already an avatar familiar to us, the artist celibate who devotes himself to the child of the woman selflessly and sexlessly adored. A surrogate parent in the Merlin mould, it will be his task to raise the 'woman guide of humanity', unsurprisingly called Marie, and train her for her future mission.

The feminist inversion of the patriarchal archetype in *Méphis* is, though remarkable in its date and its gendering, typical of the inversions and subversions which were to characterise the theme in the twentieth century. Some were entertaining but in no way remarkable, like Giraudoux' celebration of the wiles of woman in his Alcmene's manipulation of her besotted Jupiter (1929). Perhaps the most startling inversion, which, while remaining patriarchal, was profoundly oppositional in its day, was Georg Kaiser's *Zweimal Amphitryon* which appeared in 1944. It falls outside the scope of our

study, as the birth and the care of the adulterine child is shown as Amphitryon's deserved retribution for having made war, not love. The really mind-boggling feature is that Heracles is to be born as a pacifist saviour figure, redeeming the male sex from its own worst instincts and from centuries of indoctrination.[20]

'however true it is, that the child may be of the blood and seed of its parents – the parents, nevertheless, are not of the blood and seed of it; inasmuch as the parents are not begot by the child, but the child by the parents …'

Tristram Shandy, IV, 29

However, a novel has just appeared which represents the most extensive variation of the myth, Peter Carey's *The Unusual Life of Tristan Smith* (1994). It unites the most ancient and the most modern themes in a series of remarkable transformations of social and natural parenting: most ancient because the miraculous child is quite literally a monster,[21] that is, a creature which combines in one body elements of two different orders, such as divine and animal or animal and human; most modern because Tristan fulfils in the end the Freudian prophecy that modern man will eventually become a prosthetic god.[22] Tristan becomes an object of cult worship when he eventually combines his tiny mutant body with a robotic outer shell. Thus he draws together the most archaic and most cybernetic representations of divine excess.

The Unusual Life of Tristan Smith creates two wholly imaginary countries on some alternative Earth, countries with their customs, their governments, their literatures, their languages, their entangled histories. As with so many stories of virtual worlds, there is a strong ideological climate constructed. But Carey's way of avoiding the didacticism which always threatens books of this sort is that the ideological warfare takes place, not so much between two political systems, though they are adumbrated, as between the theatrical life of two countries. This permits ideologies to speak through the body. In one country, the island state of Efica, these are sexual bodies, acrobatic bodies, contorted bodies. In the other, the master state of Voorstand, falling bodies dicing with death contend with pseudo-physical images in the shimmering world of simulacra.

One culture and one architectural icon dominate Voorstand: the Sirkus and its ubiquitous domes, which are the temples of a secular religion. The Sirkus, once established as a theatre to enshrine the

strongly moral folktales of the original Voortrekers, has become what the Games were in Rome. The ideological opposition to the Sirkus which is invading Efica and its earlier popular culture is represented by yet another circus/theatre. This is the Feu Follet where the book and Tristan's life begin, and where much of the first (Efican) half of the story takes place. This theatre, centred on the body and on immense bodily control, is portrayed in a series of unforgettable scenes: the idealism, the bitchiness, the energy, the wild flashes of actor and audience rapport, the shoe-string budgets, the adrenalin and the envy; and all heightened to the point of hysteria by the sudden birth of a monstrous, misbegotten scrap of genius to the actor-manager of the Feu Follet, Felicity Smith.

For Felicity Smith gives birth to a monster, the clawing screaming figure of that other, the artist, whom most of us, eventually, strangle before it can take over our bodies and our lives. But in this case, generated from a performance of *Macbeth*, the 'birth strangled babe, ditch delivered by a drab' is saved to be raised as the new messiah of the grotesque. His mother snatches him from kindly euthanasia and staggers back to her theatre and her part. Displaying him to her stunned audience, she says: 'Thou shalt get kings, though thou be none.' Like all oracles this is true in its own way. Fierce determination and that complete disregard for the wishes or comfort of others, which characterise genius, finally enable the deformed scrap of humanity to become an actor. On the stage, behind the make-up, my God what make-up, and in an ever progressive series of masks and disguises, he does in the end generate royalty, the absolute power of the successful actor.

The account of the birth is a *tour de force* in itself, told from the point of view of the foetus. The Amphityronesque aspect emerges most clearly in the scene after Tristan's birth when the nurse confronts his three fathers, who love his mother, live with her sometimes, have sex with her, perhaps; each therefore having a different social or biological claim on the mewling scrap of life she has produced. Which, the nurse asks, is Mr Smith?

But there is no Mr Smith. Tristan bears no father's name, indeed Smith is only his mother's pseudonym, and on his birth certificate the whole question of genealogy is resolved when he is registered as Tristan Actor-Manager. What makes all three men Amphitryon figures is that the actor-manager, Felicity, is no Alcmene. She is rather the divine Other, her desire governs that of the men and the decision to conceive and give birth is hers alone. Although each father is jealously

conscious of the rivalry of the others, it is not this which governs their parenting. When they eventually learn to love Tristan, it is the fierce determination of Felicity, the Other they all worship, which provides the model.

Tristan's three fathers could well be described as 'dreimal Amphitryon'. None can lay complete claim to the child and none can give him his name. Each embodies some features of the archetype. A pseudo-Zeus figure is the presumed biological father, Bill Millefleur. Bill is a star in the mythological world of the Sirkus, descending from on high and the apparent immortality of the high wire and the trapeze to mate with the perfect woman, Felicity, and to impregnate her with the miraculous monster. Bill also helps inspire the cultivation of the acting skills which mark Tristan as the divine offspring. But Bill's incapacity to assume the role of patriarch, his uncertainty of fatherhood, his subordination to Felicity, make him rather less than god-like.

The next Amphitryon figure is Tristan's second father, Vincent. His religion is the theatre and its high priestess Felicity. A conventional adulterer, he sleeps with Felicity but is not the biological father of Tristan. So he is denied both a child of his own blood and even that embodiment of physical perfection for which he hankers. Perfection is his other religion. Yet his fatherhood is sanctified by the desire of the Other. His Other, the goddess of his temple, is Felicity, and her word is his command. If she worships the monstrous in her miraculous son, then so will he. His money and support make her dreams possible.

The third Amphitryon is Wally, the stage manager of the theatre. He lavishes a selfless love on Felicity and her child, and it is he who actually physically raises Tristan. From changing the first diapers, through years of constant care and protection of the deformed and helpless scrap of humanity, he watches over Tristan's 'unusual life' until the moment when he makes the supreme gesture of sacrificing his life to save that of his adored 'son'. We have seen his predecessors in Merlin and Flora Tristan's Albert.[23] These parents force one to rethink conventional gendering. All Carey's characters are highly sexed and freely sexually active, but as for the conventions of feminine and masculine behaviour, forget it. These people make their own lives, and the women are as likely to be fathering as the men to be mothering.

'thank heaven, fasting, for a good man's love.'
As You Like It, III,v[24]

And so to our moral. Once there was a male god – hence he fulfilled all the criteria of maleness – phallic, isolated, invulnerable, irresistible, immortal and paternal. Unfortunately he desired a perfect human son and, in order to bear him, looked around for a perfect wife. Alas, the perfect wife came only as part of a perfect couple, and we all know how hard to break up perfect couples are. And as rare as hens' teeth. Almost as rare as perfect gods. Poor Zeus.

Then there was a human husband, who conformed to all but one of the criteria of maleness. The trouble was, he was not satisfied to reproduce himself biologically as all good husbands should. Just like the god, he wanted a perfect son to confer immortality in retrospect. He got his desire in the paradoxical way that oracles fulfil desire. Never a desire without a lack ... gain a son, lose a wife, lose your macho image. Poor Amphitryon.

Then there was a breakthrough, a husband who tinged his maleness with a little of the suddenly discovered female self. He got both his still desirable wife and a divine son. Things were looking up. The trouble was no-one, including Jungians and feminists, ever quite believed in him. Just what was his true desire, and had he got his yin and yang in exactly the right proportions?

So what was left for our Amphitryon to try next? Well, he could start by forgetting his 'feminine' side, still in its schizoid box with pink ribbons, but he had to do this without reverting to the patriarch of our earlier models, the one with the blue ribbons. He could feel free to love a child for its own sake, even if his wife had borne it to another man (or god). He could take many forms: a fond parent having Heracles taught the lyre, or a Merlin carrying off the swaddled infant, the future king, or a Wally fostering his monster with fumbling maleness. In fact, in fathering, he could become a human being and forget about being a man.[25]

Can we believe that this Amphitryon was happy?

Notes

An earlier version of this essay appeared in *New Literary History*, 4, 26 (1995), 789–807. My thanks go to the Editor of that journal for kind permission to publish it here.
1   The 1909 essay on 'The Family Romance of the Neurotic'(*SE*, IX:236–41). *SE* will be used hereafter for *The Complete Works of Sigmund Freud*,

Standard Edition. See also Marie Maclean *The Name of the Mother: Writing Illegitimacy*, ch. 3. *Name* will be used hereafter for references to this work.

2 In this book I look especially at three movements in personal narratives: legitimation, the move back into society and particularly the mastery of the symbolic; relegitimation, the desire for reintegration; and finally delegitimation, the assumption of an excluded status, of alterity, of multiplicity, and of the oppositional.

3 See Naomi Segal's masterly study of the adulterine child fictionalised as the punishment of sin, in *The Adulteress's Child* (1992). I am looking at the other, more pagan, side of the coin.

4 See, in particular, Loraux, 1989, and *Name*, chs 2 & 3.

5 See Passage and Mantinband, hereafter P&M, pp. 10–16. Unfortunately we only have vase paintings as evidence. Euripides' play seems to have centred on Alcmene's trial and near death on the scaffold for adultery, from which fate she was saved by Zeus. The comedies, as might be expected, focused on the doubling and cuckoldry.

6 One might compare the two versions of the Joseph and Mary story, that of the bible in which they beget other children, and later church versions, in which Mary remains immaculate.

7 See *Name*, especially ch. 3.

8 In the very first recorded mention of Heracles, his lineage is given as that of Amphitryon. This is perhaps because he is at war with his social and part foster mother, Hera, another ambiguity, as Heracles means 'glory of Hera', yet their relationship was almost always antagonistic (Loraux:167).

9 According to Marina Warner, in *Alone of all her sex: the Myth and Cult of the Virgin Mary* (1976): 'For Matthew the Virgin birth was a symbol that gave Jesus legitimacy as a God, and was not inconsistent with his legitimacy as a social being with an official socially recognized father'(21).

10 We have no need to assume with Lindberger (pp. 34–5) that Geoffrey of Monmouth must have plagiarised the story, in order to add extra lustre to Arthur's parentage by the comparison with Heracles. Lindberger was writing in the high period of source criticism. We know now that the great narrative myths constantly reappear in archetypal variants.

11 I will not enter into the vexed question of sources, since what I am looking at are deep fantasmic structures. It has frequently been pointed out that Shakespeare undoubtedly owes elements of *The Comedy of Errors* to Plautus, but any connection with *King John* is probably unconscious.

12 My thanks to Dr John F. Knight for indicating the relevance to my study of this little known play.

13 There is a link here to the biblical validation which we examined earlier:

> At the age of twenty-five Elizabeth was crowned queen. Her coronation pageant underscored what for years had been a major element of her self-presentation and the public's perception of her: she was her father's daughter. The first show was a three-tiered arch displaying Unity and Concord. On the bottom tier were represented Henry VIII and his queen; on the next, Henry VIII and Anne Boleyn (redeemed after so many years of obloquy); and on the top, Elizabeth I.
>
> (Marcus:407)

This is a successful plagiarism of the medieval popularity of the iconic Tree of Jesse, which showed in branch form the genealogy of David with Mary and her child as its ultimate flower. This, as we have seen, was a striking example of the pairing of social and biological, or rather divine, genealogy, to reap the advantages of both.

14 In this use of warring brothers the myth belongs to a wider range of tales of illegitimate heroes. If the bastard is regal, noble or divine it is he who tends to be the exemplar of physical perfection. However, with the common motif of legitimate/adulterine pairs of brothers, there is always a factor of excess. They are never ordinary, in a different corpus of stories (see *Name*) it is the bastard who is hateful, evil and often deformed, whereas, in the Amphitryon type of tale, this lot falls to the legitimate child. See also René Girard, *Violence and the Sacred*.

15 In Tristan's *Méphis*, the hero, a painter at the time, is offered '60 francs de ma femme guide de l'humanité, à condition que j'en ferais une sainte vierge'. (I:221).

16 Janet Lungstrum (1992) has an excellent discussion of Lacan's reading of the play in his *Séminaire II*, but both are more interested in the fidelity and infidelity of the couple, mirrored in that of the reader, than the questioning of the name of the father which results.

17 For a fuller discussion of this text, see *Name* ch. 6.

18 Tristan selects the name because of an inverted symbolism and worship of an anti-god fashionable at the time of Romanticism. It characterises, for example Baudelaire's 'Litanies of Satan'. She chooses the name Méphis for the same reasons as Zamyatin some 100 years later, in *We* (1924).

19 See *Name*, pp. 9–10.

20 This play makes a really inventive use at all levels of the original Greek concept of drama as the trag-oidos or goat play and is the perhaps the most subtle of the modern 'Amphitryons'.

21 See Girard (1991) pp. 43–55. In keeping with his patriarchal standpoint, Girard regards the monstrous, especially the beast that partakes of a god, as a dangerous obliteration of difference.

22 'Man has, as it were, become a kind of prosthetic God. When he puts on all his organs he is truly magnificent, but these organs have not grown onto him and they still give him much trouble at times.' (Freud, 1929:90–2) quoted in Grosz, 1994, p. 39.

23 An earlier version of a similar non-biological father figure is Horace Dunlop in Carey's *Illywhacker*, 1985.

24 Feminists and Shakespearians will forgive this little piece of textual subversion.

25 Thanks to my husband and friends, particularly Marie Rose Auguste, Julie Solomon and Ross Chambers, for their help, support and advice, without which I could never have completed this article.

REFERENCES

Carey, Peter (1994) *The Unusual Life of Tristan Smith*, St Lucia: University of Queensland Press.
Freud, Sigmund (1981) *Complete Works*, The Standard Edition, 24 vols, (ed.) and (tr.) James Strachey, with A. Freud, A. Strachey and A. Tyson, London: Hogarth Press and Institute of Psychoanalysis.
Girard, René (1961) *Mensonge romantique et vérité romanesque*, Paris: Editions Bernard Grasset. Tr. (1966), *Deceit, Desire and the Novel*, Baltimore: Johns Hopkins University Press.
Girard, René (1977) *Violence and the Sacred*, Baltimore: Johns Hopkins University Press.
Girard, René (1986) *The Scapegoat*, Baltimore: Johns Hopkins University Press.
Girard, René (1991) *A Theater of Envy: William Shakespeare*, New York, Oxford: Oxford University Press.
Graves, Robert (1972) *The Greek Myths: 1 and 2*, Harmondsworth: Penguin.
Grosz, Elizabeth (1994) *Volatile Bodies: Towards a Corporeal Feminism*, Sydney: Allen and Unwin.
Lindberger, Örjan (1956) *The Transformations of Amphitryon*, Stockholm: Almqvist & Wiksell.
Loraux, Nicole (1989) *Les Expériences de Tirésias*, Paris: Gallimard.
Lungstrum, Janet (1992) 'A Transcendental Infidelity: Kleist, Lacan and Amphitryon', *Modern Language Studies*, 22, 4: 67–75.
Maclean, Marie (1994) *The Name of the Mother: Writing Illegitimacy*, New York & London: Routledge.
Marcus, Leah (1989) 'Erasing the Stigma of Daughterhood: Mary I, Elizabeth I, and Henry VIII', in Boose, Lynda and Betty Flowers (eds) *Daughters and Fathers*, Baltimore: Johns Hopkins University Press.
Passage, Charles E. and Mantinband, James H. (1974) *Amphitryon. The Legend and Three Plays; Plautus, Molière, Kleist*, Chapel Hill: The University of North Carolina Press.
Schondorff, Joachim ed. (1964) *Amphitryon; Plautus, Molière, Dryden, Kleist, Giraudoux, Kaiser*, München/Wien: Langen Müller. All the basic Amphitryon scripts referred to are in this volume.
Segal, Naomi (1992) *The Adulteress's Child: Authorship and Desire in the Nineteenth-Century Novel*, Cambridge: Polity Press.
Shakespeare, William (1910) *The Complete Works*, London, New York etc.: Oxford University Press.
Tolstoy, Leo (1971) *Anna Karenina*, (tr.) R. Edmunds, Harmondsworth: Penguin.
Tristan, Flora (1838) *Méphis*, 2 vols, Paris: Ladvocat.

2

Adultery and Killing in
La Mort le roi Artu

Sarah Kay

Insofar as adultery is considered wrongful, in medieval texts, it is often because it is connected in some way with an offence against property. This is either because of the importance laid on legitimate inheritance (which in turn requires wives to be faithful to their husbands), or because of the tendency to see women as themselves a form of property. In *La Mort le roi Artu* (*The Death of King Arthur*), however, adultery is presented in relation not to property but to the taking of life. How and why this is so is what this chapter will explore.

The *Mort* is the last work in the great early thirteenth-century compilation known as the *Prose Lancelot*,[1] and describes the decline and fall of Arthur's kingdom. The adultery between Arthur's queen Guenevere and his greatest knight Lancelot plays a key role in this apocalyptic narrative, since it leads to the estrangement of Lancelot and Arthur. When Arthur pursues Lancelot abroad, he entrusts his kingdom to Mordred, who usurps it for himself; Arthur feels unable to call on Lancelot to assist him against Mordred, and so his army perishes along with Mordred's.

In the early part of the *Mort*, Arthur is induced by court spies to ask himself repeatedly whether Lancelot and Guenevere are guilty of adultery. But he is also called upon to approve legal challenges against both of them for wrongful killing. For both have caused death, in episodes which present striking parallels. The victims in both cases are knights who have similar names (Guenevere kills Gaheris, Lancelot kills Gaheriet), and both are commemorated by inscriptions put up by members of the court. The brother of each victim wants to avenge his death: Mador de la Porte obliges Arthur to put Guenevere on trial; Gawain's love for Lancelot turns to implacable hostility as he pressures Arthur to go to war against Lancelot, and eventually challenges him

to single combat. Then again, each of the killings could be described as accidental. Guenevere hands Gaheris a poisoned fruit which was prepared by someone else (Arvalan) and intended for Gawain; she was completely unaware that it was poisoned. Similarly Lancelot strikes down Gaheriet, who is his dear friend, without recognising him in the confusion of rescuing the queen. Finally, when each of the avenging brothers (Mador, Gawain) obtains a judicial duel (or approximation to one, in Gawain's case), he is pitted against Lancelot who fights first on behalf of the queen and then on his own behalf, and on both occasions wins. Although much of the romance is about efforts to ascertain whether or not Lancelot and the queen are lovers, attempts to entrap them are not successful. Thus Lancelot and the queen are never required legally to defend themselves as adulterers, only as killers. The killings, it seems, function as a displacement of the crime of adultery, and also as a narrative metaphor for it.

This metaphorical dimension is established textually by the close association that exists in each case between the question of adultery and the alleged wrongful killing. In the first case, that of Guenevere and the poisoned fruit, the link is established from the outset. Arthur has returned to court from the castle of his sister Morgan, who has shown him Lancelot's paintings which reveal his love for Guenevere. And so for Arthur 'there was never a time again when he was not more suspicious of the queen than he had been, because of what he had been told' (62:14–17).[2] Only two sentences later those suspicions find an object, as Arvalan hands the fruit to Guenevere and Gaheris dies (62:21ff.). Meanwhile, Lancelot has been dismissed from the court by the queen as a result of a misunderstanding, a fact which causes Boors to curse the love between them (66:48–50). The interweaving of these episodes associates the themes of love and death.

A similar convergence of these two themes occurs in the case of Lancelot's accidental killing of Gaheriet. It is causally linked with the adultery plot, since it takes place while Lancelot is rescuing the queen from execution. When later Lancelot hands her back to Arthur, he seeks to justify himself with respect both to the queen, and to the death of Gawain's brothers, so that the issues of adultery and the killing are linked again: 'Sire, behold the queen, whom I return to you, who would earlier have been killed as a result of the disloyalty of members of your household, had I not taken the risk of rescuing her. [...] And it is better that they should perish in their treachery than that she should die' (119:22–33). He goes on: 'If I loved the queen with foolish passion, as you were given to understand, I would not give her back

to you, not for months, and you would not win her back by force' (119:35–8). But Gawain pulls the discussion back to Lancelot's guilt for Gaheriet's death: 'You can be sure that you will not lack for war [...] for you will have it, and mightier than you ever did before, and it will last until my brother Gaheriet, whom you wrongfully killed, will be avenged on your own body; and I would rather see your head cut off than have the whole world' (119:55–61).

These links between adultery and killing shift the ground on which the adultery is considered. Most characters in the text want to know whether Lancelot and the Queen are committing adultery as a matter of fact, not how to judge them if they are. For Arthur, adultery calls for automatic condemnation. Gawain, Guerrehés and Gaheriet prefer that he should not know, rather than cause enmity in the court (85:44ff., 86:48ff.). We readers, however, know that the couple are lovers; our problem, rather, is what attitude to adopt to this. As the story goes on, an increasing number of characters know the truth about their relationship, and some (such as Lancelot's kin) are clearly loyal to them. But no character, whether in the know or not, discusses the question which is uppermost in the reader's mind, namely how we should view their adultery. On the contrary, there is a gap between the discourse that maintains, of Lancelot, that he is the best knight in the world because of his love for the queen, and the discourse lamenting that, because of his love for the queen, a terrible cataclysm will engulf the Arthurian kingdom.[3] If the text seeks to evaluate the fact of their relationship, it does so via the thunderous silence between these two positions. In the matter of the killings, however, the facts are agreed between readers and characters; it is their evaluation which is in question for all of us together. Both the judicial duels address the question of whether the killers are guilty of a disloyal and treacherous act. That is, they ask with respect to the killings what the reader might ask with respect to the adultery. In this way, the metaphorical importance of the killings becomes both more obvious, and more interesting.

The Guenevere trial considers disloyalty and treachery from the point of view of intention. Before the combat, Mador makes his formal accusation to Lancelot: 'Sir knight, I am ready to prove that she killed my brother disloyally and treacherously' (83:2–3), a charge Lancelot rebuts with an important change of wording: 'And I am ready [...] to defend her on the ground that she never intended disloyalty or treachery' (83:4–5). Lancelot's formulation is, for Gawain, an illumination of Guenevere's innocence (83:9–14). Arthur agrees that

this new perspective makes it likely Guenevere's champion will win (83:14–16). And Guenevere herself repeats the winning formula: 'I never intended disloyalty or treachery,' she says (84:12–13). Win Lancelot duly does; the queen is exonerated. If, as I have argued, the trial is a metaphorical displacement of anxiety about adultery, can we infer from Guenevere's acquittal that she is also to be exonerated sexually because she 'never intended disloyalty or treachery'? Is the text driving a wedge between intention and result, and inclining us to base our moral judgements on the former not the latter?[4] The fact of Gaheris's death is undeniable, but Guenevere has been found innocent because she did not mean to cause it; likewise, although her adultery has dire political consequences, since she did not intend them, should she be acquitted of responsibility for them too?

One could feel more confident about making this inference if the text were more committed to the concept of intention. When members of the court first find Gaheris's body, the question of intent is raised, and Guenevere protests her ignorance that the fruit was poisoned, but Arthur counters: 'Whatever the circumstances in which you gave it to him, the outcome is evil and intolerable, and I greatly fear that you will suffer more for it than you imagine' (62:63–6). No one believes Guenevere to be innocent or is prepared to dishonour himself defending her (74:74–9; 74:98–103; 79:6–8). The consensus view is unambiguously expressed by Gawain: 'for we know very well that the queen killed the knight, as she stands accused; I saw it and so did many others' (79:16–18). Even Lancelot who did not see it believes her to be guilty: 'for I know truly, from what I have heard, that I shall be on the side of wrong and Mador on the side of right' (75:40–2). He fights only because he loves the queen, and her reputation is hitherto unblemished (75:36–8; 82:21–6). The outcome, not the intent, of her deed is what mesmerises everyone's attention.

So Lancelot's all-important formulation at the trial, which wins support and eventual acquittal for the queen, is curiously inadvertent; while the switch of position by Gawain and Arthur is almost somnambulistic. In fact, the text seems more inclined to dull the distinctions between intent, outcome, and responsibility than to illumine them. This obfuscation reaches a peak when Arthur, shortly afterwards, reproaches Gawain for having withheld the truth of the queen's adultery from him. Gawain's reply, 'Indeed, my treachery never did you any harm' (87:60–1), is simply mind-boggling. Has he forgotten what treachery is? His use of the term implies that he meant

no ill, had no ill effect, and bears no responsibility: the word becomes empty of meaning.

Throughout the *Mort*, the capacity of the characters to form, or respond to, intention is extremely limited. The text contains several examples of unintended killing or wounding apart from the two cases I am concerned with. They include Lancelot being wounded twice (by Boors who failed to recognise him at the Winchester tournament (19:22ff.), and a huntsman who missed his intended quarry in the forest (64:25ff.)); and Arthur killing his last-but-one survivor by hugging him too hard (192:8–11). On each occasion questions of intent and moral responsibility are dimly raised but they never get anywhere. Thus Boors tells Lancelot that he ought not to be blamed for wounding him since Lancelot was fighting incognito (47:25–30), and Lancelot agrees but nevertheless remains full of reproaches (47:35ff.). Elizabeth Edwards has described the characters in medieval prose romance as resembling 'a distinctive mark, or graving, on the surface of the text [... which is] of insufficient capacity to accommodate more than one code at a time'.[5] In the *Mort*, they seem able to focus either on intent or on outcome but not on both at the same time, as they would need to do in order to evaluate the ethical significance of one *vis-à-vis* the other. Guenevere's trial may involve the question of intent, but it no more succeeds in making it a determinate issue than these other episodes do. We cannot infer from it that intent defines the moral horizon of action in the *Mort*. Does the text, then, have anything clearer to say on the question of justice?

When Mador enters the judicial duel, he does not know who his opponent is. Only when he has been defeated does Lancelot declare his identity. Mador then protests to the king: 'Sire, you have deceived me, setting my lord Lancelot against me' (85:9–11). In the Gawain–Lancelot encounter over the death of Gaheriet, the question is again raised whether the outcome of a trial depends less on what is being fought over than on who is fighting. Gawain sends a messenger to challenge Lancelot to single combat. The messenger thinks he must be mad to fight such a 'good and seasoned knight' (144:44–5) and Arthur, repeating these same words, also fears that Gawain cannot win (146:59–65), but Gawain insists that justice will be done, for right makes a weak knight prevail, whereas wrong makes a strong one lose (144:65–9). In the course of the combat Gawain's strength grows and ebbs, so that he seems first likely to win, then headed for defeat. Does he lose because his strength declines, or because he was wrong to fight in the first place?

The Gawain–Lancelot combat echoes the concerns of the Guenevere trial. Once again, the charge involves killing 'treacherously and disloyally' (144:29–30; 147:40–1). Different opinions are expressed as to which of the two, Gawain and Lancelot, is on the side of right, and Lancelot himself, acting as his own champion, is as diffident about the justice of his cause as he was when fighting for Guenevere. He prepares himself for the duel by confession and vigil, 'for he was very afraid lest ill befall him against lord Gawain, on account of the death of his brothers whom he had killed' (150:15–17). But rather than foregrounding the status of intent in relation to the notion of right,[6] what is at stake here is the status of right itself. What is it and how do you know when you have it? Many of the *Mort*'s critics seem persuaded either that Lancelot clearly has justice on his side, or that he clearly does not. R.H. Bloch, for example, writes: 'Lancelot's victorious support of a merely adequate cause against Mador and a patently indefensible one against Gawain can only be interpreted as the triumph of might over right'.[7] Convinced that Lancelot's causes are undeserving, Bloch is obliged to see the *Mort* as a world in which belief has been lost in the efficacy of an immanent God to achieve justice through human intermediaries.[8] For other critics, however, Lancelot is just as obviously in the right, as borne out by his victories.[9]

Such critical responses, it seems to me, make too much sense of a text which (just as in the murky issues of intent and outcome) clouds and inhibits judgements; the critics are reliant on notions of right and justice being transparent whereas in the *Mort* they are at best dimly lit, at worst wholly opaque. For justice in the *Mort* is linked to an irresolvable problematic of how far the world is governed by providence and how far by chance or fortune; and how far we could possibly know which, or what that meant. This is a problem on which, as Karen Pratt has shown, the characters can shed no light.

> They are constantly 'reasoning why' – hence the frequent references by them to God, Fortune, Destiny, and their own guilt or sin. Yet they never reach a conclusion. This is because not only is it not man's place to reason why, it is also a futile activity, since it is evident that the world of the flesh is subject to laws which are far less just and predictable than those that govern the salvation of an individual's soul.[10]

It is also a problem from which the text as a whole retreats into secular gloom, reflecting 'the equivocal attitude of so many secular

writers in the Middle Ages towards the problem of explaining history and the rise and fall of great civilisations'.[11] Thus while it is true that Lancelot emerges from his second duel having apparently demonstrated to Gawain's satisfaction that he did not kill Gaheriet 'treacherously and disloyally', this duel does not clarify our ethical attitude towards Lancelot either as a killer, or as a lover. It merely leaves the whole field of ethical inquiry darker and more impenetrable.

So far I have considered the trial scenes of Guenevere and Lancelot as metaphors – inconclusive ones – for how readers might attempt to put them on trial for adultery. I now want to examine the crime with which they are charged. Why are they represented as killers? What do adultery and killing have in common?

The deaths for which Lancelot and Guenevere are tried (even if they are not found guilty) are only two among the indefinitely many to which their adultery might be said to contribute. For the *Mort* portrays an increasingly violent world, its conflicts aggravated by the rift between Lancelot and Arthur. The text opens with a series of tournaments, but these soon give way to genuine warfare in the wake of the attempted entrapment of the lovers and Lancelot's rescue of Guenevere. Arthur finds himself at war, successively, with Lancelot, the Romans, and Mordred. Armies are wiped out as civilisations crumble. Fighting dominates the text, and killing becomes necessary and unavoidable, simultaneously appalling and banal. (Bresson's 1974 film *Lancelot du Lac*, based on the *Mort*, excellently captures the frenzied meaninglessness of violence in this text.) In identifying the lovers as killers, then, the text both integrates their adultery to the *Mort*'s cataclysmic canvas, and represents it as (literally) lethal.

The sinister and guilt-laden implications of this contrast markedly with the role of the philtre in the *Tristan* story, guarantor of the lovers' innocence. As the philtre marks equality between Tristan and Iseut, so the striking parallels between the deaths of Gaheris and Gaheriet signal the parity between Lancelot and Guenevere. But while the *Tristan* lovers drink the love-potion together, Guenevere, as if in reminiscence of Eve's role in the Fall, offers a poisoned fruit to someone else.[12] And while the *Tristan* potion is a presage of the lovers' eventual death, in the *Mort* the lovers themselves are oddly immune to the fatality they are associated with. In fact, their killings are a curious reversal of the anticipated story-line, namely that *they* should be the ones to be killed. As in other Celtic-influenced texts, the penalty for adultery in the *Mort* is death, but Arthur is prevented from executing Guenevere. The couple might have shared the fate of

other literary adulterers (such as Iseut) who die of their own accord, as though in acknowledgement of society's condemnation of them, but they do not. Like all the major characters in the *Mort*, Lancelot and Guenevere are at times so overwhelmed by grief or anger that they are convinced they will die, but only the maid of Escalot, much earlier in the text, is as good as her word and actually dies from her grief whereas Lancelot and Guenevere don't. Instead the plot effects a curious exchange between killing the lovers and having them kill others. Their enemies (except for Morgan) predecease them, dying violent deaths, whereas Guenevere does not die until very nearly the end (197:10–11) and Lancelot outlives virtually everyone. In a text where death is so commonplace, the lovers are almost magically protected from it.

Not only that; the lovers also avoid deliberate killing. Lancelot does not kill Mador; he deliberately saves Arthur's life (115:129–31); and he refuses to kill Gawain ('I could not do it [...] for my heart to which I belong could not agree to it on any account', 158:13–15). Although the best knight in the world, he actually kills very few people.[13] The crimes of which he and Guenevere are accused consist in killing outside socially prescribed norms; it is not the deaths but the aberrant circumstances of them that lead to their being perceived as 'treacherous and disloyal', and if Lancelot had lost his two fights he would have been made to die a socially sanctioned death. Killing, the text seems to suggest, is inevitable and universal, and yet society polices it in such a way that accidental killing calls for legal investigation whereas killing on purpose does not. Adultery, likewise, is love in the wrong place, and thus perhaps only an arbitrarily censured instance of universal and inevitable behaviour. The guilt involved is one of social convention, not absolute value.

Indeed, the 'guilt' of the 'adultery killings' in the *Mort* begins to look quite innocent when one compares them with what could be called the 'incest killings', the reciprocal slaying of Mordred and Arthur. Mordred, the text reveals, is both son and nephew to Arthur, a child incestuously conceived with his sister. In Arthur's absence Mordred usurps his throne and tries to marry his wife, thus compounding treachery with attempted bigamy and further incest. Despite repeated warnings that this war will bring his reign and his kingdom to an end, Arthur seeks out Mordred and each deals the other his death-blow. Here is a striking instance of how sexual crime and killing can be linked: this tight-knit family drama crystallises Freudian

preoccupation by economically combining transgression of the two most sacred taboos: parricide and incest.

By contrast, both Lancelot and Guenevere (their adultery apart) show exemplary love and respect for Arthur and his authority. By sparing Arthur's life Lancelot avoids Mordred's parricide and by handing Guenevere back voluntarily desists from sexual transgression. As Méla says, because '[Lancelot] chooses to live henceforth in a state of unfulfilled desire out of respect for the Name of the Father [...] the essential achievement of *La Mort Artu* is to have integrated love for the king into Lancelot's love for the queen'.[14] Compared with the meaningful deaths of Arthur and Mordred, the killings for which Lancelot and Guenevere are tried are impressively insignificant. Their victims are neither figures of oppression (such as a father) nor are they rivals. There is no psychodrama involved: on the contrary Gaheris, recipient of the poisoned apple, has no connection whatever with the adultery plot, while Gaheriet was doing his best to keep out of it (93:66ff.). Gaheris is the medieval equivalent of today's 'innocent bystander', unheard of until killed. Gaheriet is slightly more prominent, but still a relatively minor figure. Each is simply the wrong person in the wrong place at the wrong time.

The random character of these deaths in contrast with the Arthur–Mordred confrontation seems to indicate that anyone could die at any time. And the fact that they die by accident corresponds with the lovers' lack of control over the rest of their lives. The lovers' killings, in other words, can be read as a projection of their own mortality and frailty, a condition they share with the other characters in the text. Here at last the literal and the metaphorical converge: death is literally about human mortality and frailty, while adultery is their ethical expression. The poisoned fruit serves as a textual marker of this convergence, since the Genesis intertext links sexuality with human weakness and death.

This essay has grappled with the lack of clear interpretation available to readers of the *Mort*. We are offered the trials as metaphors for our inquiry into adultery; and yet they don't lead very far, and when one trial is over, we start again with the other and a further set of questions. The equation between adultery and killing, which seems so sinister and guilt-ridden, conveys in fact a curious innocence which makes it difficult to evaluate. I think, however, that the way that the point eludes the reader *is* the point, and that we are invited, in reading this

text, to contemplate a depressing portrayal of human limitation. This is a penumbral text which, as it narrates the demise of civilisation, looks back (via the episode of the poisoned fruit) to the time before civilisation began. In the intervening shadows, lacking the light of Eden or of heaven, we are uncertain about the ethical significance of intention and responsibility, guilt and sin, justice and truth. Love and death are worked together in a pessimistic duo, ingrained in the shallow experience of humanity, arbitrarily treated by society, fraught with violence, subject to uncontrollable intent and unpredictable outcome, and resistant to moral judgement.

Notes

1   The fact that it is a part of a larger work may affect its interpretation in ways that I do not discuss here.
2   Quotations are in my own translation from *La Mort le roi Artu*, ed. Jean Frappier (Geneva: Droz, 1964), cited by paragraph and line number. An English translation, by James Cable, *The Death of King Arthur* is available in Penguin Classics (Harmondsworth, 1971).
3   '"It is true"', said Morgan, "[…] that Lancelot has loved queen Guenevere since the very first day he received the order of knighthood, and when he was newly knighted he performed all his great deeds of prowess for love of the queen"' (52:32–8). '"My only fear is lest my lord [Lancelot] is distressed at the queen's anger. A curse on the hour that love was ever begun; for I am afraid that it might yet be much the worse for us." "Indeed," said Hector, "if I ever was certain of anything, you will yet see between our kin and king Arthur the greatest war that ever was, and all because of this"' (66:48–54).
4   As argued by Tony Hunt re the Tristan story, 'Abelardian Ethics and Beroul's *Tristan*', *Romania*, 98 (1977), 501–40.
5   Elizabeth Edwards, 'Amnesia and Remembrance in Malory's *Morte Darthur*', *Paragraph*, 13 (1990), 132–46, p. 135.
6   Lancelot does rebut Gawain's charge by denying that he killed Gaheriet knowingly (147:85).
7   R.H. Bloch, 'The Death of King Arthur and the Waning of the Feudal Age', *Orbis Litterarum*, 29 (1974), 291–305, p. 292.
8   *Medieval French Literature and Law* (Berkeley: 1977), pp. 46ff.
9   Karen Pratt, '*La Mort le roi Artu* as Tragedy', *Nottingham Medieval Studies*, 30 (1991), 81–109, p. 96; cf. p. 97, where her phrase 'the accidental killing of Gaheriet and Gawain's *démesure*' implies the same judgement on the second trial.
10 Pratt, p. 92.
11 Pratt, p. 108.

12 See Sarah Kay, 'Motherhood. The Case of the Epic Family Romance', in *Shifts and Transpositions in Medieval Narrative. A Festschrift for Dr Elspeth Kennedy*, ed. Karen Pratt (Cambridge: Brewer, 1994), pp. 23–36, p. 33.

13 Only Agravain (94:20ff.) and Mordred's younger son (198:11ff.).

14 Charles Méla, 'Life in *La Mort le roi Artu*', in *The Passing of Arthur. New Essays in Arthurian Tradition*, ed. Christopher Baswell and William Sharpe (New York and London: Garland, 1988), 5–14, p. 10.

3

Adultery on Trial: Martin Guerre and his Wife, from Judge's Tale to the Screen

Elizabeth Guild

The case of Martin Guerre fascinated sixteenth-century French audiences high and low, with its questions of identity, transgression, recognition, and revelation. What happened? No-one really knows. Martin Guerre, who had abandoned his wife and son, returned after some five years away at war, a changed man, a good husband and worker. Four years later he was accused of imposture; his case went to trial, and he was condemned; he appealed and was about to be acquitted, given the judges' overwhelming doubt in the face of a mass of conflicting evidence as to his identity, when, as the original record has it, there was a 'miracle': the 'real' Martin Guerre arrived. Although he seemed much less convincingly 'himself' than did the accused, judgement finally went against the accused who was sentenced to be hanged and his body then burned, to destroy all trace of his person and crime.

This case of alleged imposture involved an adultery, which could have branded the wife as guilty co-conspirator, and destroyed her and her family's honour: but it was not initially adultery that compelled attention; rather, the enigma of identity. What interests me here is how the wife's part in this enigma has come to be represented, most recently in two films, *Le Retour de Martin Guerre* (dir. Daniel Vigne, 1982), and its Hollywood remake, *Sommersby* (dir. Jon Amiel, 1993). Where originally she was judged a victim of imposture, therefore an innocent adulteress, and her honour thus preserved (possibly at the cost of the 'truth'), these recent representations celebrate her adultery as affirmation of autonomy and authenticity, and in their desire to explain a case which was originally thought inexplicable, locate (too)

much of its meaning here. Apparently it was less the case's potential
as courtroom drama than as a love story that attracted the French film-
makers; and although trial scenes form a dramatic climax in both films,
love becomes the motor and meaning of this film and its remake.[1]
What is on trial in this essay are these representations of adultery in
relation to the original narrative.

The first account of the case, the report of the trial by one of the
presiding judges, Jean de Coras, published in 1561, became a standard
text for students of jurisprudence and was frequently reprinted.[2]
Subsequently there have been many other narrative versions,[3] almost
all of which attend much less than Coras to the wife's part, and almost
all marked by a drift from the original. This is not a drift over time:
even a cluster of early versions already differ significantly from
Coras's account in detail, fact and function. Early modern readers were
lured and disturbed by the possibility of events beyond explanation
in this case in which both ethical and judicial dilemmas demanded
resolution, whereas the films insist more on the aspect of love. But
despite this difference, what unites these films and early accounts is
the desire to master the situation's meaning, to bring it within the field
of reasonable explanation.

When the question 'why' is put to adultery, it is often a demand
both for explanation and for allocation of responsibility, if not guilt.
Yet each adultery's particular causes and meaning may well remain
obscure to all but the participants, beyond the impoverished banalities
of the usual reasons and stock speculations, less explanations than
cover stories, less sources of insight than recourse to reductive
generalities which offer little comfort – and which should interrupt
us in our futile tracking of full explanation of the mysteries of human
desire. On the other hand, it is often said that the reasons for adultery
are blindingly obvious: that may well be, if one accepts a particular
order or habit of explanation. Given this difficulty, to turn to adultery
as a source of explanation of other events does not seem, on the face
of it, the soundest move. In the case of Martin Guerre, adultery and
imposture have come to be caught in an interpretative loop, in which
the explanation of one enigma is sought in terms of another which
would in turn be explained by the first. The result (appearances to
the contrary) is confusion, opacity, mystery.

Coras's account of the case is the official record, an authoritative
judicial document, received as such; yet what marks it is epistemological crisis. Its narrative of the case is constantly interrupted,
overburdened by Annotations detailing the judge's interpretative

models, logic, and presuppositions. The mass and scope of Coras's Annotations are striking: faced by events and evidence that confound his sense of probability and natural order, no source of explanation seems too eccentric for him to exclude. The proliferation of Annotations suggests less an accumulation of conceptual authorities and ample, sound reasoning than the elusiveness of the issues of identity; and the more intractable and irresolvable they became, the more determined to close the question the judge seems to have become. Thus, for instance, when the identity of the supposed impostor seemed quite to elude Coras's capacities of explanation and distinction – for he found he could not decide whether the accused was or was not who he claimed to be – his power to deceive (if that is what it was) was explained as being attributable to the devil. And, so long as the judges could not determine the accused's identity, the preservation, rather, of the family's reputation – its good name – substituted as the deciding factor in their judgement of the case and they therefore found in the accused's favour.

Four issues stand out in this text. First, the enigma of identity – one man seemed more like another than the man himself; Coras could not tell the difference, could not identify the person with certainty, and this seemed to fly in the face of nature and of all his Humanist learning and metaphysics.[4] Secondly, the meaning of the situation for the wife, and her meaning, seem obscure, and her evidence and role remain ambiguous: she may actually have brought the charge of imposture, but Coras's account remains unclear both on this point and on her motives if this were the case, as it does on the question of her changing knowledge, over time, of the accused. Then, Coras, who wanted to believe the wife virtuous – he cast her as Penelope in his narrative – could not countenance that she might have *chosen* adultery, mortal sin, and he seems determined to exonerate her, to save her honour and her family's, thus judging that if she were an adulteress she was nonetheless innocent of adultery because, being a woman she was a blind, gullible victim of seduction. Still less could he allow that a man and woman might have joined together in an alliance which so undermined not only marriage but also the gender relations which sustained the fundamental social bond: between men (only) as subjects, exchanging woman as objects. The account seems caught between its writer's sense of what might possibly have happened, what remained unthinkable, and what he wanted to believe – which can be propped up by cultural stereotypes (such as, gullible women are men's prey).

In the two films the wife is given agency and new significance: both celebrate her resistance to orthodox constructions of femininity and the family, which strictly determined and delimited a woman's place as subject to first her father, then her husband; for a woman to challenge this was to risk being identified as deviant, unruly, without virtue. Both cast adulterous love as the realisation of her authenticity and autonomy, rather than (in early modern terms) as error, sin, evidence of women's lust and failure to resist temptation – for all women are daughters of Eve; and both represent her as a historical subject whose meaning converges on such present-day concerns as self-fulfilment, individual happiness, independence. This is to misappropriate her as a heroine, to disregard the intractable question of the historical and cultural specificity of her subjectivity, and to turn adultery and the mortal questions it entailed into romanticised fiction.

This reframing and dilution are aspects of the films' realism, which embraces mastery, authority, and authenticity. Their supposed historical authenticity seems reluctant to recognise the residue of difference and opacity in the past which remains beyond the reach of their painstaking reconstructions. Worse, the apparently realistic details which crowd the screen may lure the viewer into accepting that these reconstructions show authoritative knowledge of the past, and that such knowledge encompasses the films' constructions of their protagonists. The more historical paraphernalia – dress, objects, details – there is, the less subjectivity may seem to differ, that is, be unfamiliar, other to the viewer. Other clothes, maybe; but what passes for otherness is recognition of the same, of these persons from another time and place as if they were our contemporaries.

Film has the potential to explore issues of narrative unreliability and (self-) representation, both of which are crucial to the meaning of these events, but these films, rather, close the case. For they presuppose that the meaning of the events and identities is certain and representable, and cast us as spectators with fully centred vision and certain knowledge. These factors work together to obscure what they seem to clarify, and to diminish the significance of the wife whilst seeming to amplify it. The question of the man's identity and desire remains complex, embodying epistemological, ethical, and political issues. The woman's identity, on the other hand, crystallises around adulterous love, and only by proximity to the man is it lent something of the resonance of what he represents.

In Vigne's film, authority is both embodied as masculine, in the figures of the judge, priest, father and an often didactic voice-off, and

thematised. Also the framing of scenographic space is authoritative. Long shots open and close the film; there is a high percentage of fixed frontal scenes and close-ups of the characters, as if the steady hold of the camera could reveal whatever is hidden; a high proportion, too, of 'master shots', that is, the overall view which 'allows the scene to be dominated in the course of its reconstitution narratively as dramatic unity'.[5] Scenes are presented as spectacle and establish the spectator as unifying centre, authoritative witness, as if the lens' steady focus matched the spectator's gaze; the spectacle is offered for mastery and witness.

What insists is the power of the gaze, in a supposed coincidence of sight and insight. Yet what could be more at variance than this presumed 'transparency' of representation and its subject? Where Coras, and later, Montaigne, an eye-witness and one of the first commentators, emphasised the events' incomprehensibility, this film claims certainty and clarity: the spectator-as-witness is not to be unsettled, nor is she or he to unsettle the film's imposed meaning, as oriented by Vigne's Coras, figure of authority and benign justice.

Coras is enthralled by Guerre's wife, Bertrande de Rols, whom he first encounters as chief witness to the accused's identity, and as an enigma, a challenge to his powers of judgement. However, her potential to disturb is deflected by her being represented as the object of Coras's gaze, as spectacle, an effect abetted by her being identified, through tricks of lighting, costume, and camera angle with female figures in works by De La Tour and even Vermeer. These representations correspond to an eclectic range of cultural identifications of the feminine. Marginalised in most earlier versions of the tale, here the wife is central; but her meaning is none the less limited. If she is central, it is within the genre of the love story, where much is made of the gaze. Here the lover's gaze is required to communicate not only love and desire but also the vital truth of the person. But what of the gaze of the law, bent on discovering the truth of the matter? The film suggests that only love 'sees clearly'; meaning eludes the eyes of the law. Coras's final interview with Bertrande is represented as an encounter with meaning that falls beyond the gaze of the law; deliberately, he removes his judge's hat, must be other than judge if he is to encounter the truth. The limits to the law and to justice are dramatised by the contrast between its gaze and the lover's.

Much of the representation of Bertrande de Rols is as chaste wife and mother, conforming to the early modern – and cinematic – aesthetic demand that a woman be young and beautiful; and the

screenplay too insists on her dutifulness, fidelity and chastity; yet there is a shadow of a doubt. This stems from men's gaze within the frame, notably Coras's, and from the eroticised representation of Bertrande alone.

Eroticised, chaste – a potential source of sustained ambiguity, a disturbance of the film's economy of interpretation? However, this ambiguity dissolves because her desire is rarely represented as her own; rather, she confirms the male authority's interpretation to her, of herself. Take her final encounter with Coras. He asks her to explain her conduct (innocent? complicit?), so that he may fully understand – only to pre-empt her by telling her what he thinks she desired. Her response? To confirm *his* interpretation. At the very moment when her desire might be recognised, done justice, it has already been misrecognised: masculine authority dictates what a woman's desire could be, fails to respect and acknowledge desire, will, and meaning other than what it can tolerate.

Only at one moment might the representation of Bertrande not conform to this regulation. When 'Martin' returns to the village, he meets Bertrande last, alone. Kneeling, she 'recognises' him; and for a moment, the smooth surface of this representation is troubled. For as she affirms his identity, she glances fleetingly to camera: a glance coded for recognition by the spectator as disavowal, a knowing look, which invites us to view her as a woman whose desires we recognise as being like our own. But not with certainty a knowing look: it is just that it conforms to a filmic convention. In comparison to the overall economy of the film, this instance is almost imperceptible, and so outweighed by the film's mastered ambiguities that it can claim only slight interpretative significance, against the prevailing reluctance to problematise the relationship between sight, desire and knowledge.

The representation of Bertrande de Rols supplements the original account's silence with a variety of presuppositions and codes: women in film, the love story, all for love, and so on. The film tries to sustain a balance between authenticity – authoritative historical reconstruction of character as well as environment – and an appeal to a late twentieth-century sense of motivation. This double movement involves disjunctions and tensions quite as much as convergences, for the present's psychologising construction of the past, however driven by the desire for impossible transparency, inevitably bears traces of difference.

The film champions the love story as a source of meaning over against blind and oppressive justice. But this liberalism has its own

blindness: it fails adequately to represent that the ethical and epistemological questions of subjectivity and identity so acutely embodied by 'Martin'/Martin have their counterpart in and for the wife: her person, her 'truth' are mortal questions too, to which their love story only offers a limited answer.

That meaning could be transparent is a founding assumption and limitation here. What had been experienced as uncanny in the questions of identity is transformed by the templates of implicit anthropological and psychological conventions into explicable and representable events and behaviour. Desire, too, is treated as if it were fully accessible to consciousness and representation. Love seems to explain the enigma that confronted the judge and which had to be brought within the bounds of the law. The film tends to slide over the issues raised by this love. Could it, conclusively, have been called adultery, and if it were adulterous, what had been the wife's intentions, in all their complexity and mutability? How can we know what moved the judge to exonerate the wife, and is the film's sympathy for her appropriate in historical terms? The film's version of 'love' as an explanation ignores the unconscious and with it, what falls beyond representation and rational explanation. Furthermore, in ignoring the unconscious, trading it for explanation and representation, not only is an awareness of the subject's internal difference lost, but also an adequate recognition of the difference between subjects here and there, now and then. The film's determination to explain overrides difference and opacity, and thus it curiously reproduces the original judicial position: curiously, for its liberal sensibilities seem alert to the law's potential injustices and limits.

This version of the story of Martin Guerre and his wife exemplifies a form of reason's entanglement with power, and of both with that masculine thinking which has governed our notions of the subject, of identity and also of knowing, valuing investigation that explains and grasps its subject without excess or remainder. In sixteenth-century versions of the case, inexplicability was explicable as the devil's work; what remained in excess of the judge's scrutiny was the wife's knowledge, will and desire. Now psychology supersedes superstition, and the wife is represented in such a way that only a moment's excess is allowed, in that glance, and it is a coded gesture; nothing, it seems, remains opaque – if we accept the premises of the film's explanations and representation.

In Amiel's *Sommersby*, which transposes the drama into the post Civil War period, love is the visible source of truth and redemption.

The realist devices evident in the earlier film return here, intensified, promoting transparency, intolerant of any residue of opacity or inexplicability, and details requiring interpretation are such that a competent viewer readily identifies the 'master' text which assures their meaning. Not just the case of Martin Guerre. No: selected aspects of Homerian epic meet the familiar great American narrative of individual heroism and redemption.

Sommersby is less inventive, less strategic in its framing and its cinematography than *Le Retour de Martin Guerre*, much more inclined to operate on the level of diegesis, in terms of gesture, action or absence interpretable within the narrative framework. For instance, where Bertrande de Rols's complicity was hinted by that glance to camera, the equivalent here is more elaborately staged: the wife rushes to get ready for her husband and, in the bedroom, takes his photograph from a drawer and frantically rubs it clean, before returning it to its place on her dressing-table. The image of the husband put away, an unwanted, painful memory repressed? The rubbing clean: disguising how dusty the image, the memory had become? Or wiping out that image, in readiness for someone new? A gesture saturated with ambiguity? Or too readily readable to have sustained resonance?

This film urges that we have a right to our desires and happiness, and makes a hero of Sommersby. It represents adultery as a site of authenticity, happiness and reparation. Not adultery in the spectator's eyes, nor in Sommersby's, for we all know that the husband is dead, since the opening minutes of the film were replete with clues of this and of the imposture; but the wife does not, and whilst we are indemnified, it is on her alone that the moral burden falls. Double burden: both the guilt of complicity with the imposture and – unnecessary guilt – a relationship which, while she believes her husband alive, she believes adulterous. We are spared the burden of that guilt, or of having to condone adultery, all the more so because the film does not dwell on the potential ambiguity and complexity of her position. A morality slippery as an eel.

Amiel's version allows no mystery or opacity. Heroics replace ethical dilemmas; its 'psychology' is led by romanticism; calculated appeals to the spectator's sympathy function to absolve all concerned and dissolve away the issues. The film suggests that love changes the stakes and sets its own overriding rules; it banks on the spectator's desire corresponding with the 'happy couple' 's. Where the original case, and even, slightly, the first film, unsettled its witnesses, causing

them to doubt what they knew, liberal *Sommersby* anaesthetises its spectators to the ethical dilemmas with which it deals. If its representation of the wife is liberal, the issues which she embodies are diminished: adultery, collusion – a little banal, romantic happiness, an egoic satisfying of her desire for danger, for, as she puts it, 'something wild' (good sex). She is never allowed really to grasp 'Jack''s existential dilemma: he will die for the identity he has assumed and in his mind become; for her the 'truth' and 'solution' are simpler, her happiness not beyond repair. For her the question of identity is ultimately articulated in terms of her desire: his essence is to be the one she desires. She says: 'it was always you. I knew from the first moment I saw you, it was always you'. Any other question of his identity is not allowed sufficiently to enter her vision; he is as she identifies him: 'you'. And at that moment, it seems that she is as she identifies herself: 'I knew', as if her desire was a matter of knowledge, no mystery to her. The film's supposition that it can bring, and show, desire within the field of knowledge perhaps is most clearly revealed as a blindspot at this moment when it is given as *the* truth.

Laurel Sommersby takes after Vigne and Carriere's imaginary Bertrande de Rols in that such *topoi* as 'love at first sight' and 'all for love' prevail. Causality comes down to this. Where the representation differs is that the later version insists on that coincidence of desire and knowledge; the earlier version is more caught up in the woman's desire coinciding with what the man thinks he knows (of it). Neither version respects her opacity and difference.

'Jack' on the other hand continues to embody legal, epistemological and ethical questions until the end. What makes a person who he or she is? Is a person redeemable and what can be sacrificed to/for this? What's in a name? What is honour? And what, betrayal?

The film does not hesitate to supply answers from the American liberal emporium. Against the odds, 'Jack' makes reparation for Jack and for his former self, by bringing economic prosperity back to the family and town, through successfully growing tobacco, and by his anti-slavery stand, heroically defending a Black against assault by forerunners of the Ku Klux Klan.

In *Sommersby* there is a new twist to the plot. 'Jack' is arrested not for imposture but for murder; Jack Sommersby, years before, had killed a man after gambling at cards with him. Imposture, here, is a subplot mobilised as his defence against the charge: if he is not Jack, then there can be no trial. Where originally the wife insisted on 'Martin''s innocence until the end of the trial, here the wife must insist

on his guilt. In the trial scenes, two models of identity are in play: she testifies that 'Jack' is not her husband, and suggests that the whole community had accepted otherwise because they all wanted him to be Jack: here the desire to identify (as) determines identification. The other version, the stronger, is Jack's: identity as performance. This trial becomes a show, this is courtroom as drama, a test of virility: 'Jack', like Odysseus (the comparison is clear) has 'nimble wits'; 'Jack' like Odysseus, outshines all the other men of the community. 'Jack', appropriately, chooses to represent himself, and everything hangs on his performance. The crowd becomes his admiring audience. The wife's words are readily dismissed as a woman's words, emotional and unreliable; over against them are his performance, his reasoning. The more she insists that he is not Jack Sommersby – and there is a certain ambiguity here, because her motive for this is strategic quite as much as it is moral – the more elaborate and energetic his self-representation becomes. The woman's performance proves to be less heroic and compelling than the man's; and she cannot reason like him, or even understand what is at stake.

If there is a trace of irony in the film it is that masculine logic triumphs at the expense of the man's life. The film does not invite this reading, however; when 'Jack' exchanges responsibility for one crime for another, imposture for murder, we are urged to accept his stance: 'without my name I don't think I have a life'. Without another man's name, that is, he cannot redeem himself, become someone other than the 'coward, cheat, liar, thief, and deserter' that he had been as Horace Townsend. To die for a crime that was not his is represented as transcendant moral heroism, atonement Hollywood style.

It may be dramatically effective to defer the wife's dawning understanding of the existential dilemma of the man she has claimed as her husband until the end; but this is to insist to the end that the drama is almost all his. Her role throughout has been clarified, conventionalised; if she had doubts and fears, these are only expressed in a punctual melodramatic outburst, quickly dissolved. The reluctance to show the relationship except in terms of filmic convention – bed, standing by her man, birth – leaves her in a subordinate role, propping up the man's struggle to find identity but not sufficiently shown struggling for her own. Her story is not allowed the grand, heroic resonances of his: for her, love is happiness, what she wants, and questions of identity seem in abeyance; for him, his love story is an aspect of his more urgent narrative of redemption.

The last shot of her is final confirmation of how reduced her representation has become: she lays flowers on Sommersby's grave, the picture of the faithful widow, any ambiguities instantly readable. The closing shot of the grave, lovingly tended, in a tranquil churchyard, memory flowering, is in very determined contrast to the opening shot of a rocky, unnamed grave, on a bare hillside, an outcast's grave or the victim of some arbitrary accident, to be forgotten. The camera may dwell on the widow laying flowers, but the drama of identity and redemption, the trajectory from one grave to the other, will never be hers except by proxy. If there is any redemption allowed her, it is shabby and illusory: namely, the recasting of adultery and her 'sin' in a representation closer to a Norman Rockwell illustration than to any part of the original tale, least of all the woman in question.

Notes

1   In an interview the French scriptwriter J.-C. Carriere comments: 'il s'agissait peut-être d'une histoire d'amour et [...] il y avait ainsi la possibilité d'un film'. (See sleeve-notes to N.Z. Davis, J.-C. Carriere and D. Vigne, *Le Retour de Martin Guerre* (Paris: Laffont, 1982).)

2   The full title of Coras's text is *Arrest memorable, du parlement de Tolose, Contenant une histoire prodigieuse, de nostre temps, avec cent belles, & doctes Annotations, de monsieur maistre Jean de Coras, Conseiller en ladite Cour, & rapporteur du proces. Prononce es Arrestz Generaulx le xii Septembre MDLX* (Lyon: Antoine Vincent, 1561).

3   The most comprehensive bibliography of writings on Martin Guerre is to be found in Natalie Zemon Davis's historical reconstruction, *The Return of Martin Guerre* (Harmondsworth: Penguin Books, 1985), 127–31.

4   Witness, for instance, Montaigne, III, 3: 'La ressemblance ne faict pas tant un comme la difference faict autre. Nature s'est obligee a ne rien faire autre, qui ne fust dissemblable', Montaigne, *Essais*, vol. III. ed. A. Micha (Paris: Garnier-Flammarion, 1969), 275.

5   S. Heath, 'Narrative space', in *Questions of Cinema* (London: Macmillan, 1981), 19–75 (41).

4

Notorious Women: Marriage and the Novel in Crisis in France 1690–1710

Joan DeJean

Anxiety about the survival of family estates was high in the final decades of Louis XIV's reign, when so many forces must have seemed to be conspiring to end an era of prosperity. The last peace treaty that brought the country substantial new territorial gain was signed in 1678. From then on, the national estate was consistently eroded, as the ageing monarch lost territories conquered when he was still the rising Sun King. Family estates were squandered to maintain the ostentatious pomp *de rigueur* at Versailles. And money was drained from all coffers to finance the enormous expense of an endless series of disastrous wars, wars that made many women widows when they were still young enough to renegotiate their legacies.

The year 1678, this transitional moment for the French national estate, also witnessed the publication of what is accepted as the first modern novel, *La Princesse de Clèves*. Literary history has isolated this work as a solitary masterpiece with only the very indirect posterity of such novels as *La Nouvelle Héloïse* (1761) and *Les Liaisons dangereuses* (1782). In reality, however, Lafayette immediately inspired a generation of women novelists to develop the reorientation of the novel of marriage that she had initiated.

In *La Princesse de Clèves*, Lafayette reversed the romance model in which marriage is fiction's goal, a utopian union, the culmination of both personal quest and official hostilities, the wedding of a couple that also solidifies a national estate. Lafayette uses the marriage agreement to begin her story: she then defines the modern novel as the story of an unhappy union and in particular of her heroine's struggle to find a voice for her desire when all around her seek to

define her solely in terms of her official exchange value. Lafayette's immediate successors continue to portray marriage in crisis, an institution defined by some as an official contract uniting two family estates and by others as a union in which the partners had a right to personal fulfilment.

The novels that develop Lafayette's crucial identification between the model novel and marriage in crisis were, without exception, very quickly excluded from literary history. In the following pages, I will try to explain that exclusion by highlighting the most important variant of the French novel to develop in Lafayette's wake, the memoir novel. I will read two novels that I intend to represent the abundant production of an entire generation.[1] I will stress in particular the legal context in which these works could have been seen as controversial, a context that also helps explain why, as an essential part of their exclusion, their authors were portrayed as personally notorious. And in tandem with this vision of the woman novelist as dangerous acquaintance was developed one of literary history's essential myths, the novel as an agent of corruption, a literary plague capable of weakening society's foundation.

Lafayette's notorious successors were to an extent to blame for this vision. Adultery, legal separation, illegitimate births, even custody battles – any cause for public scandal is dwelled on in loving detail in the memoir fiction composed in Lafayette's wake. No longer do novelists distance their accounts in a historical past: for the first time, the novel is set exclusively in contemporary France. These are the first-person accounts of women who, like the Princesse de Clèves, seem designed to make their readers compare their behaviour with the conduct they would expect from someone they knew. In short, everything about these novels would seem to guarantee that their authors would be identified with their scandalous heroines. And they were.

Let me state from the outset that I quite frankly do not always know how to present either these texts or the women who wrote them. My goal is not to proclaim the notorious women innocent of 'crimes' with which they have been charged, but simply to point out the complexity of a situation hitherto read far too literally. The heroines of these works – despite their obvious similarities with their creators – are not autobiographical projections: the biographies of these women writers have been corrupted, but enough remains to make this much certain. Their heroines present their narratives as open to diverse inter-pretations. Like the narrators of autobiographies, they ask us to sit

in judgment on their lives. However, in their stories they make the process of judgment, and especially the act of condemnation, explicit. When we compile the guilty verdicts at the conclusion of each episode (the crimes with which the heroine is charged by her persecutors), the resulting portrait in every case is nearly identical to the biography that subsequent commentators present as that of the novel's creator, a reconstruction that, these novels teach us, is absolutely predictable. *Fin-de-siècle* women writers turn the novel into a notoriety trial. They show the grounds on which a woman was proclaimed notorious and the consequences of this verdict. Their texts are all the more powerful because they are situated on the level of the fantasm rather than in the domain of autobiography. Instead of the story of an individual woman, each work projects a powerful construction of gender, a period's obsession with the alleged proliferation of women judged notorious because they threatened the ruin of families.

The literary historians through the centuries who proclaim these novels unworthy because of their, and their authors', immorality have deprived readers of novels of real merit. I will present briefly the two I feel would most readily find a public today: the first, by an aristocrat, features the question of adultery; the second, by a bourgeoise, the plight of the children of a broken marriage. Both suggest that, on the eve of the Enlightenment, the institution of marriage was widely believed to be in crisis.

My involvement with these texts began with an interdiction pronounced with the full authority of Antoine Adam, the individual who surely saw himself as the principal architect of our current vision of seventeenth-century French literary history. Instead of a commentary on the *Mémoires de Madame la comtesse de M**** (1697) by Henriette de Castelnau, Comtesse de Murat, Adam turns the alleged entry in his *Histoire de la littérature française du dix-septième siècle* into something worthy of tabloid journalism: the Comtesse, he contends, was imprisoned because of her 'public scandals' (*scandales éclatantes*). He mocks the 'exertions' of her previous biographer in defence of her virtue; the (nameless) scholar was ignorant of the proof of her criminality, a lesbian sonnet that demonstrates that 'it was just as dangerous to leave her in the company of women as in that of men'.[2] He dismisses her novel categorically: 'No one would dream of reading it now' – and immediately offers a Count as substitute for the 'dangerous' Countess, the *Mémoires de la vie du comte de Gramont* (1713) by Anthony Hamilton, which 'remains even today a work justly admired' (5:317). Only those who know that Adam is not

usually given to such overt critical hostility will understand how intensely my curiosity was piqued by his attempt to guarantee the exclusion of a work to which he had experienced a powerful reaction.

The work fully justifies both the strength of his reaction and my curiosity. The *Mémoires de Madame la comtesse de M**** is a crisply written, fast-paced, extended novelisation of Woman's struggle to preserve her reputation. I say 'Woman's' advisedly, for the narrator frequently reminds her reader that she is going public with her private life to call attention to an issue of general importance for her female contemporaries, the desire to believe that women live their lives for *galanterie*. Some of the work's early editions have a second title page, 'The Defence of Women': together, the two titles convey perfectly the novel's point of view, according to which 'the faithful account of my life's adventures' demonstrates that 'most often there is more misfortune than dissoluteness in the conduct of the women whose reputation the public delights in destroying'.[3]

The narrator recounts her own life to explain why her behaviour was so publicly decried. At an early age, she is forced by her father to marry an older man to whom he owes money; he in effect sells her to pay off his debt. Her husband, apparently with some cause, is constantly jealous and mistreats her. She flees to a convent, and writes her father and her husband to request a separation. She is persuaded to return home but, when she finds herself pregnant, her husband declares publicly that it is not his child and renews his abuse. She again flees. When she learns that her mother is conspiring with her husband and his family to have her locked up, she attempts, in the manner of the Princesse de Clèves, to regularise her irregular situation in the hope of recovering control over her life. Having put herself under the protection of a magistrate, she goes public with the details of her husband's mistreatment and asks for an official separation. When her mother, speaking on her husband's behalf, tries to force her to accept a private agreement that would require her to leave Paris, she refuses the exile that would save the family's honour at the expense of her freedom and her reputation: 'I had been too abused to content myself with a private agreement, when I wanted public justification' (158–9). When her husband dies just in time to spare both families the disgrace of divorce proceedings, she has recourse to the only 'public justification' still left her and publishes these memoirs, which conclude with the threat to continue her literary scandal by editing the memoirs of other women who have been 'as harshly treated as she' (276).

With the *Mémoires de Madame la comtesse de M****, Murat made the novel go public with the story camouflaged behind *La Princesse de Clèves*'s brilliant historical façade, the story of Woman's attempt to win legal control over an unhappy marriage. I say 'Woman's' once again because the text suggests – through references to other ill-treated women and to women who have already gone public with their memoirs of unhappy marriages – that the Comtesse's tale documents the existence of a social phenomenon bigger than this case history, that this account is a response to history. It is also possible, as we will see, that the novel played a part in shaping history – and not just literary history's depiction of Murat herself, as any reader could predict, as a notorious *femme galante*.

Murat's heroine is aware of her legal rights and especially of their limitations. She realises that 'the treatment of which I was accusing my husband was not dangerous enough to authorise my separation', and that her husband is within his rights when he 'threatens to keep [her] locked up in his château' (47).[4] Thus, the ultimate scandal of her conduct is that it is just as innovative as the Princesse de Clèves's *aveu*: she refuses to accept these legal limits, just as she refuses to accept the private 'accommodation' her mother offers her. She holds out for a 'public justification', official recognition that a husband unhappily married was not allowed to act out his displeasure in violence to his wife's person and that a wife could refuse to remain a prisoner of her husband's suspicions. The *Mémoires* demonstrates that female notoriety is really not an affair of *galanterie* – this explains why the question of the heroine's guilt or innocence is treated so playfully, its evocation cloaked in innuendo that makes it impossible ever to know what really happened – but an affair of publicity and legality. The Comtesse's real crime is her request, 'in defence of [all] women', for legal change.

Two decades after *La Princesse de Clèves*, the conflict latent in that story, between what is clearly an officially accepted definition of marriage as contract and what is portrayed as an emerging conception of marriage as a means to personal fulfilment, was finally being publicly displayed.

An equally striking illustration of this conflict is provided by a most curious set of paired memoirs, the *Mémoires de Madame Du Noyer écrits par elle-même* (1709–1710) by Anne-Marguerite Du Noyer and the *Mémoires de Mr. Des N*** écrits par lui-même*, presumably by her husband, Guillaume Du Noyer.[5] The identification between author and narrator established by the titles of these memoirs suggests that

they be read as non-fiction. However, in the case of the woman's narrative, the presentation of the narrator's life has far more in common with Murat's fiction than with contemporary autobiographical texts. Du Noyer's memoirs repeat the pattern, established by Murat's, whereby the notorious woman makes her life public, thereby establishing her own notoriety, in a form of self-defence that is primarily a defence of all women who are victims of abusive husbands and unjust laws. Like Murat's, Du Noyer's memoirs cross the border between fiction and non-fiction more clearly in their depiction of the situation of Woman at the end of Louis XIV's reign than in their depiction of an individual life.

The status of their companion text, the refutation of Du Noyer's memoirs allegedly written by her actual husband, is harder to determine: the work seems too polished to have been written by a professional soldier with no known intellectual aspirations. In view of the highly polemical issue that is the focus of Du Noyer's consideration of marriage, intermarriage between Protestants and Catholics in the aftermath of the revocation of the Edict of Nantes, the countermemoirs could have been composed by a pro-Catholic faction. The blatantly controversial stance Du Noyer adopts suggests a second theory: the countermemoirs were also her work, an essential part of both her attempt to portray the destruction of a woman's reputation and her attempt to paint a full picture of religion's effects on marriage.

Du Noyer's incipit parallels Murat's: she is 'presenting herself as a public spectacle' in a *general*, rather than a personal, defence, 'to give a fair idea of myself at a time when calumny is trying to disfigure people'.[6] The personal history that follows, like Murat's, is full of misfortune. The narrator loses her mother at an early age; her father literally sells her to her mother's childless sister by means of a contract 'unique of its kind' (6:8). She is destined to be well married, when her adopted father gambles away all their money and the marriage contract is broken (6:8). This broken contract sets her on the road to another type of notoriety: she finds herself, a strict Protestant, without protection during the persecutions that surrounded the revocation of the Edict of Nantes (6:16–17). She recounts in great detail the victimisation of French Protestants and their flight into the diaspora (6:60–4, 76–7, 89–90, 112). She herself escapes the country, disguised as a man (6:116).

Upon her return to France, she is imprisoned to obtain a forced conversion; she is released when she marries a Catholic. Her

orthodoxy, however, is only apparent, for the public marriage contract is founded on a private contract, her husband's written promise never to use his authority to force her to renounce practices dictated by her religion. The marriage works until her husband violates both contracts, the public one by gambling away her inheritance (6:388), and the private one by refusing (after she has once again left the country to escape religious persecution) to allow their daughters to marry Protestants. In the face of his efforts to force her to return their children to him, she flees to Holland, then to England, where her memoirs culminate in her symbolic reception into the Protestant state: when she takes leave of her reader, she is in Westminster Abbey awaiting the coronation of a queen.

The countermemoirs, 'written by Mr. Des N*** himself', supply the negative vision that Murat's heroine integrates into her own story. When these texts are read together, one woman's private history becomes indicative of a larger, public menace. In his account, Des Noyers occupies the position of orthodoxy, political and religious: his orthodoxy is established by various outside authorities called in to confirm his view of her life. First, the anonymous author of the preface tells us that the husband was always a model of patience, controlling his 'just anger' at behaviour so 'dangerous and mad' that it merited a public flogging. The preface is paralleled by the anonymous text used to conclude the countermemoirs, a comedy in three acts, *Le Mariage précipité*, said to have been staged in Utrecht in 1713 as a satire of his wife: the alleged Du Noyer stand-in is ridiculed because of her outrageous efforts to trap a rich Protestant for her daughter.

In between these predictable proofs that Catholic (men) and Protestant (men) alike were scandalised by 'the she-devil's' conduct (1:160), the narrator presents evidence that startles, even in the context of a text as basely mudslinging as this, a 'Memoir by my daughter Constantin' (5:256–81). This document indicates the true nature of these paired memoirs: together, they function as a custody trial, at which readers are asked to sit in judgment. Which parent deserves to raise these daughters, or, in this case, to arrange their marriages? – the father who claims to have respected a private marital agreement and supervised their Catholic upbringing? – or the mother who, according to the father, has broken that contract and abducted the daughters, in the father's version of her words, 'from the arms of idolatry to lead them on the way to heaven' (5:238), that is, on the journey from Catholicism to Protestantism. This elaborately staged family drama – perhaps the first true precursor of the bloody custody

battles in today's divorce proceedings, down to the child's statement explaining why he or she wishes to live with a certain parent – is without precedent at this period and is far more vivid than the earliest examples of the parallel legal genre, the custody hearings of the first French divorce trials in the 1790s. Actual legal proceedings, recorded in the third person, lack the immediacy of these 'personal' appeals.[7] However, it is hard to reconcile this immediacy and the distanced chronological perspective on these proceedings. Neither of the paired memoirs informs us about their outcome: we can only assume from the placement of the daughter's account – she is looking back on events that took place some years before; she is writing 'because [her father] orders her to do so', and her narrative of their 'retreat' (*refuge*) to Protestant countries exactly corroborates his version of those years – that the father wins out, and that she therefore ends up a Catholic.

This family docudrama – how fictive, how staged, we will never know – calls our attention to the big picture in which all contemporary tales of female notoriety must be understood. The *Mémoires de Madame Du Noyer* define female notoriety as the woman's decision to challenge the State and its official religion in the person of the individual to whom they have delegated authority over her. They reveal important consequences for the French nation if notorious women are allowed to infiltrate Catholic families: the loss of capital (the narrator demands that her husband return her dowry, which she claims he is squandering) and the loss of children as loyal citizens. In his revenge, 'Mr. Des Noyers' becomes the spokesman for all those who feared the public cost of women's personal freedom. Nowhere was this fear more evident than in the abundant contemporary commentary about marriage and its dissolution.

La Princesse de Clèves already attests to a new interest in the potential cost to the woman married off without regard for her feelings, and to a desire to explore concrete solutions to an officially unrecognised dilemma. This interest was more intense, the solutions proposed more concrete, in *fin-de-siècle* women's writing: the difference between subsequent fictions of married women and Lafayette's inaugural fiction is thus one of degree, rather than a total change of moral register. In addition, the next generation of novelists had to position their fiction in response to an image of the married woman that was probably unheard of, or at most dimly visible, when Lafayette was creating her novels. This image, that of married women 'prey to their weaknesses', 'without heroism', was not of their creation: it was

already on the existential horizon by the time their novels began to appear.

What was its origin in reality? In all likelihood, the notion of what one commentator termed a female 'pestilence'[8] was largely fantasm, like all the most powerful fictions of female desire, from the prostitute with the heart of gold to the lesbian *femme fatale* – part wish fulfilment and part dreaded occurrence. This image – the adulterous woman seeking a 'divorce' (the contemporary term for what we know as legal separation) that would destabilise the genealogical and the financial stability of honourable families – becomes so frequent in a variety of texts both legal and literary that it is easy to sympathise with the (feigned?) bewilderment of a contemporary literary commentator, François Granet, who wondered if 'secret marriages, divorces, and abductions have really become today such common events?'[9] One may legitimately wonder, as Granet did, if the State's 'foundations' could really have been threatened by the conduct of a few women no longer willing to accommodate themselves to bad marriages?

It is possible that the threat of upheaval represented by the adulterous woman in search of a legal settlement was useful to the State since, by the 1690s, the complex legal machinery it had contrived to put in place around what was called divorce seems suspiciously like a legal fiction. In the decade that witnessed the publication of *La Princesse de Clèves*, French legal theorists loyal to the State had argued in a series of treatises in favour of the contract theory of marriage. Their proposal that a marriage functioned as a sacrament only when it was founded on a valid contract was intended to give the State the authority necessary to take control over marital disputes away from ecclesiastical courts in favour of secular courts. The primary goal of contract theory was to guarantee that the State had the last word in determining when, and if, a union could be dissolved – all in the hope of preserving secular control over the transmission of estates.

In practical terms, however, the controversy surrounding who had a right to terminate marriages and under what conditions had an unexpected side-effect: it encouraged private individuals to consider the possibility that unhappy unions could be terminated. It is in this context that the discourse in *La Princesse de Clèves*, in which Prince and Princesse meditate on the individual's rights within the institution of marriage, makes sense. Lafayette's novel and those of her notorious successors confirm a theory often advanced by marriage historians: the belief that marriage should be a means to personal fulfilment

culminates inevitably in the existence of divorce in the modern sense of the term.

When seen in conjunction with the contemporary vision of Woman seeking to destabilise the State and the Family by putting an end to the marriage they had planned for her, the memoir novels of the notorious women testify to the complex situation that had been generated in the gap between legal speculation and legal reality. On the most obvious level, I have in mind the discrepancy, noted by Granet, between the tightening of restrictions that continued to make it almost impossible for women to find a legal solution to the most disastrous marriages and the popular perception, evidenced by this entry in Furetière's *Dictionnaire universel*, that, aided by cooperative authorities, women were having their own way and making their own law: '*Separation*: Women begin *separation* proceedings against their husbands in order to live as libertines (*dans le libertinage*).'[10] It was not, of course, their living in sin that caused concern, but the possibility that women could be 'libertine' in the sense of 'femme sans aveu', woman answering to no one, woman as legal 'adventuress'.

On a less obvious level, I refer to French divorce speculation as a legal fiction because the treatises that continued to argue for the definition of marriage as contract that justifies State control over the institution also continued to encourage the belief that it was possible to dissolve a marriage and therefore indirectly to promote the desire for a new kind of marriage, what James F. Traer refers to as 'modern' marriage.[11] Nowhere is this situation clearer than in Pierre Le Ridant's 1753 treatise, *Examens de deux questions importantes sur le mariage*: Le Ridant – the most sweeping early contract theorist, who would make marriage a civil matter entirely outside ecclesiastical jurisdiction – considers only the question of annulment and lists only traditionally accepted grounds. Nevertheless, widespread public discussion of annulment and separation – along with the 1670s, the mid eighteenth century is the period of most intense debate concerning the nature of marriage – surely encouraged the perception that marriage could, according to Le Ridant's favourite expression, 'be broken'. In addition, general acceptance of marriage as a contract and as a sacrament only once the contract is valid could only have diminished the institution's moral authority. Divorce historians present this period as the point of no return: the Revolution's divorce decree was but a logical next step.[12] They have also noted that the vocabulary of 'happiness' began to enter contemporary definitions of marriage in the 1760s, immediately after this new wave of divorce commentary

(Dessertine, ch. 1). At the same time, for those unhappily married and seeking a legal solution, all talk of 'breaking marriages' was but a tantalising mirage, a legal fiction that surely made reality all the harsher.

Only one critic took the early novel as seriously as it deserved. To try to stop these women from using the novel as a public forum for such dangerous ideas as a wife's equality with her husband, Boileau was prepared to go to great lengths, even to recontour his own œuvre. The satires were a pillar of Boileau's reputation; originally, there were nine, written and published between 1657 and 1674. Everything indicates that he intended to stop the series there. Then in a 1692 letter, Racine announces his hope of seeing 'the satire on women' soon.[13] It is clear that Boileau's return to satire was motivated by the production of heirs, the scandalous women of the 1690s.

The 10th satire is most often referred to by the title Racine uses, 'Satire on Women': Boileau takes the particular example of *Clélie*, a novel by Madeleine de Scudéry (1654–1660) as the springboard for a generalisation about the dangerous behaviour of a new race of women. The satire is addressed to a young man about to marry; it is a warning about the conduct that *Clélie* promotes in its female readers. The novel's 'enchanting discourse' will put his future wife 'on the edge of a precipice'. How 'can she continue to walk without her foot slipping' when all around her 'everything is being said, and heard'? What begins only as 'the affair of a novel' easily becomes 'a début in crime'. The end is then in sight: 'One fall always leads to another.' By the end, the chaste fiancée, fused with Scudéry's chaste heroine, has become the most notorious *femme galante* of the 1690s: Boileau ends his fantasmagoria of the novel's contagion with Clélie as the new Phèdre, the new Messalina, bringing about the 'ruin' of 20 men, 'a woman without restraint and without law given up to vice' (67). The novel was making women wild; Boileau hoped to convince a new race of husbands to take the law into their own hands and put an end to the 'ruin' of families, the bleeding of their resources to finance the libertine excesses of these adventuresses.

Since Boileau was Boileau, 'lawmaker of Parnassus' and royal historiographer, this fantastic exaggeration was sure to win allegiance. The claims on which his argument is founded soon became critical principles, accepted facts of literary life that a commentator might repeat without offering proof: (1) Novels corrupted their female readers; (2) Novels were responsible for the decadence of French

society; they were a threat to marriage and to the financial stability of families. Commentators who wished to curry favour with the regime had the orthodox line thus neatly traced for them.

We should remember that Boileau never mentions the notorious women of the 1690s, even though it is evident that he had them in mind. We should also remember that, following Boileau's example, those commentators who included them never presented them as solely, or even principally, a literary threat: they were not novelists, but 'adventuresses', devouring fortunes as they devoured men. Their deletion from literary history might have been complete, without the efforts of twentieth-century critics to recover a fuller picture of the seventeenth century. These women had published so extensively that scholars such as Adam and Henri Coulet could not have excluded them from their accounts.

However, with inclusion like this, writers hardly need exclusion. Coulet dismisses them, one after another, explaining why there is no point in reading them: he mocks the 'futility' of Bédacier's presentation of history, the 'ponderousness' of La Force's argumentation.[14] And Adam ... For Adam, Murat was a shocking lesbian, La Force both sexually and politically 'compromised', d'Aulnoy (in a plot worthy of Alexandre Dumas) a would-be husband-killer.[15] In his eyes, these women were dangerous acquaintances, not fit to keep company with the great men who make seventeenth-century French literature an uplifting experience, and perhaps – who knows? – still a source of contagion for women readers.

Notes

1   Women writers were a major force in the production of novels at the end of the seventeenth century, during the period when classical theatre and poetry were on the wane and the novel was on its rise to the apex of the French tradition. Maurice Lever's *La Fiction narrative en prose au XVIIe siècle* is the most reliable barometer of the novel's production during this crucial period. If we consult his lists – and even if we eliminate the significant percentage of novels whose author is still unknown today – for the period 1687 (20 years after *La Princesse de Clèves*) – 1699 alone, 33 per cent of the novels included by Lever are by women. For certain years, especially in the early 1690s, the percentage is even higher. This essay is taken from my *Tender Geographies: Women and the Origins of the Novel in France* (Columbia University Press, 1991). Another version, 'Notorious Women: Marriage and the Novel Crisis in France (1690–1715)',

has appeared in *Yale Journal of Criticism*, 4.2 (1991), 67–85, published by the Johns Hopkins University Press.

2 Adam, Antoine *Histoire de la littérature française au XVIIe siècle*, 5 vols, Del Duca, 1949–56, 5:317 n.2.

3 Murat, Henriette de Castelnau, Comtesse de. *Mémoires de Madame la comtesse de M****, 1697, n.p., 1740, 5.

4 A treatise drawn up in 1670 for Louis XIV by the lawyers Abraham and Gomont specifies that only a man can bring charges for adultery, not a woman: 'In punishment, the woman is locked up in a monastery and her dowry is given to her husband.' (Cited by Alain Lottin, 'Vie et mort du couple: Difficultés conjugales et divorces dans le nord de la France aux XVIIe et XVIIIe siécles.' *Dix-septième siècle* 102–103 (1974):76).

5 I cannot explain why the husband's name is written 'Des Noyers' throughout the memoirs he allegedly authored, but 'Du Noyer' in his wife's text and in entries in biographical dictionaries. The husband's response seems to have been added to the wife's text for the first time in the 1720 edition, the first edition published after her death. When speaking of the account allegedly written by the husband, I will write his name 'Des Noyers.'

6 Anne-Marguerite Du Noyer, *Œuvres complètes*, 10 vols, London: Jean Nourse, 1739, 6:1.

7 Isabelle Vissière reproduces legal proceedings of eighteenth-century trials on women's issues such as domestic violence, *Procès de femmes au temps des philosophes*, Des Femmes, 1985.

8 Father Charles Porée, *De Libris qui vulgo dicuntur romanenses, oratio*, Bordelet, 1736, p. 51.

9 François Granet, *Réflexions sur les ouvrages de littérature*, 1737–1741, 12 vols, Geneva: Slatkine Reprints, 1968, p. 118.

10 Furetière's entry also reveals the extent to which separation was threatening because of its financial consequences. He quickly defines 'separation' as 'division, distribution'. His first example – 'For this inheritance the separation of property was made in several portions' – slants the reading of his second example, on women and separation. In reality, a wife could not hope to obtain a separation unless her husband's betrayals were scandalously public and with disastrous consequences: the Marquise de Sablé – La Rochefoucauld's literary collaborator, author of *Maximes* (1678) dropped from the literary history that glorifies his – was able to separate from her husband only after he had had 20 liaisons and had caused her financial 'ruin' (Adam 1:273). Other legal separations were obtained by husbands, who used this means to put away wives declared adulterous.

11 *Marriage and the Family in 18th-Century France*, Ithaca and London: Cornell University Press, 1980. See also Lawrence Stone, *The Family, Sex, and Marriage in England, 1500–1800*, New York: Harper & Row, 1977; and Dominique Dessertine, *Divorcer à Lyon sous la Révolution et l'Empire*, Lyon: Presses Universitaires de Lyon, 1981.

12 See, in particular, Jules Basdevant, *Les Rapports de l'église et de l'état dans la législation du mariage du Concile de Trente au Code Civil* (Société du

Recueil général des lois et des arrêts du Journal du Palais, 1990), pp. 58, 190–1.
13 Boileau, *Œuvres* (Paris: Gallimard, 1966, 926).
14 Henri Coulet, *Le Roman jusqu'à la Révolution*, 2 vols, (Colin, 1967) 1:290.
15 'Madame d'Aulnoy was born into one of the best families in Normandy. Married to the Baron d'Aulnoy, she wanted to get rid of him and, with her mother's help, she plotted a scheme destined to have him condemned to death for high treason. But he was acquitted, and the two women's accomplices were executed. The novelist retired to a convent' (5:315n.). The same note contains a similarly wild account of La Force's 'adventures', also ending with her forced 'retirement' to a convent. Adam offers no corroborating evidence in support of these charges, a gesture that would have been appreciated by those aware of the frequency with which wild accusations of this kind were made at the end of Louis XIV's reign.

5

'Let other pens dwell on guilt and misery': Adultery in Jane Austen

Claire Lamont

'I am proud to say I have a very good eye at an Adultress'.[1] That startling claim is made in one of Jane Austen's letters. It appears that she did not make much use of the talent in her fiction. Only one character in an Austen novel is an adulteress, Maria Bertram in *Mansfield Park* (1814). In one other novel adultery has already occurred and affects the plot: in *Sense and Sensibility* (1811) the story of the first Eliza is a tale of female adultery (205–7). Austen never makes a major plot element out of male adultery, although she refers to it occasionally. In *Mansfield Park* the uncle who was guardian of Henry and Mary Crawford moves his mistress into the house on the death of his wife (41). This is a meagre amount of material to go on, but enough, I hope, for something to be said about adultery in Austen's novels.

In the last volume of *Mansfield Park* the heroine, Fanny Price, is under pressure to accept a proposal of marriage from Henry Crawford. Her uncle presses upon her the eligibility of the offer. Even the indolent Aunt Bertram tells her that it is her duty to accept (333). But Fanny has two reasons for not doing so: she has doubts about Henry Crawford's character and she is in love with her cousin Edmund. She refuses, and the pressure on her is removed only when Henry runs off with her newly-married cousin Maria, now Mrs Rushworth. Maria's adultery removes the pressure on Fanny, and vindicates her moral judgement of Henry Crawford. It acts as a touchstone of the moral worth of Mary Crawford, leading to Edmund's final conviction as to her character, and ultimately his freedom to marry Fanny. Maria Bertram's adultery is so advantageous to the unwinding of the plot and the hopes of the heroine that it has tended to be overlooked. She

has been an unlikeable character, and her unhappy fate can be seen as one of those bitter threads that mars the ending of even a happy comedy, like the fate of Malvolio in *Twelfth Night*.

The episodes involving Maria in the early part of the novel suggest her yearning for personal freedom and sexual fulfilment. Critics have seen in the visit to Sotherton and the rehearsals of *Lovers' Vows* anticipations of her future behaviour. Her marriage to a rich but stupid neighbour, Mr Rushworth, opens up her life: she goes to Brighton and London. She has got some sort of freedom but she has not got sexual satisfaction, and when it is offered to her by Henry Crawford, keen to test his powers of seduction after his rebuff by Fanny, she sacrifices everything she has just gained in order to obtain it.

The consequences for Maria are severe. 'Mr. Rushworth had no difficulty in procuring a divorce' (464). We might remember that the first Divorce Act in England to allow full divorce through the secular courts was passed in 1857; *Mansfield Park* was published in 1814. Before 1857 marital rupture was a matter for the ecclesiastical courts, and the most they would allow was a judicial separation with no right of remarriage. G.H. Treitel has pointed out that Mr Rushworth must have taken advantage of a procedure available only to very rich men, divorce by Act of Parliament.[2] The underlying purpose of the procedure had been to protect the right of landowners to produce legitimate heirs. A man who could prove adultery in his wife could be given, though at great cost, another chance to find a wife who would be faithful.[3] Such a remarriage is predicted in the case of Mr Rushworth (464).

Divorce by Act of Parliament was not entirely disadvantageous to the woman, as it gained for her as well as for her husband the right to remarry, thus allowing her to marry her partner in adultery. Maria Rushworth, however, suffers the worst of all outcomes: Henry Crawford refuses to marry her after her divorce and she returns disgraced to her father's home.

Marital divorce is mentioned only twice in Austen's novels, in the case of Maria Rushworth, and in the case of the Eliza in *Sense and Sensibility* who had been forcibly married by her guardian to the older brother of the man she loved. Her lover went to the East Indies to be out of the way, and she in her misery had an affair with another man. Her adultery enabled her husband to obtain a divorce (206). Adultery in the wife was a sufficient cause for a divorce. The matter was unequal between the sexes: a woman would have to prove cruelty

by her husband as well as his adultery. A further inequality in practice was that few women had control of the money necessary for litigation.[4] The result was that women were under pressure to tolerate adultery in their husbands, but there was no reason for a wealthy man to tolerate it in his wife. In Austen's novels both cases of female adultery result in the husband procuring divorce. She does not give a detailed look at male adultery, but it appears that Henry and Mary Crawford's aunt had lived with their uncle's adultery (41, 46).[5]

Adultery was forbidden to both sexes by the Seventh Commandment.[6] At least since the Marriage Act of 1753 both parties to a marriage had taken a civil and religious vow which involved, in the words of the church's marriage service, 'forsaking all other'.[7] Why was breaking that vow more serious in the woman? To attempt to answer that question would involve going back beyond religious and legal codes into anthropology. In many cultures (though not all) women have paid the utmost penalty for adultery. I shall confine myself to suggesting the reasons which weighed with upper-class people in the late eighteenth century. They can be summed up under three headings: dynasty, property and sex.[8]

It was common to regard adultery in the wife as more serious than in the husband because it ran the risk of bringing into a man's family a child that was not his. When Mr Rushworth becomes alarmed at the intimacy of Henry and Maria's rehearsals of *Lovers' Vows* Mary Crawford assuages his jealousy by remarking how *maternal* Maria's manner was (169). It is stupid of Mr Rushworth to take comfort from that, as illicit maternity was one thing he, as a wealthy man in a patrilinear culture, had to fear. A child produced by male adultery would not be brought into the matrimonial home. This situation is not exactly illustrated in Austen, though she does indicate that children fathered outside wedlock were not brought into any home whether previously or subsequently established. Harriet Smith in *Emma* (1816), the natural daughter of a tradesman, is maintained at Mrs Goddard's school (22, 481). In *Sense and Sensibility* Mrs Jennings denies that Colonel Brandon's supposed love-child should prevent his marrying Marianne as the child 'may be 'prenticed out at small cost, and then what does it signify?'(196).

Another reason for taking a graver view of female adultery related to the idea of property. A married woman who was not allowed to own property, could herself be seen as property. Adultery was either trespass by another man on the husband's property, or a species of rebellion by the subject territory. The third reason why female adultery

was regarded seriously may be summed up in the one word, sex. One thing adultery did was isolate a woman's sexuality as just that. If a woman had everything to lose by adultery then only sexual appetite could explain it. That was not only an offence against modesty (meaning here reticence concerning the bodily functions), it was an offence against chastity. In *Boswell's Life of Johnson* there is a discussion of female virtue. Boswell records

> I asked [Dr Johnson] if it was not hard that one deviation from chastity should so absolutely ruin a young woman. JOHNSON. 'Why no, Sir; it is the great principle which she is taught. When she has given up that principle, she has given up every notion of female honour and virtue, which are all included in chastity.'[9]

If a wife lost her honour through adultery, so did her husband. A man would feel aggrieved at his wife's adultery because he expected to be the actor, and an act of wifely adultery would reveal at least that someone had usurped his place as sexual initiator. Mr Rushworth, whose first response to his wife's adultery was 'great anger and distress' finishes up after his divorce 'mortified and unhappy' (450, 464).

News of the adultery is conveyed to Fanny by an announcement in her father's newspaper. (The word adultery is not used in this or any of Austen's novels, incidentally.[10])

> 'it was with infinite concern the newspaper had to announce to the world, a matrimonial *fracas* in the family of Mr. R. of Wimpole Street; the beautiful Mrs. R. whose name had not long been enrolled in the lists of hymen, and who had promised to become so brilliant a leader in the fashionable world, having quitted her husband's roof in company with the well known and captivating Mr. C. the intimate friend and associate of Mr. R. and it was not known, even to the editor of the newspaper, whither they were gone.'(440)

We notice the mock-sorrow and salacious speculation of the newspaper. Austen had experience of the elopement of a woman she knew being reported in a newspaper. In a letter to her sister in 1808 she writes, 'This is a sad story about Mrs. Powlett [who had run off with Lord Sackville] ... A hint of it, with Initials, was in yesterday's Courier.'[11]

There is a critique of adultery in the reception of the news of Maria and Henry's elopement by the different characters in the novel. The first is Fanny's: it is horror and stupefaction. The elopement and what it implies is 'sin of the first magnitude' (441). Fanny's heart 'revolted from it as impossible'. When she considers the result of such disgrace on the family of the woman involved 'it appeared to her, that as far as this world alone was concerned, the greatest blessing to every one of kindred with Mrs. Rushworth would be instant annihilation' (442). Fanny wishes the family to be annihilated. When Edmund arrives in Portsmouth he greets her 'My Fanny – my only sister – my only comfort now' (444). He has annihilated not himself but Maria (and Julia who has eloped with Mr Yates) in order to claim that Fanny (his cousin) is his 'only sister'. This is echoed by Lady Bertram's view of the situation, 'as comprehending the loss of a daughter, and a disgrace never to be wiped off' (449).

The men in the family have the job of of turning out to look for the errant daughter. Maria's father, Sir Thomas, has time to reflect on his shortcomings as a father and educator: 'Wretchedly did he feel, that with all the cost and care of an anxious and expensive education, he had brought up his daughters without their understanding their first duties, or his being acquainted with their character and temper' (463–4). His daughters did not know their 'first duties'. One's 'first duties' are duties to God. The Catechism, echoing the Ten Commandments, divides one's duties into two categories, 'my duty towards God, and my duty towards my Neighbour'.[12] Sir Thomas, like Fanny and Edmund, sees Maria's defection as first and foremost the breaking of a religious vow. There is a comparable link between adultery and religion in Austen's letter to Cassandra referring to the 'sad story about Mrs Powlett'. Austen comments 'I should not have suspected her of such a thing. – She staid the Sacrament I remember, the last time that you & I did.' The point there is that the Prayer Book specifically names adulterers among those warned not to take the sacrament of Communion.[13]

The failure to see the matter as a moral fault is what condemns Mary Crawford. She has already had ample opportunity in the novel to display her casual attitude to religious observance. Mary Crawford defends her brother referring to what has happened as 'a moment's *etourderie*' and hopes it will be 'all hushed up' (437). (One notices the use of French words in this context; the other was *fracas*.[14]) During her last meeting with Edmund what shocks him most is that Mary repeatedly refers to Henry and Maria's affair as 'folly' and deplores

most its exposure (454–5). Fanny had responded to the elopement with horror, horror that seems to include physical as well as moral repugnance. Edmund laments that by contrast Mary Crawford showed 'No reluctance, no horror, no feminine – shall I say? No modest loathings!'(455).

Mary has a worldly pragmatism about what to do next:

> We must persuade Henry to marry her ... My influence, which is not small, shall all go that way; and, when once married, and properly supported by her own family, people of respectability as they are, she may recover her footing in society to a certain degree. In some circles, we know, she would never be admitted, but with good dinners, and large parties, there will always be those who will be glad of her acquaintance ... (456–7)

Mary's advice is that the Bertrams use their money and position to brave the disgrace. The only person to agree with her is Mrs Norris: 'Mrs. Norris ... would have had [Maria] received at home, and countenanced by them all. Sir Thomas would not hear of it ...' (464–5).

For the father-figures in the novel female adultery warrants punishment, not countenance. The first father to pronounce on the subject is Mr Price, Fanny's father.

> 'I don't know what Sir Thomas may think of such matters; he may be too much of the courtier and fine gentleman to like his daughter the less. But by G— if she belonged to me, I'd give her the rope's end as long as I could stand over her. A little flogging for man and woman too, would be the best way of preventing such things.' (439–40)

Sir Thomas, however, is not a Lieutenant of Marines, and his punishment for his disgraced daughter is banishment. Maria and her Aunt Norris retire together to 'an establishment ... formed for them in another country – remote and private, where, shut up together with little society, on one side no affection, on the other, no judgment, it may be reasonably supposed that their tempers became their mutual punishment' (465). The narrator adds one thing more, and that is a comment on the fact that only the female suffers public punishment for adultery:

That punishment, the public punishment of disgrace, should in a just measure attend *his* share of the offence, is, we know, not one of the barriers, which society gives to virtue. In this world, the penalty is less equal than could be wished; but without presuming to look forward to a juster appointment hereafter, we may fairly consider a man of sense like Henry Crawford, to be providing for himself no small portion of vexation and regret ... in having so requited hospitality ... and so lost the woman whom he had rationally, as well as passionately loved. (468–9)

Mansfield Park is unlike Austen's other novels in its use of religious language. Although the narrator does not presume 'to look forward to a juster appointment hereafter' the reader cannot escape the sober intimation that the novel implies a Christian 'hereafter', and that its dispensation might take a juster view of the penalties for adultery meted out to the two sexes.

'Let other pens dwell on guilt and misery.' That is the famous opening sentence of the last chapter of *Mansfield Park*. In the two cases in her novels where she looks at adultery Austen presents it as guilt whose consequence is misery. Eliza in *Sense and Sensibility* after her divorce falls into further sexual liaisons, into poverty and debt, and finally into consumption from which she dies. Maria is saved from poverty; her death is social rather than physical. 'I quit such odious subjects as soon as I can, impatient to restore everybody, not greatly in fault themselves, to tolerable comfort, and to have done with all the rest' (461). In this declaration of closure the narrator proposes 'to have done with' the faulty characters. Do we as modern readers agree 'to have done with' Maria Bertram? In one sense perhaps we do. In terms of plot *Mansfield Park* draws on the Cinderella story, and Maria is one of the ugly sisters.[15] Maria is disagreeable to Fanny, the Cinderella figure, throughout. The ugly sisters have nothing to do at the end when Cinderella is united with her prince but to go off, followed by the hatred of the reader. I suspect that in *Mansfield Park* Mrs Norris, the wicked stepmother, does elicit that hatred, but does Maria?

Is it possible to sympathise with Maria Bertram, unlikeable as she is? Could her story be told more sympathetically, as one of unrequited love, even infatuation, for a man of 'cold-blooded vanity'?(467) Having married the wrong man for the wrong reasons Maria makes a last grab for happiness when the man she loves tempts her again. Her rash elopement is 'under the idea of being really loved by a man who had

long ago made his indifference clear' (454). Pride prevents her from confiding in anyone at any stage. The women who observe her attraction to Henry Crawford while engaged to Mr Rushworth respond with jealousy or cynicism (Julia and Mary) or a reluctance to witness it (Fanny) (160–1, 168). The men who care for her happiness (Edmund and her father) both think, mistakenly, that she does not have strong feelings (116, 201). She is not helped, and she will not help herself. 'She did not want to see or understand' (44).

The sympathetic reader might point out also the speed with which errors are observed and publicised in her society. The maid of Mrs Rushworth senior has evidence against her, and a newspaper is quick to publish her disgrace (450–1, 440). Lawrence Stone in his *The Road to Divorce* mentions how many well-to-do people had their adultery revealed by domestic servants, and how keen newspapers were to report it.[16] There is, however, another kind of novel adumbrated in the attempt to sympathise with Maria Bertram, a kind which is not being written. We are asking for a later novel, one with more sympathy for sexual fulfilment, one prepared to see adultery as self-realisation. In it we would expect to see more of the woman's feelings than Austen allows, or at least be invited to sympathise with her refusal to confront her own passions. There is scope for tragedy in Maria's story, but the novelist would have to be one of the later nineteenth-century novelists of adultery – perhaps Flaubert – rather than Austen.

Mansfield Park takes a harsh view of adultery. If the novelist had wished to enter into a debate about adultery Mary Crawford's liberal views could have been founded on ideas of sexual freedom associated with the French Revolution rather than simply on worldliness. But Mary is not given the intellectual dignity of a Jacobin or a proto-feminist. The novel not only endorses sanctions against adultery, but on a couple of occasions expresses particular anxiety about its growing acceptability. Fanny's father comments that 'so many fine ladies were going to the devil now-a-days that way, that there was no answering for anybody' (440). One notices that Mr Price regards it as a particular failing of the upper classes.[17] Mary Crawford speaks as a woman of the upper class in recommending that the Bertrams brave Maria's disgrace: 'In some circles, we know, she would never be admitted, but with good dinners, and large parties, there will always be those who will be glad of her acquaintance; and there is, undoubtedly, more liberality and candour on those points than formerly' (457).

The presence of these passages probably reflects the Evangelical influence which Marilyn Butler has noted in Austen's later novels.[18]

Certainly *Mansfield Park* seems harsher in tone towards sexual transgression than its predecessor, *Pride and Prejudice* (1813). In that novel Mr Collins remonstrates with Mr Bennet for receiving Lydia and Wickham at Longbourne: 'You ought certainly to forgive them as a christian, but never to admit them in your sight, or allow their names to be mentioned in your hearing' (364). Mr Bennet comments, '*That* is his notion of christian forgiveness!' The difference may be explained, however, not only by the difference in tone between the two novels but by the fact that Lydia was not an adulteress; she was a foolish girl who thought she was eloping to Gretna Green but found herself living unmarried with a young man who turned out to require more effective bribery to make him go through with the marriage ceremony. Lydia's story is not one of guilt and misery but, almost more terrifying, of guilt and irrepressible self-satisfaction.

Mansfield Park does not invite sympathy for Maria Bertram; and yet the modern reader hesitates, haunted by her banishment at the end of the novel. One notices again the difference in tone between *Mansfield Park* and *Pride and Prejudice*. When in the latter the news of Lydia's marriage spreads through the neighbourhood the narrator comments 'To be sure it would have been more for the advantage of conversation, had Miss Lydia Bennet come upon the town; or, as the happiest alternative, been secluded from the world, in some distant farm house' (309). In that passage banishment to the country for sexual transgression sounds like some lurid and callous cliché. Maria, by contrast, is treated like contagious evil. She might hurt other young women, as her example has already damaged her sister Julia (467). The domestic values of Mansfield are one reason why adultery cannot be tolerated, as adultery threatens the family. But what about Maria herself? Her punishment is to be 'shut up' with Mrs Norris. The two fathers in the novel propose two different punishments for Maria. Lieutenant Price suggests flogging; Sir Thomas imprisons her. Flogging is associated with the armed forces, and I suppose most readers dismiss the suggestion as brutal and only appropriate to the boorish Mr Price. But Michel Foucault has taught us to take another look at the contrast between the two sorts of punishment; physical punishment and imprisonment.[19] Mr Price's punishment is punishment of the body, physically painful, and gross in its intrusiveness on the dignity of the individual. But it is brief in time. The punishment that Maria endures only indirectly touches the body; it does not intrude on her personal dignity; but it lasts for ever and, in Foucault's expression, 'punishes the soul'.[20] Foucault in describing

the development of penal practices – he is writing specifically about France after 1760 – comments, 'the expiation that once rained down upon the body must be replaced by a punishment that acts in depth on the heart, the thoughts, and the will, the inclinations.' Imprisonment is not simply a method of punishing a crime, but is the ultimate technique of control.

Marilyn Butler has pointed out that Maria Bertram is a forthright, autonomous woman in a novel which, unusually for a woman writer of the period, celebrates the compliant woman. 'The empowered woman of other novelists becomes Austen's adulteress.'[21] Maria Bertram expresses autonomy in two ways, by acting independently of the claims of others and by unlicensed sexuality. These are not forms of autonomy sanctioned by Austen. One notices that the most sympathetic aspect of Mary Crawford, whose worldly views Marilyn Butler suggests are actually more deeply entrenched than Maria Bertram's,[22] is that she is kind and considerate socially, especially to Fanny. Maria Bertram's ill-natured behaviour and aggressive superiority may define the self, but to no advantage; is her attempt to live according to the dictates of sexual passion any more successful?

Recent critics have taken another look at the question of sexuality (or the lack of it) in Austen's novels. Susan Morgan in her article entitled 'Why There's No Sex in Jane Austen's Fiction' points out that Austen is interested in women's self-realisation, but she does not look for it through the one thing which had traditionally shaped women's lives, namely their sex.[23] I have already quoted Dr Johnson's belief that all female virtues are subsumed in the physical fact of chastity. Mary Wollstonecraft had lamented that for women virtue was sexual whereas men could cultivate what she calls non-sexual virtues.[24] In creating her female characters Austen is in Wollstonecraft's camp rather than Johnson's, unlikely though that might seem. Austen's novels offer a woman the chance to be valued for non-sexual virtues, for rationality, judgement, moral independence. That is their innovation. An Austen character may stand up for herself in several ways and be admired for it, but she must not assert herself through sex, the old enslaving mechanism. The heroine of *Mansfield Park* develops moral independence against severe mental pressures. Its anti-heroine struggles to map out her life through sex. Maria Bertram offends against her creator's view of how responsible autonomy in a woman might manifest itself. Jane Austen may have 'a good eye at an Adultress', but it was not her purpose to make a heroine of one.

Notes

Quotations from Austen's novels are taken from *The Novels of Jane Austen*, ed. R.W. Chapman, 5 vols, Oxford (1923); page references to this edition are in brackets after the quotation.

1 To Cassandra Austen, 12 May 1801. *Jane Austen's Letters*, ed. R.W. Chapman, 2nd edn, Oxford (1952) 127. The adulteress is identified in Tom Winnifrith, 'Jane Austen's Adulteress', *Notes and Queries*, CCXXXV, (1990) 19–20; see also his *Fallen Women in the Nineteenth-Century Novel*, London (1994) 17–18.

2 G.H. Treitel, 'Jane Austen and the Law', *The Law Quarterly Review*, C (1984), 549–586 (572–3).

3 Lawrence Stone, *The Road to Divorce: England 1530–1987*, Oxford (1992), Chapter X 'Parliamentary Divorce', esp. pp. 322–4.

4 Keith Thomas, 'The Double Standard', *Journal of the History of Ideas*, XX (1959) 195–216 (200–1).

5 Eighteenth-century women were often advised to overlook the sexual irregularity of their husbands. Dr Johnson is explicit on this point: 'Between a man and his Maker it is a different question: but between a man and his wife, a husband's infidelity is nothing ... Wise married women don't trouble themselves about infidelity in their husbands.' James Boswell, *Boswell's Life of Johnson*, ed. G.B. Hill and L.F. Powell, Oxford (1934–50) III, 406.

6 Exodus 20:14.

7 *The Book of Common Prayer*, 'The Form of Solemnization of Matrimony'.

8 Keith Thomas, *op. cit.*; Lawrence Stone, *The Family, Sex and Marriage in England 1500–1800*, London (1977) 501–7; Annette Lawson, *Adultery: An Analysis of Love and Betrayal*, London (1988) 35–51.

9 *Boswell's Life of Johnson*, *ed. cit.*, II, 56.

10 Peter L. De Rose and S. W. McGuire, *A Concordance to the Works of Jane Austen*, 3 vols, New York and London (1982).

11 To Cassandra Austen, 20 June 1808. *Jane Austen's Letters*, ed. R.W. Chapman, *ed. cit.*, 197, and note to Letter 52.

12 In *The Book of Common Prayer* 'A Catechism' precedes 'The Order of Confirmation'. The phrase 'first duty/duties' is not used elsewhere in Austen's novels, but Lady Susan refers to her daughter 'whose welfare it is my first Earthly Duty to promote'. *Lady Susan* in *The Works of Jane Austen*, ed. R.W. Chapman, vol. VI, *Minor Works*, rev. edn (1975), 289. See *A Concordance to the Works of Jane Austen*, *ed. cit.*, I, 291–2.

13 *The Book of Common Prayer*, 'The Order of the Administration of the Lord's Supper, or Holy Communion'.

14 The *Morning Post* of 18 and 21 June 1808, which carries the announcement of Mrs Powlett's elopement, contains this sentence, 'Mrs P's *faux pas* with Lord S—e took place at an inn near Winchester.' *Jane Austen's Letters*, *ed. cit.*, note to Letter 52.

15 Derek Brewer, *Symbolic Stories: Traditional Narratives of the Family Drama in English Literature*, Cambridge (1980) 155–65; Marilyn Butler, Introduction to *Mansfield Park* in the World's Classics series, Oxford (1990) ix.

16 Lawrence Stone, *The Road to Divorce*, 211–30; 248–55.
17 Lawrence Stone asks whether there *was* an increase in wifely adultery in the period (*The Road to Divorce*, 256–60). One conclusion he draws is that the publicity given to actions alleging 'criminal conversation', which usually preceded Parliamentary divorce, gave a distorted view of the adulterous behaviour of upper-class women (259).
18 Marilyn Butler, *Jane Austen and the War of Ideas*, Oxford (1975) 162–5; 242–3; 284–5. Lawrence Stone considers the question of 'Social Ostracism' in *The Road to Divorce*, 341–4.
19 Michel Foucault, *Discipline and Punish: The Birth of the Prison* (1975), trans. Alan Sheridan, Harmondsworth (1977).
20 *Ibid.*, 16.
21 Marilyn Butler, Introduction to *Mansfield Park*, World's Classics edition, Oxford (1990) xvi–xxii, xxvii–xxviii.
22 Marilyn Butler, *Jane Austen and the War of Ideas*, 222–3.
23 Susan Morgan, 'Why There's No Sex in Jane Austen's Fiction', *Studies in the Novel*, XIX (1987) 346–56.
24 Mary Wollstonecraft, *A Vindication of the Rights of Woman* (1792), ed. Miriam Brody, Harmondsworth (1985) 146.

Part II
The High Age
of Adultery: Contexts

6

Legitimation and Irony in Tolstoy and Fontane

Felicia Gordon

— what was being said of the rights and education of women should have interested Kitty. How often had she considered the question ... how often had she wondered what would be her own fate if she did not marry and how many times had she argued with her sister on the subject. But now it did not interest her in the least.[1]

One way of reading novels of adultery, which combine social and psychological realism with melodramatic and exemplary punishments of the adulterous wife, is in relation to the issue of democratic legitimacy. In the late eighteenth and through most of the nineteenth centuries, democratic or quasi-democratic civil societies relied on some form of public consent, whilst they simultaneously excluded women from the democratic process.[2] One function of novels of adultery, it will be argued, was to legitimise women's exclusion from the public sphere by demonstrating that marriage was their only safe haven and that outside marriage they were doomed. Novelists as disparate as Flaubert and Tolstoy represent women's lapse from marital fidelity as deserving the most severe form of punishment, if not by stoning as decreed in the Old Testament, then by the death, often suicide, of the adulterous wife. In examining the philosophic subtext of *Anna Karenina*, *The Kreutzer Sonata* and *Effi Briest*, it will be suggested that one phenomenon novels of adultery may reflect is a transformation of the ancient legally sanctioned historic violence of husbands towards wives into an internally assumed violence of women towards themselves. At the very moment when in many European countries, laws affecting women were either becoming or threatening to become more liberal, novels of adultery showed the law of the father internalised in the feminine subject.[3] Tolstoy's Kitty

Shcherbatsky, the dutiful daughter soon to become the good wife, has lost all interest in 'the woman question'.

Geneviève Fraisse (*Reason's Muse*) has suggested that democratic cultures faced a new crisis of gender definition.[4] Self-evidently democracy, by its claim that legitimacy rested on the consent of the governed, raised the question of women's inclusion in the sphere of citizenship. To deny women participation in civic life required a renewed theorising of sexual differences. The idea of the moral life associated with male-only participation in the public sphere (citizenship) meant that women were necessarily excluded from the ethical realm in its highest form. This move, extensively theorised in Rousseau, Kant and Hegel produced a circular reasoning by which women were self-evidently unfit for citizenship, because they lacked the highest moral sense.

In spite of such philosophic legitimation, this visible inconsistency between democratic theory and political practice did not disappear. Even in autocratic cultures like Russia and Prussia the problem was not eliminated, since the heritage of the Enlightenment ensured that 'women's place' formed part of any discussion of social reform. Yet the gap between progressive legislation and the fictional representation of marriage is striking. For example, although Prussia had the most liberal divorce laws in Europe, the dramatic requirement for the adulterous heroine's social ostracism and early death in Fontane's *Effi Briest* remained intact.[5] Tolstoy in *Anna Karenina* ensures that his plot precludes divorce as a solution to marital breakdown, although it was permitted in law. Novels of adultery which dramatised the interplay between the private and the public sphere both legitimated women's place in the scheme of things but also, as we shall argue, served to undermine philosophic certainties.

Women were still, as Hegel suggested, tied to the old laws of the 'nether world', a necessary reminder of divinity but incomplete without male self-consciousness.[6] In a century where theories of change were identified with progress, a negative attitude towards women's participation required that inequality be figured as naturally rather than socially constructed. If women were not to function as members of the polity, arguments needed to be based on incapacity, not exclusion but on an incapacity paradoxically affirming women's special and semi-divine status. Thus from the dawn of the democratic era in philosophic discourse, as Fraisse demonstrates, women were consigned to the realm of nature. Simultaneously however, marriage and the family became a central focus of bourgeois moral orthodoxy.

The citizen was to be nurtured in the moral family. The question then arose as to how amoral or pre-moral persons, normally women, could incarnate the moral core of a society from which they were excluded. In Kant and Hegel the problem was resolved via the idea of a bridge of mutual recognition.

Kant in his *Observations on the Feeling of the Beautiful and the Sublime* (1763) and Hegel in his *The Philosophy of Right* (1817) and *The Phenomenology of Mind* (1830) attempted to wrest the institution of marriage from either the purely religious (a sacrament) or the largely material (property) to allow it to function within the ethical realm as an instrument of culture.[7] Such ideas can be clearly traced in Tolstoy, where in *Anna Karenina* the three marriages: Dolly and Stiva Oblonsky's which nearly fails but is repaired thanks to Dolly's forbearance, Anna and Karenin's which does fail thanks to her adultery and Kitty and Levin's which is difficult but successful, show Tolstoy, like Kant and Hegel, searching for an ethical bridge between the sexes. In *The Kreutzer Sonata* on the other hand Tolstoy abandons the idea that nature and culture can be harmonised, particularly as nature in the form of sexuality is figured as irredeemably evil. Marriage founded on desire becomes the destroyer of the ethical personality in husband and wife.

In both novels Tolstoy shows himself conversant with and preoccupied by the 'condition of woman question'.[8] John Stuart Mill's *The Subjection of Women* (1869) is explicitly satirised in *Anna Karenina* in a multi-layered conversation in which the proponent of liberalism is shown as irascible and foolish and the supposed beneficiary of women's emancipation (Kitty) is not able to feel any interest in the subject.[9] (See opening quotation.) Tolstoy's attacks on women's emancipation in *Anna Karenina* and *The Kreutzer Sonata* may be linked to related anxieties about the loss of faith and certainty in the post-Darwinian world.[10] He focuses on marriage as representative of the 'condition of Russia question', arguing that the problem of Russia is not primarily one of economic backwardness as the liberal or socialist reformers claimed, but a question of ethics.[11] He seeks to demonstrate that ethics are not culturally relative but universal. So in *Anna Karenina*, marriage and adultery are intended to exemplify the workings of a universal moral law. Tolstoy's abandonment of the ideal of marriage in *The Kreutzer Sonata*, however, can be seen as a logical development of the early themes associated with sexuality and desire.

In *Anna Karenina*, Levin is deeply ashamed of his early sexual adventures and wishes to marry in order to give his sexuality a moral

framework. His preoccupations appear to echo Hegelian descriptions of the marriage state.[12] For Hegel, the family rescues sexual relations from the purely natural, particular and contingent, and links them to the ethical and the universal. While all human beings desire full ethical self-consciousness which is achieved by the recognition of others, for men this recognition is achieved in the public sphere and for women in the family. The family forms part of the ethical life, but on a lower plane, being tied to nature. Yet to the extent that it is ethical, family life is intrinsically universal. Hegel, like Tolstoy, wished the family to represent more than mere nature (sex) but also to represent more than a contract of material convenience (property).[13]

> In a household of the ethical kind, a woman's relationships are not based on a reference to this particular husband, this particular child, but to *a* husband, to children *in general*, – not to feeling, but to the universal. The distinction between her ethical life [*Sittlichkeit*] (while it determines her particular existence and brings her pleasure) and that of her husband consists just in this, that it has always a directly universal significance for her, and is quite alien to the impulsive condition of mere particular desire. On the other hand, in the husband these two aspects get separated; and since he possesses, as a citizen, the self-conscious power belonging to the universal life, the life of the social whole, he acquires thereby the rights of desire, and keeps himself at the same time in detachment from it.[14]

What happens to women in the ethical household who do demonstrate particularity of desire? Considering Anna Karenina, one can appreciate how she violates the Hegelian ethical model. Not only does Anna desire a particular man, Vronsky, who is not her husband, she is physically repelled by her husband, Alexei Karenin, as a particular individual. She fails to love her husband as a Hegelian universal and wishes, but fails, to love him as a particular individual. Nor is desire validated as either authentic or happy in the novel. Kitty and Levin's honeymoon 'remained in the memories of both of them as the bitterest and most humiliating period of their lives'.[15] The consummation scene between Vronsky and Anna shows him distraught with 'lower jaw trembling' and Anna grovelling on the floor in the classic pose of the woman taken in adultery.[16] This scene, far from representing pleasure, is equated with shame and guilt, which Anna internalises, begging forgiveness from the only representative of male culture

present, her lover/seducer, Vronsky. 'She had no one in the world now but him, and so to him she even addressed her prayer for forgiveness.'[17]

A further important distinction emerges between men and women in what Hegel calls the particularity of desire. Women can only have access to the ethical realm within the family and through the mediation of the husband who participates in the universal concerns of the community. Women derive their meaning from their husbands, who function not as individual objects of desire, but in their role as ethical exemplars for the family. It follows that a wife's particular feelings of love or aversion for any particular husband are irrelevant. The husband, however, who derives his ethical significance from the public sphere, has the right to feel particularity of desire for this or that woman.

Anna Karenina's destruction is shown to proceed from her social exclusion, which in turn leads her to depend ever more heavily on Vronsky, to become pathologically jealous of him and to imagine suicide as a form of revenge. But social pressures in themselves are inadequate to explain the process of Anna's deconstruction from confident magnificence at the novel's opening to querulous misery at the end. Tolstoy demonstrates that the consequences of female adultery (male adultery is notoriously not punished in Anna's brother, Stiva Oblonsky) are not merely social ostracism or personal misery within the family. The double sexual standard is not shown to be socially just, but to exist as a transcendental law. By betraying her husband, Anna denies the universal ethical principle represented by the husband and through him, civil society.[18] In Hegelian terms, Anna loses all possibility of significant Being when she abandons her role as wife, since Being flows from the husband. Outside of marriage there is nowhere for Anna to go. She enters a parody of marriage as Vronsky's mistress but her self-confidence, warmth, and vitality vanish. As Hegel puts it: 'The individual, when not a citizen, and belonging to the family, is merely unreal insubstantial shadow.'[19] Tolstoy's ideological message is that the heroine's nemesis is the outcome, not of husbandly outrage or even of social disapprobation but of the inexorable workings of the moral law. Dolly, on the other hand, who forgives her erring husband, devotes herself to her family and rejects Anna's suggestion of birth control methods with horror, takes on added stature. However, Tolstoy, a realist as well as an ideologue, does not suggest that the good Hegelian wife will necessarily be a happy one.

Anna Karenina juxtaposes Anna's failure in marriage and adultery with Levin's successful achievement of marriage and a family. The novel closes with a return to the land and the establishment of a patriarchal family. Kitty becomes the Rousseauistic mother. Here ethics seem grounded in nature, not culture, where in St Petersburg, aristocratic life had encouraged the Anna/Vronsky liaison. But Levin's (and Tolstoy's) admiration for Kitty's spontaneous ability to respond to the realities of life and death is heavily charged with condescension as well as envy. Apart from Tolstoy's own marital difficulties, it is unsurprising that marriage which was to provide ethical salvation is subsequently denounced in *The Kreutzer Sonata* as being a gross deception. Whereas critics often focus on the overtly personal nature of this story, it is worth emphasising its consistencies with *Anna Karenina*. In both, sexuality is terrifying and distasteful. But for the later Tolstoy there is no possible bridge between nature and culture; the only mutual recognition between the sexes becomes that of hostility.

Pozdnyshev, the tormented husband, follows through the logic of those Hegelian contradictions in marriage suggested in *Anna Karenina*. The narrator's discovery that marriage encompasses nature (sex) and that even a woman's love for her children has a sensuous element, invalidates the idea that marriage can attain any degree of ethical universality. Thus the Rousseauistic family is construed as evil. Women, because they inflame men's sensuality, are also evil. It does not matter whether Pozdnyshev's wife has taken the musician as her lover or not; she is guilty on either count. Tolstoy logically undermines the very married state which had been the ethical cornerstone of *Anna Karenina*. The private sphere of the family becomes a hell from which there is no transcendence. All relations between the sexes are doomed. Tolstoy has constructed a parody of Hegel's master/slave relationship whereby each player in the dyad attained self-consciousness through the recognition of the other. In *The Kreutzer Sonata* the slave is degraded and so is the master. 'And there she is, still the same humiliated and debauched slave, while men continue to be the same debauched slave-masters.'[20] The very fact that Pozdnyshev recognises the alterity of his wife, that she is another person and in spite of his best efforts cannot simply be reduced to an object, leads him to kill her. *The Kreutzer Sonata* could be read as an ironic post-lude to *Anna Karenina* but the conflicts it treats as insoluble save through murder are already suggested in the former work.[21]

Anna Karenina while acknowledging the tragedies of the female condition, legitimates women's subjection by convincingly dramatising the horrors of social, spiritual and mental exclusion. The novel validates female oppression not by approving of it, but by suggesting that no other existence is available to women, save the even worse one of perpetual exile from the world of self-conscious Being. *The Kreutzer Sonata* legitimates oppression in another sense, by logically demonstrating the impossibility of ethical relations between the sexes. The corollary must be the requirement to contain the 'weaker' sex because, paradoxically, Pozdnyshev asserts that women are the dominant sex:

The way things are at present, the woman is deprived of the rights possessed by the man. And, in order to compensate for this, she acts on the man's sensuality, forces him into subjection by means of sensuality, so that he's only formally the one who chooses – in actual fact it's she who does the choosing. And once she has mastered this technique, she abuses it and acquires a terrible power over men.[22]

Pozdnyshev echoes Rousseau's fear that if women had the rights of desire, 'the men, tyrannised over by the women, would at last become their victims and would be dragged to their death without the least chance of escape'.[23]

Though faithful to the traditional plot of novels of adultery which requires the punishment of the wife, Theodor Fontane in *Effi Briest* (1895) offers a devastating indictment of the bankrupt nature of sexual relations based on separate spheres theory.[24] As Roy Pascal has observed, *Effi Briest*, in its account of the breakdown of a marriage, represents the 'general contradictions of the whole of civil society'.[25] The disillusionment of the deceived husband, Innstetten, with the Hegelian ethos of public service is often focused upon by critics as demonstrating the bankruptcy of the Junker class and of the Prussian State founded on Hegelian principles.[26] Effi is sometimes understood as a shallow character, demonstrating Fontane's inability, unlike Tolstoy, to portray passionate natures. I will be arguing, however, that her supposed limitations are central to Fontane's critique of separate spheres. Far from showing his incapacity to depict passionate natures, his portrayal of Effi, like that of Innstetten, represents an accurate expression of Kantian gender categories operating in this novel in the context of the Hegelian State.

Kant's *Observations on the Feeling of the Beautiful and the Sublime* (1763) was an early text, preceding his analytic works and indebted to Rousseau's *Emile* (1762) and in it Rousseau's portrait of the ideal girl/wife, Sophie.[27] In the *Observations* Kant contends that aesthetics and ethics divide on gender lines. Women have an instinctive feeling for the beautiful, men have a spontaneous facility for the understanding of principles and for the sublime. Thus women have 'a strong inborn feeling for all that is beautiful, elegant and decorated ... They have many sympathetic sensations, good heartedness and compassion, [they] prefer the beautiful to the useful.'[28] It follows that virtue is different according to gender: 'the virtue of a woman is a beautiful virtue. That of the male sex should be a noble virtue. Women will avoid the wicked not because it is unright, but because it is ugly ... I hardly believe that the fair sex is capable of principles.'[29]

Effi Briest as a young girl is the personification of the Rousseauistic/Kantian ideal. Seen first in the tamed nature of her parents' garden, she is eager to marry and to marry well. She has no hesitation in accepting a husband who is to be her mentor in the world of culture, the role Innstetten appropriately adopts. A spontaneously Kantian woman, she prefers the beautiful to the useful. In buying her trousseau, Effi would rather go without than not have the best and most luxurious items. Effi enters upon a marriage where, in a Hegelian sense, she should derive maximum significance. Her husband is the embodiment of the Hegelian commitment to the public sphere (or the Kantian sublime). In Effi, Fontane has hit on a gender stereotype which will illuminate the contradictions inherent in the gender relations implied by it.

Effi rightly senses the unbridgeable gap between herself and Innstetten even before their marriage. She remarks to her mother: 'And I think Niemeyer even said later that he was a man of fundamental principles, too ... And I'm afraid that I ... that I haven't got any ... He's so kind and good to me and so considerate but ... I'm scared of him.'[30] Kant, we remember, hardly believed 'that the fair sex is capable of principles'. Effi bears him out.

The chasm between Effi and her husband is the Kantian one of the feminine deriving spontaneous pleasure from beauty and the masculine which through laborious effort attains an abstract universality of principle, or the sublime. In Hegelian terms it is the gap between female and male, the family and the state. How is marriage supposed to allow individuals to bridge this gulf, to move from one state of being or consciousness to another? Kant's answer

is that each individual recognises the qualities of the beautiful or the sublime in the other. 'Woman has a superior feeling for the beautiful, so far as it pertains to herself; but for the noble so far as it is encountered in the male sex ...'[31]

In Fontane, this ideal of spontaneous recognition founders on the misery and loneliness of Effi, the beautiful artefact. The man of principle seeks to control the woman without principles by fear, already noted in the passage quoted above, and orchestrated with gothic embellishment by the device of the Chinaman's ghost. Innstetten's cruelty in manipulating Effi's fears, as well as his detachment, link him to the Kantian sublime: 'A man who grounds his actions on the principle of justice, for example, will subordinate all other actions and impulses to it. Love for another may still remain, but from a higher standpoint one sees it in relation to one's total duty. As soon as this feeling has arisen to its proper universality, it has become sublime, but also colder.'[32] Effi recognises this coldness in her final judgement on Innstetten's 'rightness'. Like Alexei Karenin, he is a good man, who, as she puts it 'doesn't really love'. From a Kantian perspective, the inability to love deeply is what makes him a good man.

In killing off Effi, Fontane writes the obverse of his novel *L'Adultera* (1882) where the adulterous couple are shown succeeding in an arduous but satisfying life. Yet Fontane, while offering a plot which appears to endorse Kantian and Hegelian gender prescriptions, ironically chronicles the collapse of belief systems, an almost universal breakdown in strategies for living. The sense of unease pervading all personal and social relationships relates to a sense of inauthenticity in public roles. Innstetten who goes through the motions of the code of honour knowing it to be bogus and who admits that his commitment to public service is hollow, is representative of the emptiness of social life grounded on no ability to feel or as Effi says, to love. The world of the novel is like the empty rooms in Innstetten's Kessin house, full of nothing but whispers.

Fontane exudes scepticism about the ideological structures to which his characters attempt to conform. Innstetten and Crampas, both a generation older than Effi, subscribe to the same unbending code of honour. Husband and lover equally attempt to 'educate' Effi with their fictions, Innstetten with his tale of the Chinaman and Crampas with that of Don Pedro. They are parodies of the Kantian husband–educator. Nor are their fictions shown as having a sustaining

virtue. Passion seems bloodless in this novel; Crampas dies for nothing; Innstetten decides he has killed a friend for nothing. Wüllersdorf's 'auxiliary constructions', another name for sustaining fictions, seem equally fragile. The rigidity of abstract universality and its divorce from life is ironically exposed in Effi's mother, a woman who holds to the doctrine of social acceptability above that of family affection. It is her husband, lacking any grasp of theory or principles, who affirms his right to love his daughter. In the paradise of Hohen-Cremmen, gender roles are reversed and the father, far from being a figure of patriarchal severity, exudes a kind of muddled, *unprincipled* goodness. Unlike his wife and son-in-law, he is not concerned by social status, but like Fontane, who he may resemble, he is past the age of ambition.

The fate of the adulteress in novels of adultery arguably betrays an underlying anxiety. Women, thanks to their civic exclusion, are a source of instability: they enact the revenge of the repressed. The bourgeois novel of adultery may be read simultaneously as a construction of legitimation or an ironic undermining of the ethical double standard on which marriage depended. At the very moment when women's emancipation threatened to become an historical reality and when divorce and the dissolution of marriage became a practical possibility, such novels acted as powerful agents of denial. Female adultery could be figured as calamitous, not because it caused pain and misery to individuals, not because betrayal and deceit are ethically obnoxious, but because it denied the power of abstract universality on which the very concept of ethical life was held to depend, a universality which turned out not to be universal at all, but masculine. Whether approached from a standpoint of Tolstoy's moral absolutism, or Fontane's scepticism, female adultery was an instance of reality breaking through ideology. Neither Anna nor Effi can be construed as social rebels or feminists *manquées*. They largely accept the foundational masculinist assumptions of their culture. One is reminded of the dead Emma Bovary, watched over by those two ideologically opposed individuals, whom Flaubert parodies as symptomatic of the political divisions of nineteenth-century France, the anti-clerical chemist, Homais, and the priest, Bournisien. Superficially in conflict, they speak the same language, as do the uncomprehending husbands and lovers of the novels of adultery, a language of abstract universality from which women are excluded. The nineteenth-century novels of adultery can be read as Tolstoyan

didactic warnings – 'vengeance is mine, and I will repay' – as efforts to legitimate and to render 'natural' the sexual double standard upon which all other social inequalities depended or as ironic deconstructions of the murderous artificiality inherent in gender prescriptions.

Notes

1 Leo Tolstoy, *Anna Karenin* (sic) (1878), trans. by Rosemary Edmonds (Harmondsworth: Penguin, 1978), p. 415. All subsequent references will be to this edition.
2 For a wide ranging discussion on women's exclusion from citizenship in the post-revolutionary settlement see Geneviève Fraisse, *Reason's Muse: Sexual Difference and the Birth of Democracy*, trans. by Jane Marie Todd (London: University of Chicago Press, 1994), to which this paper is much indebted.
3 For a comparison of laws relating to marriage and divorce see Roderick Phillips, *Putting Asunder: A History of Divorce in Western Society* (Cambridge: Cambridge University Press,1988), pp. 403–73. On the legitimacy of domestic violence see Carole Pateman, *The Sexual Contract* (Cambridge: Polity Press, 1988).
4 Fraisse, 'Introduction: Troubled Reason', pp. xiii–xviii.
5 Prussia was relatively liberal on the question of divorce which was sanctioned on a wide variety of grounds including adultery, desertion and insurmountable aversion (Imperial Divorce Law, 1875.) The Russian Code of 1836, on the other hand, legalised women's obedience in marriage where women had a serf-like status. Adultery was the only admissable grounds for divorce and needed eye-witness, third party testimony. See Phillips, *Putting Asunder*, pp. 428–39 and Richard Stites, *The Women's Liberation Movement in Nineteenth-century Russia* (Princeton: Princeton University Press, 1978), p. 182.
6 'Just as the family thereby finds in the community its universal substance and subsistence, conversely the community finds in the family the formal element of its own realisation, and in the divine law its power and confirmation. Neither of the two is alone self-complete. Human law as a living and active principle proceeds from the divine, the law holding on earth from that of the *nether world* [my italics], the conscious from the unconscious, mediation from immediacy; and returns to whence it came. The power of the nether world, on the other hand, finds its realisation upon earth; it comes through consciousness to have existence and efficacy.' Georg Wilhelm Friedrich Hegel, *Phenomenology of Mind,* (1830), trans. by J. Baillie (New York: 1967), pp. 478–9.
7 Kant, *Observations on the Feeling of the Beautiful and the Sublime* (1763), trans. by John T. Goldthwaite (Berkeley: University of California Press, 1960) Georg Wilhelm Friedrich Hegel, *The Philosophy of Right* (1817), trans. by

T.M. Knox (New York: 1967), *The Phenomenology of Mind* (1830), trans. by J. Baillie (New York: 1967).

8 Leo Tolstoy, *Anna Karenina*, pp. 411–14. On Tolstoy's anti-feminism see Richard Stites, *The Women's Liberation Movement in Nineteenth-century Russia*, pp. 159 and 177–8.

9 J.S. Mill's, *The Subjection of Women* (1869) had an enormous European-wide readership and was translated into most European languages (though not Russian). Russians probably read it in French. See Richard J. Evans, *The Feminists* (London: Croom Helm, 1977), pp. 18–21 and note 16, p. 40.

10 Leo Tolstoy, *The Kreutzer Sonata and Other Stories* (1889), trans. David McDuff (Harmondsworth: Penguin, 1983). All subsequent references will be to this edition.

11 Levin is much troubled by the implications of materialism (see Part 1, Ch. 7, *Anna Karenina*). Tolstoy, like Dostoevsky, took issue with the utopian and materialistic vision of social and sexual emancipation developed in Cherneshevsky's *What is to be Done* (1863).

12 For extended discussions of Hegel and the family see: Genevieve Lloyd, *The Man of Reason: Male and Female in Western Philosophy* (London: Methuen, 1984), Carole Pateman, *The Sexual Contract*, especially Chapter 5, Diane Coole, *Women in Political Theory*, (Brighton: Harvester, Wheatsheaf, 1988), Chapter 8.

13 Hegel, *Phenomenology of Mind*, 'The Ethical Life', p. 112, paragraph 163 and p. 114, paragraph 166.

14 Hegel, *Phenomenology of Mind*, pp. 476–7.

15 *Anna Karenina*, p. 509.

16 *Anna Karenina*, pp. 165–6.

17 *Anna Karenina*, p. 165.

18 The logic of Hegel's position tends to equate adultery to treason, as in English law it was once 'petit treason'). See Roderick Phillips, *Putting Asunder*, p. 130.

19 Hegel, *Phenomenology of Mind*, p. 470.

20 Tolstoy, *The Kreutzer Sonata*, p. 64.

21 See Roderick Phillips on spouse murder as a solution to marital problems, pp. 307–9.

22 Tolstoy, *The Kreutzer Sonata*, p. 49.

23 Jean-Jacques Rousseau, *Emile* (1762) trans. by Barbara Foxley (London: J.M. Dent and Sons Ltd, 1974), p. 322.

24 All references to this novel are to Theodore Fontane, *Effi Briest*, trans. by Douglas Parmée (Harmondsworth: Penguin, 1967).

25 Roy Pascal, *The German Novel* (Manchester: Manchester University Press, 1956), p. 201.

26 See: Erika Swales, 'Private Mythologies and Public Unease: On Fontane's *Effi Briest*', *Modern Language Review* (75, 1980), pp. 114–23, Stanley Radcliffe, *Fontane's 'Effi Briest'* (London: Grant and Cutler, 1986, J.P. Stern, *Reinterpretations* (Cambridge: Cambridge University Press, 1964), Henry Garland, *The Berlin Novels of Theodore Fontane* (Oxford: Clarendon Press, 1986), J. M. Ritchie, 'Embarrassment, Ambiguity and Ambivalence

in Fontane's *Effi Briest'*, in Jörg Thunecke (ed.) *Formen realisticher Erzählkunst* (Nottingham, 1979), pp. 563–9.

27   Immanuel Kant, *Observations on the Feeling of the Beautiful and the Sublime*, Introduction by John T. Goldthwaite, pp. 1–8.
28   Kant, *Observations*, p. 77.
29   Kant, *Observations*, p. 81.
30   Fontane, *Effi Briest*, p. 39.
31   Kant, *Observations*, pp. 93–4.
32   Kant, *Observations*, p. 58.

7

Adultery and
the Exchange Economy

Jo Labanyi

In one of the more humorous passages of *The Communist Manifesto*, Marx and Engels counter bourgeois fears that communism means the abolition of the family:

> The communists have no need to introduce community of women [...]. Our bourgeois, not content with having the wives and daughters of their proletarians at their disposal, not to speak of common prostitutes, take the greatest pleasure in seducing each other's wives. Bourgeois marriage is in reality a system of wives in common.[1]

The link between capitalist exploitation and prostitution has often been made; Marx and Engels also see a link between the capitalist economy and adultery. In this essay, I shall focus on Galdós's two best known novels, *La de Bringas* (1884) and *Fortunata y Jacinta* (1886–7), which are concerned with money, prostitution and adultery: Rosalía de Bringas gets her come-uppance from the prostitute Refugio and commits adultery for money; Fortunata is a prostitute who becomes an adulteress. I shall argue that prostitution and adultery are connected but that they express differing anxieties, and that, of the two, adultery is the more threatening. When Marx and Engels, writing in 1848, related adultery to the capitalist system of production, they were talking about male adultery. The classic European realist novels of female adultery – in France, Flaubert's *Madame Bovary* (1857); in Russia, Tolstoy's *Anna Karenina* (1874–6); in Portugal, Eça de Queiroz's *O primo Basílio* (1878) and *Os Maias* (1888); in Spain, Alas's *La Regenta* (1884–5) plus the two novels by Galdós discussed here – were written in the second half of the nineteenth century, when capitalism moved

into its consumerist phase. The best known example, *Madame Bovary*, makes the link between female adultery and consumption clear: adultery gets Emma into debt.[2] By 1884, when *La de Bringas* is written, things have changed: it is debt that gets Rosalía into adultery. Far from feeling obliged to commit suicide, she surmounts her debt crisis and launches into adultery as a 'career' that keeps the domestic economy afloat. Her initiation into adultery coincides with the 1868 Liberal Revolution, whose chief political demand was free trade. *Fortunata y Jacinta* takes place over the period 1869–76: the years of transition from the 1868 Revolution to the Restoration, which saw capitalism take off in Spain under the slogan, accepted by conservatives and progressives, of 'liberalism with order'. In order to understand why Galdós's two major novels of female adultery should be the ones with the most economic references, it is necessary to set them in the context of liberal political thought.

C.B. Macpherson reminds us that the ability to enter the market is the classic liberal definition of freedom. Liberal political theory talks of 'free' exchange and 'free' competition because those who engage in the market economy do so as owners of property which they are free to dispose of as they wish. One is free because one owns property, and this freedom is manifested in one's ability to alienate that property, and with it one's freedom. Macpherson argues that this somewhat crazy logic conveniently telescopes together different kinds of proprietorship in a way that allows a differential scale of rights to be set up, while claiming that all men are equal. For Locke and other classic liberal theorists define proprietorship as the ownership not just of land and wealth but also of one's person: that is, one's faculties or 'personal properties'. To quote Locke:

> By *Property* I must be understood [...] to mean that Property which Men have in their Persons as well as Goods.[3]

Or, as Kant puts it:

> The only qualification required by a citizen (apart, of course, from being an adult male) is that he must be his own master and must have some property (which can include any skill, trade, fine art or science) to support himself. In cases where he must earn his living from others, he must earn it only by selling that which is his.[4]

Until the mid nineteenth century it was taken for granted that workers
and beggars were excluded from the right to vote because, although
they were free, they had voluntarily alienated their 'property in their
persons' by entering into a wage contract or accepting alms. As
Macpherson notes, this brilliant sleight of hand places those deemed
to have freely alienated their freedom in an ambiguous position: in
civil society yet excluded from it, subject to its laws but denied its
rights. This ambiguity will come to a head when, in the mid nineteenth
century, workers start to demand the vote arguing that, if they are
free to sell their labour, they are entitled to the rights of free individuals.
The point here is that freedom and rights are seen as dependent on
one's ability to enter the market economy. And one's person is as much
a saleable commodity as any other form of goods.

In other words, freedom and rights are dependent on one's ability
to make a contract, whether of sale or purchase. Liberal political
theory is contract theory. Macpherson mentions women only twice,
acknowledging their particularly ambiguous status for, while they are
seen as human beings, they are defined as dependents and therefore
not free to alienate their own property. In late nineteenth-century
Spain, as in Europe generally, women could own property but could
not transfer it without their husband's signature, and the husband had
rights to its use and to any income from it. We are talking here of
landed property, something most women did not have. But all women
have 'property in their persons': or do they? Carole Pateman has
noted the anomaly of women selling their labour – that is making wage
contracts – when they were deemed ineligible to make contracts. She
also observes that, although women were not allowed to make
contracts, there was one contract they were all expected to make: the
marriage contract. What is this contract made by women who cannot
make contracts? If workers and beggars were ambiguously placed in,
but not in, civil society inasmuch as they were free individuals who
had freely alienated their freedom, what was the position of the
married woman, in civil society by virtue of the marriage contract,
yet excluded from it as a dependent unable to make contracts?
Moreover the marriage contract for women, even more than the wage
contract for workers, constitutes their 'voluntary' renunciation of
civil rights since they 'promise to obey'; as Pateman observes, the
marriage contract is the only contract to include such a clause.[5]

Given the equation of freedom with the ability to dispose of one's
property, and given the fact that the only property women had access
to in practice was their person, it follows logically that the only free

women were prostitutes. (The assumption that selling one's labour is a voluntary alienation of freedom helps explain why prostitutes, and not their male clients, have been held responsible for prostitution.) In nineteenth-century Spain prostitutes were called 'public women': this meant not just that they were public property, but that they were in the public sphere constituted by those free individuals able to enter into market relations. If the prostitute is deemed to have voluntarily alienated her person, she has, like the worker, forfeited her rights. But when, in the mid nineteenth century, workers start to claim that, if they have the right to sell their labour, they are entitled to the rights of free individuals, it becomes possible to argue that women who sell their persons are also free individuals entitled to full membership of civil society. A number of memorable prostitutes start to people the European novel, alongside adulteresses, at this time.

What, then, is the difference between prostitution and adultery? The prostitute, assumed to have no family, is unambiguously in the public sphere. But the wife is confined to the private sphere of the family yet in some sense, as a signatory to the marriage contract, part of civil society. Tony Tanner has suggested that what is disturbing about the adulteress is that, in her dual role of wife and lover, she is both inside and outside marriage, blurring the distinction between private and public spheres.[6] Her position is made even more ambiguous by the fact that adultery places her outside the law but, inasmuch as she has freely alienated her property in her person, in the public sphere constituted by that civil society of free individuals; while marriage places her inside the law but outside the public sphere of free individuals. Or rather, as we have seen, the marriage contract places the wife both inside and outside the public sphere, in that she is a signatory to a contract while being ineligible to make contracts and that contract signifies her renunciation of civil status. Marriage already contains the confusion of public and private spheres that adultery exacerbates. It is the difficulty of knowing where married women stand in society that makes them a subject of such interest in the realist novel.

So what exactly is the nature of the transaction that the adulteress enters into? It is an exchange in the sense in which the term is used in liberal political theory, since she is freely disposing of her property in her person. The market nature of the exchange is clear in Rosalía de Bringas's case, but she is unusual among adulterous heroines in selling herself for money. Most, even the consumption-oriented Emma Bovary, 'give' themselves for free. But consumerism is still the key. The shift in the mid nineteenth century to a consumer economy brings

women into the market regardless of their position as dependants, for this is the age when 'buying became shopping'.[7] If capitalism initially produced a split between public and private spheres by taking production outside the household, now it brings the two together again as the household increasingly becomes a unit of consumption. Female household management becomes the art of spending wisely but even the thriftiest wife is expected to spend. The adulteress is clearly a more suitable symbolic expression of this kind of invasion of the public sphere than the prostitute, who sells but cannot buy. Bridget Aldaraca has shown how late nineteenth-century Spanish women's magazines were full of articles warning of the dangers to marriage of excessive female consumption, while at the same time encouraging women to follow fashion.[8] The specialised *magasins de nouveauté* and shopping arcades that sprang up in Paris in the 1830s and 1840s were echoed in Madrid in the 1850s. By the 1880s Madrid could boast several department stores, with names modelled on their Parisian prototypes, though still on a relatively small scale.[9] If freedom is defined as participation in the market economy, female consumption is a threat not just to the husband's purse but also to his monopoly of authority (Rosalía's miserly husband is described as 'the legislator'). It has also been suggested that female consumption was found threatening because it allowed women to experience a pleasure that was not mediated through the male: they consume fashion to please not their husbands or even other men, but themselves.[10] The narrators of nineteenth-century novels of female adultery frequently describe their aberrant heroines as 'selfish' because they are concerned with their own pleasure. They give their bodies in order to 'consume' love, and are often driven to do this by their consumption of romance (Galdós's Fortunata is exceptional in the selflessness with which she gives rather than takes love).[11]

Alda Blanco and Carlos Blanco Aguinaga have shown how, by borrowing money and by committing adultery, Rosalía puts into practice the 1868 Revolution's demand for the free circulation of goods.[12] What is at stake here is not just an economic but also a political matter. *La de Bringas* expresses unease at the new capitalist exchange economy by equating it with adultery, but the equation also works the other way round to show the freedom women acquire by entering the marketplace. The novel implies that the process is irreversible: when Rosalía's husband loses his sight, he does not see darkness but 'thousands of dots of light or flickering rays, fleeting, shifting, metallic' (156), an image of the circulation of money which

even misers like Francisco Bringas cannot blind themselves to. The novel closes with Madrid locked in a giant traffic jam as all the civil servants dislodged by the Revolution move house: the city has come to a standstill not because society is static but because everything (including Rosalía) is in circulation. Rosalía's sewing-room is described as a 'swirling sea' as old dresses are re-fashioned into new in an unending movement that mirrors the exchange economy. As John Varey has noted, Rosalía's husband is ironically described as the spitting image of the French politician Thiers, whose book *De la propriété* was in Galdós's library. Galdós had earmarked the pages corresponding to Chapter 4, which discusses the notion that man's primary property is his property in his person.[13]

Georg Simmel has observed that the modern city privileges the visual, since things are displayed for potential consumption: *La de Bringas* is a novel about vision not so much because appearances are false, as because in a consumer society appearance and not use determines value. Simmel, like Walter Benjamin, saw the late nineteenth-century World Exhibitions, which put the universe in a showcase, as images of modernity.[14] Galdós made his first trip to Paris in 1867, at the time of its second World Exhibition. The Crystal Palace, where the first World Exhibition was held in 1851, was built by a designer of greenhouses; Walter Benjamin commented that the Paris shopping arcades – like greenhouses – blurred the difference between indoors and outdoors, as did the new department stores.[15] I have talked elsewhere about the significance of greenhouses and conservatories for adultery, inasmuch as they blur the distinction between the private indoors world and the public world outside.[16] The royal palace where the Bringas family live as civil servants is described as an inextricable mixture of interior and street; the resemblance of its description to Benjamin's description of the Paris arcades is uncanny. As the novel notes, Queen Isabel II had triggered the 1868 Revolution by, in 1866, offering to pay off the National Debt by putting Crown Property up for sale, keeping a quarter of the proceeds herself: an offer that met with outrage, despite the liberal opposition's demands for free trade, because Crown Property belonged to the State and not to her Royal Person.[17] Isabel II was, of course, also a notorious adulteress who, if unable to dispose of Crown Property, could not be stopped from disposing of her 'property in her person'. The novel shows that the exchange economy was already established before the Revolution (the paupers at the Maundy Thursday Royal Banquet sell off their gifts to waiting traders); after

the Revolution it becomes institutionalised in the hands of the middle classes, as the royal adulteress leaves for exile and the petty bourgeois Rosalía takes her place.

In *Fortunata y Jacinta* the consumption is done not by the adulterous Fortunata, who gives love rather than consuming it, but by the respectable wives of the bourgeois Santa Cruz family: Doña Bárbara is forever buying food; her daughter-in-law Jacinta tries to 'buy' a son. Doña Lupe, Fortunata's petty bourgeois mother-in-law, is also constantly sending her maid out to the market. Much like Engels in *The Origin of the Family*, Galdós (who never married) implies that bourgeois marriage is a commercial transaction: Doña Bárbara – a merchant's daughter and wife, with an eye for a bargain – chooses Jacinta as a bride for her son Juanito from the 'showcase' of daughters exhibited by Isabel Cordero, another shopkeeper described as a 'trader in daughters' (33).[18] Although Fortunata commits adultery with Juanito out of a love that is entirely selfless (she refuses his offer of gifts), she agrees to marry Maxi for financial gain. He in turn 'buys' her by breaking open his money box and putting its contents in circulation (a re-take of Rosalía de Bringas's adulterous putting into circulation of the contents of her husband's money box). Doña Lupe, a money-lender, tolerates her daughter-in-law Fortunata's infidelities in return for investing the money she gets from her other adulterous lover Feijoo, and the prospect of investing the income she is expected to get from the Santa Cruz family on the birth of her child with Juanito. (There is no problem about Doña Lupe being not just a consumer but a producer of wealth, for widows in Spain have always enjoyed their late husband's economic rights.)

But the novel does not set up a clearcut, if disturbing, opposition between marriage as financial exchange and adultery as love. Fortunata accepts money from her later adulterous lover Feijoo, a sign that by this stage in the novel she is learning, with the help of his liberal pragmatic advice, to play the market. Juanito commits adultery with her, and returns to his wife Jacinta, much like a female shopper attracted by the latest fashion; indeed he first seeks Fortunata out after marriage on hearing she is back from Paris dressed in the latest French fashions. His final adultery will be with Aurora, manager of a new department store specialising in imported French linen and underwear: a penetration of fashion into the most private parts. The novel suggests that the nation's shifts of political allegiance follow a similar process of change of fashion.

In the course of the novel, Fortunata is re-fashioned by a succession of bourgeois and petty bourgeois characters, male and female. Her death from a haemorrhage at the end of the novel implies that her life force has been drained by those who have consumed her. But her entry into the market as a commodity is not an entirely negative experience. Prostitution had subjected her to straightforward exploitation, but as an adulterous wife – moving in both private and public spheres – she does gain a measure of autonomy. Her final act is to dictate a will: that is, make a contract, the ultimate liberal definition of freedom. What is more, she makes the contract with another woman, Jacinta. As a result Jacinta is empowered to free herself from her husband Juanito in a *de facto* declaration of divorce (in the sense the term had in nineteenth-century Spain of 'legal separation'). At this point, Jacinta starts to have adulterous fantasies about the now dead Moreno Isla, who as a London banker represents the apex of the capitalist market system.

Fortunata's move from innocent to adulteress should not be seen as a move from original 'naturalness' to commodification. When Juanito first meets her she is eating a raw egg, but she is also in her aunt's poultry shop where he eyes her like a prospective buyer (she is explicitly likened to the chickens for sale). Her father was a market vendor and her mother also had a poultry shop. As a member of the working class and a female, she is outside society (a 'savage' or 'wild animal') but also enmeshed in the market from birth. The market is everywhere; the question is not whether one enters it but whether one can play it to one's advantage. Adultery and marriage are both part of the exchange economy. When Fortunata asks which is the real marriage, Juanito's legal tie to Jacinta or his adulterous liaison with her, she is asking a serious question, for marriage and adultery can no longer be clearly distinguished. But the novel leaves one feeling that adultery, to the extent that it gives Fortunata a degree of freedom to dispose of her property in her person (and in the person of her son), is the better option.

Fortunata y Jacinta begins with an account of the Madrid textile trade from 1796 to 1869: this is not picturesque background (*costumbrismo*) but the key to the novel's treatment of gender. Under Don Baldomero I, the Santa Cruz business is part of the domestic household, with employees and family eating and praying together. But the introduction of paper money, imperial expansion, faster transport (railways), and the progressive removal of customs tariffs (in 1849 and 1868) transform the business, with the result that Don Baldomero II

sells it off, formalising the split between the private sphere of family and the public realm of work that is intrinsic to capitalism. This belated capitalist consolidation coincides with the new consumerism, made possible by wealth from the boom in private property as a result of the earlier disentailment laws and the re-building of Madrid in the 1860s, plus the introduction of running water which encourages people to change their clothes. This development leads to a feminisation, as Isabel Cordero takes over the running of her husband's shop, transforming it into a *magasin de nouveautés*, and as the Santa Cruz firm moves from supplying army uniforms to selling ready-made female fashions. Galdós comments:

> the most interesting thing about this empire is women's fashion, the source of powerful energies that leave the private sphere for the public. (30)

Fashion, he continues, conceals in its folds:

> the whole political and administrative machine, the National Debt and the railways, public expenditure and income, the welfare State and socialist parliamentarianism. (30)

The significance of these words should be clear from the above discussion. By making his protagonist female and working class, Galdós shows his awareness that women's claims to the public sphere are linked to those of the proletariat. When read in the light of liberal political theory, with its equation of freedom and the market, the suggestion that the process unleashed by fashion leads to socialism is entirely plausible.

A noticeable feature of the pre-1868 Madrid textile trade, as described by Galdós, is its incestuous nature: everyone is related to everyone else, Baldomero Santa Cruz marries the daughter of his mother's second cousin, their son Juanito marries a first cousin (Jacinta). Just as Baldomero is opposed to free trade, so he wants to keep everything in the family. His selling off of the family business inaugurates a new era marked by the free circulation of goods and adultery. Incest, literal and figurative, occurs in several late nineteenth-century Spanish novels: for example, Valera's *Pepita Jiménez* (1874) where the hero marries his father's fiancée, and Pardo Bazán's *La madre naturaleza* (1888) where incest occurs between half-brother and sister. These novels of incest depict a closed semi-feudal society where

modernisation has failed to take place or is being resisted. In Eça de Queiroz's *O primo Basílio* and *Os Maias*, the adulterous relationships are also incestuous for late nineteenth-century Portugal's attempts at modernisation are shown to be a sham. If incest symbolically represents the pre-modern order, adultery – as Galdós perceived – is an image of modernity triumphant: an ambivalent image which presents the newly established exchange economy as a gain in freedom at the expense of commodification. It is the position of women that exposes the contradictions in the system.

Notes

1 Karl Marx and Friedrich Engels, *The Communist Manifesto* (Harmondsworth: Penguin, 1974), p. 101.

2 *Madame Bovary* directly influenced Alas's *La Regenta*, which nevertheless takes a very different psychological focus. There is no evidence that Galdós had read Flaubert's novel, though he bought and read Balzac's complete works in 1867–8, before writing his own first novel in 1870.

3 From Locke's *Second Treatise of Government* (1690), quoted in C.B. Macpherson, *The Political Theory of Possessive Individualism*, 13th edn (Oxford: Oxford University Press, 1990), p. 198.

4 From Kant's 1793 essay 'On the common saying: "This may be true in theory, but it does not apply in practice"', quoted by Jürgen Habermas, *The Structural Transformation of the Public Sphere: An Inquiry into a Category of Bourgeois Society* (Cambridge: Polity Press, 1991), p. 110.

5 Carole Pateman, *The Sexual Contract* (Cambridge: Polity Press, 1989), pp. 130–1, 6, 54–6, 111–12, 180–1.

6 Tony Tanner, *Adultery in the Novel: Contract and Transgression* (Baltimore: Johns Hopkins University Press, 1979), pp. 12–13.

7 Rudi Laermans, 'Learning to Consume: Early Department Stores and the Shaping of the Modern Consumer Culture (1860–1914)', *Theory, Culture and Society*, 10.4 (1993), 87.

8 Bridget A. Aldaraca, *'El ángel del hogar': Galdós and the Ideology of Domesticity in Spain* (Chapel Hill: University of North Carolina Press, 1991), Chapter 3.

9 Pedro Ortiz Armengol, 'El urbanismo madrileño y su evolución histórico-social' and Gloria Nielfa, 'El comercio madrileño entre "La Fontana de Oro" y "Madrid-París"', in *Madrid en Galdós, Galdós en Madrid* (Madrid: Comunidad de Madrid, 1988), pp. 67–86, 123–38.

10 Aldaraca, p. 109.

11 Rachel Bowlby notes that serialised fiction and advertisements appeared on the same newspaper pages, turning the former into another consumer commodity: see *Just Looking: Consumer Culture in Dreiser, Gissing and Zola* (New York/London: Methuen, 1985), p. 84.

12 Introduction to their edition of *La de Bringas*, 2nd edn (Madrid: Cátedra, 1985), pp. 16–40. References to the novel are to this edition, with quotations in my own English translation. A translation of the novel by Catherine Jagoe will be published in Dent's Everyman's Library in 1996.
13 John A. Varey, 'Francisco Bringas: nuestro buen Thiers', *Anales Galdosianos*, 1 (1966), 65–6.
14 Georg Simmel, 'The Berlin Trade Exhibition', *Theory, Culture and Society*, 8.3 (1991), pp. 119–23; and Walter Benjamin, *Charles Baudelaire: A Lyric Poet in the Era of High Capitalism*, 3rd edn (London: Verso, 1989), pp. 164–6. Peter A. Bly discusses the novel's interest in vision in *Vision and the Visual Arts in Galdós* (Liverpool: Francis Cairns, 1986).
15 Marshall Berman, *All That is Solid Melts into Air: The Experience of Modernity*, 5th edn (London: Verso, 1990), p. 237; and Benjamin, *Charles Baudelaire*, pp. 37, 50, 54, 170–1.
16 'City, Country and Adultery in *La Regenta*', *Bulletin of Hispanic Studies*, 63 (1986), pp. 61–2. The connection was originally made by Tanner (*Adultery in the Novel*, pp. 113–17, 156–8) with reference to Rousseau's *La Nouvelle Héloïse*.
17 See Blanco and Blanco Aguinaga's edition of *La de Bringas*, p. 13, n. 11.
18 References are to Benito Pérez Galdós, *Obras completas*, 7th edn, vol. 5 (Madrid: Aguilar, 1970); the translations are my own. A competent if sometimes irritating translation of *Fortunata y Jacinta* by Agnes Moncy Gullón is available in Penguin Classics (1985).

8

The Adulteress's Children

Naomi Segal

Women in the novel of adultery are doubly mothers – first because they function in the phantasy-triangle that brings the adultery story out of the oedipal motive, and secondly, more literally but no less complicatedly, because they actually have children in the texts, through whom they suffer and sin. The texts I will look at in this essay are all written by men; in none of them are the mother–child relations casual or tangential: rather, they work within a motivated structure that is at once filial and paternal, in which the woman stands between generations and between the positions of the implied author and the intended reader, in the place where the mother stands in the oedipal triangle, at a point that has to be surpassed. How is she used by her author as a version of that textual reproduction by which he intends to evade the use of the body? How does her desire and its punishment function in his structure of desire, designed according to the masculine mode to win pleasure out of failure? What difference does it make to all this if the text is focalised upon the figure of a man or a woman, or if the desired mother in the text has a daughter or a son?[1]

The male-authored novel of adultery can be placed at a particular moment in the family romance that brings realism out of romanticism. If any use is to be made of the genealogy of literary history, it must be, I think, by psychoanalysing its fantasy life and in particular the developmental drama it represents. The 'younger self' of the realist novel is the confessional *récit*,[2] a text in which a young man confesses to an older man, telling of a woman misloved and (directly or indirectly) murdered. The hearer receives the narrative, acknowledges the boy's failures and accepts him into the literate society of men. For confession seals and sanctions the oedipal bargain by which a young man is led across the inert body of the once-desired mother into a manhood dependent on her loss.

These texts are all premised on the childbed death of the mother giving birth to the hero. 'I cost my mother her life when I came into the world', so René begins his narrative;[3] and from then on his sister Amélie is burdened with an incestuous desire for which she must take total responsibility and which will end by killing her. Almost 60 years later we find another son's narrative, *Dominique* (1863), in which the mother dies a few days after weaning and the hero attaches himself to the youthfully married Madeleine, pursues her mercilessly until she first admits his passion, then begins to express her own, and then leaves her, nursing the nostalgia of renunciation for ever after. A few days before the climax, Madeleine takes Dominique to see a dead child whom her sister Julie had nursed: 'on the way home, she wept a great deal, repeating the word "child" in a tone of acute distress which told me much about a secret sorrow that was eating away at her life, and of which I was pitilessly jealous'.[4] This pitiless jealousy, directed towards a baby that is not even allowed to exist, is the first principle for the representation of the mother–child pair in the novel of adultery.

It is clear from the masculine business of the *récit* (like that of Freud's theory of the smutty joke) that the oedipal drama is premised not on a murderous attitude of son to father but on one directed by both of them towards the mother, who must repeatedly be 'disappeared' and reappear as text. The gesture that will make son into father is also the basis of the pattern of negotiations which is realist narrative. Narrative in the *récit* is a plot contracted between men over a woman. With the novel of adultery, something happens to put the muscle and hair of a bourgeois genre onto the slim frame of its predecessor. Authorship becomes what literary historians are prone to call mature: texts get bigger, heroes less wimpish, subject matter more manly, authors start pretending to be either God or a scientist. Two phantasies inform a man's assumption of realist authorship. One, embodied in the protagonist, is the wish to be the hero of the family romance, the Tom Thumb of the gold-paved city; the other, disembodied in the narrator, is the wish to control that child as he plays and wins and loses. The realist author wishes to be two simultaneous selves who will battle it out before our reading eyes while he floats out of sight paring his fingernails. Julien Sorel goes out on his fairytale quest to win public success and consequent sexual gratification: no matter what mistakes he makes, he cannot lose because his losing is the sweetest mode of winning. 'Stendhal' as narrator is equally blessed: he whispers over the boy's shoulder in

accents we are grown-up enough to understand, plays fairy godfather, guides him, mocks him, strokes him on his way.

With unsubtle directness I have suggested the pleasure of the implied author's fantasy of control: that the hero is playing phallus in a world for him. But by the logic of desire there is a necessary flaw in that fantasy. We know from Lacan that the phallus conceived as a whole figure cannot be masculine. Detached in his world of adventures, the hero represents castration and feminisation; if he is also to be heroic, his vulnerability must appear elsewhere, passed on to his own supplement, or double, or appendage – and that last limb appears in the text as the beloved's son, held under threat by the implied author who is God enough to hold the rights of life and death over all his characters. The woman begins to desire; the boy falls ill; he survives, but only just.

In the novel of adultery, it is still not the father-figure who is most to be feared. Fathers are husbands merely: cuckolds, comic in the very stupidity or vulgarity of their power. Like a Molière protagonist, Arnoux is all bluster, Rênal a gullible fool, Karenin saintly perhaps but irredeemably ugly. Mothers in the novel of adultery tend to be done to death as they are in the *récit*, but a little more indirectly – they die through their children.

There are two distinct genealogical positions assigned to these women. The mothers of sons are in what I call the 'patrilinear' position. Framed as icons, they play Mary, Venus, Jocasta: they stand where they are put, as the channel or seedbed that, once itself transferred from father to husband, carries *le nom du père* from husband to son. Into this conventional idyll irrupts the desiring hero – all boy, wanting and hating her in equal measure, determined to bring sexuality out of the maternal pose – and for a moment it seems that a dyadic structure of desire might replace the function of the legitimate couple. But around the time that they first have sex, her son (or her youngest son) falls ill. When this happens, the dilemma of husband versus lover, the parenthesis in which she seemed caught, changes into another: beloved child versus paternal God. Where her desire may go to from here, along with the foolish hero's, will depend on the specific mode of the paternal phantasy taken up by the author of the novel.

Mothers of daughters – the 'matrilinear' alternative – are already chastised, and whether the child is born before or during the adulterous liaison, whether she is the offspring of lover or cuckold, the very fact of self-reproduction in a mother seems a scandal that can only be read as punishment. Women in male-authored fiction do

not have daughters unless they are already transgressive: prostitutes who keep their mothers or daughters by the effort of their sin, murderesses like Thérèse Desqueyroux, mad things like Nadja, and a host of adulteresses from Atala's mother to Alissa's can produce nothing but what Sartre (in a different connexion) calls 'a virgin with a stain'.[5] There is, it seems, something so disturbing in this wilful doubling of the gendered other that it appears in fiction framed within a cell, a garden, some sort of *oubliette*. If the son as subject of desire is (as we have seen) never quite there, the daughter with her mother is always quite precisely there. Where 'there' is is a secret place that does not bear looking at – so the voyeur–author cannot help but peep – and when he does he of course does *not* see nothing. What he envies after all is not the icon whose distribution he as a man controls but the site where he is not, where only a feminised effigy of himself is possible. In representing such a pairing among females across the genealogical divide, in representing matrilinear love, the male author makes what his body cannot make. Like lesbianism in Proust, this is the place where masculine authorship stops.

I want now to turn to the novels to examine in some detail the different modes of maternity and authorship that they present. After exploring three examples of the 'sick son' plot, I shall take as a contrastive instance *Anna Karenina* (1878), in which patrilinear and matrilinear modes vie within the focalisation of the fiction and the female protagonist, for Anna has a legitimate son and an illegitimate daughter and is the desired object of both women and men. After that I shall turn to two matrilinear texts, *The Scarlet Letter* (1850) and *Effi Briest* (1895), to show how the mother–daughter pair is bound over in its cellular space; and I shall finish by returning to the case of Flaubert who, in one hominocentric and one feminocentric novel of adultery, uses irony to divide and rule not just according to a classed hierarchy from the divine down to the stupid but also by a gendered politics of discourse to do with the dread and the compulsion of copying.

Le Rouge et le Noir (1830) begins and ends with mothers and sons. At the close, Mathilde is still carrying a child everyone insists is male – that is, too good for her – and who remains unborn no doubt both in order to save him from life and to keep the space clear for Julien to return to the womb of death, not quite trapped in the world yet by paternity. At the opening of the text, we learn that Mme de Rênal has three sons, but see only the elder two, cavorting dangerously on a wall erected by their father the mayor; and we meet Julien as the over-

literate youngest of a motherless home, foundling, changeling or cuckoo in the all-male nest. At their first encounter, she takes him for a girl. As he enters the edenic scene of a loving family with her children, he becomes more exactly the image of a man she has never known before. Then they make love, and the favourite son, the one who occupies Julien's family position, falls ill.

It is at this moment that the challenge of the mother's son as rival becomes clear. Mme de Rênal discovers apparently for the first time that what she has been doing is a sin, a 'crime in the sight of God'.[6] At the boy's bedside she flings herself at her husband's feet, claiming that she has killed their child; he, fortunately, is too stupid to understand. Julien's consolations and entreaties seem to her 'the blandishments of the devil' (107). Then he has the inspiration to take up the first of a series of Christ-like attitudes:

'Oh heaven! if only I could take Stanislas's illness upon myself!'

'Oh, you love him, at least!' cried Mme de Rênal, rising and throwing herself into his arms. (110)

At this moment, we see the benignity of Stendhal's divine position: all three protagonists will survive, to pass through more vicissitudes and end up reaffirming the *Liebestod* of desire.

Flaubert is less kind. Frédéric's love is infinitely patient: it is the woman's fetishes – the arc of her dress, her lace, her black hair, her daughter – that he worships her by, and to cross these blocks would be as unthinkable as to leave her alone. This text too offers a double mother–son structure: remember Rosanette's poignant and hideous maternity, the child no sooner born than rotting away and laid, purple, in a frame of camellia petals. Both the sons in this novel have peculiar gestations: Rosanette's takes inordinately long to be born, while Mme Arnoux's is four years old when Frédéric returns to Paris after two years at home. Arnoux junior is snotty-nosed and dirty-fingered, but the young man can bear him if it will ensure the confidence of his beloved. Regular visits to enquire after the health of this or that family member make him 'the parasite of the household'.[7] Then one day the boy has a sore throat and in her distress and gratitude – Frédéric offers some platitudes about him being better in a jiffy – Mme Arnoux agrees to meet her admirer next Tuesday on the corner of the rue Tronchet.

But the author has something else in mind for his hero. Tuesday happens to be the first day of the 1848 Revolution. At the same time, little Eugène wakes his mother (with a sound she dreams as a dog barking) displaying the horrible symptoms of croup. Mme Arnoux, unlike Mme de Rênal, suffers the whole crisis alone: she performs her absurd agony before no audience and with the sole aid of the author's pitiless scalpel. After pages of detail, the boy coughs out the croupous membrane and is saved; and his mother offers up 'as a holocaust, the sacrifice of her first passion, her one weakness' (282).

The difference between these two scenes underlines the different modes of power which the author may have over a world in which he is to take pleasure. Stendhal creates a vale of happiness dependent on the greater bliss of Romantic death; Flaubert sets up a dialectic of over-material world and under-material author, the one a fistful of dust, the other hovering, hovering – and how this affects his female protagonist, we shall see later.

In Maupassant's novel *Pierre et Jean* (1887), the whole story takes place a generation after. Pierre is the black-haired, wayward elder son, just settled down to a career as a doctor; Jean is an up-and-coming lawyer, blond and pliable; both are in love with the pretty widow next door. Then a family friend, Maréchal, dies and leaves all his money to Jean. The novel consists of Pierre's gradual discovery, Hamlet-like, of his mother's long lost sexual passion, which originated unsurprisingly when, as a little boy, he caught scarlet fever – 'and Maréchal, whom we didn't know well yet, was such a help to us ... he would go the chemist to get your medicine ... And when you were better, you've no idea how pleased he was, hugging and kissing you'.[8] Even before his suspicions start growing, Pierre is outraged at this, and utters the complaint of our whole troop of insufficiently loved legitimate boys: 'If he knew me first and was so devoted to me, if he loved me and kissed me so much and I was the cause of his great friendship with my parents, how come he left his whole fortune to my brother and nothing to me?'

In romanticism, the 'gods stand up for bastards'. It is after all always a question of who inherits, how much and from whom. Let us not forget that it is not only in folktales that the youngest child ends up inheriting something bigger and better than the older, legitimate siblings. In Genesis, too, the privileged genealogy passes down via a younger son favoured by his mother and the authorial God. In the protest of Pierre we see the righteous anger of the child who is after all *only* the favourite of convention and not of passion, whose

inheritance will evade the narratives we really like to read, the desires we dream by.

The texts of the patrilinear mother are in the masculine mode not only because of the bind in which the mother finds herself but also because they are (closer in this respect to the *récit*) told from the viewpoint position of a desiring man. The matrilinear texts, in a variety of ways, are feminocentric rather than hominocentric. In *Anna Karenina* we find a woman split conventionally between husband and lover, more cruelly between lover and legitimate son, but also in a less overt way between the patrilinear and the matrilinear and the hominocentric and feminocentric modes. If Lionel Trilling admired the text for its fragrant everyday values and its comfortable paternity,[9] he has not looked too carefully at the heavy inexorability with which Tolstoy strips Anna of the charm that, in the opening pages, makes her what Virginia Woolf once called 'central ... the whole thing',[10] that is, the mother. Like Mrs Ramsay, we lose Anna with a shock during the course of the narrative, but we lose her long before her death.

Camus's cynic Clamence offers a good definition of charm: 'a way of making other people say yes to you without ever asking a direct question'.[11] At the start of the novel, Anna arrives as good fairy to a household in turmoil: her sister-in-law Dolly has discovered her husband's adultery and Anna, by sheer sympathy, induces her to take him back. Anna shares her charm with her brother Stiva – but we see how unforgiving a double standard operates here when, for passion rather than good-natured appetite, she does once what he has repeatedly done. From the moment of the first embrace, an iron divinity watches and pursues her, and she is never allowed to be 'really happy' again. The son whom she loved without rival in his infancy continues to pull her back while the daughter conceived in the fullness of desire 'for some reason [does] not grip the heart'.[12] Anna's patrilinear dilemma is clearcut; she represents it thus to Dolly:

'Do you see, I love ... equally, I think, but both more than myself, two beings – Seriozha and Alexei.

   I love these two beings only, and the one excludes the other. I cannot have them both; yet that is my one need. And since I can't have them, I don't care about the rest. Nothing matters; nothing, nothing! And it will end one way or the other, and so I can't – I don't like to talk of it.' (671–2, ellipses Tolstoy's)

Such is the inexorability of the either–or economics of the patrilinear bind. Anna's clarity of understanding, forced into the moral lacing of her author's concept of right, fails at the end of this statement: 'it must end one way or other', she stammers, and so it does. Her son Seriozha is presented more tenderly and carefully than the other sons – and he never falls ill, though it is at his bedside that she famously visits him on the morning of his birthday. While Vronsky's viewpoint is very rarely taken, on one of the few occasions it is, he is intuiting Seriozha's confusion: 'What does it mean? Who is he? How ought I to love him?' (203–4), the boy wonders, and it is in response to his gaze that both Anna and Vronsky get 'a feeling akin to that of a sailor who can see by the compass that the direction in which he is swiftly sailing is wide of the proper course, but is powerless to stop.' The stop comes with Anna's suicide at the local station; and the last time we see her lonely son he is playing the dangerous 'railway game' he has learned at his all-male school. In this text, the legitimate son, vulnerable still, also functions as righteous judge; in such films as Vittorio De Sica's *I Bambini ci guardano* (1942) and David Hare's *Paris by Night* (1988), a mother's choice of adultery over devotion to her sick son mediates via his gaze the weight of the same iconic judgement.

But what of Anna's place in the world of women? If her famous charm is first presented in her encounter with Vronsky's mother, in which they discover a mutual sympathy as the mothers of sons, this is actually the first of several woman–woman relations that shape our initial impression. Both the Countess Vronsky and Dolly's younger sister Kitty are described in the opening pages as 'falling in love' with Anna. And it is this that leads me to suggest that, where the hazy certainty of Anna's maternal value seems to be unexpectedly presented without the viewpoint of any specific man's desire, where we might be inclined at first to call it (as many critics have) the author's desire colouring the whole value-system of her world, I think its atmosphere rather resembles that of *To the Lighthouse*, the unpredatory, only dimly sexual desire of daughter for mother. Vronsky's attitude to Anna never takes the undestructive gaze-like form of Kitty's. The clever plotting of the author–God insists of course that Kitty's love should change into horror when she sees before her very eyes that the two people she adores are falling in love with each other.

Kitty grows up, through this and other useful humiliations, and marries the sensitive oafish Levin – whose probity is shown by his inability to respond to Anna's charm except in a brief drunken lapse. And Kitty has a legitimate, loved, healthy son, while Anna's daughter

is none of these things. When she is born, Anna nearly dies; she is given the same name as her mother, as if only one of them may survive; and for a while, the world is turned upside-down while Anna seeks her husband's forgiveness, Vronsky is driven to attempt suicide, and Karenin, alone of all the household, takes an interest in the innocent baby. Later, after Anna and Vronsky have left and are living together with Ani, we see through Dolly's viewpoint how incomplete their not-quite-domestic scene appears to a 'real mother'.

Anna refuses both to get a divorce and to give Vronsky any further children. In using contraception, she is choosing not to satisfy his wish for paternity (of sons?) and the chance to pass on his name. In this text, as in many of the others, parenting by choice rather than by blood is marked with favour over the genetic relation that breaks down. We have seen Karenin's selfless impulse to nurture his wife's illegitimate daughter; at the point where all her patrilinear relations are flawed by the sanction of social judgement, Anna herself takes charge of a red-haired English girl by the name of Hannah. 'You'll end up being fonder of her than of your own daughter' (731), her brother comments. 'How like a man!', Anna responds, 'In love there's no such thing as more or less. I love my daughter with one love, and this girl with another'. But Anna is held tight in a jealous bind of either–or. In the end, a quarrel with Vronsky over this girl precipitates her suicidal crisis; she visits Dolly and finds her starry-eyed over the icon of Kitty and the baby; and as she falls under the train, she thinks of her own childhood, no one else's. But after her death, it is Karenin who takes the infant child of his rival and alone is permitted to unite the son and daughter of Anna Karenina in one family.

The Scarlet Letter and *Effi Briest* both set adultery a magical seven years before discovery and punishment. Utterly different in tone – Hawthorne's text drips with the rhetoric of judgement, a discourse-world in which everything is swathed in symbolism; Fontane's is written with a sunnily light touch and a grand-paternal warmth – both nevertheless offer the extremes of a positive and negative view of the mother–daughter pair framed in a cellular space. Hester Prynne appears in the opening scene, poised at the prison-house door with her baby on her arm. The narrator identifies this couple as the anti-icon, marking by contrast that other maternity that existed 'to redeem the world'.[13] From this moment, we know the baby must be female. Pearl is the beginning and end of Hester's transgression. Where Hester wears, her daughter is, the visible mark of disgrace: no wonder

she dresses her in the wild threads of scarlet like the A, while she wears a shadowy grey. The implication is, in this text oozing signification, that the self-reproduction of the woman is tantamount to the gross display of the blood that makes her female.

Pater semper incertus est; mater certissima.[14] While the early Freud celebrates the visibility of the superior male organ, the late Freud of *Moses and Monotheism* prefers the truth of paternity which is imperceptible to the naked eye: only by inference – the 'advance in intellectuality' – can we know who our father is, while our knowledge of the mother, he argues, is primitive and blatant. *The Scarlet Letter* is about this 'advance in intellectuality', when paternity is discovered and polytheistic paganism gives way to the Judaic myth of disincarnation. Hester and Pearl are forced to shout femininity to the world, and give us the opportunity to piece out a surprising realism of the day-to-day single-parent grind with its complex mutual dependencies. Meanwhile the secret father, Dimmesdale, suffers more subtly, as the secret husband Chillingworth, probes him with the passion of psychoanalysis. By a mixture of guilts, he finally breaks, displays his own scarlet A to the world, and dies, dividing the mother–daughter couple for ever. At this moment, we are told, the child's spell is broken: 'as her tears fell upon her father's cheek, they were the pledge that she would grow up amid human joy and sorrow, nor for ever do battle with the world, but be a woman in it' (256). Pearl enters the genealogy by leaving the matrilinear cell where Hester remains. As Chillingworth shrivels up and dies, cheated of his prey after so much work in the underground, he chooses to leave all his worldly goods to Pearl, fostering perhaps not so much Hester's as Dimmesdale's child, but again ensuring that legitimacy has not lost its rights to bequeath.

Dimmesdale, first described in terms reminiscent of the Christ-child, cannot take up his place on the adulteress's bosom. His suffering is internal, while she (we are repeatedly told) has the moral advantage of the public show in which she burns blood-red. The scarlet of Hester's social sin has to do with an over-bodiedness that is never only textual. Unlike the torture-victim of Kafka's 'In der Strafkolonie', Hester is not just a written page. Her visible redness is the sign of a bleeding that emerges from inside without any wound.

Men's part in reproduction begins with alienation and ends in appropriation. At the beginning of the process, he enters the woman, gasps and leaves her his seed; the phallus emerges no longer a phallus; what has he given her? At the end of the process, he coopts the child

from the women who surrounded its birth; if it is male, he marks it with a socially prescribed bleeding and gives it his name; but the female child remains unmarked and will bleed without the need for war, ritual or 'valour'. Under this genealogy, daughters can only be copies of a fault, or reproduction as unproduction. Not castrated but rather castration itself, the mother's daughter bears witness to what the boy-child risked: she is a thing utterly removed from the man's body. When she is textualised, no wonder the letters all become scarlet.

If the adulteress is a woman who bleeds and falls, her daughter in the novel of adultery copies both these gestures. *Effi Briest* opens in an edenic garden where mother and daughter sew, talk and play; but a moment later the snobbish mother has betrothed her child to the man she refused a generation earlier because he was exactly her age. Junker genealogy requires a miscegenation of the generations, with every girl uncomfortably wedding an uncle figure who will raise her. Effi's adultery is as empty of passion as Hester's – only the most vigilant of readers will realise it has happened at all. Her doom follows seven years later when, a contented and utterly conventional Berlin hostess, her one transgression is revealed in a pile of letters she mysteriously did not throw away. The moment of discovery comes while she is staying at a spa: her daughter, another Annie, trips over and cuts her head while running to the apartment door. Thus the daughter takes the fall in Effi's stead, just as the latter got married in her own mother's. 'You are so wild, Annie, always like a whirlwind, you get that from your mother', comments the concerned father; a few days later he has killed the lover in a duel and cast off his wife. For a long while Effi lives alone, then with her daughter's former nanny, and eventually she manages to see her child again. But at the child's docile and toneless parroting of polite formulas, Effi sends her away and finally loses her temper at them all, their virtues and the docility she has always accepted. Daughters submissive to their mothers' submission, the wildness only a temporary flush on well-scrubbed cheeks, transgression in this world has little to do with passion or knowledge. The genealogical tie too is just a series of displaced repetitions, copies all too false and all too true.

I want to finish by going back to the Flaubert of *Madame Bovary* (1857). Though of course this novel was published 12 years before the mature *Education sentimentale*, it is, in terms of my interests, a more complex version of its author's obsession with the unbodied reproduction of the text. He began the novel that he loved to hate, so the anecdote goes,

after his friends Bouilhet and Du Camp advised him to drop the unwieldy *La Tentation de Saint Antoine*. Comparing the two texts, he later wrote: '*Saint Antony* did not cost me a quarter of the intellectual tension that *Bovary* demands. It was an outlet; I had nothing but pleasure in the writing, and the eighteen months I spent in writing its 500 pages were the most deeply voluptuous of my whole life. Consider, then, every minute I am having to get under *skins* that I find antipathetic.'[15] If the saint's pained continence lets Flaubert pour forth, this novel of adultery is repressive precisely as it represents the entry 'inside the skin' of the woman. Everything in *Madame Bovary* is a sexual relation: the author refuses the very entry he desires.

His godlike position – hovering not touching – is a refusal of incarnation because that would feminise. The implied author Flaubert must be what Emma is not. She consumes, is watched, fails and can only read; he is pure creativity, everywhere present and nowhere visible, pouring forth and unseen – above all, a writer. Emma can only take in the linguistic matter of others, pre-digested cliché, and (in a move copied by Joyce in his silly females Eveline and Gerty Macdowell) she is represented in *style indirect libre* by an exact computation which we work out, obedient creatures of irony, as the coefficient of knowing author to stupid character. Where foolishness is, in one of those passages, there is Emma; where control, unbodied desire and 'style' is, is Flaubert. In doing this we think we are catching up with him; but the author, like God, can never be caught up with; and after all our effort (as similarly in the *Dictionnaire des idées reçues*) we find ourselves in the character's position after all, only consumers, feeding on our own vomit, readers.

For Flaubert, then, the gender politics of the text is a mode of paternal control. But after all he exists in it also as his own daughter. Critics kindly assure him that identification hasn't made him girlish; from Baudelaire onwards, they exclaim at the 'masculinity' of Emma Bovary. But Baudelaire, as usual, sees what this means. What is this powerful dandyish woman, he warns, but the 'poet as hysteric'?[16] A hysteric, nowadays, is a woman who does not know whether to be a woman or a man. The poet as hysteric is a man who does not know how to reproduce himself.

Flaubert plagued Louise Colet with letters raging at the thought of her being pregnant: 'Me – a son! Oh no, no, sooner be knocked down by a bus and die in the gutter'.[17] But, against this horror of self-reproduction in the body via the woman, he viewed textual creativity as the 'real thing': 'We're good at sucking, we tongue a lot, we pet

for hours, but can we really fuck? can we discharge and make a child?'[18] If the child is the book, it can only be the detached phallus: 'a book about nothing, a book with no external attachment, which would stand up by itself by the internal force of its style'.[19] This disguise, this anti-incarnation as the phantasy of divinity, is the extreme opposite of the woman's self-reproduction. Emma Bovary must have a female child because she is capable only of copying. Flaubert must have no child but a text, a text in which all that is body is readerly, female and despicable, because he above all will not reproduce himself.

Notes

All translations are my own and reference is given to the original text. Further references to a cited text appear after quotations; passages without page-reference are from the last-cited page. Unless otherwise stated, all italics are the author's and all ellipses mine.

1 This article is based on my book *The Adulteress's Child* (Polity Press, Cambridge, 1992); an earlier version appeared as 'The adulteress's child', in *Spectacles of Realism: gender, body, genre*, ed. Margaret Cohen and Christopher Prendergast (Minnesota University Press, Minneapolis and London, 1995).
2 See my *Narcissus & Echo* (Manchester University Press, Manchester, 1988) and chapter 2 of *The Adulteress's Child*.
3 François-René, vicomte de Chateaubriand, *Atala; René; Les Aventures du dernier Abencérage*, ed. F. Letessier (Garnier, Paris, [1805], 1962), 185.
4 Eugène Fromentin, *Dominique*, ed. B. Wright (Garnier, Paris, 1966), 274.
5 Jean-Paul Sartre, *Les Mots* (Gallimard, Paris, 1964), 18.
6 Stendhal, *Le Rouge et le Noir*, ed. P. Castex (Garnier, Paris, 1973), 107.
7 Gustave Flaubert, *L'Education sentimentale* , ed. P. Wetherill (Garnier, Paris, 1984), 171.
8 Guy de Maupassant, *Pierre et Jean* ed. Pierre Cogny (Garnier, Paris, 1959), 97.
9 Lionel Trilling, 'Anna Karenina', in *The Opposing Self* (Oxford University Press, Oxford, 1980).
10 Virginia Woolf, 'A Sketch of the Past', in *Moments of Being*, ed. J. Schulkind (Triad/Panther, St Albans, 1978), 96.
11 Albert Camus, *La Chute* (Gallimard, Paris, 1956), 62.
12 Leo Tolstoy, *Anna Karenin* [sic], trans. by R. Edmonds (Penguin, Harmondsworth, 1978), 567.
13 Nathaniel Hawthorne, *The Scarlet Letter*, centenary edition, vol. 1, ed. W. Charvat and F. Bowers (Ohio State University Press, Columbus, 1962), 56.
14 For a brilliant analysis and contextualisation of this, see Marie Maclean, *In the Name of the Mother: Writing Illegitimacy* (Routledge, New York & London, 1994).

15 Gustave Flaubert, letter to Louise Colet of 6 April 1853, *Correspondance* vol. 2, ed. J. Bruneau (Gallimard, Paris, 1980), 297.

16 Charles Baudelaire, 'Gustave Flaubert', in *Œuvres complètes*, ed. M. Ruff (Seuil, Paris, 1968), 452.

17 Gustave Flaubert, letter to Louise Colet of 3 April 1852, *Correspondance* vol. 2, 67. This abhorrence perhaps goes some way to explain the super-scrupulous author's lapses with the two boys' gestations in *L'Education sentimentale*.

18 Gustave Flaubert, letter to Louis Bouilhet of 2 June 1850, *Correspondance* vol. 1, ed. J. Bruneau (Gallimard, Paris, 1973), 628.

19 Gustave Flaubert, letter to Louise Colet of 16 January 1852, *Correspondance* vol. 2, 31.

9

Carnal Knowledge in French Naturalist Fiction

Nicholas White

Ever since Denis de Rougemont's famous study of the representation of desire in the West, it has been a critical commonplace to assert the permanence of the theme of adultery.[1] More specifically, though, Tony Tanner's account of such transgression in the 'bourgeois novels' of Rousseau, Goethe and Flaubert is only the most famous of a number of analyses which highlight the particular urgency of the theme, which is seen as coincident with the rise of the middle classes in much of Europe and prior to the birth of Modernism.[2] What needs to be defined is the relationship between the apparent ubiquity of the form and the historical specificity identified within the bourgeois novel. Tanner suggests that a shifting of social norms around the turn of the century is reflected in a 'move from the more realistic novel of contract and transgression [...] to what might be called the novel of metaphor' (86). In his terms, 'as bourgeois marriage loses its absoluteness, its unquestioned finality, its "essentiality", so does the bourgeois novel' (15). The disaffection with the 'novel of contract and transgression' which inspires the development of Modernist prose is sketched by Tanner in terms of a triple impulse, embodied by Lawrence, Proust and Joyce respectively.[3]

This image of literary history in mutation needs to be clarified by a more exact focus on the precise manner in which bourgeois realism reaches its culmination with the advent of Naturalism towards the end of the nineteenth century, and then wanes. Our exemplary texts will be French novels written in the wake of *L'Education sentimentale*, particularly those belonging to Emile Zola's vast cycle of 20 novels which focus upon social and family history during the Second Empire, *Les Rougon–Macquart*, which he began to write just prior to the Franco-Prussian War and concluded with the publication of *Le Docteur Pascal*

in 1893.[4] Exploring how late nineteenth-century writers responded to the dominant tradition of adultery in the novel allows us to chart in historical terms the process by which this dominant form apparently comes to be viewed as kitsch. In other words, we shall investigate the ways in which enthusiasm for the form seems to be replaced by cynicism. Of particular interest in this context are the ways in which the representation of adultery relates to other forms of sexual transgression and their representation in the Naturalist fiction of the later decades of the nineteenth century. For what becomes apparent to a reader of such fiction is the conspicuously self-conscious way in which adultery is often displaced and replaced as the key sexual motif under the Third Republic.

It can be argued that the novel of adultery is not – as Tanner's study might suggest – simply terminated in the twentieth century by the shift in cultural momentum to Modernism. Instead, the particularly self-conscious nature of the invocation of the motif of adultery in late nineteenth-century French fiction already sows the seeds of dissatisfaction with the topic of adultery. What is more, those moments of apparent nineteenth-century enthusiasm for the form, on the one hand, and the cynicism of parody on the other, may not be as far apart as we might expect. Indeed, the stakes implicit in defining the historical limits of such enthusiasm ought to be tempered by an awareness that the novel of adultery is, by its very constitution, a perpetually cynical form.

So before we try to fix onto the *fin de siècle* a rigidly historicist frame whereby novelists suddenly appear to fall out of love with adultery, it is perhaps worth asking whether these expressions of dissatisfaction with the novel of adultery are not in fact also reflections of a thoroughgoing dissatisfaction to which the century as a whole bears occasional witness. As research into adulterous permutations in fiction expands, it would be all too easy to forget that the importance of Flaubert's novels lies not in the fact that they embody the motif of adulterous passion – there are plenty of other nineteenth-century novels which do that – but because they too parody the form. Emma Bovary, of course, finds in adultery all the platitudes of married life. Adultery is, in this view, just as boring as marriage. So the irony at the reader's expense is grand. In Flaubert's terms, readers are interested in part because many nineteenth-century bourgeois readers were interested in the fundamentally platitudinous 'excitement' of romantic and popular fiction. They – and we – find what is boring

interesting. It is this which places Flaubert's writing onto the edge of unreadability. As Jonathan Culler affirms:

> Boredom is a literary category of the first importance; it is the background against which the activity of reading takes place and which continually threatens to engulf it. The strategies of reading and interpretation must be understood as attempts to avoid boredom, and, on the other hand, boredom itself is a literary device whose usefulness modern literature has increasingly forced us to appreciate.[5]

L'Education sentimentale cannot quite bring itself to enact this most platitudinous of encounters, this time between Frédéric Moreau and Mme Arnoux, though even if the novel did represent the consummation of their adulterous desires, the novel would still be, in Flaubert's terms, a 'book about nothing'. Something would be as meaningful and as meaningless as nothing. Event and non-event coincide strangely, and this is in keeping with the partially eclipsed political history in the novel. We shall return shortly to the mechanism which ultimately prohibits the consummation of adulterous desire in *L'Education sentimentale*.

Centred (or rather decentred) around the non-event of Trudon's tryst with Mme Duhamain at the restaurant des Marronniers, Henry Céard's *Une Belle Journée* (1881) was clearly modelled on *L'Education*. Mme Duhamain agrees to the meeting only to find that her admirer is simply a further instance of the banality she regularly encounters, rather than an exception to the rule of tedium. In a self-conscious echo of Flaubert, 'nothing happens'.[6] Adultery seems to have lost its subversive vitality as the characteristic threat to bourgeois familialism. These novels of adultery *manqué* are complements to Zola's own novel of adultery, *Pot-Bouille* (1882). Both types of novel are forms of parody. In the Flaubert/Céard model, adultery never quite happens; in Zola's novel, it seems to happen virtually all the time, which is in keeping with the critical distinction between, on the one hand, a Flaubertian world from which materiality and experience are in some sense erased and, on the other, the world of Zola in which copia is the order of the day.[7]

Still earlier examples of this dissatisfaction with the novel of adultery also abound, as Stephen Heath reminds us.[8] In the fictional dialogue in part 3 of Baudelaire's essay on *Madame Bovary* (1857), the question is put: 'What is the most hackneyed, the most prostituted constant,

the most worn out hurdy-gurdy?' The answer is immediate: 'Adultery', with a capital A. And in a review of Musset's *Emmeline* (1837), Balzac himself writes that 'Misunderstood women have become ridiculous. Adultery in literature has been done to death for a while, though it still wends its way in the world.'

The list rolls on. So whilst stressing the intensity of the *fin de siècle*'s concern for the renovation of this cultural commonplace, it would nevertheless be misleading to depict the culture it succeeds in terms of an homogeneous investment in it. The nineteenth-century French novel exhibits an ambivalence towards the motif of adultery which is characteristic of parody. Of course, there are always innumerable examples of banal popular fictions of adultery to exploit. What happens in the kind of fictional text which literary studies have chosen to privilege is that adultery often becomes an irresistible temptation for the author just as it does for his heroine. Adultery as a literary theme is perhaps always already tired of itself, only too aware of the 'decadence' it betrays. This kind of self-conscious cultural fatigue characterises a form of the novel which is written in spite of itself.

In addition to the parodic *Pot-Bouille* another noteworthy manifestation of the *fin de siècle*'s dissatisfaction with the form is the invocation of the incest motif as an apparently more radical conjugation of human desires which functions as a contrary model of emotional ambivalence. Whereas the carnal knowledge of adultery undermines the cognitive authority of the cuckold by piercing the supposed self-enclosure of the family, the apparently transgressive motif of incest attempts to reassert the self-contained nature of desires held within the domestic arena. Consequently, it will be suggested that questions of space and knowledge reveal a particular relationship between what we might call the novel of incest (such as Zola's *Le Docteur Pascal* which focuses on an uncle/niece relationship that is viewed as incestuous) and the tradition of the novel of adultery to which it responds.

Pot-Bouille deals with the adulterous machinations of the inhabitants of a tenement block in Paris and is dominated by a Don Juan figure, Octave Mouret. The ambivalence of Zola's position is revealed in the way that he indulges in the adulterous motif as much as he parodies its cultural predominance. Extra-marital affairs are multiplied to farcical proportions as Octave runs up and down the stairs, from apartment to apartment, at certain times succeeding and at other times failing in his attempt to seduce a string of bored housewives.

This novel is only one piece amongst a vast range of evidence which suggests that there is in the wake of Flaubert's *L'Education sentimentale* a conscious revision of the investment in the novel of adultery. Of course, tales of adultery are the staple diet of many of the popular fictions transmitted by our modern media. The difference would seem to be that the novel of adultery is now viewed as kitsch, even if it can still be found in the most interesting of cultural locations. The novel of adultery was one of the major victims of the retrospection to which the *fin de siècle* subjected its own century. Other less ambivalent examples of discontent abound. In praise of Joris-Karl Huysmans's *La Bièvre* (1890), Emile Verhaeren, for instance, writes critically of novelists such as Ohnet, Bourget and Daudet: 'You feel sea-sick, pitching and tossing on the boat of eternal adultery, this irrepressible commonplace of the French novel. We are crying out for a change. We are waiting in hope for it.'[9] Huysmans himself writes to encourage Arnold Goffin in his promotion of other types of literary project which would be 'more interesting than the story of Duchess X's adultery with Count Y, following the formula of Bourget or Prévost. What dated love affairs are being served up to us!'[10] The list rolls on, but the point is that these critiques belong very much to the nineteenth century itself, and *Pot-Bouille* seems to be part of this growing dissatisfaction.

Parody is one way of having and not having the novel of adultery, and *Pot-Bouille* is therefore a fitting culmination to a cultural tradition, rather than a sudden break with the past. For parody is a way for the novelist to possess the form by which he or she is possessed. It is a way of speaking the language of adultery and, in that very same gesture, ridiculing such talk. It is a way of cheating on the novel of adultery. At a party described in chapter 5 of *Pot-Bouille*, for example, a group of men discuss a novel serialised in the *Revue des Deux Mondes*. Léon complains that: 'It's well written – but another adultery! This really is becoming tiresome.'[11] Duveyrier then argues that novelists overestimate the extent of bourgeois adultery. At that very moment, however, Octave Mouret and his partner in crime Trublot are planning their adulterous adventures which they subsequently undertake. The novel of adultery is parodied in this way by Zola's use of the Don Juan figure who enjoys a double-edged relationship to the patriarchy that the novel of adultery subtends. As a sexual peripatetic, the Don Juan figure, Octave threatens husbands with the notorious uncertainty of paternity, and yet at the same time embodies

a certain principle of virility (itself grounded in a crisis of masculinity and paternity).

Pot-Bouille is therefore both inside and outside the novel of adultery, just as its hero, Octave, moves in and out of various domestic spaces within the house of apartments on the rue de Choiseul. Manifestly important in the novel of adultery is the representation of the spatial arrangements between domesticity and the outside world. For adultery allows desire to pass between the domestic realm and the world outside. It refuses to permit the solidification of the porous interface between inside and outside, domesticity and other places, whereas fears over the uncertainty of paternity demand the petrification and solidification, the sewing up and nailing down of such boundaries. The price that the adulterous heroine often pays for denying this demand is obviously exacting in the extreme.

In *Pot-Bouille*, moreover, the subversion of the spatial order of family life by the novel of adultery is itself adulterated. Octave manipulates the concierge's warning that women are not to be brought back into the apartment block. His logic is as treacherous as his behaviour: 'If I take a woman from within this building', Octave tells himself, 'then I wouldn't be bringing her in from outside.'[12] Just as adultery is mischeviously held within the bounds of this building, so the language of adulterous paternity is haunted by the language of the family which it betrays. Believing that he is the father of the child carried by Marie who is one of his mistresses, Octave gives her forehead 'the kiss of a father who is yielding his daughter to a son-in-law'. Octave can only respond to the possibility of paternity by borrowing a gesture from the repertoire of family life. Marriage and adultery, it seems, are complicitous, just as the very notion of blasphemy requires a concept of faith. Indeed, it should not surprise us that the inside/outside binarism will not suffice, and there is clearly scope for a wider project which traces the precise vectors of desire through the ever more complex spatial arrangements of a society in the process of urbanisation, and which traces how this is represented in fiction.

Moreover, Zola's invocation of the nineteenth-century science of genetics stresses the fragility of the fidelity/adultery opposition, for the genetic bequests of family history visit the crimes of the past upon succeeding generations in the Rougon–Macquart line. Even legitimate, non-adulterous parenthood involves another family tree, another potential history of illegitimacies and uncertainties (as Coupeau discovers in *L'Assommoir* when he marries into the

illegitimate Macquart line and fathers Nana). This desire for genetic knowledge central to Zola's Naturalist enterprise supplements the desire for paternal knowledge reflected in the novel of adultery. Posed implicitly in patriarchal terms then is the question, 'How is the father to ensure the legitimacy of the line he marries into?'

This question is presented with particular acuteness in *Le Docteur Pascal*. The solution it provides to this crisis of knowledge is a perturbing one. The paradoxical answer to the father's dilemma is to be found in part in the love affair between uncle and niece – docteur Pascal and Clotilde. This love affair is the final sexual relationship in Zola's vast cycle of novels, and it produces an unnamed child who provides the focus for a positivistic hope for the future. This incestuous relationship between Pascal and the daughter of his brother Aristide allows Zola to tie up the strands of the family tree as they spread ever wider. Clotilde, like Pascal of course, belongs to the legitimate Rougon line which ultimately triumphs over the illegitimate Macquart line with the birth of 'the unknown child'.[13] Pascal appears to learn what fathers apparently want to discover, namely knowledge of the legitimacy of the blood line. This is what might be called the haemic truth of the family tree. But, of course, it in no way resolves the crisis of paternal knowledge, the perpetual crisis of uncertain paternity. Besides, Pascal's genetic background can only ever approximate to that of Clotilde.

As a young girl Clotilde was sent by her father to live with uncle Pascal. She therefore grows up under the same roof as this paternal figure. This incestuous bond contradicts the spatial arrangements in the adulterous paradigm. For whereas adultery allows desire to migrate between the conjugal realm and the outside world, and thus threatens home life with entropy, incest can force desire to remain under the same roof and thus beget the corresponding danger of implosion. The porous interface of the adulterous household is in theory solidified by incest. Consequently it is an illuminating paradox that in this case the fact of incest appears to ensure the demand for secure paternal knowledge. Incest fulfils a conservative function here and is thus no random choice of sexual bond given the cognitive insecurity and the conspicuous spatialisation to be found in the novel of adultery.

Incest is only one of a number of transgressive sexual relations represented by the novel as a genre, and one way forward for critics working on the novel of adultery might be to follow up the implications of such a complex network of transgressions. For there

is a way in which different sexual transgressions commingle and compete in the space of the novel. Take for instance Zola's *La Curée* (1872), the second novel in the *Rougon–Macquart* cycle which he plans as his own 'new Phèdre'. This novel describes how stepson and stepmother, Maxime and Renée, fall in love. Their incestuous if not consanguineous passion is foregrounded in Chapter 4 of the novel by their embrace in the salon blanc at the café Riche. This 'supreme fault' is explained as a verbal transgression: 'And everything was said'.[14] The perversion of incest, a perversion which is strictly *interdit* (forbidden or unspeakable) enjoys a particular status as a challenge to the Naturalist desire for total knowledge. For if Zola's goal is to say everything ('tout dire') then he must speak of the unspeakable. When stepson and stepmother consummate their passion, the husband Aristide is being doubly cheated on, both by his second wife, Renée, and by his son by his previous marriage, Maxime. Therefore incest is in this case also adultery. And for Maxime, indeed, this *amour* satisfies primarily the *amour-propre* of adultery: 'She was the first married woman that he had possessed. He did not consider that the husband was his father.'[15] So the internalised cultural norm of adultery postpones the return of the repressed at the level of language, consciousness and indeed conscience, even though the taboo has already been broken. Maxime is the brother of Clotilde – the very Clotilde who has a child by uncle Pascal 18 novels later – and her father is Aristide. Indeed, it is in this second novel, *La Curée*, that we learn how it is that Clotilde will come to be living under Pascal's roof in the twentieth novel in the cycle.

La Curée describes incest as one of the perversions characteristic of decadence, and perhaps one of the advantages in linking adultery and incest in the way that I have outlined is that it may allow us to make sense of the shift described by Tanner from the novel of adultery to the modernist novel. The perversions of the Decadence, of course, come to characterise the *fin de siècle* which lies between these two traditions, and there is no shortage of accounts which describe the use of the incest motif in that period.[16] In the context of *fin de siècle* France, the history of Wagnerism must be central to any comprehensive account of the topic, and this might itself take us back to neglected literary texts such as Elemir Bourges's *Le Crépuscule des dieux* (1884), designed as a novelistic *Twilight of the Gods*. The history of the representation of incest in sociology, anthropology and forms of psychology and psychoanalysis would take us back, of course, to those two great *fin de siècle* figures, Durkheim and Freud.

Let us conclude by invoking a vital moment from *L'Education sentimentale* which enjoys an emblematic force in the French tradition of fictionalising adultery. Frédéric Moreau has been vainly pursuing a married woman, Mme Arnoux. Disillusionment follows delusion. And when in the penultimate chapter the once so coveted Mme Arnoux visits Frédéric Moreau for the last time, the hero senses that she has come to offer herself to him. Frédéric considers but then rejects the possibility of satisfaction, and it is the narrator who notes: 'He felt something beyond expression, a repulsion, something like the dread of incest.'[17] In this scene the incest taboo acts as a metaphor of aversion. The 'maternal' role that Mme Arnoux has played in the desiring scenarios of the youth is crystallised. Whereas in *La Curée* it is the thought of adultery which obscures incest, in *L'Education sentimentale* it is the haunting figure of incest which halts adultery. For Frédéric, the taboo represents not only the impossibility of fulfilling desires but the untenability of desires themselves. This return to fundamental law signals the end of the novel. Such regressive circularity is mimed in the structural circularity of *L'Education sentimentale*, hence the ironic undercutting of the plot in the final sardonic retrospection of Frédéric and his friend Deslauriers, recalling their abortive trip to the brothel as 'the best that we have known'.[18] Adultery's capacity to generate narrative is built into the architecture of everyday life, and the stresses and strains of such textual and domestic structures are eloquent testimony to the failure of domestic space to hold within its walls the forces of desire. Given that it is therefore as a crisis of knowledge and as a crisis of space that the novel of adultery comes to grip the imagination, it is possible to discern a telling spatial and cognitive logic in these invocations of incest, as passion in Zola's world of ever multiplying sexual encounters and as a taboo in *L'Education sentimentale*, and just as this invocation invites the provisional closure of one type of story, so at the end of the nineteenth century it also marks the inception of another.

Notes

Unless otherwise denoted, translations from nineteenth-century French texts are my own and reference is given to the original text.

1   Denis de Rougemont, *Love in the Western World* (New York: Anchor Books, 1957); first published as *L'Amour et l'Occident* (Paris: Plon, 1939).

132 *Scarlet Letters*

2. Tony Tanner, *Adultery in the Novel* (Baltimore/London: The Johns Hopkins University Press, 1979).

3 In the first case, exemplified by *Lady Chatterley's Lover*:

> It is society itself that is receding into silence and non-Being, and the significance of adultery is drowned in the experience of physicality. Lawrence is attempting to redefine the very terminologies of contracts and relationships – a revaluation by rebaptism, in Nietzsche's terms.

In the case of Joyce, however, 'there is no example of what might be called normal sexual intercourse and perversion is the usual mode of procedure. Here familial and social problems are absorbed into an ultimate exploration of "linguicity"'. In a footnote, Tanner refers to a third case, suggested in conversation with Edward Said, of 'the "hommes-femmes"', as described by Proust. This would point to a kind of self-sealing narcissistic sexuality leading to the solitary solipsism of Proust's famous soundproof room and a life given over to endless *writing*' (13–14).

4 Emile Zola, *Les Rougon–Macquart*, 5 vols, ed. by Henri Mitterand (Paris: Gallimard (Pléiade), 1960–67).

5 Jonathan Culler, *Flaubert: The Uses of Uncertainty* (Ithaca/London: Cornell University Press, 1974), 19.

6 Henry Céard, *Une Belle Journée* (Genève: Slatkine, 1970), 260.

7 The complementary nature of this relationship between parodic models is implicitly affirmed in *Au Bonheur des Dames* which transposes Octave's private *éducation sentimentale* to the public realm of capitalist adventure. His dictum 'that everything happens and that nothing happens' (in *Les Rougon–Macquart*, III, 795) suggests that the multiple scenarios of Octave's *Bildung* cancel each other out, only to conclude in the *bonheur* of this 'fine day' ('cette belle journée', 798).

8 Stephen Heath, *Gustave Flaubert: Madame Bovary* (Cambridge: Cambridge University Press, 1992), 80.

9 Emile Verhaeren, 'Métempsychose de romancier', *L'Art moderne*, 19 October 1890.

10 Cited in J.K. Huysmans, *Lettres à Destrée*, ed. by G. Vanwelkenhuyzen (Genève: Droz, 1967), 78, n. 4.

11 Emile Zola, *Pot-Bouille, in Les Rougon–Macquart*, III, 94. Particularly pertinent in the context of parody are the songs evoked at social gatherings. At the Duveyriers' party described in Chapter 5, Octave joins in the singing of 'The Consecration of the Swords' from Giacomo Meyerbeer's opera, *Les Huguenots* (first performed at the Opéra de Paris on 29 February 1836). Meyerbeer's tragedy of misunderstanding and the dramatic irony of tardy recognition (where St Bris discovers too late that he has been the murderer of his own daughter) stands in contrast to Zola's comedy of deception. Likewise, *Pot-Bouille* implicitly ironises Grétry's *Zémire et Azor* (first performed at the Comédie Italienne on 16 December 1771) in which Octave participates in Chapter 10. The happy ending of this comic opera (the marriage of Zémire and Azor) is undermined by the cynicism of Zola's black comedy. *Pot-Bouille* sits between the tearful gravity of Meyerbeer and the blithe comedy of Grétry, both of which play

out dramas of misunderstanding between father and daughter (echoed in the family narratives of the Pichons and the Josserands). In the latter case Sandor comes to realise that his daughter actually enjoys her enforced partnership with Azor. Thus necessity is aligned with desire and the potential tragedy is averted.

12 *Pot-Bouille*, 60.
13 Emile Zola, *Le Docteur Pascal*, in *Les Rougon–Macquart*, V, 1665.
14 Emile Zola, *La Curée* in *Les Rougon–Macquart*, I, 456–7.
15 *La Curée*, 482.
16 These range from Mario Praz's classic account of *The Romantic Agony* (Oxford: Oxford University Press, 1970; first published in English in 1933) to Elaine Showalter's *Sexual Anarchy* (London: Bloomsbury, 1991) and Jennifer Wælti-Walters's history of *French Feminist Novelists of the Belle Epoque* (Bloomington/Indianapolis: Indiana University Press, 1990).
17 Gustave Flaubert, *L'Education sentimentale* (Garnier-Flammarion, 1969), 440.
18 *L'Education sentimentale*, 445.

10

Patriarchal Ideology and French Fictions of Adultery 1830–57

D.A. Williams

In the early decades of the nineteenth century the institution of marriage underwent a significant transformation: the profoundly misogynistic Civil Code, drawn up by Napoleon's lawyers, established a new legal framework for marriage in an attempt to strengthen the authority of the husband, proved profoundly inimical to new expectations relating to marriage, and ran directly counter to the principles of liberty and equality which were part of the broad cultural legacy of the French Revolution. From 1830 marriage became the focus of considerable debate and gave rise to attempts to codify its underlying logic and a wide range of literary representations. The state of marriage was a question which was urgently addressed in many quarters, a sensitive subject of virtually universal concern. Literature clearly had a vital and, in some respects ambivalent, role in this collective preoccupation with marriage: the novel, in particular, both diagnosed and contributed to the difficulties of marriage. What is of particular interest, however, is the extent to which the novel reflected or was able, in some way, to maintain a critical distance from the conventional view of marriage. This question can be posed most acutely in relation to attitudes to adultery of the wife, which remained a central concern for much of the first half of the century, providing something of a test-case for theories about the relationship between ideology and literature.

Ideology, as Terry Eagleton has recently shown, has a variable semantic content.[1] It can be used neutrally to signify 'the ideas and beliefs which symbolise the conditions and life-experiences of a specific, socially-significant group or class' but the use of the term frequently carries the assumption that the function of such ideas and beliefs is to promote and legitimate the interests of the dominant

social group. Although the word is more commonly employed in a political context, it can also be used in connection with relations between the sexes. What will be termed patriarchal ideology can be identified as a set of ideas and beliefs whose function it was to promote and legitimate the authority of men and the subordination of women: a well-regulated society depends upon the authority of the male and the submission of the female; differences between the sexes, assumed to be innate, predispose men to an active life in the public sphere, women to a more passive life in the private sphere; in marriage, which represents the royal road to fulfilment, the fidelity of the wife was supremely important, whilst that of the husband was not so critical. None of these beliefs, it need hardly be said, was borne out by the reality of lived experience. Adapting Althusser's well-known dictum that 'ideology represents the imaginary relationship of individuals to their real conditions of existence',[2] patriarchal ideology could be said to promote a certain imaginary or idealised view of relations between the sexes, the real conditions of existence, which as sexual beings, we all necessarily experience. It attributed to the man a care and concern for the woman which was frequently lacking and assumed in the woman a subservience which was at odds with the natural desire in all human beings for a measure of self-determination. It amounted to a rosy-eyed view of the benefits which each sex was likely to derive from following a certain well-worn path, beginning with courtship and ending in conjugal bliss and parenthood.

The relationship between ideology and literature is a complex matter and has been construed in various ways. One approach is to view literature as nothing more than unadulterated ideology, as an 'ideological reflex', along with morality and religion, of the life-process.[3] Such a model is reductive and makes it difficult to separate the ideological implications of literary works from the ideology of the age. On the other hand, the opposite view that authentic art can completely avoid the ideology of its time seems utopian. An intermediate position, one which recognises that literary works of necessity bear the stamp of the ideology of their age, but are not in any mechanical sense reducible to 'ideological reflexes', has been put forward by French theorists such as Althusser and Macherey and subsequently refined by critics such as Eagleton and Jameson. In a well-known statement, Althusser has suggested that literary works, even or perhaps particularly when they appear to be supporting the

ideology of their time, allow us to see ideology, as it were, 'from the inside':

> What art makes us *see*, and therefore gives to us in the form of *'seeing'*, *'perceiving'*, and *'feeling'* (which is not the form of *knowing*), is the *ideology* from which it is born, in which it bathes, from which it detaches itself as art, and to which it *alludes*. [...] Balzac and Solzhenitsyn give us a 'view' of the ideology to which their work alludes and with which it is constantly fed, a view which presupposes a *retreat*, an *internal distantiation* from the very ideology from which their novels emerged. They makes us 'perceive' (but not know) in some sense *from the inside*, by an *internal distance*, the very ideology in which they are held.[4]

In putting ideology to work, the literary text, according to Pierre Macherey, illuminates the absences, the contradictions and 'silences' of a given ideology. Macherey insists on the paradox that what is most eloquent about a work of literature is not what it says but what it does not say. The gaps and silences in the text become a way of exposing the gaps and silences which constitute the fault-lines of ideology.[5] Following Althusser and Macherey, Eagleton suggests that works of literature may display the contradictions and conflicts which exist within an ideological formation but can operate only within the constraints of that formation.[6] A limited number of ideologically permissible outcomes may be possible in a novel: the final resolution of the central conflict in the conclusion of the plot is often pre-determined by a pre-existing matrix of beliefs or prior ideological configuration.[7]

One of the most promising attempts to define the 'hold' of ideology on the literary text has been made by Fredric Jameson in his discussion of the 'elementary structure of meaning' proposed by Greimas in *Du Sens*. Since this debate is conducted in relation to the literature and period which concerns us it will be examined in greater detail. Starting from the structuralist premise that a fundamental opposition between Culture and Nature underpins all forms of social organisation,[8] Greimas subsumes permitted and excluded sexual relations under the broad headings of Culture and Nature. Further oppositions can be elaborated under these two headings on the basis of whether or not relations are prescribed or forbidden, producing four separate permutations which can be arranged into the following 'semiotic rectangle':[9]

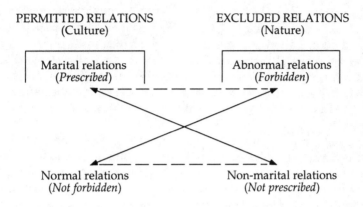

PERMITTED RELATIONS   EXCLUDED RELATIONS
(Culture)   (Nature)

Marital relations *(Prescribed)*   Abnormal relations *(Forbidden)*

Normal relations *(Not forbidden)*   Non-marital relations *(Not prescribed)*

The important thing to note about this schema is that the content of the different 'slots' can vary. Greimas suggests that what he calls 'traditional French society' puts normal marital relations in the pole position, as the prescribed permutation to which all other kinds of relations are to be related, placing incest opposite marriage, in the category of forbidden relations, and, more significantly, and in a way which can have no real justification, 'permitting' adultery of the husband as the converse of incest in the category of not forbidden relations, whilst 'excluding' adultery of the wife, as the converse of marital relations, in the category of not prescribed relations, but excluded ones. Another way of expressing the resulting configuration which emerges from this particular way of defining the various logical possibilities which the semiotic rectangle allows is the four-term homology: Marital Relations are to Incest as Adultery of the husband is to Adultery of the wife.

In *The Political Unconscious* Jameson seeks to appropriate Greimas's model, which he considers to be essentially 'transhistorical', for a historicising and dialectical criticism by designating it as 'the very locus of ideological closure':

Seen in this way, the semiotic rectangle becomes a vital instrument of exploring the semantic and ideological intricacies of a text [...] because it maps the limits of a specific ideological consciousness and marks the conceptual points beyond which that consciousness cannot go, and between which it is condemned to oscillate. [...] It furnishes a dramatic embodiment of ideological closure as such, and allows us to map the inner limits of a given ideological

formation. [...] The very closure of the 'semiotic rectangle' now affords a way into the text, not by positing mere logical possibilities and permutations, but rather through its diagnostic revelation of terms or nodal points implicit in the ideological system which have, however, remained unrealised in the surface of the text, which have failed to become manifest in the logic of the narrative, and which we can read as what the text represses.[10]

Jameson's move represents a significant theoretical advance and posits a more complex interaction between literature and ideology. Ideology may not be clearly visible in the form of explicit statements but it is always there in a sense, as a kind of silent censor, marking the limits beyond which the text cannot go, shaping the way in which certain types of behaviour are categorised. Put simply, if at a certain historical juncture the various 'slots' in an underlying scheme of oppositions are filled in as Greimas suggests, fictional representations of adultery will of necessity be predicated upon the assumption that adultery of the wife is a heinous crime. At a fundamental level, issues which a text may appear to be debating will have already been resolved and the outcome of the plot, which may appear to be uncertain, will always be pre-ordained by a kind of ideological necessity. Such a model explains why the ready sympathy which the adulterous wife elicits is frequently offset by the unhappy, even gruesome, end she experiences.

We might, however, wish to ask how, given that the content of the slots of the semiotic rectangle is not fixed in perpetuity, the ideological limits of one age change into those of the next and how what appears to be fixed proves, if one takes a long-term view, to have a degree of flexibility. Are the inner limits of a given ideological formation and those which are latent in the text necessarily coterminous or could it be that literature is partly responsible for loosening the very ideological constraints by which it is bound? More specifically, in fictions of adultery produced at a time when patriarchal values were particularly prevalent, were the ideological contours surrounding adultery of the wife in the novel as clearly defined as those within the general culture?

The dominant view of marriage in the nineteenth century was that it corresponded to women's needs, even though it involved a kind of enslavement.[11] This view was strongly contested by early feminists and utopian socialists, amongst others. Several of the major writers of the period also expressed views which were directly opposed to

the patriarchal view of marriage. Within this ideological context, the question of adultery was a key issue and all kinds of fears crystallised for obvious reasons around the figure of the adulterous wife.[12] Since marriage, under the patriarchal system, was the one and only place in which the sexual desire of the woman could be legitimately expressed, adultery of the wife represented a kind of disastrous spillage or scandalous excess of sexual desire, which threatened to undermine the very basis upon which society and the authority of the husband rested.[13] The conventional view of adultery of the wife was, accordingly, that it was 'a crime which in itself contains all the others'[14] and its dangers were forcefully spelt out.[15] Adultery of the wife exerted a strong fascination upon writers of the period, eliciting a variety of responses, ranging from firm condemnation to surreptitious expressions of sympathy, sometimes both within the same text. There is often an unresolved contradiction between a deeply entrenched sense of the catastrophic nature and consequences of adultery and a strong and at times uncontrolled urge to endorse the adulterous woman's bid for personal fulfilment. This contradiction produces highly erratic ideological readings, as novelists, not knowing whether to condemn or to condone, oscillate wildly between different value-systems and perspectives. The ideological viewpoint of the author is not always clearly presented – indeed there is a clear move away from explicit presentation – and even when it is, it is often highly confused. The act of adultery itself often undergoes a kind of repression and exists as a kind of gap or absence in the text, something which must be presumed to have taken place, but which the novelist is unable or unwilling to depict. What follows is a selective account which attempts to illustrate the variety and complexity of the mediations of patriarchal ideology found in French fictions of adultery between 1830 and 1857.

George Sand wrote her first novel, *Indiana* (1832), fired with a deep sense of the iniquity of the legal and ideological systems governing the position of women in marriage and society.[16] The harsh treatment she receives from her husband, a retired soldier imbued with the values of patriarchy and the persistent attention shown to her by the conventionally dashing aristocrat, Raymon de Ramière, do not prove sufficient, however, to tip the heroine over the brink of adultery, on which she remains precariously poised for most of the novel. Indiana proclaims her belief in a woman's entitlement to both independence and love,[17] but repeatedly resists Raymon's increasingly ardent entreaties. Rabine has argued that although George Sand may call into

question the laws which govern marriage, she reproduces the nineteenth-century ideology of the passive and chaste woman.[18] Indiana perceives sexual contact as necessarily degrading and George Sand seems to take it upon herself to act as a protective angel saving her from a fate worse than death.[19] The repression of adultery enacted in the manifest content of *Indiana* is accompanied by a powerful drama of profanation over which there seems to be little authorial control. Noun, Indiana's *soeur de lait*, functions as a kind of double upon whom Indiana's repressed sexuality is displaced. In a key scene, which takes place in Indiana's highly symbolic 'circular bedroom', Raymon makes love to Noun, who is dressed in Indiana's clothes and, as her image is reflected endlessly in the mirror, the two women become confused in Raymon's mind, leaving him with a sense of having violated Indiana through Noun.[20] The subsequent death by drowning of Noun can be read, consequently, given the system of equivalences between the two women, as a projection of the kind of fate which would await Indiana, were she to give expression to her repressed adulterous desire.[21] The suicide of Noun also prefigures the aborted suicide of Indiana at the end of the novel. George Sand steers her heroine away from disastrous sexual entanglements at one level, only to countenance them and their fatal consequences at a deeper level where Indiana and Noun fuse to convey a single image of female fate under the patriarchal system.

Stendhal was highly critical of the conventional values of the post-revolutionary period. Under no illusions about marriage under the patriarchal system, he approached the subject of adultery with scant concern for the official ideology of the time. Although *Le Rouge et le Noir* (1830) focuses mainly on the life and times of Julien Sorel, it also gives an unusually uncensorious depiction of the adulterous wife. Madame de Rênal remains blithely indifferent to the implications of her behaviour until her son falls ill and only then is filled with remorse. *Le Rouge et le Noir* diverges significantly from the common pattern in the nineteenth-century novel which involves the married woman, on the verge of adultery, being held back by the illness of her son.[22] Madame de Rênal is momentarily made aware of her 'crime': 'Although endowed with a profoundly religious character, up to that moment, she had not given any thought to the enormity of her crime in the eyes of God.'[23] Stendhal does not, however, choose to prolong her anguish: Stanislas recovers and she no longer has to face the stark choice of son or lover. The comment on her release from her torment – 'Finally the Heavens took pity on this miserable mother'[24] – is more

than a little ironic. The contradiction between the apparent acceptance of the traditional view of adultery and the final rejection of such a view could not be more glaring. The harsh punishment which adultery normally receives is abruptly suspended and the relationship once again bathes in a kind of edenic innocence. Stendhal's complete imperviousness to the pressures of the ideological formation of his age is grounded in the more powerful hold of images and instances of the maternal. It is impossible to do justice to the full complexity of Stendhal's preoccupation with the maternal element in such a short account,[25] but it is arguable that the recurrent oedipal structure based on the expression of his ambivalent feelings towards the mother leads to the demise of the configuration normally produced by the semiotic rectangle. The equation of adultery of the wife with incest loses much of its ideological power if at some fundamental level incest is valorised. Julien's over-determined act of shooting Madame de Rênal in no way stems from any residual view of adultery as crime, but is yet another example of Stendhal's compulsive expression of powerful feelings of aggression towards the maternal. Significantly, Madame de Rênal survives the shooting and is blissfully reunited with Julien in prison. In *Le Rouge et le Noir* Stendhal appears to enjoy a kind of imaginative freedom which finally allows him to project the adultery of Madame de Rênal into a realm of experience which is removed from ideological pressure.

Balzac established his reputation as a novelist largely through his engagement with the problematics of marriage under the patriarchal system. Having demonstrated in his early treatise, *Physiologie du mariage* (1829), how the logic of marriage itself pushes all women towards adultery, he went on to produce a quite extraordinary range of fictional works exploring the difficulties experienced by various types of married women. Although his view of marriage was broadly in line with patriarchal ideology, Balzac adopted a progressive stance on a number of issues.[26] His attitude to adultery of the wife is particularly contradictory. He both insists on the need for marital fidelity and recognises all the forces which make this difficult to achieve. Although on occasion he shows adultery being forestalled,[27] he is more inclined to focus on the wife whose response to the 'crisis' to which all marriages inexorably lead is to betray or attempt to break free from the husband.[28] If adultery is seen as inevitable, it is also seen to have problematic consequences in the long term, both in terms of the wife's capacity to provide for herself and her children,[29] or, more subtly, in terms of her own emotional stability or mental well-being.[30]

The ideological contradictions which run through Balzac's work are perhaps best epitomised by *La Femme de trente ans* (1842). This novel began as a series of shorter studies of different women, which were finally brought together in a single work, covering various stages in the life of a central figure, Julie d'Aiglemont, from her early choice of a totally unsuitable husband, to disastrous marriage, adultery, unhappy family life and old age. The frequently stressed disparate nature of the novel makes for a considerable degree of ideological turbulence. In one section the heroine voices a powerful critique of marriage under the patriarchal system as a form of legal prostitution,[31] whilst the authorial commentary insists on the need for wives to be bound by strict laws.[32] The pivotal section entitled *A Trente Ans*, offers a subtle and sympathetic study of the heroine as she is poised on the brink of adultery and a highly poeticised image of the first physical contact with Vandenesse.[33] The subsequent problems encountered by the heroine, in particular the murder of her adulterous child, committed by her legitimate daughter, Hélène, and, at the end of her life, her lack of credibility as a moral guide in the eyes of another daughter, Moïna, as she, in her turn, is on the verge of adultery, point to the long-term destabilising effects on the family of adultery. In order to integrate the disparate episodes of the novel, Balzac resorts to a conventional scheme of crime and punishment, one which clearly reflects patriarchal ideology. However, just as there is a good deal of understanding, even sympathy, shown for the act of rebellion of Hélène when she takes the extraordinary decision to run away with a brigand who has broken into the family home, so, in spite of the human misery to which it gives rise, Julie's adultery, which is also an act of rebellion against the same embodiment of patriarchal authority, receives a kind of tacit support. If Balzac avoids depicting the act of adultery itself but gives a full account of its causality, he gives full expression to Hélène's rebellion without making its causality explicit. The two acts of rebellion illuminate each other, allowing the novel to make a silent plea which goes some way towards circumventing the ideology to which it elsewhere subscribes.[34]

Madame Bovary (1857) differs from earlier fictions of adultery in that the narrative is shorn of the interpretative commentary which, in previous narratives, placed the adultery of the heroine within clearly defined ideological confines. Adultery which is not condemned is readily perceived as adultery which is pardoned,[35] and the novel as a whole can be seen as committing a kind of crime against the ideological image of the family.[36] Stephen Heath suggests that by

representing adultery in *Madame Bovary* as platitude, as flatly oppressive as all the rest,[37] Flaubert likewise exhausts the platitudes of the novel of adultery, leaving no hold for its habitual framework of reference and value. Thus, when Flaubert writes of his adulterous heroine that 'she found in adultery all the platitudes of marriage',[38] the opposition between relations which are prescribed and those which are not within the 'semiotic rectangle' which subtends patriarchal ideology appears to be dismantled. The scandal provoked by the novel, whilst a measure of the novel's 'undoing' of received ideas about marriage, should not lead us to overlook the implications of the heroine's untimely end, which it is possible to read within the terms of a patriarchal scheme of reference.[39] Emma's death by suicide is significantly linked through the symbolic figure of the Blind Man with her adulterous experience. The Blind Man's appearance and behaviour recall several aspects of Emma's behaviour with Rodolphe in the forest but many of the same descriptive details also anticipate her death-bed agony. For instance, Emma's *ventre*, which the Blind Man's *comédie* highlights as a symbolic site, is the locus of sexual activity and physical suffering, both subject to a similar regime of ingestion and expulsion, suggesting a deep-seated continuity between her adultery and her death. The appearance of the Blind Man as Emma is about to die paves the way for a final vision which takes on a sinister significance, as Emma, in her confused state of mind, imagines she can see 'the hideous face of the beggar rising up like a nightmare amid the eternal darkness'.[40] The text provides us with no way of knowing whether any credence should be given to the scheme of eternal damnation that such a vision suggests but it is evidence that not all the drama has passed out of the time-worn subject of adultery.

Flaubert's novel can be read as a kind of *summum* of the themes and motifs of the preceding fictions of adultery. As such it both prolongs and gives a final definitive expression to the ideological centrality of the adulterous woman. Adultery in subsequent novels, as others have noted,[41] will not have the same urgency and is rarely seen as a crime which must be punished by death. This may in part be explained by some fundamental weakening of the semiotic rectangle which, arguably, provided the co-ordinates for the ideological formation underpinning the fictions of adultery we have examined. If such a weakening has occurred, it is perhaps due in some measure to the impact of these fictions themselves. In the very process of subscribing to a greater or lesser extent to patriarchal ideology, each in one way or another has put it under strain, brought it into conflict with

alternative value-systems, until its unacceptable face, perhaps most dramatically embodied in the unseeing orbs of the Blind Man, is finally and decisively exposed. What is most striking about the relationship between literature and ideology, as exemplifed in the works which have been examined, is the latitude they enjoy; although the looming presence of patriarchal ideology can always be felt both in and through the text, it was clearly possible to offer a degree of resistance to it, to escape its stranglehold, and perhaps even to begin the slow process of its demolition.

Notes

1 T. Eagleton, *Ideology. An Introduction* (London, Verso, 1991), pp. 1–31.
2 See L. Althusser, 'Ideology and Ideological State Apparatuses' , *Essays on Ideology* (London, Verso, 1993), p. 36.
3 See K. Marx and F. Engels, *The German Ideology*, quoted in R. Williams, *Marxism and Literature* (Oxford, OUP, 1977), p. 59.
4 'Letter on Art in Reply to André Daspre' in *Essays on Ideology*, pp. 174–5 (The italics are those of Althusser).
5 P. Macherey, *Pour une Théorie de la production littéraire* (Paris, Maspéro, 1970).
6 See T. Eagleton, *Criticism and Ideology. A Study in Marxist Literary Theory* (London, NLB, 1976).
7 *Ibid.*, p. 87.
8 A.J. Greimas, *Du Sens* (Paris, Editions du Seuil, 1970), pp. 142–3.
9 *Ibid.*, p. 141 (This is a simplified version of the model proposed by Greimas).
10 F. Jameson, *The Political Unconscious. Narrative as a Socially Symbolic Act* (London, Methuen, 1981), pp. 47–8.
11 See the views quoted in C. Nesci, *La Femme Mode d'emploi. Balzac, de la 'Physiologie du mariage' à 'La Comédie humaine'* (Lexington, French Forum Publications, 1992), p. 21.
12 See S. Heath, *Gustave Flaubert. Madame Bovary* (Cambridge, CUP, 1992), p. 78.
13 J. Weeks, *Sex, Politics and Society: The Regulation of Sexuality since 1800* (London, Longman, 1981), p. 32.
14 P.J. Proudhon, *De la Justice dans la Révolution et dans l'Eglise* (1858), *Oeuvres complètes*, iv, Marcel Rivière,1935, p. 307 (quoted in Heath, *op. cit.*, p. 81).
15 See the article entitled 'Femme adultère' in *Les Français peints par eux-mêmes*, Curmer, 1840–42 (quoted C.Nesci, *op.cit.*, p. 16).
16 See 1842 Préface, *Indiana* (Paris, Folio, 1984), pp. 46–7.
17 *Ibid.*, p. 233.
18 L. Rabine, 'George Sand and the Myth of Femininity', *Women and Literature*, 4 (1976), pp. 2–17.
19 See, for instance, *Indiana*, p. 221.

20 *Ibid.*, p. 104.
21 *Ibid.*, p. 119.
22 This pattern has been discussed by N. Segal in *The Adulteress's Child: Authorship and Desire in the Nineteenth-Century Novel* (Cambridge, Polity Press, 1992), pp. 62–114.
23 'Quoique d'un caractère profondément religieux, jusqu'à ce moment, elle n'avait pas songé à la grandeur de son crime aux yeux de Dieu', *Le Rouge et le Noir* (Paris, Garnier, 1960), p. 112.
24 'Enfin le ciel eut pitié de cette mère malheureuse', *ibid.*, p. 116.
25 For a recent discussion of this preoccupation see C.A. Mossman, *Politics and Narratives of Birth. Gynocolonization from Rousseau to Zola* (Cambridge, CUP, 1993), pp. 19–71.
26 See A. Michel, *Le Mariage chez Honoré de Balzac. Amour et féminisme* (Paris, Les Belles Lettres, 1978).
27 See *Une Fille d'Eve* and *Le Lys dans la vallée*.
28 See *La Muse du départment* and *Honorine*.
29 See *La Grenadière*.
30 See *La Femme abandonnée* and *Adieu*.
31 *La Femme de trente ans* (Paris, Folio, 1977), p. 165.
32 See C. Prendergast, *Balzac: Fiction and Melodrama* (London, Edward Arnold, 1977), p. 134.
33 *La Femme de trente ans*, p. 206.
34 For a persuasive reading of Hélène's rebellion see C. Prendergast, *op.cit.*, pp. 135–7.
35 See D. LaCapra, *Madame Bovary on Trial* (Cornell, Cornell University Press, 1982), p. 56.
36 See D. LaCapra, *op.cit.*, p. 32.
37 *Op.cit.*, p. 82.
38 'Elle retrouvait dans l'adultère toutes les platitudes du mariage', *Madame Bovary* (Paris, Garnier, 1971), p. 296.
39 See for example 'Masters' by Rollie Hollstein, quoted by G. Falconer, 'Création et conservation du sens dans *Madame Bovary*' in *La Production du sens chez Flaubert* (Paris, Union générale d'éditions, 1975), pp. 395–6.
40 'la face hideuse du misérable qui se dressait dans les ténèbres éternelles comme un épouvantement', *Madame Bovary*, pp. 332–3.
41 See in particular T. Tanner, *Adultery in the Novel* (Baltimore, Johns Hopkins Press, 1979).

Part III
The High Age
of Adultery: Texts

11

No Fairy-tale: the Story of Marriage in Trollope's *He Knew He Was Right*

Mary Hamer

The first library that gave me a reader's ticket was the municipal library in Birmingham, when I was a child. Harborne Public Library offered a service which the university libraries that I use these days fail to provide. Or perhaps they have reason to hesitate before the task. In Harborne Library the books were divided strictly into two categories, fiction and non-fiction and they were issued on separate tickets. As a child, I was given a ticket for each one; they did not let us take out storybooks on the ticket meant for non-fiction. At the time I sensed an implied rebuke, without examining what might lie behind it but today, as I sit down to write about fictions of adultery, I come to a pause. I find myself asking today whether I believe that a taste for fiction is really less commendable than a taste for what passes itself off as the truth. And I wonder on what shelf and in what library I should find a book that would tell the truth about marriage.

It is the church which claims to dispense truth when it comes to Christian marriage, the church which presents its teaching as the superior version. There is a certain justice in this, for until the church invented Christian marriage in the thirteenth century, couples were left free to ask a blessing on their union or not, as they felt inclined. Yet it is impossible to avoid reflecting that when the church acted to bring sexual intimacy between men and women within the purview of its law, the law in question was the law of the father, the law that establishes men in command. It was by means of their most intimate desires, the longing women feel to know the bodies of men, their longing to give birth to their own children, that women were to be

grappled more firmly into a structure of authority and belief that was organised for their disadvantage.

Plays and novels used to end, only too many of them, with a marriage, as if that brought all questioning to a close. Trollope had been as fond as the next man of using an engagement to signal that his story had reached a satisfactory conclusion but there came a moment when satisfaction failed, when the story of public life began to go wrong for Anthony Trollope himself. Someone else was promoted to be head of the Post Office, where he had worked for more than 25 years. Before long he resigned from the civil service and within two months of that date he began work on the novel *He Knew He Was Right*.[1]

He had been planning for some time to resign, Trollope claimed in his *Autobiography*. There may be truth in this but he can hardly have been planning to be disappointed. He had risen to fame as a writer and to financial security only in middle age, after beginning his career as an awkward incompetent clerk, who became involved with unsuitable young women and could not earn enough to live in the way his education and background seemed to warrant. To the end of his life, he admitted, he was plagued by the fear that he would wake to find all his later success was a dream. When he found himself passed over at the Post Office it may have seemed that his nightmare was dangerously close to reality. The voice of Trollope's envy and fear echoes clearly in the opening of *He Knew He Was Right*.

What fairy-tale had they told him when he was setting out in the world as a young man? He knew better now: at 50, he had learned something that was not taught in school about the way the world deals with desire. He begins by speaking with a deceptive nursery charm about a specially favoured young man, a prince almost, or a hero at least:

> When Louis Trevelyan was twenty-four years old, he had all the world before him where to choose; and among other things, he chose to go to the Mandarin Islands, and there fell in love with Emily Rowley, the daughter of Sir Marmaduke, the governor.[2]

Only after that tone and other less accomplished voices full of bitterness have been explored in the opening pages is he free to move into the story of the Trevelyans' marriage.

For the first two years, as he explains, all went well: a baby was born and the house the young Trevelyans had taken in fashionable

Curzon Street was cheerful. Trouble starts, or as Trollope puts it himself, 'wrath began' only at the point where Emily Trevelyan refuses to obey her husband. When she declines to discourage the visits of a Colonel Osborne, a man of her father's age, whom Trevelyan dislikes, his wife voices an opposition that he cannot tolerate. His response is to send her away till she can learn to behave herself.

First she is sent with her baby and her sister to the country to live with strangers. Soon he has hired a detective to keep a watch on her movements. Trevelyan becomes isolated now even from his own friends, since they won't agree that this behaviour is reasonable. The reader is never sure whether he has lost all feeling for what is appropriate or if he is defying conventions he no longer respects. Because Louis misses the baby, he arranges for his son, little Louis, to be brought to visit him at an inn by a friend. At last, with the help of the detective, he brings off a plan to snatch the child from his mother and carries him off to a remote farmhouse in Italy. By this time it is clear, even to those who had been critical of Emily that Louis is severely disturbed. Trevelyan's appearance is transformed and he speaks strangely. When he is traced to the farmhouse and persuaded to give up the child, his wife, Emily, arrives to take back her baby. She sees how ill Louis has made himself and refuses to leave him there alone. Finally she succeeds in persuading him to let himself be taken back to England, where after a few weeks he dies.

It is the final movement of the tale that surprises the most. The wife comes to retrieve one baby and finds it is her husband, the adult, who needs to be taken home. By the end of the novel the father is more helpless than the infant for he can longer even walk. It had seemed merely a convention at the start of the novel that they shared the same name. By its end, the movement of the story has taught us to understand that the father and the motherless child have more in common than a name. On their reunion, Trevelyan must depend on his wife for everything, like a sick child. Perverse as this may seem, it might be precisely what he wanted, for Trevelyan has been visibly engaged in working his way back to intimacy and dependence on whatever terms. Other men, the men he might have met as an equal find his company intolerable now. By becoming an emaciated invalid, troubled by nerves and unable to get a good night's sleep, Trevelyan has put himself in need of a woman's care. At the same time he has put on a semblance of femininity in his own person. In his weakened state Trevelyan, the ideal bridegroom, could almost be taken for a woman himself.

Why else should he steal his little boy away from his wife? When she begs to be allowed to stay and sleep on the floor by the baby's bed, her husband proudly tells her 'That is my place'.[3] Was it a way for him to recreate an intimacy that he longed for but now felt was forbidden to him, to establish himself in the place of a mother to his own little boy? He fed the baby with his own hands, so he claimed, and got him to say his prayers. Isn't there more than a hint of rivalry in telling his wife this? Later, when he is in Italy, Trevelyan begins to adopt the appearance of a woman by letting his hair grow long and wearing a dressing-gown. At the moment when the other men who see him, the Honourable Mr Glascock and Sir Marmaduke Rowley, his father-in-law, are most convinced of his insanity, Louis Trevelyan seems to be absorbed in trying to represent something about mothers.

It is Luce Irigaray who remarks that mothers have been excluded from recognition in that culture that Europe has derived from the Greeks, though she puts it rather more strongly. She says western culture itself is founded on the murder of the mother.[4] In his account of what happens when the man of culture par excellence, Louis Trevelyan, poet, mathematician and scientist, breaks down, Trollope seems to concur that mothers, as the repressed, are due for a return. It is as if the figure of a mother were surfacing through the body of Louis Trevelyan. Another term for what is going on would be acting out. Trevelyan has no conceptual grasp of what he is doing or of how he is transforming himself.

But then, by this point in the novel, his mind as well as his body has surrendered some of its old habits. It is impossible to have a conversation with Trevelyan in this state. He no longer speaks the same language as English gentlemen. What he talks about all the time is himself and the wrongs that have been done him. But perhaps he is now giving expression to a truth that was formerly suppressed. After the process of transformation, does Trevelyan's speech like his body register what had previously been silenced and suppressed? In the language that gentlemen speak there is little room for emphasis on the self. Trevelyan's self-absorption and his obsession with justifying himself embarrass his friends and offer a clear sign of his aberration, in their eyes. To the reader it may seem that a truth is being spoken at last, a truth about the culture of which Trevelyan seemed almost a proprietor, a truth about self-interest and about educated men.

Breakdown, transformation, acting out; what violence has taken place inside Louis Trevelyan? We know the external factor, a recalcitrant wife. But encountering Xantippe's resistance did not spell

disaster for Socrates. There is something more to understand about
what went wrong with Trevelyan. Could it have something to do with
the problem of truth? Socrates died before his time, like Trevelyan,
but politics were involved in Socrates' case: the state condemned
him to die for the questions he asked. Louis Trevelyan, who was
expected to take up a seat in Parliament before long, was not troubled
at first by questions that might threaten the state. Questions only
started, for Louis Trevelyan, when he did not get his own way at home.
'What is my wife doing?' he asked Mr Bozzle the detective.

Trevelyan was not really like Socrates, the broken-nosed elder who
forced his pupils to think by asking them questions. He was just an
ordinary intellectual, a man who could have been a fellow of his
college. There is a Greek figure that the novel compares Trevelyan
with but it is Apollo or rather a statue of Apollo that he is said to bring
to mind. It is Apollo, 'the most Greek of all gods' as the *Oxford Classical
Dictionary* instructs us, 'the ideal of young but not immature manly
beauty', that is really, under the name of Trevelyan, the object of
Trollope's attack.[5] Trollope invites us to see through an image of the
masculine that continues to be honoured in the ancient universities
entrusted with the transmission of European culture.

> He could talk on all subjects, was very generous, a man sure to be
> honoured and respected; and then such a handsome, manly fellow,
> with short brown hair, a nose divinely chiselled, an Apollo's mouth,
> six feet high, with shoulders and legs in proportion – a pearl of
> pearls! (2)

There is just a tincture of Christianity present in this language:
wasn't it the news of the Gospel that was the pearl of great price, one
that a man might sell everything he owned to possess?[6] But the
language of faith has shifted on its axis here. Rather than the word
of the Gospel, it is Trevelyan himself in so far as he resembles Apollo
that is the object of desire. The culture that sets such store by the
idealised body and voice of the young male, although it may think
of itself as Christian, is still one structured on the pattern of Greek
thought and belief, still one marked with the trace of Greek erotics.
The principle that holds it together is worship of an image, a fantasy
set in stone, a fantasy of the male.

What does Apollo stand for? What words might be expected to come
from that beautiful mouth? Though he is often associated with
prophecy, it's not clear that he can be relied on for guidance. His oracle

at Delphi spoke in riddles and he had stolen the oracle anyway. Legend has it that Apollo took over a shrine that was not his in the first place but belonged to a female seer who was later made to speak in his name. Apollo's concerns extend beyond poetry and music, and even further than medicine, just as Trevelyan's activities do not stop at publishing poetry and writing scientific articles or being ninth wrangler at Cambridge. Apollo seems to be responsible for running civilisation itself: 'approving codes of law ... inculcating high moral and religious principles ... and favouring philosophy'.[7] It may be time to ask if he speaks in riddles there too.

It is Trevelyan's father-in-law, Sir Marmaduke, the governor of the Mandarin Islands, who is the active agent of authority; Trevelyan has played only the intellectual part, not tucked away in the seclusion of Cambridge but as a man about town.

> Sir Rowley found that his son-in-law was well spoken of at the clubs by those who had known him during his university career as a man popular as well as wise, not a bookworm or a dry philosopher or a prig. (3)

In this novel the connections between the framing of thought and the framing of political power will be very clearly set out. A violence that we now call colonialism was justified during the nineteenth century in the name of civilisation.[8] Peoples outside Europe found the administration of their own territory and their resources usurped by powers from France, from Britain, from Germany, Portugal and Spain. Does it come as any surprise to learn that Apollo was 'especially prominent in suggesting or approving schemes of colonisation'?[9] There is a sense in which women are outside the Europe of Apollo too: it is not their body or their voice that his cult honours.

One of the most universal fears, anthropologists tell us, is the dread of pollution. This calls for the last of the tasks that Apollo performs; 'In matters of ritual, especially of purification, his oracles are regarded as the supreme authority.'[10] Ritual in this story of nineteenth-century life is the province of the Church of England: what happens in church, shall we ask and from where does the threat of pollution come? The novel is ready with an answer: 'the wedding was celebrated in London by the Rev. Oliphant Outhouse, of Saint Diddulph-in-the-East, who had married Sir Rowley's sister'(3).

Is it in the marriage service that we are to search for a prophylactic against contamination? There must be danger for a man in marriage,

or it would be no concern of Apollo's. Or perhaps it might be more accurate to say that in living with a woman a man's notion of masculinity, his confidence in that male identity he has been brought up in, risks coming under threat. It certainly seems as if Trevelyan anticipates trouble, when he speaks to his future father-in-law, a man who has no fewer than eight daughters.

> 'I haven't a penny piece to give to either of them,' said Sir Rowley.
> 'It is my idea that girls should not have fortunes', said Trevelyan.
> 'At any rate, I am quite sure that men should never look for money.
> A man must be more comfortable, and, I think, is likely to be more affectionate, when the money has belonged to himself.'(2)

Sir Rowley, ignorant agent of Apollo, the colonial official who could not explain the mode of government within his own territory when brought in front of a parliamentary committee, 'could not but admire the principles of his proposed son-in-law'(3). A reader more politically alert can escape that compulsion and listen with a sceptic's ear. Trevelyan already suspects, as his language tells us, that it would be hard for him to sustain the intimacies of marriage without being sure of having the upper hand. Is that why the ceremony in St Diddulph's, the wedding service drawn up for the use of men and women in the Anglican faith, required Emily to promise to obey?

It was Virginia Woolf who wrote ironically about the magic of women, the magic power they have to reflect men at twice the natural size.[11] Emily Trevelyan comes to a moment when she will no longer perform that function, no longer help to keep her husband's image of himself as a man intact. A young woman who had escaped being brought up in the world that had structured her husband, Emily is neither diminutive nor weak, as contemporary notions of the feminine in upper-class British women would ideally require.[12] She is tall, sits her horse without tiring and dances all night. She grew up in the tropics and she is described as dark, in terms that make her close to the Islanders, with darkly glowing skin and full breasts – 'a bust rather full for her age' (6). Emily Trevelyan, daughter of Sir Marmaduke the governor, is presented as if she were a pagan black woman, with all the embodied desire and sexual vibrancy that the new 'science' of race was busy attributing to blacks.[13] There was no intent and, as Trollope demonstrates by his example, no language in which to name desire in a Christian woman.

Mary Douglas has argued that rituals of purification are directed to preserving categories, that they are involved in keeping a particular taxonomy in place.[14] Femininity, as Irigaray has argued, is an epistemological construct designed to complement and fix the supreme construct of masculinity.[15] For a husband like Louis Trevelyan, a man who as an intellectual used ideas to orient himself, physical experience of Emily and her desire might threaten to overset this most important category of all. If a woman could be like this, what did it mean about who he was himself? It was a question to give unwelcome resonance to the term 'carnal knowledge'.

When her husband angrily tells her to stop receiving Colonel Osborne, Emily Trevelyan divines that her sexuality is the focus of blame. It is by no means misguided on her part to sense this. And it is only to be expected that a woman whose life is so intensely experienced through her body will resist any such attack. Her mistake, though, is to claim immediately, that her husband suspects her: this is not the case at all when things first go wrong. Emily is being truthful, in a sense, but not truthful enough. How could she know that her sexuality in itself, a sexuality that Osborne's faded attentions acknowledge, puts her husband's sense of reality out of true?

When does he start to suspect her, if he ever really does? Trevelyan has a difficulty in naming the source of his own sense of injury. He is clear that he requires an act of submission from his wife: this is what she baulks at. The unnamed struggle between them is a struggle of will, a will that might be called desire's shadow. But in the confusion that the failure of naming entails it is not inappropriate that the spectre hovering over the scene is the unspoken word 'adultery'. For what does the word 'adultery' and its cognates mean but pollution?[16] It has not always been acknowledged, however, that it is a fiction that adultery threatens. When it brings news of women's desire, adultery puts into question an ancient fiction, European culture's old story, its myth of masculinity.

People may have exclaimed 'such a handsome, manly fellow, with an Apollo's mouth, a pearl of pearls', (3) but not everyone in the novel is entirely enslaved by the myth. Emily's mother qualifies this report: 'Only, as Lady Rowley was the first to find out, he liked to have his own way.' Lady Rowley's husband, who is father-in-law to the young man, cannot see the problem. 'But his way is such a good way, said Sir Marmaduke. 'He will be such a good guide for the girls'. 'But Emily likes her own way too', said Lady Rowley (3). Sir Marmaduke is father to Emily, not merely a father-in-law and he has watched her

grow up. How well does Sir Marmaduke understand his eldest daughter?

> Sir Marmaduke argued the matter no further, but thought, no doubt, that such a husband as Louis Trevelyan was entitled to have his own way. He probably had not observed his daughter's temper so accurately as his wife had done. With eight of them coming up around him, how should he have observed their tempers? At any rate, if there were anything amiss with Emily's temper, it would be well that she should find her master in such a husband as Louis Trevelyan. (3)

In poising the voice of a mother against a father's voice, Trollope spells out a vital connection between the ignorance of fathers about daughters and what awaits those daughters in marriage.

What Emily wants is her baby: right from the start , she never likes to leave him for long. It costs her something to maintain her distance from her husband, too. There is no resisting the thought that she is made to play the part of Mary, in this story; at first a madonna with child, by the close, the mother in a Pietà, supporting in her arms a tortured and collapsed male body. Is this another founding fantasy of the west, the fantasy of the Blessed Virgin, making itself and its function in structuring experience known? Some say there can be no such thing as a Christian tragedy but the forms that are taken by suffering in this novel seem to give that the lie. Christian marriage itself, compulsory heterosexuality, seems structured to produce tragic suffering. Trevelyan is transfixed, impaled like a butterfly upon a pin, if not crucified by what marriage has taught him about his wife. He experiences it as an epistemological crisis: the only recourse for him, other than admitting his own error, is to strain after further and yet more precise knowledge in search of proof. This is what takes him to Bozzle, the detective, for daily reports on his wife. It is not only his friends who wonder at him for associating with Bozzle and inviting Bozzle to scrutinise his wife: Trevelyan loathes the detective's company and hates himself for what he is doing.

Trollope's first title for this novel was 'Mrs Trevelyan': it is on Emily's desire that the novel dwells at its close. She longs for a sign from her dying husband that he recognises her for who she is and does not really believe that she was untrue. It is a longing he sternly refuses to gratify, right till the last moment. Emily only gets her desire then because she is willing to take her husband as an infant, a child

who has not yet learned to speak and whose signs it is up to a mother to interpret . The contact that finally satisfies her is one which brings her a sense of his mouth, the infant's primary organ, rather than his words: she takes the movement of his lips against her hand and the inarticulate sounds her straining ears can pick up from his tongue as evidence that she was believed, that she was true. 'It is all over', repeats Emily when he has died. 'Consummatum est': aren't those the last words of Christ? Does the mother have something in common with the saviour, the murdered saviour, in this novel? No wonder *He Knew He Was Right* frightened Henry James off Trollope for good.[17]

Notes

1   Trollope started work on *He Knew He Was Right* on 13 November 1867 and finished it on 12 June 1868.
2   *He Knew He Was Right* (London, 1869), 1. All references are taken from the World's Classics edition, ed. John Sutherland (Oxford, 1987). There is a buried reminder of 'A frog, he would a wooing go' in this opening that should not be overlooked.
3   Ibid., 842–3.
4   Luce Irigaray, *Le corps-à-corps avec la mère* (Montreal, 1981). See also Margaret Whitford, *Luce Irigaray: Philosophy in the Feminine* (London and New York, 1991), 75–97.
5   *Oxford Classical Dictionary*, second edition, eds N.G.L. Hammond and H.H. Scullard (Oxford, 1970), 81–2.
6   *Matthew*, 13: 45–6. Again, the kingdom of heaven is like unto a merchant man, seeking goodly pearls: who when he had found one pearl of great price, went and sold all that he had, and bought it.
7   Hammond, op. cit., 81.
8   See G.W. Stocking Jr, *Victorian Anthropology* (London and New York, 1987), pp. 35–6 and *passim*.
9   Hammond, op. cit., 82.
10   Ibid.
11   *A Room of One's Own* (London, 1929). Penguin Twentieth Century Classics Edition, 37.
12   See Lynda Nead, *Myths of sexuality: the representation of women in Victorian Britain* (Oxford and New York , 1988), pp. 13–47. Since completing this argument my attention has been drawn to the work of Joseph A. Kestner, *Masculinities in Victorian Painting* (Aldershot, 1995). Kestner proposes five key paradigms of masculinity: classical hero, gallant knight, challenged paterfamilias, valiant soldier and male nude. These coincide interestingly with the set of positions that Trevelyan, his father-in-law and Colonel Osborne could be said to take up between them.
13   See Hugh Honour, *The Image of the Black in Western Art* (Cambridge, Mass., 1989) Vol. IV, Part 2, 54 and Sander L. Gilman 'Black Bodies, White

Bodies: Toward an Iconography of Female Sexuality in Late Nineteenth-Century Art, Medecine, and Literature', *Critical Inquiry* 12, no. 1 (Autumn 1985): 213–19.

14 Mary Douglas, *Purity and Danger: an Examination of Ritual and Taboo* (New York , 1966), 159–79.

15 See *Speculum of the Other Woman*, trans G.C. Gill (Ithaca, 1985), 133–46.

16 See *OED* which offers only a speculative Latin root, consisting of *ad*, to with *alter*, other.

17 See 'Anthony Trollope' (1883), reprinted in Leon Edel ed., *The House of Fiction* (London, 1957), 103–4.

12

Machado de Assis and the Beloved Reader: Squatters in the Text

Maria Manuel Lisboa

> I was his wife
> But henceforth
> My name from his
> Be freed.
> *Aeschylus*

One of Machado de Assis' critics, John Gledson, has commented that

> Machado presents his readers [...] with the choice between two books, the one immensely readable, interesting, amusing, the other much more unsettling, giving uncomfortable insights into Brazilian upper class society, [...] its repressiveness and callousness. With immense tact and daring, with a mixture of aggression and politeness which is the hallmark of his style, Machado kept his readers, and was, in his own lifetime, a writer of considerable prestige. The only price he had to pay (and no doubt he was content to do so) was that part of his message went unperceived until long after his death.[1]

I should like to suggest that Machado was more than willing to be misunderstood and possibly delighted to be so, in his capacity as a writer who, in his own words, offered to his resisting and unresisting readers alike 'one utterance but two meanings',[2] a cryptic, Machereyan, gap-ridden posture which nevertheless did not prevent him from occasional unambiguous self-positioning as an author driven, in his own words, by the 'monomania [...] for taking art not for art's sake,

but rather as [...] a social, national and human mission'.[3] It is this delight in the encoded but, paradoxically, intermittently signposted impetus to have a political and ideological impact which will be drawn upon here as informing the present consideration of his most famous novel, *Dom Casmurro*.[4]

Briefly, the plot, a first-person narration retrospectively recounted in old age by Bento Santiago, or Bentinho, concerns his adolescent idyll with the young woman next door, Capitu. The larger part of the novel deals with the adolescent pre-marital period, in the course of which Bentinho, with Capitu's help, must contrive to release himself from his pre-ordained enrolment into the seminary and the priesthood, a destiny originating in a promise made by his mother, Dona Glória. Following the miscarriage of her first child years before Bentinho's birth, Dona Glória vowed to offer up her next son, if vouchsafed one, to the priesthood, and in due course conceives Bentinho. The latter's father dies just before the birth, and Bentinho grows up as an only child.

The priesthood vow is eventually circumvented, largely thanks to Capitu's initiative in finding a solution to the problem, and also through her deliberate arousal of Bentinho's prospective jealousy, by means of her vivid description of the likelihood that if Bentinho does not marry her, someone else will, and beget a child upon her. This episode is possibly crucial since, at this early stage in their lives, Capitu plants in Bentinho's adolescent mind the image of herself as the mother of another man's son. This image will subsequently return to haunt them both. In the event, Bentinho and Capitu marry, and after two childless years, a boy, Ezequiel, is born. For a variety of reasons Bentinho comes to suspect the child of being not his but his best friend's, conceived adulterously and, after the accidental death of this friend Escobar he charges Capitu with adultery and banishes her to Europe where in due course she dies. Dona Glória and Ezequiel also die in quick succession, and Bentinho is left in old age to write his memoirs of these events, which constitute the narrative we read, and in which Capitu emerges as a deceitful temptress, seen, through the optic of the retrospective male character's first-person narration and with the advantage of hindsight and monopoly of speech, to have been corrupt from an early age. Capitu herself is deprived by the nature of the first-person narration of the opportunity to present her case and to defend herself. The adultery itself, moreover, is never unambiguously ascertained, merely stated to be a fact by Bento's

narrative, whose primary structuring device is the reorganisation of pre- and post-marital events to the purpose of reinforcing his case. The consequences for Capitu of her continuing silence will be marital separation, exile and death. Less clearly, but no less importantly, however, as I shall argue in the remainder of this paper, the alleged adultery and the ambiguity accruing to the actual likelihood of its occurrence nonetheless become, through a series of coded narrative sleights of hand, the pretext in the course of the novel for the enlisting of, among other unlikely bedfellows, mothers-in-law and daughters-in-law in a larger counterplot, whose objective and effect, as will be argued, is the hijacking of a series of linguistic puns and literary metaphors whereby the previously excluded female voice and presence are forcibly imposed upon the canons of a variety of master discourses, and, in particular, that of the first-person narrator.

The speaking male subject – in this instance the husband self-presented as deceived to a reader whom he seeks to convince of his marital misfortune – resorts for the shoring up of his crumbling subjectivity to a series of literary metaphors and self-affiliations, frequently invoking ancient and modern classics of various denominations for the purpose of self-accreditation in the eyes of the reader. Thus Bentinho, for example, has recourse to, insistently misreads and *is shown* to misread Plato, Socrates, Shakespeare and the Bible, which he uses as backing traditions, only to find, curiously, that the canonical text will in the end insist upon having the last stubborn word, and a last word, moreover, which, by undermining the male in favour of the female voice, would appear sometimes to contravene its own expected orthodoxy. For example, when already to all appearances convinced of Capitu's guilt, Bentinho goes to the theatre to see a production of *Othello*. At the end, remarking upon the audience's furore at the moment of Desdemona's death he remarks: 'how would the public react if she were truly guilty, as guilty as Capitu?' (*DC*, 933). What is omitted from the parallel Bentinho draws between his own and Othello's plight is of course the admission of another obvious possible similarity between Desdemona and Capitu, namely that of their analogous innocence. The omission on the part of a narrator who early on in the exposition of his *ars poetica* exhalted the advantages of the gap-ridden text ['livro omisso,' *DC*, 868] and the advantages for the reader of filling in the gaps for the purpose of a full understanding of the whole, allow here for a moment of self-undoing which requires no intervention on the part of either Machado as author or his female characters as objects, but speaks for both. By

a curious paradox, furthermore, while the classical plots of Aeschylus, Sophocles and Euripides, and of Shakespearean and Biblical scenarios, reject the obeisances of the male in this narrative and preserve their integrity in the face of his subservience to them, ultimately, in fact, undoing his credibility as speaker, in the hands of the plot-controlled female protagonist they appear willingly to lend themselves to a variety of reversals and distortions of their original plots; and in doing so, they self-defeatingly allow the heroines – Capitu and as will be seen Dona Glória also – to arrive, notably almost entirely without the advantage of direct or indirect speech, at effects which aid and abet a female re-writing of the established canonical fates of a variety of Medeas and Clytemnestras, in the original texts defeated and condemned, but here possibly and surprisingly morally victorious at the end.

Thus, what the obedience of the male voice to the orthodoxy of the classical text is unable to achieve, namely the purchasing of support for its own version of reality and for the *status quo* which it serves, the contrasting silence of the female character *does* achieve. The deconstructive difficulty at the heart of the male character's first-person narration in the end unwittingly leads to a revision of previously sacred plots which newly redefine the parameters of textual truth. And by the same rationale, the extradiegetic author, Machado, as well as the textual critic, in particular perhaps the feminist critic – his beloved (female) reader ('my dear friend,' 'my lady [...] whom I admire'[5]) in contrast with the unqualified male one (*EJ*, 954, 971) – whom he invites into the fictional and fictitious world of his male protagonist's first-person narration, become joint squatters in these multiple texts, that is, in both the narrator's text and in the canonic classical tradition which the latter recruits, but whose territory both Machado as author, his female protagonists as actors and the critic as reader variously invade, newly to unlock within them hitherto forbidden female textual spaces. In the process, and as regards the issue which specifically concerns us here, the female character, and in particular the machadean mother and mother-in-law, wife and daughter-in-law, may die, but in the words of Machado himself, albeit losing their lives, they win the discursive and literary battle of posterity (*DC*, 863–5).

The male protagonist's penchant for classical allusion, his need to frame his argument within the perceivedly comforting parameters of a tradition of authorship which he sees as complicitous in his own misogyny, leads to the deployment within this novel of an array of

intertextual literary cross-references which at first glance appear to encode a gender separation unfavourable to the female protagonist. Thus, Machado's male characters invoke Greek philosophy and world literature, Christian dogma and pagan wisdom in a manner which excludes the woman from language, thought and text, casting her instead as either compulsorily silent within the dominant culture, or as venturing into speech as an act of wary transgression, deprived of a shared tradition of representation, alienated from sources of power and definition, and always guilty *a priori*, whether according to a post-lapsarian, post-edenic or an Aristotelian or Platonic vocabulary of lost Grace. Curiously, however, in antithesis to this project of negative female representation, what emerges beneath the gaze of the mystified male protagonist is a gallery of newly cast, newly cleansed heroines, modern but endowed with an array of lost and regained classical mothers or foremothers, Jocastas, Antigones, Iphigenias, Electras, a recovered tradition which now permits their accession to a right to speech which Machado himself seemingly consciously allows in them, while disallowing it in his male would-be heroes.

The classical metaphor persists throughout this author's novels, in particular *Dom Casmurro* and later works, so that at one point Bentinho, admitting that he is 'proficient in Latin but virgin of women' (*DC*, 821), relates an adolescent episode in the course of which, in true biblical fashion, he associates the temptation to sin with his own knowledge or awareness of womanhood and of female sexuality, and desires the generic fall of all women, in an accurate modern replay of Genesis and the expulsion myth (*DC*, 867–8).

Unsurprisingly then in view of this, Capitu, slandered, debarred from the possibility of self-defence, textually and divinely condemned by her blessed lover (his name after all *is* Bento, or 'Blessed One'), and later, indeed, banished and figuratively murdered by him, on a number of occasions experiences a strong desire to learn Latin, the language from which she is particularly and explicitly excluded by masculinity, as embodied in the figures of her husband and her priest, the language of culture and of the *status quo*, and of their associated religion or God. Latin is the language which, if infiltrated, might grant her a platform for self-representation, the power of self-definition and the possibility of acquittal from a charge of adultery which will otherwise silence her and lead to her expulsion and death at the hands of Bento, the representative of the Law of God-the-Father/God-the-Son, a law which Latin articulates (*DC*, 838–40).

Capitu is condemned as an adulteress, excluded from speech, Latin or otherwise, denied the opportunity of self-defence and banned from the hegemony of the masculine universe whose monopoly over language, wisdom and truth she inconveniences. The metaphor for this denial of her rights is the prohibition of her acquaintance with Art as well as the classical languages and other subjects seen as the prerogative of the male, symbolic of his supremacy, and therefore his exclusive sphere. Bentinho, in his adolescence a seminarist vowed into the priesthood by his mother and the recipient of a classical education, has the command of Greek and Latin; furthermore, through his self-identification with Othello the Moor, to whom he variously refers and with whose plight he compares his own (without, however, at any point arriving at the obvious conclusion of Capitu's innocence, analogous to that of Desdemona[6]) he must also be seen to speak Arabic, the language through which the classicals re-entered and influenced Western thought.[7] He can thus be seen to operate from a privileged position *vis à vis* language and knowledge, an advantage from which Capitu as a woman is excluded. Nevertheless, as will be seen, the decodable text of Bentinho's would-be incontrovertible truth (which at another level might be read as Machado's invitingly deconstructible plot), will result in the undoing of the former within its own chosen frame of reference, since it will be by means of enlisting the self-same classical texts, pagan and Christian alike, that the messianic heroine will be revived, reinstated and recast as victorious after death.

The reinstatement initially requires the bonding of the two female protagonists, Capitu and her mother-in-law, Dona Glória. After Capitu's marriage to Bentinho, she is attenuated in the role of *femme fatale* attributed to her by her husband and temporarily reassigned to the roles of virtuous wife and mother, just as Dona Glória's function as mother surrenders to a more obvious narrative necessity as the figure of the loving, protective mother-in-law. The latter event, all the more unusual in a Brazilian nineteenth-century context as forcing the interests of blood and lineage to surrender to those of gender, might be taken as an example of bold feminist alignment on the part of the author. All the more so since it is a ploy which is repeated even more explicitly, in both the novels that followed this one, the last two that Machado wrote before his death.[8] In all these instances, whatever revision the lovers and husbands might bring to their perception of their women, the virtue of the latter, interestingly, and strikingly in the case of Capitu, remains untainted to the end in the eyes of the

mothers-in-law, as grudgingly admitted by the accusing males. Early on in *Dom Casmurro* it is suggested that Dona Glória's experience of love in marriage was a unilateral one. On one occasion Bentinho contemplates two portraits of his parents which face one another on the walls of the family home, and interprets their gazes as signifying the following, respectively: 'I am all yours, my handsome gentleman' (in Dona Glória's case) and 'See how this girl adores me' (in her husband's) (*DC*, 815). Love, then, originates in the woman towards the man, and results in the death of either one. If Dona Glória guesses that in Capitu's case it will be the latter, not Bentinho, who will die, and in the light of her realigned loyalty (or maternal duty) to gender rather than blood (or to a daughter-in-law rather than to a son now clearly co-opted into the Law of the Father) as suggested above, following the marriage she takes on the established classical guise of the two-faced, Janus woman, two-faced, that is, in the literal sense, since the mother (in-law), like the classical tragic Greek one, here displays two distinct facets. First, the loving, avenging function of a stricken Clytemnestra faced with the sacrifice of her daughter to an exclusively male enterprise of offended marital honour (in the Homer version and in the first play of the Aeschylus trilogy[9]). And second, in the light of her own husband's early demise, the murderous wife/mother whose slaying of her husband is duly punished in the last two plays of the Aeschylus version by the son and heir of the Law of the Father. The revisionary writing, therefore, begins in Machado in apparent obedience to Aeschylus' plot of female fiendishness, with the symbolic disposal of Dona Glória's husband through death, and her assumption of possession over the body (and soul) of her son. This supposition accounts also for the numerous widows elsewhere in this writer's fiction, in which the disappearance of the head of the family signals the coming-of-age of the wife within the family circle, and the transfer of power into her hands following the death of the spouse. In Dona Glória's case, the death of her husband leaves her effectively in sole control of a household moreover conspicuous by the number of male dependents which otherwise inhabit it: her young son, an impoverished uncle kept by her charity and an even more impoverished *agregado*, an ambiguous combination of servant, errand-runner and unpaid adviser, also kept out of charity. Widowhood in Machado, therefore, introduces a reversal in domestic power relations and an altered *status quo* which vouchsafes women's access to a position of control over a variety of males to whom they were previously subjected. This new order more than once results also in

Machado in an alliance between the newly empowered mother and her daughter-in-law.[10] In Dona Glória's case her relationship with Capitu, initially grounded in mutual suspicion, is curiously altered only when the latter is recast from girl-next-door into prospective daughter-in-law. In this new context of marriage and admission into a family in which arguably, in Dona Glória's experience, women either stand as unilaterally loving wives or as powerful widows, the two women are recast as protective mother and vulnerable daughter, in defiance of the actual mother–son blood tie. This new *status quo* will only be undone by Bento when he succeeds in discrediting his wife and bringing about her death – and therefore that of his mother as the latter's functional avatar – through accusations of immorality, and, more specifically, adultery.

The upsetting of the matriarchal household, however, takes place only after the widowed mother has variously attempted to dispose of her male lineage, metaphorically or literally, as a means of safeguarding primarily her own domestic rule, but presciently, as it turns out, the life of her daughter-in-law, threatened by marriage to the son. In *Dom Casmurro*, Dona Glória miscarries one male child, and her next autonomous act, just before her husband's death – one which she conceals from him and which he would almost certainly have forbidden as implying a threat to the male succession within the family – involves the promise of their unborn son to the priesthood, a promise tantamount to castrating and silencing him in a context where the importance of clerical power, however great, must be seen to be eclipsed, in the terms of the novel, by that of the male imperative to beget a son and perpetuate the male secular lineage. By vowing to make her son a priest, Dona Glória deprives him of the possibility of marriage, sexual expression and paternity within a literary paradigm in which sexuality and paternity signal voice, and voice is power. Moreover, she reverses the gender of the burnt-offering in the Aeschylean sacrifice of Iphigenia by Agamemnon, thereby rewriting the classical original. Her promise defuses the future patriarchal threat which her son will personify to herself and secures her own familial power and dynastic control. In her now matriarchal household only unthreatening males (her submissive adolescent son and a series of impoverished male relatives and economic dependents) are suffered to remain, on condition of obedience to her rule. The sexless, childless, disempowered, ideologically void male relatives are adult versions of the adolescent Bentinho, and Dona Glória, therefore, by miscarrying her first son, emasculating and marginalising the second, becoming

a widow and thus technically usurping familial power – in a patriarchal context in which no other trajectory to autonomy outside that of a *coup* is available to the woman – effectively ensures the continued negation of masculine supremacy within the family, and the impossibility of reinstating the male rule. She also, albeit unbeknown to herself at this point, secures for a while Capitu's deliverance from the unforeseen dangers of marriage to Bento. In this instance it is interesting to note that early on in the novel Dona Glória becomes associated, through an allusion made by Bentinho himself, with Pandora, who also appears elsewhere in Machado's fiction as a paradigmatic inimical mother, malevolently intentioned toward her male offspring (*DC*, 814–15).[11] The array of murderous, Medea-like mothers in Machado's novels, indeed, sets up an agenda of monstrous maternity threatening, in classical form, to exterminate or be exterminated by the son in his pursuit of patrilinear rights. In the original myth Pandora did permit control over the fated box, symbolic of contained evil, to slip out of her hands into those of her husband, Epimetheus. In *Dom Casmurro*, too, Dona Glória in the end allows power to revert back to the male line by deciding not to proceed with Bentinho's symbolic castration, releasing him from the priesthood and allowing his marriage and eventual paternity, tantamount to a recuperation by him of masculine power at other levels, and culminating, as we shall see, in Capitu's death and her own in a novel where the continuation of marriage leads to the death of the wife. Her decision thus inaugurates the reinstatement of the Law of the Father in the person of his son and successor, and, once again, as per the classical strictures, the Oresteian son will rise to power and vindicate the father through a matricide at first glance exculpated by the restored *status quo*. Bentinho's effective murder of his wife, as I shall argue below, is also the murder of the mother who is that wife's alter ego, and their deaths will be seen to become narratively contiguous, contingent and interchangeable.

If Dona Glória's promise of her son as sacrificial victim is a rewritten classical betrayal of offspring by parent (for example a gender reversal of the Iphigenia sacrifice by Agamemnon), Dona Glória's identification with Capitu, echoing that of Clytemnestra and Iphigenia, equally inaugurates a cycle of murder and revenge which will culminate in the deaths of the two female protagonists at the hands of the husband/son. The linking of the two deaths – and the assertion of a common causality, the agency of the son/husband as murderer – relies here upon a chain of similarities and analogies which connect the two

women, and in particular the imagery surrounding their deaths, their epitaphs, and the implications of the latter. Dona Glória's death, coinciding chronologically with Capitu's, and identifiable with it through the similarity of their epitaphs, not surprisingly is dealt with even more elliptically than the latter's, since it is matricide, and clearly the more serious of the two crimes in antiquity as in nineteenth-century Brazil, both societies whose conventions condoned the murder by a husband of a wife guilty or merely suspected of infidelity.[12] The downfall of Capitu, moreover, coincides diegetically with the decline of Dona Glória who, until the loss of her younger self, had been insistently described by Bento as someone whom old age did not affect. When Capitu is exiled by Bento, Dona Glória according to him rapidly ages by all the years she had not done before and the two women's deaths follow each other in close succession, concluding the fusion of their two characters. Each woman is dismissed by the narrator in one sentence, Capitu as an afterthought – [Capitu] I believe I have not mentioned, was dead and buried' (*DC*, 939–41).

Their analogous epitaphs, perhaps more clearly than any other aspect of the novel, signal the moment of authorial contradiction of both the narratorial verdict of guilt and the prescriptions of the classical foretexts. In an inversion of the Aeschyllean sequence whereby Clytemnestra's initially understandable murder of her husband, motivated by maternal grief and the desire for vengeance, is quickly reformulated by the Greek playwright as unforgivable homicide punishable by death, Machado begins by presenting us with heroines of seemingly dubious character. Controversially, however, but I would argue consciously and with the deliberation of an intended political purpose, he proceeds to reappraise and redeem them in the moment of their deaths at the hands of the Oresteian son upon whom, in contradiction to the prescriptions of the paradigmatic tragedy, the burden of blame is authorially imposed at the end. In an echo of his male protagonist's own favoured self-accrediting strategy, but clearly with the purpose of the latter's undoing, Machado, like Bento, has recourse to canonical philosophy from both pagan and Christian sources to validate his own authorial conclusions, the two women's analogous epitaphs providing the material clue to the process of apportioning blame or innocence in this novel. If Capitu is Dona Glória's alter ego, the latter's epitaph – 'a saint' (*DC*, 937–8) – chosen (significantly and against considerable opposition, by Bento himself, who insists upon its descriptive accuracy), must be seen equally to apply to the former and therefore to confirm the

unlikelihood of her adultery and criminal motherhood, since even Machado would presumably balk at the canonisation of an adulteress. Furthermore, Dona Glória's epitaph effectively rephrases Capitu's own – 'she died beautiful' (*DC*, 940) – an accolade bestowed, significantly, by her own son Ezequiel, and which, according to the Platonic contingency frequently drawn upon by Bento (for instance when he repeatedly draws the reader's attention to Capitu's eyes, represented as shifty and symptomatic of a general deviousness), equates physical with spiritual worth, and must therefore be seen to assert Capitu's bodily and moral soundness alike, and to acquit her of essential blame. Similarly, the description of Dona Glória by Bento, elsewhere, as being 'candid as the first dawn, prior to the first sin' (*DC*, 73), further reinforces the suggestion of spiritual blamelessness, phrased now not in Platonic but in Christian prelapsarian terms, which, according to the alter ego extrapolation, must be seen to encompass her daughter-in-law too. In the case of both women, therefore, their sanctity and their beauty, according both to Biblical symbolism and to the Platonic strictures which Bentinho himself evokes and then hastily revokes at critical moments, refer also to their moral status and override the possible negative connotations of their disobedience, thereby reaffirming their innocence at the end, and becoming causally linked to the fact of their deaths, here reformulated as martyrdoms.

The two women, therefore, emerge as twinned heroines, their alter ego status and the Oresteian script alike being further echoed through the fact that in both women's case it is the birth (or at least, in the case of Dona Glória, the *fact* of having) a son – Bentinho himself and Ezequiel, the child Bentinho suspects of being conceived adulterously – which leads to their downfall. Motherhood, therefore, kills Capitu as well as Dona Glória, the latter because in her capacity as her daughter-in-law's mirror image she must stand or fall with her at the hands of the same opponent. Bentinho, like Orestes, thus becomes guilty of matricide as well as of the murder of his wife. In the end, nevertheless, Machado is in the business of revising, rather than simply rewriting the classical texts, and the pairing of mother and daughter, or in this case mother-in-law and daughter-in-law which he deploys must be seen to contest the original defeated Clytemnestra/Iphigenia duo, and to rethink the original myth's conclusions. Thus, when Dona Glória releases Bentinho from his priest-in-training status, she may deliver both Capitu and herself to the death which follows Bentinho's suspicions of Capitu's adultery,

but the verdict surrounding their deaths remains as problematic as the irresolvable question of Capitu's guilt or innocence.

Finally, therefore, Bentinho, Oedipal son in his love-hate fixation upon the mother, Oresteian in his matricide, is betrayed not by her, nor even by his allegedly adulterous wife, but in effect by his author, who deals with him in the only way in which the speaker of the dominant discourse of the Symbolic Order can be dealt with, that is, through the removal of his voice's transcendental impunity, and the withdrawal also of the various traditions upon which Bento as the mouthpiece of masculinity draws for credibility. Bentinho, therefore, would-be priest, Blessed One, the son of God,[13] rewrites the edenic script in a manner which accentuates the female guilt intrinsic to it, thereby creating a new, aggravated textual truth, but by this act he, like Adam, also partakes of forbidden knowledge and becomes implicated in the enjoyment thereof. Moreover, since as far as Machado's male character is concerned, knowledge is tantamount to sexual initiation, by attempting to become the originator of a new textual truth he becomes sinful, and sees this truth, or his claim to truth, in the end snatched from him not by the earthly mother whom he murdered but by the Divine Father here deployed as agent by the extradiegetic author. Both the Divine and the literary father, therefore, or the former as the means to the latter's narrative end, can be seen to indict Bentinho for his lost innocence and to forsake him at the last.

The possibility of Machado having been able to step outside the sexual political assumptions of his epoch to pose instead the illegitimacy of those assumptions, need not resort for example to a Marxist principle of internal contradiction[14] or to the assertion of an unconscious dimension to the author's text.[15] Already in his early chronicles Machado readily engaged in or pioneered important literary and political debates in Brazil, including his polemics on nationalism in literature, naturalism, and, more pertinently here, his texts on the relations between the sexes in the second half of the nineteenth century in Brazil and the importance of education for women.[16]

In *Dom Casmurro* Machado, as the extradiegetic author of this first-person narration, in the end betrays both his narrator/hero and the classical texts to which the latter has recourse for support, and returns us instead to the untruth of the diegetic text, as well as to *a* truth in it, a female truth which that narrator originally silenced. Dona Glória and Capitu, therefore, at the end become truly mother- and daughter-in-law, *in law*, acquitted in the eyes of a new, reconstituted tribunal,

revisionary of former ones both contemporary and antique. In this way, moreover, a further provocation is enacted, and in this novel, as in others, Machado, glancing retrospectively at the classics, unseats the possibility of the empirical truth of his male speaker. By doing so he simultaneously dislocates the Brazilian Positivist moment which the latter, like other of this author's heroes – for example the pseudo-Darwinian Brás Cubas of *Memórias Póstumas de Brás Cubas* – represent and involuntarily caricature, gesturing instead backwards, to a (now unstable) realist certainty, and forward, to modernist uncertainty, to disturbing lost possibilities in Homer and Aeschylus, in Genesis and in Shakespeare, then and now.

Notes

1   John Gledson, 'Brazilian Fiction: Machado de Assis to the Present', in *Modern Latin American Fiction: A Survey* ed. by John King (London: Faber and Faber, 1987), 21.

2   Joaquim Maria Machado de Assis, *Obra Completa*, 3 vols (Rio de Janeiro: Editora José Aguilar, 1962), III, 398.

3   Quoted by Astrojildo Pereira, 'Instinto e Consciência da Nacionalidade', in *Machado de Assis*, ed. by Alfredo Bosi (Rio de Janeiro: Livraria São José, 1959), 43–85.

4   Machado de Assis, *Dom Casmurro*, in *Obra Completa*, I, op. cit., 807–942. All subsequent references and quotations from *Dom Casmurro* will refer to this edition and will be indicated by a page reference in the text and the abbreviation *DC*.

5   Machado de Assis, *Esaú e Jacó*, in *Obra Completa*, I, op. cit., 980–1. All subsequent references will be to this edition and will be indicated by a page reference in the text and the abbreviation *EJ*.

6   For a discussion of the links between Bentinho and Othello, and the identification of Bentinho as *being* Othello, see Helen Caldwell, *The Brazilian Othello of Machado de Assis: A Study of Dom Casmurro* (Berkeley and Los Angeles: University of California Press, 1960).

7   Ibid.

8   Machado de Assis, *Esaú e Jacó*, op. cit., 943–1091. *Memorial de Aires* in *Obra Completa*, I, op. cit., 1093–198.

9   As will be discussed later, the second play of the *Oresteian Trilogy* appears to contradict the initial understanding reading of Clytemnestra's murder as the result of a mother's grief, and to re-cast her as simply the unforgivable slayer of her husband.

10 For example in one of his early novels, *Iaiá Garcia* in *Obra Completa*, I, 389–507.

11 See also the notorious figure of Pandora in *Memórias Póstumas de Brás Cubas*, in *Obra Completa*, I, op. cit., 509–637. All subsequent references will

be to this edition and will be indicated by a page reference in the text
and the abbreviation *MP*.

12 For a discussion of Brazilian legislation on crimes of passion see Ingrid
    Stein, *Figuras Femininas em Machado de Assis* (Rio de Janeiro: Editora Paz
    e Terra, Coleção Literatura e Teoria Literária, 1984), 29.
13 See Helen Caldwell, op. cit., 32–61 for a discussion of Bentinho's status
    as Divine Son and Fallen Angel.
14 K. Marx and F. Engels, *On Literature and Art*, ed. by L. Baxandall and S.
    Morawski (New York: International General, 1973).
15 Both Engels and Marx separately debate the notion of an unconscious
    dimension to a text. Engels does so among other writings in his letter to
    Margaret Harkness and Marx in the text 'The Holy Family' on Eugène
    Sue, both discussed in Terry Eagleton, *Marxism and Literary Criticism*
    (London: Methuen, 1983), 46–8.
16 Machado de Assis, 'Queda que as mulheres têm para os tolos' in *Obras
    Completas*, III, op. cit., 965–72. 'Cherchez la femme,' ibid., 1003–4.

13

The Need for Zeal and the Dangers of Jealousy: Identity and Legitimacy in *La Regenta*

Alison Sinclair

La Regenta (1884–5), by Leopoldo Alas, is a narrative which parades seductively as one of adultery, yet is replete with forms of desire other than that of sexual desire, whether this be legitimate, or associated with the accomplishment of an adulterous union. In this novel a surface text of sexual desire can be read as being constructed as a defence against the apprehension of decay. This is a strategic and defensive construction in the face of a psychotic apprehension of a world that is collapsing and dissolving and the desperate need to erect a framework, a bulwark against it. The framework erected is the fiction of sexual desire, produced in heightened form as the fiction of adulterous love. The text is thus one that, viewed from a Lacanian framework, articulates the intention to answer the hysteric's question of 'What sex am I? Can I reproduce?' in preference to facing the obsessional's question of 'Am I alive or am I dead?'.[1] What parades as a desire that relates to specific objects (desire *for* a particular lover, for example) can in the light of this be construed as a longing or a need more primitive than a stage at which the ego can be deemed to relate to others as whole beings. Desire is predominantly orientated not towards precise objects but, consonant with the Freudian understanding of impulses or drives as expounded in his 1915 essay, 'The Instincts and Their Vicissitudes',[2] towards particular forms of satisfaction or appeasement. Forms of desire are linked throughout the novel to preoccupations about identity, uncertainties of definition, the need for legitimation, the lack of a proper place in the social

structure. The working through of desire emerges in the course of the text as a process by which individuals, rather than seeking one another, are involved in orientating themselves in relation to one another, and, for the majority of them, in finding some type of foothold in the insecure social and familial frameworks of the city of Vetusta.

Much of the material relating to desire in *La Regenta* concerns thoughts about the satisfaction of desire, rather than strategies for its consummation. It is significant, in relation to this, that the predominant expression given to desire in the novel is in the form of envy, a type of desire which can gain no satisfaction, and further that it is one of the forms of desire most consistently associated with women and the clergy, carrying connotations of sinfulness and illegitimacy, and contrasting with the 'accepted' and 'legitimate' masculine lexicon of desire claimed by a number of the prime male characters of the novel.[3]

Envy is a state frequently viewed as little distinct from jealousy, and thus its presence in an adultery novel might not strike us as particularly unusual. In *La Regenta*, however, envy and jealousy are clearly distinguished from one another, both in their distribution and their dynamic import. Envy's characteristic presence is in characters who stand to the side of the adultery narrative, producing a feeling which suffuses the whole ground of the text. Jealousy, meanwhile, is the emotion which emerges dramatically and yet predictably in the figure of the final adultery, albeit in an inappropriate quarter. An understanding of the underlying relationship between the two feelings in the novel can be gained by examining the distinctions made between them in two fields, theology and psychoanalysis. The distinctions in both fields will help to reveal the dislocated aims and trajectories of desire in the novel, and in particular they have a crucial role in our understanding of the characterisation and motivation of Fermín de Pas, the character who is bystander to the adultery and yet central in its dynamic. The line of the argument to be followed will take us from Aquinas to the Oedipus complex.

As a framework for this discussion, a number of initial points need to be made. Firstly, *La Regenta* is a novel only apparently about adultery. The expected act of adultery finally occurs off-stage, off the page, between Chapters 28 and 29 of a 30-chapter book. This reduction to a tantalising absence of the very act which would seal the identity of *La Regenta* as a novel of adultery is highly significant, and one which confirms the illusory nature of the importance given to adultery in the novel. It is worth noting that although the absence of an on-stage act of adultery is not unusual in novels of adultery, the degree of

emphasis and innuendo in the narrative about the act to be accomplished is unusual. The reader is thus not the recipient of a decorous narrative, but a narrative of sexual teasing. The narrative is furthermore one where sexuality is both used and avoided. It is used in a desperate attempt to evade, through the creation of a narrative of suspense and excitement, a fate of death, dissolution and annihilation. It is avoided by Ana, until the accomplishment of the adultery, and by Alvaro after it, ever conscious of his waning potency.

Secondly, the narrative of adultery is part of a strategy to secure the boundaries of gender, a defensive move in the face of the difficulties in securing the boundaries of the identity. That is, the securing of gender-boundaries, which relates to our positioning in a social world, is called upon to shore up the boundaries of a self not publicly defined in terms of gender relations. The vital need for this process can be deduced from the framing of the novel which consists in layers of confusion, and in which crumbling and insecure boundaries, figured in terms of mud, nausea and dizziness, threaten the self with dissolution. The attraction of entering into an established narrative where gender figures dramatically is that there are clearly distinguished characters playing out set parts which establish simultaneously the boundaries of gender and identity. The illusory nature of this strategy in *La Regenta*, of course, is revealed by the high level in the majority of the characters of gender ambiguity and of ambivalence both about sexual orientation and the experience of sexual desire in general. The adulterous triangle, with its established principals of husband, wife and lover, is one in which it is presumed that gender is a known quantity. Hence engagement in the activity of adultery can be construed not simply as proof of desire between the lover and wife, and the nature of that desire as masculine or feminine, but also as a proof that those characters are established in their roles as men and women. More than this, they exist. The husband, meanwhile, is in a sense metaphysically compensated: his status is legitimated by his position of loss, and the loss in its turn confirms his possession of identity, since to have suffered loss, he has to be presumed to exist. It is as if he were able to say 'I have lost my wife, my possession, therefore I am, and I am masculine.'[4]

Thirdly, desire in *La Regenta* is all over the place, in two senses. On the one hand, there is a great deal of longing, wanting, feeling deprived – and there is more of this than there is sexual desire. On the other hand, the novel is chock-a-block full of desire which is dislocated, disowned, perverted, denied, as though independent of either subjects

or objects. Fourthly, and as a complication of this, the definition of 'deseo' as given in María Moliner's *Diccionario del uso del español* indicates that *desear* is always used in relation to an object. There is only a brief mention of *desear* in the sense of sexual desire, with a significant use of a food-related noun: 'to feel sexual appetite for someone' (sentir apetito sexual hacia alguien).[5]

The topic of desire is not treated with evenhandedness in the novel, and most comment has been about the nature of desire in Ana Ozores.[6] Significantly less has been said about the desire of Alvaro, who, as lover – indeed, as man – one might have viewed as a subject of desire. But his desire, apart from the accumulation of sexual conquests, is more overtly related to social power and class-prestige than to sexual feeling (see his relationship with Paco Vegallana (I. 235)).[7]

The nature of desire is arguably most complex in Fermín de Pas, priest and confessor to Ana Ozores; he is the character prohibited even by the adultery narrative from the ownership of or the right to own sexual desire. As priest, an expected celibate, Fermín is the character best qualified as the ground on which the difficulties and vicissitudes of masculine desire may be figured. He is, as it were, forbidden territory, where more dangerous issues in the elusiveness of masculine desire can be explored, both the implied male narrator and the implied male or masculinised reader being relieved of the need to identify with him.[8]

The nature of Fermín's desire undergoes a number of changes in the novel, and his trajectory can be viewed as a wish to move from illegitimate desire to legitimate, from desire associated with his mother to desire associated with something or someone not his mother. We can view him as moving within two schemes: that of the church and that of the family (presented in that order in the novel), and within both of these he is involved in a struggle. In theological terms his position is that he would like to manœuvre himself from the position of *envidia* (envy) to the position of *celo* (zeal). In psychoanalytic terms, and in the structure of familial dynamics, his need is to move from the dyad to the triangle. What actually happens is that he moves from *envidia* not to *celo* but to *celos* (jealousy). This is despite his attempts to escape the family constellation into which he is born (and which he subsequently tries to reconstruct through the families of others). Further, his position in social terms is exacerbated by the ecclesiastical structure into which he has moved. His misfortune is that when his desire is revealed for all to see (or at least for Ana to see), it is in the form of *celos*, precisely that class of desire for which

he is socially and professionally disqualified by his position within the church, since *celos* is a husband's emotion, the feeling of a rightful possessor, and what he feels *celos* about is precisely what he cannot have. Nothing is resolved, beyond the impossibility of his relationship with another being where desires sexual and emotional might be gratified.

First, let us look at the theological transition, and the distinction that underlies it. Traditional Catholic understanding of envy is based primarily on the work of Aquinas. In his account of envy, the emphasis is not on the good that is longed for, but on the lessening of personal esteem: 'another's good may be reckoned as being one's own evil, in so far as it conduces to the *lessening of one's own good name or excellence*. It is in this way that envy grieves for another's good ...' (emphasis mine). He goes on to indicate that envy is found between people whose condition is comparable.[9] Examples of such comparability are found in *La Regenta*, for instance, in same-sex relationships, and among the clergy.

In its account of Aquinas's view, the *New Catholic Encyclopedia* states that while envy is a grave sin, jealousy may not be so: 'jealousy implies a sense of right, on the part of the jealous person, to the exclusive possession of something'. It further elaborates that 'jealousy, in spite of all the pejorative connotation that is usually attached to the term, is not necessarily evil, so long as the right is well founded and the reaction to its violation is expressed in a reasonable manner'.[10] A first reaction to this exception made for jealousy is to read it as symptomatic of the patriarchal culture that produced the encyclopedia. But before we become diverted by this apparent defence of jealousy into an exploration of patriarchal assumptions, let us return to Aquinas.

In his discussion of envy, Aquinas himself does not actually talk about jealousy: he talks about *zeal*. The word in the Latin original is *zelus*, the term used in the Vulgate for the jealous/zealous God, who fiercely states his rights of possession over his people. It is quite distinct from *zelotypia*, used by Jerome, the translator, for marital jealousy (as in Numbers 5: 14, 30). What Aquinas actually says about zeal implies that the possession does indeed belong to someone else: 'we may grieve over another's good, not because he has it, but because, the good which he has, we have not: and this, properly speaking is zeal'. If the 'zeal be about virtuous goods' it is 'praiseworthy', whereas if about temporal goods it is not necessarily sinful. In sum, the *Encyclopedia* outlines a justification for jealous action which is not

present in Aquinas. While one might surmise that there is a potential philological confusion in either the Vulgate or the Hebrew of the Old Testament, this is clearly not so. Jerome discriminates carefully in his choice of words for the translation of zeal/jealousy, while in the original Hebrew of the Old Testament the root word *QN'A* is used throughout, but with a variation of grammatical structure which distinguishes decisively between zeal, jealousy and envy. Thus *QUIN'AH* is jealousy, *EL QUAN'A* a 'jealous' God, and the *QAN'AIM* the Zealots.[11]

For Aquinas then, zeal is permissible, even good, and from Fermín's relationship to desire and its expression we may construe that this is the feeling which he would like to characterise himself as possessing. One of the major conflicts and areas of tension in the novel, however, is the difficulty in so doing without being implicated in the complex desire of his mother, Doña Paula. Not only does Fermín have to disentangle himself from her *codicia* (covetousness – an illegitimate desire, pertaining in the novel only to women and priests), but the *ambición* he would like to own in its place as his is tainted by the fact that he is, in his career-moves, only carrying out what she has wanted for him. The position of *celo*, by contrast, is associated with his feelings about possessions which might be truly *his*.

There are complications in Fermín's position in relation to both *envidia* and *celos*. First, *envidia*. What is remarkable is the degree to which Fermín manages to stay clear of suffering *envidia* as subject, thus contrasting with the other clerical figures of the novel. But from the first he is himself an object of *envidia* (see for example I. 115, 132, 417, 481; II. 199, 336). The emphasis on the suffering of envy being related to the object rather than the subject is a traditional one, in a framework in which the object suffers through having the evil eye of envy cast upon him. In *La Regenta* this emphasis is reiterated in the case of Fermín, where male gazes relate not solely to female objects, but also to other males in *La Regenta*, in a dynamic of *envidia* about virility which exists between men. Hence Fermín's reluctance, for example, to be associated with the *envidia* of Celedonio (I. 120). He fights against being the object of *envidia* precisely because it comes too close to his own experience of it as subject.

Fermín's desire is to see himself as a subject of *celo*, a feeling so elusive it is rarely named. An exception is when Fermín thanks Petra for her zeal in ensuring that Ana's letter comes directly to him (I. 412), the *celo* denoting the fierce guardianship over a piece of property (the letter) passing secretly, as might a love-letter, between woman and

priest). The sexual and amorous connotations surrounding the *celo* attached to the safe delivery of the missive are consonant with the meaning *celo* bears in Spanish which is additional to its function as the exact term to translate Aquinas's *zelus*, that is, its association with animals who are on heat and ready for mating. Further, the verb *recelar*, in addition to the meaning of 'to fear' is used to denote the action of taking the 'teaser' to a mare to prepare her to receive the mating of the stallion,[12] a connotation which has a wealth of suggestion for the dynamic subtext of dislocated desire in *La Regenta*, not least indicating the function Fermín will actually have in 'preparing' Ana for the affair with Alvaro.

Tellingly, the first description of Fermín's zeal about his property comes in Chapter 1, where he regards Vetusta as his prey (fighting off rivals, as does the jealous God in Deuteronomy. 5: 9). *Celo* is revealed most strongly, and most dangerously (in terms of the legitimate status of Fermín's desire) in his fiercely proprietorial relationship with Ana as his confessional daughter. It peaks in Chapter 17, and is clearly displayed to public view when she takes part in the Easter Procession in Chapter 26. From Chapter 18 onwards, however, Fermín comes to be dominated by *celos,* as he moves increasingly towards the position of regarding himself as the true husband of Ana. To look at the possible dynamic of *celos,* we need to move to the psychoanalytic model for envy and jealousy.

The distinction made by Melanie Klein is that envy, beyond being 'the angry feeling that another person possesses and enjoys something desirable – the envious impulse being to take it away or to spoil it', derives from the subject's relation to one person only. Jealousy, by contrast, exists in a three-person relationship. It is mainly concerned with 'love that the subject feels is his due and has been taken away, or is in danger of being taken away, from him by his rival'.[13] Klein's further observation that in envy the boundaries between the two people involved are extremely unclear is relevant to the degree to which the over-riding anxiety in *La Regenta* is with the lack of adequate boundaries of identity and gender. Envy will necessarily occupy pride of place as the symptom of the inaccessibility of identity and/or gender-definition.

Recent work which has contested the status of Oedipal theory and has argued that it does not describe a natural route to gender acquisition, but rather acts as agent for the construction of compulsory heterosexuality within a patriarchal society, reinforces the points made above about the link between the three-person relationship

and concepts of the acquisition of legitimate masculine desire within a patriarchal society.[14] In the case of Fermín there are particular complications. He consistently tries to move himself into Oedipal situations which will be satisfactory (in terms of conferring a sense of self, rights and possession). Unfortunately, while he would wish to be lover (the role of the son in the Oedipal triangle, and in which he would be able to express his (albeit transgressive) desire), the role most closely related to his social position as priest is that of father, a position which will be replicated when his involvement with Ana moves him into the place of husband. The position of father/husband carries a further disadvantage. Though he prohibits illicit desire, the father will himself be subject to ageing, doomed to relinquish power to the son, to suffer *celos*, and – like all others – to die. In Fermín's case he will be obliged to make that symbolic relinquishment with little chance to have experienced the filial moment of desire.

The arrival or the presence of the father can be viewed as breaking the mother/child dyad, or introducing space by creating a triangle. By this, if the child is a boy, incestuous desire is prohibited, identification with the parent of the same sex occurs, the bond of love for the mother is broken, and the child is able to be engaged in a new form of desire, having before it the example of the father's desire for the mother. The increased differentiation of the self that results is accompanied by speculations about possession: if the mother is an object, there is the issue of whether the child or the father possesses her. Oedipal theory is bounded to patriarchy in the way that it nicely confers rights of possession on men, while providing an unsatisfactory theory for the gender-acquisition of women. Jealousy becomes clearly the province of the boy, since the rivalry with the father for the mother is what sows the seeds of jealousy in future relationships. Jealousy will then be available to be experienced, so that other, less tolerable feelings, such as loss or insecurity, do not have to be felt.[15]

If the Oedipal process had been satisfactorily resolved for Fermín, then theoretically the path to desire, indeed to zeal, would have been opened up. Fermín, however, is impeded by the general lack of anti-incest boundaries in Vetustan society. In his case the absence of his father does not simply leave him the prisoner of his mother, but leaves him without the example of permitted desire.[16] Much play is made in the novel, especially in the Vegallana household, of the idea that everyone is family, everyone related to everyone else (I. 264). We might recall the myth of Fermín and Ana that they can be 'almas hermanas' (sibling souls), as though sibling love will render sexual

desire out of court, and as though such a relationship had the decorum of the *compadrazgo* so acutely analysed by Pitt-Rivers.[17] This mirage of sibling love turns out to be no more than the willed non-differentiation that dominates the novel, a non-differentiation that allows the characters to pretend to act as children, with games with lights out, and romps in the hay and on swings, and which for the most part dulls the possibility of the excitement of sexual difference.

Fermín is further impeded by the unsatisfactory nature of his own Oedipal history. As a result, he is forced, as are others in Vetusta, into the playing out of triangular games which will give him some differentiation, through the desire for which another will have to act as his agent, the cost of this being that what he experiences will necessarily be *celos* and not *celo*. The triangles he is involved in, besides those of his past, are those in which he acts as father, and those adulterous triangles, partially but not wholly Oedipal in nature, in which he figures. The problem with these triangles is their number, their complexity, and their lack of absolute geometric integrity, since repeatedly there are possible alternates or substitutes at different angles. This, added to the degree to which they overlap, will dictate the inaccessibility of desire. As structures to construct or allow desire, triangles in *La Regenta* are decidedly unsafe.

Fermín's deficient or complicated Oedipal constellation is that he has two fathers, a real one, who dies, and a patron. In addition there is a host of other phantasy ones, unnamed, uncouth, and beyond acknowledgement. Fermín's real father is Francisco de Pas, a local wastrel who dissipates his life in gambling and other pursuits deemed masculine in the society of the region, and dies in Fermín's youth. He is retained by Fermín, nonetheless, as a symbol of 'real' masculinity, formulated and emulated in the image of the huntsman. Paula finds a substitute father for her son in Camoirán, the bishop, but as cleric, the bishop cannot provide an obvious model of potent sexual masculinity, and indeed has an emotional 'feminine' style from which Fermín disassociates himself. Finally there are the numerous, faceless phantasy fathers, the miners. They provide the material for a troubling, possibly negative family romance that Fermín does not articulate but that the reader is given evidence for entertaining.[18] In Chapter 15 we are given graphic information about Fermín's adolescent awareness of his mother's relationship with the miners. He is required to keep himself separate from them, yet cannot fail to be aware of their presence and their possible activity (I. 555).

In relation to this Oedipal background so deficient in models for identification, we can see the logic in the way Fermín moves to become to others the father he was lacking himself, acting in adult life as the substitute father in a number of triangles. Yet the position he adopts is to be the father to daughters, rather than the father to sons. While this is in accord with the social unlikelihood of his acting as father confessor to a man in Vetusta (the menfolk traditionally standing in opposition to the Church and its practices), it holds a symbolic significance for his own gender-functioning: he can be neither source nor recipient of a model of masculinity. All he can do is to usurp the place of weak fathers. Thus he stands in place of Olvido Paez's weak father Francisco (I. 473), and in place of the father of Rosita Carraspique (Chapter 12). Whereas Francisco is the name of 'real' masculinity in Fermín's Oedipal triangle, heavy allusions occur in relation to the other Franciscos to undermine that. The Hotel de Páez is dated 1868 (I. 471), the date of the revolution which dethroned Isabel II and her consort Francisco de Asís. It is not by chance that Carraspique's full name is given at the start of Chapter 12 as Don Francisco de Asís Carraspique: the historical Francisco de Asís was renowned for his homosexuality, and for *not* having fathered the children who bore his name. The trail leads back to the casting of doubt on Fermín's own parentage.

If Oedipal triangles do Fermín no service in the search for *celo*, the option of the jealous lover remains. The difficulty is that he is discovered. In Chapter 25, Fermín declares that he is the 'preso', or prey. His outburst reveals all. Ana finally articulates to herself that what Fermín has is not brotherly love, but passion, love, jealousy, rage (II. 322). His desire for her is 'outed', made public, by the indecorum of jealousy.

Fermín continues to try to go through the illusion of being the subject of *celo*, until the point at which, in the final two chapters, he finds that in the adulterous triangle he is not the lover, but the husband, a position of loss, humiliation, shame and jealousy. Thus having desired to escape from the discomfort of being the object of *envidia*, an emotion it is imperative to him *not* to own, Fermín is simultaneously 'outed' and ousted. His *celos* declare his vain attempt to be the subject of *celo*, and leave him in an impasse as unnegotiable as the net of envy from which he had desired to escape.

Notes

1   See Jacques Lacan, 'The Hysteric's Question', in *The Psychoses: The Seminar of Jacques Lacan*, ed. by Jacques-Alain Miller, Book III (1995–96), translated with notes by Russell Grigg (Cambridge: Cambridge University Press, 1993), and Gregorio Kohon, 'Reflections on Dora: the Case of Hysteria', in Kohon, ed., *The British School of Psychoanalysis: The Independent Tradition* (London: Free Association Books, 1986), 376.

2   Sigmund Freud, 'The Instincts and Their Vicissitudes' (1915), in *On Metapsychology: The Theory of Psychoanalysis*, trans. under James Strachey, ed. Angela Richards, Pelican Freud Library, vol. 11 (1984), 113–38.

3   See Alison Sinclair, 'The Gendered Language of Desire in *La Regenta*', forthcoming in *Journal of Hispanic Research*, vol. 3 (1994–5), 231–49.

4   On some of the connotations of the triangle, see René Girard, *Deceit, Desire and the Novel: Self and Other in Literary Structure* (1961), translated by Yvonne Freccero (Baltimore: Johns Hopkins, 1965), Eve Kosofsky Sedgwick, *Between Men: English Literature and Male Homosexual Desire* (New York: Columbia University Press, 1985), Berta López M., 'El deseo triangular en *La Regenta*', *Estudios Filológicos* 22 (1987), 59–76, and Alison Sinclair, *The Deceived Husband: A Kleinian Approach to the Literature of Infidelity* (Oxford: Oxford University Press, 1993), 199–217.

5   María Moliner, *Diccionario del uso del español*, 2 vols (Madrid: Gredos, 1966).

6   See James Mandrell, 'Malevolent Insemination: *Don Juan Tenorio* in *La Regenta*', in Noel Valis, ed., *'Malevolent Insemination' and Other Essays on Clarín*, Michigan Romance Studies 10 (Ann Arbor, University of Michigan, 1990), 1–28; Noel Valis, 'On Monstrous Birth: Leopoldo Alas's *La Regenta*' in *Naturalism in the European Novel: New Critical Perspectives*, ed. Brian Nelson (New York/Oxford: Berg, 1992), 191–209 and 'Aspects of an Improper Birth: Clarín's *La Regenta*', in *New Hispanisms: Literature, Culture, Theory*, ed. Mark I. Millington and Paul Julian Smith, Ottawa Hispanic Studies 15 (Ottawa: Dovehouse Editions, 1994), 96–126; Lou Charnon-Deutsch, 'Voyeurism, Pornography and *La Regenta*', *Modern Language Studies* 19 (4) (1989), 93–101, and '*La Regenta* and Theories of the Subject', *Romance Languages Annual* 1 (1989), 395–8.

7   Page references to *La Regenta* are from the edition by Gonzalo Sobejano, 2 vols (Madrid: Clásicos Castalia, 1981), and will be given in the text.

8   See Lou Charnon-Deutsch, *Gender and Representation: Women in Spanish Realist Fiction*, Purdue University Monographs in Romance Languages 32 (Amsterdam/Philadelphia: John Benjamins) on the masculinisation of the reader and 'Voyeurism, Pornography and *La Regenta*', 94 on the male narrator.

9   Saint Thomas Aquinas, *Summa Theologica*, trans. by the Fathers of the English Dominican Province, 2a 2ae 2 36.1 (London: R. and T. Washbourne Ltd, 1917), 473. See also Aquinas's awareness of the primitive and early nature of envy in his quotation from Augustine's *Confessions*: 'I myself have seen and known even a baby envious, it could not speak, yet it turned pale and looked bitterly on its foster-brother' (36.3, 477).

10 *New Catholic Encyclopedia* (1957–67), 17 vols (Washington: Catholic University of America).

11   I am indebted to Dr Graham Davies and Dr Ben Segal for this information.

12   María Moliner, *Diccionario del uso del español*, 2 vols (Madrid: Gredos, 1966).

13   Melanie Klein, 'Envy and Gratitude' (1957), in *Envy and Gratitude and Other Works 1946–1963* (London: Virago, 1988), 181.

14   See John Brenkman, *Straight Male Modern: A Cultural Critique of Psychoanalysis* (New York and London: Routledge, 1993), and Nancy J. Chodorow, *Femininities, Masculinities, Sexualities: Freud and beyond*, (London: Free Association Books, 1994).

15   Ernest Jones, 'Jealousy' (1929), in *Papers of Psychoanalysis*, 5th edn (London: Baillière and Cox, 1948).

16   Jessica Benjamin, *The Bonds of Love: Psychoanalysis, Feminism, and the Problem of Domination* (London: Virago, 1990), 95.

17   Julian Pitt-Rivers, *The People of the Sierra* (London: Weidenfeld and Nicholson, 1954), 107–10. The *compadrazgo* is the relationship of *compadres* between the parents (*padres*) and the god-parents (*padrinos*) of a child, the latter conventionally being a married elder brother and his wife. The relationship is one of extreme formality and seriousness, and introduces further levels of incest taboo, since it is forbidden by popular terms to marry either one's *padrino* or *compadre*.

18   Sigmund Freud (1909), 'Family Romances', in *On Sexuality: Three Essays on the Theory of Sexuality and Other Works*, ed. Angela Richards, Pelican Freud Library, gen. edn James Strachey, vol. 7 (Harmondsworth: Penguin Books, 1977), 221–5.

Part IV
Films and Fictions

14

No Second Chances: Fiction and Adultery in *Vertigo*

Michael Wood

Many of Hitchcock's films have moments of farewell to reason, points where an amiable, unobsessed person leaves the movie for good. This person is often a woman, and in *Frenzy*, for example, she is about to be brutally murdered. These departures are always stylistically marked, lingered over, so that we feel their weight even if we scarcely seem to notice them, and perhaps we don't need to notice them consciously. *Vertigo* has one of the most beautiful and enigmatic of such moments.

Barbara Bel Geddes as Midge, our hero's wry and faithful friend, visits him in hospital. He is James Stewart, playing Scottie, a former police detective who has seen the woman he loves plummet to her death from a high tower. He was unable to save her, unable even to reach the top of the tower, because of his fear of heights, established at the outset of the movie when he dangles from a high roof while a fellow policeman dies falling into an alley. The coroner at the inquest on the woman's death has spoken less like an instrument of the law than like the voice of Scottie's own conscience at its most sneering and devastating. Neither Scottie nor Midge nor we know at this moment that the woman Scottie saw fall past him through the air was not the woman he loved, but someone else, the victim of an elaborate murder plot. The moviegoer's problem is compounded by the fact that the falling figure we saw was visibly a dummy, thus neither the woman Scottie loved nor any other human being, only a movie prop. I'm not suggesting that Hitchcock needed or went out of his way to design this implausibility; only that it entirely serves his purposes.

In the hospital, Midge has put some Mozart on the record-player, explaining that this is the music therapist's idea. 'Mozart's the boy for you', Midge says. 'The broom that sweeps the cobwebs away.' No

189

response from Scottie, who is catatonic throughout the scene. Midge continues diffidently, 'Well, that's what the lady says.' A little later Midge goes to see the doctor, one of those horn-rimmed stooges Hitchcock is so fond of, placed in the films to make clear that professionals are the least likely of all people to understand what is going on in Hitchcock's world. The doctor tells Midge that Scottie is suffering from 'acute melancholia, together with a guilt complex' – not just guilt, we note, but a guilt complex. Midge informs the doctor that Scottie was in love with the woman who died, and the doctor sagely nods and says, 'That does complicate the problem, doesn't it?' Midge adds that Scottie still is in love with the woman who died, and adds further, making a little face of pain, that she doesn't think Mozart is going to help at all. At this point she leaves the movie, departing down the hospital corridor along which we recently saw her approaching the doctor's office; except that when she arrived she walked briskly down the middle of the corridor, and now she walks way over to the right, very slowly, almost leaning on the wall; like a defeated person, of course, but also like a person whose defeat means there is no middle any more. This shot is held for a long time, and then fades before Midge leaves the corridor, so that for all we know she may be there still. Or rather, she is there still, this is her sign in the movie, sanity baffled and abandoned.

But then we need to ask what kind of sanity this is, and the joke about Mozart is pretty complicated. Asking Scottie to 'please try' and make contact with the world and his old life, Midge says 'You're not lost. Mother's here.' Their relationship has always been like this, although not through any choice of hers. An early bit of dialogue establishes that he proposed to her once, and was turned down. The implication is that he needed to persist to show he was in earnest, but he doesn't see this even now; and has taken her refusal as his alibi, as a guarantee that their relationship will not commit him to anything more than her company and her protection of him. Mother's here; always was. He asks her not to be 'so motherly', but he doesn't expect her to stop. Midge couldn't have saved Scottie from obsession because she has allowed herself to be placed in a zone too far from romantic craziness. The cosy sanity of their friendship may well be another pathology; but it is mild enough to look like reason. When she leaves the movie, she doesn't take with her any real possibility of rescue for Scottie. What she removes, from the film rather than from him, is the availability of any perspective other than Scottie's. That is why Hitchcock needs to linger as she goes. It's all obsession from now on.

When Scottie finally leaves the hospital Hitchcock twice shows him in a frame with a road sign that says 'One Way'. The only alternative to obsession is to play the fact of the movie against the movie itself; the fact that *Vertigo* is a movie against the movie that *Vertigo* is.

The joke about Mozart is not just that it's foolish to think music, any music, could help with melancholia; it's that Mozart is about as far from the rest of Bernard Herrmann's Wagnerian score as you could get. A looping cello strain accompanies Midge's walk back down the corridor, the voice of romantic mourning and departure, as if one missed marriage is ending and another is about to start. When Lesley Brill writes of the 'adulterous harmonics' of *Vertigo*,[1] the phrase does not refer to Herrmann's music, but it could. The music of the movie is not only haunting, it is haunted, a *Tristan and Isolde* for morbidly swinging, or falling lovers. If you hear it away from the film, on the radio for example, you immediately experience the dips and dizziness of a story that won't let go, as if the music were the film's (all too palatable) madness. It is true that the score clings, at the high points of the story, to the hero's idea of a woman rather than to any actual female, even fictional, but this puts the music even more intensely at the service of the entanglements of (someone's) desire. What we hear in the soundtrack is the lush and piercing romance of obsession, and this obsession is through and through adulterous: our man is in love with his own reinvention of another man's wife.

There are many complicated stories in *Vertigo*, and I want to concentrate on two of them: that of the woman refashioned into her own image, and briefly, that of the conspiracy so elaborate it can only serve some purpose other than its own. These stories are well buried and very devious, so a certain amount of straightforward description is needed in order to show their contours – description as straightforward as I can make it, that is, since like all description it will be tugged by the interpretation it implies or seeks.

'There is something statuesque about her,' Donald Spoto writes, 'something eminently desirable and yet infinitely remote, the quintessence of the mystery of Woman'.[2] Before we start laughing or crying over this nonsense, we should pause over the possibility that this is just the effect Hitchcock is after. The person in question is Kim Novak, and Spoto is thinking of an early scene in *Vertigo*, where we see her for the first time. She is the mistress of a man called Gavin Elster, and she is impersonating his wife Madeleine, for the benefit of Scottie, whom Elster wants to employ to keep track of his supposed wife's mysterious disappearances. The settting is a restaurant which

is all red plush and glitter, she is wearing a long dark dress with a stole and her ash blonde hair is swept up behind her head. The camera finds her on the far side of an inner room, holds her in long shot, seen from the back and then from the side, and the music rises in romantic ripeness, dark strings insisting on the promise of mystery. Kim Novak gets up from her table, walks towards the camera and towards Scottie. The camera holds her in two separate profile shots in emphatic close up. She leaves the restaurant and our view. The music dies away. We have seen what we have seen.

We have not (of course) seen the quintessence of the mystery of Woman, but we have seen a fraught and powerful deployment of the myth of such a quintessence, and it's worth noting how much essentialising has gone on, and in what directions. This idealised object of male desire is blonde and distant, dressy, solid, and most important, married to someone else – at least as far as the viewer, in and out of the film, knows at this stage. Spoto's 'and yet' makes the myth look casual where it's working hardest. This woman is desirable *because* she is remote; matrimony is just the name of her remoteness. She is something like desire itself in this strangled fantasy: safe because unavailable, free for whatever obsession wants to make of her. She is statuesque because she is Kim Novak, and because Hitchcock wants her to look like a work of art, but that too serves the myth: a little later we're going to follow out a grisly version of the story of Pygmalion. We also know that the supposed wife is strange, haunted, given to 'wandering'; that the husband is worried about her. It may be that for Scottie (and for many male viewers) this particular story just doubles the fact of the marriage, enhances her remoteness. Already forbidden, she is someone who keeps going away.

Scottie, initially reluctant to have anything to do with Elster's problems, is now hooked, of course. He follows the person he thinks is Madeleine all over San Francisco and the surrounding area, until one day she jumps into the Bay and he rescues her. He has fallen in love with her – with her beauty and her wandering, her near-magical disappearances – and she seems to respond. After the rescue, the adulterous ground of this love is recalled by the ringing of the telephone as the lovers' hands meet for the first time: the husband, right on cue.[3] Madeleine's dilemma, as Scottie pieces it together, is that she believes she is possessed by the spirit of her great grandmother, the unfortunate Carlotta Valdes, who was abandoned by the man she loved, and committed suicide. Madeleine has a recurring dream, and insists 'there's something I must do'. Scottie

recognises the landscape of the dream, an old Spanish mission some miles south of San Francisco. He takes her there, in the hope that reality will exorcise the troubled fantasy; but finds that it fulfils it instead. Madeleine throws herself from the mission's high tower, Scottie panting on the stairs below, unable to go any higher, and we arrive at the situation I have already described: the inquest and Midge's visit to the hospital.

Two things now happen, or rather two stories now open, independently of the infinite complications of the murder plot. In a familiar but compelling romantic trope – that of Heathcliff, say, insisting that although young Hareton Earnshaw reminds him of Catherine there is nothing special about this, since *everything* reminds him of Catherine – Scottie tries to start his life again but sees Madeleine everywhere, that is, keeps seeing women who are like her and turn out not to be her. These are not illusions but uncanny foreshortenings of the visual world, especially suited to the film medium. The women do look like Madeleine, from a distance, and one of them actually has her car, as well as a hairdo and grey suit just like hers. 'The entire world', Scottie might say as Heathcliff does, 'is a dreadful collection of memoranda that she did exist, and that I have lost her'.[4] It's not clear where such a story can go, what reward such grief could possibly find, except a reunion in another world. But before this story settles in *Vertigo*, it is interrupted by a further, stranger one. Scottie latches on to a woman who, to us, looks nothing like Madeleine, that is, matches none of the codes that have signified Madeleine to us: blonde hair, expensive clothes, loneliness, lost, aristocratic look. The woman is Kim Novak, so on one level she just is Madeleine, or Madeleine was her, but there is an interesting criss-cross in our moviegoing responses here. We know it's Kim Novak, because we have recognised her. Why couldn't Scottie do the same? Yet we feel this is not Madeleine, and can't see what resemblance he can see – after all, he doesn't know she's Kim Novak, and the signs are all wrong. The story set up for us now is not that of a man finding resemblances to his lost love everywhere, but of a man making a resemblance where there is none, determined that his love cannot have vanished from the world, must be represented by some sort of reincarnation or refashioning, not condemned only to those shadows and echoes.

This is the spookiest and cruellest section of the film. Scottie makes friends with the woman, takes her out, and gradually begins to make her over into Madeleine as he remembers her. He buys her clothes, gets her to wear a trim grey suit like Madeleine's. 'It can't make that

much difference to you', he says, as if any woman's looks were only a function of some man's fantasy, and as if the mere reality of her life had no claim of any kind to make against the imperatives of his necrophiliac dream. He is pursuing, not a ghost and not exactly a simulacrum, but something like the resurrection of an ideal appearance which is itself the reality, the movie version of his phantasmatic love. If this woman can be got to look exactly like Madeleine, then Madeleine will have been brought back to life, but not in her own flesh, only in the perfection of a repetition. For this the resemblance has to *be* perfect; no longer a resemblance, but an identity, at least a visual one, which is all a movie can actually show us. It can hint at other things, of course, but those hints are always complications or questionings of the visual. Hitchcock is the master of this material, and at one point in his conversations with Truffaut, explaining why he decided not to make a movie of John Buchan's *The Three Hostages*, which involves kidnapping and hypnotism, he offered the following oracular remark: 'Visually speaking, there would be no difference between someone who is really hypnotised and someone who's pretending.'[5] Just as in Hitchcock's *Suspicion*, there is no difference, visually speaking, between a glass of milk that is poisoned and one that isn't. When shooting that film, Hitchcock put a light bulb inside the milk to highlight this lack of difference. What he is paradoxically saying in his remark about the Buchan novel is that movies are made of such lacks of difference in the realm of the visual, such collisions of possible meanings in a single visual space, but that the lack of difference has to matter on the screen – it can't just make no difference that there's no difference. In *Vertigo*, as we shall see, there is both all the difference and no difference.

The extremity of Scottie's obsession is revealed first by a look, then by a devastating remark, a re-run of 'It can't make that much difference to you'. He has bought Judy clothes and shoes like Madeleine's, but seems to be arriving at a possible abatement of his fantasy, perhaps about to begin to be able to think of Judy as a person rather than the embodiment of a phantom. Then his eyes freeze and whiten as if he were a crazed scientist in a much older movie; the obsession music rises. He doesn't need to speak, but he does. 'The colour of your hair', he says. She says, 'Oh no', and he brutally pleads, 'Judy, please. It can't matter to you.'

Even when she has dyed her hair, she makes one last small gesture of resistance, a different styling of the hair. Scottie insists, and she gives in, goes to the bathroom, and returns, her hair up, now looking

exactly like Madeleine. The couple embrace, the room spins round them, turning at one point into the coach house of the mission where Madeleine is supposed to have met her death. It is one of the eeriest moments in the cinema. Literally, an actress playing one part reverts to her appearance in another part, but the visual authority of the thing suggests the total fulfilment of Scottie's dream, sheer miracle, not so much the defeat of death as an illustration of its docility, its revealed lack of finality. Scottie has regained everything a character in a movie (or indeed a movie viewer) could regain or want to regain, because Kim Novak has shed what looked all along like a false self and turned before his and our very eyes into … Kim Novak.

What is unusually phantasmagoric here is that Kim Novak is Kim Novak on the level of the plot too. There was no Madeleine, or rather we have never seen Madeleine except as a falling dummy: the rich, absent and then dead wife of Gavin Elster. Kim Novak is Judy Barton, her hair undyed, and her accent slipping back from California haughty to Kansas demotic. She was Elster's mistress, and part of his elaborate plot to get rid of his wife. When Scottie asks him at the beginning of the movie how he got into the ship-building business, he says 'I married it', and faithful to his stark pronoun, Elster murders the human hidden in the 'it' and keeps the money. At the top of the tower Scottie couldn't climb, Elster was waiting with the already dead Madeleine, whom he flung down, knowing Scottie would not be able to climb high enough to see the deception – he'd read in the newspapers about Scottie's acrophobia and retirement. Elster and Judy then waited till the coast was clear, and took off.

'I was intrigued', Hitchcock told Francois Truffaut, 'by the hero's attempts to re-create the image of a dead woman through another one who's alive'.[6] Another one. Hitchcock himself speaks the language of Scottie's understanding, for the viewer knows, as soon as Scottie leaves his new-found friend after their first meeting, that there is no other, only the one and the same, since Judy confesses this in a letter the viewer sees and hears. Scottie, whatever he thinks he is doing, is in reality, that is, in a story which is simultaneously Hitchcock's, Elster's and Judy's, recreating the image of a woman he thinks is dead through that of one he thinks is alive, while all the time there is only one woman, a single physical presence and a complicated matrimonial and familial fiction, Carlotta Valdes and all.

There are many ways of describing this situation. The film itself, like Hitchcock's remark, takes Scottie's view, at least at the moment of Judy's transformation into Madeleine. Every source of Hitchcock's

and Bernard Herrmann's art is dedicated to making us feel that a miracle is taking place: the real vertigo is here, in the delirious music, in the room spinning behind the lovers. Judy moves towards Scottie in a haze, and in slow motion: back from the dead, where else? The title of the Boileau–Narcejac thriller Hitchcock based the film on was *D'entre les morts*. And yet we can't forget what we know: bluntly, that even within the story the miracle is a matter of make-up and coiffure. Outside the story, it's exactly the same thing, of course, since Kim Novak has to be turned into Judy Barton as Madeleine in just the way Judy Barton has to be turned (back) into the false Madeleine. The fiction of the film and the fiction of the conspiring characters are identical.

It is here that we need to think about the plot of the plot, Gavin Elster's elaborate subterfuge within which his wife's real death will take place. Most pieces of narrative fiction work according to several different logics at once, and we are not always as clear as we might be about these differences. In *Vertigo*, as in many thrillers, there is a logic of faint but crucial verisimilitude, driven by a series of implicit maxims about human behaviour: grief can traumatise a person; a man who wanted to get rid of his wife but keep her money might decide to kill her. These maxims don't tell us much, but our consent to them is important, mainly because they distract our attention from other, deeper logics that we might not like to contemplate openly. The chief of these other logics in *Vertigo* is that of Scottie's psychic needs, or more precisely the logic of the story which will allow those needs their unhappy fulfilment. 'You're my second chance', he keeps telling Judy late in the movie, but there are no second chances here, just the one delusive appearance of chance, always ending in the same image: that of the man who watches others fall to their death. Gavin Elster's plot for the murder of his wife doesn't make any real sense as a murder plot; only as the plot Scottie needs to stray into. 'You think I'm making it up', Elster says to Scottie when he first tells him about his wife's wanderings. 'I'm not making it up. I wouldn't know how.' Within the logic of verisimilitude this line, if we remember it, makes Elster a particularly clever villain: he has not only made it all up, he has included a plausible picture of himself as a man who can't make things up. According to the darker logic, he hasn't made it up, he is merely the instrument of whatever agency ministers to the orchestration of Scottie's fear and desire. We could call this agency Hitchcock, but it might more plausibly be thought of as the demands of the metaphor Hitchcock wishes to deploy. In Elster's story, Scottie's acrophobia is a convenience, a crucial ingredient in his fiendish plot.

In Scottie's story Elster and his whole murder plan are a convenience, a means of allowing Scottie to fall in love with the inaccessible and imaginary Madeleine, of losing her (as he thinks) and finding her again (as he also thinks) and losing her yet again (as he finally does, when she falls to her death from the place where the real Madeleine Elster was thrown down).

I'm afraid the quintessence of Woman makes its reappearance here, all the more so because Midge and mother and all other less essential women have been banished from the film. What Scottie has remade and lost again is not only his dead love but a wife/mistress, and an adulterous affair; he has brought us back to where the story started, with a glimpse of a woman who was what women are supposed to be: beautiful, enigmatic, haunted, a little crazy, tied to someone else; statuesque at the beginning and dead (for real) at the end. We both forget and remember all this, just as we forget and remember that the miracle is a mirage. Slavoj Žižek is right, I think, to see in Scottie's rage when he discovers his error, learns that he hasn't resurrected the dead, merely returned a conspirator to an old impersonation, 'an authentic *Platonic* fury: he is furious at discovering that he was *imitating the imitation*'.[7] In this special sense there are *only* second chances. Scottie himself says as much when he takes Judy back to the mission tower. 'You played the wife very well, Judy. He made you over, didn't he? He made you over just like I made you over – only better. Not only the clothes and the hair, but the looks and the manner and the words.' Even there, though, Scottie is not confessing the full extent of his displacement from the real. It's not that Elster did the job better, it's that he did it first, and it was the job itself Scottie fell in love with, the play wife, not Judy the mistress, and not Madeleine the actual wife. His Platonic fury concerns not only the double secondariness of his imitation, but the revelation that there was nothing but illusion for him to love, that he was in love with illusion itself.

We can learn what Žižek calls the Lacanian 'lesson' of *Vertigo*: that the subject is a 'virtual image', something that will have been but never is. 'It is always-already "past", although it never appeared "in the past itself"; it is constituted by means of a double reflection, as a result of the way the past's mirroring in the future is mirrored back in the present'.[8] But we also need to see what Scottie has not quite allowed himself to see, even in his final lucidity: that adultery is something like the fiction of the fiction, that he was in love not only with another man's wife, but with another man's invention; that his own invention

was a travesty of another's, a recreation of another's possession. Just as Sarrasine, in Barthes' reading of the Balzac work, is erroneously in love with a castrato and unconsciously in love with castration, so Scottie is naively in love with a wife and unconsciously in love with the impossibility of marriage. Even his illusion, so to speak, is adulterous, a figure for an obsession with arriving too late.

I'm not suggesting that Hitchcock intends or unintentionally effects any kind of elaborate deconstruction. On the contrary, I think he means to envelop us in the fullest, most dream-soaked mystification. But the fact of the movie stares us in the face even as we immerse ourselves in its swooning illusion. Scottie has repeated Elster's gesture, which in turn mirrors Hitchcock's or any director's in his manipulation of a female star – in his manipulation of a male star, too, although the resonances are entirely different. But the spectacular simplicity of what we have seen resists these anxious competitions. There is an alternative to obsession, which allows us to see the obsession for what it is. When Kim Novak turns into Kim Novak – is it possible not to feel that her role as Judy is accidental, her life as the imaginary Madeleine the real, the essential thing? The cinema itself seems to be talking to us. It says not that there are only fictions but that fictions are often what we need, that there is a place where secondariness is home, all Platonic fury spent or not even aroused in the first place. No deception. This is where we came in, and why we came in. What we see is what we get; but we only get to look at it, and no one is asking us to believe it is true, except to appearances.

Notes

1   Lesley Brill, *The Hitchcock Romance* (Princeton University Press, 1988), 210.
2   Donald Spoto, *The Art of Alfred Hitchcock* (Fourth Estate, 1992), 282.
3   It is at this point that Brill speaks of 'the adulterous harmonics of [Scottie's] first furtive embrace'.
4   Emily Bronte, *Wuthering Heights* (Penguin, 1985), 353.
5   François Truffaut, *Hitchcock* (Panther Books, 1969), 383.
6   Ibid., 303.
7   Slavoj Žižek, *For They Know Not What They Do* (Verso, 1991), 16. Žižek's italics.
8   Ibid., p.15.

15

The Fatal Attraction of *The Piano*[1]

Naomi Segal

All fictions of adultery rely on the structure of triangularity. Their principle is that desire is always circuitous, that either disruption or indirection is its very essence. But triangularity is an extremely complicated and variable phenomenon. In the discussion that follows, I want to compare two fictions produced in the last ten years. Both were immensely popular films, breaking box-office records in the USA and elsewhere, and provoking critical and general interest beyond anything their directors had received before. Prior to *Fatal Attraction*, Adrian Lyne was known for *Flashdance* and *9½ Weeks*, both reckoned to be glossy and essentially superficial exercises. Jane Campion's *Sweetie* and *An Angel at my Table* had won critical acclaim and awards, but were unpopular or unknown by the general public. *Fatal Attraction* (1987) and *The Piano* (1991, 1993) caught the attention of the moment and speak, it seems, very powerfully to the preoccupations of the last two decades of this century.

What I shall examine in this essay is how the principle of triangularity works differently, both in structure and in a more general psychological functioning, in these two films. At the risk of starting over-simply, I want to work inward from a symmetrical assumption: that *Fatal Attraction* is a powerful negative myth of contemporary masculinity and *The Piano* is an equally powerful positive myth of contemporary femininity. Both their residual enigma and their production of over-determined explanations (the BFI offers an at-a-glance list of around 70 longer articles and reviews on each) attest to their resonance. What exactly is it they do?

Again, to start simply: what are their common elements? Both films have a plot that turns upon the question of adultery and each uses a triangle as its basic form. In both, the trio of adults is supplemented by the addition – which, however, I would suggest, makes for a more complex triangularity rather than some other figure

– of a female child and, parallel or supplementary to her, other objects or creatures intermediate between the 'fully human' and the land- or cityscape.[2] In an earlier article in this volume, I have represented the 'matrilinear' function of the mother/daughter pair in nineteenth-century fictions written by men. There the daughter stands as the signal of a maternal sexuality which is by definition excessive and therefore represented by a redundant reproduction: already-too-much feminine produces 'only' more feminine. The apparent repetitiousness of the woman incapable of making what is not herself expresses the – for her male author – enigma of an Eros that omits, evades and thus exceeds the masculine. And the story of Anna Karenina, Effi Briest or Hester Prynne can only be brought to a stop when that overflow is rechannelled into its assigned place: the daughter is coopted by fostering or marriage – either way, by re-legitimisation – back into a genealogical and hereditary system presided over by men.

In 1980s and 1990s mainstream cinema, particularly USA films, sons appear as the third person in unhappy families where the wife is to be ejected from a domesticity which runs better without her. *Kramer v. Kramer* is only the most popular of these myths.[3] They roll comfortably on from an oedipal origin and what Leslie Fiedler identified as long ago as 1960 as a peculiarly American alienation from adult sexuality and nostalgia for the ostensibly unsexed bonds of boyhood.[4] More recently we find the male body feminised in increasingly comical (read: safe) ways to take over further areas of women's space. Robin Williams and Arnold Schwarzenegger, with a little technology, will make better mothers than their wives ever could, and the latter is undoubtedly a more reliable kindergarten teacher than the Nicole Kidman character in *Malice*.[5]

Given this vocabulary of the sympathy-for-father genre, it is perhaps surprising to find that *Fatal Attraction*'s Dan Gallagher (from whose viewpoint the film is wholly presented) has a daughter – more still, we might think, that his perfect wife has one. Good mothers in male-authored fictions generally have sons and lose them only when they cease to deserve them. That Beth Gallagher has a daughter, however short-haired, suggests something of the prehensile ambiguities of her role in the triangular plot in which she will be in turn the reject, the haven and the killer.

Much more ink has been spilled over Dan and Alex, and I will return to them. But let's begin with the surprisingly matrilinear wife. Most reviewers, whether grudgingly or with relief, recognise that Beth is

no dish-rag. We must believe that Dan has little reason to cheat on her, and that he can enjoy a pleasant future with her, even if they avoid baths for a few months. She must be not so much less as differently sexy from the excessive Alex, who thrills for only a very short time, after which she begins to spill. Beth differs not by being unattractive but by offering, feature for feature, hair, eyes and mouth which invite rather than threaten – her gaze is dewy, her smile humble, her hair flowing, whereas Alex's are respectively demanding, knowing and controlled.[6] Yet the wife is, paradoxically, less sexually available than her rival. He can have her but he can't have her (a planned nude scene between them was never shot) because first the (male) dog and then the child are placed in between them. This same dog is mutely included in the adulterous weekend: in a day, he witnesses outdoor frolics and indoor grapples, two plays at death and their outcomes, and he eats the evidence in a plate of cold spaghetti sauce; later, the daughter and her (female) rabbit will be brought similarly into the drama of Alex's invasions after first having taken the place of sexual intimacy between the husband and the wife.

Crucially, triangularity is presented in *Fatal Attraction* as invasive. True to the tradition of adulterous plots, it is the story of an outsider breaking in and breaking up. Like the scapegoat in tragedy or detective fiction, that outsider is finally dispatched in order to save (or perhaps simply patch) the original unit, whose inner faults s/he has less exposed than disguised. Alex Forrest, as her name suggests, is the wild by which the safe is demarcated. Whether in the cluttered New York apartment or the well-acred suburban homestead, she presents the black hole that forces itself into completion. What she invades is warm, cosy, threatened and imperfect. Implosion is also explosion. To return to Beth, we need to look again at how her desirability is represented. Not available but enclosed.

We frequently see Beth half-undressed, making up or getting ready for her bath. But she always seems complete because she is in her right place, in front of a mirror. Applying lipstick, she reproaches her daughter for parodying women's titivations. Before the glass, she checks the colours on her skin: rouge, bruises. At one point, the most erotic moment they share, Dan comes up behind her and gazes (he at her, she at herself and both at the couple they make) upon the mirrored image of their marriage. In parallel, much later, while he is downstairs making a conciliatory cup of tea,[7] she examines her reflection again, twice in his shaving mirror, then in her larger one; and in the latter frame, as she wipes away the steam, Alex's face

appears behind her. Of course this types the outsider as both intervening on and belonging inside the scheme she ruptures. Beth is potentially the same sort of woman as Alex: less libidinous perhaps but more sadistic, for we witness only Alex's attacks on herself, whereas it is the two goodies, male and female, who threaten murder,[8] and while he rehearses it with detailed ferocity, she carries it out.

If triangularity is conceived as invasion in this myth, we have seen that it is not just Alex who threatens the closure of the framed space. It is already disrupted internally by the stops which its domestic 'extras' present to desire. Dan, as the truism goes, seeks something outside the marriage that he doesn't find inside it. That it is something he only fleetingly or superficially wants is unimportant; he is not happy in the frame as Beth, we are constantly assured, is happy. Beth moves from one enclosure to another. She is a *femme d'intérieur* in every sense (except in the extraneous pun of her offering an inside to others: no one enters her). When she is outside her gilded cage and set in motion, she very quickly shatters.

While Beth is engaged in the panicky drive that will break her into the pieces that only her own violence can mend, the narrative intercuts to Alex whizzing up and down the big dipper with Beth's daughter. Side by side and perfectly safe, they are on the rails while the mother is driving off them. The increased pace of Alex's wickedness has been marked in a number of inroads. First she had borrowed the husband without the wife's knowledge, harassed him and entered their space by means chiefly of the telephone, whose fetishistic audibility gets louder as it creeps nearer and nearer to the no longer properly monogamous bed. Soon she herself arrives at their flat posing as a buyer, and takes away the new phone number. In her next attack, the acid burns but does not penetrate the car: only the skin of the Volvo is marked, but her abusive cassette is taken first into his car, then his 'den' – where it is Beth who scares the life out of him by her gentle arrival. Then the boiled rabbit, comi-tragically transferred from hutch to pot, and the moment of confession which has Dan ejected from the family space, Ellen lifted, and Beth hospitalised.

Alex's wish to be included begins to become pathological only from the point at which she lays claim to a good reason for it. She tells Dan she is pregnant. Despite the views of some critics, we never know for sure if this is true – her vomiting in the garden after watching the schmaltzy scene of family and pet is surely justified psychologically as much as physically, and could *you* imagine voluntarily riding the big dipper in the first trimester? But it does not really matter. She

claims it and Dan and Beth believe it. This child is both rival and sibling to Ellen; it could explain such uncertainties as why she does no harm to her baby's older sister and why Dan tries repeatedly to kill them both but only his unrelated wife can take over that filicide. More importantly, it makes her a doubled threat to the family. Her child offers the negative image of their legitimacy. Her attack is no longer that of the simple outsider but of the inversion of relatedness that upturns theirs.

Who has penetrated whom? For all Alex's come-on, Dan enters her body (this is a movie about unsafe sex) and cannot ever wholly come out again. Whether literally in the foetal residue – 'How do you know it's mine?' he predictably stutters – or in the need that she retains, he is in Alex as much as she is in him. He repeatedly breaks into her flat, though it is not locked. If she always rises up again when injured like a cyborg or a vampire, so does he, after teasing her with a faked heart-attack in the park. Alex's pregnancy is, as Karen Durbin points out, really Dan's.[9] It is she, not Beth, who has a mother's rights over him. It is she who practises the kind of sex that impregnates, ignoring the props and fetishes that, by contrast, Beth arrays between herself and Dan. Alex's child makes her more immediate, Beth's makes her less.

Her child makes her uncanny because Alex is the enclosure of the pre-oedipal, pre-sexed, the more-herself-half-his. Beth's role is to be contained, not to contain. She alone of all the four protagonists is secure in the joint affection of living parents. Her child is no longer in her and, androgynously short-haired, ungainly in girly costume, aged somewhere between five and six (the parents do not agree on this) hangs ready like a fruit to drop into the oedipal moment where her father waits hungrily. She practises the proposal scene from a play, watches junk TV and learns card tricks from her grandfather; she can already answer the phone and pass messages to Mommy. She is on the way to being a mediator and seems to hold the marriage together, but actually, like the other 'third persons', she holds it apart.

Too much has been written about the ending of *Fatal Attraction* for me to want to add much here. Mandy Merck unusually stresses its consistency with the rest of the film, all of which can be read as a representation of the child's eye view of the primal scene. At earlier moments, she argues, both Alex and Ellen have been lookers-in on the couple; now in the final frames, the daughter

is safely offstage. As first Father, then Mother, attempts to kill the woman who has come between them, the child who has come

between them – a child who was previously aroused from bed by raised voices – fails to appear at the primal scene. As the camera surveys the film's bloody climax, the reverse look we expect to be given, Ellen's look, is withheld. Instead, I would argue, we are invited to take up her vantage point, to watch another white-clad lover struggle and die in the intimate surroundings of the family bathroom, and to be as shocked as a child. The exaggerated and implausible horror of Alex's death (a Grand Guignol finale which displeased realist critics) is rendered psychologically appropriate by our own infantilized viewpoint, which replaces that of the little girl, seen only in the film's final, notorious close-up of the Gallagher family photograph. (210–11)

This is surely a correct reading of the psychological buzz which the climax gave viewers, not least the good wives of bad men, and which Sherry Lansing and Adrian Lyne justify in clearly orgasmic terms.[10] But there is another, if only momentary, viewpoint within the final scene – that of Alex through whose (dead or undead?) eyes we witness her drowning. We shall see another resurrection from drowning in our other film, also viewed from the lower depths upwards and also marking the limits of the disposal of female desire. Alex is being finished by the nuclear family, Ada is about to start one. How differently does triangularity function in our declaratively 'women's film'?

To recapitulate: *Fatal Attraction* is provocative because it both uses and inverts the familiar version of the adulterous triangle. An outsider threatens an established dyad; but because that outsider is a woman she threatens it differently. In this traditionally penetrative fantasy of sexual irruption, the subject of forced entry is female and familial: she enters more insistently because she is an already containing unit, herself both penetrated by and penetrative of the man's psychological space.

I use the term 'penetration' reluctantly because I would like to enter the continuing 'sex wars' debate without getting caught in its most common traps. I do not want to identify the two modes of desire represented by these two films with male and female practice – that would be patently simplistic. I am not sure that the consequences of gendering them masculine and feminine are altogether useful either, leaving unbroached as it does the question of same-sex desire and *its* place in any gender binary. But it is on the whole true that *The Piano*

moves more women more powerfully than it seems to move men, and that this effect (which I share) requires explanation.[11] Clearly, the music, visual sweep and erotic build-up is part of it. But I think there must be something more to explain why this film appears to transcend the bounds of the masculine images of desire with which our culture so massively familiarises us, women and men, gay and straight.

So let me try to distinguish the two modes in other ways. In *Fatal Attraction* the sex represented is avid, noisy and violent. Quite deliberately, we know, the three most violent scenes, all taking place in kitchens and bathrooms, the most 'bodily' parts of a house, set up an analogy between the choreography of sex and murder. The only moments of missionary-position *corps-à-corps* are Dan's two attempts to kill Alex, in which shot-reverse-shot shows the equally contorted faces of murderer and murderee in such a way that we can neither distinguish homicidal from sexual violence nor the status of aggressor and victim. Let us call this mode of desire 'invasive', noting that it is the mode most commonly presented to us in cultural products hitherto. The triangle of invasion, desire as breaking and entering, the colonisation of resistant space by an outsider who might be ejected. Love and death in the western world.

In *The Piano*, it is also a question of the entry into a person's protected space and of colonisation. Desire is triangulated and cooptative but differently so. The key differences are temporal and spatial, using the inevitability, the step-by-step of desire in a way that replaces sadism with curiosity, and showing how bodies can reach each other in a mode that somehow resembles the playing of a piano.

The adulterous triangle in this film consists of a woman and two men, the most common pattern in traditional representations of adultery which, with their oedipal freight, tend to show an already assigned woman sought by a younger man. But here the married woman stands at the apex of the triangle, insistently focalised, alongside neither of the men. And, somewhat like Alex and very much like Hester Prynne, she starts out doubled by an illegitimate daughter whose existence declares her sexuality and represents one mode of access between her and the world.

Ada's muteness is not explained and is presented in the first frames as a state that she has both chosen and is powerless to reverse.[12] 'Not a handicap but a strategy', a multiplication and dissemination of the possible resources of communication,[13] her silence marks out very clearly the way in which an originating choice (or 'will', as the characters describe it) both frees up and restricts the actions that

follow. This film, like the other, multiplies and fetishises the channels between subject and object; but it reverses the triangulation which sees the 'third' element as invasive, and presents it instead as a putting out, a means towards the other. Where Beth's daughter was a possession that could be stolen from her, Ada's daughter is an extension of herself that is broken from her. It is not surprising that when Beth is hurt it is by a shattering of the whole body, and when Ada is hurt it is by the cutting off of one of her fingers, the spoiling of a complete set, what her mutilator calls 'clipping her wings'.

There are many other objects and modes of mediation – indeed, what some viewers dislike about the film is the relentless (oddly, simultaneously over-obvious and over-arty) stylisation of these devices. Bonnets resemble scallop-shells 'designed to concentrate acoustic information',[14] crinolines are tents, skirts leading-reins, shirts dusters, the wooden slats of a packing-case or a rough-hewn cottage let sound out or voyeurism in, and the visual sweep of the camera combined with the concentration of close-up brings together natural lighting, predominance of forest-greens and subaqueous blues to alternate the fantasies of being-lost-in and emerging-out.

The piano is, of course, the main fetish-object: both desired thing and part of self, it is bulky, inert, biddable and sensual; its cumbersomeness and beauty make it the possession no one can hold with certainty, like their own body.[15] It ends the film imagined undead beneath the sea and still, even after Ada's graphic birth out of the amniotic bubble, keeping one version of her body suspended umbilically above it. In the opening moments of the film, there is a shaft of red, a colour only rarely seen,[16] and through which (like the light seen through fingers, behind which a child might hide its face, thinking that makes it invisible) a piping voice identifies itself as Ada's 'mind's voice', and announces that she stopped speaking when she was six. This, we will discover, is just after or just before she began to play the piano. Thus the instrument allows the child's preservation as voice inside her body and its voluntary–involuntary expression, a model of psychoanalytical *Aufhebung*.

We are tempted perhaps to think it is Flora's voice. Unlike the Maoris, whose difference is marked fairly carefully in superiority and mimicry,[17] her doubling of her mother is both functional and reciprocal. It is a double Venus that is brought forth and landed on the beach, and the adequation and exploitation of the child as substitute for speech is shown when she pronounces Ada's aggressive message to the sailor and only escapes his fist by hiding in her

mother's skirts. She has the rights of monogamous enjoyment of her mother: like Ellen, she is there in the bed when the husband visits at the end of the day and it is her he offers to kiss rather than the woman.

The child and the piano are alternative communicators of the woman's physical desire. For Stewart both Ada and her piano are his to buy and sell; Baines at once recognises its mediatory function. He first takes her to it, standing as audience to the complete unit of mother/child/instrument on the beach; then he uses it to bring her to him, listening silently as she reappropriates it by playing. From this point, the child as mediator becomes redundant to the newly formed unit of woman, piano and man. It is of course essential that Baines cannot read, so that the instrument is at first the only means between them. Gradually, through the simultaneously comic, threatening and reassuring eroticism of Baines's clumsy 'bargain', the woman's body re-enters the communicative circuit, replacing both piano and child.

I will return to the development of dyadic communication in a moment. First, there is more to say about the human mediators. Flora, cast off as she becomes the object rather than the interpreter of her mother's will and coopted by the patriarchal–symbolic society of the Scottish colonisers, makes an expected move from the mother/daughter cell into the fostering oedipal. Continuing to wear her angel-costume – the Hebrew for 'angel' means 'messenger' – she will act as transmitter of judgment and carrier of keys. But before the story is over, she will undergo a second transfer, from Ada's bed to Baines's and she will end up turning healthy cartwheels in another triangular family, the least traditional of all.

Stewart plays his assigned role as disruptor of adulterous love; but he too is also used as something peculiarly connective. In the interlude of her imprisonment, Ada plays only in her sleep, and when she makes an unexpected move towards her husband, seems to 'play' on his body in a similarly somnambulist way. What makes this moment so affecting is that it remains in excess of what it proposes. Ada's erotic approach is not simply the redirection of a sexual appetite that Baines has aroused and Flora cannot satisfy. Two scenes represent her night visits: in the first, the screenplay describes her motive as 'a separate curiosity of her own'; in the second, she is 'moved by his helplessness, but distanced, as if it has nothing to do with her'.[18] With a detachment hanging somewhere between compassion and cruelty, Ada touches but will not let herself be touched. But what unmans and maddens the husband most is *how* she touches him: with the back of her hand

upon the back of his body. This special mode of caress is reserved elsewhere only for the sea, the child and the piano.

In many European languages, the word used for the keys of a piano is associated with the faculty of touch (French *touches*, Italian *tasti*, German *Tasten*) and connected with a verb of blind or quasi-blind feeling, groping (*toucher/tâtonner, tastare, tasten*). In describing Ada's silence as strategy rather than disability, Campion is both right and wrong: she has extended the reach of her senses, transferring voice into an extra modality of touch. Stewart is unmanned by this, Baines understands and reciprocates. It is this which makes the sexuality of this film unusual.

George Baines's mediation between cultures is etched on his brow, and it is not simply what makes him a cross between Tarzan and Mellors, it is also the sign of his bilingualism, the ability, like Ada's, to transfer himself and his desire from one mode to another. She cannot speak, he cannot read; she plays, he listens; he touches, she touches. Like Stewart, Baines talks stiltedly – here, Harvey Keitel's struggle with the accent came in useful – and, like him also, he struggles to hear Ada speaking, but whereas the former intuits her wishes 'in his head', Baines helps her to move her voice out onto the surface of her skin.

Colonisation comes from and operates by the structures of capitalism: grading, marking and counting out. Analogous to piano keys and fingers, numbered territorial stakes measure out the landscape and buttons are supposed to pay for it. These are Stewart's coinage. Baines and Ada begin with black and white keys, black overclothes and white underclothes; but at a certain moment, the bargaining stops and with it the grading of access which is undoubtedly one mode of the erotic, creating an appetite in both the heroine and the audience. Baines is after all, like the husband, a colonial exploiter, but less absolutely, not so much an owner as a mediator and interpreter. Implicated nonetheless, he buys the piano and expects to buy Ada; but let us not forget that Ada is as hard a bargainer as he is and it is he who stops the negotiations first.

Erotic violence is not always chaotically invasive: Sade, quite the reverse, creates an atmosphere of *graded* cruelty by his obsessive enumeration, space within space, sectioning off of days, cells or tortures. It is no chance that Stewart cuts off just one finger: he can then grade the threat on into the future, 'another and another and another'. Thus the gentle strip-tease of the un-erect Baines is also potentially coercive, but he stops when he has reached her skin. What

follows is the transformation of the temporal erotic onto a multiplied surface which is the whole extent of the person (inside and out, we may understand) now accessible without destruction.

In *The Piano*, then, adulterous triangularity is reinterpreted: not as the other who invades or irrupts into an enclosed thing that can be punctured or shattered. It becomes instead the condition of the complex movements of desire through its own involuntarinesses into diverse forms which meet other forms at the tips of the fingers. Both these fictions are post-AIDS: *Fatal Attraction* is indeed about the perils of penetration, of man by woman and woman by man, of hallowed spaces by their own fracturability and violence, and of frames by the seduction of a false imaginary. *The Piano* is about the extensability of desire upon a surface that is its own mediation.

Notes

1 My title refers to Mandy Merck's excellent article 'The fatal attraction of *Intercourse'*, in *Perversions* (Virago, London, 1993), 195–216.
2 Both films, interestingly, attach a male dog to the female child, and use the dog for humorous or even *louche* moments based on the animal's propensity to lick.
3 In 'The Mirror Cracked: the career woman in a trio of Lansing films', *Film Criticism*, 12, 2, Winter 1987/88, 28–36, Roslyn Mass observes the representation of strong women who meet a bad end in films produced by Sherry Lansing; among these are *Kramer v. Kramer* and *Fatal Attraction*. Betty Caplan points out that, for a Single Working Woman, Alex is seen very little at her job ('In work but out of sense', the *Guardian*, 12 May 1988, 25).
4 Leslie Fiedler, *Love and Death in the American Novel* [1960] (London: Jonathan Cape, 1967).
5 See Colleen Keane, 'Recent thrillers: postmodern play and anti-feminism', in *Metro Magazine*, no. 97, Autumn 1994, 20–2.
6 See Hilary Mantel, 'Mad, bad and dangerous', *The Spectator*, 23 Jan 1988, 43–4.
7 In a generally excellent article, Jean Désobrie points out the recurrence of steaming liquids in the invasion of Alex into the Gallagher family: *Cinémascopie: propos sur le cinéma contemporain* (Roger, s.l., 1989), 139–40.
8 This is pointed out by Shaun Usher, in 'The *Great* Attraction', *Daily Mail*, 15 January 1988, 26. A similarly cynical view of the yuppy couple and their like is given by Michael VerMeulen in 'Manhatten transfers', *Sunday Telegraph*, 7 Feb 1988, 21.
9 See 'The cat's meow', *Village Voice*, 15 December 1987, 90: 'What Douglas experiences as a result of his fling with Glenn Close reminded me of

nothing so much as that classic female nightmare (and luckless female reality), the unwanted pregnancy: a huge, distressing, apparently endless consequence he cannot rid himelf of. And all because the poor guy had a little fun. Hey, is life unfair or what? He even tries to get an abortion but Alex is having none of it. Sorry, fella, she says, *you can't get an abortion*. O role reversal! O bitter joy!'

10 See Adrian Lyne, in an interview with Brian Case ('Out of Lyne', *Time Out* 13—20 January 1988, 31): 'You see, if you build up a lot of empathy for the married man and his family – and I based a lot of it on mine – and then say, sorry fellas, he's going to jail, you're left alone, that's it – I don't think that's fair. I mean, you're giving the audience the foreplay and then ...' Or Sherry Lansing, less graphically, in Mass, op. cit., 33: 'I love the ending we have. It is eminently satisfying.'

11 See Lizzie Francke, *Sight & Sound*, Nov. 1993, 224: 'For a while I could not think, let alone write, about *The Piano* without shaking. Precipitaing a flood of feelings, *The Piano* demands as much a physical and emotional response as an intellectual one ... Not since the early days of cinema, when audiences trampled over each other towards the exit to avoid the train emerging from the screen, could I imagine the medium of film to be so powerful.'

12 Kate Pullinger, who wrote the book of the film (abandoned by Jane Campion after a couple of chapters) explains that 'Ada is mute because at six, when she contradicted the adults, she was ordered not to speak again that day and she decided to stay silent for ever' (see Marianne Brace, the *Guardian*, 18 April 1994, 11). Whatever the originating event – and why should it not be the smallest of traumas? – a result is necessarily something more than its occasion.

13 See Campion's interview with Ian Pryor, *Onfilm*, 10, 9 October 1993, 25; and Valerie Hazel, 'Disjointed Articulations: the politics of Voice and Jane Campion's *The Piano*', paper delivered to the Centre for Women's Studies, Monash University, in March 1994.

14 Adam Mars-Jones, 'Poetry in motion' in the *Independent*, 29 October 1993, 26.

15 Campion, who cites one of her motives as the wish 'to explore the relationship between fetishism and love' (Katherine Dieckmann, *Interview*, 27, 1, January 1992, 82), stresses the characteristics of the piano as inert object, and a number of critics note the analogy with the ship of *Fitzcarraldo*. But it is interesting to remember that her original title was *The Piano Lesson*, which has been followed exactly in the French version, while the Italian pluralises it into *Lezioni di Piano*.

16 For example, here, in the patterned curtain behind which Baines waits naked, in Flora's Red Riding Hood cloak and in the blood which splashes on her white apron.

17 Campion has claimed that the original interest in making a film set early in New Zealand colonial history arose from her fascination with the 'European cross-dressing' of Maoris in the mid nineteenth century (see Geoff Andrew, 'Grand entrance', *Time Out*, 20–27 October 1993, 24). More generally, she contrasts her 'strange heritage ... as a *pakeha* New

Zealander' with the Maori sense of history (*Piano* screenplay, London: Bloomsbury, 1993, 135). She has since been accused of orientalism and her portrayal of the Maoris in the film criticised as too simplistically based on a noble savage/repressed Britishers contrast. See for example the debate between Richard Cummings and Stella Bruzzi in the letter pages of *Sight & Sound*, February 1994, 72 and March 1994, 64.

18 Screenplay of *The Piano*, 90 and 93.

16

Dissolving Adultery: Domesticity and Obscenity in *The Game*

Jonathan Smith

I

This final essay deals with a novel that is relatively little known, partly because it is a first novel published in 1994.[1] It was chosen because it explicitly or implicitly questions the significance of adultery in relation to a variety of kinds of contemporary context. In this opening section I attempt some additional contextualisation which should show why this is important.

As I write in mid-decade, the 1990s appear at least as grim as the 1980s, not least because of the difficulty of grasping the sense of contemporary situations, let alone changing them.[2] One facet of this problem is the voracious appetite of allegedly informed or even radical opinion (which waxes increasingly careless of anything else) for the direst products of what used sometimes to be called the culture industry.[3] This may be illustrated by reference to the limited but significant critical as well as popular acclaim enjoyed by a recent middlebrow copping-off movie set in the Med.

Kenneth Loach's *Land and Freedom* (1995) contrives to reduce the Spanish Civil War to the occasion of a wholesome English youth's meeting a dusky beauty. This happens in circumstances sufficiently tragic, exotic, and remote to legitimate all at once the lachrymose masochism of the unhappy ending, the fix of soft porn that gets us there, and the denial of all this by the vindictive sadism with which our hero is eventually characterised as being such an irredeemable dim-wit that we postmodern sophisticates could not possibly have been identifying with him all along, however much his earthy Northern accent and decent sentiments egged us on. All this is in flashback, intercut with events at the time of his death 60 years later.

Central among these is his burger-chomping, cola-slurping grand-daughter's historical education by perusal of his yellowing collection of 1930s press clippings (although these must presumably either be from the capitalist press, or from a socialist press as ill-informed and inept as the film suggests its original audience was). At least the film ends in an appropriately self-cancelling fashion, with the girl slipping her grandfather's most treasured mementoes of Spain into his grave for burial with him. Things are then nicely rounded off by the piety with which the grand-daughter joins a pair of ragged veterans in a graveside scene of clenched-fist saluting that very effectively purchases an atmosphere of populist unity, but only at the cost of eliding the sense of sexual and generational difference without which it is difficult to imagine any future politics. I have laboured this point somewhat in order to underscore from the outset the degree to which the 1990s appear to be losing a distinction that might be considered valuable, between political radicalism on the one hand, and fantasies of sexual tourism on the other.

Having established this we can see how the cult status of another recent film that is closer to our immediate theme of adultery points to similar conclusions. *The Piano*'s Sunday-supplement photography of wild and exotic landscape and seascape is perhaps sufficiently innocuous in itself. But modulating as it does into sub-Jungian racism in the characterisation of the heroine's lover Baines as white-man-gone-native, it might have been expected to raise more critical discussion than it generally has. So too might the nineteenth-century *papier-mâché* that clogs the film so densely. If this is compatible with the film's celebration of a certain contemporary conception of sexuality, then it would appear apposite at least to enquire as to the substance of the latter, as well as its politics.

I take the intellectual interest of the fictional theme of adultery to reside chiefly in its potential as a figuration of the pursuit of illicit sexual fulfilment in general, and then, by a crucial semantic slide, of subversive autonomy as such. Discussion of such patterns of figuration might therefore assist in the kind of enquiry into the substitution of fantasy for politics just envisaged. There is however a significant overlap between the implied (and real) audiences for the cinematic spectacles I have mentioned on the one hand, and for the academic genre to which the present essay belongs on the other. There is therefore also an overlap between the political questions the two genres raise. It has accordingly seemed important, if the issues surrounding the problem of the theme's current significance were to be grasped, to consider some

less familiar exhibit in a contemporary *artistic* genre than those already mentioned. I stress the word 'artistic' because although *The Game* appears to echo many of what have become the commonplaces of the academic discourse known as poststructuralism, it is doubtful whether their significance or significations in this context are amenable to effective elucidation by reference to canonical theoretical texts, or in terms derived directly from them. This is so principally because the latter have in many cases recently been suffering such an erosion of meaning, in the positive as well as the negative referencing, as to be largely neutralised, intellectually and politically.

This last problem is of course part and parcel of the more general one to which I refer above in the first two sentences of my second paragraph, and it is therefore by no means clear that it can be resolved by the mere taking of thought or acts of the will. The accompanying footnotes supply some token references, and these must suffice for the present because this whole topic, which probably defies adequate treatment absolutely, certainly defies it within the limited scope of the present essay. However, the most significant aspect of the question from the present point of view is perhaps the widespread notion that Foucault is to be lauded or damned to the extent that his writings are or are not held to deny human autonomy in general and female autonomy in particular. These views have often been broadcast without pause to assess his theoretical formulations' sense, their architecture, or their force (including their carefully nuanced implications for the question of the continuing viability of the Freudian and Marxist traditions). But problems such as those of autonomy and heteronomy cannot be resolved by demonstration, much less by the *fiat* of authority figures, whatever *soi disant* radical as well as liberal academics may wish,[4] and it is a large part of Foucault's achievement to have preserved them as complex, open, dilemmas. *The Game* is a work of fiction within which a story of adultery is framed, unframed and reframed in a series of different interpretative contexts, permitting us to see it as the figuration of a dilemma of this type in all its complex irresolubility.

II

Consider this passage from the second page of *The Game*:

we've been doing this since January. Generally we drive around for a couple of hours, stopping furtively in lay-bys and leafy side-

streets. Anyone who saw us on that roundabout – him so much older and glummer than me, me snapping at him – would think I was telling him to leave his wife if it weren't for the sign on the roof, PASS WITH GRAHAM STILGO. I could still be telling him that, of course. The sign is perfect cover. In fact, I think Graham's quite glad he's got that sign, judging by the suggestive way he leans over to murmur 'Gas, gas, angel', or 'Watch that bike', into my ear. (4)

The 18-year-old narrator, Sarah Finney, presupposes here that adultery is widely considered to be the norm. She mentions this in connection with the hypothetical example of Graham Stilgo and herself, and therefore with the adulterous relations of married men and younger unmarried women. At this stage, the example screens by inverting it a theme which will return in the shape of Sarah's memories of Genevieve, married female lover of a younger unmarried man. What might seem normal to the point of banality for a man is for a woman the height of transgression, whether this is interpreted heroically (and therefore also normatively), as it will be through much of the novel by Sarah, or as verging on participation in the demonic, by Genevieve's sister: 'Juliette refused to entertain the idea of Genevieve's body in the family grave. Murderess, suicide, adulteress, it would be impermissible. She would not even discuss it with the priest' (153). But *The Game* eventually questions the very definition of adultery, as well as various characters' evaluations of it.

After Sarah snaps at Graham on the roundabout, the driving lesson repeatedly suffers further disruption, and each time, the theme of adultery develops further. From the countryside, he directs her into the outskirts and then the centre of Portsmouth, and her objections to this route redouble when he reminds her she once expressed a nostalgic wish to go that way because she lived in Portsmouth as a child:

for a basically nice man he must have a record number of annoying habits. The 'angel' stuff is one, the pipe-sucking at high speeds another. His watch must be set to bleep the quarter-hour, it goes off so often, and he can never turn it off. And then there's the brilliantine; I mean, it's 1982 and he can't even be forty and he wears brilliantine. And, *and*, he takes me literally, all the time, as if everything I say is cast-iron intention and gospel truth. (4)

Initially, Graham's literalism occasions a relatively trivial rift, which Sarah tries to narrow as they cross the city towards the docks; but she does this with an irony that elicits a literal response, so that the rift widens. During this exchange, the question of adultery resurfaces: '"Le Havre or Cherbourg – which would you prefer, darling?", I asked him. One last attempt to make a joke of it. He began to explain how the driving school and his wife and boys would object to our leaving the country' (6).

While adultery may be considered (as it is here by Sarah) to be as much a norm in itself as the transgression of a norm, it nonetheless coexists with the proprieties in relation to which it still also figures as transgression. Graham personifies these proprieties as well as those of literal meaning, and the structured field of coexisting but contrasting marital and adulterous normalities informs these early references to the theme. Later, Sarah's worldly wisdom will stand to be upset, and this structured field to be dissolved, by the discovery that the possibility of transgression has been restored right where we have learned to expect it least – on the side of marital relations. One effect of this will be to suggest that the basis of sexual propriety has come to reside elsewhere than in the legal form of marriage.

The novel will corrode received criteria of linguistic as well as of sexual propriety. The bumpiness of Sarah's driving lesson and dialogue with Graham in Chapter 1 figures the antagonistic alternation, throughout almost the whole of her narrative, of a voluntary recollection bordering on invention, and an associative involuntary remembering approximating to forgetting. Informed and deformed by this antagonism, Sarah's narrative deviates conspicuously from the criterion of 'cast-iron intention and gospel truth' that she imputes to Graham: this phrase designates a quotidian version of archaic doctrines of free will and divine revelation that marble and haunt the contemporary lives the novel narrates. These doctrines constitute the spectral armature of a propriety which is the more difficult to identify or transgress, sexually or verbally, because they place so high a value on the self-evidence of truth and of autonomy as to be deaf and blind to all else. The force of the novel's mode of narration is to question these values.

Here, at the beginning of the book, as it will be again at the end, remembering is figured by southward travel: as a child, Sarah lived in a series of houses on the south coast, while her naval officer father moved from posting to posting – Dartmouth, Hayling Island …; then the family moved inland, so that at the novel's opening, as she drives

south toward Portsmouth and the coast, she also drives towards her past. Meanwhile, her ironic fantasy of elopement from English banality to exotic France heralds an extended treatment of the imaginative dimension of national identities and differences articulated in the novel's language as well as its plot and its vivid evocations of landscape and seascape. England figures as something like the type of identity, and France of alterity, with its mixture of baffling opacity and exotic allure, although these polarities too melt away as the plot unfolds. The possibility of vicarious tourism, sexual or otherwise, is largely eliminated here by a creeping awareness that elsewhere is to a substantial but scarcely quantifiable extent a mirage of differential relation to where one is, glimpsed from nowhere in particular in a desert without landmarks: come the closing page, a 'flat southern voice' heard by chance in the English countryside is 'a voice from another country' (264). But a further disruption of the driving lesson poses all these questions in ways that link them together, and develop them as a context for the novel's thematisation of adultery.

At the entrance to the docks, Sarah exclaims, swerves, and accelerates wildly. Graham never receives any explanation, but already within the next four pages this mystery begins to be resolved for the reader. On returning home Sarah tells her mother she had thought she had seen, or had seen someone like, Genevieve – who is then rapidly identified as Mrs Finney's French sister-in-law Juliette's sister. Conversely, the questions of why Sarah reacted so abruptly, and why she remembers her mother's reaction to the news as having been so drastically blank, persist through much of the novel. Sarah's hectic narration of childhood and adolescent memories in which Genevieve looms large is punctuated by a series of equally staccato returns to a present time which only really achieves primacy in the closing chapters, where Genevieve's adulterous heroism will be subjected to drastic reinterpretations triggered by the onset of war with Argentina and the departure of Sarah's father for the South Atlantic. In my next two sections I shall therefore outline Sarah's story and Genevieve's place in it, before considering the theme of adultery in more detail and in relation to that context.

III

From the age of eight, Sarah has known that Genevieve had a gun. She remembers finding it, at their first meeting, in the bathroom of her mother's brother's London flat, where Genevieve was then staying,

and hiding it in order to establish a relation of complicity by protecting her newfound aunt from the family's curiosity. She also remembers seeing Genevieve point the gun at her estranged husband Paul Belar three years later, while snatching their daughter Naomi from his flat in Toulon. Sarah was in the meantime being brought up and educated at convent and boarding schools in Christian, military, and domestic traditions befitting the daughter of a naval officer. In reaction, she had come to idolise Genevieve as a uniquely forceful and undomestic woman. However, this feeling is qualified by some reserve on Sarah's part towards the unfamiliarity that makes Genevieve attractive to her, by a sense of betrayal when Genevieve eventually settles into a more domestic existence with her lover Jean-René, and by Sarah's sense that her ambivalence towards Genevieve is reciprocated. We notice at their second meeting (and the point is then developed) that this is partly because Sarah's complicity perpetuated whatever guilty secrets there were in Genevieve's life, somehow confirming her as an outcast and disqualifying her as a mother, so that she temporarily lost custody of Naomi, and partly for this reason turned to drink.

Sarah's usefulness to Genevieve is apparently that during three successive summer holidays in France, between the ages of 11 and 13, she befriends Naomi and helps reconcile her to her mother's new life with Jean-René. Sarah even remembers the initially hostile and fractious Naomi, who was barely less jealous of Sarah than both girls were of Jean-René, eventually referring to Genevieve as 'our mother' (137). However, memory traces from different epochs of Sarah's life, articulating disparate interpretations of her relations with Genevieve, are overlaid, interwoven and melted together by the shocks of the story she tells, so that it combines this domestic overtone with others. These are sometimes compulsively idealising, and sometimes modulate towards the erotically charged insistence with which, towards the end of the novel, she will recollect accompanying Genevieve a second time to Toulon, and to a final confrontation that ended with the older woman shooting dead first her husband, then herself. This happened the summer after Sarah was expelled from her boarding school for acts of sacrilege and arson that she fancies inspired Genevieve, but which seem also to have been inspired by the heroic aura in which she saw Genevieve veiled. However, although Sarah accompanied Genevieve to Toulon, she rapidly lost her memory of what happened there. Instead, she remembers experiencing entry into a new school at the end of that same summer as a surgical operation:

'my outlaw's heart had been excised as swiftly and painlessly as if they had used a laser-beam' (128).

What raises Genevieve from the dead in 1982, or lifts Sarah's repression, is the imminence of war, together with the friction it generates between the traditional military loyalties of Sarah's family and its domestic peace, and the exacerbation of this friction by the arguments of her friends and contemporaries as to the propriety of the Task Force's departure for the South Atlantic. Genevieve's enigmatic fascination reasserts itself, sending Sarah raving off to Jean-René in France, and then back just as abruptly to England and her family in the time of its critical need of stability. This time, her mother has her see a psychiatrist, whom she finds as inanely moralistic as Graham Stilgo, although this seems by no means to frustrate his work. The story Sarah tells is not naturalistically framed in this therapeutic situation, but from this point – the twenty-second of twenty-three chapters – Genevieve is replaced as Sarah's major focus of interest by the flat, brittle harshness of a service-family life perpetually overshadowed by wars past, present and future. Her rebelliousness subsides into pained ambivalence.

> My father came back and we stood there overcome by, I wish I could leave it at joy and relief, but it was also pride.
>
> My mother is as strong as a kicking mare. I keep comparing her to animals which is regrettable, distracting since I am trying to describe the strength of a human being. The strength of my grandmothers too; they're all three of them the same. I would be tempted to say it is strong stock if I hadn't seen, over thousands of days, how it is not passed on, how you have to make it each time for yourself ...
>
> I saw Suzanne in the street two months after it happened. She invited me home and there were no dark clouds in their house, their house was ablaze with Matthew's absence as if the war had gone through it and left it blasted and shining. Suzanne gorging herself, alone, on puddings she can't stand, yes Julian I know it's a crime, that Matthew is finished for her and for all of them and will never come back. (261–2)

At the beginning of the final chapter Sarah drives south again towards the coast, partially retracing the route of her driving lesson. She is alone now, free from the control of instructor and psychiatrist alike, because she is in control of herself, and her memory, as well as

her motor. But this Stilgoesque sense of control has been established with the assistance of the psychiatrist, and purchased at the cost of reinterpreting her enthralment to the adulteress Genevieve as a homoerotic relation that compensated the younger woman for the absenteeism of a naval officer father and the elder for that of a naval officer husband.

IV

In the context of the crisis framed by first and final chapters, driving south is an important object rather than a figure of memory. Twice, on the day she first met Naomi and then again two years later, Sarah was driven by Genevieve towards Toulon. Sarah's memory of the first of these journeys culminates in a parallel between the two settings, England and France, that will recur:

> … just as we came into Toulon I opened my eyes to see a ship on the sea turning in a blaze of light, a warship so heavy but weightless in the water, a wedge in the haze like a thundercloud, and seeing that, feverish still and just woken, I thought for an instant that I was at home. (57)

In conversation with Jean-René during her visit to France in 1982, Sarah recovers her memory of the end of her second drive south with Genevieve, and recalls entering Belar's flat to find him dead and Genevieve dressing him in his uniform to fake a ceremonial suicide. Only here, in the chapter immediately preceding the one in which Sarah enters therapy, are we told that Belar, like Sarah's father, was a naval officer. A whole series of parallels between the English and French settings gradually dissolves much of the exotic fascination of the French one. No less gradually it comes to appear that what France and Genevieve alike have represented for Sarah is a fantasy of escape from the world of her upbringing and schooling, and that Genevieve may have been something other than the forceful (because adulterous, and by that token independent) heroine Sarah has taken her to be.

The parts played in this story by Belar, by Jean-René, and by Henri Palastrier (Genevieve's second partner, whom Sarah never meets), make adultery a persistent theme, although it is gradually supplemented by the homoerotic one and eventually, in the course of Sarah's therapy, comes to be subordinated to it. However, the

significance of Genevieve's adultery is withheld from Sarah by the complexities of their relations, and by the dense stratification and unpredictable surges of her memory. It is withheld also from the reader, for whom an opaque enigma materialises out of Sarah's staccato recollections of her own pre- and early-adolescent fascination, bafflement, and insecurity.

This involves the brusque opening and gradual resolution of other mysteries similar in structure to the initial one that arises from Sarah's revealing in Chapter 1 what made her accelerate so abruptly, most of which will be at least partially maintained until near the end, since Genevieve's characterisation as an adulterous and then bisexual heroine depends on them as well as being the novel's central axis. For instance, in Chapter 2, Sarah tells how as an eight-year-old she discovered the shocking object in the bathroom cabinet, but does so without immediately saying what it was. When she reveals that it was a pistol, this in turn raises more questions than it answers: right to the end of the book, the continuing interplay between Sarah's ignorance and fantasy on the one hand, and Genevieve's secretiveness on the other, is crucial.

Something similar happens in Chapter 12, when Sarah narrates the way she remembers, four years later in the French countryside, hearing Genevieve explain her reasons for having the gun in her possession.

> the truth came out in the middle of it all like an arrow ... almost before I recognised it, but when it hit me I comprehended everything from the beginning. It's like the facts of life, I thought slowly. Once you find out, you realize that you always knew. (112)

This is perhaps the crux of the novel, since what Sarah recollects Genevieve saying will eventually be undermined by other depositions as to the facts of Genevieve's sexual life, and indeed, effectively, as to the 'facts of life' themselves. Sarah understands Genevieve to have said the purpose of the gun was to frighten Belar, and 'teach him a lesson' (112). Although this phrase is initially related to a context of routine, husband-on-wife, domestic violence, Sarah will later, during the Falklands War, explain the 'lesson' to her psychiatrist as punishment meted out to Belar for leaving Genevieve behind when posted abroad (236, 254, 262). This is, however, a novel where some naval uniforms are more imagined than real: Sarah remembers that on the day she first met Genevieve, her brother Jonathan went to

'Sunday School where he drew a picture of God in a naval uniform (Ha ha ha, what a killing little boy you have, Mrs Finney)' (11).

The nihilist or postmodern signification (that God is dead) of the lapsus Sarah attributes to the Sunday-school teacher lends her memory of Jonathan's drawing an Oedipal sense that resonates through the entire novel. Years earlier again, when Mrs Finney's brother Nicholas married Genevieve's sister Juliette, the sisters of the bridal couple 'had run off together after the wedding into the woods and climbed up a tree, and had to come down in a hurry for the photo session' (10). In consequence, they were photographed so hastily re-shod in their party shoes that neither had a matching pair. Thus from the moment when the disruption of Sarah's driving lesson leads her to re-examine the photograph at the end of Chapter 1, the real or imagined parallel between Captain Finney and Belar is already matched by one between their wives, who are also both blonde, and repeatedly imagined preternaturally youthful by Sarah. We shall see in due course that the manner of this latter parallel's continuing development will be crucially important.

Combined with Sarah's memory of Jonathan's 'killing' drawing, these parallels retrospectively introduce a spectral but heroic image of Genevieve and her gun into the Finney household years before the event of her own and Belar's deaths, and indeed right from the beginning. After her psychiatric cure, on the final page of the novel, Sarah will even reinterpret the confusion of her mother's and Genevieve's shoes in such a way as to establish that the homoerotic element in Genevieve's history dates back to before her own birth, and therefore cannot be of her own or her psychiatrist's imagining. But it is no more clear that Belar was a naval officer than that Genevieve returned from the dead; and the novel's deviation from illusionistic narrative convention also invites us to question her heroic stature and her bisexuality. This in turn will eventually lead to a questioning of the definition of adultery itself.

V

At the end of the novel, Sarah still has yet to hear Jean-René's version of Genevieve's life, which offers crucial clues to the meaning of the enigma-riddled story she herself tells. These are, however, available to the reader because Sarah's story is earlier suspended for 70 pages out of 264 (147–217), where Jean-René himself narrates. Nothing

guarantees the truth of Jean-René's story. Its descriptions of climate and landscape, like its characterisations of Palastrier and Genevieve, have a mythic and parodic resonance that sows seeds of unspecifiable but ineradicable doubt. His narrative also consists largely in hearsay, itself on occasion second-hand, and is no less fraught with mourning than Sarah's own, whose decentred character tends in any case to discredit narration as such. The relation between the two accounts is important, however, for it is here that we can find the crux of the novel's thematisation of adultery.

Jean-René's guiding thread is a series of conversations between himself and Palastrier that took place after Genevieve's death. The two men's relationship is scarcely less ambivalent than Sarah's with Genevieve, and the information about Genevieve (if such it is) that Jean-René suggests he was teased by Palastrier into teasing out of him is in Jean-René's view 'obscene' (202). Jean-René has a personal stake in this judgement, but its wording resonates across the novel with Sarah's use of the same term while in her relatively conformist and domesticated mode, shortly before the Task Force departs for the South Atlantic. Sarah, who has now twice seen Genevieve in the streets of Portsmouth, is about to be triggered into joining the anti-war demo where she will see her a third, decisively disquieting, time. However, she protests initially on a smaller scale, against a family lunch she expects to be a 'bloody ra-ra send-off', at which 'we'll probably toast the bloody Queen': it is at this point that Sarah's mother comes closest to enacting the parallel between herself and Genevieve upon which Sarah dwells repeatedly, claiming not to care, since it will not affect what happens, whether 'we toast the Queen …'. She gave a tiny scratch of a laugh. 'Or whether we drink to the Argentine Air Force' (125). This exchange precipitates rebellion and flight in Sarah; but her immediate reaction is to use the word 'obscene' twice: 'I gulped snot. "That's obscene", I said. "That's an obscene thing to say"' (126).

The parallel with Jean-René's reaction to Palastrier's tidings underlines their importance: on each occasion the word marks a climactic moment where the edifice of domesticity is rocked to its foundation in the traditions and dogmas the novel questions. When Sarah uses it, it marks the vulnerability of the Finney's family life to the realities of the military career it has up to this point supported; in Jean-René's mouth, it signals the fragility of the sense of his domestic existence with Genevieve once the significance of adultery is put in question. This suggests that an interpretation of Genevieve's adultery as a gesture of transgressive autonomy is part and parcel of the same

atavistically Christian and profoundly moralistic dominant discourse that motivates Captain Finney's abandonment of wife and children for the sake of his country. Much the same is true of Sarah's reinterpretation, under therapy, of her enthralment to Genevieve as having been their common recourse, beyond the pleasure principle, to homoeroticism.

What Palastrier reveals to Jean-René, and therefore to us (but not to Sarah, who is still only just about to hear it from Jean-René when the novel ends), is Genevieve's reason for resisting the divorce Belar was seeking at the time of both their deaths. This revelation comes at the end of a narrative of Genevieve's life with Palastrier told at a dozen meetings over a period of three years, dramatising the work of mourning. Palastrier's revelation brings Jean-René, from a grief of mythic depth, to hate Genevieve's memory. Further, Jean-René reflects on the displacement of his grief by hatred, and also discusses it with Naomi, in metaphorical terms of salvation, and redemption from a state of damnation (163, 175, 205). This Christian tonality resonates with that of Sarah's upbringing and education. It also demonises Genevieve in death far more effectively than she ever was in life: even Jean-René is at last persuaded of Juliette's view, voiced after Genevieve's death, that marriage to Belar had given her a 'doomed quality which she never lost after she left him' (156). At first, Jean-René was angered by Juliette's resignation, and the way she encouraged Naomi to anaesthetise herself against mourning (rather as Sarah is anaesthetised twice over, once on changing schools and a second time under therapy: the difference is that in Naomi's case the robotic, traumatised adolescent is described in other characters' words). Now, however, Jean-René himself secretes a shell of anaesthetic doctrine.

Genevieve had to the end remained attached to Belar in a way she had gone to extremes to conceal. The gun was a prop in a lethal sexual game begun at their first meeting and continued until his attempts to dissolve their marriage were cut short by death. Palastrier claims to have had Genevieve's secret from Belar himself, whom he visited in search of enlightenment after proposing marriage to Genevieve and finding that she then began to slip away from him: apparently, her shame at what Palastrier discovered by thus violating her privacy was what caused her to leave him. The triple relay that allegedly conveys this information from Belar via Palastrier and Jean-René to the reader leaves it crucially unclear who leads whom – or indeed that either party leads the other – in the gradually escalating

violence of this power game within which something all parties appear to acknowledge as sexual deviance is followed, accompanied and indeed compounded by marriage, infidelity, separation, and temporising debate over the question of a divorce that is overtaken by death. It therefore becomes equally unclear that Genevieve's subsequent adulterous liaisons with Palastrier and with Jean-René represent the transgressive face of her sexual being, which cannot either be considered to find expression in the alleged homoeroticism of her relations with Sarah: this is postulated during Sarah's therapy as part of a reinterpretation of her past whose whole purpose is to make possible her mental and moral recuperation.

Jean-René's complaint is that his domestic existence with Genevieve and Naomi had been 'living a lie' (203); he and Palastrier had been 'cuckolders cuckolded' (202), victims of a sexual infidelity which this phrase reinterprets metaphorically as adultery. Genevieve's metaphorical adultery, which is metaphorical because committed with her legal husband, is no less offensive to Jean-René than a literal one would have been. This is partly because it violates a domesticity the novel evokes only to destroy it as forcefully as it evokes landscape and seascape, the friction of French with English idiom, and the atmosphere of a middle-class 1970s childhood, but also because, in its indecipherable compulsiveness, it violates the criteria of 'cast-iron intention and gospel truth' which Jean-René, with his horror at 'living a lie', personifies no less than does Graham Stilgo. These values and dogmas are aligned with each other by being associated in this double personification; but in the case of Jean-René they are also dissociated from legal marriage. They are grounded instead in an atavism sufficient to dissipate the nominal illegitimacy of the domesticity they support. Thus the theme of adultery dissolves into others: intention deflected by desire (which shows itself in Palastrier's account of Genevieve's misery at her compulsion), and truth qualified by the impact of desire on the operations of discourse (which shows itself in Jean-René's claim to have been 'cuckolded', and in Sarah's heroic characterisation of Genevieve, here also dissolved along with the autonomy her infidelity supposedly betokened). This is the provocation of Genevieve's story: the sexual bond with her legal husband is her offence. Worse, it is neither a matter of choice nor, even, of her subjection to his deliberately exercised domination, which would at least entail some logical possibility of reversal. It is therefore a provocation not just for the values Jean-René espouses, but for any voluntarism (be it a feminism) that fails to reckon with the distinction

between intention and desire, and with the permanent risk of its own deviation by their being taken one, or each, for the other. The significance of all this is developed by means of another repetition comparable to that of the word 'obscene' discussed above.

VI

Palastrier's final attempt to convince Jean-René that Genevieve's love for each of them in turn was not compromised by her game with Belar ends thus: '"Jean-René", said Henri Palastrier, "she was a fantastic girl"' (217). Emphasised by its appearance here in the very last line of the section narrated by Jean-René, the word 'fantastic' echoes and is modulated by its use on two occasions by Sarah. The enthusiasm of the first, in the midst of Sarah's narration of her original childhood encounter with Genevieve, is marked typographically, by italics: 'she was *fantastic*' (12). Conversely, although Sarah employs the word in the same colloquial sense on another occasion, it here describes an event she also likens to a dream, and this has destructive implications. In the closing pages, whose bitty inconclusiveness marks the waning in therapy of Sarah's engagement with the particularities of persons and places, her younger sister Flora and she are drinking coffee 'with sugar in it ... for shock' after watching a video documentary about the Falklands War, when Flora recalls seeing Father Christmas winched down from a helicopter at a party for children of naval families, and believing in him – something Sarah says 'must have been fantastic' (260). When, in the last line of the novel, Sarah invites Jean-René to tell his story, she is about to hear that Genevieve's heroism was no less fantastic than the domesticity of her existence with Jean-René, which to him, now, is itself as fantastic as the existence of Father Christmas: Genevieve will be betrayed again, as she was twice before, when Belar told Palastrier his story, and when Palastrier repeated it to Jean-René.

We have already seen that Sarah has by this stage reinterpreted Genevieve's heroism in her eyes as their mutual homoerotic *pis-aller*, and reinforced this interpretation by fantasising a comparable encounter, earlier in Genevieve's life, with her sister's sister-in-law, Sarah's own mother. The implication of Sarah's somewhat sarcastic invitation to Jean-René – '"Talk all you like, Jean-René", I said. "Tell me about her"' (264) – is that she is about to see this fantasy of

homoeroticism forced back, along with adultery, to the side of a sexual normality that can incorporate such deviations because of their compensatory function. Conversely, the scandal of Genevieve's history, as Sarah now stands to hear it told, is that it has no such function, being consonant neither with what the novel represents as being a dominant discourse, nor with fantasies of its subversion.

That she does stand to hear it told is the novel's closing note of hope. After all, Genevieve's heroism in Sarah's eyes has up to this point frequently been expressed in metaphors of masculinity whose terms range, crucially, from the chivalric through a military register to the paramilitary. Consider for example Sarah's introduction to Chapter 21, in which, during her visit to Jean-René at the time of the Falklands War, she will narrate the day of Belar's and Genevieve's deaths:

> When I was a kid I thought she should have a sword. I thought she was like a prince or a knight, but she wasn't. She was a guerrilla, like me, taking to the hills or fighting undercover. We used to be outlaws together – we had to be outlaws. And if we fought each other it was only out of love, Jean-René. We were two of a kind. She might have laughed at me and called me a Spartan in front of you but we both knew the truth. The true colours. We were perfect, we did the sword-dance with each other, step-step-pirouette, feint, parry, *touché*, as well-drilled as show-gladiators. Except of course we didn't have any swords. (236)

This is still not the sense of the novel, since it reconciles Genevieve's heroic standing in Sarah's eyes, and the ascription of bisexuality that cancels and preserves it, with the symbolism of the traditions in which Sarah grew up, and because these traditions' founding dogmas of revealed truth and free will have by now been well and truly shredded.

The book's physical appearance and jacket synopses present it as an exhibit of popular culture, and convinced at least one reviewer, who took it for a 'therapeutic romance',[5] but it is not that: it is a work of great, and discomfortingly thoughtful, tenderness which it is to be hoped, against hope, will prove susceptible of being rebroadcast without being easily domesticated.

Notes

1 Frances Liardet, *The Game* (London, Macmillan, 1994). For their helpful and encouraging remarks on preliminary drafts of this essay, thanks to David Bellos, Ann Caesar, Peter Hainsworth, Nicholas White, and, especially, Frances Liardet and Naomi Segal. For any defects in the final version, I am of course to blame.
2 For all the questions they raise, the pioneering English-language analyses by Fredric Jameson are still among the most incisive. See especially *Postmodernism, or, the Cultural Logic of Late Capitalism* (London: Verso, 1991).
3 On public opinion at the turn of the decade, see Jacques Derrida, 'La démocratie ajournée', in *L'autre cap* (Paris: Minuit, 1991). I do not, of course, wish to suggest that this material is easily compatible with that cited in note 2 above. The disjunction between Jameson's work and Derrida's would need to be charted by reference to their different responses to Sartre, Althusser and Lyotard.
4 See Perry Anderson, 'A culture in contraflow', in *English Questions* (London: Verso, 1993), 193–301, for a classic statement of the view that there is some meaningful sense in which British academia swung to the Left while society in general swung to the Right in the 1970s and 1980s. It didn't feel like that if you had your undergraduate and postgraduate education, as well as your apprenticeship in university teaching, all since 1979. Nor is it easy to make sense of Anderson's position in abstract principle, since a meaningfully politicised academy would presumably by definition exert some influence.
5 Roz Kaveney, 'Playing with murder', *TLS*, 25 March 1994, 21.

Index

Adam, Antoine, 58–9, 67, 69n.
Adolph Friedrich, Duke of
    Mecklenburg, 19
adultery, representation of
    Brazil, 7, 160–73
    England, 3, 6, 21–4, 70–81 149–59,
        212–28
    France, 1, 2, 6, 8, 25–6, 34–69,
        113–14, 119–21, 123–45
    Germany, 24–7, 91–5, 112, 117–19
    New Zealand, 199–200, 204–9
    Russia, 6, 18, 22, 85–91, 94, 98,
        111, 112, 115–17
    Spain, 6, 98–108, 174–85
    United States of America, 1, 45–6,
        51–5, 189–205, 209
AIDS, 209
Alas, Leopoldo, 7, 98, 174–85
Aldaraca, Bridget, 102
Althusser, Louis, 135–6
Anderson, Perry, 208n.
Aquinas, Saint Thomas, 178–80,
    184n.
Armstrong, Judith, 4
Arthurian legend, 4, 21, 34–44
Augustine, Saint, 184n.
Aulnoy, Marie-Catherine Le Jumel
    de Barneville, comtesse d', 67,
    69n.
Austen, Jane, 6, 70–81

Balzac, Honoré de, 6, 141–2, 198
I Bambini ci guardono, 116
Barthes, Roland, 198
Baudelaire, Charles, 32n., 120,
    125–6
Bazán, Pardo, 106
Bédacier, Catherine, 67
Benjamin, Walter, 103
Béroul, 8–9
Blanco, Alda, 102
Blanco Aguinaga, Carlos, 102

Bloch, R.H., 39
Boileau-Despréaux,nicolas, 66–7
Boswell's Life of Johnson, 73, 79, 80n.
bourgeoisie, see middle-classes
Bourges, Elemir, 130
Bowlby, Rachel, 107n.
Breton, André, 112
Brill, Lesley, 191
Bronte, Emily, 193
Buchan, John, 194
Burmeister, Johannes, 19–20

Campion, Jane, 199, 210n.
    see also The Piano
Camus, Albert, 115
Caplan, Betty, 209n.
Carrière, J.-C., 55n.
Carey, Peter, 27–9, 32n.,
Castelnau, Henriette de, *see* Murat,
    Comtesse de
Céard, Henry, 125
Chateaubriand, François-René,
    vicomte de, 110, 112
Cherneshevsky, Nikolay
    Gavrilovich, 96n.
children in fictions of adultery, 3, 6,
    10, 13–33, 109–22, 152, 157–8,
    167, 183, 199–200, 202–4, 206–7
Cinderella, 76
Civil Code, 134
classical references, 4, 7, 13–33,
    152–5, 162–72, 172n., 197
Clinton, Bill, 1
Clinton, Hillary, 1
Colet, Louise, 120
The Communist Manifesto, 98
Conservative scandals, 1
contracts, 6, 64–5, 100–1, 105
Coras, Jean de, 46–51
Coulet, Henri, 67

D'entre les morts, 196

DATE DUE

GAYLORD   PRINTED IN U.S.A.